Educational Leadership for America's Schools

Educational Leadership for America's Schools

Allan R. Odden
University of Wisconsin–Madison

WITH THE ASSISTANCE OF

Eleanor R. Odden
Madison, Wisconsin

McGraw-Hill, Inc.

*New York   St. Louis   San Francisco   Auckland   Bogotá   Caracas
Lisbon   London   Madrid   Mexico City   Milan   Montreal   New Delhi
San Juan   Singapore   Sydney   Tokyo   Toronto*

This book was developed by Lane Akers, Inc.

This book was set in Palatino by ComCom, Inc.
The editor was Lane Akers;
the production supervisor was Richard A. Ausburn.
The cover was designed by Tippit/Woolworth.
Project supervision was done by Tage Publishing Service, Inc.
R. R. Donnelley & Sons Company was printer and binder.

EDUCATIONAL LEADERSHIP FOR AMERICA'S SCHOOLS

 This book is printed on recycled, acid-free paper containing 10% postconsumer waste.

1 2 3 4 5 6 7 8 9 0 DOH DOH 9 0 9 8 7 6 5

ISBN 0-07-047489-3

Library of Congress Cataloging-in-Publication Data

Odden, Allan.
    Educational leadership for America's schools / Allan R. Odden, with the assistance of Eleanor R. Odden.
      p.   cm.
    Includes bibliographical references and index.
    ISBN 0-07-047489-3
    1. School management and organization—United States.
2. Educational leadership—United States.   3. Educational change—United States.   I. Odden, Eleanor R.   II. Title.
LB2805.033   1995
372.2'00973—dc20   94-40278

About the Authors

ALLAN R. ODDEN is a professor of educational administration and co-director of the Finance Center of the Consortium for Policy Research in Education (CPRE) in the School of Education at the University of Wisconsin–Madison. The CPRE Finance Center is one of 25 federally funded research and development centers. He is the principal investigator of the CPRE Teacher Compensation Project. His areas of specialization are education policy, education finance, school-based management, and education policy implementation. His current research focuses on integrating education reform, with changes in education governance and finance for the purposes of tranforming schools into high performance organizations. He was a professor of administration and policy in the School of Education at the University of Southern California from 1984 to 1993, and worked with the Education Commission of the States for nearly a decade from 1975 to 1984, serving as director of policy analysis and research and director of its education finance center. He was president of the American Educational Finance Association in 1979–80.

Professor Odden has written widely and published more than 150 journal articles and book chapters. He is the editor of *Rethinking School Finance: An Agenda for the 1990s* (1992), coauthor with Lawrence Picus of *School Finance: A Policy Perspective* (1992), and editor of *Education Policy Implementation* (1991). He received a Ph.D. and M.A. degree from Columbia University, a Master of Divinity from the Union Theological Seminary and a B.S. from Brown University. In the mid-1960s, he was a mathematics teacher and curriculum developer in New York City's East Harlem.

ELEANOR R. ODDEN is an education consultant in Madison, Wisconsin. She formerly was assistant professor of teacher education at Occidental College in Los Angeles. For serveral years, she was an adjunct professor at the University of Southern California teaching courses on the educational change process. She was coordinator of staff development for the Glendale Unified School District in California, and before that was Coordinator of Reading for the Jefferson County School District in Colorado. She has been a consultant and trainer in numerous school districts. Her areas of specialization include teacher and administrator professional development, school based management, and curriculum implementation. She has trained teachers and administrators in effective teaching, effective school strategies, training of trainers, clinical supervision, peer coaching, the educational change process, and school based management.

She received an M.A. in psychology with a focus on remedial reading, an Ed.D. in special education with a focus on learning disabilities from Teachers College, Columbia University, and a B.A. degree from Brown University. She was a teacher in New York City's East Harlem public schools in the mid-1960s.

For our children, Sarina Elizabeth and Robert Allan Myung Soo

Contents

Preface

This book is designed as an introduction to education leadership for America's public schools. It provides an overview of the organization and governance of the American public school system with a particular focus on the new directions in which the system is moving and the new types of leadership required.

Rather than organized around structural and functional topics, the strategy taken by more traditional introductory texts, it is organized around the objective of creating, implementing and leading high performing schools. It includes chapters on educational goals, learning theory, curriculum and assessment, organization and education change (restructuring), as well as chapters on teachers, school leadership and management, the courts, school finance and leadership and policy at the local, state and federal levels.

The book assumes that education reform is an enduring feature of American schools. From the rhetoric of the early 1980s reports that the nation was "at risk" from a "rising tide of mediocrity" to the teacher professionalism and school restructuring proposals of the end of that decade, to today's systemic education reforms, as well as other reform emphases and periods, the book sets educational leadership in a context of continuous efforts to make the country's education system better. Rather than criticizing pressures for change, the book implies that these pressures are almost endemic to education in America.

Therefore, the book is focused on the education reform agenda of the 1990s—the imperative to teach "hard content" to all students, i.e., to raise all student achievement to levels attained by only a fraction of students today. The book is structured to identify the knowledge and issues related to the country's goal of educating all students to high levels of proficiency in thinking, problem solving and communication in core curriculum areas. The purpose of the book is not to probe in depth all of the complex issues raised, but to identify the wide range of issues education leaders of tomorrow's schools need to understand, and to summarize key aspects about what is known in those different issue areas to provide a beginning basis for informed leadership of the public schools.

In many universities, the book could be used for the introductory educational administration course and the topics covered in each chapter could then be addressed more fully by other courses. Indeed, the book was designed while Allan Odden was a professor at the University of Southern California. It was conceived as a text for a new introductory course for a revised Ed.D. Program designed to prepare education leaders who could transform schools into high performance education organizations. The revised doctoral program included a core of new courses on such subjects as learning theory, curriculum and instruction, instructional leadership and the educational change process, teaching diverse students, as well as courses in politics, finance, personnel, and governance.

Rather than just describing the development of educational administration, management and governance, the chapters succinctly summarize key issues of the past and then move on to the thorny issues related to the curriculum change, school restructuring and leadership required to accomplish the nation's bold education goals, that were first agreed to by then President Bush and the nation's governors in 1990 that became codified into law by the Clinton Administration's Goals 2000 program enacted in early 1994.

The book takes seriously the backward mapping approach to policy and leadership (Elmore, 1979–80) and is sequenced to reflect that perspective. Chapter 1 argues the case for dramatically improving the results of the nation's education system—student achievement. The next chapter discusses the conditions of students in public schools and their current state of achievement, and identifies student mastery of the complex subject matters of mathematics, science, language arts, history and geography as the primary goal for the country's education system. Following the backward mapping strategy, the book targets classroom and schools as the key service delivery units in the education system, i.e., the place where teaching and learning take place. Then, drawing heavily from advances in cognitive science research, the next chapters identify current understandings about learning, pedagogy, curriculum standards, and performance assessment that, combined, can develop advanced cognitive expertise in all students, including those from poverty backgrounds, with limited English proficiency, and other special needs.

The book then discusses what teachers need to know and be able to do to work in schools where these pedagogical strategies, curriculum standards and assessment procedures represent the core of learning activities. Again following the backward mapping approach, the next chapters begin the process of identifying organizational and other policy dimensions that can reinforce and support the previously discussed school practices. One chapter identifies the new logic of organizing for high performance, leadership and management in school restructuring activities; other chapters articulate implications for local, state and federal policy and leadership; and the last two chapters discuss the role of the legal system and how a school finance system might be restructured to support these new directions.

Throughout the book, the chapters summarize historical changes, identify traditional practices, and suggest future directions and the potential new changes they might require. Although forward looking, the book draws heavily from research conducted in actual school settings. Thus, while sanctioning new directions required by the systemic education reform in which the country seems to be moving (Smith & O'Day, 1991; Pechman, & Laguarda, 1993), suggestions and recommendations are derived from research on how this can actually happen in genuine school settings in actual school districts or in real local, state and federal political and policy settings. Thus, the book attempts to be forward looking while remaining grounded in the realities of life in schools, districts and legislatures.

Because the book is an introductory overview, it does not provide the micro-level information needed to fully implement suggested new directions. Further probing of the related research literature perhaps through other course work in a leadership preparation program, or through detailed planning in schools and districts or intense collaborative interactions with colleagues and education leaders at the local level are needed in order to design and implement such strategies. We hope the book convinces new education leaders and policymakers that a much improved American education system is possible, energizes those individuals to develop the new professional expertise and practice that will be required to put this new vision in place, and encourages them to assume a wide variety of leadership roles in the U.S. education system.

McGraw-Hill and the author would like to thank the following reviewers for their many helpful comments and suggestions: Fred Carver, University of Georgia; Gary Crow, Louisiana State University; Cecil Miskel, University of Michigan; and Gail Schneider, University of Wisconsin at Milwaukee.

Allan R. Odden

New Challenges for American Education

Change and dramatic improvements in student performance are required for the nation's schools in the 1990s. The nation's ambitious education goals, agreed to by the President and governor of each of the 50 states (National Education Goals Panel, 1991) and codified into law by the federal Goals 2000 legislation approved by Congress in early 1994, set a very high level of expected student achievement (Table 1-1). Producing these new and higher levels of achievement will require substantial change in local schools, including hard decisions about how to use resources. These demands for higher productivity are pressuring other public and private sector organizations. Today, all organizations need to improve quality in a relatively short time period and with existing resources, although many private sector companies must meet these performance demands with resource cuts.

There are numerous schools stepping up to these productivity challenges. The Hollibrook Elementary School in Houston, Texas is one example (Hopfenberg et al., 1993). A school of about 1000 students and 100 staff, it sits in a community surrounded by government-built subsidized housing. Its students are representative of 35 different countries, with 90 percent from Hispanic immigrant families. About 85 percent start school with limited proficiency in English. Ninety-one percent of students are eligible for free and reduced breakfast and lunch. In 1988, students scored in the lowest quartile on norm referenced standardized achievement tests. Three years later, test scores were up from 3.7 in reading and language arts to 5.2 and 5.6 respectively, and to 6.6 in mathematics.

With a vision focused on results (raising the achievement of all students to grade level by the sixth year), the school decentralized its decision making and organizational restructuring, encouraged collegial work among teachers and with the community, upgraded its curriculum combining it with high expectations for student learning, invested heavily in ongoing professional development, and worked hard to produce these results. Funding was not increased but resources were reallocated and used to fund new activities that

1

had a payoff in student learning. Hollibrook is one of many examples of public schools in real (and tough) settings that show how all students can be taught to high levels, even without large infusions of new dollars.

Abbotsville Elementary School in Baltimore, Maryland is another example. In 1989, it became the first Success for All School with the goal of producing all students at high levels of reading proficiency by the third grade (Slavin et al., 1994). A school of about 600 African-American students and nearly all of whom are eligible for free and reduced lunch, it also reallocated resources on programs likely to produce results, restructured the entire school organization, brought in the community as a full partner, and worked hard to accomplish its ambitious but attainable goal. It provided a preschool program for its 4-year-olds, a full-day kindergarten for its 5-year-olds, one to one tutoring for first and second graders who did not keep up in reading, cross-age but homogeneous grouping for small classes of language arts instruction, a manipulatives problem-solving-oriented mathematics program, heavy use of cooperative learning, and cross-age tutoring. These programs were provided by major resource reallocation and some modest funding infusion. Within three years, it had virtually attained its results. Over time, moreover, the initial group of third graders have maintained their learning accomplishments and each year the achievement of the new group of third graders is above that from the previous year.

The Edison Project of the Whittle Corporation in Tennessee, while as yet untested, provides another vision of how school resources might be restructured to provide more educational services and produce higher levels of student learning. Each Edison School proposes to develop mastery of the complex subject matter domains of mathematics and science, humanities and the arts, character and ethics, health and physical fitness, and practical arts and skills. Its school buildings will be organized with small groups of children placed in schools within schools called *academies*. It will devolve substantial authority and responsibility to teachers, who together will run the curriculum program. It will provide small class sizes with lead teachers and teacher assistants. It will make heavy use of telecommunications computer technologies. And it proposes to stay open for longer, an eight-hour day (even for four- and five-year-olds) and an eleven month school year, all at the current national average educational expenditure per pupil (The Edison Project, 1994). This design makes a dramatically different decision about how education dollars are used to provide educational services. Edison Project schools will be implemented in Massachusetts beginning in 1995; only time will tell whether such schools deliver the level of student performance promised. If they do, they will represent yet another strategy for improving productivity in education.

Similar productivity pressures have impacted the private sector. In the mid-1970s, the Xerox Corporation in New York faced a problematic future. Having led the world in producing photocopying machines for the previous 20 years, Xerox was losing market share and profits to Japanese firms, which not only were selling machines at a lower cost but also producing machines of higher quality. In initial meetings with key division leaders, Xerox corporate executives were told that the Japanese had a competitive advantage because of government help and lower wages, Xerox suppliers were the source of lower quality Xerox machines, and producing the types of machines the Japanese did would take time and require more resources. In a national economy without worldwide market competition, Xerox might have responded with money, time, and placing pressure on parts suppliers. Instead, corporate leaders said that the company would need to produce better machines in less time and at a significantly lower cost or Xerox simply would be out of business.

Over the next ten years, Xerox did exactly that. It regained its market leadership position and has remained as a world leader in the photocopying machine business. Its market continues as a highly competitive one, so Xerox cannot rest on past accomplishments. Each year the company needs to reduce the time to design, make, and market new machines, make higher quality machines, and sell them at lower prices. Doing better with less is the cold, hard reality of the international marketplace.

The government sector more generally is facing similar productivity pressures. Governments at the federal, state, and local levels across the country today confront citizen needs and social problems far beyond their resources to resolve. Yet political realities require that they respond. In part as a result, governments are beginning to redesign and reinvent themselves (Barzelay, 1992; Osborne, 1988; Osborne and Gaebler, 1992). Doing more with less, or at least doing more with the same is becoming the norm. For example, Osborne and Gaebler (1992) found that many local governments have contracted out sanitation services to private vendors—costs usually dropped while collection services improved. Sometimes the public agency competed for and won the contract, and also improved quality at the same or lowered costs. Visalia, a city in California created an entrepreneurial fund to encourage city agency heads to make purchases and start activities on their own. St. Paul, Minnesota rebuilt its downtown with private money, spurred by the government's creation of a redevelopment agency which quickly began to make money. And the Defense Department, that quintessential bureaucracy, implemented lump-sum budgeting for many of its bases around the world, cutting 1200 pages of regulations to 44 pages and even letting base commanders roll end-of-the-year fund balances into the next year's budget.

Osborne and Gaebler (1992) found that large, centralized government bureaucracies maintaining their rules and regulations and treating all situations the same were not working in the 1990s. The best governments—local and state—were decentralizing authority, flattening structures, creating partnerships with businesses (both profit and nonprofit) and even creating profit-making enterprises of their own. In fact, they reported that Orlando, Florida created so many profit centers that their earnings soon outstripped their tax revenues!

These new approaches to government focused on outcomes instead of rules. They looked for new ways to meet the government's obligations to citizens that both increased the quantity and quality of services but without commensurate tax hikes. They strived to empower citizens and provide then more choices rather than just "serve" them. They saw the choice not as tax more or spend less, but to govern better and manage resources more creatively. They looked for ways to make money rather than to raise taxes.

As stated above, schools have similar demands for creativity and change. On the results side, the nation has ambitious education goals. The national goal is to raise all students to a level of learning attained by only a small majority of students today. Under normal circumstances, these aspirations would be difficult. But as Chapter 2 shows, today's students pose more complex educational challenges even for meeting older and lower achievement aspirations. Meeting the new goals will be a tough task, and no doubt require additional resources (Casserly and Carnoy, 1994).

Many education leaders feel this challenge cannot be met. They claim that parents do not support schools enough, and that students bring bigger problems with them to school—more students come from families with incomes below the poverty level, speak a language other than English, live in single parent or merged/blended families, or have both parents out of the home working most of each day. The public as well as educators believe that the schools need more money, that teacher salaries need to be raised, and class sizes lowered. Just as the Xerox division leaders, the public and educators seem to believe that schools need perhaps more modest aspirations, and certainly more time and more money.

Luckily, education funding per pupil, after adjusting for inflation, has an historical record of continuous rises. Education funding increased by at least 25 to 65 percent during each of six decades preceding the 1990s (see Chapter 13). But there is no fail-safe insurance that resources will continue to rise. Even if educational resources in many states rise at the levels matching historical patterns, raising student learning to such new levels will still be a challenge. But, real funding per pupil in several large and growing states such as California is unlikely to increase during the 1990s and likely will drop (Guthrie, Kirst, and Odden, 1992). Nevertheless, the national goals still apply to these states. To accomplish these goals for all students, these education systems must produce higher levels of student learning with lower levels of real resources.

In addition, as this chapter will argue, there are other pressures that require large improvements in what students know and are able to do. The skills needed by the economy and improvements in educational equity are two such demands. Movements within education to restructure schools (Comer, 1980; Goodlad, 1984; Levin, 1988; Sizer, 1992; Slavin, 1990) and upgrade the curriculum (e.g., National Council of Teachers of Mathematics, 1989) represent other demands. In short, education simply must do more—produce higher levels of student learning—with the resources they have, just as governments in general and most businesses in the corporate and private sectors. In other words, the 1990s is likely to be another decade of education reform with intense pressures to increase outcomes whatever the level of inputs and resources.

Reforming America's schools is not just a phenomenon of the 1980s and 1990s. Education reform has been on the leadership and policy agenda since the common school movement in the eighteenth century (Cuban, 1985, 1992; Tyack, 1991; Tyack and Hansot, 1982). Our country has always wanted to make the schools better—to improve schools as places in which to teach and learn and to increase student learning. Thus education reform is not a stranger to those in public or private elementary and secondary education.

During the 1990s, the nation's schools are again caught up in a reform environment. Indeed, education reform is an international phenomenon, with nearly all the major country's working on implementing or creating new, comprehensive education reforms (Warren, 1990; Jacobson and Berne, 1993). The purpose of this chapter is to (1) summarize the various rationales for reforming and dramatically improving the American education system; (2) discuss the various education initiatives of the 1990s that will sustain and advance reform momentum; (3) put the 1990s reforms in historical perspective; and (4) briefly describe the current education organization and governance structures within which these reforms have been developed and from which new practices need to flow.

PERSPECTIVES ON THE NEED FOR EDUCATION REFORM

There are many different perspectives on the need to improve the country's schools, each in part deriving from alternative views of the conditions of the American education system. Three different assessments of the conditions of education in the nation are presented below, together with their implications for change.

The Schools are Better than Ever—The Complacency Perspective

One view of the American education system—with which it is difficult to disagree completely—is that it is better than it has ever been. The claim is that despite pessimism in reform reports and commission recommendations, American public schools are educating more and a greater diversity of students than ever before. Graduation rates are the highest they have ever been and thus drop out rates are at an all time low. It has also been shown that student performance is at or near all-time highs (especially if learning in college is included) at least our top students generally perform at competitive levels in international comparisons, the number of students scoring above 600 on the Scholastic Aptitude Test (SAT) is at its highest level, and nearly 60 percent of all students attend college or have a postsecondary education experience.

Two 1991 studies (Bracey, 1991; Carson, Huelskamp, and Woodall, 1991, 1993) amassed research to support the above claims. First, according to several governmental documents (Frase, 1989; NCES, 1991) the percentage of 17- to 18-year-olds completing high school rose from 10 percent in 1910 to 75 percent in the mid-1960s and then held steady until 1990. Moreover, by their mid-20s, fully 87 percent of all individuals either had graduated from high school or earned general education development (GED) certificates. In other words, the drop out rate did not rise significantly during either the 1970s or 1980s and, in fact, most students ultimately graduated from high school.

Similarly, raw data supported a rosier picture of student achievement. While falling in the 1960s and early 1970s, student performance on standardized testing began to rise in the mid-1970s and continued to rise into the 1980s, some scores reaching all time highs by the mid-1980s (Congressional Budget Office, 1986). Data from the National Assessment of Educational Progress (NAEP) also supported a more positive view of student achievement, and certainly showed that student achievement had not plummeted. In summarizing findings from 20 years of NAEP testing, Bracey (1991) quoted Mullis, Owen, and Phillips (1990) who wrote:

> Across all three ages assessed, overall reading performance in 1988 was as good as, if not slightly better than, it was nearly two decades ago. . . . In 1986, mathematics had changed very little from the levels achieved in 1973. . . . Viewed as a whole, science achievement in 1986 remained below levels attained in 1969. Trends at ages 9 and 13 are characterized by decline in the early 1970s, stable performance at that lower level of achievement through the 1970s, and improvement in the 1980s. With these gains, average proficiency at age 13 remained slightly below the 1970 level. At age 17, science performance dropped steadily from 1969 to 1982, but improved significantly from 1982 to 1986.

Moreover, achievement levels of minorities, both African-Americans and Hispanics, had risen relative to achievement of whites. Indeed, by 1990, the achievement gap between minorities and nonminorities had nearly been cut in half (Mullis, Owens, and Phillips, 1990).

These studies even showed that the top students were doing well, contrary to popular perception. While the general pattern was for a declining average score as the percentage of students taking SAT-type tests rose, the statistics for the top students defied the overall trend. The percentage of students scoring over 600 on both the verbal and mathematics portion of the SAT fell in the early 1970s but then rose again and has remained constant since about the mid-1970s. The percentage of high school seniors taking the College Board achievement tests has risen since 1977 as have their average scores. And the number of students taking the College Board advanced placement tests rose while the average scores remained about the same (Bracey, 1991).

In short, these studies provided data showing that the conditions of the American education system were not all that bad, in many categories were quite good, and in some cases at their highest level in history. Subsequent reports reached the same conclusions (Bracey 1992, 1993). How could national commissions (e.g., National Commission on Excellence in Education, 1983) or critics (e.g., Finn, 1991a) characterize the nation's education system as a "rising tide of mediocrity" or claim that the public schools were failing? Sure the schools could always be made better, but improvements would be made to a successful system in order to make it better and not to a failed system that needed a complete restructuring.

Proponents of the complacency perspective are not opposed to changing or improving the education system. But they provide "soft" pressures for change. They believe schools *could* be better, but do not necessarily believe they *must* be better. Indeed, this perspective often leads to a laissez-faire approach to change: if parts of the system need improvement individuals will respond and make the changes. The complacency perspective is closer to the adage: If it ain't broke, don't fix it.

But this perspective, as will be argued below, is the basis for a false complacency. It is like saying the Chrysler of 1985 was vastly superior to the Chrysler-Ford-Chevrolet of 20 or 30 years ago. That was absolutely true. The problem was that in the 1980s American cars were not as good as many foreign cars, which often were not only better but also lower priced. The issue is not whether the U.S. education system is better than it was years ago. The issue is whether it educates students to levels needed for *today's* economic and social demands and whether the U.S. education system produces high enough levels of learning for all students, those in the bottom half as well as those in the top half.

In fact, our students generally do not achieve at a level for today's economic and social requirements and the country's schools do not do a good enough job of educating the bottom half. Although the education system has improved over time, and while on some indicators it is better than ever before, the fact is that it is not good enough, as the next sections argue.

The Economy and Job Skills Requirements—The Economic Perspective

Rather than comparing current conditions to past conditions, the economic perspective on the need for education reform compares current conditions to future economic and work force requirements, and to trends in the distribution of income. According to this perspective, the future health of the U.S. economy, the future standard of living for American citizens, and the nature of the distribution of income across all citizens (which has become more unequal during the past 20 years) hinges on the level of learning produced by the nation's K–12 education system. This linkage has been argued by a wide range of individuals and groups including, among others, chief executive officers of the nation's largest companies (National Alliance for Business, 1990), commissions and studies created the U.S. Secretary of Labor (Johnston, 1987; Secretary's Commission on Achieving Necessary Skills, 1992), the nation's governors (National Governors' Association, 1991), economists (Reich, 1991; Thurow, 1992), and education policy analysts (Marshall and Tucker, 1992; Murnane and Levy, 1992a, 1992b; National Center on Education and the Economy [NCEE], 1990). The rest of this section details these arguments.

There is widespread agreement that during the twenty years from 1970 to 1990 the country experienced both a decline in the average wage of production workers and an increasing inequality in income distribution. Indicators of these realities are many but sorting out what caused them is complex. Burtless (1990a) is a good source that analyzes these realities and also, includes several studies from economic, demographic, welfare policy, job structure, and job behavior perspectives.

Burtless (1990a) made the following major points. First, there was only small growth in per capita income and average wages for all workers over the 20 years from 1970 to 1990, and that growth was a combination of large growth for the top fifth and decline for all other income levels. Second, average wages for production workers in the United States, after adjusting for inflation, fell from 1973 to at least 1987, meaning workers were worse off economically at the end of the 1980s than at the beginning of the 1970s. Third, productivity growth of the economy also declined over this time period and was the major cause of wage decline. But fourth, and even more disturbing, income inequality rose throughout the 1970s and 1980s. While decline in productivity was the reason behind the drop in average wage gains, it did not explain the growing inequality of wages and incomes (see also Murnane and Levy, 1992a, 1992b on these points).

What then is causing rising income inequality? The answer is not straightforward and is the subject of some controversy. One argument is that the U.S. economy is simply producing—some argue by design (Levin and Rumberger, 1983, 1987)—a proliferation of low-wage jobs, indeed using technology to "dumb down" jobs to low-skill levels and thus low-wages (Burtless, 1990a; Bluestone and Harrison, 1986). This argument persists despite several studies showing that the future economy will require a higher level of job skills (e.g., Berryman & Bailey, 1992; Bishop and Carter, 1991; Johnston, 1987, 1991; Murnane and Levy, 1992b). A second and demographic argument is that the entrance of the baby-boom generation into the labor force caused a one time, though significant, bulge in the percentage of entry level, and thus workers with lower wages. This situation will correct itself as that generation matures (Burtless, 1990b). Burtless (1990a) also assessed claims that the proliferation of part-time jobs caused income inequality and the welfare state was the culprit for income inequality. He found neither convincing. Neither was the dalliance in unionization.

What Burtless (1990a) found throughout the studies reported was a growing wage gap between skilled and unskilled workers. Underneath this phenomenon was not the desire of business to create low-wage jobs nor a change in demand across different companies and industries (from high-skilled to low-skilled). The critical factor was a structural change in the demand for labor—companies were changing production techniques to require a higher level of skilled workers (see also Packer and Wirt, 1991).

The result was that labor market demands for skilled workers grew faster than supply, thus bidding up high-skilled wages. Simultaneously, labor market demands for unskilled workers fell faster than supply, thus bidding down low-skilled wages. This marketplace reality produced rising returns to higher education and skill levels, and a widening gap between highly trained and less-trained individuals, such as high school dropouts (Blackburn, Bloom, and Freeman, 1990; Murphy and Welch 1989). Less-skilled workers suffered in two ways—a growing earnings differential relative to high-skilled workers and increased unemployment. The problem, in other words according to Burtless (1990a), was not a surplus of lousy jobs, but a surplus of unskilled and a shortage of higher skilled workers in a market demanding increasingly higher skill levels (Levy and Murnane, 1992).

The implication of this conclusion is clear for education reform. Burtless (1990a) argued that if the demand for low-skilled workers has dropped, the policy implication is to improve the skill levels of those workers, and of new workers graduating from high school and entering the labor market. "If the nation has too many unskilled workers, rather than too many bad jobs," Burtless (1990a:30) concluded, "both efficiency and equity will be served by improving the skills of workers now lodged at the bottom."

This conclusion suggests that no matter how much progress the education system has made during the past century, it cannot be complacent. It needs to substantially raise the skills and knowledge of individuals in the bottom half, thus expanding the pool of talented labor who can function in the evolving high-skilled, and thus higher wage, economy. Without such a policy, the nation could have growing upper and lower classes, divided by income and perhaps an overall declining average standard of living.

The link between education, jobs, and wages has been argued as a large part of the solution to the country's economic productivity stagnation as well (Berryman & Bailey, 1992; Murnane & Levy, 1992b). In order to compete in the world economy and continue to pay high wages, the United States needs to create and sell products and services that have high profit margins. Since large scale, standardized production quickly migrates to lower wage countries, the U.S. cannot depend heavily on such products for economic growth. It will always be undercut in price by lower wage countries.

Thus, advanced countries like the U.S. need to operate in niche markets and produce more customized products and services. Such products and services require workers to add more value than standardized commodities. These goods command both higher prices and produce higher profit margins, which allow companies to pay workers higher wages. The jobs created give workers more responsibility, wider arrays of discretion and broader decision-making authorities. Such jobs, moreover, also require higher skill levels than most front-line workers currently have. Several economic analyses have outlined this approach to economic productivity (e.g., Johnston, 1987; Marshall & Tucker, 1992; Murnane and Levy, 1992a, 1992b; Packer & Wirt, 1991; Reich, 1991; Thurow, 1992). This approach is supported by the nation's governors (National Governors' Association, 1990) and companies that have implemented this strategy have both raised wages and become more productive (Bailey, 1990; Blinder, 1990; Kochan and Osterman, 1990; Lawler, 1986).

Such a perspective on the economy also has clear education reform implications—the K–12 education system must produce individuals who can enter the work force with thinking, problem solving, mathematics, science, and technological skills far beyond what most schools produce today. Berryman and Bailey (1992) call this the "double helix" of education and the economy by arguing that the skill requirements of the reorganized workplace and our knowledge of how people learn effectively (see Chapter 3) imply similar strategies for education reform. In short, according to this argument, education reform is in the strategic, economic interest of the country and the objectives sought would be salutary for all students.

Appropriate Cautions. This strategy for improving economic growth is not without challenge. Levin and Rumberger (1987) argue that many companies use technology to "dummy down" and not "upskill" jobs and that managers want to control workers rather than give them more responsibility. Levin and Rumberger identify many examples of these practices in corporate America. Rather than being comfortable in hiring increasingly smart workers and giving them more autonomy and discretion, companies prefer to narrow job tasks, reduce worker involvement and autonomy, and pay wages that are as low as possible to low-skilled people.

This perspective views workers as cost items and the money spent on wages and training as simply cost increases; this approach does not see money spent on education and training as investments nor high-paid, skilled workers as critical—and even cost effective and productive—human capital (Reich, 1991). However, in the long-term, this strategy is viewed as a low-wage, low-standard of living approach (Magaziner and Clinton, 1992; NCEE, 1990; Marshall and Tucker, 1992).

In another caution, Balfanz (1991) argued that an education reform that simply increased student scores on current tests will unlikely increase individual or group productivity largely because the types of skills measured by typical testing programs are not related to job performance (see also Levin and Kelly, 1994). Standardized testing programs assess isolated bits of information that rarely require application to real life problems. Further, the abstract kinds of skills taught in most classrooms is usually used neither on the job nor for personal matters. Thus, the focus of education reform might be off the mark, if its success is measured by the array of tests most school districts and governments currently use.

Work Organization and Education Implications. The points of Levin, Rumberger and Balfanz need to be taken seriously in order for the economic growth argument to stimulate a productive type of work organization and education restructuring. Packer and Wirt (1991) begin to make more precise what is known about the new productive work organization and its connections to the school's curriculum, instruction, and learning strategies. They outline, as have others (Berryman and Bailey, 1992; Levin and Rumberger, 1987; Lawler, 1986, 1992), how high performance work systems need to be organized, the type of skills workers need to function effectively in those organization, and thus the types of curriculum and teaching that need to be imbedded in the elementary/secondary education system.

According to Packer and Wirt (1991), the high performance work organization has several characteristics. Responsibilities for day-to-day decisions are taken from managers and given to workers. Workers function in teams. Teams, not individuals, are rewarded for performance. Workers focus on outcomes and customer satisfaction. They emphasize customized products and services, flexible production schedules, timeliness, use of microcomputer-based technologies, combined with the ability to produce "craftlike" products on the scale of mass production. Workers must have broader and more complex technical skills—to work up or down the production line or to deliver a sophisticated service. Over time, work becomes technologically more complex and requires a higher level of cognitive knowledge and interpersonal skills to perform tasks well (Packer & Wirt, 1991). Workers also assume responsibilities for organizing and coordinating work tasks as well as allocating resources to perform those tasks, responsibilities that are traditionally reserved for management (Zuboff, 1988). These characteristics are very different from the typical bureaucracy and require a substantially new set of work skills (see also Packer, 1992 as well as Chapter 6 in this book).

Packer and Wirt (1991) articulate the implications of these work skill requirements for the schools. Schools need to teach students how to think and solve real world, practical problems, and they need to accomplish these tasks cooperatively in work groups. Teaching such skills to all students is aided by the evolving view of learning emerging from cognitive science (see also Chapter 3). Cognitive scientists have concluded that to be useful, knowledge should be learned in the context of problems and social situations that are similar to those in which the knowledge will be used. Knowledge, thus, is more than inert tools and algorithms. Knowledge is active, something that can be used in real situations to solve problems and resolve dilemmas. The main characteristics of knowledge emerging from cognitive science is that higher level thinking skills can be taught to all students, knowledge is actively and socially constructed, and learning takes place in a meaningful context (Resnick, 1987; 1989). Finally, cognitive science finds that the mental processes associated with thinking are not restricted to the most able or oldest students, that all students can successfully engage in learning how to think, and that these mental processes begin almost at birth. Thus, this type of learning should be grafted appropriately into the elementary as well as the secondary school curriculum.

In short, the link between the economy and education reform is symbiotic. The way to improve the U.S. economy is to focus on high value-added jobs that exist in high performance work organizations. This requires a major restructuring of how corporate America is organized and managed, entailing substantial decentralizing of the organization, coordination, and implementation of job tasks. Such jobs require a higher level of cognitive skills as well as a new set of interpersonal skills that enable individuals to work effectively in work teams. The focus of education reform should be to restructure schools to develop these new types of skills for all students, especially those in the "bottom half." If this challenge was impossible to accomplish years ago, rapidly emerging findings from cognitive science suggest that a "thinking" oriented curriculum can be created, and indeed can not only be more focused on developing thinking skills than is today's curriculum but also can be as successful for lower ability students as for higher ability students (see Maloy (1993) and [Chapter 3]).

As some have put it, the economic rationale for reforming public schools is a rationale for having schools do what the best teachers have always wanted to do—develop high levels of cognitive and social skills for all students.

Unequal Access and Unequal Learning—The Equity Perspective

Developing high levels of cognitive and social skills for all students has rarely if ever been an explicit agenda for the American public school system. Indeed, the history of American public schools, despite its successes, has been to treat various groups of students differently and in many cases explicitly to educate some students to higher levels than others. The equity perspective on the conditions of education and the need to reform schools devolves from these realities.

The United States is and always has been a diverse nation, and as Chapter 2 shows, is becoming more diverse in the 1990s. But for a variety of reasons, our education system historically has worked better for some groups than for others—Anglo Saxons, upper income individuals, and males have tended to be better served by the public education system than have minorities, lower income students, immigrants, and women (for mathematics and science).

The NAEP reports (Mullis, Owen, and Phillips, 1990) provide extensive data documenting the varying levels of achievement across different groups and classes of students in the United States. Minorities achieve at a lower level than nonminorities. The learning of students from higher income families substantially exceeds that of students from lower income families. Women and girls do less well in mathematics, science, and technology subjects. Further, there are significant differences across regions and states (Mullis, Campbell, and Farstrup, 1993). The causes of these differences are numerous, but variable expectations on the part of the education system and tracking practices have contributed substantially to these inequalities (Latimer, 1958; Oakes, 1985; Oakes and Lipton, 1990).

While achievement inequalities have been reduced during the past 20 years (Smith and O'Day, 1991a), unacceptable levels remain. Moreover, while higher levels of achievement are required for all students, the increasing diversity of American public school children (see Chapter 2) and the less than admirable treatment of lower ability students throughout our history suggest that overcoming the racial, income, ethnic, sex, ability, and regional divides on student learning will not be easy (Casserly and Carnoy, 1994).

One reason our new aspirations to raise the learning of all students to new, high levels will be difficult is that, despite our rhetoric about equal outcomes (Table 1-1, #3 and #4), our equity orientation has been one primarily of access which began only in the 1960s, and throughout most of the twentieth century we have not had uniformly high learning expectations for all students. The special needs programs developed in the 1960s and 1970s (see Chapter 2) sought to provide poor, language minority and handicapped students with greater access to educational services. The programs never explicitly sought to make high levels of educational achievement the same for all students. Even in supporting equal access we usually succumbed to differential expectations for outcomes.

For example, the late nineteenth century Committee of Ten created by the National Education Association envisioned a rich education for all students. It recommended that every core subject taught in high school should be taught to all students, irrespective of their ultimate career. This was a high point for equity. But these aspirations were soon superseded by the Cardinal Principals promulgated by a 1918 Commission on the Reorganization of Secondary Education which sanctioned a tri-part school system—tracking the top students into a college preparatory course, the middle group of students into vocational education, and allowing the bottom basically to drop out.

This strategy reflected to a large degree the needs of the emerging indus-

TABLE 1-1. National Education Goals

1. All children in America will start school ready to learn.
2. The high school graduation rate will increase to at least 90 percent.
3. American students will leave grades four, eight, and twelve having demonstrated competency in challenging subject matter including English, mathematics, science, history, and geography; and every school in America will ensure that all students learn to use their minds well, so they may be prepared for responsible citizenship, further learning, and productive employment in our modern economy.
4. Students in the United States will be first in the world in science and mathematics achievement.
5. Every adult in America will be literate and will possess the knowledge and skills necessary to compete in a global economy and exercise the rights and responsibilities of citizenship.
6. Every school in America will be free of drugs and violence and will offer a disciplined environment conducive to learning.
7. The Nation's teaching force will have access to programs for the continued improvement of their professional skills and the opportunity to acquire the knowledge and skills needed to instruct and prepare all American students for the next century.
8. Every school will promote partnerships that will increase parental involvement and participation in promoting the social, emotional, and academic growth of children.

trial economy. In the early twentieth century, the beginning of the industrial age and a period of rapid immigration, there were good, well paying jobs in heavy industry—steel, automobiles, and manufacturing. Only basic skills were required for these jobs. Even drop outs had these basic skills. Moreover, the new bureaucratic form of work organization had managers at the top making most of the strategic and operational decisions that required a high level of skills. Managers constituted a small proportion of the workforce and the percentage of students tracked into a higher learning curriculum provided a sufficient supply of college education and skilled management talent.

An integral part of this economic and education strategy was a psychological theory that highlighted ability and learning differences across students, thus "justifying" the explicit and what became an implicit tracking structure. The result was unequal access to a rich curriculum, unequal levels of learning, and in the longer run, unequal access to the labor market and thus unequal wages. The system worked for the economy of the day, but was far from an equitable system for all.

As a result, one of the deep-seated tenets in the education system is that achievement cannot be the same since students will master different amounts of knowledge because of differences in ability. A deep-seated practice that supports the expectation of differential outcomes is the academic tracking of students that systematizes unequal access to curriculum and thus exacerbates learning differences (Oakes, 1985; Oakes & Lipton, 1990). Uprooting these practices will take Herculean efforts; producing higher levels of learning for all students will not be possible, though, unless these pernicious practices of differential expectations are eliminated.

From the equity perspective, therefore, the education reform imperative is to reconstitute the educational system so that it expects all students to learn complex subject matter, exposes all students to a rich curriculum and brings all students to high levels of learning and problem solving. This new vision is not only equitable, but also the democratic, American approach to schooling.

Summary

All three perspectives on the state of the American education support the need for dramatic improvement. Student achievement overall needs to rise to new levels, and all students need to become more proficient in mastering complex subject matter and applying that knowledge to practical problems in the world of work and home. As the Chapter 3 outlines, moreover, we now have the instruments in the education tool kit to move forward on these bold new education objectives. And as the next section outlines, several national initiatives already have been launched to begin this new journey of education reform.

A Final Note

The three rationales for education reform share our assumption that schools and the education system exist to improve the performance and educational conditions of children. The thrust of this book is essentially based on this assumption.

But there are other, more skeptical, perspectives on the purposes of schooling. Spring (1988; 1994) poses several other purposes. One is that the structure of the educational enterprise works to benefit and improve the conditions of those working in or on the system—teachers, administrators, political leaders, book publishers and test makers, and sellers. Under this view, the school system seeks to raise teacher salaries and lower their class sizes, to implement policies that make politicians look good, and to increase profits for companies making books and selling tests. While these purposes are not inherently "bad" they are not necessarily focused on or in the best interest of students.

Under this more critical perspective, another purpose of school is to reproduce the current social and economic order and not to provide equal opportunity for all. Indeed, this purpose can be seen in the Cardinal Principles that explicitly sought to use the schools to sort students into their roles in the economic order. Further, Tyack (1974) argued that in the name of education reform and progressive government, the creation of school boards as entities divorced from general government and "professional" administrators who ran school systems also gave control of school systems largely to white Anglo Saxon Protestant male managers, thereby curtailing the influence of minorities, Jews, Catholics, immigrants, workers, and those in poverty (see also Apple, 1990; Spring, 1994).

A related third view is that several politically disenfranchised groups have never had significant influence over the education system and have not been served well by the school system (Apple, 1991, 1993). Indeed, the persistent lower achievement of low income, minorities, and limited-English-proficient and immigrant background student (see Chapter 3) provides empirical support for this view. Adherents of this perspective, thus, have a hard time believing the current goal of teaching *all* students to high standards.

Final, anecdotal, and unpublished stories are emerging from several focus group and local reform groups around the country suggesting that not everyone wants the education system to teach all students to high standards. Many individuals in advantaged school districts allegedly state that such an accomplishment would make it more difficult for their children either to get into the best colleges or to get the best jobs. They like schools as they are and the education system as it is.

In short, there are other perspectives on the purposes of schooling that question the focus of this book, and of government policy at the federal and most state levels, of teaching all students to high standards. Having the educational system actually deliver on this ambitious goal would help to overcome these more critical and skeptical perspectives. But this goal accomplishment can be attained only if the political forces undergirding these other perspectives are overcome in restructuring the education system to serve all students well.

NATIONWIDE INITIATIVES

All perspectives on the conditions of the country's education system support the need to change the nation's schools. While there are different rationales for change, and different intensities to the impetus for change, all urge major improvements in public education. In part as a result, the country is experiencing a dizzying array of initiatives to change, improve, and restructure the nation's K–12 education system. These reform initiatives likely will continue to evolve during the 1990s. The overall thrust is to expose *all* students to ambitious curriculum programs and dramatically improve the cognitive skills of *all* public school students.

Although education in the United States has traditionally been under local and state control, the initiatives that began in the late 1980s are focused on developing a national, though not federal government, education policy. By the mid-1990s, these initiatives likely will have a major impact on states and localities across the U.S. This policy-making shift will represent a major contrast from the 1980s, when the states dominated education reform (Murphy, 1990b) and increased education expenditures 30 percent in real terms over the decade (Odden, 1992b).

The key concept of the 1990s education strategy is "nationwide" as contrasted with "federal government" policies. Neither a large array of mandated federal policies, nor a gigantic increase in federal aid (which currently provides only about 6 percent of total K–12 education expenditures [Odden and Picus, 1992]) is expected. Instead, the federal government will have a more indirect role, focused on supporting state and professional development of content, performance, and opportunity to learn standards, as embodied in Goals 2000 (see Chapter 10). By the end of the 1990s, the United States will *not* have a detailed national curriculum like that of France in the 1930s (Smith, O'Day and Cohen, 1991) but it very likely *will* have nationwide curriculum standards and subject matter frameworks (Smith, Fuhrman, and O'Day, 1994).

Before the new 1990s initiatives began, many examples of nationwide policy already existed, such as the SAT, the American College Testing (ACT) program, school accreditation (e.g., the North Central Association of Schools and Colleges), and the efforts of such organizations as the Education Commission of the States and the American Association of Colleges of Teacher Education. Although these policy-setting organizations did not represent a specific group of educators, they possessed the legitimacy to recommend or administer nationwide policies. In addition the United States, unlike many foreign nations, has a long tradition of voluntary, nonprofit, tax-exempt organizations, such as the College Board and the National Collegiate Athletic Association (NCAA), with the ability to administer nationwide policies. Nonprofit organizations likely will be the catalysts and designers of national curriculum, examination, and school restructuring experiments that will dominate the 1990s.

An Overview of the Major National Initiatives[1]

Several inter-related national initiatives have begun since the late 1980s. They tend to be focused on student outcomes, curriculum, and testing policies. They reflect both a rising professionalism within education as well as increased concern for the health of the public school on the part of state, federal, political (governors, legislators, Congress, and the President), and business leaders (e.g., the National Business Roundtable). Further, the key leaders of each tend to be integrally involved in many of the other initiatives as well, which both gives force to the impetus of the initiatives and provides informal coordination (Kirst and Odden, 1992–93). The major initiatives include the following.

Professional Group Creation of Curriculum Standards. In 1989, the National Council of Teachers of Mathematics (NCTM) issued ambitious curriculum standards of what students in grades 1–12 should know and be able to do in mathematics. Their report (NCTM, 1989) represented a breakthrough consensus among educational and mathematical professionals on standards for a national mathematics curriculum. The report set ambitious, high—some would say world class—standards, not watered down agreement on a minimalist mathematics program. The report called for all students to develop mathematical problem-solving and reasoning abilities, understanding of the basic mathematics principles, and the ability to use and apply mathematical knowledge. The report did not identify day-to-day mathematical tasks, but identified what students should know and be able to do after certain longer term time periods, such as after grades 1–4, 5–8 and 9–12. Several other professional groups are now developing curriculum standards for other content including the National Science Teachers Association (1989), the National Council of Teachers of English, as well as Project 2061 of the American Association for the Advancement of Science (1989). History standards are being developed by the Center for the Study of History at the University of California, Los Angeles, California. In the early 1990s, a second round of content standards

---

[1]Portions of the following appeared in Kirst & Odden (1992–93).

activities were begun (Massell & Kirst, 1994); standards are being developed in mathematics, science, language arts, history, civics, geography, social studies, foreign language, the arts, and economics.

These initiatives are important for two critical reasons. First, they are national and represent a developing professionalism within education. The experts within each field are, through a widespread but expert-lead consensus developmental process, identifying standards for what students should learn in school in the different content areas, and the standards they are developing are ambitious. Second, the standards become the linchpin around which many additional initiatives are connected. Put differently, high quality curriculum standards are the professional and substantive drivers of most of the other national actions, such as new student testing strategies.

National Certification of Teachers. Beginning in 1994, a new National Board for Professional Teaching Standards (NBPTS) will begin a national program of board certification of teachers. The NBPTS, based in Detroit, Michigan, is an outcome of the Carnegie Report to professionalize the teaching profession (Carnegie Forum on Education and the Economy, 1986). NBPTS has a 60-some member board, two-thirds of whom are teachers. NBPTS certification will be based on evidence of what teachers know and are able to do, defined as being able to teach the various national curriculum standards that are being developed. Board certification will be different from any current teacher evaluations and will feature demonstrated competency in school settings and the ability to adapt subject matter to diverse students (e.g., teach fractions to sixth graders in poverty impacted areas or who have limited English proficiency). NBPTS assessments stress teachers' knowledge of their students and demonstrated ability to work with other teachers to improve local schools.

New Forms of Student Testing. Several efforts have been inaugurated to transform the way student learning is assessed from moving away from standardized testing of fragmented pieces of knowledge to performance testing in which students demonstrate through projects and portfolios what they know and can do. One effort is the New Standards Project, in Rochester, New York (NPS, funded by the Pew Memorial Trust, in Philadelphia, Pennsylvania, and the MacArthur Foundation in Chicago, Illinois. NPS is charged with building a national consensus for educational assessments, that would be taken by all students, in five core subject areas (the same as national Goal 3). NPS is codirected by Marc Tucker of the National Center on Education and the Economy and Lauren Resnick of the Learning and Research Development Center at the University of Pittsburgh (Resnick, 1992–93). Tucker had been a major education reform leader (O'Neil, 1992) and Resnick a prominent cognitive psychologist (Resnick, 1987). NPS is also designing examinations that will have "high stakes" and compatibility with national curriculum standards. Mathematics will most likely be the first subject area developed, and the examination will be based on the NCTM standards.

Another testing activity is the National Assessment of Educational Progress (NAEP). NAEP has conducted periodic national assessments of student achievement in core subject areas since the 1970s (Mullis, Owen, and

Phillips, 1990; National Center for Educational Statistics, 1993c, 1993d). NAEP is funded by the federal government and is overseen by the U.S. Department of Education. The Educational Testing Service (ETS) is the federal contractor that through the "nation's report card" has identified student achievement changes in curricular subjects like science and foreign language using three-year updates from a national sample of students.

While NAEP has *not* been based on national curricular standards or frameworks, key members of the various curriculum professional associations have participated in the development of NAEP tests. For the first time in 1990, moreover, NAEP provided state-by-state comparisons on student achievement in eighth grade mathematics (interstate NAEP). In 1992, state comparisons were provided for eighth grade mathematics and reading, and fourth grade mathematics. In 1994, science was added and three grade levels were assessed. NAEP will continue at least in the short run as an overall measure of educational attainment at the national and state level, and likely will evolve to be more aligned with national curriculum standards. Its increasingly comprehensive state comparison data will give it strong influence on states and the directions of a national curriculum.

There are several other interstate compact consortiums developing new approaches to testing what students know and can do. One is coordinated by the Council of Chief State School Officers, the national organization of the chief education official in each state. The overall goal of this and all other projects is both to transform how student achievement is assessed and to link student testing to high quality curriculum standards, hopefully those embodied in national curriculum frameworks.

Reinforcing Political Initiatives. Several initiatives started by political leaders undergird as well as stimulate these more professional activities. The most prominent is the National Education Goals Panel (NEGP) which resulted from the 1989 Summit that brought together the President and the 50 state governors to discuss the national interest in education. One key outcome of the Summit was the first ever national education goals (Table 1-1).

NEGP was created to monitor the nation's progress towards the goals. As originally constituted, the Panel included six members from the Bush Administration, six governors (three Republicans and three Democrats), and Congressional leaders but only as ex officio members. In 1992, the NEGP was expanded to include members of Congress and other public members. The National Governors' Association (NGA) had been active in elaborating national education goals, and played a major role in measuring and reporting how well the U.S. was meeting these goals (NGA, 1991). In 1991, the NEGP issued its first report on the status of the nation in accomplishing the national goals, including state-by-state progress reports (NEGP, 1991). Reports were also issued in 1992 and 1993 (NEGP, 1992, 1993).

A second political body was the National Council on Education Standards and Testing (NCEST) created by Congress to determine the feasibility and desirability of establishing national curriculum standards and national student assessment programs. NCEST consisted of a thirty-member bipartisan board co-chaired by the same governors who initially led the NEGP: Roy Romer of Colorado and Carroll Campbell of South Carolina. The NCEST Board members, Table 1-2 were an example of the emerging national coalition of political and education leaders at the forefront of these national initiatives. NCEST's January 1992 report (NCEST, 1992) advocated establishing national curriculum standards and student examinations, but linked to the curriculum standards

TABLE 1-2. Members of the Original National Council on Educational Standards and Testing

Co-Chairs

Governor Carroll A. Campbell, Jr.	Governor Roy Romer
South Carolina (R)	*Colorado (D)*

Members

Gordon Ambach	Council of Chief State School Officers
Eva L. Baker	University of California, Los Angeles, Calif.
Brian L. Benzel	Edmonds School District, Washington
Mary Bicouvaris	Hampton Roads Academy, Virginia
U.S. Senator Jeff Bingaman	Committee on Labor and Human Resources (D-New Mexico)
Eve M. Bither	Maine State Department of Education
Iris Carl	National Council of Teachers of Mathematics
Lynne V. Cheney	National Endowment for the Humanities
State Senator Carols Cisneros	New Mexico Senate
Ramon C. Cortines	San Francisco Unified School District
Chester E. Finn, Jr.	Vanderbilt University, Nashville, Tenn.
Martha Fricke	Ashland School Board, Nebraska, former President National School Boards Association
Keith Geiger	National Education Association
U.S. Representative William Goodling	Committee on Education and Labor (R-Penn.)
State Senator John Hainkel	Louisiana Senate
Sandra Hassan	Beach Channel High School, New York
U.S. Senator Orrin Hatch	Committee on Labor and Human Resources (R-Utah)
David Hornbeck	David W. Hornbeck and Associates
David Kearns	U.S. Department of Education, former CEO Xerox
U.S. Representative Dale E. Kildee	Committee on Education and Labor (D-Michigan)
Walter Massey	National Science Foundation
Edward L. Meyen	University of Kansas, Lawrence, Kans.
Mark Musick	Southern Regional Education Board
Michael Nettles	University of Tennessee
Sally B. Pancrazio	Illinois State University, Normal, Ill.
Roger B. Porter	The White House
Lauren Besnick	University of Pittsburgh, Pittsburgh, Pa.
Roger Semerad	RJR Nabisco
Albert Shanker	American Federation of Teachers
Marshall S. Smith	Stanford University, Stanford, Calif.

being developed by groups such as the NCTM. Unlike NEGP, NCEST had Congressional authorization and participation, thus expanding the coalition beyond the 50 governors and the former Presidential Administration.

NCEST recommended that it be succeeded by a new entity, the National Education Standards and Assessment Council (NESAC), with responsibilities for oversight and quality assurance for the development of curriculum standards and a national student examination system. This panel, under a slightly revised name (the National Education Standards and Improvement Council [NESIC]) was enacted in early 1994 when the Congress passed the Clinton Administration's Goals 2000 federal education reform program, which also made the national goals formal education policy for the U.S. (see Chapter 10).

Another prominent political initiative was creation of the New American Schools Development Corporation (NASDC), as a follow-through project of President Bush's America 2000 program (The White House, 1991). In that program, the President supported world class curriculum standards, high-stakes testing, federal funding for break-the-mold schools to be developed by NASDC, and a continuation of NAEP. President Bush also contended that private or public school voucher programs were compatible with national standards and examinations; parents could make more informed choices using vouchers in public or private schools if they could compare schools on results from a national examination. But while the voucher proposals did not gain support, NASDC was created and began functioning in late 1991.

NASDC's board was composed primarily of large American businesses that were funding several "break-the-mold" school design experiments aimed at producing dramatically different school organizations. All schools funded must implement the world class curriculum standards in the core subject areas specified in NEGP and NCEST and being developed by the professional associations. NASDC hoped to provide $200 million in privately funded school experiments between 1992 and 1996, and in 1992 committed about $25 million for 11 teams to design break-the-mold schools. The NASDC schools were supported by Bill Clinton after he became elected President in 1992 and by early 1994 NASDC was more than half towards its fund raising goal.

Finally, in 1994, the Congress enacted President Clinton's Goals 2000 systemic education reform initiative, which puts the federal government officially behind the development of many of the above initiatives (see Chapter 10). This action carries with it federal support for the nation to design and implement a systemic education reform program (Smith and O'Day, 1991), all designed to produce new and high levels of student achievement.

The political momentum behind these national efforts is impressive and growing. The pressure for national changes is *not* solely top-down, but rather is coming from all directions including political leaders, business, professional associations, universities,[2] and school districts. Political support for these initiatives is broad and included both 1992 presidential contenders, the past and

[2]Systemic reform was coined by the Consortium for Policy Research (CPRE), a collaboration among Rutgers, the State University, New Brunswick, N.J. University of Southern California, Los Angeles, Calif. Harvard University, Cambridge, Mass. Michigan State University, East Lansing, Mich. Stanford University, Stanford, Calif., and the University of Wisconsin-Madison, Madison, Wis.

current President, the Congress, the nation's governors, both teachers unions (National Education Association and American Federation of Teachers), as well as the National School Boards Association.

Despite this momentum for national reform, obstacles remain significant. Although resistance based on local control of schools appears to be crumbling, the organizational issues associated with coming to consensus on curriculum standards are complex. The technical issues of designing examinations of student learning linked to the curriculum standards are more than complex and require new advancements in psychometrics. Maintaining political support and funding will not be easy at either the federal or state levels.

Nevertheless, these national initiatives reflect an emerging consensus on what will be emphasized nationally by several bodies during the 1990s as an overall strategy for accomplishing major school changes designed to produce measurable improvements in student learning, and advance the nation's bold education goals (Business Roundtable, 1991; National Alliance for Business, 1990; NGA, 1990; 1993; Smith and O'Day, 1991):

- Clear student-learning outcome goals (i.e., what students should know and be able to do).
- A high-quality curriculum.
- Site-based management, allowing teachers to exert substantial influence over implementation of education programs.
- A monitoring system, calibrated to world class standards, that indicates the degree to which objectives are being accomplished.
- A sharp-edged accountability system with real rewards and sanctions.

How the specifics of these strategies affect the course of education will evolve only as the 1990s unfold.

But the above national, professional, and political initiatives represent several new departures for education policy, especially at the state and local level, and suggest that education leaders will need to contend with and contribute actively to these activities throughout the 1990s. In fact, one purpose of this book is to help prepare school leaders to aggressively engage in these issues and to embrace the need to overhaul the nation's school systems. To do so, leaders need to be informed and knowledgeable. They need to know the breadth and depth of these complex issues, and must possess a wide array of knowledge in order to make substantive contributions towards their resolution.

THE TRADITIONS OF EDUCATION REFORM IN THE UNITED STATES

While the national initiatives just discussed arguably represent new departures for education reform, they follow a century and a half-old tradition of education reform in this country. In the United States, interest in education reform often is a symbol for wrestling with national problems and even redefining national purpose (Popkewitz, 1988; Tyack, 1991). For example, education reform often emerges as a policy topic when the United States is falling behind in international competition, such as in response to the growing power of Germany at the turn of this century, the cold war and rise of the Soviet Union in the 1950s, and the economic might of the Japanese in the 1980s (Tyack, 1991). At other times, education reform derives from broader issues internal to the United States, such as business calls for centralization and bureaucracy to reflect the growing industrial economy at the beginning of the twentieth century and the focus on civil rights in the 1960s (Tyack, 1991).

In other words, education reform often is one of the vehicles through which the country addresses broader issues. The national initiatives discussed above reflect this pattern since its key proponents view better education as a key to restoring the productivity of the U.S. economy. Since the nation always is addressing problems, education reform becomes a recurrent theme, never fully off the policy agenda. Thus, each period of education reform, including that of the 1990s, follows in a long tradition of linking education improvements to improving the nation; the specific emphases may represent new departures for that reform period, but reform in general is not a stranger either to the educational community or to the country. Put another way, the history of education is the history of education reform (Warren, 1990).

This long, persistent, and somewhat predictable history of education reform, nevertheless, has produced several reactions among educators. Some respond to ever present reform proposals with cynicism, often arguing that current proposals were tried years ago with no major impacts. Such individuals continue to implement current practice believing that reform momentum will pass and the impetus for change will abate. Others respond with some degree of enthusiasm, arguing that many current proposals are new and different, would substantially improve schools and make education better for kids. They seek to implement reform proposals by working hard to change classroom and school practice. A third response is characterized by the "silver bullet" approach; this response argues that a specific program can resolve the school systems' problems. A fourth approach claims that not only schools but the total society does not work, and a societal restructuring must occur before schools can hope to change. And there are numerous responses in between these different viewpoints on reform.

A reasonable question to ask is whether reform ever makes a difference. Does reform ever "work?" Does the persistence of education reform rhetoric mean the schools change dramatically as each period of reform programs are enacted or have educational practices remained constant despite periods of new policy talk? Much research has been conducted to answer this question.

In his analyses of reform, Cuban (1988; 1990) makes a distinction between first- and second-order school changes. First-order changes entail improvements in the current system; an example would be the increase in high school graduation requirements typically part of reform packages in the early 1980s (Fuhrman, Clune, and Elmore, 1988). Such reforms are easier to implement because they require only modest changes in the current structure. Second-order changes, however, require fundamental changes and turn out to be more difficult to implement. A current example would be teaching a thinking-oriented curriculum. An example of the past would be the mathematics and science curriculum reforms proposed after the Russians launched the Sputnik satellite in 1957; few of these programs remain (Atkin and House, 1981). Cuban

(1985) suggests that changes in pedagogy and curriculum face the most difficult implementation challenges but that both pedagogical and structural reforms can succeed, such as for example, kindergarten (Cuban, 1992).

Anecdotal evidence suggests that some reforms work and others do not. It is possible to argue that schools have not changed that much; further, there are many examples of failed reforms such as the Dewey-based schools of the Progressive Era, the 1950s National Science Foundation mathematics and science curriculum reforms, career education, nongraded classrooms, open classroom schools, differentiated staffing, and merit pay. The classroom still includes 20–30 children with one teacher, usually lecturing. The textbook is the key determinant of the curriculum. The emphasis is primarily on basic skills. Children are pretty much organized into grade level, same age classes (see Cohen, 1993). Districts have elementary (K–6), junior high (grades 7–9) and high (grades 10–12) schools. Districts make most of the educational, personnel, and fiscal decisions.

But other evidence suggests that some reforms did work and produced substantial change. In 1910 high school attendance was not mandatory with only 10 percent graduating from high school. In 1990, about 85 percent graduated from high school and attendance was mandatory and had been for over 50 years. Today, handicapped students are entitled to a free and appropriate education whereas 50 years ago most were not allowed to enroll in public schools. Schools today must be integrated; sports activities and resources must be made available equally to girls and boys. Free kindergarten is provided by all states. On the curriculum side, there also are changes. Most school campuses have computers. Cooperative learning groups are expanding. Teaching for thinking is at least the goal. Many textbooks have been substantially changed and now include real literature, historical documents, and include contributions reflecting the diversity of the American culture. In short, the answer is that American public schools can be characterized by both change and constancy (e.g., Cuban, 1985).

Kirst and Meister (1985), Tyack (1991), and Cuban (1992) suggest that while not all reforms succeed, reforms that last have several characteristics. First, they usually are structural add-ons that do not disturb the standard operating procedures of the regular program. Examples are vocational and physical education which literally became housed in new structural wings of schools. Second, they have constituencies who provide political support and who lobby for their continuation. Examples from the past include driver's education which originally was supported by both car manufacturing and insurance companies. More current examples are categorical programs such as special and bilingual education. Third, reforms designed by teachers and administrators themselves such as graded schools and increases in teacher certification requirements tend to last. Fourth, reforms that last can be easily identified and measured, such as counts of pupils eligible for different categorical programs. Fifth, reforms that last usually become part of state laws and regulations. Home economics, physical education, and special education again are examples.

In general, Cuban, Kirst, and Tyack argue that structural changes are easier to make than curriculum and pedagogical changes, but all three argue that over time many reforms, even pedagogical (Cuban, 1985), have changed schools substantially. Tyack (1991) makes a distinction between "policy talk," the period of reform discussion, policy proposals, and new program development, and "institutional practice," the period over which change can occur. His key point is that policy talk can occur in distinct periods, such as the education reforms of the 1980s, but the impacts of those policies take decades and, thus, assessment of change in practice must occur over a much longer time period.

This conclusion by an education historian is bolstered by longer term assessments of education policy implementation (Kirst and Jung, 1980; Odden, 1991a). Implementation studies show that while the structural reforms of the 1960s and 1970s categorical programs were initially battered on the implementation shoals of local districts by the end of a decade they were firmly in place. Moreover, while most pedagogical reforms have faced difficulty in being implemented, the curriculum and teaching reforms of the early 1980s changed practice much more quickly than most predicted (see also Fuhrman, Clune, and Elmore, 1988).

The latter finding provides some basis for optimism for the proposed 1990s reforms, which at heart are curriculum and instruction-oriented. Even using the Cuban, Kirst, and Tyack criterias for reforms that last, one could be optimistic. First, as the above section on national initiatives shows, the substance of many of the 1990s reforms are being designed by education professionals themselves. Second, the constituency lobbying for the reforms are the political elites of the country—the President, the 50 state governors, chief executive officers of the largest corporations, and even the Congress and state legislators. Surely these groups represent a powerful reform lobby. Third, the standards being developed for new curriculum frameworks and the new forms of performance-based student assessment being developed to track progress represent measures that both describe the reforms and indicate impacts. Fourth, new curriculum standards and new student assessments are being enacted into state laws and regulations at relatively rapid rates, at least in the early 1990s. Finally, the 1990s reforms also include new structural elements—school restructuring, site-based management, public school choice, national board teacher certification from a new professional organization, etc. While optimism can be justified, the reforms also represent second-order changes that require fundamental alternations in professional practice within schools and classrooms, reforms that have the most difficulty being implemented.

Whatever the course of previous education reforms, institutionalizing the 1990s reforms will require hard work. Evidence of change in institutional practice will at best, according to Tyack (1991), gradually emerge over the next decade or two. As Elmore and McLaughlin (1990) eloquently state, education reform is "steady work."

THE CURRENT STRUCTURE OF EDUCATION GOVERNANCE

One reason education reform takes time to change school and classroom practice is the fragmented and, some might argue, unwieldly education governance structure. Unlike most other countries in the world which have a national education system, education in the United States constitutionally is a state function. Thus, the country has 50 different state education systems; even territories and commonwealths have their own unique education systems. In addition, all states except Hawaii have delegated administration of education to local districts. Each local district, moreover, has a local school board consisting primarily of individuals from the public at large, usually without substantive expertise in education, who have the authority and responsibility to make education policy. In September 1991, there were 15,344 local school districts (National Education Association, 1992) governed by about 100,000 school board members, most elected by the public.

This fragmented structure has produced a relatively conservative and slow moving system. Neither the national government nor even state governments can summarily "mandate" changes. Indeed, nearly all federal education initiatives must move through each of the 50 state systems before they reach local districts. Before they finally affect schools and classrooms, therefore, they are administered by three governmental bureaucracies—the U.S. Department of Education, the state education department, and the local district central office. Each bureaucracy adds its set of rules, regulations, and requirements to such initiatives, which often can make the programs look quite different once they reach either the district or school level.

This complex, federal structure was consciously designed to limit the influence of state and federal governments on local education programs. In the early years of this country, schools were primarily private and church run; state education systems did not exist and there was no federal education role. Beginning in the midnineteenth century, the country, through the efforts of such education leaders as Horace Mann, the chief education officer in Massachusetts, created the Common School. This was an effort to develop, through education, a common core of learning and common set of cultural understandings among the nation's young children. In the latter half of that century, those events culminated in the creation of state education systems, with state constitutions requiring the provision of free, public education and creating a common set of requirements for teacher certification, school accreditation, and school financing.

Since schooling began as a local and private responsibility, these system creating efforts were always accompanied by support for "local control" of the curriculum program. Indeed, the centralizing thrusts were by design offset or curtailed by creation of local school districts which were given explicit control over curriculum and responsibility for actually providing educational services. As the history of governmental incursion into education policy evolved from 1850 to 1950, and even into the latter half of the twentieth century, however, the story is one of increased control by higher level governments, first local districts, then states, and in this century the federal government (Kaestle and Smith, 1982). Until the Education Summit of 1989, however, rising centralization was counter balanced by continued support for local control over curriculum, instruction, and testing.

As this chapter has argued, this tacit agreement was rewritten during the 1989 Education Summit and its progeny of national initiatives. Today, the country has its first ever national education goals, seems to have embarked on a course to develop national curriculum standards, and may even create a national student testing system (National Council on Educational Standards and Testing, 1992), which certainly represent a modification of, if not a major break with traditional notions of local control. As one pundit opined, "At the 1989 education summit, the President and 50 state governors looked local control in the eyes and local control *blinked*." Unless the national initiatives discussed earlier in this chapter significantly abate, local control as conventionally understood is a reality of the past.

These sea changes significantly alter notions of the traditional roles of different levels of government, but again follow in the footsteps of continued education reform and gradual centralization of education governance. In the first half of the twentieth century, the tacit governance agreement was that local districts administered education programs and controlled the curriculum; states licensed teachers, accredited schools, and provided a base-funding level; and the federal government did quite little—gathered and published educational statistics and supported research. At times, the federal government undertook new educational initiatives in the national interest, such as creating a vocational education program in the early twentieth century to spur development of the industrial economy.

This common understanding of the roles of the various government levels began to change again in the 1950s and 1960s, but new federal initiatives were still justified as being in the national interest. The National Defense Education Act and related programs were rationalized as a response to the growing threats of the Cold War, and the 1960s new categorical programs, such as the Elementary and Secondary Education Act of 1965 and desegregation requirements, were part of the national equity agenda to reduce poverty and eliminate discrimination.

In the 1970s, a rising state role was reflected by major changes in state school finance programs, which redefined the state fiscal role from simply providing a base funding for all districts to addressing the fundamental causes of resource differences across districts and even the equity of the overall state and local tax system (Odden & Picus, 1992). The 1970s also saw states designing their own versions of categorical programs for special needs students, such as students from low-income families, limited English proficient students, handicapped students, etc. Nevertheless, federal and state initiatives from the 1950s to 1970s still kept an arms length from curriculum, which at least rhetorically remained under local control.

The 1980s education reforms, spurred by a federal report but led by state actions (Fuhrman, Clune, and Elmore, 1988), began the process of piercing the armor of local curriculum control. These reforms contained substantial new requirements for curriculum and instruction, including increased high school graduation requirements, toughened curriculum standards, and new student testing programs (Firestone, Fuhrman, and Kirst, 1989). The Education Summit at the end of the decade continued the assault on local curriculum control by creating a national set of education goals, which was followed early in the 1990s with proposals for national curriculum standards. This bursting of the local curriculum control bubble, moreover, was not just the result of political actions but also, as discussed in previous sections, caused by a rising professionalism within education, exemplified by the publication and wide dissemination of national standards for school mathematics (National Council of Teachers of Mathematics, 1989).

Despite these centralizing and curriculum-oriented national initiatives, the formal education governance structure remains the same—50 state education systems, 15,344 local school districts, and a national government with strong interests and no formal education control mechanism. Thus, one of the additional issues that must also be tackled during the 1990s is the governance of the education system. Can the current federal, fragmented system withstand the nationalizing assaults? How will it and how should it change? Will more choice characterize the education system in the near future? What are the new roles of local districts when education goals, curriculum standards, and testing systems are developed outside of their control and even influence?

In short, the 1990s should be an exciting period of continued changes in education. Goals, curriculum, testing, and governance likely will be different in the year 2000 than in 1990 which was certainly different from 1980. Whether for economic or equity reasons, the push for dramatic change in public schools will continue. Ultimately, these restructurings could produce large changes in educational governance as well (Elmore, 1991), since the country's long-standing notions of local curriculum control already have been altered. As the next chapter shows, moreover, the students also will be different which in itself requires significant changes in education.

American Students: Who They Are and What They Know

For years, America equated the term "family" with an idealized Norman Rockwell version: a working husband, mother at home, and two to three children, generally Caucasian. Most schools organized programs assuming that family structure was in place. In 1950, 60 percent (only) of households were characterized by these qualities. By 1980, those characteristics applied to only 11 percent of families, a percentage which dropped to only 7 percent by 1985 (Hodgkinson, 1985). In the 1980s, the country began (finally) to understand that the nature of the American family had changed.

Further, the country also became more aware of the declining conditions of children. In 1985, Hodgkinson wrote that for every 100 children born, 12 would be born out of wedlock, 40 would be born to parents who would divorce before the child was 18, five would be born to parents who would separate, two would be born to parents one of whom would die before the child was 18, and only 41 would reach the age of 18 in a family unit defined traditionally as a husband and wife with children.

In addition to these conditions, the changing nature of student ethnicity became more known as the student population became characterized by rising numbers and percentages of minorities and immigrants. These new realities about the nature of family life and the conditions of children will continue to evolve during the 1990s. Schools must recognize and consider these changed conditions as they create educational experiences, especially those that connect the school with the home.

As the changing conditions of children solidified more clearly in the minds of the American public, so also did the realities of student achievement. The declining test score phenomenon of the 1970s was paralleled by similarly dismal results of international comparisons of student achievement in the 1980s. Nearly all reports (e.g., LaPointe, Mead, and Phillips, 1989) showed American students scoring at the bottom of international assessments of student achievement, not only below Japan, but also below developing countries such as Korea and then-communist bloc countries such as Hungary.

This chapter reviews these conditions of children. The first section profiles the demographics of school age children from 1960 to 1990, and provides some projections into the twenty-first century. Section two places rising student diversity into an historical perspective. Section three provides a quick overview of policies and programs created for special needs students and the types of programs that could accomplish the national goal of making all five-year-olds "ready to learn" by the year 2000. The last section provides an overview of the status of student achievement in the early 1990s, the baseline from which the country must work to dramatically increase student achievement by the year 2000.

CHARACTERISTICS OF THE SCHOOL AGE POPULATION

Growth characterized public school enrollments in nearly every decade of the twentieth century until 1970 when suddenly enrollments began to drop and continued dropping throughout the decade. Even though these changes surprised school people, they were predictable and known to demographers who predicted future school enrollments from information on publicly available birth data. In the 1980s, again to the surprise of many school people, enrollments began once more to rise in some states such as California which grew about 200,000 students per year (Guthrie, Kirst, and Odden, 1991) but were stable or declining in other states. The 1990s will be characterized by growth at the beginning of the decade and then decline as the country moves into the twenty-first century. This section profiles these and other characteristics of the school age population.

Table 2-1 provides total population and school age population data from 1960 to 1990. While the total population grew during each ten-year time period, the school age population grew during only one decade—the 1960s. The school age population dropped from 1970 to 1980, and then declined again (although only slightly) from 1980 to 1990. As a result, the school age population as a percent of total population declined each decade. While the school age population was 24.7 percent of the total population in 1960 and rose to 25.8 percent in the 1970, it dropped to 20.8 percent in 1980 and down to 18.2 percent in 1990. As the percentage of children dropped, the percentage of older

TABLE 2-1. Total Population and School Age Population 1960 to 1990

Population (thousands)	1960	1970	1980	1990
Total[a]	179,979	203,984	227,255	249,415
School age				
Age 5–17	44,177 (24.7)[a]	52,593 (25.8)[a]	47,238 (20.8)[a]	45,310 (18.2)[a]
Age 5–13	32,966	36,672	31,096	31,999
Age 14–17	11,211	15,921	16,140	13,311

[a]Percentage of total population.
Source: From NCES (1992), Table 14.

Americans grew. Since numbers in part reflect political power, the political ramifications of these demographic realities were increased political power for older Americans and decreased political power for children.

While the total school age population grew during the 1960s and declined during the 1970s and 1980s, there were different patterns for K–8 versus high school students. Elementary age students initially followed the overall pattern, rising in the 1960s and then falling in the 1970s. But the number of children aged 5 to 13 began to rise in the 1980s producing growth for elementary schools. On the other hand, high school enrollments grew in the 1960s, continued to grow in the 1970s, but then declined in the 1980s.

Thus, overall patterns of the school age population camouflage variations underneath. Indeed, not only are changes in the school age population different for elementary versus secondary students, but also they are different across the states. For example, student enrollment growth (and also growth of the total population) is a phenomenon primarily for southern and western states, while nearly all of the midwestern and eastern states continue to experience decline. In fact, over half of total population and most of the school age population growth during the 1980s occurred in three states: California, Florida, and Texas (Hodgkinson, 1992).

Differences between elementary and secondary, and public versus private school growth patterns are shown in Table 2-2. In terms of total enrollments, Table 2-2 shows that enrollments dropped from 1976 until the mid-1980s, and then should increase throughout the 1990s until the year 2000. The projected change between 1995 and 2000 is small and suggests relative enrollment stability (growing a very small amount). The patterns are somewhat different for K–8 versus grades 9–12 enrollments. K–8 enrollments declined from 1976 to 1980, and then stayed relatively constant (growing a tiny amount) during the last half of the 1980s. They are expected to grow between 1990 and 1995 and then stay about the same (declining a small bit) through 2000. Grades 9–12 enrollments, on the other hand, fell over the entire 15-year period from 1976 through 1990, but reflecting the aging of the elementary cohort, are predicted to rise throughout the 1990s, reaching a new peak by the year 2000. Thus, while enrollments overall in the latter half of the 1990s will be relatively stable, they

TABLE 2-2. Public and Private School Enrollments with Projections, Fall 1976 to Fall 2000 (thousands)

	Total	*Total* K–8	9–12	*Public* Total	K–8	9–12	*Private* Total	K–8	9–12
1976[a]	49,484	33,831	15,653	44,317	30,006	14,311	5,167	3,825	1,342
1980[a]	46,249	31,669	14,581	40,918	27,677	13,242	5,331	3,992	1,339
1985[a]	44,979	31,225	13,754	39,422	27,030	12,392	5,557	4,195	1,362
1990[b]	46,192	33,765	12,427	40,801	29,546	11,255	5,391	4,219	1,172
1995[b]	49,431	35,496	13,935	43,682	31,061	12,621	5,749	4,435	1,314
2000[b]	49,976	35,145	14,830	44,186	30,754	13,432	5,790	4,391	1,398

[a]Actual years.
[b]Projected years.
Source: From Gerald and Hassan (1991a), Table 1.

will be a combination of a slight elementary decline and a solid secondary increase.

These patterns are somewhat different for both public and private schools. First, while total enrollments dropped from 1976 to 1985 and then are projected to increase until 2000, Table 2-2 shows that private school enrollments grew at the end of the 1970s, throughout the 1980s and are projected to continue growing during the 1990s as well, suggesting that more students will be attending private schools. Converting private school enrollments to a percentage of total enrollments, the results show that the percentage of students attending private schools rose from 10.5 percent in 1976 to a peak of 12.4 percent in 1985, and then should stabilize at about 11.6 percent throughout the 1990s. While this reflects an increase, it is small and the bulk of students will enroll in public schools, as has been the pattern during the twentieth century.

Public school enrollments fell from 1976 to 1985, and then began to slowly increase and are expected to increase during the decade of the 1990s. But the overall increase is projected to be a combination of K–8 enrollment increases that will peak in 1995 and then fall somewhat during the last half of the decade, and grades 9–12 enrollment increases throughout the decade, after decline during the 15-year period from 1976 to 1990.

Table 2-3 shows that student enrollments also have changed their ethnic composition during the three decades from 1960 to 1990. In 1960, white students comprised 86.8 percent of all school age children; that figure had dropped to 80.1 percent by 1990 and is projected to fall throughout the 1990s. African-American school age children rose from 12.2 percent in 1960 to 15.3 percent in 1990. Other races also are increasing as shown in Table 2-3.

Using census figures and official government projections, Hodgkinson (1992) shows that by the year 2000, while total children aged 0–17 will continue to increase, white children will decrease by 3.8 million, while minority children will increase by 4.4 million, a combination of 2.6 million children of Hispanic origin, 1.2 million African-American children, and 0.6 children from other races. Thus, school enrollments will be even more heavily minority at the close of the 1990s than they are today.

Again the minority characteristics of youth changes dramatically by state. According to Hodgkinson (1992), while minorities will constitute 10 percent or less of all youth in 11 states by the year 2010, minorities will constitute large, *majority* percentages in 11 states and the District of Columbia: 93.2 percent in

TABLE 2-3. School Age Population by Ethnicity, 1960 to 1990

Population	1960	1970	1980	1990
School Age (Age 5–17)				
Total	44,177	52,593	47,238	45,166
White	38,336 (86.8)	44,783 (85)	39,001 (82.6)	36,221 (80.2)
African-American	5,366 (12.1)	7,108 (13.5)	6,996 (14.8)	6,894 (15.3)
Other Minorities	446 (1.1)	703 (1.5)	1,238 (2.6)	2,051 (4.5)

Note: Values in parentheses are percentages of the total population.
Source: From NCES (1992), Table 15.

Washington, DC, 80 percent in Hawaii, 57 percent in California and Texas, 53 percent in Florida and New York, 50 percent in Louisiana and Mississippi, and between 40 and 49 percent in Illinois, Maryland, New Jersey, and South Carolina. These states, it is interesting to note, include seven of the nine states in which half of the population of the entire United States resides.

To the degree numbers of people translate into political power, nationally there could be political power behind the policies needed to address the rising minority characteristics of youth in general, as well as children enrolled in schools. But most African-American children live in central cities, which have lost power to the suburbs, and the South, which also has lost political power. Hispanics, however, are concentrated in California, Florida, and Texas, three of the largest four states which alone by the year 2000 are projected to have 112 of the 435 seats in the U.S. House of Representatives, a sizable political bloc (Hodgkinson, 1992).

Table 2-4 shows that the family context of children and students, in addition to their ethnic character, also has changed over time. First, the percentage

TABLE 2-4. Family and Poverty Status of Children Under 18, 1960 to 1990

	1960	1970	1980	1990
Families with children under 18				
Percent of married couples				
Total	N/A	89	80	76%
White	N/A	N/A	N/A	81%
African-American	N/A	N/A	N/A	45%
Hispanic	N/A	N/A	N/A	72%
Percent of female-headed				
Total	N/A	10	18	20%
White	N/A	N/A	N/A	16%
African-American	N/A	N/A	N/A	51%
Hispanic	N/A	N/A	N/A	24%
Percent of married couples with income below poverty level				
Total	26.5	14.9	17.9	19.9
White	20.0	10.5	13.4	15.1
African-American	65.5	41.5	42.1	44.2
Hispanic	N/A	33.1[a]	33.0	37.7
Percent of female-headed families with income below poverty level				
Total	68.4	53.0	50.8	53.4
White	59.9	43.1	41.6	45.9
African-American	81.6[b]	67.7	64.8	64.7
Hispanic	N/A	68.4[a]	65.0	68.4

[a]1975
[b]1959
Source: NCES (1991), Table 17; NCES (1992), Table 19

of children in families headed by a married couple has fallen, from 89 percent in 1970 to 76 percent in 1990. The percentage in 1990 was less than 50 percent for African-American children. Since many married couples in 1990 had previously divorced and remarried, the figures overstate the stability of a two-parent family for children. Over the same time period, the percentage of children in single, female-headed families doubled, moving from 10 percent in 1970 to 20 percent in 1990. The 1990 figure was nearly one-fourth for children in female-headed Hispanic families and just over 50 percent for female-headed African-American families. In short, the trend is for fewer children to live in families headed by married couples, and for more children to live in families headed by females. The numbers are larger for minority children.

Table 2-4 also shows that these trends in conditions of families have economic consequences as well. While family poverty declined from 1960 to 1970, largely because of the War on Poverty programs of that time, it has increased every decade since 1970 and was up to 19.9 percent in 1990. The rate was significantly higher for African-American and Hispanic families, at 44.2 and 37.7 percent respectively. Further, the data show that family poverty was a significantly worse reality for female-headed families. In 1990, 53.4 percent of all families headed by a female had an income below the poverty level. The figures were 64.7 percent for African-American and 68.4 percent for Hispanic female-headed families. Other data show that the percentage of children in poverty nearly doubled between 1960 and 1990, and that in 1990, over 20 percent of children lived in a poverty context with the concentration expected to rise to 25 percent during the 1990s (Reed & Sautter, 1990; Children's Defense Fund, 1994).

These figures paint a disquieting picture of the conditions of children in the 1990s. The family structure is less stable, half of all students will live through a divorce situation some time before they are 18, increasing numbers of families have no father and are headed by the mother, poverty is on the rise, and the situation is worse—by large margins—for minority families. The figures in this table do not indicate other conditions. As Hodgkinson (1992) notes, in 1990, 82 percent of children under 18 had a mother working outside the family, 13 percent were regularly hungry, 19 percent had no health insurance and thus poor medical services, and many were born to mothers addicted to drugs (including the so-called "crack" babies) and/or alcohol, or to mothers infected with the human immunodeficiency Aids-inducing virus. All these children attend school, and bring with them more and tougher social, emotional, health, and education problems which must be addressed by the school.

These conditions have prompted many to wonder about the incidence of "special needs" students in the country's schools and the future incidence of such students. Pallas, Natriello, and McDill (1989) surveyed the conditions of the "educationally disadvantaged" or "at-risk" students in the mid-1980s and made projections to the year 2020. They identified five factors correlated with educational disadvantage: minority ethnicity, poverty, living with a single parent, having a mother with less than a high school education, and living in a home where a primary language other than English is spoken. Their analyses showed a rising incidence of each of these five factors. For all children aged 0–17, they projected that by the year 2020 minority ethnic status would grow from 17 to 45 percent, poverty status would grow from 21 to 27 percent, the percentage living in a single or no parent household would grow from 26 to 29, the percentage having a mother with less than a high school education would grow from 20 to 29, and the percent living in homes where a primary language other than English was spoken would grow from 2.5 to 7.5. They concluded that conditions typically associated with educational disadvantage would grow from about 25 percent of all children in the mid-1980s to at least 30 percent in 2020 and possibly even higher. Other analysts have reached similar conclusions on the potential size of the at-risk population (Levin, 1989; Reed and Sautter, 1990).

In part as a result of the conditions of children, programs for special students are increasing as are their costs. Table 2-5 provides a glimpse of the impact of special needs students on school systems in 1988. The information shows participation rates in a variety of special programs in both public and private schools. While some students can be enrolled in more than one program, the data show that 5.4 percent were in programs for limited-English proficient students, 19 percent in remedial mathematics or science programs, 7 percent in handicapped programs, and 12 percent in vocational/technical programs. While these percentages cannot be simply added to indicate the percentage of all students in special programs, they nevertheless indicate a high percentage. Moreover, the figures only show official participation rates. Many students who need such special programs are, for a variety of reasons, not enrolled in them. Thus, even the participation figures in Table 2-5 underestimate the need for special student programs in the late 1980s. Further, while also not shown by these data, participation rates for minority students were systematically higher in all categories. As the conditions of children are expected to decline throughout the 1990s, these figures should rise.

All but one of the participation rates were lower for private schools. Indeed, private school participation in handicapped and vocational programs, generally the most expensive, were less than one-third and one-sixth, respectively, of that in public schools. Private school participation rates for special programs exceeded that of public schools (6.85 percent to 6.5 percent) only for gifted and talented programs, the least expensive programs.

TABLE 2-5. Participation Rates for Special Programs, 1987–1988

Programs	Public (%)	Private (%)
Bilingual Education	2.77	1.77
English as a Second Language	2.61	1.12
Remedial Reading	10.77	6.31
Remedial Mathematics	7.14	4.37
Programs for the Handicapped	7.17	2.12
Programs for Gifted and Talented	6.50	6.85
Vocational/technical Programs	11.97	1.74

Source: From NCES (1991), Table 53.

Summary

This section has attempted to portray only briefly the troublesome conditions of children in America. Although there are many advantaged children in this country, they represent only a small portion of the total. Most children experience difficulties within the family, including divorce and periods of neglect. The poverty rate for children is reaching 25 percent on average and more than twice that for children in the country's largest cities. The health conditions of large percentages of children are below that in many developing countries. Growing numbers of children are homeless, too many still suffer from hunger and poor diet, and violence including death is a rapidly emerging problem for many youth, not just those in the inner city (Children's Defense Fund, 1994).

The public schools must cope with the challenges these declining conditions of children present to the classroom teacher. Remedying many of these conditions is well within the reach of the country, both programmatically and economically, as discussed below, but until they are resolved, the children attending our country's schools require more than just educational services if they are to perform at the high cognitive levels needed for the high wage jobs in the evolving economy.

STUDENT DIVERSITY IN HISTORICAL PERSPECTIVE

The increasing diversity portrayed in the above section is not a new phenomenon in America. While there is a racial dimension to the increasing diversity today, the diversity the country faced with the waves of immigration in the early twentieth century from eastern and southern European countries, though primarily white racially, nevertheless represented major differences for that time period.

The controversies regarding the current influx of immigrants (the 20-year period from 1981 to the year 2000) are often fueled by the following misconceptions: (1) the country has never had to cope with as many immigrants as it has now, (2) immigrants have never been as different from "American" customs and values as they currently are, (3) earlier immigrants started using English more quickly, and (4) the United States, rather than continuing to welcome immigrants, has to finally begin closing the door. Platitudes such as "we were all immigrants once" are of little help to educational leaders in schools which are becoming more and more diverse. This section briefly discusses each misconception from a historical perspective.

Misconception #1: The Country Has Never Had As Many Immigrants. Federal record-keeping of immigration began in 1820. These records document the astounding numbers of newcomers that arrived over the next 100 years, from 800,000 in the 1820's to close to 9 million between 1901 to 1910. The largest number of *legal* immigrants to this country in any decade thus far arrived between 1901 and 1910 (Kellog, 1988). The current influx is comparable, and when illegal immigration is added, probably exceeds the migration that occurred at the turn of the twentieth century. But too few American citizens appreciate that the early history of the country had comparable numbers of immigrants (and larger percentages) given the population of the country in the 1700s and 1800s, and that in absolute numbers the first decade and the ninth decade of the twentieth century are comparable.

Misconception #2: Immigrants Have Never Been As Different from American Customs and Values Than They Currently Are. The largest number of immigrants to the United States prior to the 1900s were from Great Britain, Ireland, Germany, and Scandinavia. Although language was an issue for the Germany and Scandinavian immigrants, these four large groups considered themselves ethnically similar and were primarily Protestant. The large influx of immigrants from central and southern Europe who arrived between 1901 and 1910 were not considered similar in ethnicity, few of them spoke English and most were Catholic.

These differences were met with strong negative responses to nearly every aspect of the lives these immigrants were attempting to start—from housing to religion to employment to schooling. Current local negative reactions to the different traditions some current immigrants bring with them (such as early marriages, different diets, different forms of parental discipline) are identical to the horror with which some of the analogous cultural practices of the central and southern Europeans were viewed in the early 1900s.

Two differences which are significant to educators today are the younger age of many current immigrants and the different nature of some of their languages. Muller and Espenshade (1985) estimate that 60 percent of recent immigrants are between the ages of 16 and 44. Kellogg (1988) notes that while the median age of the U.S. population is 32.1 and rising, the median age of Hmong and Vietnamese immigrants is 13 and 21 respectively. The median age of Mexican immigrants is 23. With regard to the language differences, the Cambodian, Laotion, and Thai languages do not use the Roman alphabet (which all the European languages did) and have different sentence structures than English. Some languages such as Haitian and Hmong have had a written language for just a few decades. While some of today's immigrants arrive with no literacy and no education, many more arrive with some English and higher levels of education than earlier immigrants.

Misconception #3: Earlier Immigrants Set About to Learn English Faster. In the 1750's Benjamin Franklin wanted to reduce the widespread amount of German instruction in the schools of Philadelphia. An Ohio law of 1839 recognized that German was as effective a means of instruction as English. A similar statute in Louisiana in 1847 said the same thing for French. Immigrant groups with political power in local communities pushed for and gained either foreign language instruction or separate classes in a foreign language. This occurred for Italian, Polish, Czech, French, Dutch, and German (Crawford, 1989). It is also true that many immigrants chose not to permit their children to retain fluency in their language of origin, but it is inaccurate to think that was standard practice and that bilingual education and the drive to maintain native fluency is a sign of our time rather than an issue with a long history.

Misconception #4: Rather Than Always Welcoming Immigrants, the United States Must Begin to Finally Close Its Doors. Systematic exclusion of certain groups is part of this nation's immigration history. The earliest example of exclusion is the displacement of Native Americans which began in the 1600s and continued for the next 200 years. The involuntary, brutal nature of African migration which also began in the 1600s is an important facet of North American immigration history. Large numbers of Chinese laborers (more than 200,000) arrived between 1860 and 1880. The first federal law to limit immigration by nationality was the Chinese Exclusion Act of 1882. The Second Immigration Act of 1917 was designed to exclude Asians and others by requiring a literacy standard for admittance. The National Origins Act of 1924 established quotas based on representation in the 1890 census for each country outside the Western Hemisphere. This policy of exclusion was not changed except in small ways until the Immigration Act of 1965. This act was designed to "open (the United States) up not merely to the tired and the poor but to the racial and ethnic balance of the wide world." Under this act, Europeans constituted only one quarter of new immigrants. Additional laws giving refugee status to individuals fleeing political repression further increased the diversity of immigrants.

The history of immigration and diversity in this country is both a story about how the United States has been a haven for newcomers, as well as a story about resistance to each surge of new arrivals. This resistance stems from many sources: perceived economic threat, disdain for language, culture or ethnicity, racism, residual ethnocentric beliefs which are retained in a new setting. The school is one of the first institutions where immigrants live out their hopes, fears, defeats, and successes. We would hope that schools in the 1990s, clearly in the twenty-first century, would understand the complex history of immigration and diversity in this country and seek to make life, and clearly education, better for the immigrants who populate the schools today. The next section describes existing and proposed programs to meet the needs of the nation's children.

PROGRAMS NEEDED TO ADDRESS CURRENT AND FUTURE CONDITIONS OF CHILDREN

The positive side of the country's historical Janus-faced attitude towards immigration and diversity has produced a fairly strong lineage of education programs focused on educational needs in part caused by diversity. This programmatic and policy response matured in the latter part of the century.

In the early part of this century, immigrants and their children had rough lives but, with minimum basic mathematics and language skills, most could find jobs in the industrial world. A sound, 12 years of education was not then a critical ingredient to economic success. Nevertheless, several education initiatives were undertaken. First, in 1917 a new federal vocational education program, the Smith-Hughes Act, was created to ensure that the education system produced students with the "practical" skills needed for the developing industrial economy. Shortly thereafter, secondary school education became mandatory in most states, reflecting a belief that even a production worker needed the basic skills developed in a high school education. But a comprehensive range of special-needs programs did not begin to emerge until the latter half of the century, except for state-run institutional schools for small numbers of handicapped students.

From 1950 to 1970, beginning with the U.S. Supreme Court decision in the 1954 Brown v. Board of Education, which outlawed de jure segregation, many new programs were created by federal and state governments to address issues related to student diversity and special education needs. Desegregation related court decisions, regulations, laws, and programs were developed over a 20-year period from 1954 to at least 1974 at the federal level, and accompanied by programs in many states as well. In 1992, for example, desegregation assistance in California was the second largest education categorical program.

In the mid-1960s, the federal government enacted the Elementary and Secondary Education Act (ESEA) of 1965, Title I of which focused new attention on the education needs of children from poverty and low-income backgrounds. Funded by a full $1 billion, the largest ever federal education program, it marked a turning point in education's attention to the needs of students whose divergence from the "norm" profile required additional educational services in order to achieve at acceptable levels. After a few years, ESEA was expanded by Title VII to provide a federal program for limited-English proficient (LEP) students who needed an alternative education environment to learn not only English but also the subject matter in the various content areas in the school curriculum.

These initiatives were followed (and in some cases preceded) by legislative actions in many states creating state programs targeted on the same student needs. By the late 1970s, 20 states had compensatory education programs for low-achieving or poor students, and about 20 states that at that time enrolled the bulk of all LEP students had bilingual education programs. By the late 1980s, 28 states had compensatory education programs in addition to federal Title I program, and 22 states had bilingual or English as a Second Language program (Odden & Picus, 1992).

Programs for the handicapped also expanded dramatically during the 1970s. While most states had some version of programs for physically and mentally handicapped prior to that time, more comprehensive service of handicapped students was stimulated in 1975 by Congressional enactment of the Education for All Handicapped Children Act (Public Law 94-142) which required schools to provide a free appropriate education and related services for all students, regardless of handicapping condition. In addition, the law required a detailed plan from each state indicating how it would ensure that appropriate services were provided to all eligible students, including a plan to write rules and regulations for local districts and a strategy for overseeing local compliance with them. In part as a result, state special education programs expanded dramatically during the latter half of the 1970s. In the early 1990s, the Congress enacted The Individuals with Educational Disabilities Act. This act made it a civil right for all handicapped students to be fully included in classroom activities, a standard higher than that in P.L. 94-142 which conditions service on educational needs and results.

In addition to these large programs, over the years the federal government and the states have created targeted education programs for immigrant students, Indian students, gifted and talented students, and several other categories including remedial reading and mathematics. Further, other programs and laws (e.g., Title VI of the Civil Rights Act of 1964 and Title IX of the Education Amendments of 1972) have been enacted to make discrimination in providing education services to various categories of diversity—race, ethnicity, alien status, and sex—illegal.

While it took several years for many of these federal and state programs to become fully implemented (Odden, 1991a) and while not all poor and LEP students yet receive the extra services they need (Doyle & Cooper, 1988), by the beginning of the 1990s the country nevertheless had an array of programs designed for the special needs of a variety of students. Although the path of program enactment, implementation, and impact is strewn with bumps, wrong turns, and unfinished business, the programs, nevertheless, reflected a comprehensive policy on the education needs deriving from the diversity of students enrolled in public schools. While far from perfect, this side of the country's behavior towards diversity is commendable.

Policies and Programs for National Education Goal 1

While public schools in general enroll only students aged 5 to 17, increased policy attention is being focused on younger students. National Education Goal 1 is that all students (at age 5) should come to school ready to learn by the year 2000. Three key objectives were attached to this Goal:

- All disadvantaged and disabled children will have access to high-quality and developmentally appropriate preschool programs that help prepare children for school.
- Every parent in America will be a child's first teacher and devote time each day to helping his or her preschool child to learn; parents will have access to the training and support they need.
- Children will receive the nutrition and health care needed to arrive at school with healthy minds and bodies, and the number of low-birthright babies will be significantly reduced through enhanced prenatal health systems.

The general intent was to ensure that students starting their formal K–12 education experience would have the requisite social and education skills to perform well in a school environment. The goal was written in part because many students from diverse backgrounds—low income, immigrant, neglected, handicapped, different culture, or ethnicity—did not have those skills and thus had difficulty with, or were not able to benefit fully from, an elementary school experience.

As a result in part of these goal statements, policy interest centered on health, parental, and education experiences of young children. The objective was to produce healthy students who were socially and developmentally able to engage fully in a kindergarten program. Health issues included both prenatal and postnatal concerns. Numerous studies have shown the potential negative impacts of low birthweight, prenatal alcohol and drug exposure, maternal smoking, and malnutrition on children (Newman & Buka, 1990). Thus one aspect of policy initiatives related to goal one is to help pregnant women provide the healthiest environment for their children. For example, the federal Special Supplemental Food Program for Women, Infant, and Children's (WIC) program helps ensure an appropriate diet both before and after the child is born, for families with incomes below 185 percent of the poverty level. While proven cost-effective, in 1994 it served only between 50 and 70 percent of eligible women across the states and would have required an increase of just over $1 billion to about $4.5 billion to fully fund. Such a program is a first step accomplishing Goal 1. The expansion of Medicaid in 1986 and 1987 to provide larger numbers of pregnant women with prenatal and maternal health services is another initiative that could have salutary, long-term impacts on the conditions of children.

After birth, children need continued attention to their nutritional, health, social, and education developmental needs. WIC-type programs also assist at this stage. But other programs are needed as well. All children need to be fully inoculated against infectious diseases, whereas in the early 1990s large numbers, including many immigrant students and students from poverty families, were not. Moreover, students in the millions of American families in 1994 not covered by health insurance also had inadequate health services. While the expansion of Medicaid in 1986, 1987, and 1992 potentially made all poor children Medicaid-eligible, thus potentially providing access to an appropriate level of health and medical services, how implementation of this strategy (and other strategies to provide children just above the poverty level with medical insurance) resolves the inadequate health conditions of children in 1994 will become known only as the 1990s progress.

Many young children also live in families where they are abused, neglected, ignored, homeless, or otherwise mistreated in ways that do not foster either their social or educational development. A variety of family support programs could be funded to insure that their children's social needs are more fully met (Carnegie Task Force on Meeting the Needs of Young Children, 1994).

Finally, early childhood development programs, such as the federal Head Start program, have been shown by several research studies to significantly enhance both the education and social skills development of young children. Preschool programs for children from low-income families help them learn basic skills in their early elementary years (Slavin, Karweit, and Wasik, 1989, 1994). Cost-effectiveness studies, moreover, show large, positive ratios (Barnett, 1985). Fully funding the federal Headstart program for eligible (i.e., low income) three-, four- and five-year-olds would have required $7.6 billion in 1991, or $5.6 billion more than the $2 billion then appropriated for the program (Odden and Kim, 1992).

As the first NEGP report concluded (1991), the country pretty much knows the types of programs that need to be in place in order to meet Goal 1, i.e., to insure that all children start school ready to learn. The strategies just discussed represent the comprehensive set of programs the country needs to enact and fully fund in order to meet this goal. All that is needed is the political and fiscal will to do so.

School-Linked Social Services

Once the increasingly diverse group of young American children come to school ready to learn, however, many still will need follow through social services to keep them healthy, homed, and socially sound in order to fully benefit from educational activities. Although several federal and state programs have been created to address these needs, the overall system is incoherent and fragmented (Kirst 1989; McLaughlin & Heath, 1989) and does not work very well for children. Programs are administered by several different governments—counties, cities, and school districts at the local level—and literally dozens of agencies. At-risk children, who generally need services from several programs and agencies, face a dizzying and complicated array of applications, eligibility requirements, service locations, scheduling complexities, and structural requirements that make the parts of the system add up to much less than a coherent and workable whole. While some services might be in short supply, the solution according to Kirst (1991), is not to expand existing programs, but to overhaul the total structure and reorganize how the programs are administered and provided.

His proposal was to provide "one-stop" shopping for a variety of children's services by locating multiple services in one place at the local level, which could be a school, but also could be another institution. The agency where the multiple services are located would be "in charge." All agencies would allocate funds from regular administrative funding in order to provide an overall service coordinator for that location. The coordinator would work with all the agencies to collaborate in a process to make the delivery of services not only more convenient locationally but also more coordinated and streamlined. For example, the agencies could agree on one application and a common set of eligibility requirements. Thus, one set of paper work would open-up service delivery from several agencies. Some agencies could even subcontract with others to provide their services. The lead agency, through the coordinator, would become the broker or case manager for the child. This structural collaboration and collocation would overcome the complexities and fragmentation of the extant structure of children's social services at essentially no extra cost (Kirst, 1991; 1992a).

In the long run, Kirst (1991) argued, educators and social service providers must be trained differently, and the overall policy structure changed to make the system of children's services, including education, more coherent and easier to access by children who need the services. At heart, though, is the notion for greater school collaboration with other social agencies providing support services for children and their families. The idea is not to add another role for schools, such as breakfasts were added in the 1960s. The strategy is for school/social service agency collaboration to streamline the panoply of services for children and make them easy to use and, therefore, more effective (see also Adler and Gardner, 1994).

CURRENT STATUS OF EDUCATIONAL ATTAINMENT AND STUDENT ACHIEVEMENT

From the data on the deteriorating conditions of children and the patchwork quilt approach to providing children's social services, one might predict that educational attainment and student achievement would be at all time lows. But the facts show that not to be the case. Educational attainment, i.e., graduation from high school, has been rising during the past forty years and achievement has recovered from the lows in the 1970s. Nevertheless, there are significant concerns about the status of student achievement in America. This section discusses these and related issues.

Educational Attainment

Educational attainment is one of the broadest measures of how students do in the nation's schools, colleges, and universities. Table 2-6 provides data by race on years of schooling completed for the adult population from 1960 to 1990. The numbers reveal a consistent pattern of increasing educational attainment. For example, in 1960 only 41.1 percent of adults aged 25 and older had an education equal to four years of high school or more. By 1990, this figure had risen to 77.6 percent. While the figures for African-American and other minorities were lower, the rate of change from 1960 was much greater for minorities, ris-

TABLE 2-6. Years of Schooling Completed, 25-Years and Older, by Age, Race, 1960 to 1990

	All Races (%)	White (%)	African-American and Other Minorities (%)
Four years or more of high school			
1960	41.1	43.2	21.7
1970	55.2	57.4	36.1
1980	68.6	70.5	54.6
1990	77.6	79.1	68.7
Four years or more of college			
1960	7.7	8.1	3.5
1970	11.0	11.6	6.1
1980	17.0	17.8	11.1
1990	21.3	22.0	16.5
Median school years completed			
1960	10.5	10.8	8.2
1970	12.2	12.2	10.1
1980	12.5	12.5	12.2
1990	12.7	12.7	12.5

Source: NCES (1992), Table 8. Used by permission.

ing over three-fold from just 21.7 percent in 1960 to 68.7 percent in 1990. The data show that for all groups the median years of schooling continually increased over this 30-year time period.

Table 2-7 begins to focus more closely on data commonly associated with the high school graduation or dropout rate. The data show, by race, the percentage of the population completing high school by the age of 29 for each decade since 1940. There are several trends shown in the table. First, the percentage of this age group completing high school has increased each decade, and was a full 85.7 percent in 1990. This table shows that whatever percentage physically dropped out of high school, by age 29 only 14 percent of adults had not completed high school, or its equivalent. Second, the percentage for minorities is lower than that for whites, but the gap has decreased and was almost eliminated in 1990. In 1940, by contrast, while 41.2 percent of all whites aged 29 had completed high school, only 12.3 percent of minorities had, a difference of over three to one. In 1960, 63.7 percent of whites aged 29 had completed high school, but 38.6 percent of minorities, a difference of less than two to one. By 1990, the percentage of 29-year-old minorities completing high school stood at 82.5 percent, only 3.8 percentage points below that of whites.

**TABLE 2-7. Percent of Population Completing
High School, Age 25–29, by Race, 1940 to 1990**

Year and Race	Persons Age 25–29 Completing High School
1940	
Total	38.1
White	41.2
Minority	12.3
1950	
Total	52.8
White	56.3
Minority	23.6
1960	
Total	60.7
White	63.7
Minority	38.6
1970	
Total	75.4
White	77.8
Minority	58.4
1980	
Total	85.4
White	86.9
Minority	77.0
1990	
Total	85.7
White	86.3
Minority	82.5

Source: NCES (1992), Table 8. Used by permission.

Two conclusions can be drawn from these data. First, in 1990 the high school completion rate was 86 percent and the long-term dropout rate just 14 percent for Americans aged 29, much different from the more commonly understood rates of 75 and 25 percent, respectively. In other words, while a large number of students might drop out of high school in their teenage years, over half re-enroll and earn the degree or its equivalent.

The fact is that the high school drop-out rate is one of the most discussed and misunderstood measures of educational attainment. The reason it is so misunderstood is that it is a phrase that can be measured many different ways. One measure of the dropout rate is the percentage of students in a particular grade, usually grade 9 or 10, who do not graduate from high school four or three years later. Clearly, the selection of either grade 9 or grade 10 will alter the drop-out rate, with the rate being higher for grade 9 than for grade 10, simply because there are more years in which a student can drop out. Some measure the dropout rate as the percentage of high school seniors who do not graduate, which is a figure much smaller than either the grade 9 or grade 10 cohort drop-out rate.

Whatever measure is used for individuals in school, it is very different from the percentage of students who do or do not eventually earn a high school diploma or its equivalent such as a GED as shown by Table 2-7. The fact is that many who drop out of high school often re-enroll into a variety of programs and eventually earn a high school degree.

Distinguishing which concept of graduation is considered is a major issue in discussing the dropout rate. The conventional understanding is that the drop-out rate is about 25 percent, suggesting that 75 percent of students graduate from high school (Frase, 1989). But new NCES reports on the high school dropout rates (Frase, 1989; Kaufman and McMillen, 1991) shed new light on this conventional notion and discuss various measures of this phenomenon. They suggest that there are three different measures:

1. *Event* dropout rates measure the proportion of individuals who have dropped out of school over a particular time period, typically 12 months. In 1990, the event rate was 4.1 percent, i.e., 347,000 students of all high school students aged 15 to 24 dropped out of grades 10–12. The event rate has declined since the early 1970s (Kaufman & McMillen, 1991).
2. *Status* dropout rates measure the proportion of individuals who are dropouts at any one given time, regardless of when they dropped out of school. In 1990, the status rate was 12.1 percent, i.e., about 3.8 million persons aged 16 to 24 had dropped out of high school (Kaufman & McMillen, 1991).
3. *Cohort* dropout rates measure what happens to a single group, or cohort, of students over a time period. There is no single measure because it depends both on the age at which measurement begins and the age at which measurement ends. Kaufman & McMillen (1991) showed that the cohort dropout rate for the sophomore class of 1980 (followed in the High School and Beyond study) was 17.3 percent in their senior year and that the cohort rate for the eighth grade class of 1988 (the National Education Longitudinal Study of 1988) was 6.8 percent in their sophomore year of 1990.

Kaufman and McMillen (1991) also reviewed the high school competition figures from various U.S. census reports and reached similar conclusions to those discussed at the beginning of this section. In other words, while the convention notion is that 25 percent of freshmen high school students drop out and only 75 percent graduate with their class, the fact is that over half re-enroll and earn a high school diploma or its equivalent by their mid-20s.

Student Achievement

In addition to the general measures of education attainment, parents and policymakers are keenly interested in what students know, i.e., levels of student achievement and changes in student achievement over time. Many states and local districts give average achievement test scores of schools to local newspapers which publish the results with large headlines indicating whether student performance is up or down. Policymakers closely follow trends in measures of student test scores such as the Scholastic Aptitude Test (SAT), the National Assessment of Educational Progress (NAEP), and other commercialized standardized achievement tests with great intensity, hoping their policies cause the scores to rise and wanting continued increases. Average test scores of whatever stripe have become the public report card for the nation's schools.

But as study after study concludes, different tests measure different aspects of student performance. Some, such as NAEP, are good overall indicators of student achievement; others, such as the SAT are not. This section discusses the nature of different tests, changes in student achievement over time, the current status of student achievement, how U.S. students compare to their peers in other countries on tests of mathematics and science, and how the achievement gap between minorities and nonminorities have changed over the past 20–25 years.

Types and Purposes of Tests. Tests can be divided into several categories but three will be discussed: tests predicting college success, tests indicating knowledge in a content area, and tests comparing students to each other. The most well known tests predicting success in college are the SAT and American College Testing (ACT) program. Declines in SAT and ACT scores during the 1970s became leading indicators of the deteriorating condition of the U.S. education system, at least in the press.

While declines in these scores obviously had substantive meanings, SAT and ACT scores themselves were not good indicators of student achievement in elementary and secondary schools. First, the tests were designed to predict student success in the first year of college, not to measure past achievement. While success in college can be correlated somewhat with achievement, neither the SAT nor the ACT is or ever was meant to be an achievement test. Second, only a small portion of students take the SAT; indeed, the bulk of students taking these exams are high school seniors applying to college. Thus, at best they indicate something only about these students but certainly not about students in general, nor about elementary and junior high school students.

Third, across districts and states, a different percentage of students take these tests depending on whether the colleges they want to attend require the test scores for admission. Thus, for example, in 1990 only 5 percent of students in Iowa took the SAT while in Massachusetts only 72 percent. Fourth, as the percentage of students taking the test in a state or district increases, the average score generally drops simply because more lower achieving students become part of the test taking pool. Similar shortcomings apply to the ACT, although the types of questions on each test differ substantially. In short, neither the SAT nor ACT, despite their popularity in the press, are good indicators of level or trends in student achievement.

Criterion Referenced Tests. NAEP is probably the most well-known criterion referenced test, although many state testing programs use this type of test. The purpose of a criterion referenced test is to indicate the degree to which students know the content matter in a particular subject area. Such tests include items that cover the range of content matter in, for example, the eighth grade mathematics curriculum program, or the fourth grade language arts/reading program. Scores on the test indicate how much of the subject matter, and which aspects, students have learned. The validity of the test score turns on the degree to which the test items cover the appropriate content in a subject area. If for example, the test included only basic mathematical skill test items, it would not be a good indicator of student knowledge of mathematical principles or of mathematical problem-solving.

Criterion referenced tests can be given to all students to produce scores for individual students. The more common procedure, used in NAEP and many state testing programs, is to give the tests to just a sample of students and report scores by grade levels, schools, districts, regions, states, or the nation. Such scores are relatively good indicators for answering such questions as: What is the mathematics knowledge of eighth graders, or what do 17-year-olds know about U.S. history? The proposals for a national testing system, discussed in Chapter 1 and Chapter 3, however, generally include testing for all students.

Standardized Achievement Tests. The California Test of Basic Skills (CTBS), the Iowa Test of Basic Skills (ITBS) and Stanford Achievement Tests (SAT) are some of the well-known tests of this genre. They have several characteristics. First, they tend to be produced and sold commercially and the test cost per student is quite small, less than $10 per pupil. Second, they generally are used to provide achievement data for individual students, although they can be aggregated to grade, school, and district levels. Third, and most important, their purpose is not to indicate mastery of a subject area but to compare student achievement in that subject area. They are best used to answer such questions as: How does Mary's achievement in eighth grade mathematics compare to other eighth graders in the country, or how does fourth grade student achievement in science in one state or district compare to other fourth graders across the country?

Because standardized tests are designed primarily to compare student achievement, they assess only isolated bits of knowledge, those areas that best predict different levels of knowledge. Further, different tests measure different aspects of content areas. Moreover, many aspects of a subject might not be included in the test. Thus, knowing a content area well might not result in good scores on such tests. As a result, norm-referenced standardized achievement tests are poor indicators of how much of a subject a student has learned. Further, commercial standardized achievement tests have varying connections to the content taught in commercial textbooks; the larger the mismatch, the less the test is a good measure of student achievement, even in a comparative sense.

Despite these significant shortcomings, standardized achievement tests are used pervasively by local school districts across the country. They were mandated for use in evaluating the impacts of the federal Title I program for low-achieving, poor students, although two committees recommended eliminating that recommendation for the 1993 reauthorization of the program (Independent Review Panel, 1993; United States Department of Education, 1993).

Trends in Student Achievement. Student test scores changed dramatically during the 15 years prior to the 1990s. While holding fairly steady from the mid-1950s to the mid-1960s, the scores began to decline in the 1960s and generally continued to decline during the 1970s. These trends caused considerable concern among parents, policymakers and educators. Although the drop in the SAT scores became the leading public indicator of this downward trend in achievement, even though it was not a sound measure of achievement, subsequent analyzes have documented the reality of drops in student achievement during this time period.

Koretz's studies for the Congressional Budget Office (1986; 1987) were the most detailed, comprehensive, and substantive analyses of tends in student achievement and causes of those trends for the period from 1965 to 1985. Koretz concluded that there was indeed a decline in average test scores that probably indicated a decline in student achievement. He concluded that the declines occurred for all students, at all age levels except the early elementary grades, in all content areas, in public and private schools, and in all regions of the country. Further, he concluded that the declines were documented by all types of tests—SAT, ACT, and NAEP scores and scores on standardized achievement tests. He found that the declines were the greatest for older, high school students and worse for items assessing the ability to understand and solve problems than for items that measured basic skills. However, he also found that the test score decline, which lasted about ten years, was immediately followed by a widespread and significant rise in test scores, so that by the mid-1980s achievement in some grade levels was at an all time high!

Koretz identified several patterns to and causes of these rapid changes in student test scores. First, contrary to public understanding of test score decline that was framed more strongly during the 1970s when the SAT scores of high school students began to drop, Koretz (1986; 1987) showed that the decline actually started earlier in time, during the mid-1960s, and at the elementary level (grade 5). He showed that the decline was a "cohort" rather than "period" phenomenon. A cohort effect produces changes one grade level at a time as a cohort moves through the education system, one grade each year. A period effect indicates a change in all grade levels at a particular point or period of time.

Koretz showed that student achievement began to decline when the cohort of students born in the 1950s, i.e., the baby boom generation, entered fifth grade in the mid-1960s. Scores for each successive cohort of students declined until the cohort of students born in 1962 to 1963 entered grade 5 in the mid-1970s when the scores of fifth grade students began to rise again. By the mid-1980s, fifth grade scores on a variety of tests had regained the loss from 1965 to 1975, and in some cases were at the highest levels they had ever been.

Scores for other grade levels followed these patterns. Thus, it was not until the early 1970s that the 1950s cohort of students completed high school and caused high school test scores, as well as the SATs, to drop. High school scores continued to drop until the early 1980s when they also began their rebound.

Koretz's last major substantive finding was that during this time period the test scores of minority students had fallen less than those of nonminority students, and then had risen at a steeper rate, thus over time reducing the achievement gap between minority and nonminority students. While a significant gap remained, there had been important progress in closing that gap over this long time period. The gap was reduced more for African-American students than for Hispanic students. Further, the results were not due to large rise in affluent minorities because some of the largest increases occurred in schools with the highest minority concentrations (greater than 40 percent) and in many of the most economically disadvantaged urban schools.

Published in 1986 and 1987, Koretz's reports were partially directed to the education reformers of that time; he strongly argued that policies created in the mid-1980s had very little to do with either the past test score decline or the rise that then was occurring. His 1987 report also probed the reasons behind the cohort phenomenon. His sharpest conclusion was that the changes were a complex interplay of both educational and noneducational factors, which were difficult to sort out. Nevertheless, he concluded that several factors in both areas were the cause of both decline and rise. The primary non-education factors were family size and ethnicity. Family size increased for the baby boom generation of the 1950s, but then began to decline for the baby bust generation of the 1960s and 1970s. Also, the ethnicity of students, and thus their general income level, began to change in the 1960s which lead to decline at that time. To a lesser degree, he found that changes in student use of alcohol and drugs contributed first to test score decline, as use and abuse were on the rise, and then to test score rise, as use declined. Interestingly, he found that television watching had no effect, because there was no change in behavior during this time period. He also found little effect of single parent families, which increased only modestly during the time period analyzed.

Several education factors contributed to the test score changes. First, a watered down curriculum and proliferation of electives probably contributed somewhat to the decline, as did requirements for less homework for high school students. Koretz also concluded that Title I and other compensatory education programs, as well as desegregation-related programs begun during the late 1960s, helped contribute to increased test scores for minority students, especially African-American students.

He repeatedly cautioned against reaching clear cut and simple conclusions on causes of changes in average test scores. First, as just discussed, the potential education and noneducation factors that could cause change are difficult to measure let alone analyze as to their individual effects. Second, many other factors could be operating. For example, average test scores could decline if the high school dropout rate was reduced because more lower achieving students then would be staying in school and taking tests. Average SAT scores also could drop if a higher percentage of students, and thus more lower achieving students, took the test. On the other hand, average scores could rise if the reverse happened.

Further, as another report (Canell, 1987) found, standardized test scores can change if the "norms" are not updated. In order for standardized test scores to provide accurate comparisons, norms must be developed to indicate how low, average, and higher achieving students score. Norms need to be updated, however, to give an accurate current comparison. In the 1980s, many districts were showing that the bulk of their students were scoring "above the average." But often times, the average was based on norms created several years earlier. Comparative scores often plummeted when new norms were used, even with the same test.

Koretz's conclusions were drawn from one of the most comprehensive analyzes of test score changes over time. His findings were corroborated by many other studies, including the overview of Linn & Dunbar (1990) and the two NAEP reports that summarized the findings of 20 years of NAEP testing (Applebee, Langer, and Mullis, 1989; Mullis, Owen, and Phillips, 1990), which are discussed next.

NAEP Reports on Student Achievement. The NAEP was created in the mid-1960s as the first, and still today, the only national system of educational testing. Funding is provided through the U.S. Department of Education. It was designed from the beginning to give the country objective and sound data on student achievement. It was initially designed to test in ten areas: reading, writing, science, mathematics, social studies, citizenship, music, literature, vocational education, and art, but testing has concentrated on reading, writing, science, mathematics, and social studies. Initially, the program was designed to prohibit comparisons among the states; results were provided for the nation as a whole, for city, suburb, and rural areas, and for broad regions of the country—the Northeast, South, Midwest, and Far West. In 1990, NAEP began a trial state assessment that provided results on a state-by-state basis and, as discussed in Chapter 1, that approach is expanding in both subject areas and grade levels being tested.

NAEP is a criterion-referenced test taken only by a sample of students within and across states. Its results indicate what students at age 9, 13, and 17 (generally grades 4, 8, and 12) know in different content areas especially reading, writing, mathematics, science, and social studies. The 21-year NAEP data base provides one of the most comprehensive data bases on student achievement in America, and as Chapter 1 argued, will be used at least during the first part of the 1990s to gauge the nation's progress towards increasing student learning.

In 1989 the previous 20 years of NAEP reports were synthesized (Applebee, Langer, and Mullis, 1989) and, with one additional year of results, the

NAEP data were again summarized in 1990 (Mullis, Owens, and Phillips, 1990). Both books provide concise summaries of student achievement. Table 2-8 provides trend data from the early 1970s to 1990 for reading, mathematics, science, and civics. The data exhibit the following trends:

> *Reading* scores were higher for all four age groups by the end of the 1980s compared to the beginning of the 1970s. The average proficiency of nine-year-olds increased from 1971 to the mid-1980s and then dropped off a bit. 13-year-old scores rose throughout the 1970s and then stayed constant throughout the 1980s. Reading scores of 17-year-olds were stable over the 1970s and then rose consistently in the 1980s.

> *Mathematics* average proficiency scores changed but only modestly. For all three age levels, scores dropped a bit in the late 1970s and then rose marginally during the 1980s. In 1990, nine-year-old and thirteen-year-old scores were higher than they were in 1973.

> *Science* scores generally were about the same in 1990 as they were in 1970, although the pattern again was a drop over the 1970s and then a rise during the 1980s.

> *Civics* average proficiency scores remained basically the same, but exhibited a small drop for 13-year-olds from 1976 to 1988 and a very small gain for 17-year-olds.

Overall, the data indicate modest changes in student achievement over the 20 years from 1970 to 1990. The bottom line finding, however, is that what students knew in these key content areas as the 1990s began was about the same as what they knew in 1970, despite the fact that funding per pupil rose 25 percent in the 1970s and 48 percent in the 1980s after adjusting for inflation (see Chapter 13).

TABLE 2-8. National Trends in Average Proficiency on NAEP Assessments: Ages 9, 13 and 17

Content	Age	Year					
Reading		*1971*	*1975*	*1980*	*1984*	*1988*	*1990*
	9	208	210	215	211	212	209
	13	255	256	259	257	258	257
	17	285	286	286	289	290	290
Mathematics		*1973*	*1978*	*1982*		*1986*	*1990*
	9	219	219	219		222	230
	13	266	264	269		269	270
	17	304	300	299		302	305
Science		*1970*	*1973*	*1977*	*1982*	*1986*	*1990*
	9	225	220	220	221	224	229
	13	255	250	247	250	251	255
	17	305	296	290	283	289	290
Civics				*1976*	*1982*	*1988*	
	13			61.7	61.3	59.6	
	17			49.1	49.1	50.0	

Source: Applebee, Langer, and Mullis, 1989; Mullis, Owen, and Phillips, 1990; Mullis et al., 1991; NCES, 1993b.

In the late 1980s, NAEP began to analyze their data and characterize results according to proficiency levels that would give more concrete meaning to the results and indicate what students knew and could do when they scored at different levels on the NAEP test items. That type of analysis was particularly relevant to the national goal that required all students by the year 2000 to leave grades four, eight, and twelve (approximately age 9, 13 and 17) demonstrating competency in challenging subject matter such as English, reading, mathematics, science, history, and geography.

Tables 2-9, 2-10, 2-11 and 2-12 provide proficiency information for reading, mathematics, science, and civics. NAEP identified five proficiency levels.

TABLE 2-9. Reading Proficiency Levels: 1988

Proficiency Level		Percent Scoring at or Above		
		Age 9	*Age 13*	*Age 17*
350	Can synthesize and learn from specialized reading materials	0.0	0.2	4.8
300	Can find, understand, summarize and explain relatively complicated material	1.2	10.6	41.8
250	Can search for specific information, interrelate ideas, and make generalizations	17.0	58.0	86.2
200	Can comprehend specific or sequentially related information	62.5	95.1	98.9
150	Can carry out simple, discrete reading tasks	93.0	99.8	100.0

Source: From Mullis, Owen, and Phillips, 1990.

TABLE 2-10. Mathematics Proficiency Levels: 1990

Proficiency Level		Percent Scoring at or Above		
		Age 9[a]	*Age 13[b]*	*Age 17[c]*
350	Reasoning and problem solving involving geometry, algebra and beginning statistics and probability	0	0	5
300	Reasoning and problem solving involving fractions, decimals, percents, elementary geometry and simple algebra	0	14	46
250	Simple multiplicative reasoning and two-step problem solving	11	67	91
200	Simple additive reasoning and problem solving with whole numbers	72	98	100

Source: From Mullis et al., 1991.
[a] = grade 4
[b] = grade 8
[c] = grade 12

TABLE 2-11. Science Proficiency Levels: 1986

Proficiency Level		Percent Scoring at or Above		
		Age 9	*Age 13*	*Age 17*
350	Can infer relationships and draw conclusions using detailed scientific knowledge	0.4	0.2	7.5
300	Has some detailed scientific knowledge and can evaluate the appropriateness of scientific procedures	3.4	9.4	41.4
250	Understands basic information from the life and physical sciences	27.6	53.4	80.8
200	Understands some basic principles, for example, simple knowledge about plants and animals	71.4	91.8	96.7
150	Knows everyday science facts	96.3	99.8	99.9

Source: From Mullis, Owen, and Phillips, 1990.

TABLE 2-12. Civics Proficiency Levels: 1988

Proficiency Level		Percent Scoring at or Above		
		Age 9	*Age 13*	*Age 17*
350	Understands a variety of political institutions and processes	0.0	0.3	6.0
300	Understands specific government structures and functions	0.1	12.7	49.0
250	Understands the nature of political institutions and the relationships between citizen and government	9.6	61.4	89.2
200	Recognizes the existence of civic life	71.2	94.4	98.8

Source: From Mullis, Owen, and Phillips, 1990.

Levels 150 and 200 can be characterized somewhat as the basic skills in the content area. Level 250 represents an intermediate proficiency level. Level 350 represents the types of skills needed to do first year college level work. Across all four figures, two major findings are clear. The good news was that by the age of 13, nearly all students had mastered the very basic skill levels in all subject areas. The disconcerting news was that only a very small percentage of 17-year-olds achieved at a level to do first year college level work; the figure for the percent scoring at or above the 350 level were 4.8, 5.0, 7.5 and 6.0 percent for reading, mathematics, science, and civics, respectively. These were not outstanding levels of achievement. They reflected the stark reality of why many college and university presidents argue that, today, the first two years of college is really remedial high school level work.

In addition to the above comments on student achievement in 1990, Mullis, Owen, and Phillips 1990 stated the following:

- In *reading*, students responded correctly to specific informational questions about reading passages, but only half to two-thirds got the overall "gist" of the passages. Students also were much less successful in extending the meaning of various passages and only a small percent gave elaborated responses to open-ended questions. Generally, students were not able to organize evidence in a coherent way to support meanings they inferred from material they have read.

- In *mathematics*, students performed the basic arithmetic calculations but had difficulty applying them to one-step problems, let alone multiple step or open-ended problems. Smaller percentages really understood mathematical principles and had sound problem solving capabilities. NAEP found that less than 6 percent of 17-year-olds had a firm grasp of algebraic concepts, the basic mathematics knowledge needed to engage in any kind of quantitative analysis above arithmetic.
- In *science*, the results were more disappointing. Although all students had some grasp of the most basic scientific principles, even though science was taught only sporadically in elementary schools, less than half of the 17-year-olds had a sound knowledge of basic science and understood the scientific process, nor of how the scientific process could be applied to everyday issues such as the environment and technology. Smaller percentages had detailed knowledge of subdisciplines such as physics, chemistry, and biology.
- The *civics* results also fell short of what students should know. While over 60 percent of 13-year-olds understood the basic nature of U.S. political institutions, less than half of high school seniors knew about specific government structures such as legislatures, the courts, governors, etc. When this test was given in 1988, for example, during the height of the 1988 presidential primaries, only 57 percent of twelfth graders knew that presidential candidates were nominated at national party conventions!

In the early 1990s NAEP began collecting data to provide scores for the nation, regions, as well as each individual state (National Center for Education Statistics, 1993c, 1993d) and to score results by the percentage of students achieving at basic, proficient and advanced levels. Tables 2-13 and 2-14 provide the results for both reading and mathematics for 1992. The striking finding from both of these tables is the small percentage of students at any grade scoring at or above the proficiency level. Indeed, the results again show that American students are doing relatively well at basic achievement but need substantial improvement in order to show "mastery of complex subject matter," the level of achievement hoped for in the national goals. The data in these two tables also show that mathematics performance is consistently below that in reading.

In summary, NAEP showed that whatever test score decline occurred in the 1960s and 1970s, the gains made in the 1980s pretty much wiped out those declines and students entered the 1990s achieving at about the same level as those in the 1960s. Although there was no net achievement loss over the 20-year time period from 1970 to 1990, the absolute level of student achievement was not sufficient. The results show conclusively that students in our country's schools do not achieve at a level that would represent competency in chal-

TABLE 2-13. Reading Proficiency Levels: 1992

Proficiency Level	Percent Scoring at or Above Proficiency Level	Anchoring Description
Basic		
Grade 4: demonstrate an understanding of the overall meaning of what is read, make obvious connections.	59	Understand uncomplicated narratives and high information texts, identify themes, locate explicit material, summarize parts of texts, and make judgments about characters' actions.
Grade 8: demonstrate a literal understanding of text and make some interpretation	69	Understand passages representing familiar genres. Identify literal information, recognize central themes and topics, and identify central purpose of practical documents. Interpret and describe character traits.
Grade 12: demonstrate overall understanding and make some interpretation.	75	Develop interpretations from a variety of texts. Understand overall arguments, recognize explicit aspects of plot and character, respond personally to texts, and use document features to solve real world problems.
Proficient		
Grade 4: demonstrate overall understanding of text, including inferential as well as literal information. Able to extend meaning by drawing conclusions.	25	Understand and interpret less familiar texts. Provide textual support for interpretations and generalizations, understand some subtleties in story, relate texts to background experiences.
Grade 8: show overall understanding of text, including inferential and literal information. Extend ideas in text to make clear inferences and connections to own experience and other reading. Identify some devices authors use in composing material.	28	Able to move beyond surface understanding of a text or multiple texts. Make inferences about characters and themes, link generalizations to specific details, support their opinions about text, recognize an author's intention, and use a document to solve simple problems.

Proficiency Level	Percent Scoring at or Above Proficiency Level	Anchoring Description
Grade 12: show overall understanding of text, including inferential and literal information. Extend ideas in text to make clear inferences. Clear connections between inferences and textual information. Analyze authors use of literary devices.	37	Integrate background experiences and knowledge with meaning from a variety of texts. Can interpret characters' motives and consider different points of view. Can interpret literary devices, identify text structure and writing style, and use document information to solve complex problems.
Advanced		
Grade 4: generalize about topics in reading selection and demonstrate awareness of how author compose and use literary devices. Judge texts critically, give thorough, thoughtful answers.	4	Interpret and examine meaning of text. Summarize information across whole texts, develop own ideas about textual information, understand some literary devices, beginning to formulate more complex questions about text.
Grade 8: able to describe more abstract themes and ideas of text. Analyze both meaning and form and support analyzes with explicit examples from text. Thorough, thoughtful and extensive responses.	2	Compare and contrast information across multiple texts. Connect inferences with themes, understand underlying meanings, and integrate prior knowledge with text interpretations. Demonstrate some ability to evaluate limitations of documents.
Grade 12: able to describe more abstract ideas and themes in overall text. Analyze both meaning and form in text. Explicitly support analyses with specific textual examples. Able to extend information in text by relating it to own experiences. Thorough, thoughtful and extensive responses.	3	Construct complex understandings of multiple passages of different genres. Can interpret multidimensionsal aspects of characters and connect discipline specific knowledge to text. Examine authors' devices, judge the value of information sources, suggest improvements to text.

Source: From NCES (1993c).

TABLE 2-14 Mathematics Proficiency Levels: 1992

Proficiency Level	Percent Scoring at or Above Proficiency Level	Anchoring Description
Basic		
Grade 4: Should be able to show some evidence of understanding the arithematical concepts and procedures of the five content areas of: 1) numbers and operations, 2) measurement, 3) geometry, 4) data analysis, statistics and probability, and 5) algebra and functions.	61	Able to estimate and use basic facts and compute with whole numbers; show some understanding of fractions and decimals; and solve simple real world problems in all five content areas. Minimal written responses presented without supporting data.
Grade 8: exhibit evidence of conceptual and procedural understanding in all five content areas, including an understanding of arithmetic operations on whole numbers, decimals, fractions, and percents.	63	Complete problems with the help of prompts of diagrams, charts, and graphs. Able to solve problems in all areas through appropriate selection of strategies and technical tools. Use fundamental concepts of algebra and geometry in problem solving. Able to determine which data necessary and sufficient to solve problems.
Grade 12: demonstrate procedural and conceptual knowledge in solving problems in all five content areas.	64	Use estimations to verify solutions. Use algebraic and geometric reasoning to solve problems. Recognize relationships presented in verbal, algebraic, tabular, and graphical form. Apply statistical reasoning in organization and display of data. Generalize from patterns in algebra, geometry and statistics. Use correct mathematical language and communicate mathematical relationships and reasoning processes.
Proficient		
Grade 4: consistently apply integrated procedural knowledge and conceptual understanding to problems solving in all five content areas.	18	Use whole numbers to estimate and compute. Conceptual understanding of fractions and decimals; solve real world problems in all five content areas. Written solutions should be organized and presented with supporting information and explanations of how solutions were achieved.

Proficiency Level	Percent Scoring at or Above Proficiency Level	Anchoring Description
Grade 8: apply mathematical concepts and procedures consistently to complex problems in all five content areas. Gather and organize data and be able to calculate, evaluate and communicate results within domains of probability and statistics.	25	Able to conjecture, defend ideas and give supporting examples. Understand connections between fractions, percents, decimals, algebra, and functions. Able to compare and contrast mathematical ideas. Make inferences from data; apply properties of informal geometry and accurately use technology tools.
Grade 12: consistently integrate mathematical concepts and procedures to the solutions of more complex problems in all five content areas. Judge and defend the reasonableness of answers to real world situations.	16	Demonstrate understanding of algebraic, statistical, geometric, and spatial reasoning. Analyze and interpret data in tabular and graphical form. Understand and use elements of the function concept in symbolic, graphical, and tabular form. Make conjectures, defend ideas and give supporting examples.
Advanced		
Grade 4: apply integrated procedural knowledge and conceptual understanding to complex and nonroutine real world problem solving in all five content areas.	2	Solve complex and nonroutine real world problems. Draw logical conclusions and justify answers and solutions processes explaining why. Go beyond obvious interpretations and communicate thoughts clearly and concisely.
Grade 8: able to reach beyond recognition, identification and application of mathematical rules to generalize and synthesize concepts and principles.	4	Probe examples and counterexamples to shape generalizations and develop models. Use number sense and geometric awareness to consider reasonableness of answer. Use abstract thinking to create unique problem-solving techniques and explain reasoning process.
Grade 12: consistently demonstrate integration of procedural and conceptual knowledge and the synthesis of ideas in the five content areas.	2	Understand the function concept; compare and apply the numeric, algebraic, and graphical properties of functions. Apply knowledge of algebra, geometry and statistics to solve problems in continuous and discrete mathematics. Able to communicate math reasoning through clear, concise and correct use of mathematical symbolism and logical thinking.

Source: From NCES (1993d).

lenging subject matter. They know the basic skills, but have a hard time using those skills. They are weak on thinking, problem solving, and application of knowledge to complex problems, the types of skills needed in the evolving economy and society as discussed in Chapter 1. Finally, less than 10 percent have the knowledge and skills needed for the first year of college. In short, these results outline the difficult challenges facing the country in upgrading student achievement.

Casserly and Carnoy (1994) identify the enormous task, and likely costs, for the country of teaching all students to high standards. Their logic is three-fold. First, small percentages of students on average score at or above proficiency or at advanced levels. It will take a large effort to boost average achievement. Second, the percentage of low-income and minority students, and other students at-risk, achieve at even lower levels, thus requiring even greater educational and fiscal efforts to get their achievement above proficiency. Third, given the declining conditions of children (described in the first section of this chapter), increasing numbers of children will require extra educational services in order to achieve at proficient and advanced levels. Casserly and Carnoy laud the goal of teaching all students to high standards but are clear that it will take extraordinary political and fiscal resolve to do so. They also argue that policies focused on substantially improving the conditions of children would benefit this large educational goal.

International Comparisons of Student Achievement. The low-level of student achievement would not be that much of a potential macro-economic problem if they achieved above their peers from around the world. But the several international assessments of student achievement that have been con-

TABLE 2-15. Rankings on the 1988 Mathematics International Assessment

Country	Average Proficiency Score	Percent Scoring at or Above Scale Levels				
		Add & Subtract	Simple Problems	Two-step Problems	Understand Concepts	Interpret Data
		300	400	500	600	700
Korea	567.8	100	95	78	40	5
Quebec (French)	543.0	100	97	73	22	2
British Columbia	539.8	100	95	69	24	2
Quebec (English)	535.8	100	97	67	20	1
New Brunswick (English)	529.0	100	95	65	18	1
Ontario (English)	516.1	99	92	58	16	1
New Brunswick (French)	514.2	100	95	58	12	<1
Spain	511.7	99	91	57	14	1
United Kingdom	509.9	98	87	55	18	2
Ireland	504.3	98	86	55	14	<1
Ontario (French)	481.5	99	85	40	7	0
United States	473.9	97	78	40	9	1

Source: From Lapointe, Mead, and Phillips, 1989.

ducted since the 1960s generally show that U.S. students perform at the bottom in these international academic "Olympics." While there are numerous technical problems in comparing student achievement across different countries, including language, culture, curriculum, length of school day and year, family and retention differences, the general findings across all the assessments are quite similar (Lapointe, Owen, and Mullis, 1989; Lapointe, Askew, and Mead, 1992a, 1992b; Medrich and Griffith, 1992). First, U.S. students generally perform in the bottom quartile on both mathematics and science tests. Second, Asian countries, particularly Korea and Japan, score at the very top. Third, the "best" U.S. students usually score below the best students from other countries. Fourth, such results have occurred on international assessments from the mid-1960s to the early 1990s.

The international assessments conducted by NAEP in 1988 (Lapointe, Owen, and Mullis, 1989) and 1991 (Lapointe, Askew, & Mead, 1992a, 1992b) provide some of the best data on U.S. students for international comparisons because the assessments used test items that NAEP had used in their United States assessment program, thus at least giving neutral, objective data on the achievement of students in this country.

Table 2-15 displays the results for the 1988 mathematics assessment, and Table 2-16 provides results for the 1988 science assessment. For both subjects, U.S. 13-year-old students generally scored at the bottom. In mathematics, the United States ranked last among the 12 country scores given; Korea scored at the top by a large margin. In science, the United States scored a bit higher, but still with the lowest third of all countries and Korea again was in the top group, although second to British Columbia.

Similar to the NAEP results in the previous section, the results from the

TABLE 2-16. Rankings on the 1988 Science International Assessment

Country	Average Proficiency Score	Know Everyday Facts	Apply Simple Principles	Analyze Experiments	Apply Intermediate Principles	Integrate Experimental Evidence
		Percent Scoring at or Above Scale Levels				
		300	400	500	600	700
British Columbia	551.3	100	95	72	31	4
Korea	549.9	100	93	73	33	2
United Kingdom	519.5	98	89	59	21	2
Quebec (English)	515.3	99	92	57	15	1
Ontario (English)	514.7	99	91	56	17	2
Quebec (French)	513.4	100	91	56	15	1
New Brunswick) (English)	510.5	99	90	55	15	1
Spain	503.9	99	88	53	12	1
United States	478.5	96	78	42	12	1
Ireland	469.3	96	76	37	9	1
Ontario (French)	468.3	98	79	35	6	<1
New Brunswick (French)	468.1	98	78	35	7	<1

Source: From Lapointe, Mead, and Phillips, 1989.

international assessment showed that only 40 percent of U.S. eighth graders could correctly solve two-step mathematics problems while nearly double that level (78 percent) of Korean students could. Fully 40 percent of Korean students understood mathematical concepts compared to only 9 percent of students in the United States. In science, again not unlike the results from NAEPs U.S. assessments, the international data showed that only 42 percent of U.S. eighth graders could analyze experiments while 73 percent of Korean students could, and 33 percent of Korean students could apply intermediate scientific principles compared to only 12 percent of American students.

The 1988 international assessment also showed that, in all countries, greater amounts of time spent watching television were associated with lower test scores, and that in nearly all countries less than 50 percent of 13-year-olds spent more than one hour per day on homework (Lapointe, Mead, and Phillips, 1989).

The NAEP 1991 international assessments (Lapointe, Askew, and Mead, 1992a, 1992b) produced equally dour results. In science, U.S. students ranked 13 out of 15 countries. Students in Korea, Taiwan, Hungary, the Soviet Union, Canada, France, and Spain outscored U.S. students. Only students in Ireland and Jordan scored below U.S. eighth grade students in science. In mathematics, the results were less distinguished with U.S. students scoring 14th out of 15 countries, outpacing only students in Jordan. Again, Korean students scored at the top in both subject areas.

While the general pattern of low-student achievement has been consistent for nearly all international comparisons of student achievement in mathematics and science, giving surface credence to the results, international comparisons of student achievement are not without criticism (Rotberg, 1990; Medrich and Griffith, 1992). In addition to the sociocultural differences across countries, nearly all surveys suffer from a variety of sampling problems. Nevertheless, several conclusions about why achievement differs have been drawn (Medrich and Griffith, 1992).

First, curriculum exposure (opportunity to learn or the enacted curriculum) is a major factor for achievement differences across countries. Countries that include more content in the curriculum tend to have students who perform at higher levels. This conclusion reflects both a stronger mathematics and science curriculum in most other countries, as well as the relatively weak American curriculum. The U.S. mathematics K–8 curriculum emphasizes arithmetic calculations, is relatively shallow and narrow, and devotes substantial time to review and repetition (Medrich and Griffith, 1992; McKnight, et al., 1987). Cohen and Spillane (1993) and Westbury (1992) also concluded that the enacted curriculum is a key determinant of differences in student learning across countries, as well as states, districts, schools, and classrooms.

Second, the *within* school tracking that is generally practiced in most American schools (Oakes, 1985) is negatively associated with achievement whereas tracking across schools, as practiced in many other countries, is associated with higher levels of achievement. However, the sample selected for international comparisons from other countries often is taken from their more academic schools, thus biasing up their overall results. At the presecondary level, though, these systems, including Japan, do not track and systematically expose all students to a rigorous curriculum. By contrast, McKnight et al.

(1987) found the most variation in curriculum exposure occurred for students in the United States, with students generally given either remedial, regular, enriched or algebra classes, and only the small percentage of students in the latter doing well on international comparison tests.

Medrich and Griffith (1992) reached three other conclusions:

- Across countries, family background characteristics affect learning. In nearly all countries, the higher the family socio-economic status, the greater student achievement.
- Countries committed to keeping students enrolled in school, such as the United States, tend to score less on international tests, but formally educate a larger percentage of their student population. Japan is the exception, as well as perhaps Korea, which educate nearly all their students who still perform at the top.
- Generally, the best students in the United States do not perform as well as the best students in other countries. Again, the curriculum, i.e., opportunity to learn is the culprit. The best students in other countries tend to be exposed to a more rigorous curriculum.
- Students in developed countries tend to score higher than those in developing countries.

For the purposes of this book, and perhaps overall education policy as well, the most important findings on the causes of achievement differences are the differences in curriculum. Opportunity to learn cuts across all other variables. When students are exposed to broader and deeper curriculum content, they learn more. This conclusion holds for all students, both across and within countries. It is a key issue, as latter chapters will argue, for improving the achievement of students within this country, as well as for making any country's student achievement more equitable.

Although the above conclusions and analyses on international comparisons of student achievement have held for several years and across many different studies, a recent assessment of reading achievement conducted by the International Association for the Evaluation of Educational Achievement (Elley, 1992) provided more optimistic findings about American pupils. U.S. fourth graders scored second highest out of the 31 countries that participated in the assessment. U.S. eighth graders tied for eighth place in the 31 country reading assessment. U.S. students achieved particularly well in both the narrative and expository portions of the test. These findings clearly imply that this country is doing a better job in developing reading competence than in developing mathematics and science competence. The above comments on the unacceptably low level of achievement in these and other content areas nevertheless still hold. The international reading assessment merely implies that, relative to other countries, the level of reading achievement disadvantages the country less than the level of mathematics and science achievement. Cognitive competence in all content areas still need to be dramatically improved, and the challenge is particularly urgent for low-income and minority students.

The Achievement Gap. In reviewing NAEP scores in the 1970s and 1980s, Mullis, Owen, and Phillips (1990) showed that the scores of minority students have consistently fallen below that of white students. The general pattern, they stated, is that the achievement of 17-year-old African-American and Hispanic students is about equal to that of 13-year-old white students. While an achievement gap between minorities and nonminorities remains, the more positive news is that gap had declined in every assessment given between 1970 and 1990, and that on average by the end of the 1980s the achievement gap had been halved.

For reading, the results showed that the gap between African-American and white students not only had dropped, but also became smaller as students progressed through school. In 1988, the gap for students age 9 was 29 points, but only 20 points for students age 17. By contrast, in 1971, they showed that the gap for 9-year-olds was 44 points and 53 points, i.e., higher, for 17-year-olds. Not as much progress was made in mathematics, but the gap nevertheless dropped. The same trend showed for science. The achievement gap for Hispanic students generally have shown the same trends, but generally were not as large as those for African-American students and did not decline as much.

The overall results, though, are a silver lining in the otherwise less than shining facts on student achievement. While still unacceptably large, the achievement differences between minority and nonminority students in this country has been on a consistently declining path. The reason, moreover, is increased learning on the part of minority students since achievement levels of white students were the same in 1990 as they were in 1970.

SUMMARY

To produce students in the year 2000 who show proficiency in the complex subject matter of reading, literature, writing, mathematics, science, history, and civics is a stiff challenge for America's schools. Student achievement is not what the country would like it to be, and we would like to score at the top in international assessments of student achievement rather than the bottom. While student achievement has a long improvement road to travel, two pieces of good news should be kept in mind. First, the schools have produced a 20-year track record of improving the learning of minority students. We need to keep the achievement of minorities on this improvement track during the 1990s.

Second, the major factor for low-student achievement is the curriculum. The curriculum in the country's schools has not been rigorous enough. Changing the curriculum, moreover, is within the control of education professionals and policy makers. As Chapter 1 discussed, several national initiatives now seek to revamp the country's K–12 school curriculum to a much higher level of standards. As the next chapters argue, moreover, we now have strong knowledge of how students learn to think and solve problems in the different content areas that can be used by teachers to lead students through a set of experiences in a more complex curriculum that results in a much higher level of learning for each individual.

New Understandings About Student Learning

In 1966, the federal government released a major study on inequality of educational opportunity, commonly called the Coleman Report (Coleman et al., 1966). The report concluded that "schools bring little influence to bear on a child's achievement that is independent of his background and general social context" (Coleman et al., 1966: 325). According to headlines in newspapers around the country, the report found that schools did not make a difference in student achievement but that socio-economic status determined learning.

Educators were hard pressed to believe such findings since they were counter intuitive. After all, students did not learn science by sitting under a tree or by playing basketball on the street corner. Mathematical principles were not consciously developed simply by playing with blocks, marbles, and dice. Even writing was not an effortless product of good conversation. These cognitive skills had to be taught, worked on, and learned. Schools had to make a difference; the study's conclusions were wrong.

On the other hand, skeptics of government programs and even many policymakers gravitated to the Coleman Report findings. At worst they would relieve pressures to reform society through big investments in schooling. At best they would focus attention on broader social inequities that needed resolution.

Despite these cross currents, work continued to improve the schools. From the back to the basics movement of the 1970s, to the education reforms of the 1980s, and the education goals of the 1990s, the country, policymakers, business leaders, educators, parents, and the public have continued trying to make schools better in order to advance learning. Are these efforts doomed to failure? Was the Coleman report right or wrong? Can schools make a difference? If so how?

Answers to these questions are crucial especially given the educational aspirations for the 1990s. The goals we want the American education system to accomplish during the 1990s have been set at a high level. We seek to raise the learning of all students to a level that only a small fraction attained in 1990.

We want to produce high school graduates who can "think" for a living, individuals who can solve problems, analyze data, draw reasonable conclusions from incomplete information, and as importantly, can apply these thinking and analytic skills to challenges of everyday life—in the workplace, at home, and in personal contexts. We seek to produce these new high levels of learning for a student population that is very diverse and has increasingly high concentrations of students who historically have not performed that well in public schools.

By articulating these goals, we do not mean to imply that individuals now do not think. All individuals think. "When we say we want to teach students to think, we really mean that we want to improve the quality of their thinking. We want to teach them to think more deeply, more consistently, more productively, and more effectively than they otherwise might" (Nickerson, 1988: 4).

Are these expectations reasonable? Aren't these aspirations actually elitist? Don't they apply only to the "bright" students? Can students in the "bottom half" master thinking skills? Do we know how children, especially the diverse children who attend public schools, develop high level cognitive capabilities? Can schools really make such a big difference? How do we know if we are being successful? Can teachers realistically organize classrooms with these high aspirations? Can policy play a role in attaining these goals? Was Coleman actually wrong? Positive answers to such questions are key to dramatically transforming America's schools.

These questions raise the issues that should be the driving forces behind all high performance schools: how children learn, what they need to learn, how teachers guide the learning process, and how student performance is assessed. This chapter as well as chapter 4 begin to answer these questions. This chapter addresses new understandings of how all children—young and old, poor and rich, language minority and majority—develop cognitive expertise in thinking and problem solving in core content areas. It draws heavily from the emerging findings from cognitive research that is transforming our knowledge of how children learn, and the roles curriculum, teaching, and assessment play in that process.

The chapter has three major sections. The first summarizes new understandings of how children learn to think, setting that knowledge in an historical context that starts with the Coleman Report (1966). Section two discusses how the new approach to learning works in the various curriculum, content areas. The third section applies these new understandings of learning to special student populations including the poor and language minorities.

THE DEVELOPMENT OF COGNITIVE CAPABILITIES

The educational vision for the 1990s from both the economic and equity perspective is to teach all students how to engage in high-level learning processes—to think, solve problems, communicate clearly, work in collegial groups, and apply these cognitive skills to everyday problems, or as Porter,

Archbald, and Tyree (1991) put it, to teach "hard content" to all students. Arguing for schools to raise all student's achievement to a level that only a small percentage reach today is good political rhetoric but substantively meaningless unless the promise can be fulfilled.

This section discusses the knowledge base for accomplishing this bold educational vision. It begins with the "low point" of school effects that surrounded release of the Coleman report in the 1960s, moves through the effective teaching and schools research that emerged in the 1970s, and emphasizes the more recent findings from cognitive research that began to blossom during the 1980s and are central to discussions of learning in the 1990s. While the roots of educators' attempts to teach thinking skills reach back to the end of the nineteenth century and the Dewey influence during the Progressive Era of the 1920s and 1930s, we focus on the more modern post-1950s era.

The 1966 Coleman Report

As part of the 1960s emphasis on educational equity, a large federal study was commissioned to describe and analyze racial and ethnic disparities in resources and student achievement. One goal of the study was to document, with a large national data base, the inequities in educational opportunity and to show how those inequities caused differences in student achievement. The hope was to show with "hard data" the reasons for low performance of poor and minority students in low-spending school districts.

The study created one of the largest national data bases of quantitative information ever gathered into one statistical file. It gathered a range of data on student achievement, socio-demographic, educational expenditure, and other data for hundreds of districts across the country. Data analysis was conducted by study group headed by James Coleman at the University of Chicago, Chicago, Illinois. The study was one of the first to use advanced statistical techniques, specifically multiple regression analysis, to analyze the individual impacts on achievement of several causal factors in a large data base. In part because of its large data base and use of advanced statistical analysis, the study's results assumed an aura of "authority" once released.

The report was issued in mid-1966 (Coleman et al., 1966) at a major press conference. The results were not as predicted. Coleman and his study team documented wide variations in student achievement, educational expenditures, and concentrations of minorities across school districts in the country. But the study concluded that socio-economic factors accounted for the bulk of variation in student achievement, and that only a small portion of student achievement difference could be attributed to schools, once socio-economic factors were included in the analysis. Expenditures also were unrelated to achievement differences. In the popular press, the results were interpreted to mean that "school didn't make a difference," that family income and other socio-demographic factors were the key determinants of student learning.

These findings had major implications for education policy. The results suggested that wide variations in education expenditures per pupil, a major focus of school finance policy (Odden and Picus, 1992), could be ignored because they did not cause differences in student achievement. Further, the results implied that education policy also would not be very effective in reducing achievement differences because noneducation factors were the key factors that affected learning. Released in the midst of a major expansion of the federal role in education as well as increases in state education spending, the report raised important questions about the allocation of government resources to education. If schools did not make a difference in student learning, why invest scarce governmental revenues in new educational programs or school finance equalization formulas?

In the wake of the report's release, there were two major research responses. One was a series of projects that attacked the study's statistical methodology (Guthrie et al., 1971; Mayeske, 1969; Jencks et al., 1972) and thus questioned its major conclusions. But insider researcher debates over statistical procedures, however important or valid, were not able to penetrate and change press and public understandings that schools didn't make a difference in student learning, the legacy of which is strong in many places even today.

The other research response, begun in the early 1970s, was organized by the National Institute of Education (NIE), then the educational research arm of the federal government. NIE largely reflected the response of many educators that the public had been misled by the Coleman report which had dramatically understated school effects. NIE organized several related research programs to determine what teaching and school effects were related to higher student achievement. Over the next decade, numerous researchers conducted scores of studies to identify what teachers and schools could do to improve student performance.

The Effective Teaching and Schools Research

One of the major concerns of the 1960s, that in part was a stimulus for the creation of the Coleman research project, was the depressed achievement of low-income and minority students, many of whom attended school in big city school districts. At that time, the policy concern was that these students were not learning the "basic skills" of reading and mathematics. Two federally supported research programs, one on effective teaching and one on effective schools, were launched to find teachers whom and schools which were more effective than others in teaching low-income and minority students the basic skills. The research objectives were to identify what teaching processes and what school characteristics produced higher than average levels of student learning.

The research programs were quite successful. By the 1980s they had begun to produce a set of findings that many argued formed the base of professional knowledge of how to be an effective teacher and an effective school. Both sets of research, often called process-product research, were synthesized several times during the 1980s. Comprehensive reviews of the effective teaching research include Brophy (1983), Brophy and Good (1986), Cohen (1983), Doyle (1986), Gage and Needles (1989), Kyle (1985), Porter and Brophy (1988), and Rosenshine and Stevens (1986). Comprehensive reviews of the effective schools research include Edmonds (1979a, b), Cohen (1983), Good and Brophy (1986),

Hawley and Rosenholtz (1984), Kyle (1985), Lipsitz (1984), Purkey and Smith (1983), Wilson and Corcoran (1987, 1988).

The findings from both the effective teaching and schools research were basically at odds with the Coleman report findings. Across the many studies conducted, this research found that both classroom management and pedagogical strategies as well as school organization variables were linked to higher student learning (Cohen, 1983). In terms of classroom management, the more effective teachers maximized the time available for instruction. They were well prepared and maintained a smooth pace during lessons. Transitions between activities were organized, brief, and smooth. Students were taught at the beginning of each school year the rules governing classroom conduct, classroom procedures, and how materials would be used (Brophy, 1983; Emmer, Evertson, and Anderson, 1980; Evertson, 1985, 1989; Evertson and Emmer, 1982; Evertson and Harris, 1992). Making the details of classroom management the content of instruction during the first weeks of school was a key finding from this research. The bottom line was that classroom management practices made a difference in student learning.

Effective teachers also engaged in several important classroom teaching processes. The most effective teachers viewed teaching academic content as their primary task. Their days were well-planned and organized. They emphasized student mastery of the curriculum and allocated most of their classroom time to active instruction. The best teachers engaged in active teaching which entailed structuring the presentation of content, using advance organizers, summarizing key points, and reviewing main ideas. Active teachers often presented information through interactive lessons, provided feedback through sequential questioning, and prepared students for seatwork during which they experienced success on 80 to 90 percent of academic tasks. The most effective teachers provided numerous opportunities for student practice with feedback, through classroom recitation, seatwork and homework. Furthermore, effective teachers asked all students both basic and advanced questions, turned incorrect student answers into opportunities for instruction, and focused attention and praise on genuine student achievement and mastery. In short, the most effective teachers maximized student opportunity to learn and academic learning time, i.e., the amount of time devoted to instruction during which students experienced a high success rate (see also Odden and Odden, 1984).

In summary, what teachers did mattered. Through a combination of different classroom management and pedagogical practices, some teachers produced higher levels of student learning than others.

Effective schools characteristics complemented these teaching strategies. Effective schools were characterized by: (1) strong instructional leadership, usually provided by the principal; (2) consensus on school goals which had an academic focus; (3) realistic but high expectations for student learning on the part of teachers as well as students; (4) emphasis on active instruction in the curriculum; (5) a system for monitoring progress towards academic goals; (6) ongoing staff development; and (7) an orderly and secure environment with a strong and consistently enforced student discipline program (see also Odden and Odden, 1984). In other words, how schools were organized and managed also made a difference in student achievement.

These research findings were important because they represented a major movement beyond testimonials and anecdotal evidence on what effective teachers and schools did. Indeed, some claimed the research was broad enough to serve as a beginning knowledge base for professionalizing educational practice (Berliner, 1990; Brophy, 1992).

Nevertheless, the research had several shortcomings. First, while it distinguished more from less-effective teachers, it did not identify what the best teachers did (Brophy, 1992). Second, it based effectiveness on higher scores on standardized achievement tests, which measured only basic skills and isolated bits of knowledge. Third, it did not show what teachers did nor how schools were organized to produce students who were capable of thinking and problem solving in content areas.

In short, although the effective teaching and schools research represented significant advances in understanding how schools could make a difference, it was insufficient for addressing the more complex issues of how students learn to be thoughtful users and constructors of knowledge, which characterize the education goals of the 1990s. Indeed, just as the school effectiveness research was maturing, the needs of the changing economy for thinking and problem-solving skills, as discussed in Chapter 1, began to emerge throwing into some question the usefulness of this burgeoning base of professional educational knowledge. But just as the shortcomings of these research traditions were becoming clear, another body of educational research findings began to appear, namely the research on learning primarily from cognitive scientists.

Cognitive Science Understanding of Learning and Thinking

For years, the primary objective of most educational programs was to teach the basic skills and to cover the curriculum so students would be exposed to a wide array of content. As the National Assessment of Educational Progress (NAEP) results showed in Chapter 2, the American education system can claim some success in accomplishing these objectives. But American students fall short on tasks that require deep understanding, thinking, application, use of knowledge in new contexts, or more generally, higher order thinking skills. But just what is higher order thinking? And hasn't higher order thinking always been part of the school curriculum?

In 1987, Lauren Resnick, Director of the Learning Research and Development Center at the University of Pittsburgh, Pittsburgh, Pennsylvania, wrote a book entitled *Education and Learning to Think,* that not only defined higher order thinking skills but also synthesized the research on how to develop thinking skills and outlined the implications for the public school curriculum. She argued that higher order thinking has been part of the American curriculum, but primarily for "bright" students. One point of her book was to show that the emerging research provided strategies for teaching higher order thinking to all students, especially those in the "bottom half." Resnick (1987:3) defined higher order thinking in the following ways:

- "Higher order thinking is *nonalgorithmic*. That is, the path of action is not fully specified in advance."
- "Higher order thinking tends to be *complex*. The total path is not 'visible' (mentally speaking) from any single vantage point."
- "Higher order thinking often yields *multiple solutions*, each with costs and benefits, rather than unique solutions."
- "Higher order thinking involves *nuanced judgment* and interpretation."
- Higher order thinking involves the application of *multiple criteria*, which sometimes conflict with one another."
- Higher order thinking involves *uncertainty*. Not everything that bears on the task at hand is known."
- Higher order thinking involves *self-regulation* of the thinking process. We do not recognize higher order thinking in an individual when someone else "calls the plays" at every step."
- Higher order thinking involves *imposing meaning*, finding structure in apparent disorder."
- Higher order thinking is *effortful*. There is considerable mental work involved in the kinds of elaborations and judgments required.

While no single definition of higher order thinking can capture all its flavors, these nine aspects illuminate the nature of what is meant by higher order thinking, or as others have noted, problem solving, thoughtfulness (Brown, 1991), or understanding (Elmore, 1991). We should also note that higher order thinking is not generic but occurs in a context, usually a discipline based context. Higher order thinking in schools, therefore, would be taught in each subject area, not as a separate, cross-cutting skill.

Higher order thinking obviously includes a set of activities far beyond the basic skills. Moreover, higher order "thinking is not a skill to be learned in a single course; it is a way of life that needs to be practiced daily" (Bransford, Goldman, and Vye, 1991:147). But if only a small portion of American students today can engage in higher order thinking, increasing that portion to a much higher level will firstly require fundamental change in our understanding of student abilities. If higher order thinking can be taught to all students, it seems to challenge traditional definitions of intelligence.

Intelligence and Higher Order Thinking. Traditionally, intelligence has been viewed as a static or fixed phenomenon and most intelligence tests included "academic" tasks, i.e., tasks that often had only one answer and tasks individuals generally would confront in their schoolwork. Bransford, Goldman, and Vye (1991), in reviewing advances in cognitive science research during the 1980s, argued that these understandings are now under going rapid transformation. There are several dimensions to emerging understandings of intelligence. First, intelligence is multidimensional (Gardner, 1983, 1991; Sternberg, 1985). Second, intelligence can be performed in everyday settings and that, indeed, intelligence in daily settings, e.g., one's job, is at least as important as academic intelligence. The key aspect of this new understanding is the identification of practical as well as academic intelligence, the fact that one individual could do well in school but poorly in carpentry, while another could be an excellent business entrepreneur but have low grades. Every day intelligence is a key component of the modern understanding of intelligence. Third, intelligence is not a property fixed at birth but can be developed, enhanced, and expanded over time (see also Nickerson, 1988). Bransford and colleagues discussed research that showed the interaction between an individual's beliefs about intelligence and their own intelligent capabilities; those who believe they can learn tend to make much more progress.

There are several implications of these new understandings. First, schools should switch from relying heavily on academic tasks to using everyday tasks. Such a shift would entail, as Bransford and colleagues suggested, writing to a particular audience, reading to learn concepts and information needed to solve problems, and analyzing data from experiments in everyday settings. Vocational education programs could be used to teach advanced thinking skills, not just low-level basic skills (Raizen, 1989). The result would be to enhance the possibilities for everyone to advance their intellectual capabilities and develop thinking skills.

Second, the new understandings of intelligence expand teachers' and parents' notions of what it means to be smart. There now are several arenas, including everyday arenas, in which being *smart* is a legitimate claim to being *intelligent.* Knowing how to make or fix things is intelligent, just as is knowing how to design things.

Finally, the notion of intelligence shifts into a development arena. The issue becomes how to develop everybody's intelligence over time not simply to identify and take as fixed intelligence differences at some point in time.

Bransford et al., (1991) and others (Brophy, 1989, 1991; Elmore, 1991; Maloy, 1993; Resnick, 1987, 1989; Resnick and Kolpfer, 1989) identified several key new understandings of how advanced cognitive knowledge and thinking skills develop. Eight precepts about learning emerge from these writings:

- Learning is constructivist; learners must actively construct new knowledge. Knowledge can not be taught by teachers; it must be created by learners.
- Learning best develops when individuals grapple with everyday, practical tasks and problems that require the active management of different types of knowledge, constructs, and processes.
- Learning begins at very early ages. Elementary school and preschool children and even babies have abilities to construct knowledge.
- Learning does not occur alone but through social interaction. There is a social aspect to cognitive development which is at odds with most school notions of learning.
- Thinking is not an "advanced" skill but part of all learning tasks. Learning requires the development of 'basic' and 'higher order' knowledge simultaneously.
- Learning is not content free but occurs in the context of specific bodies of knowledge.
- Individuals bring very different understandings, knowledge, and preconceptions to learning tasks, which must be recognized, understood, and

used in order to help them further develop their cognitive capabilities successfully.

- Learning and thinking, therefore, is not a course to be added, but an orientation to be infused throughout the day and a disposition to develop in the classroom, school, office, and at home.

Each of these topics is discussed in more detail below.

Learning Is Constructivist. Learning goes beyond memorizing facts and knowledge and seeks to find the underlying relationships and constructs that bind and interrelate a subject area. It is an act of discovering or constructing the infrastructure of a discipline and using that knowledge to solve problems, resolve dilemmas, and accomplish complex tasks. Learning entails building hypotheses and connections from facts, ideas, and prior strategies that a learner brings to the problem or task. "Knowledge construction, the bridging of knowledge gaps, requires learners to reason with incomplete information. They must begin with what they already know, target what they want to learn, and think their way to truly 'educated' guesses to the skills and information that will connect the two (Maloy, 1993:2)."

Teaching students how to learn is very different from covering the curriculum and having students pass tests, even with high marks. Learning to understand means that students not only solve problems, but also can reflect on the solutions they have derived. Students need to learn facts, but they must also be able to see implications from facts, develop solutions to new problems which facts may present, and link the solutions they develop to the broader constructs of the content domain in which they are working (Resnick, 1989). While intentional learning might seem a lofty, unattainable goal, it has been shown that it is a learning that can be taught to all types of students (Bereiter and Scardamalia, 1989) and that children taught with these goals in mind approach and construct problem solving in different and more powerful ways (Elmore, 1991).

The constructivist approach to learning is especially important given the problem of "inert" knowledge that plagues many students. Inert knowledge is knowledge that an individual might have studied and memorized and in the process perhaps even earned a high grade for performance, but when needed to address problems and issues in a nonschool context, this knowledge is not tapped. It is knowledge that was "known" or was "learned" at some point in the past, but remains inert or unused even when it is needed.

The problem is that in order to be useful, knowledge must be learned, i.e., constructed, in the context of problems and dilemmas. When so learned, knowledge tends not to be forgotten and is stored in long-term memory, able to be retrieved and used in future problem settings. In constructing knowledge, moreover, individuals not only learn new knowledge but also when and how to use that knowledge. These dimensions of knowledge are not attained when it is passively received; they are learned only when knowledge is actively constructed (Maloy, 1993; Resnick 1987).

Knowledge is useless (worse than inert) if individuals do now know when and how to use it, i.e., know how to match principles and facts with the conditions at hand. These characteristics of knowledge have been termed conditionalized knowledge. Research on experts (in curriculum content areas, chess, etc.) has shown that they have conditionalized knowledge, i.e., they know not only "what" but they know "why," "when," and "how" (Bransford et al., 1991). Further, experts have metacognitive awareness, i.e., they know what they know. Metacognitive awareness is a byproduct of the knowledge construction process.

Bransford et al. (1991) and many others believe that inert knowledge and the typically low levels of conditionalized knowledge and metacognitive awareness among American students are largely a problem of the traditional teaching and learning process. Too often teaching requires memorization rather than understanding the conditions under which that knowledge is significant and relevant. Secondly, teaching often does not make connections with students prior misconceptions about topics. When new knowledge does not change the misconception, the misconception determines how the individual addresses the next encounter with the problem not the new knowledge. To have new knowledge replace misconceptions, teachers need to make explicit the conflicts between the old perceptions and the correct understandings, and to show why the new understandings are valid. Third, teachers often rely too heavily on textual materials that tend to provide academic exercises. This makes it difficult for students to see how the new knowledge works in practical everyday situations and thus decreases the probability of the student's using the knowledge in an everyday context.

Traditional teaching also (Barnsford et al., 1991; Resnick, 1987):

- Stresses the mastery of isolated bits of knowledge that rarely add up to a whole knowledge base or set of constructs (Resnick, 1987; 1989)
- Emphasizes declarative rather than procedural or conditional knowledge
- Is fact and skill rather than problem oriented
- Uses decontextualized problems in workbooks rather than real problems from everyday life.

The result might include short-term success in earning a high grade, but development of a knowledge base that often is inert, and if not inert, too often used in the wrong contexts for the wrong reasons in the wrong ways.

Bransford et al. (1991) and Resnick (1987) also argued that traditional testing reinforces this mode of teaching and the creation of inert knowledge because it:

- Emphasizes recall of low-level skills, factual data and memorization of isolated information
- Rarely includes doing something that entails constructing knowledge such as writing an essay, conducting an experiment, and solving a problem.

In summary, the active construction of knowledge is a critical ingredient of new understandings of how individuals learn how to think. The challenge is that too little of current teaching and learning fosters knowledge construction. As a result, students have too much inert knowledge and too little conditionalized knowledge and metacognitive awareness. Shifting teaching and assessment to activities that have students engaged in active projects to solve problems, resolve dilemmas, and otherwise construct knowledge is a clear implication of modern knowledge about how to develop thinking and cognitive processing capabilities for all students. Moreover, "students who see beyond the facts and procedures to the principles that bring them to life are likely to regard themselves as effective thinkers, people who can generate sound solutions to unexpected problems (Maloy, 1993:2)."

Learning Occurs Best When Everyday Problems Are Tackled. This precept follows from the above, especially the new appreciation for everyday intelligence and cognition. As nearly all researchers have argued that (Bransford et al., 1991; Resnick, 1987, 1988; Resnick and Klopfer, 1989) the only way learning can become useful is if it is developed in a context where it will be used. Thus, rather than relying primarily on textbook examples, the wide range of problems, dilemmas, and issues in everyday life must become the medium for learning.

This approach certainly argues for using manipulatives in the mathematics program, a hands on approach to science, writing for particular purposes, etc. Such real life opportunities not only allow individuals to develop cognitive capabilities in contexts that they actually will encounter outside of school, but also facilitates their ability to use that knowledge in new and unfamiliar contexts they inevitably will encounter.

In the real world, moreover, problems and issues are not "content" bound, but cut across discipline domains. Addressing such complex problems requires the learner to apply strategies and procedures from multiple content domains to the issue at hand. Using everyday problems as the focus of instruction requires the teacher and student to work, think, and construct knowledge in a multidisciplinary way, but as is developed below, a first step is developing knowledge with each content area.

Learning Begins Early. Another emerging finding is that learning is not just an advanced skill that is developed by older students, but also a capacity that begins to develop at the earliest of ages. Bransford et al. (1991) found numerous examples of understanding the concept of numbers, and of problem solving, search behavior, hypothesis testing, and a variety of other thinking skills among young children. The young children studied made errors and their thinking processes were in need of development, but they showed a surprising breadth and depth of thinking capacities. An example is the toddler's attempts to generalize grammar rules calling the plural of fish "fishes" or the past tense of go "goed." This is not an example of poor grammar, but of very young children generalizing a grammatical rule and applying it, incorrectly it turns out, in a new context. The error is not in the application of the general rule, but in the exceptions to the rule that are unknown to the child.

Research in science, mathematics, second language acquisition, and several other disciplines has unearthed similar capacities to generalize and apply principles and concepts in new contexts among young children (see Kennedy, 1991; Maloy, 1993; Resnick and Klopfer, 1989). Children are constrained primarily by lack of specific content knowledge and insufficient opportunities to refine their thinking expertise in the specific content domain, not in their ability to engage in the thinking, knowledge construction, and cognitive development process.

Learning Occurs Through Social Interaction. A perhaps somewhat surprising aspect of learning concerns its social nature (Bransford et al., 1991). In the 1970s and 1980s, Piaget (Piaget and Wadsworth, 1979) was the dominant theorist of the learning process. While he stressed the constructivist nature of learning, his view usually was of children working in isolation. His writings included little emphasis on social interactions which now have become associated with the development of learning capacities.

The new understandings are that children develop learning skills through mediators, i.e., parents, teachers, and peers. Through social discourse—conversations, debates, discussions, and cooperative work groups—students learn what to notice, how to interpret events, and what is counted as thinking for a particular culture. Talk, public reasoning, and shared problem solving become characteristics of classrooms that foster effective learning activities (Bereiter, 1994; Bredo, 1994).

The social nature of learning undergirds the important roles teachers play in the learning process. The teacher's job is not to get out of the way of the learning process, but to take an active role in guiding students through that process. Resnick and Klopfer (1989) suggested that cooperative problem-solving and meaning constructing activities were effective and that such interactions between teachers and students, and among the students themselves:

- Provided opportunities for modeling effecting thinking strategies.
- Refined each individual's knowledge and skills through mutual criticism.
- Informed the students of and socially valued the elements of critical thinking, including interpretation, questioning, trying possibilities, and demanding rational justification.
- Helped create a disposition to engage in the thinking process.

In classes characterized by such public learning discourse, Leinhardt (1992) found that teachers and students worked together to monitor the group's understanding (metacognition), to accept or refute interpretations of others, to propose their own hypotheses, and jointly to increase the demand of the task and reduce its difficulty by sharing it. Using the classroom as a social arena for public examination of thinking, she suggested, accomplished three important goals:

- Students learned the terminology of and gained competence in generating knowledge of a particular discipline, such as mathematics or science.
- Students built on or refuted preconceptions as they built new knowledge
- Students merged actions, discussions, and tasks with the concepts, principles, and factual knowledge in a specific subject matter.

The result, in part, was transforming inert knowledge into "generative, usable knowledge" (Leinhardt, 1992:24).

Finally, the social nature of learning reinforces current emphases on cooperative learning (Slavin, 1990). Championed in many quarters as a way to provide for successful learning in untracked, heterogeneous classroom organizations as well as ways to successfully overcome barriers across races and ethnicities, cooperative learning now becomes a necessary ingredient for developing thinking skills as well.

Thinking Is Not an Advanced Skill but a Capacity Integral to All Learning. The constructivist approach to learning does not separate basic from "higher order" thinking skills. In the constructivist approach, knowledge and skills are needed to solve higher order problems. The two go hand in hand (Resnick, 1987). For example, research shows that mastering reading comprehension, understanding mathematical principles, and learning how to write, which are goals of the elementary curriculum, entail a variety of thinking skills (Resnick, 1987; Resnick and Klopfer, 1989). Further, Peterson, Fennema, and Carpenter (1991; Fenema, Carpenter and Peterson, 1989) showed that when elementary students were taught several strategies for solving mathematical problems that also required arithmetic calculations, they become more proficient not only at problem solving but also at the basic arithmetic skills.

The implication is that schools should infuse thinking into the earliest elementary school curriculum including even preschool programs. Traditionally, schools teach the basic skills before thinking skills—phonics before comprehension, grammar before writing, arithmetic before mathematics. With the new understandings of how children learn, the traditional approach can be altered to include cognitive development and learning strategies from the outset and throughout the school day.

Learning Is Content Specific. Pedagogical approaches to teaching learning skills, moreover, are not "generic" but must occur within different content domains, such as mathematics, science, history, geography, and english (Kennedy, 1991; Resnick, 1987). For example, "knowing" long division entails more than knowing how to divide one number by another; it entails knowing when division is needed to solve a particular problem, as well as knowing that division is the reverse of multiplication (Putnam, Lampbert, and Peterson, 1990). Teachers who "aren't very good at math" have a hard time teaching such mathematics. Being an expert thinker in history entails different knowledge than being an expert in science. In short, learning to think is heavily content dependent. Therefore, teaching students intentional learning requires teachers who know well, at a deep level, the constructs associated with different subject matter areas (see also Chapter 5).

The content-imbedded nature of learning also follows from a long tradition of research on experts and novices (Bransford et al., 1991; Resnick, 1987). Experts not only know more, but they organize and categorize knowledge within the principles and constructs of a content domain. Thus, they can quickly take specific information and set it into a broader structure that allows them to analyze the information in quicker and more profound ways. Further, these capabilities are "automatic," they are a natural way the expert assimilates new information and acts on it.

For example, expert chess players can reconstruct a chess board after viewing the board for only a few seconds. They see the pattern of play that has evolved and thus place what looks like a complex puzzle of pieces to the novice into a set structure. On the other hand, when shown a chess board with pieces placed at random, the expert is no better at placing the pieces than is the novice.

Finally, the style of thinking can differ by content domain. For example, Bransford et al. (1991) concluded that physicists reason towards a goal, while computer programmers reason backward from a goal.

While there is strong agreement that learning is content specific, Nickerson (1988) suggested that recent research results showed there was some transfer across content areas from teaching basic thinking processes such as classification, generalization, seriation, deduction. He also argued that teaching normative thinking (Latin, logic, statistics, geometry) did not impact thinking when the content was taught as just an abstract rule system. But when the study of these disciplines focused on their *principles* of reasoning, they did impact reasoning in general. Despite these findings, Nickerson (1988) concluded that domain-specific knowledge was important and critical to the development of thinking capabilities. Further, a variety of content knowledge must be tapped to wrestle with practical problems in the real world, which are not constrained by disciplinary boundaries.

The clear implication is that schools must infuse thinking into the entire curriculum, and teach the principles of analysis within each content domains. Teachers must teach not only content but the strategies required by that content to make learning meaningful, integrated, and constructed. Teachers, therefore, have a dual agenda: (1) to teach strategies students need in order to learn content and (2) to teach students how to learn to use those strategies.

Students Bring Different Knowledge and Preconceptions to the Learning Process. Learning is not only a product of the knowledge a teacher brings to the teaching process, but a product of the knowledge and understandings individual students bring as well. Effective cognitive development strategies require that teachers understand the variety of constructs students might bring to the learning task and the types of common but intelligent "errors" they can make. Teachers need to know and understand how students learn to be constructivists in different content domains because the types of prior strategies and errors students bring to learning vary by content area (Bransford et al., 1991; Brophy, 1989; Kennedy, 1991; Resnick and Klopfer, 1989).

Research on common errors students make or the incorrect hypotheses students have created, at least informally, has advanced especially in mathematics and science (Anderson, 1991; Ball, 1991; Brown and Burton, 1978; Carpenter and Fennema, 1991; Clemons, 1991; Fusan, 1988; Lawson, 1991; Riley, Greeno and Heller, 1983). Knowing these errors gives teachers a strategic advantage. When teaching a particular concept, they know beforehand the errors many students might make, and are able to structure learning experiences to expose the errors, diagnose them, show how an alternative hypothesis or concept is both different and appropriate, and thus foster student progress in advancing conceptual and factual knowledge in that content domain.

These precepts of teaching and learning, argues Elmore (1991), require that individual differences be recognized and used in constructing effective classroom learning activities. All students bring a different set of experiences, knowledge, conceptual understandings, and problem-solving strategies to new learning contexts. This variability is not unusual but should be expected, for all students regardless of the heterogeneity or homogeneity of the classroom on other variables. "Exploiting" these differences to advance the learning of all students is not only the "right" way to structure the classroom, but also the most successful.

Good teachers, therefore, must understand both the learner (what she/he knows about the subject and about learning) and the material to be learned, and bring to the teaching situation a collection of strategies for linking each student with the next appropriate set of conceptual underpinnings of a content area.

Learning Is a Disposition and Part of Organizational Culture. As the previous discussion implies, learning cannot effectively be separated from what occurs during the normal hours of the school day, or during the hours at home, on the play field, at the dinner table, or at the office. Learning is not a separate activity, course, time period, or topic. Learning is an orientation, a disposition, a way of approaching situations, perhaps a new way of approaching work that occurs in schools (Bransford et al., 1991; Leinhardt, 1992; Nickerson, 1988; Resnick, 1987; Resnick and Klopfer, 1989).

This reality has several implications. First, intellectual dialogues that occur at home or in school provide messages about how learning is viewed and valued. If alternative viewpoints are respected, if hypotheses are jointly probed and evaluated, if alternative ways to solve problems are encouraged, if the topics for analysis come from real world contexts, and if emphasis is placed on both the conceptual and factual elements of constructing "answers," then a constructivist notion of learning is reinforced. If practical problems are disparaged, if single solutions are emphasized, and if factual information is valued over conceptual and procedural, then a different notion of what it means to learn is connoted.

Second, if learning is part of the overall culture, then learning must be infused into the entire school curriculum. An emphasis on understanding and conceptual development, together with factual and skill enhancement, must become part of each content area taught, as well as other activities such as physical and vocational education, and even student discourse during lunch. For parents, the implication is to encourage their children to discuss what they read, explore their natural environment, and talk about their thoughts, opinions, and ideas.

The third implication is that a learning disposition can be created and that a culture that supports a learning disposition can be created. By infusing into the entire school day behaviors that encourage thinking, hypothesis testing, public discourse, and cooperative activities focused on real problems, a dimension of organizational culture is created that acknowledges and supports an active, thinking, constructivist approach to all issues. In short, not only is learning itself constructivist, but also a culture that supports learning can be constructed.

An Example of Learning in Mathematics

Understanding the general dimensions of 1990s notions of learning is an important first step in understanding how school curriculum and teaching need to be restructured to develop learning among all children. Lampert (1991) provides several concrete examples for how this is accomplished for mathematics. Unique among nearly all cognitive researchers, Lampert teaches elementary mathematics to young children and uses her classroom as a laboratory for integrating research on teaching and learning mathematics.

To help fourth grade students develop advanced mathematics understandings appropriate to their age, Lampert (1991) posed the following problem: "Using only two kinds of coins, make $1 with nineteen coins." The problem provoked animated teacher-student discussion that both revealed how students thought about mathematics and the procedures she wanted to teach them. While simplistic at first blush, this kind of example was ideal for structuring interactions that communicated to students important elements of mathematics: developing and defending strategies, making hypotheses, articulating and defending the principles students used to make their guesses. Through this and other similar examples, students reasoned with the mathematical principles of additive composition, commutativity, associativity, place value, and distributivity (Lampert, 1991).

There are several attributes that make this a good example. First, it places students in familiar territory; they are used to dealing with money. Second, it is directly related to the mathematical principles to be developed. With coins, students have experience with taking numbers apart and putting them back together again. They can prove two quarters equals fifty cents, and two nickels is a dime. Third, students can make conjectures about these relationships because they have a ready means to prove them. Fourth, they have high potential for leading students into more unfamiliar and important mathematical territory, such as in this case, for example, multiplication and commutativity. Fifth, this problem allows teachers to elicit students' assumptions about how some portion of mathematics works and to have the students test, defend, and perhaps change these assumptions but in a familiar territory. Sixth, as students reveal their assumptions and prior knowledge, it provides teachers with language and strategies to lead students into less familiar mathematical territory, thus allowing the teacher to bridge old knowledge with new. Finally, this type of problem has many paths to solutions, and does not depend on a routine application of an arithmetic algorithm.

In summary, this one problem shows how examples from student's everyday life can be used as a powerful medium to develop advanced cognitive skills. The example reflects nearly all of the precepts of the cognitive approach to learning, provides a natural and comfortable setting for teachers and students to engage in complex intellectual dialogue, and in the process not only connotates a new view of mathematics as a field but also helps advance student understanding of mathematical principles. It should be noted that this example and its attributes would work as effectively in a classroom in low-income communities as well as higher income communities.

DEVELOPING LEARNING IN THE CONTENT AREAS

While the eight general precepts of the cognitive approach to learning discussed in the previous section provide a good overview, the content-imbedded nature of learning, which is one of the precepts, suggests that it is appropriate, even mandatory, to identify the specific characteristics of learning in each of the content domains (see Kennedy, 1991; Resnick and Klopfer, 1989). As Bransford et al. (1991) concluded, both the style and substance of learning is different across content domains (see also Kennedy, 1991; Resnick and Klopfer, 1989). While a general understanding of how learning today is different from past notions of learning or schooling, the texture of learning in each content domain also needs to be understood. This section briefly discusses what learning means in several content domains: reading, writing, mathematics, science, and history/social studies. Although the school curriculum includes topics beyond these four (e.g., art, music, health, physical education, vocational education), these five areas illuminate how learning is specific to key content areas. In developing a school program, the specifics of learning in each content domain would need to be stipulated and the school program organized to capitalize on the unique nature of learning in each content area.

Reading

Traditionally, reading or language arts has been taught as a set of different subjects: phonics, decoding, spelling, grammar, writing mechanics, comprehension, and expository writing (Adams, 1990; Goodlad, 1984). The content for reading comprehension has typically not included materials from nonlanguage arts content areas, even though comprehension and writing capabilities are crucial for science, mathematics, and other subjects. Reading and reading comprehension has been taught as a set of subskills that could be taught in isolation (Resnick, 1987; Smith, 1992). Many curriculum programs, therefore, included a series of subskill exercises; it was assumed that when all subskills were mastered, reading comprehension would emerge.

Cognitive approaches to reading view it quite differently. To begin, reading is done for a purpose or for pleasure, not just as an isolated task (Brophy, 1992). In addition, reading is viewed as a sense-making process of finding meaning, or through social discourse, conversation, negotiating meaning from text. Further, good reading is developed not by reading artificial stories in school reading books, but by reading real literature—novels, poems, and stories as well as passages from history, science, and mathematics. Finally, in these processes, the traditional skills of phonics, spelling, grammar, and writing mechanics are developed in the context of reading authentic materials. In short, reading becomes an activity that uses real not artificial text, has extracted meaning from the text as the primary goal, and embeds skill development within this sense-making process (Smith, 1992).

In reviewing 20 years of research on reading, Dole and associates (1991) reinforce these cognitive notions of reading. Reading comprehension, they concluded, is an interaction of reading and the construction of comprehension. All readers, it turns out, use the knowledge they already have and the cues or information in the text to build, or construct, meaning from the text. Indeed, Dole et al. (1991) conclude that even novice readers can act like experts if they are given texts and tasks for which they have the appropriate background information, and experts can function like novices if given poorly written textual materials.

The key to the construction of meaning, i.e., reading comprehension, depends on two entities: the background knowledge (Bransford, 1979) the reader brings to the task and the set of strategies they use to garner meaning from the text. Background or prior knowledge is a critical component of reading comprehension for prior knowledge is the filter each individual uses to determine importance, draw inference, elaborate text, and construct understanding or comprehension (Dole et al., 1991).

Knowledge, however, can be inert, incomplete, fragmented, or in conflict with the information in the text. Students are unlikely to change their understanding or fill in their knowledge voids unless they become aware of the conflicts or inadequacy of their current information and realize the validity of the new information in the text. In order for those processes to occur, individuals need a set of strategies to make sense of text and put new knowledge into a restructured and active (v. inert) knowledge base.

Good readers, thus, have more than good reading skills; they have a set of powerful reading compression strategies. Further, they use those strategies intentionally, they use them to extract meaning from what they read, they use the strategies flexibly by deploying different strategies in different situations, and finally, they are metacognitively aware, i.e., they reflect on their sense-making activities as they read text. In short, good readers attack reading comprehension quite sophisticatedly, and actively and consciously construct meaning from text (Dole et al, 1991).

Helping students become more proficient at reading comprehension, then, becomes a task of helping them to develop strategies they can use to extract meaning from text. Dole et al. (1991) identified five effective reading comprehension strategies:

- Determining importance, including main idea, the distinction between author-determined importance and reader-determined importance, and how to differentiate important from unimportant information
- Summarizing information, which includes the ability to differentiate more important from less important information, and to synthesize text to a set of key ideas
- Drawing inferences, which is at the heart of comprehension, and includes making inferences from what is read and filling in details to elaborate and make more clear what is read

- Generating questions, often in public settings, to probe their understandings and to test the understandings that they have constructed
- Monitoring comprehension which includes being aware of the quality of one's textual understanding and knowing when, how, and what to do as comprehension is inadequate or fails to emerge.

Dole et al. (1991) elaborated on these strategies and also cite research in which these strategies have been explicitly taught to students.

The example of reciprocal teaching illustrates these implications (Palinscar and Brown, 1984). Reciprocal teaching is an instructional procedure in which teachers and students take turns leading discussions about shared text in order to achieve common understanding through the flexible application of four comprehension strategies:

- *Question generating.* Text is read silently, orally by the student or orally by the teacher, depending on the reading ability of the class. The dialogue leader (either teacher or student) begins the discussion by asking questions about the text. The group discusses these question, raises additional questions, and resolves disagreement by rereading and coming to agreement.
- *Summarizing.* The dialogue leader offers the initial summary, and discussion follows to achieve consensus. The idea is to summarize and synthesize the gist of what was read.
- *Clarifying.* This occurs throughout the discussion whenever a concept, word, piece of information, or phrase is misunderstood. Both students and the teacher can contribute to clarification.
- *Predicting.* The discussion leader generates individually and asks members of the group to make predictions of what might appear in the next portions of the text. The members of the group are guided in this process by using priori knowledge of the topic and clues provided in the text.

Reciprocal teaching not only reflects the types of instructional strategies Dole et al. (1991) suggest for teaching reading comprehension, but also the constructivist and social nature of reading. Reciprocal teaching is a research proven effective strategy for developing reading comprehension expertise (see also Palinscar and Brown, 1989).

There are several implications of the new understanding of reading for the teaching of reading. First, reading should always be done for a purpose—enjoyment or to get information. Thus, reading passages could include content from all subject areas including science, mathematics, or history. Sustained, silent reading of books of choice for pleasure also becomes an appropriate school activity. Second, reading materials in school should be authentic and not artificial; students should read actual children's literature, poems, newspapers, and other materials. Third, reading comprehensive instruction needs to focus on helping students develop the above strategies to enable them to actively, successfully, and consciously make meaning of text.

In summary, our understanding of how individuals become good readers has changed dramatically over the years. Reading comprehension, a higher level strategy, is not the sum of a set of discrete skills that can be developed individually and in isolation. Reading comprehension is an action of making sense out of real, textual materials. The sense-making process is a combination of the background knowledge a student brings to the task and a set of strategies the individual uses to consciously make meaning out of the text being read. Teaching these sense-making strategies, thus, becomes a primary objective of new instructional approaches toward developing reading comprehension capabilities.

Writing

Traditionally, writing has emphasized mechanics: grammar, punctuation, capitalization, spelling, and handwriting. To be sure, schools offered expository writing classes and good writing was required in numerous classrooms around the country. But the emphasis of instruction, and what was tested, tended to be on the mechanical skills involved in writing (Goodlad, 1984).

Today, writing also is viewed as a complex, cognitive activity. Writing is understood as an act that is conducted for a purpose. The cognitive view of writing is that it is the way individuals organize and communicate their thinking to a particular audience for a particular purpose, by consciously using a set of writing strategies.

Writing is not only viewed as a quintessential cognitive process, concludes Hull (1989) but as a set of processes (planning, writing, rewriting, etc.) that occur recursively, in no particular order. Thus, while a complex cognitive activity, writing is not necessarily a "neat" activity. It is, however, an activity that entails organizing, structuring, putting text to paper, and revising several times. In the process of creating authentic compositions, students develop and revise outlines, create a series of drafts that are revised over time, and thus polish their final writing product (Brophy, 1992; Englert and Raphael, 1989; Scardamalia and Bereiter, 1986).

Hull argues that expert writers give more attention to some of these processes than do novice writers. Beginning writers usually have incomplete or flawed understandings of what writing entails, but research shows all individuals can be taught writing skills and can become good writers (Hillocks, 1991; Hull, 1989).

Good writing also is a product of social construction, in which writers receive feedback from either individual students and/or teachers. Indeed, the feedback often occurs through one-on-one or group dialogues as each reader recites the meaning they have garnered from the text, identifies areas where clarity is needed, and discusses with the writer mechanisms for making key points clearer.

These findings suggest several implications for how to teach writing (Hillocks, 1987; 1991). First, students must be given opportunities to write; good writing is a product of writing over time. Second, teachers must provide instruction in the processes of writing: planning, organizing, outlining, drafting, obtaining feedback, rewriting, and editing. Third, classroom opportunities must be structured to have each writer receive feedback on each successive draft, through whole or small group discourse. These activities, it should be noted, help socialize students into a discourse community over writing (Hull,

1989), which becomes another component of an organizational culture that has a disposition toward learning.

Mathematics

Most individuals perceive mathematics as a discipline characterized by rules, calculations, formulas, quantitative manipulations, and single answers. Mathematics is viewed as a discipline of linear reasoning and deductive logic conducted by individuals usually in isolation. It is formalistic, rarely or simplisticly related to real life problems, and few people "are good at math."

The cognitive view of mathematics is that it is a discipline characterized by exploring, conjecturing, reasoning, and using mathematical and quantitative principles to solve nonroutine problems (Carpenter, Moser, and Romberg, 1982; Ginsburg, 1983, 1989; Lampert, 1991; Resnick and Omanson, 1986; Schoenfeld, 1989). Lampert (1991) argued that mathematics is produced by testing assertions in a reasoned argument, and that development of mathematical knowledge emerges from a community of discourse in which individuals (students) make generalizations and hypotheses and defend or change them through the course of the discussion. Classrooms that develop this type of mathematical capacity are characterized not by students working alone on worksheets that provide drills in arithmetic skills, but by students working in groups and with the teacher to solve real life problems that require simultaneous development of computational skills and reasoning with mathematic principles (Brophy, 1992). In short, mathematics too is a discipline that is learned through constructing knowledge.

There is a rapidly growing body of research documenting children's natural mathematical inclinations, i.e., the informal understandings and problem-solving strategies they bring to problems at even the earliest ages (Carpenter, Moser, and Romberg, 1982; Ginsburg, 1983, 1989; Resnick and Omanson, 1986; Schoenfeld, 1989). Young children have informal ideas about values of more and less, numbers, adding, subtracting, multiplying, commutativity, and distributivity. For example, young children could multiply 3×4 by adding 4 and 4 and getting 8, then saying for the other 4, which is a combination of 2 and 2, that 8 plus 2 is ten, and ten plus 2 is 12, so 3 times 4 is 12. This example shows remarkable mathematical reasoning, and a finesse with mathematical reasoning that would surprise most adults or teachers.

When confronted with new or somewhat more complex problems, however, students might apply their repertoire of concepts or procedures incorrectly and produce "bugs" in their analysis that lead them to make systematic errors. Research shows that students at all ages and for all mathematical topics up to and including algebra have developed these informal conceptual reasoning tools which they use to attack new mathematical problems (Resnick, 1987; Schoenfeld, 1989). In other words, research shows that even without formal mathematical instruction, children naturally engage in the cognitive construction of mathematical knowledge.

Resnick (1987) concluded, moreover, that most student errors in doing mathematics derive not from careless mistakes but from systematically applying incorrect procedures. The problem is that most mathematical instruction does not engage students in meaning-construction activities, but stresses routine application of rules that leads to errors when students confront nonroutine problems. Research on how individuals successful in mathematics attack problems concludes that they engage in several identifiable strategies (Resnick 1987; Schoenfeld, 1985, 1987, 1989):

- Planning to identify the nature of the problem and the alternative strategies that could be used to solve it
- Task analysis to test alternative strategies for attaching the problems as well as generating solutions to subproblems
- Checking their manipulation of symbols by referencing the meaning of those symbols and not just a rote following of rules
- Metacognitive checking in which they monitor their own understanding, check for consistency, relate new material to prior knowledge, and probe the degree to which their solution "makes sense."

Developing these strategies within the mathematics class, thus, becomes a prime goal of mathematics instruction (Ball, 1991; Clemons, 1991). In order to accomplish this goal, teachers need knowledge of mathematics with an emphasis on its underlying principles, knowledge of students' mathematical knowledge and the types of errors they are likely to make, and knowledge of pedagogical strategies that can be used to help students link new strategies with their priori knowledge and, thus, further their development of mathematical understanding. Problem solving should characterize the mathematics classroom. This focus is now made more possible by the availability of low-cost, portable, and powerful calculators that can liberate mathematics from its historic emphasis on number and symbol manipulation (Schoenfeld, 1989).

The goal of instruction in mathematics needs to follow the general precepts for cognitively generating knowledge (Ball, 1991; Clemons, 1991). Teachers need to help students persist in their constructivist behavior by providing them with a set of quantitative reasoning strategies that allow them to correctly connect their prior knowledge with the problems presented in the new context and, thus, advance their mathematical understandings. This process requires teachers to make students aware of the errors imbedded in the informal strategies they have developed, the differences between the strategies that are being taught and their prior strategies, and why the new strategies lead to correct solutions of the problems being addressed.

Science

The findings in science parallel those for the preceding three topics. First, too many students are taught science as a deterministic subject characterized by vocabulary, rules, and single answers. As a result, little scientific knowledge is developed, much science remains as inert knowledge, and student performance is characterized by incorrect and ill-guided application of formal rules that lead to answers that make no sense. While there are exceptions to this summary, it holds as a broad generalization.

Recent research in science, however, is quite similar to that in mathematics. Students bring to the science class a vast reservoir of scientific knowledge from their experience of scientific phenomena in everyday life. Indeed, they have even developed hypotheses and theories about how the scientific world operates (Driver, Guesne, and Tiberghien, 1985; Larkin and Chabay, 1989). Second, there is a difference between experts and novices in scientific problem-solving. Novices, often students in advanced science classes, focus on finding the correct equations and a way to join them correctly. Experts, usually scientists, spend much time on scientific reasoning: their talk is qualitative and centers around the "big" concepts in science such as force, momentum, velocity, conservation, energy, and the relationships among these concepts and sub-concepts.

The solution to improving science instruction, then, is to capitalize on the array of natural scientific knowledge students bring to the classroom, even at a young age, engage students in a variety of scientific phenomena that exists in everyday life, and structure learning experiences in which the teacher helps students, usually in groups, make connections between their prior knowledge, the new concepts being taught, the misconceptions of their informal constructs, and the reasons why the new concepts led to appropriate problem resolutions (Anderson, 1989, Anderson & Roth, 1989; Brophy, 1992; Lawson, 1991; Minstrell, 1989). To be sure, the specific scientific activities, and the concepts that will be developed are particular to science, but the overall process is generically constructivist and follows the eight general precepts discussed in the preceding section.

History/Social Studies

The themes for social studies again are similar. Although there is debate over the purposes of the social studies curriculum, which have changed over the years (Brophy, 1990), the debate is one of content and more political than cognitive. Whatever the particular goals, the findings about current practice, how students can learn higher order thinking in social studies, and implications for classroom instruction are becoming clear.

Although traditional social studies classes are characterized by emphases on isolated facts, dates, persons, events, and places (Newmann, 1988), the social studies curriculum must be organized around the "big ideas" in social studies (Brophy 1990, 1992; Newman, 1991) in order to develop higher level thinking in social studies. Current trends suggest those ideas will come from history, geography, and civics (California State Department of Education, 1987; Ravitch, 1987). The big ideas could include, for example, change, citizenship, conflict, diversity, environment, freedom, interdependence, justice, morality, causation, power/authority, resources, and control.

Social studies instruction to produce complex thinking would consist of structuring readings and activities around discourse in which these ideas are probed and the content specifics of history, geography, and civics are used to deepen understanding of these concepts (Leinhardt and Beck, 1994). While research on student understanding of these concepts and how teachers can develop these notions is at a more beginning phase than for the preceding subjects, current understandings and implications for teaching that would foster understanding and higher order thinking are quite parallel.

Summary

Research in the content areas on how thinking is developed both parallels in general thrust the overall findings from cognitive research on how thinking is developed, and injects the specifics of each content area into that development. The big ideas and general principles that become the focus of instruction vary in mathematics, science, and social studies. But the strategies for developing understanding and use of those ideas are similar: focusing on authentic materials or problems, exploring alternative ways to address the problems, confronting prior knowledge and strategies particularly those that lead to incorrect conclusions, developing new concepts, and showing how and why they are used to reach new understanding (see also Prawat, 1992). These classroom processes are usually done in group work or other social interactive settings. Such classrooms characterize both elementary and secondary schools. And the result is both the firming of thinking and problem solving, the advancement of conceptual knowledge and the learning of facts and basic skills. Finally, as the next section argues, these strategies are particularly effective for the bottom half of students, students who historically have not been taught, and thus have not learned thinking and higher order problem-solving strategies.

DEVELOPING LEARNING AMONG SPECIAL-NEEDS STUDENTS

Chapter 2 outlined the changing nature of public school students and reviewed achievement differences among groups of students. The data showed that achievement of the low income, ethnic and language minority, and immigrant students who are increasingly populating the schools has been at lower levels than the majority population. These achievement differences must be reduced if not eliminated, and all students must develop thinking and problem-solving skills. An important issue, therefore, is whether this chapter's summaries of how children learn to think also apply to the student populations increasingly enrolling in public schools.

We will argue that the development of learning for special populations evolves in the same way as it does for students without special needs. Further, this section suggests that the explicit teaching of learning skills, generally and in the content areas, is of particular benefit to diverse student groups, especially students in the "bottom half." From a cognitive perspective, all students daily engage in the construction of knowledge. Some are more successful than others, but knowledge construction is an ongoing activity for all students. Further, basic skills are developed best in concert with thinking skills. The implication is that the teaching strategies discussed above should "work" for special-needs students, including students in the bottom half. This section probes the evidence for this implication.

Economically Disadvantaged

Although the country has a 25-year history of providing compensatory education programs to poor children, with funds from both federal and state governments, there is little evidence that the types of compensatory education programs schools typically provide have much of an impact on the achievement of economically disadvantaged students. In reviewing 20 years of research on the effects of compensatory education programs, Odden (1991b) concluded that students who received compensatory education services did marginally better than similar students who did not, but the impact often eroded within a short time period after students left the program. Put bluntly, there was a small achievement effect but it did not last very long.

The reason for these small programmatic effects is not that the programs were not implemented, nor implemented incorrectly. Indeed, the implementation literature shows that by the late 1970s, compensatory education programs and most other state and federal categorical programs for special-needs students, were implemented in compliance with their accompanying rules and regulations (Odden, 1991a). The major reason for small program effects was probably poor program design, in both a micro- and macrosense, i.e., both in terms of what happened in the classroom and in the overall sequence of programs provided.

More Effective Classroom Strategies. Due in large part to periodic Congressionally mandated studies of the federally funded Title I program, we have considerable knowledge about the nature of compensatory education programs. Children selected for service are usually identified by scores on standardized achievement tests. The dominant form of extra service is remedial reading. Students most often are "pulled out" of regular classes and given drill and practice on reading skills—phonics, vocabulary, and decoding. Often, their classmates receive instruction in reading comprehension during this pull-out period (Allington and McGill-Franzen, 1989; Birman et al., 1987; Milsap, Moss, and Gamse, 1993; Odden, 1991b). For mathematics, the second most prevalent compensatory content focus, students generally receive drill and practice in the basic arithmetic operations of adding, subtracting, multiplying, and dividing (Milsap, Moss, and Gamse, 1993).

Compensatory education students thus receive extra-educational services, but its instruction focused almost entirely on the basic skills. Surprisingly, some classroom research even found that compensatory education students received less actual time than their peers on instruction in both reading and mathematics (Allington and McGill-Franzen, 1989). There was little if any evidence of a concerted effort to teach thinking skills, nor of the types of instructional practices suggested in the preceding sections of this chapter (Birman et al., 1987; Milsap, Moss, and Gamse, 1993; Odden, 1991b; Rowan and Guthrie, 1989). While there was modest evidence that compensatory education students' scores improved in the basic skills, there was evidence that their achievement, not surprisingly, on thinking and other "advanced" skills was below par.

Despite the persistence of this basic skills focus, there is increasing evidence that it is possible to develop advanced cognitive capabilities for disadvantaged students. For example, when teachers understand how thinking skills develop, and alter their classroom strategies to explicitly help students develop those capacities, student performance, including disadvantaged student performance, improves—not only on thinking and other "advanced" skills but also on the basic skills (Carpenter et al., 1989; Kennedy, 1991; Peterson, Fennema, and Carpenter, 1991).

Garcia and Pearson (1991) argue that good reading instruction for children in poverty is similar to that for all children and should include a focus on developing six research-based reading comprehension strategies: (1) determining importance, (2) synthesizing, (3) drawing inferences, (4) asking questions especially on the part of students, (5) comprehension monitoring, and (6) a fix-up strategy to "repair" errors in comprehension. They identify three research-based pedagogical strategies to accomplish these objectives: explicit instruction in which the teacher models how meaning is determined from authentic text, cognitive apprenticeships from the work of Collins, Brown, and Newman (1989), and whole language.

Reciprocal teaching is a particularly effective pedagogical technique for helping all students, including disadvantaged students, become better at reading comprehension. Palinscar and Brown (1984, 1989) and Palinscar and Klenk (1991) showed that disadvantaged students and students in the "bottom half" developed substantially more advanced reading comprehension skills when teachers used reciprocal teachings as their instructional strategy and focused on developing reading comprehension.

Bryson and Scardamalia (1991) and Calfee (1991) have documented how the cognitive approach to teaching writing, discussed in the previous section, can be successful for compensatory education students. They showed that students could perform sophisticated writing tasks even before they had mastered writing mechanics such as spelling and punctuation.

Peterson, Fennema, and Carpenter (1991) showed how teacher metacognitive awareness of the knowledge and skills disadvantaged students brought to the learning experience helped teachers structure instructional strategies that were successful in having students advance their mathematical understanding. They demonstrated that young children had sophisticated understandings of basic mathematical concepts even though they lacked computational expertise. Their cognitively guided instruction model has produced large increases in student performance on both advanced and basic mathematics skills, including large increases for disadvantaged students (Villasenor, 1990). The results showed that all students, including those from low-income backgrounds, learn advanced mathematical concepts the same way.

Resnick et al. (1991) also have demonstrated how a cognitive approach to teaching elementary mathematics is successful in developing thinking skills for students from disadvantaged backgrounds. Results from their research have shown that the impact is so powerful that, in some instances, the lowest achievement level of economically disadvantaged students can be raised to the 66th percentile.

Finally, several broader strategies have been successful in developing advanced skills among economically disadvantaged students. Collins, Hawkins, and Carver (1991) show how the cognitive apprenticeship model can be used to develop such skills in several content areas for disadvantaged students. The key to this model is teaching the processes experts use in the different content areas by having teachers guide students through a series of activities in which those skills are explicitly the focus of instruction. Slavin

(1989) has extensive data on the positive effects of cooperative learning on the achievement of all students, especially students with lower abilities and/or from disadvantaged backgrounds. At a more general level, Presseisen (1987) and Adams (1989) have identified several instructional strategies that have been successful in developing thinking skills for Chapter 1 students. Pogrow (1990) has had considerable success in using Socratic teaching techniques with a variety of commercial computer programs to not only enhance the thinking skills of Chapter 1 students but also to improve their scores on both the reading and mathematics portions of standardized tests. In short, the evidence for our capacity to develop thinking skills for disadvantaged students is relatively comprehensive and rapidly increasing.

Means and Knapp (1991) and Kennedy (1991) summarized the general understandings teachers must have to be successful in teaching thinking skills to students from poverty backgrounds. The most important is to realize that disadvantaged students, just as all students, bring to school an array of intellectual accomplishments that include a reservoir of knowledge about language, mathematics, science, and the social world together with a series of informal theories about how those domains work. These learner conditions, thus, need to be understood and tapped as instruction is provided. Just as nondisadvantaged learners, the teacher must be aware of the intellectual state of the child and through a set of educational activities bridge that knowledge with the new knowledge to be learned.

Approaching disadvantaged students as having a knowledge deficit, a prevalent practice, simply is inappropriate. The fact is that *all* students bring to school a reservoir of knowledge and thinking skills, including informal theories about how the physical world and its social systems work. Further, *all* students have misunderstandings and errors in their theories, and knowledge gaps. In all classrooms, these intellectual predispositions need to be understood, explicitly addressed in the instructional program, and students must be helped in reconceptualizing prior theories with new understandings. Good teaching understands these variations and incorporates them into appropriate instructional strategies.

This perspective means that a complex, thinking-oriented curriculum should be part of the schooling experience for all students, especially those from disadvantaged backgrounds. If thinking skills are not part of the curriculum, advanced cognitive capacities will be underdeveloped. Once a part of the curriculum, teachers then need to use a series of instructional techniques that are effective in helping students be successful in this curriculum. Means and Knapp (1991) identified several key elements of instruction for disadvantaged students that various authors have suggested for developing thinking skills:

- Focus on complex, meaningful problems, including problems and issues from students' everyday lives
- Embed instruction in the basic skills in the context of developing improved thinking and problem solving skills
- Make connections between students' prior knowledge, or out-of-school experiences, and their culture with the intellectual objectives of the classroom.

- Use a variety of small and whole group discussions of hypotheses, strategies, and conclusions in all content areas, which underscores the social nature of learning
- Focus on developing thinking skills from the earliest grades, which reinforces the notion that all intellectual capacities develop at early as well as later ages
- Draw on everyday issues, problems, and dilemmas as the "stuff" for intellectual development, which undergirds the importance of everyday as compared to schooling intelligence.

These suggestions should have a familiar ring since they parallel the precepts of the cognitive approach to learning discussed earlier in this chapter.

More Effective Program Strategies. In addition to these classroom practices, there is an emerging understanding of broader programmatic structures including school and classroom organizations that have been successful in dramatically improving the achievement of compensatory education eligible students. Slavin, Karweit, and Madden (1989) and Slavin, Karweit, and Wasik (1994) summarized the research showing the following as particularly successful for compensatory education:

1. Early childhood education for three- and four-year-olds. Such programs have long-term impacts and future benefits when discounted to present values have positive benefit-cost ratios (Barnett, 1985; Slavin, Karweit, and Madden, 1989: Chapter 4; Slavin, Karweit, and Wasik, 1994: Chapter 3).
2. Extended day kindergarten. Students from poverty backgrounds who receive a full day kindergarten program, perform from 0.5 to 1.0 standard deviations better in the early elementary grades (Puleo, 1988; Slavin, Karweit, and Madden, 1989: Chapter 5; Slavin, Karweit, and Wasik, 1994: Chapters 4 and 5).
3. Focused one-to-one tutoring in the early elementary grades to prevent reading failure, rather than overall reductions in class size (Odden, 1990a; Slavin, Karweit, and Madden, 1989: Chapter 8; Slavin, 1989: Chapter 10; Slavin, Karweit, and Wasik, 1994: Chapter 7).
4. Continuous progress programs in reading and mathematics, with cross-grade homogenous grouping for reading and within class grouping for mathematics (Slavin, Karweit, and Madden, 1989: Chapter 8; Slavin, 1989: Chapter 6; Slavin, Karweit, and Wasik, 1994: Chapter 6).
5. Cooperative learning across all grades (Slavin, 1989: Chapter 5).
6. Peer or volunteer tutoring (Slavin, Karweit, and Madden, 1989: Chapter 2; Levin, Leitner, and Meister, 1987).

All of these programmatic strategies have been packaged into a program called "Success for All" and implemented in several schools around the country (see Chapter 6). Many of the schools have students who are all eligible for Title 1 services, i.e., from low-income backgrounds. The impacts on student achievement have been documented in a series of well-designed, longitudinal evaluation studies. The results are impressive. The program sends nearly all students into the third grade performing at or above grade level in reading, writing, and mathematics. Students in the bottom quarter show particularly large achievement gains compared to similar students who do not receive this array of services. Further, the achievement gains hold up over time (see Madden et al., 1992, 1993; Slavin et al., 1994).

Summary. The paltry impact of past compensatory education programs on both basic and advanced cognitive skills can be improved during the 1990s. By making explicit the teaching of thinking and problem-solving skills in all classrooms, all students should improve their advanced cognitive skills, and students in the "bottom half" as well as students eligible for compensatory education, i.e., low-income students, also should dramatically improve their thinking skills. New understandings of how learning develops applies to all students, including low-income and low-achieving students, as do the instructional strategies that would enhance learner development of thinking skills.

The way to improve the education program and learning outcomes for disadvantaged students during the 1990s is to make achievement in advance cognitive areas the instructional objectives of the classroom, engage students in meaningful but complex problems drawn from their everyday life and culture, link the instructional strategies used to the prior knowledge all students bring to the classroom, make students aware of the errors in their informal constructs, and guide them in the processes that lead to understanding the new knowledge and its conceptual underpinnings. A considerable array of research shows that these lofty goals are possible for all students, including those eligible for compensatory education services. The 1990s should be a period of implementing these strategies in all classrooms and infusing them into all compensatory education programs.

Language Minorities

Language minority students differ from other students mainly because they come from families who speak a primary language other than English and often, themselves, have limited-proficiency in English (LEP). Before the *Lau v. Nichols* (414 U.S. 653) case in 1974, many language minority students were not given special language help, were "immersed" in classes taught only in English, and usually had a very difficult, if not unsuccessful, educational experience. Under Title VI of the 1964 Civil Rights Act, *Lau* required that the LEP students needed to be given special services related to their limited proficiency in English.

Since then, intense debates have surrounded policy and practice discussions of how bilingual education should be structured. The key finding of Lau is not that a particular approach to bilingual education must be taken, but that as a legal requirement, the language capability of children must be considered in designing an appropriate instructional environment.

Research on the impact of bilingual education programs shows modest impacts, just as was the case for compensatory education programs (Willig, 1985; Odden, 1991b). There are numerous reasons for small program impacts. But just as for compensatory education, a key reason for small impacts particularly on thinking and problem-solving skills is that these learning objects are rarely the goal of instruction. In other words, classes for language minority students also emphasize the basic skills often in the belief that language minority students must learn basic skills and/or English before they can master more advanced cognitive strategies.

These assumptions, however, are inappropriate for language minority students, just as they are inappropriate for economically disadvantaged students and all other students as well. Current understandings of how cognitive capabilities are developed do not pertain just to English-speaking children. Cognitive development and the learning of thinking skills in content domains are the same, regardless of the primary language spoken. Thus, for example, children in France learn thinking and problem-solving skills in mathematics and science just as do children in the United States, Korea, or Spain; the only difference is that the language of discourse is the language of the country—French, English, Korean, or Spanish (Cummins 1981, 1983).

A second and related point is that thinking skills transfer across languages, i.e., they are interdependent (Cummins, 1981, 1989; Krashen and Biber, 1988). In other words, if an individual has learned advanced cognitive skills in mathematics, science, reading, and writing in, for example, Spanish, then all those thinking skills would transfer to another language, for example, German when the individual learned the German language, particularly the German language that is imbedded in the academic discourse of the content area (Cummins, 1983; Cummins and Swain, 1986). Put differently, if you can think in one language, you can think in another as soon as that other language is learned. As a late 1980s review of the literature concluded:

> [T]here is general agreement that knowledge transfers readily from one language to another, so that students do not have to relearn in a second language what they have already learned in a first. In fact, it is clear that the ability to transfer to English what is learned in the native language applies not only to content-area subjects like science and math, but also to skills in reading and writing (Association for Supervision and Curriculum Development, 1987:22).

A specific example is the program developed by the Kamehameha School in Hawaii for native Hawaiian students. The program emphasized reading comprehension skills and was taught initially in a Polynesian language; the program also advanced reading comprehension skills in English (Au and Mason, 1981; Cazden, 1988; Tharpe, 1982).

An additional, important point is that knowledge and the ability to think in subject matter content areas also makes it easier for language minority children to learn English. This argument flows from current understandings of how language is learned. Language is developed when individuals receive understandable messages, i.e., when they understand what is said to them or what they read (Krashen 1981, 1982, 1985a, 1985b, 1992; Krashen and Terrell, 1983). Krashen claims that when individuals receive messages they understand, or are given "comprehensible input," language learning is inevitable; the brain simply makes it happen (Krashen and Biber, 1988). A powerful way to make language input comprehensible, and thus facilitate language acquisition, is to provide background knowledge. Background knowledge, it should be remembered, is a major ingredient in developing all cognitive skills (Bransford, 1979; Bransford, Goldman, and Vye, 1991). Background knowledge helps produce comprehensible input which leads to language acquisition.

A major role of instruction in the individual's primary language, then, is to provide more background knowledge (Krashen and Biber, 1988). The argument is that when students learn subject matter in their primary language, they expand their background knowledge. When students then try to learn a second language such as English, the teacher is able to draw on this background content knowledge to make more comprehensible English instruction and thereby is more successful in helping the student learn that second language. In order to make this work, however, the teacher must be knowledgeable about the background knowledge of the student in order to draw on it and use it in the instructional process.

In short, subject matter instruction in the student's primary language expands background knowledge (content area thinking and problem-solving knowledge). Background knowledge helps make more comprehensible the use of English in teaching that subject matter. The result is faster acquisition of a second language, in this case, English, as well as continued learning of the subject matter itself. The process accomplishes the two major goals of bilingual education—acquisition of English and acquisition of subject matter knowledge.

Krashen and Biber (1988) give the example of two fourth graders, one of whom has good knowledge of third grade mathematics, taught in his primary language, and one who does not. If fourth grade mathematics is taught in English, they ask: Who will do better? The answer is the first child. She/he will not only learn more mathematics in fourth grade, but also more academic English because more of the instructional input will be comprehensible. The second child will struggle with both mathematics and English.

There are several implications of these arguments, which are based on theories from both cognitive development and linguistics. First, the language of learning is neutral with respect to learning itself. No matter what language is used to develop advanced cognitive skills, those skills transfer to another language once it is learned. Second, content instruction in a student's primary language not only advances the student's thinking abilities in that content area but also helps that student learn English faster. Third, student acquisition of English as a second language progresses faster when the student has more knowledge, even if that knowledge has been developed in a nonEnglish language. Fourth and finally, instruction in both the student's native language and in English makes sense: it both advances the student's knowledge and understanding in subject matter courses and over time it accelerates the student's learning of English, including the academic English specific to each content domain.

Krashen and Biber (1988) conclude from the above arguments that the structure provided in Table 3-1 should be the practice for educating language minority students. The table shows that the student's primary language should be the language of instruction in all the core subjects for beginning English level students, who should also be taking a course in learning English as a second language. When students learn some conversational English, however, they should not immediately be transitioned into mainstreamed English class-

TABLE 3-1. Language of Instruction by English Language Proficiency by Subject Area

Student English Language Proficiency	Mainstreamed English	Sheltered English	Student's Primary Language
Beginning	art, music, PE	ESL	language arts, science, social studies, math
Intermediate	art, music, PE	ESL, math, science	social studies, language arts
Advanced	art, music, PE, math, science	ESL, social studies	language arts
Mainstreamed	all subjects		enrichment

Abbreviations: PE, Physical Education; ESL, English as a Second Language.
Source: Krashen and Biber, 1988: 25. Used by permission.

rooms, as is traditional practice (Cummins, 1989), but transitioned into to sheltered English subject matter classes. In sheltered classes, teachers have two objectives: continued development of content knowledge but also development of the academic English particular to the content itself. Science and mathematics become the first sheltered English classes because those subjects have more of a language of their own. Social studies is the next sheltered English class. Only when students are proficient in conversational and academic English should they be transitioned into mainstream English taught classrooms.

Krashen and Biber (1988) identify several California bilingual education programs that have followed this strategy with considerable success. Other researchers have found similar examples in other parts of the country. The key to this more complex structure, however, is that both instruction in the primary language and sheltered English instruction are necessary to provide increasingly complex but comprehensible English input so students, over time, learn both English and also content knowledge. Once academic English is learned, the learning in all content domains easily transitions into continued learning through the English language.

Recent studies (e.g., Ramirez, Yuen, and Billings, 1991) have shown that there are a variety of ways schools and classrooms can be organized to provide successful learning experiences for language minority students. Although instruction in a student's primary language is the preferred approach for providing comprehensive input for beginning English students, in many classrooms in some parts of the country, there is not one but many primary languages that students speak. For these classrooms, sheltered English instruction must be provided at the start. Such an approach can be successful, but it takes skilled teachers, who are comfortable with multiple language classrooms and have the pedagogical expertise to develop both English skills and content knowledge in the same classroom.

The heated policy debates over bilingual education seem somewhat unnecessary given our knowledge of how learning develops. The language of instruction makes no difference. Learning can be developed in any language. For language minority students who enter American schools, the wise course is to continue their learning in their native language while also starting instruction in English as a second language (ESL). Successive transitions to sheltered English content classes with continued ESL instruction accomplishes two major goals: the learning of English and the continued learning of content knowledge. When instruction in the student's primary language is not possible, sheltered English instruction can still be possible even for beginning English students. If such pedagogical approaches were taken consistently, all language minority students would master content knowledge and learn English in 3 to 6 years. The result would be an educated, English-proficient language minority individual and a successful schooling experience.

Curriculum and Assessment for Learning to Think

In order to develop thinking and problem-solving expertise among all students, a curriculum and assessment strategy must be used that stresses the construction of knowledge in different content domains. To develop cognitive expertise, Chapter 3 argued that teaching must emphasize the big ideas and interconnecting concepts in a content domain, and then use the following strategies to guide students in building his/her understandings in that domain: focus on authentic materials or problems, explore alternative ways to address the problems, confront prior knowledge and strategies particularly those that lead to incorrect conclusions, develop new concepts and facts, and show how and why they are used to reach new understanding. These classroom activities can occur in group work or other social interactive settings, and at both elementary and secondary schools. The result is both the development of context and content-specific thinking and problem-solving strategies, the advancement of conceptual knowledge, and the learning of relevant facts and basic skills.

The purpose of this chapter is to explore the curriculum and assessment programs that would be appropriate for such a thinking-oriented curriculum. Section one discusses current notions of school curriculum in several of the key curriculum areas. Section two provides an overview of authentic or performance assessment, a student testing system that requires more than responses to multiple choice questions. The last section then summarizes issues surrounding the notion of national curriculum standards together with a national testing system. These ideas have grown rapidly as the country's education and political leaders have been shaping strategies to accomplish the country's education goals of teaching all students how to develop advanced cognitive expertise in the core content areas. This section includes a review of the concept of school delivery standards, also called opportunity to learn.

A key principle should guide teaching for understanding in key content areas (Brophy, 1992), namely a focus on indepth study of fewer topics. Teaching for understanding and application to higher order tasks means teachers need to structure their teaching around the "big ideas," or principles and concepts of a content area, and develop an understanding of those principles through indepth probing of a limited number of topics. Thus, for example, if one big idea in U.S. history is how wars start, studying one, two, or three major wars could suffice, rather than a more superficial study of all the wars (of which there are many) in which the United States has been involved. This section summarizes national, state, and professional initiatives to rewrite school curriculum by identifying the "big ideas."

The National Curriculum Reform Context

During the 1980s and early 1990s, national attention centered on the content of the school curriculum—the knowledge, skills, and competencies that students must learn. Several national curriculum reform reports, covering the core subjects of science, mathematics, social studies, and language arts, reflected common new directions within and across content areas. Many new state curriculum frameworks, such as those in California, Kentucky, Maine, South Carolina, and Vermont as well as those in other countries such as Victoria, Australia, embodied much of what was recommended in these broader, national reports. The national curriculum reports reflected an emerging professional consensus that education restructuring needed, in part, to include a major overhaul of school curriculum.

These new curriculum efforts are not the first time the country has embarked on a curriculum change agenda. In the late 1950s and 1960s there were major efforts, with large governmental funding, to improve mathematics and science education in the country. While these efforts floundered during the implementation process (Conference Board of the Mathematical Sciences [CBMS] National Advisory Committee on Mathematical Education, 1975; Atkin and House, 1981), research showed that where they were effectively implemented they had the intended impacts: students learned more—both of the conceptual underpinnings of the discipline and the facts needed to solve problems.

The 1990s version of curriculum reform is different from past efforts in at least four ways. First, the new curriculum is proposed as a common core for all students, at least up to grade 10; the 1950s reforms were more elitist and focused on the upper half of students. Second, the new emphasis on thinking and problem solving is somewhat of a backlash to the basic skills movement of the 1970s and its alleged "watering down" of the overall curriculum program. Third, research from cognitive science is producing a knowledge base for how to successfully teach thinking and problem solving in the content areas

[1]Parts of this section are adapted from Guthrie, Kirst, and Odden (1991): Chapter 6.

to *all* students; thus proposed curriculum changes have a stronger knowledge base that can be used for implementation. Finally, the business community increasingly is arguing that workers, even high school graduates who do not engage in postsecondary education, need thinking, analysis, communication, and team skills to engage in high-wage, high-skill job activities, not just the basic skills needed for previous, standardized production jobs.

Today, and largely under the direction of national professional content groups, such as the National Council of Teachers of Mathematics, Science, English, and social studies, as well as state governments such as California, Kentucky, and South Carolina, a new version of curriculum frameworks or standards are being created. They are designed in part to identify the major concepts and intellectual strands underpinning the content area, to provide an ordering of the conceptual matter and possible sequencing of topics, to identify themes with applicability across a range of issues and areas, and often also to suggest teaching strategies. The frameworks tend not to be mandated for use but, nevertheless, have assumed professional as well as political importance and influence. The following sections quickly describe several of the national curriculum reform efforts in the core content areas of language arts, mathematics, science, and history. While other content areas, e.g., art, foreign language, music, vocational education, also are important components of the school curriculum, this chapter concentrates on the subjects mentioned in National Goals #3 and 4 (Chapter 1).

Reading/Language Arts

The National Council of Teachers of English's (NCTE) long-standing concern about the dominance of basal readers was openly raised in its *Report Card on Basal Readers* (1988). The next year, the NCTE issued its first major reform statement in 20 years, *Democracy Through Language* (1989), which responded to some school reforms that had narrowed the curriculum and constricted instruction. The report indicated both that teachers should coach students rather than dispense information and judge answers, and that students should be actively engaged in learning through constant use of language in meaningful ways. Recommendations included integrating oral language, writing, and literature; using literature works rather than basal readers; eliminating ability tracking; and emphasizing consistent authentic assessment by classrooms teachers. By the end of 1991, the NCTE was actively engaged in developing professional curriculum standards for English/language arts and had a completed, but draft set of standards by the end of 1993.

The goal of new approaches to English/language arts is to develop a literate, thinking society. The assumption is that language is fundamental to the ways humans learn and make sense of things. Language should not be seen as the sum of particular parts, such as vocabulary, spelling, grammar, sentence structure, and writing neatness, but as more holistic. As a result, a major debate is whether the curriculum should be meaning-centered because the purpose of reading is comprehension (whole language) or whether curriculum should be skill-centered because recognizing words is a prerequisite to reading (skills or phonics) (Adams, 1990).

Most new language arts curricula represent a compromise between the whole-language approach and the skills approach. Proposals call for a literature-based, meaning-centered instructional program in which integrated language arts instruction is to stem from core literary works and skills are to be taught in meaningful contexts. Students are to learn to read and write by reading and writing. Extended reading of works that emerge from class study as well as recreational/motivational reading are to be used to immerse students in reading followed by stimulating discussions and writing experiences. Literary collections in school libraries are to be easily accessible to students. Further, this core curriculum is meant for all students, at least up to grade 10. The new language arts includes the following emphases (see for example, California State Department of Education [CSDE], 1988):

- A literature-based program that encourages reading, exposes *all* students to significant literacy works, and teaches skills in meaningful contexts.
- Integration of listening, speaking, reading, and writing in meaningful contexts and integration of language arts across subject areas.
- A writing program that follows the stages of the writing process from prewriting through postwriting and from content through form and correctness.
- An oral language program in which all students experience a variety of speaking and listening activities that are integrated with reading and writing.
- A simple phonics program taught in meaningful context and completed in the early grades.
- Guidance of students through a range of thinking processes as they study content and focus on aesthetic, ethical, and cultural issues.
- A school environment where teachers of all subjects encourage students to read widely, write frequently, and speak effectively, thus developing communication knowledge in all content areas.
- A school environment where adults support and model effective use of all the language arts, including reading, writing, listening, and speaking.

Kucer and Silva (1989) indicated that the departure from past language arts beliefs and practices appears so great that a "paradigm shift" is required for many teachers. While the debate over the whole language or phonics approach is not completely over, the trend seems to be toward the paradigm shift suggested by Kucer and Silva, including a greater emphasis on reading and understanding literature, writing, and communicating both within the language arts and across all other key content areas. Interestingly, nearly all these new notions of what should constitute the themes and intellectual constructs for language arts appeared in one form or other in the previous chapter on how individuals acquire language facility and learn reading comprehension strategies.

Mathematics

In the late 1980s, major reports by the National Research Council (1989) and the National Council of Teachers of Mathematics (NCTM) (1989) outlined a new vision of mathematics curriculum and set standards for instruction grounded in the principle that students learn mathematics by doing it in purposeful contexts. The reports recommend that elementary students develop number sense, geometry, measurement, probability, statistics, and algebra, all within a focus on problem solving. At the secondary level, the reports recommended that students study a common core of mathematics to acquire symbol sense and develop understanding of mathematical models, structures, and simulations that are applicable across many disciplines. The reports also recommended that calculators and computers should be available to all students at all times. There was growing professional consensus that mathematical knowledge should develop from individual and group experience with problems as students are guided to search for answers to questions related to real world situations.

Mathematics has received some of the most intense curriculum reform attention, both historically and today. The major emphases of the new school mathematics standards (NCTM, 1989; CSDE, 1992) are on developing quantitative concepts and the ability to use them, teaching for understanding, developing expertise in the communication of mathematics and science issues, and applying mathematics to everyday personal and professional life. The new mathematics "content" or "big ideas" are different from the traditional arithmetic objectives of adding, subtracting, multiplying, and dividing and include

- Sense of numbers, quantity
- Measurement and geometry
- Algebra and algebraic concepts
- Patterns and functions
- Statistics and probability
- Discrete mathematics
- Logic and language.

The traditional arithmetic algorithms are included, but within this broader framework of quantitative concepts.

The new mathematics curriculum standards also emphasize mathematical understandings that all students need to develop such as:

- Problem solving, i.e., on *using* mathematics for real life issues, versus doing exercises. Problem solving is not just word problems, nor just one type of problem. Problem solving is *application in new contexts.*
- Facility with various approaches to computations and knowledge of how to select the most efficient approach.
- Ability to use calculators so in classrooms teachers can emphasize number sense, estimation, and appreciation for/understanding of quantities rather than arithmetic algorithms.
- Facility with use of computer technologies.

The new pedagogical emphases incorporated into the mathematics curriculum are much broader than traditional direct instruction and include the need to:

- Teach problem solving by providing instruction in formulating problems, analyzing problems and selecting strategies to solve them, finding solutions, and verifying and interpreting solutions. The teacher's major role is to encourage and help students "attack problems" by thinking about possible strategies and solutions. This fits nicely into the new understanding of how students learn, as discussed in Chapter 3.
- Teach for understanding (including mental arithmetic and estimation) versus teaching for memory, thus emphasize understanding, teach a few generalizations rather than numerous rules, develop conceptual schema of interrelated concepts, and take more time to develop understanding.
- Use concrete, manipulative materials widely, especially in the early elementary grades to develop underlying quantitative concepts. This especially fits the "concrete" cognitive development stage of young students.
- Use situational lessons, i.e., lessons in which groups of students solve problems in which numerous quantitative concepts and arithmetic calculations are required.
- Use cooperative learning groups.
- Use questioning and responding techniques that emphasize critical thinking skills.

Science

As in language arts and mathematics, science instruction began to transgress the traditional boundaries among its academic disciplines of biology, chemistry, and physics. Project 2061 (named for the year Haley's comet will return) is a bold, comprehensive three-phase plan of action by the American Association for the Advancement of Science (AAAS) designed to contribute to the development of science, mathematics, and technology education. Phase 1, *Science for All Americans* (1989), defined a conceptual base for science reform by outlining the knowledge, skills, and attitudes that all students should acquire as a result of their experiences from kindergarten through high school. The report identified the following scientific literacy that should be acquired by all students:

- Being familiar with the natural world and recognizing both its diversity and its unity
- Understanding key concepts and principles of science
- Being aware of the important ways in which science, mathematics, and technology depend on one another
- Knowing that science, mathematics, and technology are human enterprises and knowing what that implies about one's strengths and limitation
- Having a capacity for scientific ways of thinking for individual and social purposes.

In Phase II, AAAS funded several project sites around the country to develop alternative curriculum models to put the Project 2061 scientific literacy into the public schools. Implementation of the recommendations of the project will occur in Phase III which will span the entire 1990s.

Science curricular reform was also on the action agenda of the National Center for Improving Science Education (1989) and the National Science Teachers Association (NSTA) (1989). The National Center's report on elementary science called for an emphasis on science that equaled that of the other core subjects. It also recommended that science instruction should focus on fewer topics in more depth and on the skills needed for investigating and problem solving. NSTA's (1989) report, *Essential Changes in Secondary Science: Scope, Sequence, and Coordination,* indicated that formal, integrated scientific study should begin in the seventh grade with emphasis on the description of phenomena that prepares students for more abstract concepts in high school. The report also recommended that biology, chemistry, and physics be taught at all grade levels beginning in seventh grade and thus that the content in these subjects, and their interrelationships be developed in an integrated manner over the course of six years.

While work continued on the AAAS Project 2061, in early 1991, the National Research Council, the operational arm of the National Academy of Sciences and the National Academy of Engineering, was asked by the NSTA and several other professional and governmental bodies to coordinate the development of curriculum standards for science. With funding from the U.S. Department of Education it set an ambitious agenda to complete development work by the middle of the decade.

The new directions in science curriculum also reflect a change in the intellectual substance of science. These advances have undergone two transformations, once in the early 1980s, when California began its reform efforts, and again during the early 1990s as the Project 2061 proposal was made, as the NSTA standards were published, as the NRC began its work on developing science curriculum standards, and as the California science framework was revamped. For example, in the California framework, the content of science was organized by its three subject matters—physical, earth, and life sciences, and the subtopics of each:

- *Physical science:* matter, reactions and interactions, force and motion, energy sources and transformations of energy, heat energy, electricity and magnetism energy, and light energy sound energy,
- *Earth science:* astronomy, geology and natural resources, oceanography, and meteorology,
- *Life science:* living things, cells, genetics and evolution, and ecosystems.

For each subtopic, the curriculum was built around a central principle, such as conservation of matter, or the three Newtonian Laws for force and matter. Key questions that are pursued at all grade levels are then build around these central principles. The framework recommends thematic units related to real issues as the topics for teaching the content.

These new efforts see scientific literacy as the marriage of concept and content knowledge, scientific process skills, attitudes about science, and the ability to use that expertise to understand the relationship of science to issues and problems of everyday life, such as air pollution, the world's ecosystems, destruction of rain forests, and ethical issues in biomedical research. Again, the focus is on scientific literacy for all students and individuals and the use of science in practical situations of real life. The most recent notions of the key concepts of science, however, changed the typical "layer cake" approach to physical (chemistry and physics), earth, and life sciences into a much more integrated approach.

Specifically, many new science frameworks including Project 2061 (see also CSDE, 1990) emphasize major "big ideas" or "concepts" of science: energy, evolution, patterns of change, stability, systems and interaction, and scale and structure. Project 2061 argues that a thematic approach to science instruction makes the important connections that exist among the various disciplines of science and enables students to understand the rapidly changing world. Through a thematic approach, the new science approach shifts the emphasis of science education from memorization of isolated facts and concepts in different science areas to an integrated understanding of the natural world. The themes go beyond facts and concepts; they link the theoretical structures of the various scientific disciplines and integrate the overarching concepts of science into a curriculum.

Through the use of themes, students can be shown how the parts of science fit together logically and how the information they are learning is used to describe other kinds of phenomena. Themes can be used to direct and connect the design of classroom activities following a logical scope and sequence of instruction. Rather than strict repetition of facts learned in chapters and units, student explain the connections among the facts according to the theme studied.

To achieve scientific literacy for all students, new approaches to science curriculum outline the following expectations for science programs:

- The major themes underlying science should be developed and deepened through a thematic approach.
- The three basic scientific fields of study—physical, earth, and life—should be addressed each year, and the connections among them developed.
- The character of science should be shown to be open to inquiry and controversy, and free of dogmatism; the curriculum should promote student understanding of how we know what we know and how we test and revise our thinking.
- Science should be presented in connection with its applications in technology and its implications for society.
- Science should be presented in connection with students' own experiences and interests, frequently using hands-on experiences integral to the instructional sequence.
- Students should be given opportunities to construct the important ideas of science, which are then developed indepth, through inquiry and investigation.
- Instructional strategies and materials need to allow several levels and pathways of access so that all students can experience both challenge and success.
- Printed materials need to be written in an interesting and engaging narrative style; in particular, vocabulary should be used to facilitate understanding rather than as an end in itself.

- Texts should not be the sole source of the curriculum; ordinary materials and laboratory equipment, video and software; and other printed materials, such as reference books can provide a substantial part of student experience.
- Assessment of student learning should be aligned with the instructional program in both content and format; student performance and investigation play the same central role in assessment as they do in instruction.

A comparison of these suggestions with the precepts for how students learn the conceptual underpinnings of any discipline found by recent cognitive science research (see Chapter 3) shows how the modern understandings of good school science curriculum reflect the most current understandings of how students acquire knowledge. Engagement in problems designed to probe and expand the key "big ideas" in science and constructing solutions to those problems not only is the preferred way to teach science by the school science experts but also has a research base developed by those who study how children learn (Anderson, 1991; Lawson, 1991).

History/Social Science

In 1986, a national assessment of history and literature was funded by the National Endowment for the Humanities, a federal agency, and conducted by the National Assessment of Educational Progress (NAEP). Nearly 8,000 17-year-old students were tested on their knowledge of history and literature. The history portion of the assessment tested the knowledge of American history. The average student answered 54.5 percent of the questions correctly. Ravitch and Finn's (1987) analysis of the results rated students' overall performance as extremely weak and suggested that ignorance of basic knowledge may seriously handicap the generation entering adulthood, citizenship, and parenthood. They proposed the following strategies for improving the teaching and learning of history:

- Teach history in context so that people and events are portrayed in relation to consequential social and economic trends and political developments. Richly drawn portraits of times and places must include a sense of many dimensions of life—ideas that influenced people's behavior; their religious, philosophical, and political traditions; their literature, art and architecture; their knowledge and technology; their myths and folktales; their laws and government.
- Study history from the earliest grades through high school.
- Study world history at least two years, including study of the evolution of the democratic political tradition and historical interconnections among different nations and societies.
- Recognize chronology as a basic organizing concept that helps make sense of events in the past and the relationships among them.
- Incorporate geography in the study of history at every grade level in order for students to understand how people and the places they inhabit influence each other.

- Enliven the study of history by using narratives, journals, stories, biographies, and autobiographies to tell the story of men and women whose decisions, beliefs, actions, and struggles shaped their world.
- Stress the human dimension illumines the characteristics of individuals who have shaped events through their struggles, accomplishments, and failures.

In addition to history and geography, the social sciences include sociology, anthropology, psychology, political science, and economics. While the social disciplines all seek explanation of the same phenomenon—human social life—and have grown out of the attempt to interpret, understand, and control the social environment, each field formulates its own questions and develops its own system of concepts to guide its research, resulting in a vast confederation of separate areas of study, modes of thinking, and analysis (Bellack, 1970). In addition to the social science disciplines, the National Commission on Social Studies in the Schools (1989) defined social studies to include government and civics, as well as subject matter drawn from the humanities—religion, literature, and the arts. From this perspective, curriculum builders face an enormous task of determining the concepts and methods to include in the social studies curriculum.

Three projects were developed after these reports. The National Center for History in the Schools, at the University of California, Los Angeles, received a U.S. Department of Education grant to develop a history curriculum framework; the head of the center, Charlotte Crabtree, had been instrumental in developing the California History-Social Science Framework. The National Council for the Social Studies also received education department funding to create more general social studies curriculum standards. Finally, the National Council for Geographic Education and the Association of American Geographers began to set geography standards for grades 4, 8 and 12. Draft reports from all these groups were sent out for review in late 1993.

Although there is still a tussle within the social studies community as to whether history or social studies more broadly will be emphasized, one view, reflected in California (CSDE, 1987) and the National History Center, puts history at the center of the study of the social sciences and humanities. In those documents, history is perceived as the glue that makes the past meaningful and provides the lens through which children and adults can come to understand the world they live in and how it is shaped. In this approach, history is placed in its geographic setting to establish human activities in time and place. Such an approach establishes a sequential curriculum that integrates history and geography with the humanities and the social sciences. Students would: (1) study the interrelationships among domestic and international politics, economic changes, technological advances, demographic shifts and stress of social change, currently, in the past and in the future and (2) develop understanding of the connections between ideas and behaviors, between values and ideals people have and their consequences in order to understand that values and ideas have consequences, and that history is not the passive ebb and flow of events but can be and has been shaped and changed by the ideas and actions of individuals and governments.

The "big ideas" for such a curriculum approach (see CSDE, 1987) would include

- Knowledge and cultural understandings such as historical, geographic, sociopolitical, economic, cultural, and ethical literacy
- Democratic understandings and civic values such as national identity, constitutional heritage, and civic values, rights, and responsibilities
- The chronological study of history, but placed in geographic settings. History and geography form the two disciplines that must be integrated. Events and changes occur at specific times and in specific places.
- Integration of the teaching of history with other humanities and social science disciplines such as religion, culture, art, architecture, law, literature, science, diplomacy, politics, economics, and sociology.
- Emphasis on studying and understanding *major historical events* and periods *in depth* rather than skimming broad ranges of events and times, i.e., depth and understanding over breadth and simple coverage.
- A specific focus on values and ethical issues to encourage development of civic and democratic values, frequent study and discussion of fundamental principles and rights embodied in the U.S. Constitution and Bill of Rights, inclusion of importance of religion in human history, and presentation of controversial issues honestly and accurately within their historical or contemporary context.

Common Themes

The end of the 1980s and early part of the 1990s witnessed a renewal of activity focused on dramatically changing the core curriculum in U.S. public schools. Although the various professional reports were developed by independent groups focusing on specific academic disciplines, Lewis (1990) found that they included the following common themes:

- Emphasis on thinking and problem-solving skills. The inability of students to go beyond basic skills to elaborate, synthesize, and solve problems was a consistent finding of NAEP. The curriculum reports indicated that this failing was related to dull content and uncreative instruction strategies. Thus, the new frameworks emphasized problem solving, complex thinking and depth over breadth.
- Development of basic skills, facts, and knowledge in context by engaging students in problem solving, rather than in isolation through direct instruction.
- Adding more content and substance in the elementary grades in all content areas but especially in science and history.
- More rigorous content for all students. Remedial programs have been criticized for putting students at a disadvantage by repetitious, dull content, instructional strategies that do not match learning styles. All the reports suggested that more rigorous curriculum content, including an emphasis on thinking and problem solving, should be provided for all students.

- Integration of curricula. Proposals included reading and writing across subject areas; interdisciplinary teaching; even integration of separate content (biology, chemistry and physics) within subject areas; and thematic units that required knowledge from two or more content areas.
- Incorporating ethical issues, controversial topics and values, both past and present.

Common pedagogical emphases give significant attention to cognitive development and to new understandings of how to enhance children's cognitive capabilities and include

- Active, constructivist student learning.
- Engaging students in issues, problems, and dilemmas in a real life, practical context.
- Reading, listening, discussing, and writing across different content areas as ways to learn basic skills, facts, and knowledge as well as solve problems.
- Reading, listening, discussing, and writing about great books in literature, history, mathematics, and science.
- Cooperative learning.

These notions of curriculum and pedagogy represent a new understanding of knowledge that constitutes a substantive domain. Rather than school subjects being conceived as an enumeration of facts, figures, vocabulary, and algorithms that can be memorized, knowledge is represented as connections among major concepts that must be explored and applied in real situations in order both to understand and use them. These proposals for the organization of the content of new curriculum, together with suggestions for how to teach the content, are almost a direct reflection of the evolving research on how to teach for understanding that has developed by research in cognitive science (Chapter 3). For perhaps the first time in the history of the country, there is a strong connection between the research knowledge base for how to teach thinking and problem-solving skills in different content domains, and the curriculum approach recommended by both professionals and supportive governmental bodies.

Putting the New Curriculum in Place

As noted above, the country does not have a stellar history of putting new curriculum in place in the nation's classrooms and schools. Twenty years after the fact, there was little "residue" of the post-Sputnik mathematics and science reforms of the 1950s and 1960s (Atkin and House, 1981; CBMS, 1975). Kirst and Meister (1985) argued that general curriculum reforms tend not to have the structural components needed to be sustained. Throughout the twentieth century, the reforms that lasted were categorical programs for special-needs students, vocational and physical education, and kindergarten. Nearly all curriculum reforms had a short life and failed over time.

Implementing the new curriculum envisioned above, therefore, will be difficult but hopefully will have a more successful implementation history during the 1990s. There is strong, positive teacher response to the 1990s curriculum reforms. Marsh and Odden (1991) and Cohen and Peterson (1990) found that teachers supported the California mathematics curriculum change efforts, and were willing to engage in the professional development needed in order to learn new content and develop new pedagogical expertise. Odden and Kotowski (1992b) found the same for the California language arts framework. In a national survey of teachers in schools where substantive reform of mathematics education had been achieved, Secada and Byrd (1993: 7) found that 86 percent of teachers indicated "strong support for their school's efforts to reform its mathematics program."

Today, moreover, there is clear understanding that attention to the process of local change (McLaughlin, 1991b) and more systemic professional development (Little, 1993) are needed in order to produce successful curriculum change this time. Cohen (1991) and Cohen and Peterson (1990) found that deep change of classroom practice would take a long time to occur. From indepth observations of teachers attempting to teach new mathematics and language arts programs, they found that changed classroom practice lagged behind teachers support of the new efforts. While teachers exerted great effort to alter both content and pedagogy, and while significant changes were produced, Cohen and Peterson found a melange of new mixed with old behavior; progress was clear but an assessment of overall classroom practice suggested that the new curriculum had not been fully implemented. They concluded that much more ambitious and extended professional development was needed in order for teachers to completely implement the new type of mathematics envisioned by the mathematics education professional community. Ball (1992) reached the same conclusions, including those for more extensive professional development. Chapter 5 discusses more fully the type of teacher professional development that is needed in the 1990s and beyond, and Chapter 11 addresses current knowledge of the policy implementation and local curriculum change and school restructuring processes.

Some Alternative Views

Although there is widespread support for the new curriculum notions discussed above, there also are some alternative views that should be noted. Even though most of the new curriculum standards or frameworks do not provide day-to-day detail on the school curriculum and outline the major conceptual strands around which the new curriculum should be organized, most nevertheless identify a considerable amount of specific content. Although strategies to teach this content is left to teachers, the frameworks assume the specified content is taught.

There are several alternative and new curriculum viewpoints, and all reflect cognitive approaches to learning. Sizer (1992), for example, questions curriculum frameworks; he believes that schools should simply commit to the nine principles of his Coalition of Essential Schools, which stress deep understanding and multidisciplinary approaches, and let teachers choose the specifics of curriculum content. Project 2061, moreover, while it often is discussed as an example of the new science curriculum, could be implemented with large projects and emphases that could last over several years. Schools following Project 2061 could teach the underpinnings of science but with varying specific content. For example, schools could focus for several years on the continent's ecosystem, pollution or space exploration, all of which entail the six key scientific concepts but include quite different specific content.

Some schools, for example the Open School in Los Angeles (Kay, 1991; Kirp, 1992) have adopted such thematic emphases which include, for example, having the entire upper school put on a major musical each year, a two-year program on the ecosystem in the marine kelp forest for grades 4 and 5, and a year long activity in designing and building a city in grades 3 and 4. While these curriculum approaches reflect generally the concepts included in the California curriculum frameworks, they cover different specific content. They could be as effective in developing thinking, problem-solving, application, and group skills, but the content covered would be different from that in most new curriculum frameworks.

There are several other alternative approaches, all reflecting the cognitive approach to learning, but differing from the typical new curriculum framework. These differences in curriculum approaches were explored by an *Education Week* (1992) special report. There may be no "right" answer to how the new curriculum should look. The dilemma is that most school curriculum now does not stress conceptual understanding nor development of thinking and problem-solving expertise within content areas. The curriculum needs to be changed. A statewide approach such as California has adopted, which is sanctioned by the National Science Foundation in its state systemic initiative, might be the approach needed to get sufficient curriculum transformation. How equally powerful alternative approaches will be handled is a policy decision for each state and district to determine.

AUTHENTIC OR PERFORMANCE-BASED STUDENT ASSESSMENT

A revised school curriculum logically needs a revised student testing and assessment approach. Indeed, the early 1990s witnessed unprecedented action in rethinking the way students are tested in most classrooms, schools, districts, and states. A new language emerged calling for "authentic" or "performance-based" tests. "Beyond the bubble" conferences were organized, urging new testing approaches that went beyond having students fill in the correct bubble on multiple choice, paper, and pencil examinations. Educators and policy-makers wanted tests that indicated not only what students knew but also what they could do; an emerging consensus was that this information could only be provided by revamping the nation's student testing mechanisms. By the mid-1990s, pundits began to claim that the profession was "reinventing" the technology for assessing student achievement.[2]

---

[2]See Office of Technology Assessment (1992) for a comprehensive overview of testing in American schools.

Problems with the Nation's Current Testing Program

Although there currently is no formal national testing system per se, except for the periodic monitoring of student achievement by NAEP, the tests nearly all states and districts use to assess the impact of their educational programs constitute an informal national system and generally include some form of commercial, standardized, norm-referenced tests such as the California Test of Basic Skills, the Iowa Test of Basic Skills, and the Metropolitan Achievement Tests. Nearly all students in the country take some form of these tests at least once or twice a year (Office of Technology Assessment, 1992). For many years, such tests were required for Chapter 1 evaluations.

In assessing the appropriateness of these tests for evaluating student performance in the new curriculum standards, or in reflecting current understandings of how students acquire knowledge, or for producing equitable results across students of different ethnic and gender characteristics, Resnick (1991), Resnick and Resnick (1992) and Resnick in *Education Week* (1992), among others, claimed that there were two major problems with "standardized" tests. The first was that those tests reflect an outmoded form of learning, at least a form of learning and knowledge that is at odds with the understanding of learning discussed in Chapter 3. The second was that norm-referenced tests imply a "bell curve" of performance which posits that some students achieve at the high end, many in the middle, and some at the low end; this clearly is inconsistent with the national goal of raising *all* students to much higher levels of achievement.

Norm-referenced tests are comprised of nearly all multiple choice or true/false items. Mathematics sections emphasize arithmetic calculations; science emphasizes facts, terms, and vocabulary; writing is tested by correct spelling and grammar; reading passages are rarely longer than 500 words; and history questions are replete with dates, places, and people. Students often have to answer two items per minute in order to score well. There is only one right answer to each question. Questions that nearly everyone can do, as well as cannot do, are excluded. All testing is individual.

Norm-referenced testing, therefore, connotes that knowledge is decontextualized and composed of bits of information that do not add up to any body of content. It suggests that learning should focus on facts and data, and not concepts and connections. It implies that there is only one solution to problems. It suggests that problems require single, rather than multiple steps to solve. It signals that learning is individual and not social. And it indicates that knowledge and learning are abstract and academic, rather than connected to the real world.

In short, the current and dominant approaches to testing are at odds with the kind of learning in which we now want students to be engaged. If such testing is not changed, students at best will get mixed messages about the learning goals of schools—one from the curriculum taught and another from how their performance is assessed. It is quite likely that most students would succumb to the message imbedded in the tests, under the belief that test scores lead to grades and opportunities. Unless schools, school districts, and states want to continue a mixed message or support a disjuncture between the curriculum it teaches and the knowledge it tests, a restructuring of testing mechanisms is required.

The second flaw of current norm-referenced tests is that they reflect a "bell curve" ideology, i.e., that scores must reflect the variation in student abilities. Thus, some students must score high, most will score in the middle, and some must score at the bottom. The bell curve usually occurs with letter grades as well, with most receiving a C, only the brightest receiving an A and the slowest receiving Ds and Fs. Indeed, if a teacher gives too many As and Bs, she/he is often reprimanded for being too "soft" on grades.

The bell curve notion of scoring tests reflects the current organization of most schools that provide essentially the same amount of instruction to all students, with student achievement varying (National Commission on Time and Learning, 1994). But it is at odds with the inherent tenets of the learning outlined in Chapter 3 which holds that all students can attain high levels of thinking expertise in the core content areas. Some students might need more time and/or more explicit instruction than others, but all students can achieve considerable thinking and problem-solving expertise in the content areas of reading, writing, mathematics, science, and history. A new testing system, therefore, must include a scoring rubric that could show all students performing at certain levels of behavior, and connoting that that reality is attainable. The sorting metric of most norm-referenced tests, which compare one student's performance to another, simply is out of sync with the notion that all students can achieve at high levels. While criterion-referenced tests always have been able to respond to this new notion of performance, rooting out the notion that performance must vary because ability varies is a key imperative if the national education goals are ever to be met.

An Overview of Performance-Based Assessment

Performance-based testing seems to be emerging as the alternative to norm-referenced testing practices. Performance-based testing seeks to determine student knowledge by assessing student performance in using knowledge to solve a problem, conduct an experiment, or engage generally in some complex task. A student might need to explain historical events, perform a science experiment, write a persuasive essay, or solve a multiple-step mathematics problem. Several strategies can be used. Open-ended or extended responses usually require students to explore a topic orally or in writing. Extended projects require sustained work on a topic carried out over several hours, or even days or weeks. Portfolios are selections of a variety of a student's performance-based work. All these methods require students to construct their responses in the knowledge that their work will be evaluated according to agreed-upon criteria.

Multiple correct answers are possible. The tasks can include some component of group interaction. The tasks usually require the assimilation of concepts and facts for the purpose of performing the task. Often, students need to explain and justify their responses, rather than just provide answers.

Trained scorers judge student performance. Scoring generally reflects the expertise level of the student's performance: basic, proficient, advanced. Sometimes the scoring rubric includes 5 or 6 performance levels, or just novice, apprentice, proficient, and distinguished levels. Such tests also assume implicitly that with enough of appropriate instruction, all students can achieve at the basic level and nearly all at the proficient level.

The key principles that guide creation of such student testing are that they must be tied to the curriculum taught and that they must reflect the type of learning and knowledge embedded in that curriculum. Baker, O'Neil, and Linn (1993), directors of the nation's largest center researching how such assessments can be created, information they can and cannot provide, and uses to which they can be put, suggested, therefore, that such tests should:

- Use open-ended tasks
- Focus on higher order or complex skills
- Employ problem-focused and context-sensitive strategies
- Generally be performance-based and provide significant student time to complete
- Consist of both individual and group activities
- Involve a considerable degree of student choice.

To provide valid student results, moreover, Baker, O'Neil, and Linn (1993) also recommended that such tests should have meaning for students and teachers that motivate high performance, require the demonstration of complex cognitive tasks (problem solving, knowledge representation, explanation, and application to problem areas), be tightly linked to curriculum standards or frameworks, and reflect explicit standards for rating or judgment. They also said the tests should be constructed to treat all students fairly.

Developing and implementing performance-based assessments, though, is a complex task and requires considerable advancement in testing technology (Baker, O'Neil, and Linn, 1993). There are many issues to address only some of which are discussed. The first is that validity on a performance test, especially if some consequence is attached to the result, depends on whether the student has had the "opportunity to learn" the curriculum (Porter, 1993b). Opportunity to learn depends largely on teachers who have the expertise to teach the curriculum and actually do teach the curriculum. As the curriculum implementation section above and Chapter 5 suggest, while teachers want to teach the new curriculum, the expertise to do so has not yet been developed for most teachers. Thus, extensive professional development and altered preservice training must be created (see Chapter 5) in order to have the new curriculum taught well in all classrooms and, thus, fulfill a precondition for making performance assessments valid.

The issue raised by this definition of validity is that the new type of curriculum to which a performance assessment program will be attached is not now taught in most school systems. The short-term dilemma may not be the validity issue just described but a strategy issue of whether the testing system can "lead" practice in the short-term. If the testing system is tied to current curriculum and instruction, it will not reflect much thinking and problem solving. But if it reflects the new curriculum standards, it likely will not be taught well in most schools today. Perhaps the accountability component of new, performance-based assessments could be postponed so that new assessments can function as a beacon about the future desired condition of curriculum and instruction. When those conditions are obtained in schools, then consideration could be given to holding students, schools, or teachers accountable for the assessment results.

Second, there are a series of technical issues related to designing and scoring performance tests, such as internal and external validity, scoring reliability, inter-task reliability, equity across ethnic and gender lines, and scoring norms and metrics that need to be resolved. Basically, performance testing requires the development of almost an entire new body of testing technology, some of which is at advanced stages and some of which is still at the research stage. The work of the National Center on Student Testing at the University of California, Los Angeles, and its newsletter chronicles the development of these issues. The New Standards Project also is working on these issues. All technical issues pose major problems, particularly at the individual student level (Baker, O'Neil, & Linn, 1993; Guskey, 1994).

A related issue is under what conditions assessment results can be used for accountability and under what conditions that it is problematic. If assessments include tasks that are "imbedded in the curriculum" throughout the school year, a goal in many states, teachers will probably need to score students' performance. But it will then be difficult for the education system to use the results for accountability purposes because teachers may consciously or unconsciously use higher or lower standards in rating each students performance. The curriculum-imbedded assessment strategy, though, allows for the gathering of more performance tasks for each student, thus enhancing the reliability of the combined results and providing immediate feedback to the teacher on the success of his or her instructional practices (Guskey, 1994).

To provide results that could be used for accountability purposes might require more "on demand" assessment procedures, which would require about a week in which a series of state-determined performance tasks would be administered to all students. State evaluators could then assess individual students' performance and thus provide neutral, objective data that could be used for accountability. But the restricted time period would reduce the number of performance tasks each student would perform and thus impact reliability. Further, unless the performance of each student were left with individual teachers to also score on their own, an "on demand" assessment would be of little use for instructional improvement.

Leaving behind the tasks would also mean new tasks would have to be created each year. Making the tasks public each year, however, could also lead to interesting public discussions of what the education system expects students to know and be able to do. Making the tests public would also help to cool the heated public debate about what is in such new tests such as occurred over the new California assessments administered in 1994.

Third, there are practical issues of administration. Maeroff (1991) and Guskey (1994) review many of these practical issues which range from the sheer amount of time real performance testing takes in order to obtain scores for all students, how even straight forward tasks can become complex in students' minds, skills needed by students to put their "best" rather than first or favorite work in portfolios, and the management and expense of structuring real laboratory activities. Given the multitude of these mundane practical issues, comprehensive performance-based testing likely will need to be phased-in methodologically and carefully.

Finally, the knowledge to implement performance testing varies by content area. Assessing writing and mathematics is at more advanced stages, and being done in several states. Performance testing of history is at the beginning stages (Baker, Freeman, and Clayton, 1991; Baker and Niemi, 1991). Science is at an intermediate stage but only a few tasks have been validated and only at selected grade levels (Shavelson and Baxter, 1992; Shavelson, Baxter, and Pine, 1992). In other words, while performance-based testing seems to be preferred to traditional assessment practices in most states and districts, considerable research and development still needs to be conducted in order to fully implement a performance-based testing system across all content areas, especially if it is to replace current testing practice in schools and districts (Guskey, 1994). For example, the first evaluation of the Vermont portfolio system of student assessment concluded that more knowledge about how portfolio assessments works is needed before they can provide comparable and valid data about student achievement (Rothman, 1992b; Koretz et al., 1992).

Uses and Purposes of Tests

Another issue to consider in selecting an appropriate testing system is that tests can have several purposes (Baker, O'Neil, and Linn 1993). They can serve as models of curriculum reform connoting both a way of learning and a conceptualization of knowledge simply by the nature of the test. Tests can be used to provide data for instructional improvement, staff development, and student diagnosis and remediation. Test results can be used for grading students, certifying students as having completed certain requirements, or for selecting students into programs, colleges, jobs, or whatever. Tests also can be used to monitor the performance of an education system—a school, district, state, or even the country. Finally, test results can be used for accountability purposes—as a basis for rewards for improvement, sanctions for nonimprovement, or job tenure.

The conventional wisdom is that a separate test should be developed for each specific purpose. And in many instances that would be correct. But, if a test is to be used to make decisions about individual students, each student must take the test. Since a large component of the total cost of any test is the number of students taking the test, costs rise as more students take the test. On the other hand, if a test is to be used only to judge the performance of a system—school, district, state, or nation—sampling techniques could be used to have only a small portion of students taking the test. If both purposes are to be met and both strategies used, some set of students, therefore, must take two sets of examinations.

In some circles, there is growing belief that broadly designed, performance-based tests could possibly serve multiple purposes; the new systems being developed in California, Kentucky, and Wisconsin will be multipurpose tests. All three states are administering an "on demand" assessment that will be scored outside the district by state-sanctioned raters. All children at specified grade levels (generally grades 4, 8, and 10) are being tested, and thus the results could be used for individual decisions. The individual results also could be aggregated to the school, district, and state level to indicate the overall performance in a subject, at a grade level, in a district, region, or whatever.

Time is another variable to consider in choosing a testing approach. Since performance-based tests require considerable time to administer, they are not suitable to be given over the course of two or three days in the spring or fall as is the practice for many current norm-referenced multiple choice tests now given for monitoring and accountability purposes. England tried this approach and discovered it required over three weeks to administer; local opposition quickly grew to such a test administration procedure. A way to reduce such time requirements is to give portions of performance-based tests over the course of the academic year as part of the regular instruction and testing activities a teacher normally would provide. As a result, the tests would not consume extra time, or at least much extra time. Further, the results could be used both to grade individual students, and by teachers for immediate instructional improvement purposes. Thus, "curriculum-imbedded" performance-based assessments, which are given incrementally to all students in grades and subjects tested over the course of the entire year, offer the potential of providing data for multiple purposes and reduces the amount of testing now conducted by simply replacing many if not all of the old tests, including some teacher-made tests. But the knowledge to implement this approach is still in the development stage; even when developed, the results might not be usable for accountability purposes.

Rapid progress is being made in developing performance-assessment programs. The psychometric issues are challenging but several states and national projects are moving forward on this agenda. It is very likely that by the year 2000, there will be numerous performance-based testing systems being used around the country.

Performance Testing: The California Approach

California's strategies and experiences in designing a full-blown performance testing system indicates the scope of such new testing approaches. Its new testing was designed to serve multiple purposes including scores for individual students, monitoring of school, district, and state performance, instructional improvement and even Chapter 1 evaluation. The main components of California's new performance assessment system included

- Individual pupil scores
- Common statewide performance standards
- Phased-in performance-based items
- An integrated assessment system.

The system will be given "on demand," will take about a week to administer, will be scored outside the district, and will provide individual scores.

Individual Pupil Scores. The assessments will provide individual scores for students in reading and writing (known as language arts), history/social science, mathematics, and science in grades 4/5, 8, and 10. English/language arts and mathematics are tested in grade 4, and history/social science and science in grade 5. The middle school test assesses grade 8 students in all five content areas. The high school performance test assesses all tenth grade students. High school students will have the opportunity to take the test again in grades 11 and 12 either to earn a proficiency score if their tenth grade performance was below proficiency or to improve their tenth grade performance, whatever its level. Overall, the tests are designed to have students demonstrate their ability to think, solve problems, and communicate in these five core content areas.

In addition to the high school performance test, high school students will be encouraged to take a variety of specialized end-of-course examinations called Golden State Examinations which in 1993 were available in six subjects: (1) beginning algebra, (2) geometry, (3) U.S. history, (4) economics, (5) biology, and (6) chemistry. California also is developing end-of-program career-technical assessments in occupational clusters within career areas or industries.

Partial implementation began in 1992–93. In 1994, the program was vetoed by the governor who wanted faster implementation of individual pupil scores, which had been delayed because of technical problems. Hopefully, it will be reconstituted in early 1995.

Common Statewide Performance Standards. The State Department of Education also developed common statewide student performance standards—carefully worded descriptions of what a student should be able to do at different levels of proficiency in each subject area. These standards replaced the use of numerical scores in reporting student results. All new tests reported student performance using the five or six levels included in the statewide standards. School and district results indicate the percentage of students who have reached each level of proficiency. These results can be used to set improvement targets for each school and district.

Student and parent reports included individual student results by level of accomplishment in each content area, indicating how the student scored with respect to the statewide standards. In addition, student reports included qualitative descriptions of the typical performance at the different standard levels, so parents will know how to interpret the results. Supporting documents, including examples of student tasks, also will be included. By the end of the twelfth grade, each student will have compiled a rich individual Record of Accomplishment which will indicate what that student knows and is able to do.

Phased-in Performance-based Items. As discussed previously, performance-based assessment requires students to demonstrate what they actually know, how well they can think, and what they can do, in other words, to perform a "real-life" task rather than passively select prewritten answers to questions. California is phasing in a variety of performance assessment methods over several years. First, individual student scores were a function of end-of-the year testing using "enhanced" multiple-choice questions—more complex questions that required students to make choices among topics or use more than one strategy to reach an answer. Additional essay questions and performance items were phased-in through an "on demand" administration. Gradually, data from curriculum-"embedded assessments" will be blended into the new testing system. Curriculum-embedded assessments are evaluations of student performance given by teachers over the course of the school year as part of the regular classroom instruction process. This type of information provides: (a) information on student progress, (b) more valid and reliable estimates of students' overall achievement at the end of the year, and (c) immediate feedback to the teacher on the effectiveness of curriculum and instruction strategies. Over time, the students' records also will include portfolio projects in language/arts, mathematics, and science; indeed, portfolio projects were piloted as early as 1993.

An Integrated Testing System. An integrated testing system means a testing system that can serve multiple purposes, providing information for student, classroom, school, district, and state performance. For the new California Assessment system, integration also meant crossdisciplinary, aligned with the state's curriculum frameworks, and embedded in the regular instructional program so the tests cease to be an "add-on" activity. The expectation is that with both types of integration, the number of tests can be reduced and the overall classroom, school, district, and state testing system can become both more cost-effective and more useful.

Long-term, achieving integration between the state assessment program and other tests districts might use, such as commercial tests, requires development of new forms of commercial tests that are aligned with the state's curriculum frameworks, based on the same performance standards in the state assessment program, and reported in similar formats to students and parents. Integration also depends on postsecondary institutions using the new test results, especially the end-of-course results for high school students, in making admission and course placement decisions.

Achieving integration between assessment and instruction, however, depends on large scale staff development—both in the skills required to implement performance assessments and the expertise needed to fully implement California's new curriculum for all students. As discussed in the above curriculum section, massive ongoing professional development is needed to accomplish these objectives, issues addressed in a section in the next chapter.

Summary. California launched an aggressive new student testing strategy in the 1992–93 school year. The new plan was requested by the Governor, mandated by the 1991 legislature, coordinated by the State Department of Education, designed by a group that included all major education professionals, and developed by both commercial, research, and state department staff. It is a "break-the-mold" testing program, that over time will replace paper and pencil, multiple choice tests with assessments that have students perform tasks that show their understanding of content areas, their ability to use knowledge to solve problems, and their skill in communicating results. The vision is to combine ambitious student outcome goals, with powerful new assessment instruments that are integrally linked to California's high quality curriculum standards. It is hoped that this vision is continued in 1995 after the legislature reconstitutes the program in response to the late 1994 veto.

California is not the only state rapidly moving down the performance assessment highway. Kentucky developed the first stage of a performance test and administered it statewide to all students during the 1992–93 school year; as expected and as found in other research, overall scores on such tests are dramatically lower than current tests. Only about 20 percent of Kentucky students scored at the proficient level in the 1992–93 administration (Rothman, 1992a). In early 1993, the Council of Chief State School Officers organized a consortium of states to collaborate in developing new student assessments that would be linked to common curriculum standards (Rothman, 1993). Also in 1993, Wisconsin began developing an "on demand" performance assessment that will be given in four content areas (mathematics, science, language arts, and social studies) to all students in grades 4, 8, and 10, and Missouri enacted a systemic reform that also required development of a performance-based assessment system linked to new state curriculum frameworks. And the New Standards Project of the National Center on Education and the Economy is working with 17 states and 6 large districts, enrolling over half the students in the country, to develop both new standards in core curriculum areas and an entirely new examination system linked to them (*Education Week,* 1992).

NATIONAL STANDARDS FOR CURRICULUM AND TESTING

As the several initiatives on the curriculum and assessment front unfolded, there also were calls to develop *national* curriculum standards and a *national* testing system, although there were few proponents for one national test. In January 1992, a prestigious national body, the National Council on Education Standards and Testing (NCEST) (1992), issued a report that called for development of national curriculum standards and testing system. This report was the culmination of a series of events that occurred between January 1992, when the report was issued, and the October 1989 educational summit that led in early 1990 to the promulgation of national education goals.

To be sure, there is no clear consensus on whether the nation should have national standards. At no time during our history have there been national education standards, and indeed the localism that characterizes the United States generally mitigates against such a development. Nevertheless, arguments for national standards are compelling and include the following according to the NCEST (1992: E6–E7) report:

> The international standing of the United States and the competitiveness of the United States economy, system of security, and diplomatic influence are national, not state or local. They require national attention to the development of the nation's human capital.

> National education standards will help assure that our increasingly diverse and mobile population will have the shared knowledge and values necessary to make our democracy work.

National standards will improve the quality of schools and of teacher professional development by providing a clear, common set of challenging goals and criteria for the allocation of scarce resources.

National standards applicable for all children will help provide the impetus for realizing equality of educational opportunity across the Nation.

The establishment of challenging national standards will encourage states and localities to raise their educational expectations and standards.

The states have scarce resources of talent and funds for the task of establishing their own standards and assessment systems. It would be far more efficient for the several states and localities to cooperate in a national approach than to create their own standards and assessment systems separately.

These arguments generally reflect the view that education reform is a key national concern that cannot be left solely to the discretion of the 50 states, and that national standards could be a spur not only to improved education quality but also to enhanced equity of education and achievement for all students (see also Smith, Fuhrman, and O'Day, 1994).

Arguments against national standards are equally compelling (NCEST, 1992: E7):

Our Nation's experience with centrally established standards (e.g., at the state level in education and at the state and national level in other sectors) is that they are generally "minimum standards" which act to drag down the entire system. If such happened with national education standards, the entire system would suffer.

If challenging national standards are established, but the strategies and resources for enabling students and schools to meet them are not put into place, the result will be a disservice to the Nation's students.

The establishment of national standards would draw attention and resources away from the many, very positive state and local reforms that are now underway throughout the Nation.

National standards will lead to a national curriculum, which will inhibit local and state creativity and initiative.

The great diversity of the Nation, culturally and ethnically, and in regional traditions, make it impossible to have a single common set of education standards that would have widespread acceptance.

In short, when national standards have been tried, they usually have been "dummied" down to some low-minimum level and thus serve as a deterrent to improved quality (see also Shepard, 1991); unless resources are distributed equitably national standards cannot be implemented fairly; and beyond the tradition of localism, the great diversity of the country make support for common national standards difficult if not impossible.

While there is no obvious answer to the question of national standards, the trends seems to favor at least attempts to create national standards. First, nearly all national curriculum content groups, such as the NCTM, NCTE, and

NSTA are in the process of developing professional curriculum standards; these actions will provide de facto national content standards. Thus, despite strong arguments to the contrary, it appears that professional organizations, not political leaders or the traditional education interest groups, will establish national curriculum standards that, to date, reflect high, rigorous, and ambitious (not minimal) standards. Leading analysts also have made strong statements on the feasibility and desirability of a national curriculum, that would be based on the curriculum standards these professional groups develop (Smith, Fuhrman, and O'Day, 1994; Smith, O'Day, and Cohen, 1991).

Second, the National Board for Professional Teaching Standards, which seeks to create high and rigorous standards for certifying the best teachers, is designing their assessments around the curriculum standards being developed by the professional associations. And revisions in the accreditation standards for schools of education (Richardson, 1994) are more strongly linked to the evolving curriculum standards, standards for Board certification, and evolving standards for new teachers (see also Chapter 5).

Third, several states and large school districts that enroll substantially more than half the nation's students, are on parallel tracks designing common curriculum standards and assessments for them, both through the New Standards Project and the Cooperative of the Council of Chief State School Officers. Although the success and quality of the efforts of any of these groups remains to be seen, they represent considerable activity on the side of creating some set of national education standards.

Finally, the new federal Goals 2000 program, enacted in early 1994, has launched the country formally on a systemic education reform journey. Although national content standards officially will be voluntary, this federal initiative will give states money to develop their own versions of content standards (hopefully following the lead of the various professional groups), as well as performance-based assessment programs linked to them. Moreover, a revised federal Elementary and Secondary Education Program likely also will require the use of performance-based assessments linked curriculum standards for Chapter I program evaluations.

The Equity Issue—Delivery Standards and Opportunity to Learn. Although political, historical, and cultural arguments against the likelihood of national standards can be compelling, the most vigorous voice challenging the notion of national standards has been framed by those raising equity issues. Especially in the context of attaching "stakes" to a national testing system, such as promotion from elementary to middle school, promotion from middle to high school, graduation from high school, admission to college, or selection for a job, strenuous objections have been raised unless other conditions are assured that make the use of national standards fair and equitable.

The basic argument is that if tests have high stakes, the education system must ensure that all students equally have the opportunity to learn the curriculum. Such opportunity to learn means that the curriculum must be fully taught to all students, and taught by teachers with the expertise needed to teach it well. The problem is that students tend to be quite systematically exposed to a different curriculum, with students in more affluent districts receiving a more thinking-oriented curriculum and students in poorer districts too often experiencing a dummied down, basic skills, and facts curriculum (Gamoran, 1987; Hallinger and Murphy, 1983; Lee, Bryk, and Smith, 1993; MacIver, Douglas, and Epstein, 1990; Oakes, Gamoran, and Page, 1992). Holding all students to high performance on a common test would be unfair, given this unequal exposure to curriculum.

Research further shows (Ball et al., 1994a, 1994b, 1994c; Cohen and Peterson, 1990) that few teachers can teach the new type of curriculum well; again, holding any student accountable for performing to high standards on a curriculum that was not taught well is also simply unfair.

Finally, educational resources vary substantially across schools and school districts in the country (Hertert, Busch, and Odden, 1994; Wykoff, 1992). These resource inequities further reduce the possibility that all students are exposed to a common, high quality curriculum taught by equally skilled teachers, thus making high-stakes testing difficult to implement.

Until these inequalities in school delivery practices are remedied, the argument is that high-stakes tests would be palpably unfair. In short, in order to implement national curriculum and testing standards with consequences attached to them, many conclude that school delivery or opportunity to learn standards would have to be ensured as a necessary prerequisite.

The logic behind delivery standards or opportunity to learn is that all students should be given the opportunity to achieve to high standards; this is required not only for equity purposes but also for the needs of a democratic society and the requisites of the current workplace. The problem is that rhetoric on this topic exceeds practice. O'Day and Smith (1993) offer three rationales for creation of delivery standards:

- To protect students from misuse of high-stakes tests
- To underscore society's obligations to provide equal resources for all schools for the services necessary to allow all students to achieve high levels of performance
- To guide technical assistance to places that are not providing full opportunity to learn.

O'Day and Smith (1993) also suggest that there should be three kinds of standards: resource, practice, and performance standards. Performance standards simply mean that schools need to show improvement from year to year. Practice standards, however, could be much more complex.

Porter (1992, 1993a, 1993b) opts for parsimony and concludes that the focus should be on providing opportunity to learn. He suggests three categories of practice standards: measures of the enacted curriculum, measures of teacher pedagogy, and measures of curriculum-imbedded resources (such as computers, manipulatives, laboratory equipment, etc.). Darling-Hammond (1993a, 1993b), on the other hand, casts a much wider net and claims practice standards would need to run the gamut from school culture, attitudes toward children, personalization of instruction, grouping policies, and other curriculum and pedagogical measures. For both, however, the methodology for obtaining measures of the enacted curriculum and the pedagogy used is at just the beginning stages, and might not be sufficient for ensuring comparable practice (McDonnell et al., 1990; Guiton and Burstein, 1993). Resource standards are somewhat straightforward, although the dilemma is that there is no simple linkage between dollar resources and curriculum and instruction resources, so deciding on resources standards that have real meaning might not be easy (Odden, 1994c).

Only future practice will determine how the debate over opportunity to learn standards will be resolved. Since designing and implementing new, performance-based testing programs likely will take until the close of the decade, there are ample opportunities for the education system to provide the professional development and training needed to ensure opportunity to learn in all schools. Hopefully, the education system will be closer to teaching the curriculum envisioned in this chapter when "high-stakes" performance assessment is implemented in the future.

CONCLUSION

Curriculum change is likely to be an enduring process for the country's education system during the 1990s and even into the twenty-first century. A new curriculum is needed as the basis for developing advanced cognitive capabilities for *all* students. Support for such a curriculum restructuring derives from many corners, including education professional groups and national and state political and education policy leaders. Concurrently, it appears that a revised approach to student assessment and examination likely also will evolve during the 1990s. The trend seems to be movement away from "standardized" norm-reference testing to more performance-based testing that is imbedded in the curriculum over the course of the year and provides information not only on what a student knows but can do. While much research and development work is needed before a full-fledged performance testing system can be deployed, districts, states, and the nation seem to support this new direction in student testing.

Finally, a component of local control of education that might give way this decade pertains to curriculum and testing. Education-content groups are developing professional curriculum standards, other organizations want to restructure teacher training around these standards (see chapter 5) and other groups want to certify advanced, expert teachers on being able to teach these standards well. Concomitantly, there are numerous calls to develop a national, not federally controlled, education system with national content and testing standards. While the arguments for and against national standards are each persuasive, the momentum seems to favor development of at least voluntary national standards. If such movements carry with them new student tests that have "high-stakes," i.e., have consequences tied to them, the education system might also need delivery standards as well that would indicate whether all children were given equal opportunity to learn a thinking-oriented curriculum.

While there is merit and excitement in these ambitious curriculum and testing reform agendas, caution and some skepticism is justified. The country has embarked on curriculum reform before with little, long-term impact. Although the new curriculum and testing reform discussed in this chapter are needed in order to teach all children thinking and problem-solving skills, getting them fully in place in all the nation's classrooms and schools will require major professional development efforts, a subject of the next chapter.

CHAPTER 5

Teachers for a
Thinking-Oriented Curriculum

Teaching is a substantively complex activity (Rowan, 1994). In an early 1992 conference organized by the U.S. Department of Education, Lee Shulman described the kinds of teaching required by the curriculum and assessment standards discussed in Chapter 4. He said that teaching all students to high standards "in the core subject areas requires of the teacher an increasingly deep and flexible understanding of the subject matter." Teachers will need to know how children learn such content and develop a set of teaching strategies that coach children through such a knowledge construction process. He suggested that new assessment strategies would over time be imbedded into the day-to-day and weekly curriculum and include performance assessments, portfolios, carefully documented projects, and more than traditional examinations (U.S. Department of Education, 1993a). These behaviors represent high standards for effective teaching practice. They would need to include strategies that worked for the diverse nature of students enrolling in the nation's public schools. If such teaching were representative of teaching across the nation, we would soon graduate students who knew content and could use it to think, solve problems, and communicate effectively. Unfortunately, this type of teaching is not representative of the typical classroom (Goodlad, 1984; Powell, Ferrar, and Cohen, 1985).

Indeed, as Cohen and Peterson (1990) demonstrated in one of the first reports of teacher efforts to implement the new mathematics curriculum standards, teachers confront significant difficulty shifting from the former basic skills, fragmented knowledge curriculum to a conceptually oriented, content-based, integrated, and thinking-focused curriculum. Four years later, they reached the same conclusion (Ball et al., 1994a, 1994b, 1994c). Further, only a small proportion of beginning teachers are being prepared to teach these new versions of curriculum.

Thus, the country faces a major challenge for teachers and teaching. Teachers' knowledge and expertise must be dramatically enhanced in order to "deliver" the aspirations identified in the previous four chapters. There is knowledge from which one can draw to teach all students how to think and solve problems in the different content domains (see Chapter 3). But the challenge is to imbed that knowledge and the skills to use it in the current teaching work force, as well as new entrants into the profession.

In other words, the key teacher issue for the 1990s is the following: How do we recruit, train, retain, and provide ongoing professional development for teachers so that they can effectively use pedagogical approaches to teach the curriculum discussed in the previous chapters and be successful in producing high levels of achievement for all students, especially the poor, LEP, culturally different and diverse students who increasingly populate American schools? Enhancing what teachers know and are able to do is one of the most important issues surrounding teacher policy in this country for the remainder of the decade. Likewise, the school's role in ongoing teacher development, a step child of the current system, rises to the forefront as a critical responsibility for school leaders in this decade.

This chapter addresses these important topics in four sections. The first provides an overview of teacher demographics, the structure of it as an occupation, issues related to teacher recruitment, and teacher policy initiatives taken during the 1980s. Section two discusses the notion of professional training, and outlines what should be expected in preservice training, including the knowledge and skills schools reasonably should expect from competent beginning teachers. The third section tackles the important topic of professional development for individuals already teaching, which includes the vast bulk of teachers who will constitute the faculty for the nation's schools throughout this decade. Section four provides new roles for teacher unions in helping to dramatically upgrade the professional expertise of the country's teachers.

TEACHERS

Demographics, Recruitment, and Policy in the 1980s

Recruiting and retaining high-quality teachers is important for the nation's public schools. Smart, highly trained, and professionally competent teachers are needed to allow all schools to produce students proficient in thinking and problem-solving tasks. Recruiting able individuals into and retaining them in the profession, therefore, are key policy objectives. This is a vast undertaking, however, because the nation's schools need large numbers of teachers and the competition for high-quality talent is stiff. The country's teaching workforce is about four times that of doctors and lawyers, and about one-half that of managers and executives; all of these professions compete with education in recruiting talent. Education needs to recruit its share of top human talent.

Table 5-1 shows key demographic characteristics of the nation's teachers and changes over time. In 1988, there were approximately 2.3 million teachers in public schools, an increase of 900,000 from 1961. Over this time period, the gender composition of teachers did not change that much, hovering around one-third male and two-thirds female. The data show a slight decline in the percentage of males since 1971 and a slight increase in the percentage of

TABLE 5-1. Selected Characteristics of Public School Teachers, 1961 to 1988

	1961	1971	1981	1988
Total number of teachers	1,408,000	2,055,000	2,184,000	2,323,000
Sex (percent)				
Male	31.3	34.3	33.1	29.3
Female	68.7	65.7	66.9	70.7
Race (percent)				
White	—	88.3	91.6	85.8
African-American	—	8.1	7.8	8.1
Other	—	3.6	0.7	6.1
Median age	41	35	37	41[a]
Median years of experience	11	8	12	15
Highest degree held (percent)				
Less than Bachelors	14.6	2.9	0.4	0.6
Bachelors	61.9	69.6	50.1	52.2
Masters or Specialist	23.1	27.1	49.3	46.3
Doctors	0.4	0.4	0.3	0.9

[a]1986

Source: National Center for Educational Statistics (1991).

females, which is interesting in part because other career opportunities opened up for women during this same 20-year time period. The percentage of minority teachers was still quite low, although it increased a small degree during the 1980s. Although not shown in the data, Hispanics constituted 3.4 percent of all teachers in 1988.

The median age of teachers fell during the 1960s, when enrollments were growing and many new teachers were hired, but since then rose to 41 in 1988. The age figures in part reflect the average years of experience, which also fell from 1961 to 1971 and then increased to 15 years in 1988. Given the modest enrollment increases for the remainder of the 1990s and thus modest numbers of new hires, the average age of teachers should continue to increase, unless larger than expected numbers leave teaching before normal retirement age.

Table 5-1 also shows that the teaching workforce became more educated over the past three decades. In 1961, 14.6 percent of teachers had less than a bachelor's degree, the bulk of which probably were either older teachers who had been trained in two-year normal schools before a bachelor's degree was required or vocational education teachers for whom a bachelor's degree often was not required. In 1988, only 0.6 percent of teachers did not have at least a bachelor's degree. Training beyond the bachelor's also has increased. While 61.9 percent of teachers had just a bachelor's degree and only 23.1 percent had a master's degree in 1961, fully 46.3 percent had a master's degree by 1988 and only 52.2 percent had just a bachelor's degree. The numbers clearly show that the average number of years of training increased noticeably over this time period.

Other data show that the average class size has fallen considerably over the years, from a high of 28 in 1961 to about 24 in 1988, and the actual pupil/staff ratio is even lower (National Center for Educational Statistics

[NCES], 1992). The figures show that there were 19 more teachers for every 1000 students in 1991 than there were in 1961, and that the country has invested money in expanding the staffing of its public schools. Research on use of money undergirds this finding; higher spending districts tend to spend 50 percent of each additional dollar on teachers, and of that, 40 cents is used to hire more teachers (Picus, 1993).

Economically, the trends for teachers have been more mixed. Average teacher salaries increased from 1960 to 1990, but the largest gain occurred from 1960 to 1970, when average salaries, after adjusting for inflation, increased by nearly 50 percent, from $23,495 to $31,560 (Table 5-2). Although average teacher salaries increased in nominal terms throughout the 1970s, when adjusted for inflation, they dropped by about 10 percent. Average teacher salaries then increased again during the 1980s, in both nominal and real terms. In 1992, real, average teacher salaries were at an all time high at $34,413. Despite these increases relative teacher salaries have not changed that much over time. Although substantially above the average for many blue-collar job classifications and some white-collar job categories such as bank tellers and insurance agents, teacher salaries are still below many other jobs that have similar education requirements (NCES, 1991; Sedlak and Schlossman, 1986). But, compared to other occupations, the relative teacher salaries today are about what they were 50 years ago.

Beginning teacher salaries, however, were targeted for policy action during the 1980s and were increased significantly. Competitive starting salaries play a key role in recruiting able individuals into teaching (Ferris and Winkler, 1986; Odden and Conley, 1992). By the end of the decade the beginning teacher salary in many states was equal to or higher than the beginning salary for all individuals who entered the workforce with a liberal arts bachelors degree (Odden and Conley, 1992), thus making education economically competitive in early recruitment into the profession. These policy initiatives and the higher beginning salaries they produced, assuming they are maintained, should help education systems hire an increasingly able workforce during the 1990s. Although there has been progress in raising beginning teacher salaries, the average beginning salary was a high percent of the overall average (65.4 percent in 1991 [NCES, 1991]) suggesting that salary advancement after entering the profession was still relatively limited, clearly implying that higher aver-

TABLE 5-2. Teachers Salary Data, Selected Years

	Average Teacher Salary	
	Current Dollars	Constant 1991–92 Dollars
1959–60	$ 4,955	$23,495
1969–70	$ 8,626	$31,560
1979–80	$15,970	$28,431
1989–90	$31,350	$34,123
1991–92	$34,413	$34,413

Source: National Center for Educational Statistics (1992): Table 73.

age salaries should be a policy target for the 1990s. These and other teacher compensation issues are discussed later in the text.

Teaching as an Occupation

Another contextual factor related to teaching and its attractiveness (or unattractiveness) as a job is its structure as an occupation. Research does not paint a very inviting picture. Teaching has been described as a semiprofession characterized by low status, easy access, absence of a body of technical knowledge, and a low degree of self-monitoring (Conley and Cooper, 1991; Lortie, 1975). Teachers generally have little or no role in important decisions, particularly those related to curriculum and instruction; too often, teachers are viewed as "workers" who implement policy made by others not as professionals who have discretion over their actions in the workplace. Teachers are portrayed as isolated in their classrooms and not engaged collegially with others in their schools (Johnson, 1990; Lortie, 1975; Rosenholtz, 1989). Their day is spent primarily interacting with children and not adults. Further, they have a careerless occupation (Johnson, 1990; Lortie, 1975), they teach. If they want other educational responsibilities, they leave teaching and enter administration, counseling, or other roles which rarely include continuation of classroom teaching (see also Carnegie Forum on Education and the Economy, 1986).

This rather dour portrait of the structure of teaching as an occupation was the focus of many reform proposals during the 1980s and early 1990s (Carnegie Forum on Education and the Economy, 1986; Johnson, 1990; Murnane et al., 1991) and many state reform efforts (McDonnell, 1991; see next section). This chapter and subsequent chapters in the book posit a very different notion of teacher, as an individual with a high level of professional expertise who can successfully teach all students to high standards, administer performance-based assessments, participate in numerous school-based decision-making teams, and function generally as a professional rather than just a cog in the education bureaucracy. We would hope that such a new vision of teaching can both help to restructure teaching into these new roles and simultaneously serve to make teaching a more attractive occupation for able and bright individuals.

Teacher Policy During the 1980s

While always part of the ongoing policy agenda, political concern about the nature, quality, and tasks of the teaching workforce began to intensify during the late 1970s with a series of policies designed to "weed out" incompetent or illiterate teachers (Darling-Hammond, 1984; Darling-Hammond and Berry, 1988). But after the first wave of education reform reports in the early 1980s, which were somewhat negative towards teachers, it dawned on policy makers that skilled and motivated teachers were critical to accomplishing the changes envisioned in the reform reports and a more developmental policy focus began to emerge.

To begin, an alarm was sounded with a series of reports documenting the decline in quality of teachers entering and remaining in the profession (Schlechty and Vance, 1983, for example). Another set of reports showed that the supply and demand forces for teachers were moving in opposite directions (see for example, Darling-Hammond, 1984), further threatening the ability of education to recruit and retain able individuals in the profession. Enrollments were rising and increasing percentages of teachers were retiring, thus pushing up demand. But supply was dropping as there was a decline in the numbers entering teacher training. Also as teacher retirements increased when post-World War II teachers reached 65 and as new opportunities for women and minorities in service jobs developed, the pool that had been a major source of able teachers throughout the twentieth century began to erode.

Then another batch of reports were released, sometimes called the "second wave" of the 1980s reforms (for example, Carnegie Forum on Education and the Economy, 1986). These reports focused on improving the knowledge, status, and power of teachers, with some proposing to "professionalize" the teaching occupation. The response was an array of dual-focused policies seeking both to recruit more individuals into teaching and to upgrade those in teaching. States enacted stiffer requirements for admission into teacher training programs, placed more emphasis on liberal arts and content courses and less on pedagogy and "education" courses, enacted programs to provide assistance to new teachers, and even required more recertification by eliminating life-time credentials. These efforts were designed to upgrade the quality of those in the professions but in the short-term, they were a deterrent to supply.

In part recognizing this short-term impact, states also approved a variety of "emergency credentialing" policies to allow easier access into the classroom, and in addition, designed new alternative routes into certification that often times bypassed formal school of education training altogether. By the end of the 1980s, nearly half of the states had some type of alternative certification program, nearly all of which de-emphasized development of professional knowledge related to teaching.[1] As Darling-Hammond (1988) wrote, it seemed that for every move to "tighten up" the profession in order to upgrade quality there was a countermove to loosen entry to expand short-term supply. These policy initiatives not only reflected a schizophrenia towards supply and demand, but also a bipolar view of teachers, with one view seeing teachers as reflective professionals and the other as semiskilled employees.

Darling-Hammond and Berry (1988) concluded their analysis of the evolution of teacher policy in the 1980s by recommending the following. First, the education system needs to identify the content and nature of effective teaching, i.e., what teachers should know and be able to do in order to be successful in the classroom, especially with the diverse students now in the country's schools. Second, the system needs to focus on how to develop that professional expertise, both in preservice programs for individuals, who will enter the profession in the future, and in ongoing professional development of teachers in the profession, who constitute the bulk of teachers for the short to medium term. Third, the system needs new strategies for assessing whether teachers had and could use the requisite professional expertise. Finally, the education

---

[1]Not all alternative credential programs ignored formal teacher training. Programs in Connecticut and Maryland, and other programs that provided alternative routes to certification but maintained high-certification standards, had considerable merit (see Darling-Hammond, 1992).

system needs to identify policies that would fairly deploy teacher expertise across schools and classrooms, an issue implicit in the concept of school delivery standards discussed briefly in Chapter 4. A restructured compensation structure could be added to this list. The next sections begin to address these issues.

PROFESSIONAL TRAINING

What It Is and How It Applies to Teaching

Professional training has several attributes, but four major characteristics will be discussed here in the context of education. The first is the codification of a body of knowledge that would be included in all teacher training programs and which would constitute the core of what all beginning teachers would be expected to know and be able to do. The second would be inclusion of the workplace, i.e., schools, in the training and development of new entrants into the profession, both as part of the university-based preservice training program and as part of school-based, postuniversity, clinical skills development program. The third is some type of an intern or apprentice year, including a probation period, which would constitute a transition between preservice training and full-fledged professional practice, during which time an individual solidifies the professional expertise needed to assume full responsibility in their profession—to take responsibility for a classroom teaching in education. The fourth is a disposition towards career long, ongoing training both to keep current with developing knowledge and expertise in the field, and to continuously hone and expand ones repertoire of professional skills.

These components of a profession are beginning to more strongly influence teacher training and development. Smith and O'Day (1988) argued that the a key for seriously addressing the first dimension is identifying content standards that would constitute the school curriculum; school curriculum content standards would then substantially determine the content knowledge teachers needed to know in order to teach it well to students. The movement towards national accreditation of teacher training institutions is another component of the evolving identification of a core set of knowledge and skills for teachers (Wise and Leibbrand, 1993). The slowly developing notion of professional development schools, i.e., school sites devoted to helping with preservice teacher training is an indication of education's response to the need to include the workplace in the development of clinical teaching skills (Darling-Hammond, 1993a). Several states have begun to require some type of internship or residency year in order to qualify for a teacher license. And the growing acknowledgment of the need for ongoing professional development, or capacity building, as a long-term component of ambitious reform reflects the fourth dimension (Fuhrman and O'Day, 1994; Little, 1993).

Beginning Teachers: What Should They Know and Be Able to Do?

Although nearly all states license teachers on the basis of their taking an approved set of university or college courses, i.e., on the basis of courses taken with passing grades, there is ferment across the country about whether this strategy is good enough. In part as a result, numerous attempts have been created to define in performance terms the skills, competencies, and dispositions beginning teachers should have and be able to use in classrooms and schools. A notion rapidly gaining support is that state licensing should gradually shift from its current input criteria to one which would include actual assessment of what beginning teachers know and can do, in general, shifting teacher licensing to a performance base similar to the shift of student assessment to a performance base.

However much teacher licensure is changed, work continues on a variety of fronts to identify the competencies that beginning teachers should possess. While hopefully these exercises will have some impact and be a stimulus for improving preservice teacher preparation, the import of these activities for schools is two-fold. First, since schools likely will become more involved in the training of beginning (as well as experienced) teachers, especially the clinical skills needed to teach successfully, school leaders must know, be able to develop, and also be expert in assessing the initial skills and expertise teachers need. Second, such knowledge should help schools both recruit and select new teachers; in recruiting one would expect school leaders to search for individuals who could demonstrate that they possessed the requisite beginning knowledge, skills, and dispositions.

The difficulty surrounding these efforts is that research has not yet provided a solid set of beginning teacher skills. Nevertheless, there is research that has probed this topic, or come close to probing it (see Houston, 1990; Reynolds, 1988). Reynolds (1992: 26) reviewed this literature and concluded the following would be reasonable to expect from beginning teachers:

- Knowledge of the subject matter they will teach.
- Knowledge of pedagogy appropriate for the content area they will teach.
- Knowledge of strategies, techniques, and tools for creating and sustaining a learning community and the skills and abilities to employ these strategies, techniques, and tools.
- [Knowledge of how to] assess student learning using a variety of measurement tools and adapt instruction according to the results.
- The disposition to find out about their students and school, and . . . the skills to do so.
- The disposition to reflect on their own actions and students' responses in order to improve their teaching, and the strategies and tools for doing so.

Several practical efforts to identify what beginning teachers should know and be able to do reflect these general findings. For example, the Council of Chief State School Officers convened a Task Force (Interstate New Teacher Assessment and Support Consortium, 1992) with representatives from 17 states and identified standards that could be used for teacher licensure; they further suggested that licensure should be based on assessment of teacher performance on the 10 standards areas. The standards spanned the range from the constructs of the disciplines the individual would teach and how children learn those constructs, to pedagogy used to teach the curriculum with an emphasis on pedagogical skills for diverse students, to expertise in conducting and using the results of a variety of student assessment techniques. An additional ingredient of the proposed standards is that they were designed explicitly to be compatible with the standards the National Board for Professional Teaching Standards would use to certify experienced, expert teachers.

The California Commission on Teacher Credentialing (1992) also published a framework for the knowledge, skills, and abilities that could be used for performance-based licensing of new teachers. It proposed standards in five areas: knowing content, planning and designing instruction, delivering instruction to all students, organizing and managing the classroom, diagnosing and evaluating student learning, and participating in and creating a learning community.

Likewise, the Educational Testing Service began developing its PRAXIS system designed for state use in a new performance-based licensing structure. PRAXIS has 19 criteria in four broad areas: organizing content knowledge for student learning, creating an environment for student learning, teaching for student learning, and teacher professionalism.

These proposals and new programs not only agree generally with the conclusions of Reynolds (1992) but have the following 10 commonalities for expertise that should be developed in preservice training and expertise that schools and education systems should expect of beginning teachers:

1. Understanding the constructs, key concepts or "big ideas" in the content domain a teacher will teach, how the constructs interrelate, and how experts in the domain use those understandings to construct knowledge advances in the domain.
2. Understanding how students learn this knowledge, including student misconceptions in the content domain and how they can be used to structure effective learning situations.
3. Appropriate pedagogical strategies focused on thinking skills within content domains, that engage students in activities that help them construct the concepts and their linkages in the domain, and to use that knowledge to solve problems.
4. Knowledge of additional pedagogical strategies that are effective with diverse students.
5. Understanding appropriate classroom organization and management strategies.
6. Recognition of the social nature of learning both in how classrooms are organized, including the use of cooperative learning, and in how teachers work collaboratively and collegially in schools.
7. Knowledge and ability to administer and use a variety of curriculum-imbedded assessment strategies, including performance-based strategies, both for assessing student performance against professional standards and improving classroom instruction.
8. Linkage to standards and performances required for advanced certification by the National Board for Professional Teaching Standards, thus implying a continuum of teacher development over time.
9. Knowledge of the broader demographic, organizational and policy system within which particular classrooms and schools exist.
10. Use of performance-based strategies to assess teacher expertise, i.e., direct assessments of what teachers know and can do rather than indirect assessments through reviewing higher education courses taken.

Research shows, moreover, that teachers who receive preservice training are more effective teachers than those who do not. Several reviews of this literature (Ashton, Crocker, and Olrjnik, 1986; Darling-Hammond, 1992; Evertson, Hawley, and Zlotnik, 1985; Greenberg, 1983) concluded that across several dimensions, individuals with a preservice training program that emphasized the content learning, how students learned that content, pedagogical strategies used to teach that content, and included opportunities to perfect those knowledge and skills in actual classrooms produced teachers who had a richer array of teaching practices, were more successful in developing student achievement, and were more reflective on the effectiveness of their practices. Further, teachers with good preservice training were more able to see learning problems from the perspective of the student, and thus modify their teaching strategies to fit better with the diversity of student needs (Grossman, 1989).

Although these developing understandings of what should be expected of new teachers are only in the process of being implemented in systemic ways across the country, school leaders need to be aware of these directions for two major reasons. First, the 10 commonalities echo themes developed in Chapters 3 and 4 on how children learn thinking skills and the type of curriculum and assessment program that should be part of their school experience. New teachers with the above expertise are the type of teachers needed to teach the curriculum described in Chapter 4 and to develop the kinds of thinking skills discussed in Chapter 3. Second, both the emerging concepts of professional development schools and the need to provide significant assistance even to fully licensed but novice teachers suggest that most districts and schools will become involved to some degree or another in professional development focused on these areas.

These directions in initiatives concerning licensing beginning teachers, if fully implemented, would help bring another piece of the education policy system into the puzzle of structuring the education system, so that student achievement goals, curriculum, and assessment, preservice training, ongoing professional development, and advanced recognition of expert professional teaching (discussed in the next section), and even teacher compensation (also discussed later) can mutually reinforce each other in a systemic manner (Smith and O'Day, 1988; Smith and O'Day, 1991).

ONGOING PROFESSIONAL DEVELOPMENT

What Experienced Teachers Should Know and Be Able to Do

Several factors suggest that substantially enhanced ongoing professional development in schools and education systems could be one of the most important new initiatives education leaders must support in the 1990s. First, it is clear that the current teaching workforce will need intensive professional development in order to have the expertise needed to teach a thinking-oriented curriculum. Indeed, from intensive studies in several states of teachers in classrooms struggling to teach a new curriculum from a cognitive learning approach, Cohen and McLaughlin (1993) and Ball et al., (1994a, 1994b, 1994c) concluded that the key implementation problem was not resistance to change (the key implementation problem of the past [Odden, 1991a]) but a teacher learning problem. The issue was how to structure opportunities for teachers to become involved in discourse communities that not only engaged them in issues of defining the new curriculum approach and the elements that constitute new forms of student learning, but also in developing the new teaching expertise required to teach that curriculum effectively.

Second, it is clear that competent beginning teachers are only novices and require access to substantial opportunities over several years in order to develop the array of teaching skills that allow them to be competent, effective teachers; put differently, there are real differences between novice and expert teachers (Reynolds, 1992). However reorganized or redesigned, schools of education simply cannot turn out full-fledged, expert teachers. Just as in every other profession, preservice professional training provides the conceptual and knowledge underpinnings for the profession and a beginning set of clinical skills to practice the profession, but the skills of practice must be expanded, revised, and honed over many years before the novice can claim to be an experienced, full-fledged member of the profession. This reality means that school systems must reconsider their role in professional development, from one of a "nice extra" if extra funds are available to a major emphasis that must become a mature component of the overall set standard programs the district finances. Intensive professional development and assistance must be provided to new teachers in order to increase their chances of becoming successful teachers, and ongoing professional development needs to be provided for all teachers so that they can continually enhance and expand their professional expertise.

Third, substantial ongoing investments in continuous professional development is one of the four key components of effective approaches to decentralized management, which, as discussed in the next chapter, seems to offer the highest potential for improving the performance of the education system and simultaneously empowering teachers and improving teacher satisfaction. Indeed, if the private sector can serve as an example, the best firms, including service and knowledge production firms, invest between 2 and 4 percent of revenues in ongoing training of the key service providers (Bass, 1990; Lawler, 1992). That would suggest that education, too, should consider investing 2 to 4 percent of revenues (about $120 to $240 per pupil in 1991–92 dollars) in ongoing staff development, which is a level far above that for nearly all districts in the country (Monk and Brent, 1994 forthcoming).

Fourth, opportunity to expand one's professional repertoire is viewed by teachers as a highly valued reward and key to a teacher's continuing to be a contributing member of the profession (Johnson, 1986; McLaughlin and Yee, 1988; Rosenholtz, 1989). Providing such rewards are much less expensive than overall teacher salary increases, a policy more often suggested as a significant teacher reward. While salaries may need to be increased, expanding teachers' opportunities to develop their professional skills could very well be a low-cost, high-gain strategy that both enhances teachers' commitment to education and their ability to produce higher levels of learning for *all* students.

Fifth, the National Board for Professional Teaching Standards is not only identifying what the best advanced, experienced teachers should know and be able to do, but also will begin "board certifying" such teachers beginning in 1994. By the end of the decade, "board certification" will be available in 30 different areas. This professional movement likely will stimulate demands for professional development because the high standards it will identify for expert teaching practice will serve as a "benchmark" for assessing all teachers' professional expertise, and career-oriented, professional teachers will want opportunities to enhance their knowledge and skills so that they can become "board certified." Further, as discussed in the preceding section, several complementary efforts were launched in the early 1990s to begin licensing teachers on a set of knowledge and skills that would be linked to those required for board certification, thus offering a continuum of teacher development from preservice to inservice leading to board certification.

Finally, ongoing professional development is a characteristic of all professions. Knowledge changes and new techniques are constantly created. Both must enter the realm of professional practice. The only way to stay current and continually reflect the highest standards of the profession in the practice of the profession is through participation in ongoing professional development activities.

In short, ongoing professional development should emerge as a solid component of school district programs by the end of the decade. From its weak cousin status today which is among the first activities to be dropped when resources are tight, it must grow to a high-status position by the year 2000 and merit a substantial allocation of dollars, up to four percent of total revenues.

The content of professional development generally should be guided by the 10 commonalities for beginning teacher expertise previously listed. These generally cover the full range of what teachers should know and be able to do. If schools become substantially restructured, however, teachers might also need expertise in counseling students, providing professional development, and a variety of management skills required for school-based management. Further, teachers in a high-involvement managed school will need group and team skills to engage successfully in the collaborative decision-making part of that management approach. Since all these skills and expertise will be included to at least some degree by the National Board for Professional Teaching Standards in what it will require for board certification, targeting ongoing professional development to that needed for board certification could also be a clear signal about the broad reach of the skills and competencies that could become the focus of these activities.

To reiterate, districts first need to give a priority to and budget support for new teachers. Despite recommendations to the contrary, new teachers in nearly all school systems are given a full-teaching load, and thus have no formally sanctioned time to observe expert teachers and receive the help they need to "firm" their professional knowledge and skills. A few districts provide new teachers with a mentor who is available if "the teacher needs help." But the common practice is to assign new teachers to the most difficult classes, those classes with students who have the most complex learning needs. In most secondary schools, new teachers also tend to have multiple preparations.

The political nature of the rationales for these teacher placement procedures reflect only senior teacher privilege and not a professional approach towards structuring schools to increase the probability of successful experiences in the first years of teaching.

A major point of this chapter is that professional development during the early years is a critically important function of schools. High-performing schools cannot be created or sustained without heavy emphasis on ensuring that the new entrants into the complex job of teaching are provided with the training and support required to make them confident, effective practitioners.

But professional training during the first years is only the beginning. Effective teachers are always in a process of becoming more expert; a final stage is never reached. The imperative for schools in the 1990s is to elevate ongoing professional development to a key component of school activities that has priority draw on the regular school budget and fits with the career stage, development needs of teachers. The parallel challenge is to structure the processes of professional development in a way that will make it work.

Structuring Teacher Professional Development

Designing a professional development structure that works is both aided and frustrated by the research on effective staff development that accumulated and became synthesized into a "theory and body of knowledge" in the 1980s. Although the bulk of staff development is comprised of awareness conferences and one-shot-one-day training programs which tend to have few if any long-term impacts (Little et al., 1987; Fullan, 1982, 1991), Joyce and Showers (1988) framed a theory for how training models of staff development could work, which was supported over time by several empirical research studies (see Sparks [1983] and Sparks and Loucks-Horsley [1990] for reviews of this research). For training programs to work, Joyce and Showers (1988) concluded that training should include exploration and presentation of theory, demonstration and modeling of the skills being taught, practice of the skill by those being trained, feedback to the practitioner about their performance, and then coaching in the workplace, usually the classroom. The combination of all these components produces change in teacher behavior. Coaching is a critical ingredient (Joyce and Showers, 1982). While there is some teacher change if coaching is not part of the process, the degree of teacher behavior change increases by a factor of four with the addition of coaching (Joyce and Showers, 1982, 1988).

If more professional development followed these precepts, the impact of funds spent on training programs would increase dramatically. With this one shift, a wide range of new teacher practice could become incorporated into and improve the education system. Indeed, school leaders seeking to make their schools high-performance organizations would be wise simply to restructure their professional development activities that include training to include these five key Joyce and Showers components.

Certainly more good training will produce substantial teacher behavior change. But, research on the effectiveness of the training approach to staff development grew from attempts of schools and districts to make focused, targeted, or single changes, for example, to develop pedagogical skills based on the effective teaching literature, install one new curriculum program often over the course of many years, or to start an effective schools program. Further, these changes tended to be based on research-proven effective programs; indeed, the educational change literature in the 1980s was firm in suggesting that change efforts should focus on selecting and implementing programs that already had a proven track record of success (Huberman and Miles, 1984; Odden and Marsh, 1989). But, the objectives of education reform in the 1990s are more ambitious. Further, effective professional practices often need as much to be created as to be implemented well. Thus, staff development consisting just of good training will be insufficient to accomplish the vast array of changes now expected of the American education system.

As Little (1993) concluded, there are at least four aspects of the 1990s reforms that suggest effective professional development will need to be more grandiose than training. First, curriculum and instruction reform, as described in both Chapters 3 and 4, require greater teacher expertise, from content understanding to pedagogy. The required new expertise represents a major departure from past practice and development of new paradigms of instruction. Moreover, elementary teachers must change curriculum and instruction in four to five areas simultaneously, and secondary teachers face school restructuring as well as calls for interdisciplinary approaches to curriculum and teaching. However analyzed, according to Little (1993), these changes are simply more comprehensive, more complex, and require more change than the innovations on which the effective staff development research was based.

Second, current reforms are more insistent on an equity agenda of raising *all* students to high levels of cognitive expertise. Thus, teachers not only have to shift their core curriculum and instruction approaches, but they have to do it for heterogeneous classes comprised of students with increasing diversity and background knowledge. Understanding multiculturalism and how to teach all students to high standards is another demand for teachers to be successful in the new contexts of schools.

Third, Little (1993) argued that teachers face major reforms in the nature and uses of student assessment, as discussed in Chapter 4. Alternative and performance-based testing not only requires development of a new understanding of testing and examinations, but a yet additional set of clinical skills that few teachers possess today. Further, licensure and advanced recognition involves teachers in a new evaluation and assessment environment for their own performance.

Finally, the organization of schools and management of school systems is also experiencing fundamental change, which pose a set of additional, albeit interesting, and engaging challenges for teachers (see also Chapter 6). For example, the Coalition of Essential Schools (Sizer, 1992) sets out nine principles for high-performing schools; teachers not only have to invent the curriculum but also run their schools. Other schools are embracing school-based management more directly, which thrusts teachers into the unfamiliar roles of actually managing a school, from budgeting, to hiring and supervising, in addition to new curriculum and instruction. Cooperative learning, peer tutoring, reading recovery, and a host of other school organizational changes also complicate the work environment for teachers. Finally, teachers are faced with marketing issues in states and localities that are implementing public school choice programs, now operational in over one-fourth of all states.

In short, the new tasks in which teachers are required to engage in the 1990s are simply "greater" than any on which the traditional professional development knowledge was based. Teachers are often required to create new professional practices and learn how to use them, all of which occurs in a context in which nearly all components are being changed simultaneously—educational objectives, student diversity, curriculum, instruction, student assignment and grouping, school organization, education management, and even compensation. Clearly, as Little (1993) concluded, more good training programs are needed but they are insufficient for the enormity of the task. What is needed is professional development for the task of "reinventing" teaching.

Nearly all studies of effective professional development focused on long-term comprehensive school changes finds that the most successful efforts are characterized by site teachers playing the lead and key roles (Marsh and Odden, 1991; Little, 1993; Massell and Goertz, 1994). This also fits with findings in the private sector (Mohrman and Wohlstetter, 1994). McLaughlin (1991a, 1992b) further supports this strategy both in reassessing the Rand Change Agent studies and in showing how effective teaching especially for developing thinking and problem-solving capabilities depends on knowledge that is situated in the daily context of specific schools and classrooms. Viewing teaching and learning as a co-constructed practice, McLaughlin (1992a) argued, requires the system to recognize both the team-oriented nature of practice and the fact that it is situational and constructed on an ongoing, daily basis. This suggests that effective staff development should be team-oriented and imbedded in collective and interdependent action at the site. However, this a rare form of professional development which usually is individualistic, bounded, and short-term (Little, et al., 1987).

These findings suggests that the bulk of professional development dollars needs to be invested in collegial and collaborative activities at the school site. This investment strategy somewhat counters the expansion of district-based professional development offices that occurred during the 1980s. While district-provided professional development can play a role, perhaps more directly in preparing school leaders than teachers, the long-term substantial changes required by the current education reform agenda can only be sustained if the leadership and expertise are created at the site level, and the needs of the site simply are too vast to be provided by a district professional development office.

At the site level, emphasis also needs to be given to creating and sustaining a culture that sanctions an ongoing focus on continuous improvement of the faculty's professional expertise. This type of culture is associated with schools that are more effective in improving student achievement (Little, 1982; Rosenholtz, 1985, 1989). When schools set clear student achievement goals and tie professional development initiatives directly to school-identified needs to accomplish those objectives, teachers are usually more satisfied, more supportive of the professional development efforts, learn more new professional practices, and the school is usually more effective in meeting its educational goals (McLaughlin, 1992a; Little et al., 1987; Little, 1993).

This conclusion could be especially important for effectively teaching diverse students to achieve at high levels, which given the information in Chapter 2, is a particular challenge for the country's education system. Rosenholtz (1985) found that one component of effective schools (schools with large concentrations of poor and minority students who successfully learned the basic skills) was teachers working collaboratively to create a set of teaching strategies that "worked" in their school; one key product of collaboration was producing a set of curriculum and instructional strategies that were effective for the poor and minority students in those schools.

The National Center for Research on Teacher Education (1991) also reached this conclusion for how teachers could be effective in teaching a multicultural student body. In most teacher training programs, teachers only became aware of different cultures and their attributes, but tended not to learn the pedagogical strategies that would enable them to develop advanced cognitive capabilities in such students. What the Center proposed was engaging teachers in site-based professional communities in which collectively the appropriate strategies for that school were collaboratively created. What both these studies suggest is that engaging site faculties in the task of creating professional practice is not just a good idea generally, but perhaps is the best strategy for raising the probability that such a battery of professional practice being identified and used in schools with high concentrations of poor, minority, and culturally different students (see also McLaughlin and Talbert, 1993).

The curriculum and instruction focus for professional development could be on developing the skills and competencies needed for Board Certification by the National Board for Professional Teaching Standards. The Board is linking its assessments to the developing curriculum frameworks produced by the various professional groups, which also are the linchpins of current education reform initiatives (see Chapters 1, 9, 10). Indeed, James Smith (Sparks, 1994: 59), Vice President of the National Board made the following comments on how professional development for Board Certification was related to the nationwide directions of education reform:

> A quick read of any of the NBPTS's standards will immediately reveal that our vision of accomplished teaching is entirely consistent with the kind of teaching that will be required to deliver a "thinking curriculum" to students. National Board-certified teachers will have demonstrated that they possess the skills, knowledge, and dispositions necessary to teach such a curriculum. Staff development aimed at preparing teachers for Board certification should be virtually the same as that aimed at enabling them to teach a "thinking curriculum". . . . This implies staff development of a nature and scale not common in schools in this country. It will have to be goal driven, coherent, focused, and of sufficient duration to allow teachers to acquire the necessary skills, knowledge, and habits of the mind.

In terms of design and structure, Adams (1992), Cohen and McLaughlin (1993), Lieberman and McLaughlin (1992), and Little (1993) argued that successful professional development strategies for the 1990s should have the following characteristics:

1. Heavy investment in concentrated, indepth training for a small but critical percentage of teacher experts in a school. Training must concentrate indepth on content and pedagogy.
2. Conscious decision to also train these individuals to become teacher trainers and lead teachers. Thus, the training must also include indepth development of leadership and adult training skills. Teachers selected to be participants in such indepth and concentrated training need to be aware of their expected subsequent leadership roles and training responsibilities.
3. Creation of "professional/social organizations" such as networks to help the trainers both continue to expand their professional expertise on the topic and over time to spread that knowledge and expertise to other teachers in at least their sites and districts. Massell and Goertz (1994) termed these "professional learning communities" and suggested them as a potentially powerful form of professional development for implementing the Project 2061 approach to new science.

These principles suggest that educators implement at least three new strategies of professional development for current educational challenges: summer institutes, subject matter associations, and teacher networks. Special summer institutes and centers offer potential for engaging teachers in long-term communities that over time help change professional practice. Such entities that actually use the teacher participants themselves to develop ideas, materials, teaching practices, and change strategies seem to be the most successful, according to Little (1993). These activities usually entail 2 to 3 weeks of intensive work during the summer, and then periodic meetings of those who attended during the course of the academic year. Many such institutes have been supported by the National Science Foundation, but several states also are beginning to support subject matter institutes, the largest program being in California which has projects in writing, literature, mathematics, science, and history. Often participants in the institute return to their school where they become trainers for the remainder of the faculty.

Subject matter associations, such as the National Council of Teachers of Mathematics and other *national* groups, but also state associations with the same focus, also increasingly are becoming influential mechanisms for developing professional practice. As stated in previous chapters, leaders in these national groups are playing the key roles at the national, state, and local levels in creating standards for curriculum, assessment, and other components of the restructured education system (Fuhrman, et al, 1993 core report). Odden and Odden (1994) also found that professional subject matter associations were critically important in both developing curriculum standards and changing professional practice in Victoria, Australia. To the extent that leaders of these associations also hold leadership roles in schools, Little (1993) concluded, their professional influence is extended.

Teacher networks are collaborative and collegial associations that provide the opportunity for teachers to experience professional growth through "deepened and expanded classroom expertise and new leadership roles (Lieberman and McLaughlin, 1992: 673)." Networks are professional discourse and development communities. Teachers in collegial networks are involved in talking about and constructing professional practice and expertise and not merely consuming it or learning it from some trainer. Networks also tend to require long-term commitments, often years, provide for meetings and collaborative interactions often times during the year, and entail considerable experimentation, development, trial and evaluation, successes, and failures as teachers in the network jointly create new curriculum, instruction, organizational, and management strategies that work with their students in their schools. The Bay Area Writing Project, the Urban Math Collaborative, the Puget Sound Educational Consortium, and the California Math A Network are networks that are well-known and often mentioned in writings (Lieberman, McLaughlin, 1992; Little, 1993).

Networks also usually include teachers from several schools and often several school districts as well. They can meet after school, in the evenings, and on the weekends, depending on the inclinations of those in the network. Often they include groups of teachers from any one school, and are aided if those teachers can be scheduled for common planning time during the regular school day. Some networks have been handsomely funded, with the planning time provided by "buying out" a teaching period and/or paying teachers for the time involved in network meetings and activities. Lower funded networks can exist if common planning time is provided through imaginative scheduling. Resources are provided for meeting and materials development costs.

Networks can have powerful impacts on teacher classroom practice. Adams (1992) found that teachers in networks focused on California's Math A for noncollege-bound high school students implemented more change in practice in line with teaching that curriculum than teachers in districts that provided lots of good training staff development. Lieberman and McLaughlin (1992) also found that networks were powerful professional development vehicles, were successful in developing profound professional discourse communities, i.e., communities of learners, and could lead to substantial change in classroom practice, but also raised a series of issues for ensuring the stability of networks and their focus on key system objectives. Marsh and Odden (1991) found that teachers involved in such networks often became the trainers and sustainers of school-site curriculum change, overshadowing the impact of district staff development.

In short, district leaders need to support professional development that is concrete, intensive, ongoing, includes follow through assistance, and is provided in collaborative and collegial structures (McLaughlin, 1991a; 1992a). Districts often cannot directly provide staff development that meets these requirements. Thus, the key role of district leaders is to enable site leaders and teachers to identify, address, support, and sustain professional development focused on needs related to key education system goals.

TEACHERS AND TEACHER UNIONS IN THE 1990S

The engagement of teachers in ongoing professional development outlined in this chapter, the transformation of teaching and curriculum discussed in the preceding two chapters, and the roles of teachers in managing schools that will be described in the next chapter seem, at first blush, to be at odds with the behavior associated with teacher unions. Teacher unions were legalized first with 1959 legislation in Wisconsin, which adopted a variation of the National Labor Relations Act into a state law governing education unionism. Education unionization was accelerated with the successful 1962 teachers' strike by the United Federation of Teachers in New York City. By the mid-1970s, over two-thirds of the states had collective bargaining laws and almost 90 percent of districts with more than 1000 students had teacher unions.

Since the National Labor Relations Act was based on the industrial union model that had evolved for labor-management relationships in the country's large-scale production organizations, that model became the structure, some might argue unfortunately, for unionism or collective bargaining in education as well. In that model, workers and managers are separate and have different roles and jobs. Management decides and labor works; managers think and workers do. Jobs are narrowly defined and supervised closely by managers. Stated differently, management acts and unions grieve, or as Kerschner and Mitchell (1986: 460) put it, "boards deliberate, managers implement, unions grieve, and teachers teach." In other words, the interests of management and workers are different; collective bargaining is adversarial almost by definition.

This model of unionism has in part helped to create a stereotypically unattractive notion of teacher-management behavior in education. In this view, teacher unions are viewed as obstructionist, self-centered, "greedy," and concerned primarily with higher salaries, better working conditions and political power and not with the learning and achievement of students. Among some, there is anger that teachers and teacher unions are so actively engaged in the politics of education, specifically school board elections. Among this group, there is skepticism about whether teachers and their unions could and would move beyond these parochial concerns (see for example, Grimshaw, 1979 and Lieberman, 1980). Those holding this view of teachers and their unions would be cynical at best about the role teachers and unions might play in education reforms; they might not bet highly on teacher support for restructuring, engaging in the hard work of professional development, or being willing to take responsibility for the results of schooling.

But this sterotypical perspective is somewhat at odds with the roles unions, especially the national unions, actually have been playing in education reform and even further at odds with the evolution of the nature and role of many state and local teacher unions. For example, in a study of the role of teacher unions in the early 1980s comprehensive education reforms, McDonnell and Pascal (1988) found that unions generally were accommodating to reform. At the local level, unions were accommodating because they felt their key issues were material benefits which were not obviously on the reform agenda; there was little incentive to oppose or actively engage in reform activities. At the state and national level, however, the general trend was to engage in helping to shape reform substance and direction, although this stance took somewhat longer to develop for one union, the National Education Association, than for the American Federation of Teachers.

In a seminal assessment of the evolution of teacher unions Kerschner and Mitchell (1988) argued that the "idea" of a teachers' union simply has been continuously changing. In the early years, the key idea was "meet and confer" and structures and norms were created around making that successful. In the second generation, the key idea was "good faith bargaining," what is typically associated with unions, and structures and expectations were created around that notion. By the 1980s, the authors argued, the idea of a union was changing to one of "negotiated policy" in which unions were beginning to play central roles in decisions on the overall education system, far beyond just the salary and working conditions that dominated negotiations during the second generation. Kerschner and Mitchell (1988) in fact provided recommendations for how to develop a professional union that could dominate the third generation.

A 1993 report on the evolving nature of unions (Kerschner and Koppich, 1993) included indepth studies in nine big city schools systems around the country (including Cincinnati, Louisville, Pittsburgh, and Rochester) of what can be called the precursors to professional unionism. Each case documented a wide range of new practices, supported by all parties, teachers, unions, administrators, and board members, that were dramatically changing traditional notions of unions, collective bargaining, and labor-management relations in education. All cases were characterized by new forms of teacher-management collaboration, concern with the quality of the overall education system and each school within it, and work on the core issues of curriculum, teaching, professional expertise, and system outcomes.

It is clear from these analyses and studies conducted over the past 10 years that there is a significant evolution of teacher unionism. The evolution is characterized by two new features. One is a new focus on professional education issues—learning, student achievement, curriculum, pedagogy, and assessment—as a key if not the preeminent concern of unions and their teacher members. This focus means that a new role of unions is to enhance and improve the quality of the actual work of teachers in order to improve the education system and raise student learning. This focus moves union concerns far beyond the salary and working conditions emphasis of industrial unionism.

The second characteristic of the evolving unionism is collaborative and collegial teacher involvement in all aspects of the functioning of schools and education systems. In the new view, it is not only appropriate but imperative that teachers take responsibility for the quality of the entire school as an organization and, in addition to teaching, engage collaboratively in a wide range of schoolwide decision-making activities.

These new behaviors begin to blur the traditional distinction between labor and management. Implicit in the studies and their conclusions also is a need for teacher engagement in ongoing professional development, in part to accomplish the goals of education reform but also to develop the skills needed for their broader decision-making roles in schools.

Kerschner and Mitchell (1986; 1988) and Kerschner and Koppich (1993) propose that teachers should consider creating a new form of unionism, which they call professional unionism. In one version, they suggest that professional unionism is characterized by union support for rigorous requirements for entering into and remaining in the teaching profession, emotional engagement of teachers in the act of teaching, and teacher responsibility for determining the nature of the teaching work that is conducted and the student outcomes of the education process. In the most recent version, Kerschner and Koppich (1993) argue that the emerging union of professionals would:

1. Emphasize the collective aspects of work in schools, by blurring the line between managing and teaching through joint committees, designing and carrying out school programs in teams, and flattening hierarchies through decentralization and even school based management,
2. Emphasize the interdependency of workers and managers on the quality of the system by organizing around the need for overall education improvement and enhancing the skills and capacity of both management and teachers, and
3. Emphasize the protection and development of good teaching practice through internal quality control and ongoing professional development.

Such new directions for union activity would dramatically change the nature of teacher unions, which have been overly influenced by (some might say mired in) the industrial model of a union. They also would connect teacher unions more directly to the nature, substance and requirements of current efforts to reform the country's education system.

We endorse these general suggested directions. We agree with Kerschner and Mitchell (1986; 1988) that teaching is complex and constructed on a day-to-day basis, indeed sometimes a minute-by-minute basis, and thus ill-suited for industrial unionism which assumes clear cut definitions of jobs and controls for individuals in those jobs. Because of the complex, collegial, and uncertain nature of good teaching, we argue in the next chapter that an even more comprehensive decentralized management structure, high-involvement management, is appropriate for education (Mohrman, Lawler, and Mohrman, 1992).

This more comprehensive form of decentralized management entails all the restructuring of teacher roles detailed by Kerschner, Mitchell, and Koppich. However, it devolves even more responsibility and roles, both technical and managerial, to professional educators in each school site (Bernstein, 1994). We follow Lawler's (1992) lead and suggest that the role of the union in a high-involvement managed organization is to insure: (1) that the high-involvement management structures remain in place and are strengthened each year; (2) that sufficient resources are invested in ongoing professional development which is site-determined and managed; and (3) that teacher compensation is restructured to emphasize individual skills and competencies, and group-based performance awards (see Chapter 13).[2] Thus, our proposals emphasize less direct union involvement in core education issues and more direct involvement of site teachers in those issues, and more involvement of the union in ensuring that management creates, sustains, and over time improves a decentralized management structure that devolves major responsibility and authority to teachers in schools and their important subunits.

---

[2]This strategy to blur the traditional distinction between union and management, including the notion of self-managing work teams, was recently endorsed by a major report of the AFL-CIO union (Bernstein, 1994).

Both proposals, ours and those of Kerschner, Koppich, and Mitchell undergird the need for the role of teachers and their unions to change dramatically over the 1990s. As Koppich (1993: 196) concluded, the status quo is not an option because we are "desperate to make public education work."

CONCLUSION

Teachers are the key to accomplishing the nation's bold education goals. The professional knowledge, skills, competencies, and dispositions of teachers will determine whether the education system educates all students to high levels of proficiency in the core content areas. To support, continuously improve, and sustain a skilled and energized teacher workforce, school leaders need to recognize their critical importance to the new directions of the education system and must protect the large investments that need to be made in supporting new teachers by investing in ongoing professional development, and as the next chapter will argue, devolving greater decision-making authority and responsibility to teachers. The dramatic curriculum and school restructuring that are required to achieve the national education goals must be lead by expert, more professional, and better skilled teachers. One of the key functions of school administrators is to help lead a system in which this devolution of power is accomplished effectively and which finally places a high-priority value on continuous professional learning because only a continuous learning system can develop the expertise to teach all students how to think, solve problems, and communicate effectively.

High-Performance School Organizations

The school is the key organizational unit in education, not the central office and certainly not the state legislature, state department of education, President's office, or Congress. All education strategies and programs eventually must be worked into a cohesive schoolwide design that works for the site as an organizational entity.

This chapter attempts to identify the characteristics of high-performing school organizations, i.e., schools that produce high levels of student learning. The first section draws on research and proposals in the education arena. The goal of this section is to describe various models of schoolwide programs that have taken the goals, instruction, curriculum, assessment, and teacher policies described in preceding chapters and made them work. Although there are few if any proven-effective strategies in that research literature, there are lessons to be learned from: the effective schools literature, Slavin's Success for All Schools (Slavin, et al., 1994), Comer's (1980) Developmental School, Levin's (1988) Accelerated Schools and Sizer's (1992) Coalition of Essential Schools. The text focuses on describing the key elements of these schoolwide programs, discussing the common elements across such programs, and identifying differences across elementary, middle, and high school levels.

The next section draws on the organizational behavior and decentralization literatures in the private and public sectors to describe and analyze issues related to organizational performance in those settings. Setting goals at the top of the system and decentralizing operations to the service delivery level, schools in education, have been shown to dramatically improve organizational effectiveness. Past research on site-based management in education covered only a small portion of the organizational issues that are involved in this approach to management and leadership (Wohlstetter and Odden, 1992). More recent research in education (Mohrman and Wohlstetter, 1994; Odden and Odden, 1994; Wohlstetter, Smyer, and Mohrman, 1994, forthcoming) and in the private sector (Lawler, 1986, 1992) found that more effective decentralization moves the following four resources down to the work teams providing the service or making the product:

- Information about how the system is doing, which in education would include information on student outcomes, teacher performance, and school as well as system fiscal data.
- Knowledge about how to provide the service, engage in collaborative work team activities, and skills in making management and budget decisions.
- Power, that is, authority over budget and personnel.
- Rewards, i.e., the compensation structure. This component usually includes skills-based pay as well as team-based performance awards. Rewards are the incentive portion of accountability, e.g., rewards for accomplishing system and organization objectives.

Each section discusses these issues in more detail, compares them to findings on school based management, and begins to apply them to schools.

ORGANIZATIONAL FEATURES OF PRODUCTIVE SCHOOLS

In order to work, the notions discussed in the previous chapters—ambitious student learning goals, high-quality curriculum standards, new forms of student assessment including performance assessment, and comprehensive, ongoing professional development programs—need to be woven into high-performing school strategies. Given the diverse character of the more than 100,000 schools that constitute the American public education system, the fabric of school organizations that are created likely will vary considerably. Nevertheless, there also likely will be common threads that run through each school organization. This section reviews the literature on current and proposed school organizational and management strategies that offer high potential for dramatically improving student learning and thus increasing educational results.

The Effective Schools Literature

Beginning in the 1970s and continuing into the 1980s, several studies were launched to identify characteristics of effective schools, i.e., schools that were producing greater student learning than other schools, often schools with similar student and community demographics. Edmonds (1979a, 1979b, 1982) produced some of the seminal work. He identified five key characteristics of effective schools: (1) clear school goals focused on academics, and a pervasive and broadly understood instructional focus with a common curriculum for all students; (2) principal leadership focused on the instructional program; (3) high teacher expectations for all students to achieve at least minimum mastery of the schools instructional program; (4) frequent monitoring of student performance and use of measures of student achievement as the basis of program evaluation; and (5) a safe and orderly climate conducive to teaching and learning. While these five characteristics might not seem that dramatic from the lens of the 1990s, Edmonds' findings were new and powerful at that time. His research showed that schools could make a difference, and that more effective schools had clear academic goals, held high expectations for all students, offered a common core curriculum program to all students, were led by principals who focused activities and resources on the curriculum and instructional program, and provided a safe and orderly environment. While how to produce such characteristics was not made necessarily clear from this research, the studies nevertheless identified several important organizational characteristics of schools that worked.

Over the 1970s, moreover, there were numerous studies of "effective" schools, although effectiveness was defined in a wide variety of ways. Purkey and Smith (1982, 1983) produced one of the most comprehensive and influential syntheses of this research. They identified 13 characteristics of effective schools, nine organizational and structural variables, and four process variables, which combined shaped the nature and character of an effective school. The four process variables that helped define and shape the school culture were:

- Establishment of clear goals and high expectations for student success, that were commonly shared by all teachers and staff. Clear goals and continual monitoring of individual, classroom, and school progress towards accomplishing those goals, were key ingredients for nearly all of the effective schools in their review.
- Collaborative planning and collegial relationships which emerged as strong factors not only in the effective schools studies, but also in the educational change and program implementation research.
- Order and discipline which provided an environment conducive to learning.
- A sense of community, i.e., a feeling of belonging to a group that had common purposes, shared common values, and provided needed supports—both technical and symbolic—for all in the community.

The nine organizational and structural variables were:

- Site management, which was necessary to determine the context-specific strategies for developing the academic program and creating a distinctive school culture.
- Instructional leadership, usually provided by the principal but which could be provided by teachers or other administrators. Effective schools had strong leadership that focused on the school's curriculum and instruction program.
- Curriculum articulation and organization, including a core curriculum related to the school's key goals and that was provided to all students.
- Maximized learning time, allocating as much time as possible of the school day to instruction in the core curriculum.
- Schoolwide, not just individual, staff training to develop the knowledge, skills, and attitudes necessary to implement the school's overall program. The most effective staff development was linked to needs of teachers that emerged from collaborative planning and collegial interactions.
- Schoolwide recognition of academic success, a mechanism that symbolically reflected the school culture's focus on academics and learning success.

- District support that guided and aided the school in accomplishing its academic objectives.
- Staff stability which helped the school create a cohesive faculty that shared expectations and norms.
- Parental involvement and support.

The contributions of this article to the understanding of the characteristics of effective schools were threefold. First, it was the most comprehensive review of the literature and included nearly all the studies that had been conducted up to that time. Second, it separated process/cultural variables from organizational/structural variables, and thus began to "unpack" the ingredients of schools that worked. Third, the review began to incorporate the educational change and program implementation literature, thus foreshadowing how to create rather than just to identify effective school organizations.

Many other reviews of effective schools were produced in the 1980s (e.g., Cohen, 1983; Fullan, 1985; Wilson and Corcoran, 1987). While the conclusions of each varied marginally, the majority of their findings were quite consistent with those of Purkey and Smith. One of the problems related to this work, however, was that it generally defined effective as achievement related to basic skills. This focus was generally driven by the dominant curriculum then in schools. Effective schools today must have the goals, curriculum, and student performance directed to the thinking skills discussed in the first chapters of this book. Another problem with the effective schools research was that most of it was based on elementary and not secondary school research. While the Purkey and Smith review incorporated some secondary school studies (e.g., Rutter et al., 1979) the bulk of empirical work was at the elementary level which led to criticisms and cautions of not applying elementary findings without thought to the larger and organizationally more complex nature of secondary schools (Corcoran, 1985; Firestone and Herriott, 1982).

Fortunately, several studies of good high schools were published at about the time these criticisms appeared (Goodlad, 1984; Lightfoot, 1983; Sizer, 1984), including some reviews of effective secondary schools (Corcoran, 1985) and effective middle schools (Lipsitz, 1984). Then, using the large sample of secondary schools recognized by the U.S. Secretary of Education, moreover, Corcoran and Wilson (1986) produced one of the most extensive assessments of effective secondary schools. Their study identified nine key themes:

- Clear goals and core values. The goals not only exist, but they are clear and specific, known by faculty, students and parents, used to guide day-to-day actions, and lead to development of a specific school vision and the core values of the school culture.
- Active, strong school leadership focused on the instructional program and usually implemented by the principal who offered the school vision, clarified the site's mission, and worked well with all the school's major constituencies. Most principals also created leadership teams which expanded the number of leadership roles in the school, and the individuals who performed those roles.
- Control and discretion, i.e., simultaneously loose and tight. Principals aggressively monitored the school's operations with respect to goals, coor-

dinated the curriculum across grades and subjects, and supervised and evaluated teachers. Teachers also had considerable autonomy in how they did their work, but within a culture of collegiality directed by a common set of goals and values. The autonomy was within the framework of faculty being collectively responsible for the accomplishments of the school.

- Good people and good environment. Effective secondary schools were effective in recruiting and retaining skilled teachers, and engaging them in ongoing professional growth opportunities. One factor related to retention was the sense of belonging to the school community that was created by the collegial school culture.
- Recognition and rewards for teaching, from symbolic to monetary. Teachers in these schools felt known and recognized for hard work and tasks accomplished.
- Positive student-teacher relationships, which enhanced student motivation and expanded task-oriented teacher-student interactions outside the classroom.
- High expectations for and recognition of student achievement, including the strong conviction that all students can learn to high levels.
- Orientation towards problem solving and school improvement. Effective secondary schools identify problems and then seek creatively to solve them. Such schools are "can do" organizations.

One of the obvious features of this set of themes is how similar they are to the Purkey and Smith (1983) findings, even though these findings are derived from secondary schools and Purkey and Smith's pertain more to elementary schools. This finding suggests that many of the key organizational characteristics associated with effective schools are common across education levels. To be sure, high schools tend to be larger, have more organizational units such as departments, and more individuals who can provide instructional leadership such as department chairs, but the organizational features of what makes them effective share many characteristics with those in elementary schools.

In one of the most recent efforts identifying effective secondary schools, Hill, Foster, and Gendler (1990) studied 13 high schools in New York City and Washington, D.C. Their sample included Catholic schools and special purpose high schools, both of which they called focus schools, as well as the more typical zoned neighborhood public high schools. They found important similarities between Catholic high schools and special purpose high schools, but dramatic differences between these two and zoned public high schools. Focus schools had two distinctive features related to: (1) mission and (2) organizational strength:

> Uncomplicated *missions* centered on the experiences the schools intend to provide its student and on the ways it intends to influence its students' performance, attitudes and behavior. . . . strong *organizations* with a capacity to initiative action in pursuit of their mission, to sustain themselves over time, to solve their own problems, and to manage their external relationships (Hill, Foster, and Gendler, 1990: vii)."

By contrast, zoned schools had fuzzy missions defined by demands of external funders and regulators. They also had weak organizations with little capacity to initiate action to solve problems, define their own character, or manage relations with external audiences.

In terms of *mission,*

- focus schools concentrated on student outcomes above all else, while zoned schools concentrated on implementing programs and following regulations.
- focus schools had strong norms and cultures that define the reciprocal relationships among students, teachers and administrators, while zoned schools let staff and students define their own behaviors.
- focus schools had a strong interest in "parenting" by working to shape attitudes and disposition, while zoned schools saw their role as transmitting information.
- focus schools offered a core curriculum that it expected all students to learn, while zoned schools differentiated by tracking, different course-taking patterns and holding variable expectations for low, average, and high ability students.

In terms of *organization,*

- focus schools operated as problem-solving entities, whereas zoned schools were constrained by regulations and mandates of their external environment.
- focus schools protected and sustained their internal character through recruiting staff who accepted the school culture and norms and socializing them into their culture, while zoned schools rarely had the choice of selecting staff and tended not even to attempt to socialize them into the school culture.
- focus schools saw themselves as accountable to their clients—students and parents, while zoned schools saw themselves accountable to the bureaucracy and outside auditors and compliance monitors.

Finally, Bryk and Driscoll (1988), Bryk, Lee, and Smith (1991), Lee, Bryk, and Smith (1993) and Bryk and Lee (1993) raised and emphasized the additional important notion of the communal aspects of effective organizations. They argued that the elements of community such as shared goals, collegial work, effective communication, good personal interactions, and a sense of "belongingness" are not only instrumental aspects of high-performing school organizations but ends in themselves of strong, functional organizations, including schools. Their work grew from not only a strand of the general organizational theory literature but also from studies of good schools. Indeed, one of the key characteristics of Catholic schools, especially those that are successful in urban communities, is their communal nature (Bryk and Driscoll, 1988; Bryk and Lee, 1993). They argued that the creation of large, bureaucratic, comprehensive, and generally impersonal urban high schools (the typical zoned school in the Hill et al. [1990] study) produced school organizations that generally did not work. Their research showed that more effective schools have communal organizations, which are small and caring, provide common learning experiences for all students, create positive faculty and student inter-relations, and are characterized by collegial, cooperative work, and shared values, such as those called focus schools by Hill et al.

Synthesis

From a reading of the above, it is clear the studies and reviews produced many overlapping findings. Even the secondary study results were quite consistent with elementary school findings, the differences primarily being size, more organizational units (e.g., academic departments), and a wider array of instructional leadership roles performed by both teachers and administrators other than the principal. The following synthesizes the various characteristics into 10 categories, and following Purkey and Smith (1983), separates them into process/culture factors and organizational/structural factors. The key process/culture factors from the last 20 years of effective schools research include

1. *Clear goals focused on results, particularly student achievement.* Effective schools know what they are doing and where they are going. They have specific goals which are related primarily, though not exclusively, to student achievement in the core curriculum, which today would be thinking and problem-solving capabilities for all students. Clear goals often lead to creation of a unique, context-specific school mission.

2. *Collaborative planning and collegial shared decision making.* Effective schools are characterized by teacher involvement in all aspects of school operations, especially those pertaining to curriculum and instruction. Collegial relationships between teachers and administrators and among teachers characterize the working style of faculty within effective schools. This is supported by other research findings (Little, 1982; Lieberman and McLaughlin, 1992; Rosenholtz, 1989; Talbert and McLaughlin, 1994).

3. *A strong culture* characterized by: (a) *high expectations* for all students and an assumption that all students can achieve to high levels, (b) a strong schoolwide *focus on the curriculum and instruction program,* (c) an expectation for *continuous improvement* including finding and creatively resolving problems, and (d) a *communal notion of organization,* that in addition to the above, creates a caring and personal culture trait.

The culture leads to the development of a set of core norms and values that are shared and known by all and constitute informal guideposts for behavior and decision making. This culture produces a strong sense of community for the school and a feeling of belonging to that community on the part of teachers, administrators, students, and parents. While the technical part of the school is focused on curriculum, instruction, and student learning, the strong school culture helps shape attitudes, dispositions, behaviors, and a strong sense of "belongingness" of those in the school, all of which work in pursuit of the technical goals (see also, Deal and Kennedy, 1982; Rosenholtz, 1985).

Seven organizational/structural variables devolve from a synthesis of the above:

4. *Site-based management.* It is clear that these schools run their own affairs. They recruit and select staff. They allocate scare resources, including time. They make their own decisions in pursuit of their goals. While few schools had complete budget authority, they acted as if they were in charge of their destiny and took initiative to make decisions to accomplish their missions.

5. *Core curriculum,* organized and articulated across subjects and grades, and *provided to all students,* even at the secondary level. Effective schools did not hold different expectations for students of varying ability. Their assumption was that all students could achieve at high levels, and they organized and provided a core curriculum to all students.

6. *Instructional leadership,* usually provided by the principal, but also provided by other teachers and administrators, especially in secondary schools. In effective schools, leadership focused on implementing the school's curriculum; the instruction program was a clear and present reality, recognized and experienced by everyone in the school. This leadership reflected the tight coupling of goals, vision, mission, and implementation, all focused on the curriculum program.

7. *Recruitment of staff and socialization of them into school norms.* Nearly all schools actively recruited and hired individuals who "fit" with the norms and values that characterized the particular school culture, and aggressively socialized new recruits into the school's values and ways of operation. This was another component of the tightly coupled nature of these school organizations (see also Rosenholtz, 1985).

8. *Schoolwide professional development,* that evolved from collaborative assessment of school issues and training needs. Ongoing development of professional expertise required to accomplish the school's curriculum and instruction mission characterized most schools. Professional development, moreover, was schoolwide and not individualistic in nature; the objective was to create the expertise to accomplish schoolwide goals.

The attention to recruiting, selecting, and developing faculty who fit the norms of the school and had the expertise to accomplish school objectives, together with the sense of belonging to a community provided by the strong school culture, helped to produce *staff stability* in most schools. More is possible with a stable staff than one that overturns substantially each year.

9. *Monitoring of student achievement,* together with a sense of *collective responsibility for school results.* Effective schools continuously monitored student and teacher performance as they related to accomplishing school goals. Faculty within the school knew whether progress was, or was not, being made. The sense of responsibility for school outcomes was collective not individualistic, and the faculties as a whole felt accountable to students and parents, i.e., the "clients" of the system.

10. *Recognition of teacher and student accomplishments.* Effective schools gave attention to and provided rewards for outstanding accomplishments, in both symbolic and substantive ways, and sometimes including monetary bonuses. Rewards and schoolwide knowledge of rewards played important roles in these schools. When individuals, both students and teachers, did well, rewards were provided.

All studies also found that effective schools created safe and orderly environments, with disciplinary programs fairly and consistently administered. This factor was almost a precondition for the other conditions. Without a disciplined and orderly school, it was difficult to turn to curriculum, instruction, and learning tasks. Indeed, one of the first tasks accomplished in many "turn around" schools was creation of a safe and orderly school environment.

As will be shown later in this chapter, the above 10 process and organizational factors "stack up" well with the findings from the broader literature on high-performing organizations. Organizations that "work" have many common attributes, and the commonalities are greater than their differences (Barzelay, 1992; Lawler, 1986; Osborne and Gaebler, 1992, Peters and Waterman, 1982). Further, these findings fit well with the economics of organizations literature (Cyert, 1988; Cyert and March, 1963; Finnan and Levin, 1993) which suggest efficient organizations have an objective function (i.e., goals), use incentives, provide information to workers and managers, adapt to meet changing conditions, and use the most productive technology. Before moving to that broader literature, however, the next section describes the key characteristics of some of the school programs of the 1990s that hold high promise for dramatically improving student learning, and shows that their organizational features are similar to the above 10 factors.

Well-Known School Programs in the 1990s

Four school-based programs developed by creative individuals attained recognition in the early 1990s for being potential models of school organizations that could produce high levels of student learning: Comer (1980), Levin (1988), Slavin et al. (1994), and Sizer (1984, 1992) (see also King, 1994).

Comer's Developmental School. Developmental schools were designed primarily for elementary students in poverty-impacted urban districts. The diagnosis of the school problem was that children from low-income backgrounds had underdeveloped social skills or exhibited behaviors that might have been appropriate in some contexts but were inappropriate in school. This behavior was interpreted by teachers as indicating the child either was unmotivated or intellectually unable to learn. But this interpretation was inaccurate. The problem for teachers was that they in fact lacked an understanding of the social development of these children and thus misinterpreted their behavior. Comer (1980, 1987) believed that all students could learn at high levels in a school in which the staff were secure and motivated and had knowledge and skills related to both the social and intellectual development needs of the students.

The solution was to design a school-based program that could effectively respond both to the children's dual developmental needs and teachers professional developmental needs. Thus, the Developmental School was created. It consists of nine components: three mechanisms, three operations, and three guidelines. The first mechanism is a collegial and collaborative governance structure for the school that includes teachers, parents, and administrators as partners. The second mechanism is a mental health team that attends to both the health needs of individual students and the "health" needs of the school's organization, culture, and climate. The third mechanism is a parent's involvement program that works with parents both on their responsibilities to and behaviors with their children, and on their broader roles in school governance.

The three operations of Developmental Schools are mainly a responsibility of the school governance group. It must create a school developmental plan with specific goals for both the social climate of the school and student academic performance. It must also design a professional developmental program linked to site-identified faculty and school needs for implementing the school improvement plan. Finally, it must produce periodic assessment of factors related to school goals—student achievement and school climate—to measure progress and readjust program strategies when progress in any area is insufficient. Although not explicit about the type of curriculum that should be part of the school, and probably more basic skills-focused when the program began in the 1970s, the organization and focus of Developmental Schools would provide an hospitable context for a thinking-oriented curriculum that builds on the background knowledge the school's students bring to the classroom.

All six of the above school strategies functions under three guidelines: (1) participants on the governance team cannot paralyze the school leader from taking action and the school leader cannot dominate and turn the governance team into a "rubber stamp" body; (2) there is a "no fault" attitude towards problem solving thus encouraging problem identification and resolution; and (3) all decisions in the school are made by collegially and by consensus.

Comer's Developmental Schools take great care in recruiting, socializing, and training teachers for the school culture that the school creates; Developmental Schools hold that only teachers who believe in the developmental approach and have the skills to be implement it can be successful. Further, Comer schools have a very strong orientation towards parental involvement; parents are almost as much of the school's overall strategy as the strategies themselves. Results from the first Developmental Schools indicated that they substantially improved student achievement (Comer, 1987).

Levin's Accelerated School. Accelerated Schools are also a school-based reform that seeks to dramatically improve the achievement of urban, economically disadvantaged students (Hopfenberg and Levin, 1993; Levin, 1987, 1988). The problem addressed by Accelerated Schools was the slower paced and less rigorous curriculum program often provided to students from poverty backgrounds. Since such students generally enter school with academic and social skills behind middle class peers, Accelerated Schools believe that their instruction must become faster paced so that they can catch up. The primary goal is to bring all students up to proficiency by sixth grade so they can have a normal and successful secondary school experience.

Accelerated Schools begin by establishing a unity of purpose among all members of the school community—teachers, administrators, parents, and sometimes representatives from the community. This goal includes developing a school-specific vision for success and an action plan for implementing it.

A second tenet of Accelerated Schools is to empower members of the school community to make all the essential decisions that affect school operations. This is accomplished through collegial and collaborative planning and decision-making. The decisions pertain to the school's curriculum program, instructional strategies, and instructional materials, as well as recruiting and selecting personnel, and allocating within school resources. Accelerated Schools make a heavy investment in professional development of the entire school staff. Accelerated Schools seek to change central office actions from command and control to support of school-based decision making.

A third tenet of Accelerated Schools is that all school activities should build on the strength of students, staff, and parents. Their programs treat all students as gifted and talented, and assume that all students have the capabilities and knowledge that can be built on and used to help them learn to high levels of proficiency. This perspective fits well with the cognitive perspective that all learning needs to build on the specific background knowledge of each individual child.

The curriculum in an Accelerated Schools reflects much more directly the type of curriculum described in Chapter 4 and the assumptions of learning blend well with those summarized in Chapter 3. An Accelerated School's curriculum is heavily language-based, even for mathematics. It includes an early introduction of reading and writing. It stresses active learning, problem solving, and applying learning to concrete situations in real life. It emphasizes development of thinking and advanced cognitive capabilities.

Accelerated Schools also include major and central roles for parents focused both on their child and their roles in the school. Accelerated School's parents sign a contract that specifies their responsibilities related to the academic achievement of their child, and they are encouraged to play a variety of roles in the governance and management of the school.

By late 1993, the Accelerated School movement had gained substantial momentum, with estimates suggesting that hundreds Accelerated Schools existed in school districts across the country. Although formal evaluation the effects of Accelerated Schools were not yet available, early indicators suggested that they have major impacts on student learning (Hopfenberg and Levin, 1993).

Slavin and Associates' Success for All School. Success for All (Slavin, Madden, Dolan, et al., 1994; 1989; Slavin, et al., 1990) is a school-based reform design created to produce students achieving at grade level by the third grade. Its designers saw the problem as one of too few urban, minority, low-income children achieving at acceptable levels of proficiency, falling further behind each year, with intervention provided too late and with insufficient intensity. Success for All Schools assume that all students can achieve school success and learn to read well. Their goal, focus, and mission is very clear: to make all student's successful readers by the third grade.

The program has several components. The first few are called prevention and include (1) a half day, quality, i.e., developmentally focused preschool program for children aged 4; (2) a full-day kindergarten program for children from poverty backgrounds at aged 5; (3) a high-quality curriculum and instruction program that focuses on language development, writing, reading comprehension, and a manipulatives-based, problem-solving oriented mathematics program; and (4) frequent assessment of student performance.

The second set of strategies are called early intervention. Success for All Schools provide one-to-one tutoring for children in grades 1, 2, or 3 who are reading below proficiency levels. This intensive tutoring is based on the Reading Recovery model (Slavin, Karweit, and Wasik, 1994: Chapter 7). Tutoring is provided by licensed reading specialists; each student that needs it receives 20 minutes of tutoring a day. The tutors also teach a regular reading class during the 90-minute daily reading/language arts period; this helps the school lower class size for reading instruction. Reading instruction is provided in small, often times numbering 15 students, cross-age, ability grouped classes; class compositions change with the periodic 6 to 8 week student assessment program. Students are in heterogeneously grouped classes for all other subjects, including mathematics for which the teacher might have two within class mathematics groups.

Early intervention also includes attention to social and family needs of students. The schools work actively with the social agencies in the community to ensure that students receive the family, health, psychological, and other supports needed to allow them to focus on learning in schools. Each Success for All School has an individual who works primarily on these social service outreach activities. This individual also helps coordinate a major parent and family outreach program of the school.

Each Success for All School also has a facilitator, who is essential to the overall operation of the program. The facilitator is responsible for scheduling all activities, providing assistance to reading teachers and tutors, as well as to all other teachers. This individual helps, in collaboration with teachers, to provide substantial initial and ongoing professional development for the faculty. The professional development is linked to process of identifying school problems, generating solutions, and developing the expertise to implement the solutions.

A third set of strategies for Success for All Schools could be called maintenance. It includes use of cooperative learning in all classrooms (Slavin, 1990) and cross-age peer tutoring in which upper elementary students tutor primary grade students in reading and mathematics.

All school strategies were based on synthesis of research that identified school interventions that produced large increments in student achievement (see Slavin, Karweit, and Madden, 1989). The package of Success for All strategies constitute one of the most explicitly research-based school intervention programs developed. Initial and long-term evaluations, moreover, document the substantial short- and long-term success of Success for All (Madden, et al., 1993; Slavin, et al., 1994). Success for All has been substantially able to accomplish its objectives of developing all students as proficient readers by third grade.

Sizer's Coalition of Essential Schools. The Coalition of Essential Schools is a nationwide network of schools, often schools within a school, that subscribe to the philosophical underpinnings of the Coalition and the nine principles that guide operations of a coalition school (Sizer 1984, 1992). It is a secondary school-based reform for both middle and high schools. It is an intensively collegial and site-based reform strategy.

Its philosophical basis includes four tenets. The first is that a good school reflects its community and the convictions of its central staff. Thus teachers, what they know and what they want to do, are key to the success of a Coalition School. The second belief is that there is no one "model" of a good school;

good schools can subscribe to common, guiding principles, which the Coalition offers, but the practical form each school takes can vary. Tenet three holds that in a democracy *all* citizens must be able to use their minds well and be able to function as thoughtful members of the workforce and society. The fourth philosophical underpinning is that the relationship between teacher and student should be student as worker and teacher as coach, which blends nicely with the constructivist approach to learning which was the focus of Chapter 3.

Coalition Schools, then, are created collegially and collaboratively by the faculty and administration of each school and subscribe to the following nine principles:

1. Students must learn to use their minds well. Unpacked, this means that students must learn to think and solve problems, to assimilate information and make sense of it, to be analytical, and to construct knowledge.

2. School goals should be simpler; students should master a limited number of essential skills and areas of knowledge. This principle links well to the notion of learning the "big ideas" in content areas, what they mean, how they connect, and how the knowledge can be used in real life settings. The Coalition also stresses the interdisciplinary nature of knowledge.

3. Goals should apply to all students. Coalition Schools assume all students can learn and seek to develop advanced cognitive capabilities, and a thoughtful approach to learning, for all students. Several Coalition Schools, moreover, are being developed in urban communities with concentrations of low-income and minority students.

4. Students entering secondary school should be competent in language and mathematics; those who are not should be given intensive remedial work. This principle helps to make practical the goal of teaching thinking skills to all students; it recognizes that some students will enter a Coalition School underprepared in the requisite skills and that it is the responsibility of the School to provide the extra instruction in order to develop those knowledge and skills.

5. Teaching and learning should be personalized. The specific ramification of this principle is to limit teacher responsibility for no more than 80 students, as compared to the typical 150 students that evolves from a teacher teaching five classes of 30 students each day. The personalized component also fits with the cognitive approach to learning which requires teachers to structure learning opportunities to the background knowledge of each individual student; 80 students are easier to know than are 150 students.

6. The prominent pedagogy is coaching. Teachers in Coalition Schools are not seen as dispensers of knowledge. Rather they are seen as individuals who guide students in their own construction of knowledge. Teachers are not passive, but their job is to structure environments in which students can successfully develop cognitive skills and knowledge.

7. Diplomas should be earned by demonstration of mastery. This principle is the Coalition's way of defining performance-based assessment; indeed, the Coalition is more comfortable with using portfolios as indicators of what students know and can do.

8. Teachers must have time for collective planning. How this is accomplished can vary by school. This principle underscores the teacher-centered aspect of a Coalition School and the critical importance of collaborative and collegial activities. This principle also subsumes a focus on professional development.

9. The cost per pupil should be no greater than 10 percent more than a traditional school, a principle which seeks to ensure that Coalition Schools are affordable. Accomplishing the 80 student-teacher contact ratio requires that Coalition Schools are staffed differently than traditional high schools, usually substituting teachers for more specialized staff (counselors, dean, coordinators, department heads) and administrators (assistant principals) and expanding teacher roles.

The Coalition of Essential Schools began in the mid-1980s after the first round of education reform programs in the wake of the *Nation At Risk* (National Commission on Excellence in Education, 1983) report. By 1993, it had grown to scores of schools. Early 1990s reports showed that creating and sustaining such schools was difficult (Prestine, 1994).

Other School-based Reform Proposals. There clearly were other school-based reform programs and proposals that were preferred around the country. One of the most prominent was *Turning Points* (Carnegie Council on Adolescent Development, 1989), a comprehensive proposal for middle school reform, which helped launch a major national drive to transform grade 7 to 9 junior high schools into grade 6 to 8 middle schools. This proposal also fit well with research on effective schools for young adolescents (Lipsitz, 1984). The *Elementary School Journal* (1993) devoted an entire issue to the research supporting these proposals, including research on how thinking skills in the content areas are taught to early adolescent students.

While there are many different proposals for restructuring elementary and high school programs around the country, the four programs profiles above reflect several of their common features. The profiled school reform programs represent some of the most well-known school reform programs that were implemented in several places across the country during the early 1990s.

Connections with Organizational Features of Effectiveness. At first blush, the key attributes of these school programs might seem to be substantially different from those of the effective schools of the 1980s. One reason for a potential difference is that the above programs emphasized much more strongly their curriculum and instruction approach than their organizational features. Indeed, many of their key organizational and management aspects tend not to be discussed at great length. Nevertheless, there are substantial similarities in the organizational features of these schools and those from the effective schools research, as Table 6-1 shows.

To begin, they all have clear goals focused on student achievement. The goals are quite specific: to develop both social and academic skills (Developmental), to bring all students to reading proficiency by the third grade (Success for All), to bring all students to mathematics and reading proficiency by

TABLE 6-1. Assessment of Comer's, Levin's, Slavin's and Sizer's Schools on the Organizational Dimensions of Effective Schools

	Comer	Levin	Slavin	Sizer
1. Clear goals, focused on achievement	Yes	Yes	Yes	Yes
2. Collaborative planning	Yes	Yes	Yes	Yes
3. Strong culture characterized by:				
High expectations	Yes	Yes	Yes	Yes
Focus on curriculum	Weaker	Yes	Yes	Yes
Continuous improvement	Yes	Yes	Yes	Yes
Communal nature	Yes	Yes	Yes	Yes
4. Site-base managed	Yes	Yes	Yes	Yes
5. Core curriculum for all students	Yes	Yes	Yes	Yes
6. Instructional leadership	Somewhat	Yes	Yes	Yes
7. Active recruitment of staff	Yes	Not clear	Not clear	Yes
8. Socialization of staff	Yes	Yes	Yes	Yes
9. Professional development	Yes	Yes	Yes	Yes
10. Monitoring student achievement, goals	Yes	Yes	Yes	Yes
11. Recognition of accomplishments	Not clear	Not clear	Not clear	Not clear

the sixth grade (Accelerated), and to develop inquiring minds (Coalition). Further, the academic achievement expected includes problem solving and advanced cognitive capabilities.

Each of these school designs pertains to a school that is site-managed. Further, all schools include substantial collaborative planning. Not only are the programs school-based (not district-based) designs, but also they all emphasize very strongly the need for widespread collaborative decision-making that includes parents, and collegial relationship among teachers and between teachers and administrators.

Each school design also takes seriously the climate and nature of the school organization. They each seek to create a definitive school culture that includes high expectations for all students, a strong focus on the curriculum program, continuous improvement, and a distinctive sense of community. The high expectations for all students is an exceedingly strong aspect of each school. Each of these schools also reflect the communal character of high-performing organizations; they tend to be small, place a high value on caring, and give attention to the personal nature of all interactions, whether or not directly related to the technical goals. These are schools which were designed from a "drive" to show that low-income, minority, urban students could achieve at high levels. There is growing evidence, both quantitative and anecdotal, that these schools are working.

Although the Comer Developmental Schools have a stronger focus on the social, affective curriculum of the school, academic and instructional leadership is a prominent feature of the other three and is included in the Comer program. Indeed, each of these schools has given considerable attention to the "core" of the enterprise—the curriculum and instruction program. And the core curriculum and instruction approaches each has created is what gives central meaning to their school design.

While there is active socialization of staff to the norms and expectations in these schools and substantial schoolwide professional development, it seems that Developmental Schools and Coalition Schools also give explicit attention at the front end to recruiting and selecting teachers who "fit" with the school's philosophy. Since schools in most districts are not allowed to recruit and select staff on their own, lack of attention to this aspect of staffing is understandable. But as will be discussed later in this chapter, recruitment and selection can be as important as socialization and training of staff in high-performing organizations.

All of these schools monitor student performance and have explicit assessment systems related to measuring key school outcomes. These schools pay close attention to results. They want to know the impacts of their program. Put a different way, not only do these schools have explicit goals related to academic achievement, but they measure, sometimes periodically throughout the school year, progress towards these goals, for each individual student as well as the school as a whole. These schools are comfortable with being accountable. They want to produce high levels of student achievement and they want documented evidence that they are doing so.

Finally these schools might recognize student and teacher accomplishment but this behavior did not seem to be a central tenet of any of their program descriptions. Thus, while willing to be accountable, they may under emphasize the role that the recognition and reward structure can play in a high-performing organization.

Four features of these school designs are not included in Table 6-1. First, the three elementary programs profiled have a strong parental outreach and involvement strategy that is central to their design. While this factor was included in the Purkey and Smith (1983) and Lee, Bryk, and Smith (1993) effective schools reviews, it was not a prominent feature of most other literature syntheses and not included in Table 6-1. Second, at least two of the school designs have a strong emphasis on the nonacademic, social service needs of students, which tend to be quite high for urban, minority students from poverty backgrounds. While this component is not directly educational, it is a program element that addresses the broader needs of children from low-income backgrounds that might be given more explicit attention from schools in poverty-impacted urban areas. Third, except for the Comer Developmental Schools, the curriculum in the school designs previously discussed was not basic skills-oriented, but much more explicitly thinking and problem-solving oriented, and included the notions of students as active learners, a focus on the big ideas in the content domains, and student construction of knowledge. Finally, except for Accelerated Schools, the programs tend not to be explicit about the role of the district in helping to create and sustain these site-based programs. As will be argued below and in the next chapter, this issue must be centrally addressed.

Indeed, while too often ignored in descriptions of high-performing school organizations, the system and organizational contexts in which they exist are important. One possible reason why the curriculum focus of the schools previously mentioned has been profiled more than their organizational features is that the education system changed the goals for and expectations of student achievement in the late 1980s and early 1990s, as discussed in Chapter 1. Today, basic skills are not enough. Everyone needs to know how to gather and analyze data, use it to solve problems, and apply it to everyday life—including the programming of a videocassette recorder! Levin's, Slavin's, and Sizer's school designs include these enhanced curriculum expectations; they are thus offered as school designs for the 1990s and beyond. Their programs include the basic notions covered in Chapters 1 through 4.

But, schools must exist in organizations as well as local and state educational systems that allow all their critical features to be implemented. Put another way, there is more to a good school than its curriculum and instruction program. Even a good curriculum and instruction program needs appropriate organization, management, and system structure to attain high performance. The above analysis shows that indeed, when probed a little more closely, the profiled school designs also include many of the organizational features, both process and structure, that were identified in the effective schools research of the 1970s and 1980s.

The next section of this chapter begins to show how organizational and management design, more generally speaking, are critical to organizational performance. This section discusses organizational issues linked to high performance in the private sector and then applies the findings to educational organizations—schools.

FEATURES OF HIGH-PERFORMING ORGANIZATIONS

The search for the components of high-performing organizations has characterized the private, nonschool sector for the past many decades, especially given the internationalization of the private economy that has produced intense competition for high-quality products and services at low prices. Although there are clear differences between the public and private sector organizations, between schools and manufacturing plants, and between schools and private sector services, this section will discuss the emerging understandings of strategies for improving organizational effectiveness in the private sector and show how they can be applied to education. Moreover, some of the additional components that have been identified in the private sector offer potential to further strengthen our understandings of high-performance organizational design in education.

One of the most popular, 1980s studies of private sector strategies that characterized higher performing corporations was the Peters and Waterman (1982) book entitled *In Search of Excellence*. They identified eight characteristics of high-performing companies:

1. A *bias for action* by both managers and workers including financing experimentation form the smallest work units.

2. Staying *close to the customer* with an obsession for service and high quality.
3. *Providing autonomy and supporting entrepreneurship* for individuals through out the organization.
4. Getting *productivity through people,* by increasing the effectiveness of the rank and file worker.
5. A *hands on, value-driven* management system, characterized by management not through meetings but by walking around the company.
6. *Stick to the knitting,* i.e., focusing on the core business of the company.
7. *Simple form, lean staff* that decentralizes operations to small units that can respond to a changing environment and eliminate layers of staff for top management.
8. *Simultaneous loose-tight organization culture,* with decentralized operations but centralized values.

By challenging the complex organizational forms and strategies of the day, such as matrix, financial and strategic management, Peters and Waterman were part of a sea change that began to question the growth of large organizations, the holding company corporation, and especially the traditional bureaucratic approach to management, which still characterizes most corporations and public education systems. Implicit and well as explicit in their initial eight points as well as more recent modifications of them (Peters, 1992) was the need to decide and then focus on the core business, keep in close contact with the customer by having him/her define function, quality and satisfaction, and depend on the front-line service providers and workers to conduct the business of the company. Staff was out and line was in; stable, complex organizational structures were out and fast-paced, ad hoc teams were in; centralization was out and decentralization was in.

At about the same time, other notions about how to make organizations more effective also emerged. William Ouchi (1981) wrote *Theory Z Management* suggesting that Americans could learn about more effective management strategies from the Japanese. Quality circles gained prominence and popularity (Lawler, Ledford, and Mohrman, 1989; Lawler, Mohrman, and Ledford, 1992). Complementary discussion centered on the nature of the work itself in many organizations, especially large-scale production plants; the implication was that tedious, low-skilled work was boring (and being shipped to other countries) and that the route to better quality was work redesign to re-engage the rank and file in high-skill, high-wage jobs (Lawler, 1986; National Center on Education and the Economy, 1990). Indeed, during the 1970s and 1980s there were numerous proposals for improving quality and productivity and companies implemented versions of nearly all of them (Lawler, 1986). Underlying all of these innovations was the notion that management and organization could be a determinant of organizational effectiveness. Put differently, what evolved during the 1970s and 1980s was the thought that new approaches to organization could enhance the effectiveness and performance of the enterprise, a thought shared by the research on effective schools as well. This broader research on new organizational forms is still evolving but several new directions already have been identified.

The New Logic of Organizations

Galbraith, Lawler and Associates (1993) and Byrne (1993) identified several elements of the evolving new logic of organizing and Lawler and Mohrman (1993) identified their implications for education; the organizational issues they raised can be applied to elementary/secondary as well as higher education. These authors identified eight new characteristics of the evolving logic of the high-performance organization.

Learning Organizations. The first concerns the dynamic and changing nature of today's effective organizations, compared to the stability of traditional organizations. Today's organizations including schools, face both rapidly changing environments and expanding technical tools that can be used to do organizational business differently and better. Thus, how best to organize cannot be found in a book or yesterday's structure (Lawler and Mohrman, 1993).

Successful organizations are those that can continuously engage in a process of change and reinvention to take advantage of the new tools and meet the needs of the changing environment (Byrne, 1993). The bureaucracy, with its clear hierarchy and structure, and resistance to change worked in previous times when demand and technology changed incrementally. Today's more effective organizations, termed "learning organizations" (Senge, 1990), not only must continuously respond to their ever changing environment, but also must change as they learn how to accomplish tasks differently and better (Cummings and Mohrman, 1987). Organizations that take a learning approach to structure and form, substantially improve their chances for producing ongoing high levels of performance. Only continuous improvement and constant organization redesign is likely to succeed in the fast paced environment of the future.

Education organization at the elementary, secondary, and tertiary levels are remarkably the same as many years ago. Schools today look remarkably similar to schools of 10, 20, 30, and 50 years ago; they may be running more programs with more functional and programmatic units, but the organizational structure has not changed much (Cohen, 1993). However, schools face a rapidly changing environment, both demographically (Chapter 2) and in terms of policy demands and directions (Chapters 9 and 10). Schools also face pressures to dramatically improve performance, and the need to incorporate sophisticated technology into their ongoing operations. Perhaps the time has come to change the typical school organization. Heavy investments in professional development and freeing the school to change organization and structure to accomplish goals would characterize the education system if it assumed a "learning organization" stance.

Thinking Global. Another pressure influencing private sector companies' approach to organization is the globalization of the market place (Galbraith, 1993; Lawler and Mohrman, 1993). After focusing for years almost exclusively on the domestic market, this economic change is causing many corporations to refocus themselves by developing products and sales strategies for international markets, and by creating design, production, and operational structures overseas. While universities could follow this corporate lead and expand foreign operations, the implication for the public schools has more to do with goals and expectations than with developing overseas operations.

The global market means that a country's competitive position depends heavily on the quality of its workforce, the knowledge and skills of which is largely determined by its K–12 elementary/secondary education system (Reich, 1991). As argued in Chapter 1, this means the ability of students in this country to think, solve problems, and apply knowledge in real contexts must be at or above the level in other countries in order to handle tasks in the workforce needed to maintain our position in the global economy. Thus, it is no longer acceptable to compare student achievement to that of other American children of the same age; the issue is how our students compare to their peers from other countries. As a result, the long tradition of localism within American public education is being challenged; decentralizing education goal setting and curriculum and instruction to local districts might no longer be viable. Today, there may be a real need for national education goals, (although professional) curriculum standards, and an examination system, all components of the Goals 2000 program enacted by the 1994 Congress (see also Chapter 10). After all, the education reform reports of the 1980s claimed the nation was at risk, not just particular districts or states (see also Chapter 1).

Thinking Big and Acting Small. Another component of the evolving logic of organization is the need simultaneously to be both large and small. The trick is to learn how to think big and when to act small. Although the trend line in education is for ever bigger and larger school systems (Guthrie, 1979) and more control by central governments (Kaestle and Smith, 1982), large bureaucracies are not that effective in the rapidly changing environment of the twenty-first century. According to Galbraith (1993) and Lawler and Mohrman (1993), there are advantages to bigness in the private sector which include finance, research and development, purchasing, and perhaps accessing large markets. But, they claim, bigness is not that successful in all aspects of an organization, especially in exercising control, coordinating performance, motivating employees, getting employees involved in making good business decisions, or relating to customers. Thus, large corporations are creating smaller units around products/services or customers (Byrne, 1993). These are the new mechanisms for improving involvement, motivation, and satisfaction and, in the right context, lead to enhanced system performance (Blinder, 1990).

The implications for schools are that "thinking big" might include setting goals, curriculum standards, assessments, and system direction at the top of the system, which could be the state or national level. These notions are now part of what is called systemic reform (Smith and O'Day, 1991: Chapters 9 and 10) and included in the Goals 2000 legislation. But "acting small" suggests decentralizing implementation of systemic reform to the school level, and perhaps even to schools or "houses" within schools (Fuhrman and O'Day, 1994; Odden, 1994a). While the role of the district office would need to be reconsidered, a topic addressed in Chapter 8, the school, and clearly schools smaller than the many 5,000 to 6,000 student urban comprehensive high schools, is the implied key operational unit within education. This would counter both the tendency within education for creating larger school districts as well as larger school organizations, and fits with the literature reviewed in the first section of this chapter. This notion of thinking big and acting small means the country would have created national goals and standards earlier and would never have created districts as large as Los Angeles or New York.

The End of Functional Units? Related to the notion of acting small is the type of operational units organizations create. Most corporate bureaucracies have been divided into functional units—design, engineering, manufacturing, marketing, sales, and personnel. But, the new logic of organizing is to create organizational units around customers or products; the new units, moreover, generally include all of the old separate functions (Byrne, 1993). The result is that employees within the new organizational units need both a greater array of technical skills, because they now engage in cross-functional activities, and a new set of team skills because working together becomes much more crucial.

The implication for schools is straight forward. Instead of organizing education by grade level and function, with individual teachers in classrooms and specialized staff either in separate school offices or the central headquarters, schools could be organized around cohorts of students and groups of teachers could provide the full array of services, from instruction, to guidance, counseling, discipline, and family outreach. This would require education systems to stop the expansion of specialized positions, not only for teachers in particular content areas but also for individuals in support areas such as curriculum development, training, counseling and even administration. Proposals such as those from the Carnegie Council on Adolescent Development (1989) and Comer, Levin, and Sizer Schools recommend putting a group of students together with a group of teachers for a number of years; teachers would not only teach a multi-disciplinary curriculum but also provide the bulk of other services and supports now provided in schools, as well as manage their operation. Such changes reflect the trends within the private sector to de-emphasize functional specialty and move to team-based organizations focused on clients.

Performing for Supervisors or Satisfying Customers. A fifth new trend in organizations entails the focus of evaluation, and who or what determines quality. The trend is away from performing for the internal supervisor and towards satisfying the external customer (Byrne, 1993; Lawler and Mohrman, 1993). In the traditional bureaucracy, including most schools, employee performance tends to be oriented towards satisfying expectations of the supervisor. Employees work according to job descriptions and are evaluated by supervisors on the quality of their work. As long as the entire system is designed and coordinated well, this approach can and has been effective.

As the environment and, therefore, customer needs and wants change, however, this internal orientation becomes strained, often becomes dysfunctional and requires a shift in focus from internal job performance to external customer satisfaction (Lawler and Mohrman, 1993). This reorientation has been behind the total quality management movement with its intense emphasis on customer needs (Deming, 1986; Lawler, Mohrman, and Ledford, 1992).

Applying these notions to the schools is not that straightforward. One challenge is defining the customer. One approach would be to define a variety of customers: universities that enroll and companies that hire graduates, parents who send children to school, middle schools that enroll students leaving elementary school, high schools that enroll middle school students, and students themselves at least in terms of their achievement. This posits that customers exist not only within the public education system itself, but also outside the system, including parents. This identification of customers both within and outside the organization is also a trend in private sector companies (Lawler and Mohrman, 1993) and public sectors experimenting with decentralized organizational structures (Barzelay, 1992).

Another challenge is common understanding of goals and expectations. Not all parents or companies (National Center on Education and the Economy, 1990) want all students to be able to think and solve problems; they might be satisfied with proficiency in the traditional basic skills. Nevertheless, more widespread support seems to be building for a high level of cognitive proficiency.

Finally, more choice of school attended might also be a concomitant of a customer orientation. It is hard to respond to customer needs if the system offers only one site where the child can attend school. Giving students the option of *public* school choice, an approach now adopted by several states, could be a policy responding to this dilemma (Odden and Kotowski, 1992a).

The bottom line, though, is that the customer focus would at least have schools focus on their most direct customers, students, and assess the impact of what they do in terms of student outcomes. "We taught the students and it's their fault they can't read," a refrain too often heard in education, clearly is incompatible with a customer focus.

Doing What You Do Best. Traditional organizations have often integrated themselves vertically as well as horizontally. Indeed, the public school system is quite strongly vertically integrated, from kindergarten to twelfth grade, and public schools tend to administer all the functions themselves, from financial accounting, to transportation, school building, food services, and publishing in addition to instruction. Many schools, especially urban schools, are now even providing breakfast, day-care before and after school, preschool, and a variety of children's social services including health, family, psychological and other support services (Odden, 1993a).

But this expanse of vertical and horizontal organization is coming under attack in the private sector (Galbraith, Lawler and Associates, 1993; Lawler and Mohrman, 1993). In the complex and fast paced environment of today, it is becoming increasingly hard, if not impossible, for organizations either to have all the expertise they need to do all these functions well, or to be able to sufficiently coordinate all of them.

This has led to many organizational innovations including "outsourcing" and "networked" organizations in which other companies do tasks or make products or provide services at which they are expert. Computer companies often buy chips from one company, disk drives from another, and screens from a third, and put their energies into assembly, marketing, and sales. Some organizations that sell products, such as Nike, literally are not engaged in any manufacturing and focus solely on design, marketing, and sales.

Schools could do well to take some lessons from this evolving logic of organizing. As just noted, schools have taken on nearly all tasks. This way of organizing puts tremendous pressure on teachers, who not only need the expertise to perform these nonteaching tasks well but also need new expertise for a tougher curriculum and instruction program. It might be time for schools to focus on just curriculum and instruction, and only coordinate the performance of other tasks and provision of other services, many of which could be "outsourced." Transportation perhaps could be done more efficiently by a public transportation system, especially if public school choice were widespread. Food services could possibly be outsourced more. Financial accounting and the computer systems that support them, especially if the information were made available on-line to schools, could be designed and maintained better by outside companies. Preschool perhaps should remain outside the public school budget. This notion here is more than the "stick to the knitting" advice of Peters and Waterman (1982). For schools it might mean a stronger focus on the core instructional program, but it also means an assessment of other entities that more effectively could provide services and functions now provided by the public school structure.

Control Through Involvement and Organization in Teams. Traditional bureaucracies have individual job descriptions and individuals are accountable to their supervisors for just their own performance as specified in the job description. This individualistic organizational approach is now changing to a focus on teams, control through involvement of the individuals who comprise the teams, and team responsibility and accountability for products, services, and even profits (Byrne, 1993; Galbraith, Lawler and Associates, 1993; Lawler and Mohrman, 1993). While traditional bureaucracies coordinate the business of the organization through the supervisors and managers in the hierarchy, this approach becomes problematic when performance needs to address quality, speed, and cost at the same time (Barzelay, 1992; Lawler, 1992).

The alternative to the traditional command and control approach is called high involvement. This approach entails moving information, knowledge, power, and rewards to the lowest levels of an organization, to work teams responsible for particular products, or customers. Such work groups generally are given: (1) financial resources and the authority to recruit, select, and train a team, (2) the training to develop needed knowledge and skills, and (3) information about revenues, costs, profits, sales, and customers. They also tend to move to a skills-based compensation structure (Lawler, 1990) and in addition earn rewards on the basis of how well as a group they make the product or please the customer.

High-involvement management provides the potential for organizations and work teams to accomplish several of the dimensions of the new logic of organizing. High-involvement work teams can redesign both the organization in which the work is conducted (either a product made or a service provided) and can redesign how the work is conducted. Moreover, high-involvement management is the management structure many organizations are adopting as they restructure to implement the new logic of organization (Galbraith, 1993; Hammer and Champy, 1993; Katzenbach and Smith, 1993; Lawler, 1986, 1992). Schools implementing a comprehensive approach to site-based management also reflect the high-involvement model (Mohrman and Wohlstetter, 1994).

The Key Elements of High-Involvement Management

One key concept of high-involvement management has been greater worker involvement in and management of the workplace. By the end of the 1980s, research was suggesting that greater worker involvement of nearly any sort was a route to improved organizational effectiveness and system productivity (Blinder, 1990). The fabric of worker involvement included a wide range of strategies such as quality circles, worker surveys, continuous improvement, and new starts, some lasting longer than others, and some more effective than others, with the high-involvement approach the most effective (Lawler, 1986). As the section on effective schools documents, this finding also appeared in the school organization literature—teachers involved in curriculum, instruction, and management issues at the site represent an important dimension of effective schools.

High involvement, however, is not appropriate for all types of organizations. An organization's management strategy should be selected on the basis of the nature of the work conducted. The nature of work can be characterized along three key dimensions: its complexity, whether it is best done individually or in groups or teams, and the degree of uncertainty that is faced in doing the work. Simple, individual, and highly certain work lends itself to hierarchical organizations; the old AT & T or Ford Motor Company of the 1950s reflected this type of organization and were very productive. Complex, collegial, and uncertain work, however, lends itself more to decentralized, employee involvement strategies, most visibly reflected in many new high technology organizations, such as Apple Computer and the restructured AT&T and Ford Motor Companies.

In the private sector today, however, Lawler (1992) and Lawler and Mohrman (1993) generally argue that an increasing amount of work is complex, is best done in teams, and exists in a rapidly changing environment (technically and otherwise) that is thus best organized through a high-involvement management approach. In a seminal article that began to apply the knowledge on high-involvement management to education, Mohrman, Lawler, and Mohrman (1992) argued that the nature of teaching strongly suggests that high involvement is appropriate for education as well. Teaching is substantively complex (Rowan, 1994), is best done collegially, faces uncertainty both in its day-to-day tasks, and exists in a rapidly changing demographic and policy environment. Their arguments are persuasive. Moreover, the conclusions of the effective schools literature reinforces this finding from an alternative education perspective.

The above argument, then, suggests that high involvement is an appropriate organizational/management strategy for schools. The school version of this approach, which has been called school-based management, in the past has taken a narrower view of what decentralized management should include, and has focused almost exclusively on just a school-based council (Malen & Ogawa, 1988; Odden and Picus, 1992). But high-involvement management is more comprehensive than just a school council and its broader features can be quite readily applied to schools (Mohrman and Wohlstetter, 1994; Wohlstetter and Odden, 1992; Wohlstetter and Mohrman, 1993; Wohlstetter, Smyer, and Mohrman, 1994, forthcoming). Lawler (1986, 1992) and Mohrman (1992) "unpack" the key components of high-involvement management and show that it works best when four resources are present in the decentralized service providing or manufacturing unit:

Information

Knowledge and skills

Power

Rewards, the compensation structure

Information about organizational goals, objectives and levels of performance, and about the key parameters of the work processes is required in order for the workforce to make good decisions that foster organizational goals and high performance. This would include information on system and unit revenues, costs, sales, profits, cost structures, etc., customer satisfaction, benchmarks with other companies, and data on the environment. In high-involvement organizations in the private sector, the work team actually makes numerous business and technical decisions. A wide range of information is needed by these teams in order to help make their decisions wise ones.

Although public schools have attempted to implement versions of decentralized management, they have not focused much attention on sharing information among participants within the school site. Indeed, the major focus in districts under school versions of decentralized management appears to be how information, such as test scores, is shared vertically between individual schools and the district office, and whether schools are adhering to regulatory policies.

Since schools are expected to meet districtwide goals, however, they need information about their performance relative to those goals. But in addition, schools, like companies, must have information about their performance relative to other schools in similar circumstances—benchmarks. Finally, schools need information about the extent to which they are meeting their clients', parents and students, needs.

Effective school-site high-involvement management policy would need to develop systematic and varied strategies for sharing information at the site, as well as with the district office and with other educational institutions serving similar student populations. It would further encourage sites to develop mission statements and make a variety of information available to their current and potential new clients.

Knowledge and skills are required for employees in high-involvement managed organizations to optimally enact their new roles in such a way as to achieve high performance and continually improve outcomes. Knowledge and skills are needed in at least four areas: (a) interpersonal or team skills for working together effectively in a group setting; (b) technical knowledge and skills for providing the service; (c) breadth skills for engaging in multiple tasks especially tasks decentralized to the work team as a result of the flattened organizational structure; and finally, (d) business knowledge and skills for managing the fiscal aspects of the work team. Developing these skills and competencies is a necessity for the work team to function effectively, and implies a large, ongoing investment in human resources development, that for the most productive companies approaches 2 to 4 percent of revenues (Lawler, 1992). Indeed, the private sector literature emphasizes in the strongest language the need to make these investments in worker training. The point is that unless the work team has the needed knowledge and skills it is difficult for them to perform their new and multiple tasks well (Lawler, 1986).

Public education has given some but insufficient attention to human resources development as discussed in the previous chapter (Little, 1993; Little et al, 1987). Such efforts usually provide much less professional development than is needed, focus more on depth skills, often ignore breadth and team skills, and are not necessarily considered part of an effective decentralization strategy. Schools have done even less to develop general business skills among site staff, a serious shortcoming, given the focus in many districts on decentralizing managerial tasks, such as budgeting and personnel. If the practice of the most effective companies can serve as an example, states and schools would allocate between 2 and 4 percent of total education revenues for human resources development in order to be able to develop the wide range of new skills teachers and administrators would need to engage successfully in high-involvement management, including the skills needed for new ways of teaching a thinking-oriented curriculum and determining what students know and can do through performance-based testing (see Chapter 5).

Power is required in order for a well-informed, competent workforce engaged in high-involvement management to have the authority to make decisions about the optimal application of resources and optimal processes to be used. Power in the private sector includes decision-making authority over the budget *and* personnel. It means the work team is given a lump sum budget to spend any way they decide, subject only to a constraint on the total amount. Further, the work team also is given authority to recruit, select, develop and, if necessary, fire personnel (Lawler, 1986).

In education, the main focus of decentralization has been decentralizing power (Mohrman and Wohlstetter, 1994). Power is most often shifted from the central administration to a school-site council. Councils usually are composed of administrators, teachers, parents, community members, and sometimes students. In this way, decentralized management empowers groups who typically have not had much power in managing schools (Odden and Picus, 1992). The idea of using decentralization as a vehicle for giving more authority to classroom teachers also is common. Most districts that instituted school-based management through collective bargaining, such as Dade County, Florida, and Los Angeles, provided teachers with majority representation on site councils (Mohrman and Wohlstetter, 1994).

A related issue concerns the powers given to school sites. Traditional school-based management programs generally delegate at least some control over budget, personnel, and curriculum decisions, however, some programs limit control to only one or two of these areas (Malen, Ogawa, and Kranz, 1990). Modest budgetary powers usually are the first to be decentralized. But, some private sector organizations have increased performance by establishing small self-managing production units with full authority over resources, including budget and personnel. Following this model, the most effective high-involvement managed schools would be given lump-sum budgets to allocate according to local needs and the authority to hire and fire school staff, including principals and teachers.

The transfer of power in the private sector, moreover, occurs through decentralization to a variety of groups. One strategy is self-contained teams, made up of employees who produce a defined product or deliver a service to a defined set of customers. Within schools, teams might be defined by grade level, academic department, a cohort of students or a school priority issue (see Odden and Odden, 1994). A second private sector strategy is creation of mini-enterprises. Mini-enterprises in schools could be groups of students organized into "houses" or "cadres" and taught by teams of teachers, similar to Developmental, Accelerated, and Success for All school designs discussed in the first section to this chapter. A third approach is to use special purpose, or "parallel" structures. Quality improvement teams, often made up of employees at varying levels, and union/management committees have been used to build consensus among employees with different responsibilities on what organizational improvements should be made and how changes should be designed. Finally, companies in the private sector have used representative task teams to enable operating units to have input into decisions that are best done uniformly throughout the organization for reasons that include economies of scale, demands of the marketplace, or legal requirements.

As education further restructures school-based management to include the components of high-involvement management, it should consider devolving more budget and personnel authority to schools as well as creating additional mechanisms for participation and involvement. Each is suitable for a different purpose. If improving the performance of schools is the focus, high-involvement approaches should create participative mechanisms that are specifically geared toward this outcome, student achievement, and perhaps put teachers in the dominant decision-making roles on curriculum and instruction issues. In a study of several districts and schools experimenting with decentralized management strategies, Wohlstetter, Smyer, and Mohrman (1994) found that the decentralization worked best when schools created several teams that involved nearly the entire faculty in collaborative decision-making, not just the school-site council.

Rewards is the final resource that is decentralized in high-involvement managed organizations (Lawler, 1986, 1992). Rewards mean that the employee compensation structure must be redesigned to align the self-interest of the employee with the organizational objectives. Companies usually shift to a knowledge and skills-based pay system, in which workers, teachers in the case of education, are paid on the basis of the knowledge and skills needed in that work environment to get the job done. Firms shift from seniority based-pay system to pay based on direct assessments of knowledge and skills. A second new component of pay could include performance-based pay, but allocated on a group or team but not an individual basis. This would include such approaches as profit sharing, cost reduction gain sharing, employee ownership, and group-based salary bonuses (Lawler, 1990).

This type of compensation structure aligns organizational goals with individual pay in several ways. First, the knowledge and skills that are developed through investments in training become the core components of the compensation system; as individuals work hard to develop new skills and competencies in different skill block areas, they qualify for salary increments. Put differently, salary increases, training, and the skills the work team decides are necessary to get the job done are interrelated. Second, since skill acquisition is fostered by collegial interactions, the pay structure indirectly reinforces individuals engaging in group efforts to expand the competency of the group as a whole. Third, since more skill acquisition is associated with higher pay, a skills-based pay structure stimulates the continuous development of knowledge and skills. Finally, since a portion of compensation is derived from group-based, performance awards, some portion of compensation is linked to the actual attainment of performance goals. In short, workers are paid individually for what they know and can do, and collectively for the organizational performance they produce.

Education has not yet decentralized financial rewards very much. Teachers continue to be paid on a standardized salary scale and education reward systems tend to use indirect, proxy measures of knowledge and skills, namely the years of education and experience a teacher has accumulated. As the National Board for Professional Teaching Standards Board certifies the most expert, experienced teachers, and other states move to license beginning teachers on the basis of what they know and can do. It would be possible to implement this component by shifting from the unitary salary schedule to one based on knowledge and skills. Kentucky was one of the first states to require redesigning teacher compensation as part of education reform; Mohrman, Mohrman, & Odden (1993) outline in more detail how a skill-based compensation structure could be designed as a component of systemic reform.

The typical career ladder program statutes designed in the 1980s, though, are neither skill-based pay schemes nor provide group-based performance rewards, but are strategies for increasing the pay of teachers who do more work. Their goal can be better accomplished through decentralized management in which the skills required of teachers and included in the skills-based portion of the compensation structure are not only deeper but broader (Conley and Odden, 1994).

Performance-based rewards are more complicated. Most past school attempts to use these strategies made the fatal error of rewarding individuals rather than groups (Murnane and Cohen, 1986); even in the private sector, individual incentive and merit programs do not work (Lawler, 1990). But group-based performance rewards, such as profit sharing, bonuses, and employee ownership are effective. Schools could consider providing performance awards to all faculty in schools that meet improvement targets. Rewards could include a salary bonus, school improvement funds, or opportunities for professional growth. But, monetary rewards are not the only extrinsic motivation available. Other possibilities include sabbaticals or opportunities to pursue full-time studies. In addition, mentor teacher positions could be reserved only for teachers in schools that met improvement targets. Another possibility would be to provide teachers with opportunities to further their education through professional conferences, classes at local colleges and universities, or involvement in teacher networks focused on some aspect of curriculum, teaching, and assessment. A final possibility would be to provide schools and faculty with more decentralized authority, including full deregulation from state education rules and regulations.

In summary, to make high-involvement management work in education, school faculty teams would need extensive information, a new array of knowledge and skills, power over budget and personnel, and a compensation structure based on skills and knowledge and group-based performance awards. Mohrman and Wohlstetter (1994) provide many additional details about how to tailor high-involvement management to schools. The ongoing reports from their study of school-based management (Odden and Odden, 1994; Wohlstetter, Smyer, and Mohrman, 1994, forthcoming) have shown that the high-involvement framework is useful for assessing education efforts to decentralize management and those attempts that decentralize the four resources (information, knowledge, power, and rewards) tend to be the most effective. As this devolution of power and authority to schools occurs, education systems should also consider several of the district implications of the new logic of organizing education systems, as well as be specific about what specific authorities are given to the site and which retained at the district level, an issue raised again in Chapter 8.

New organizational and management forms such as high-involvement work only when organizational outcomes are defined and measured, and the work team is held accountable for results. In private sector companies, the goal generally is profits and that is relatively easy to measure. Until recently, key education outcomes were not well-defined and often poorly measured. Today, as the first chapters in this book have argued, education goals related to outcomes have been adopted for the country, and student achievement has been identified as the key outcome. Systemic reform, moreover, is becoming a consensus reform strategy that includes not only clearly defined student achievement results that reflect the national education goals but also a restructured governance system that makes school sites the critical organizational unit implementing systemic reform. Chapter 10 discusses systemic reform in more detail. To insure that a decentralized management strategy such as high involvement provides clear signals about valued system results, either systemic reform or some other policy proclamation, such as the new federal Goals 2000, needs to accompany this approach to managing the education system. The remainder of this chapter assumes that systemic reform and high involvement are strategies that will be pursued in tandem by the education system.

The New Logic of Organizations and Traditional School Effectiveness

Although the new logic of organization in the private sector might, at first blush, appear to be significantly different from the 10 components of effective school organizations identified in the first section of this chapter, on further analysis the similarities outweigh the differences, especially when high-involvement management is linked with systemic reform.

According to the new logic of organizing in the private sector, a high-performing school would:

1. Be a learning organization.
2. Be attentive to global imperatives for high student performance.
3. Think big and act small.
4. Replace functional organization with teams of teachers working with cohorts of children.
5. Be attentive to school customers: children, parents, higher level education institutions, and the labor market.
6. Focus on curriculum and instruction, and outsource some functions.
7. Organize through teams and control through high involvement. High involvement would include decentralizing information, knowledge, power, and rewards.

Schools would not exist in an organizational or system vacuum. They would need to have clear notions of key student outcomes to produce, be committed to implementing a thinking-oriented curriculum, and provide performance measures of student achievement, i.e., exist within a systemic reform context. When combined with systemic reform, then, such schools would have clear goals focused on student achievement (see Table 6-1, #1). The standards for student achievement, as argued in Chapters 1 and 3, would be set to world class levels, and would hold for all students across the country, thus requiring the provision of a common, high-quality core curriculum for all students (see Table 6-1, #10). Performance assessment would provide new, robust measures of such student learning (see Table 6-1, #10). In this sense, the education system could take cues from the international arena in setting expectations for schools; the education system would think "big," i.e., by positing national standards and expectations for outcomes, curriculum, and assessment. Traditional localism over curriculum and instruction would give way to national standards, but traditional localism would be enhanced by decentralizing to schools the operational responsibility for delivering education services and attaining system outcomes.

The system could "act small" by decentralizing implementation and operations to the school site, both entire faculty in schools as well as groups of faculty in departments, houses, or other schools within a larger school site. Schools would be site-managed (see Table 6-1, #4). The site management could be structured according to the principles of high-involvement management approach, thus giving specific meaning to site management. Information, knowledge (professional development, i.e., see Table 6-1, #9), power, and rewards (see Table 6-1, #11) would be developed and/or provided to school-based teams. The teams would have the freedom to develop organizational structures and instructional strategies to enable them to accomplish system outcomes for the specific students in their particular school. In this way, each school site would be able to become a learning organization (aided by the emphasis on professional development and by not requiring a specific organizational structure) and would be able to organize the provision of services by groups of teachers working with cohorts of students by focusing on the student, parent, upper school, and business environment for that site. Such schools easily could adopt the Comer, Slavin, Levin, Sizer or any new models of schools, which dramatically reduce the functional specialization of school staff and broaden the range of activities in which teachers would engage.

As the next chapter will show, high-involvement management also includes active recruitment and socialization of staff into schools (see Table 6-1, #7 and #8). Finally, the above components of the new school organization would include collaborative planning (see Table 6-1, #2) which is almost by definition key to high-involvement management, instructional leadership as the faculty teams would emphasize teaching a thinking-oriented core curriculum (see Table 6-1, #6) and a strong culture characterized by high expectations (by setting goals at world class levels), a focus on curriculum and instruction (through emphasizing high-quality curriculum standards and teaching that curriculum to all students), continuous improvement (a stimulus of group-based performance awards), and a communal tone (see Table 6-1, #3), the school equivalents of the culture in high-involvement organizations (Lawler, 1992, Lawler and Mohrman, 1993).

The reward system in such an approach could also change to one based on knowledge and skills and group performance (see also Chapter 5). Odden and Conley (1992) and Mohrman, Mohrman, and Odden forthcoming discuss several strategies for basing teacher compensation on professional expertise and for designing group-based performance awards, that can range from school improvement dollars to salary bonuses.

Thus, schools arguably could take cues from these evolving understandings of the more general organizational characteristics associated with enhanced outcomes and improved productivity in the private sector, crossruff them with more specific aspects of effective school organizations, and potentially design new forms of high-performance school organizations. Indeed, many of the proposed school programs match both the effective school characteristics and the new logic of high-performing organizations. Further, with the conscious inclusion of the goals, curriculum, assessment, expectations, professional development, and teachers discussed in the first five chapters, school leaders and policymakers would be wise to focus on organization and management approaches, in addition to curriculum and instruction, as critical components of raising the achievement of all students to new high levels.

Organizational form and structure matter. Bureaucracies and the command and control approach to management increasingly work less efficiently today in both education and noneducation organizations. Through high-involvement management, teachers must be more involved in running and managing schools and be accountable for results. Information, knowledge, power, and rewards need to be devolved and developed at the school level, and set within a systemic reform context. Such an approach combines the core aspects of the effective schools of the 1970s and 1980s, enhances them with the new findings about effective organization in the private sector, and sets them in an ambitious systemic reform context. Such an approach, while grandiose, offers high potential for dramatically transforming schools into the types of high-performance entities the country needs them to be in the near future.

System and School Leadership

In many ways, this chapter is a continuation of the preceding chapter. It seeks to identify the types of system and school leadership needed for schools to engage in effective, site-based high-involvement management, where the goal would be to create and sustain a school successful in teaching all students how to think and solve problems in the core-content areas. This chapter focuses on leadership roles that must be played by principals, central office staff, and superintendents for the high-performance schools needed during the 1990s and beyond.

The chapter begins by reviewing theories of management and leadership as they evolved over the twentieth century. It then summarizes how conceptual knowledge of the leadership roles of principals and superintendents has evolved over this same time period, and ends with descriptions of new principal, central office, and superintendent leadership roles in schools engaging in various types of "restructuring." The last section sets the new types of educational leadership evidenced in school restructuring into a broader framework of management functions in high-performance, high-involvement organizations, and suggests a range of new roles for educators leaders trying to create and implement the types of high-performance school organizations described in Chapter 6.

EVOLUTION OF MANAGEMENT AND LEADERSHIP THEORIES

Over the course of the twentieth century, our understandings of management and leadership, generally and in education, have changed substantially. The argument developed in the preceding chapter is that current notions of the appropriate organizational form for effective schools today and in the near future appear to be quite different from the past. Since what leaders do is in part determined by the nature of the organizations in which they work, it is likely that the roles and functions of the managers and leaders of these new school organizations also will change. Although the interconnections between organizational form and leadership roles have not always been consistently delineated, this section attempts more deliberately to make those connections. It first describes the tenets of management theory that evolved for hierarchically structured organizations and then discusses how leadership theory, essentially for the same type of organizational structure, has changed over time.

Management Theory

Historically, there have been three basic schools of thought on management and organization: classical or scientific management, human relations, and open systems. These three approaches basically have offered different though complementary views of managers in bureaucracies. Within these three perspectives, the concept of organization depicted in the preceding chapter is an evolution of organizational form within open systems theory because it has been the nature of the external environment, for both nonschool and school organizations, that has been the driving factor in producing change in organizational form in the recent past. The needed management and leadership behaviors for this type of organization are discussed in the latter portions of this chapter. This section outlines how current changes in both organization and management can be viewed as part of a continuous evolutionary process.

Classical Theory of Organizations and Scientific Management. This approach was developed at the turn of the last century and perfected during the first decades of this century, and has had tremendous impact on the organizational form of private and public sector organizations as well as most schools. This type of organization evolved from the needs of an economy turning from agricultural to production. While most farms were run by a few individuals working alone, production facilities were characterized by many individuals working together. A new form of organization was needed to make this new process work effectively. In part out of this need, the bureaucracy was born.

Max Weber (1947) is the most well-known scholar of the bureaucracy. Bureaucracies are hierarchically structured organizations, with service providers or workers at the bottom and managers at the top of the organizational structure. Workers provide the service or make the product (do the work) and managers supervise and control workers (do the thinking). Each higher level office in the system has control and supervisory authority over a lower office. Work tasks are divided into various broad categories, usually functions, and within each functional area, work tasks are more finely delineated. Individuals are hired for specific jobs and need to have expertise just for the job they performed. Salary is earned on the basis of years of experience, and promotion usually occurs out of one work task to another, or up to an administrative position, but only if the requisite expertise has been learned. Explicit rules and regulations control behavior in the bureaucratic organization. Supervisors and managers have the authority to direct the work of those they manage and supervise, but only according to the rules and regulations developed for that bureaucracy. The goal is to reduce the personal and social factors that can affect behavior, by requiring individuals to behave according to the policies imbedded in the rules and regulations, thus making the organization function fairly for everyone.

Capitalizing on this new way of predictably orchestrating the behavior of many individuals in a large and complex social organization, the bureaucracy worked well for the dawn of the industrial age. For companies like the old Ford Motor and General Motors Companies, all of which produced large numbers of standardized products, as well as the old AT & T, which produced large numbers of standardized services, the bureaucracy proved to be incredibly efficient. Further, for governments seeking to eliminate the influence of politics on the delivery of governmental services and to improve their efficiency, the bureaucracy also worked well (Reich, 1983; Skowronek, 1982; Wilson, 1987; Wilson, 1989). Indeed, the bureaucracy helped create a "professional" class of managers, highly paid individuals whose job was to allocate resources efficiently, control the work of large numbers of individuals, and have large organizations provide services or make products in cost-effective ways.

Schools clearly have many bureaucratic characteristics. Education systems are organized hierarchically, with each level having supervisory and managerial control over the next lower level—superintendents over principals, principals over teachers. Individuals are hired for specific jobs—superintendent, business officer, curriculum coordinator, principal, dean, and teacher—which have specific job descriptions (job tasks) each with a different set of skills and competencies, and many times a separate license. There are a set of rules and regulations written to direct and control the behavior of all individuals in the school system. For many years, the system was protected from direct political intrusion by lay boards of education which set policy and were the legal authorities running the education system. Indeed, one of the major reasons separate school boards were created apart from general city, town, or other local governments was to keep "politics out of education" (Tyack, 1974; Wirt and Kirst, 1992).

The management theory most closely associated with the bureaucracy was scientific management, whose best advocate was Frederick Taylor (1911). He believed that there was a "one best way" to perform any job, and that both the interests of management and workers could be advanced if these ways could be discovered and implemented. Doing research primarily in production facilities (the Bethlehem Steel corporation, for example), he sought to relieve the fatigue of workers engaged in activities that required muscular exertion, which characterized many jobs in large scale production plants. By so doing, working conditions could improve, workers would have more energy and make more products in a given time period, sales could rise, and managers could both increase profits, and worker wages. While the notions of Taylor were not adopted by all managers or workers, his influence was substantial during the early part of the twentieth century.

Schools also came under the influence of scientific management (Callahan, 1962). For years, educators have been accused of trying to create the "one best system" and to proscribe the behavior of teachers (Tyack, 1974). The teacher proof curriculum of the postWorld War II era is a modern example of this phe-nomenon, as are the close and, many would say, heavy-handed supervision of teachers and the inclination to grant teachers very little control or influence over important school matters. The rise of the professional education admin-istrator and the control of school systems by those "professionals" was a prod-uct of this perspective (Tyack, 1974).

School of Human Relations. Close on the heels of bureaucracy and the scientific management approach was the school of human relations. While the former stressed the formal and technical side of organizations, the human rela-tions school stressed the informal and social components of organizations, arguing that individual social and psychological needs were critical aspects of organizational productivity. The work of Elton Mayo (1933) in the Hawthorne plant of the Western Electric corporation is perhaps one of the most well-known studies from the human relations school. Rather than addressing how the work was done, the focus of Taylor and scientific management, the human relations school focused on changing the conditions in which work was done. In the Hawthorne experiment, they improved the illumination of the work environment. Subsequently, productivity increased. But then they also decreased illumination and, surprisingly, productivity also increased. Further, when other factors were changed, such as room temperature and length of breaks, productivity again increased. The conclusion was not only that work-ing conditions could matter, but also that workers responded positively to the simple reality of attention being given to them.

The Hawthorne Effect is now identified in research as an effect produced not by some specific act or experiment, but simply by paying attention to the social or psychological needs of individuals in the workplace. Other researchers showed that many other informal components of organizations, group norms, worker participation in decision making, etc., impacted worker productivity. The overall contribution of this school of thought was that work-ing conditions and social factors, broadly conceived, could affect worker moti-vation, productivity, and satisfaction, in addition to the more formal tenets of scientific management.

However, although the human relations school identified a wide range of informal/social factors that affected worker motivation and thus organiza-tional effectiveness, the human relations school did not directly challenge the key notions of the hierarchical nature of the work organization. Attention to worker concerns helped improve the work of individuals in a production plant. Social norms mattered in how a bureaucracy ran. Worker participation in decision making helped supervisors and managers gain worker-teacher-acceptance of system goals, objectives, and procedures (Conley, 1991). In other words, the human relations school added elements to the more formal notions of the bureaucracy created by Weber, but only for the purpose of making the bureaucracy work better, not for the purpose of altering its basic structural form.

The Open Systems Approach. While bureaucracy and scientific manage-ment dominated organizational thinking during the first quarter of this cen-tury and the human relations school in the second quarter, the open systems approach became the dominant influence on organization and management thought roughly during the third quarter of the century. The advance made by the open systems approach is that organizations do not exist in a vacuum, but exist in a context, i.e., in an environment that also affects how they function. Indeed, it is from the environment that organizations obtain information, customers, materials, and numerous other factors critically necessary for their existence. Systems theories were developed in a wide range of the social sciences, including not only organizations (Lawrence and Lorsch, 1969) but also politics, including the politics of education (Wirt and Kirst, 1992).

Writings at this time were replete with charts showing how inputs from the environment penetrated the boundaries of the organization, the reactions of the organization to these new inputs, the subsequent outputs of the organization, and then (to complete the cycle) a mechanism feeding back the results to the input portion of the chart (Guthrie and Reed, 1986). A good example for schools of how the open systems approach worked is the political upheavals during the 1960s and 1970s that lead to community involvement in the schools. During this time period, many communities, often in low-income neighborhoods, began to demand more input into school operations. Initially, these demands encountered resistance from the professionals running the schools, who felt such involvement was inappropriate. But over time, and in part as a result of systems theory, many schools altered the way they functioned to not only solicit this new input but also to structure acceptable responses to the many new concerns that this input from the "environment" raised.

The open systems approach also expanded the social science understandings of the operations of the formal and informal subsystems within an organization, arguing that the overall organization was composed of a variety of subsystems. While some more complex organizational forms, such as the matrix organization, began to evolve during this time, the open systems approach also basically accepted the hierarchy of the bureaucratic structure. As such, the contributions of both the human relations schools and the open systems approach was to make the basic, bureaucratic, hierarchical organization work better. What was learned was that to be efficient, organizations needed not only good formal rules and regulations, but also needed to pay attention to working conditions and the social needs of employees, as well as signals and demands from its environment. IBM became the quintessential hierarchical organization by paying close attention to all these aspects of how complex organizations operate.

Leadership

On a somewhat separate track, leadership theories evolved over this time period. There have been several leadership theories that have developed chronologically: traits, power, behavior, situational, and visionary.

Leadership Traits. As leadership came to be studied in the latter part of the first half of this century, the first approach centered on more or less fixed traits of individuals—age, sex, personality, etc.—as the important components of leadership. Reviews of this early research, however, found no consistent pattern between personal traits and leadership effectiveness (Stodgill, 1948). Although more recent research has claimed more power for the trait approach (Stodgill, 1974; Yukl, 1981, 1982), the definition of trait has been expanded from physical or more fixed aspects of an individual to actual behaviors (interpersonal skills) or things that can be developed (technical expertise). As shown below, these more malleable factors can make a difference but, we would argue, are beyond the original conception of the trait approach to leadership.

Power Approach to Leadership. A second school of leadership developed in the 1950s and 1960s and centered around power and various definitions of power. Etzioni (1961, 1964) and others postulated several alternative concepts of power—coercive, remunerative and normative, formal, and informal, etc.— and how they were deployed by leaders and responded to by employees. Of course, legitimate power was an issue raised by Weber who argued that because of the acceptance of the supervisor/employee relationship, managers in bureaucracies had the authority to exercise legitimate power.

Behavioral School. Ohio State University, Columbus, Ohio, was the center of a series of research studies on leadership behaviors and leader effectiveness in the third quarter of this century. The basic concept of this approach was that effective leaders considered both the needs of the individual and the tasks of the organization in the way they deployed their leadership behaviors (Stodgill and Coons, 1957). Likert (1961) coined the terms "employee-centered" and "job-centered" to depict these orientations. Research showed that various leaders tended to score higher or lower on each of these dimensions. Halpin (1966) concluded that leaders who were more balanced in their approaches tended to be more effective. One can see in this school a blending of the scientific and human relations approach to management.

Contingency Approach to Leadership. Yet another lens on leadership has been the contingency approach. This school postulated that there was no one best leadership style, but that effective leadership behavior depended on the context. Hersey and Blanchard's (1982) theory that leadership style should vary with the maturity of the group has received much attention in education. They defined maturity as both job ability and psychological willingness. They argued that leaders should be more directive and task-oriented with immature groups, by "telling" for groups unable and unwilling, or "selling" for groups unable but willing. They suggested more relationship-oriented behavior with more mature groups, "participating" for able but unwilling or insecure groups, and "delegating" for groups both able and willing. There were other contingency scholars but the point of all was that leadership style should vary with the context in which leadership behaviors were exercised.

Visionary Leadership. More recently, a series of studies and books have focused on the importance of visions for effective leadership (for example, Bennis, 1985, 1989). A key to effective leadership found by this research is whether the leader has a vision for the organization, can communicate that vision to the members of the organization, and then can empower service providers or production workers to implement the vision. Vision would include not only a definition of "the business" of the organization, but also the values and norms that would guide implementation of the vision.

Concluding Comments. In reviewing most of the research on leadership, it is interesting to note the lack of commentary on the form of the organization in which the leadership is exercised. It is relatively safe to assume that most theories were developed for leadership behaviors in hierarchically structured organizations, and over time tended to incorporate the human relations concerns for the needs and capabilities of individuals in addition to tasks that needed to be performed. It also appears that leadership theories cut across nearly all types of organizations, public and private, product producing or service providing, including the schools. Moreover, little emerges in the leadership literature on how leadership should vary by the nature of the work that is done in the organization, an important perspective today which will be discussed later in this chapter.

Theories on leadership behavior have been largely determined by how the worker is viewed: as incapable and unwilling and thus needing control and detailed supervision, or as capable and willing, and thus ripe for delegation and involvement. Weber, Taylor, and others generally held the former view, while other writers and theorists held, but to varying degrees, the latter view. In the 1960s, McGregor (1960) labeled the former Theory X and the latter Theory Y. Theory X postulated that authority and control were necessary to motivate individuals to accomplish organizational goals. Theory Y postulated that individuals intrinsically want to perform well and accomplish organizational goals, a view held by McGregor. These polar perspectives on workers and management tended to dominate thought until quite recently, when American firms (as well as schools) were shown to be not as productive as firms in other countries, especially Japan. In the early 1980s, William Ouchi (1981) added several new dimensions to the above divergent views. Ouchi argued that most American organizations were based on principles that tended neither to involve the worker nor provide for their development, practices that dominated in many successful Japanese firms.

This new perspective spawned many worker involvement and quality circle programs, which were precursors to what Lawler (1986) terms the "high-involvement" approach, the basis of the new logic of organizations described in the preceding chapter. This perspective on workers and what they can and want to do, the appropriate types of organizational structures, and the requisite leadership and management roles are different from traditional views of organizational structure, worker expertise and motivation, and leadership functions. As Chapter 6 noted, the new approach engages workers and managers in an ongoing process of redesigning organizational systems to enhance system performance defined as higher quality, lower costs as well as shorter time lines (Lawler, 1992). We take up the leadership and management roles for such a system in the next section of this chapter, which first reviews the evolution of principal and superintendent leadership, including emerging roles in school restructuring, i.e., organizational redesign, efforts.

There is a long tradition of research on what the average school leader does. Over the past two decades, however, there has been an increasing amount of research on what more effective school leaders do. Currently, we are at a juncture in research on effective school leadership. Extant research on effective school leadership has focused primarily on individuals attempting to strengthen schools with traditional goals, organization, and management systems. But the critical issue today is for leadership for a restructuring or transformation that takes schools to much higher levels of performance, with attendant changes in organization, teacher involvement, and teacher leadership. The first part of this section reviews knowledge of what the average principal and superintendent does. The second part contrasts that with what more effective principals and superintendents did in the 1970s and 1980s. The third part summarizes recent research on leadership actions in schools and districts engaging in a series of fundamental change activities focused on restructuring to a higher performance school organization.

The Work of Managers

There is a great divergence between conventional wisdom or stereotypic views about what managers do compared to what they actually do. The uninformed might believe that leaders spend much time in reflective activities by conceptualizing strategic plans, being involved in meetings at which plans are discussed and modified, perhaps writing up the plans or the vision of what the organization should be, and then allocating time to facilitate the work of individuals who implement the plans. The normative view is that managers engage in planning, organizing, staffing, directing, and controlling. Behavior is at odds with this vision.

A wide variety of studies show that the work of managers consists primarily of unplanned interactions with people (Mintzberg, 1973, 1977). Managers live a complicated and fragmented life. They work at an unrelenting pace with chronic interruptions. They prefer action over reflection, and verbal over written interaction. They spend the majority of their time with subordinates. They seem always to be interacting with other people, not in long meetings but in numerous, unplanned, and relatively short encounters focusing on a wide range of practical issues, often not directly related to the central business of the organizations operations. Managers are busy. They have little time to think. They are always "on call." They have little time for desk work. On the surface their activity is mundane and seems not to approach the "ideal" of leadership.

The nature of principal work is not that dissimilar to what managers do in the private sector. Research shows that school administrators spend 80 percent of their work day in brief, fragmented, and diverse encounters with students, staff, teachers, parents, central office staff, and the public (Peterson, 1982). Desk work takes up only 12 percent of their time, and phone calls 8 percent (Manassee, 1984, 1985). Principals tend not to spend much time in planning meetings or "reflective" activities. They seem to be almost always interacting with people and having to make fast decisions. Generally, moreover, their interactions do not relate to instruction but focus on managerial tasks such as discipline, parental concerns, roof leaks, covering classes, getting supplies, etc. (Deal and Celotti, 1980; March 1978; Weick, 1982).

The life of the superintendent is not all that dissimilar. Superintendents spend much of their time on finance, building and maintenance of facilities, collective bargaining and union-management relationships, school board relationships, school community relations, and many other important and complex activities generally unrelated to the instructional program. They work in a world of where uninvited verbal interactions and externally imposed deadlines disrupt planned schedules. They are inundated with problems and short term "crises." While they spend some time in planning, the bulk of their activities are spent in interpersonal interactions with a variety of individuals generally on issues not related to the technical core of schooling, i.e., curriculum and instruction (Duignan, 1980; Hannaway and Sproull, 1978–79; Pitner and Ogawa, 1980; Willower and Fraser, 1979–80).

Effective Principals and Superintendents

It turns out that the shape of the typical workday of more effective principals and superintendents is not substantially different from the average, nor from managers in the private sector. Effective principals also live a life characterized by numerous, fragmented, and brief encounters with a wide variety of individuals at the school site. But effective principals carry a vision of what they want the school to be, know the values that their school organization needs to create in order to support that vision, and have keen understandings of what all individuals need to do to implement the vision and accomplish school goals. And they communicate these ideas in their various interpersonal interactions.

In other words, effective principals "make something" out of the myriad but brief encounters that characterize their everyday life. In their multiple albeit brief encounters with all key actors in the school and district, they remind people of the school's vision and cultural values, they monitor progress towards the school goals, teach people in the school how to interpret various efforts towards implementation, and help to develop a common language to communicate about these issues.

Key to effective principal leadership is a compelling vision. The vision is what determines the substance of their activities and communications. Their vision tends to be focused on the core activity of the school—curriculum and instruction. Effective principals communicate that vision to everyone in the school. They set specific school goals. They announce expectations for students and teachers, and model new norms and values. They develop structures to carry out their visions, such as redesigning the curriculum, implementing more effective teaching strategies, providing professional development, and creating a collegial environment.

Effective principals build a culture that embodies norms of high expectations, collegial interactions, and continuous improvement. The culture also identifies what is of prime importance in that school amidst all the conflicting and competing pressures, and governs informally how people should feel and behave. Through technical and symbolic actions, effective principals create, build, and nurture that culture.

Effective principals reward teachers who improve, and protect and facilitate teachers attempting to put changed practices into place. They track progress towards goal accomplishment by monitoring curriculum and instruction implementation, supervising and evaluating teachers, and reviewing data on student achievement (DeBeuoise, 1984, Deal and Peterson, 1990; Manassee, 1984; Rutherford, 1985; Sergiovanni, 1984). Interestingly, these types of actions are similar to what effective managers do in the private sector (Kotter, 1982).

Just like the actions of the average superintendent mirrors those of the average principal, so also the behaviors of the effective superintendent are similar to those of the effective principal. Hallinger and Murphy (1983) found that effective superintendents differed from "average" superintendents by becoming directly involved in setting a curriculum and instruction vision for the district, by ensuring consistency and coordination of a wide variety of district activities (from recruiting, selecting, and supervising staff to textbook and assessment selection) in support of the curriculum and instruction approach, and by monitoring internal processes and inspecting outcomes, for both teachers and students, related to those curricular and learning expectations.

These actions are quite similar to those of leaders in the nonschool sector. Bennis and Nanus (1985) found that leaders had a vision for where the organization should go, communicated that vision to members of the organization, enabled others to reach the goal, were persistent in making goal accomplishment a priority, and continually monitored and adjusted as they learned of changes that needed to be made to continue progress towards the goal.

Principal and Superintendent Behaviors in Restructuring Efforts

The above findings on behaviors of effective principals and superintendents in the past are important, and several aspects of these behaviors can be found in the behaviors of principals and superintendents engaged in the more complicated agendas of current school reforms. Today, however, schools as well as most organizations in both the private and public sectors today, are under intense pressure to *dramatically* improve outcomes, often times at lower costs and sometimes even over shortened time periods. Being successful in this environment generally requires more than making the old organization more efficient. It often times requires a complete restructuring of the organization itself, including its personnel selection and development system, its use of core organizational technologies, how people are organized and grouped, the rewards and personnel systems, and cultural norms (Mohrman and Wohlstetter, 1994). These are the kinds of fundamental organizational changes that many private sector companies have experienced, and are at least indicative of the kinds of changes the public schools might need to undergo in order to achieve the ambitious outcomes postulated in the national education goals.

We are beginning to identify the new leadership roles this requires of principals and superintendents. This section presents initial findings from research on a variety of restructuring efforts that were being undertaken in *schools* across the country in the early part of the 1990s. The section first describes the focus of these restructuring efforts, and then discusses the new roles that such efforts have created for principals, central office staff, and superintendents. Interwoven into the presentation are suggestions for additional roles for principals and superintendents implied by research in the private (Lawler, 1992) and governmental sector (Barzelay, 1992) which has identified evolving roles for managers and system leaders in those portions of the economy. The concluding part of this section synthesizes the results within the framework of high-involvement management, the conceptual lens for issues to address in restructuring efforts.

The Focus of Current School Restructuring. Schools across the country are implementing a variety of restructuring programs generally aimed at dramatically improving student achievement. Although the late 1980s versions of school restructuring tended not to focus strongly on the technical core of the school, curriculum, instruction, and learning, this focus seems to be stronger in more recent restructuring efforts (Murphy, Joseph, 1991; Murphy and Hallinger, 1993).

Casting a wide net for restructuring efforts that included various choice programs, different versions of school-based management, and alternative teacher empowerment programs as well as other efforts, Murphy and Hallinger (1993) came to four general conclusions about such efforts. First, the focus of restructuring tends to be at the site; the school is the key organizational unit in education restructuring. Second, restructuring today is not trying to do the same things better, but represents efforts to produce deep change in the education system. They found that restructuring is reconfiguring human interactions at all levels in the education system. In short, restructuring is about fundamental rethinking of the education system and its school organization. Third, they found that restructuring proceeds along multiple fronts, all interconnected, and that the most successful efforts work occurs simultaneously on all fronts. Fourth, they found that restructuring occurs in context, both a general context of attempted change in the education system (which in the past has had a spotty record) and in the context of each specific local district and school site. The context, moreover, shapes both the substance, pace, and style of the restructuring efforts.

In terms of the substantive foci of restructuring efforts, Murphy and Hallinger (1993) found four major emphases. The first was that teaching and learning tended to be the focus of most restructuring efforts. While the door into restructuring efforts could take many shapes, e.g., choice, empowerment, site management, the activity itself ultimately focused on the core of the education enterprise—curriculum, instruction, and student learning. Moreover, while previous restructuring efforts often made the specific impetus for restructuring the end—choice, school based management or teacher empowerment—the more recent and more successful efforts saw these as a means to an end of better curriculum, improved teaching and higher student learning. Further, the efforts tended to be directed by a set of guiding principles (such as all students can achieve to high levels), grounded in the constructivist notion of student learning (developed in Chapter 3), and centered on a small but interconnected set of interventions focused on these ends (e.g., systemic reform).

Second, Murphy and Hallinger (1993) found that recent restructuring efforts focused on the ongoing nature of restructuring, stressing the "ing" of restructuring and assuming it would be a continuous process. The efforts were centered on the work of restructuring, not on getting sometime to a shortly "restructured" state.

Third, they found that school faculty had to create site-specific approaches, and that both the paths taken and the specific programs and strategies implemented varied across schools. The focus was less on importing solutions (although sites combed the universe for programs, ideas, and knowledge) and more on creating the capacity (a learning organization) to continuously craft solutions that worked for the ever changing conditions of one's own school site.

Finally, Murphy and Hallinger found that the efforts needed to work *systematically* on changing *all* core parts of the organization *simultaneously*. As will be discussed in a later chapter, schools often found themselves buffeted by conflicting policies from local, state, and federal governments, and Murphy and Hallinger recommended that policy needed to become more coherent and systemic (Smith and O'Day, 1991; Fuhrman, 1993b).

These findings are quite similar to the large scale change efforts taking place in private sector corporations today. They must focus on their core activities—making a copy machine, a car, or providing health care; the most successful efforts entail changing all aspects of the organization from top to bottom including cultural norms and values; and they need coherent systemic policy support from the top, including the board of directors (Mohrman et al., 1989). Further, change exists in a rapidly and constantly changing environment (Lawler, 1992).

Changing Roles for Principals. Given the centrality of the site to school restructuring, one would expect dramatic changes in the role of principals involved in such efforts. Murphy's (1994a) synthesis of numerous empirical studies of the impact of school restructuring efforts on the principal is an excellent summary of these changes (see also for example, Chapman, 1990; Christenson, 1992; Goldring and Rallis, 1993; Hallinger, 1992b; Leithwood, 1992; Leithwood and Jantzi, 1990; Prestine, 1991). In terms of an overall impact, Murphy concluded that restructuring produced a nearly overwhelming workload for principals, demanded that they work both harder and differently, and created considerable stress in the short-term (see also Bredeson, 1993). More specifically, Murphy documented changes in four major areas: leading from the center rather than the top, enabling and supporting teacher success, managing a constellation of change efforts, and extending the school community.

The first change was that principals in restructuring efforts led from the center of a network of human relationships, rather than from the top of an organizational pyramid. On reflection, these role changes should be expected and even required as the organizational structure itself changes away from a bureaucratic structure to the more decentralized structure described in Chapter 6, and is also found in most restructuring efforts (Barzelay, 1992; Goldring and Rallis, 1993; Murphy and Hallinger, 1993). Put differently, rather than being the key decision-maker and "thinker" in the school as the person holding the top position in the hierarchy, principals in restructuring schools facilitated the activities of a myriad of groups and subgroups all engaged in decision making on a variety of fronts.

Murphy found that principals engaged in substantial delegation of leadership responsibilities by pushing power and decision-making authority to teachers. In order to make this approach work, the principal spent time developing numerous collaborative decision-making processes and mechanisms. Moreover, the principal participated in these collaborative processes but not as the chair of the group or the most active or most knowledgeable member, but in the background as a facilitator and thus allowing others to assume leadership and decision-making roles. The principal's role was to orchestrate the effective and substantive functioning of the groups, not to be the leader of all the groups (see for example, Odden and Odden, 1994).

Second, principals in restructuring schools worked to enable and support teacher success in their new roles. Principals worked with teachers to jointly develop a school vision, to cultivate a series of networks that supported collaborative decision-making, to allocate resources consistent with the vision, to give staff access to information critical to effective decision-making, and to promote substantial professional development and staff training. As discussed below, these activities strongly parallel the need to develop power, knowledge and information in successful decentralized management, high-involvement efforts in the nonschool sector (Lawler, 1986, 1992).

Third, principals in restructuring schools had a substantially enhanced management role largely because they had much more to manage. The school now was responsible for managing a budget, new school community relationships, parental involvement, a school improvement plan, and the many activities associated with designing and implementing a new school organization.

Importantly, Murphy (1994a) found that while principals assumed an enhanced management role they simultaneously experienced a diminished instructional leadership role. This finding is particularly important given the centrality of the instructional leadership role for principals that emerged during the 1980s (Beck and Murphy, 1993; Greenfield, 1987; Murphy, 1990a). This shift fits with findings from implementation research on major curriculum change. For example, Marsh and Odden (1991) found that teachers assumed the key leadership roles in schools making more progress in implementing new, thinking-oriented curriculum, and that the effectiveness of these teacher roles depended on support and sustenance from the principal. Odden and Odden (1994) also found that principals moved away from direct involvement in instructional leadership in locally managed schools in Victoria, Australia. If this shift from instructional leader to reform facilitator and manager holds across other restructuring efforts, it will represent a major altercation in the assumed role for a school-site leader in the 1990s.

This change of the principal role follows a continuous evolution of the key roles principals have played over the course of the twentieth century. More-over, Beck and Murphy (1993) found that the metaphors used to describe the principal role have shifted each decade from those that stress the importance of technical expertise to those that stress human relations. While a "label" of metaphors cannot yet be attached to the principal role during the 1990s, that of "transformational leader" could be one nominee (Leithwood, 1992), a role that blends technical expertise with human relations. Indeed, in another series of studies of restructuring efforts, Prager (1993) also concluded that a blend of collegial process and curricular focus was important to advance the effectiveness of school restructuring efforts.

Finally, Murphy found that principals in restructuring schools played important roles in extending the school community to broader communities. Principals engaged in promoting the school through marketing in school choice policy environments, which were rapidly expanding in nature and scope. Principals began working more directly with the variously structured boards governing the school. Further, principals played more intense roles interacting with parents, the broader neighborhood community, the local business community, and social service agencies. "Community" in restructuring efforts seemed to connote a dramatically expanded notion of school community, and the principal is a key individual at the vortex of these new and sometimes complicated interactions.

These substantial changes, while exciting in many ways, also posed challenges for the individuals involved. Principals faced difficult work challenges and nearly overwhelming workload that required great energy and faith that the effort exerted would produce the hoped for results and satisfaction from goal attainment. These challenges were deepened because, in each restructuring case, new territory was being charted; by definition, restructuring means creating a new school organization that has not been created before. Such a challenge can be both an opportunity and a burden. Whatever, it certainly raised the stakes for the individual leading the effort.

Finally, many principals had to change how they managed schools if they were to be successful in the restructuring efforts, switching from command and control styles appropriate for a bureaucracy to facilitative and background leadership roles appropriate for a decentralized management effort in which teachers assume both leadership and decision-making roles. At a minimum, this produced substantial stress for the individual principals involved, and considerable uncertainty as the process itself unfolded (Bredeson, 1993). Finally, throughout this process, the principal was still the individual whom the system held accountable for school results, even though others were making decisions in key areas.

In short, the principal's role in schools that were restructuring was very difficult and complex. The good news is that the role seems to be changing in ways to make decentralized management in a flattened organizational structure work more effectively. The "difficult" news for individuals in these positions is that they must have tremendous energy, be willing to shift from a control to a facilitative orientation (which many cannot do), and have faith that the work will pay off in better teaching and learning because they will be held accountable for what results.

Principal Leadership for High-involvement Managed Schools. Research on the behaviors of private sector middle managers in high-involvement managed organizations (Lawler, 1992) suggest additional leadership behaviors for principals related specifically to decentralizing the four key resources of information, knowledge, power, and rewards. For *information*, Lawler states that it entails several information flows and suggests mechanisms for providing downward, upward, and horizontal information flows. For schools, *downward* flows of information would include data on current and past student performance, on district and state education goals and curriculum standards, on revenues, expenditures, and costs, on new district, state, and federal policies and regulations, on community opinion about the schools, and other important system indicators. Such data could be shared both in regular meetings on the state of the school districts as well as in small regular meetings of work groups, such as grade levels in elementary school, houses in middle school, and departments in high school.

Horizontal information flows would be across content areas in high schools, across grades and functional areas in all schools. Principals could arrange for information flow across school levels—elementary, middle, and high school. An important component of this information flow would be communication with customers—parents and upper school levels, including the business community and universities and suppliers, lower school levels and schools of education. The goal would be to develop a sense among teachers that they were serving the external needs of their customers and a sense among suppliers that they were serving the internal needs of the school. These mechanisms would need to place teachers inside the channels of information flow, thus developing a tradition of getting direct feedback from customers and suppliers, rather than indirectly through supervisors, such as assistant principals and principals.

Finally, principals also could develop upward flows of information, sending data on the school, curriculum and pedagogy implementation and change, student needs, parent demands, and supplier strengths and weakness to individuals in the central office including the superintendent. The upward information flow also would include collecting information from teachers on the behavior of their site leader.

In terms of *knowledge,* principals could ensure that there is a sufficient budget for ongoing professional development and training, including off-the-job opportunities for intensive training and skill development, such as teacher networks. Principals could help teacher teams obtain the technical, crossfunctional, and business skills needed to engage in running and managing the curriculum and instruction program of the school. In addition, the principal needs to assist teachers to obtain knowledge of how the school, district, state, and overall education system operates, including general program policies, fiscal structures, governance requirements, and education politics. The goal here would be to develop understanding of the system and policy context in which the local school functions. The goal also would be to provide strategic knowledge, such as the role and influence of national education goals, and the skill needs of the evolving economy.

Principals also need to work closely with teachers on decisions related to *power* over budget and personnel. In addition to helping teachers make decisions over curriculum, instruction, and the budget, principals need to involve teachers centrally in key personnel decisions: who gets hired, who gets assigned to different work groups including developing the process for that assignment, who gets promoted and into what positions, and in evaluating the principal. Indeed, teachers would be key players in all of the important personnel functions in schools.

Lawler (1992) suggests that managers also should involve workers in setting goals for the organization, which in education would mean having teachers, within the context of national, state, and district goals, decide on the specific student achievement and other goals for their school. Goal setting can be a powerful motivator; goals would become "owned" by the teachers and viewed as achievable. Research in the private sector has shown the efficacy of this goal setting involvement (Lawler, 1992).

Lastly, principals need to involve teachers in creating and allocating *rewards* at the school site. A key aspect of this new component of principal work is ensuring that the rewards structure developed is fair and that the specific rewards provided are viewed as valuable by members of the work team. This principle means that site administrators need to involve teachers centrally in developing the process for creating and allocating rewards, and in creating the specific rewards themselves. If a skill-based compensation structure is designed (Mohrman, Mohrman, and Odden, 1994), principals need to involve teachers throughout the process of its design, including the specific performance measures. They also need to place teachers as central players in assessing the knowledge and skills of fellow teachers both for placement in a skills-based pay structure and for ongoing evaluations.

Because training is seen as a reward in both the private sector (Lawler, 1992) and education (McLaughlin and Yee, 1988), principals should encourage teachers to designate opportunities for engaging in professional development activities, including intensive and long-term programs, as part of the portfolio of school level rewards. Further, rewards could include improvements in the work itself, with principals devolving more decision making to teachers as their knowledge and skills about the entire operation of the school increases.

Finally, because the work in high-performance schools is conducted by teachers as members of the school faculty and performance is a result of schoolwide effort, rewards and recognitions for good performance should be shared by everyone in the school. No individual performance rewards should be part of the system. But group rewards could include school improvement grants (Richards and Shujaa, 1990; Richards & Sheu, 1992) as well as salary bonuses, as long as they were made available to everyone and based on school not individual performance.

In short, a wide range of new principals' roles flow from efforts to redesign school organizations and implement a decentralized, restructured, high-involvement management structure. While this process changes the nature of principals' roles and who makes key decisions at the school, it should be clear that the changes enhance the leadership functions of the principal position.

Changing Roles for Central Offices. Although not as extensively studied, central offices and superintendents' roles also appear to be changing in school systems implementing a decentralized management school structure. Murphy (1994b, forthcoming) studied the impact on superintendents and central office operations of the comprehensive, Kentucky systemic education reform program (see for example, Adams, 1993), a program that includes ambitious student achievement outcomes, major curriculum reform, and substantial school-based decision making. Murphy identified several new roles central offices have begun to undertake. Generally, the change has been from a bureaucratic control to a service orientation. Central office roles changed from controlling site actions to brokering of services, providing more consulting assistance, and becoming an advisory body. Central offices began sharing more with building personnel in a collegial, cooperative mode, rather than telling building personnel what to do in a directive mode. Central offices characterize these changes as devolving power and decision making to school sites, and then working to facilitate schools engaging in those new activities.

Central offices became engaged in two other specific new activities. First, central offices were involved much more in getting information to schools. As Murphy put it, central offices were becoming more of a transmitter of information, than a developer of strategies. What Murphy did not state explicitly was that this role was being played because schools needed more information so they could develop school improvement strategies.

In addition, Murphy found that central offices became much more involved in providing professional development and training to school personnel, both in the technical areas of curriculum and instruction, and in team skills needed by site individuals to engage in more collaborative decision-making processes. In short, central office functions changed to providing information and providing training. These new roles fit well with research from the private sector (Lawler, 1992) on new staff functions needed to make decentralized management work effectively.

Changing Roles for Superintendents. Superintendents' roles also began to change dramatically during implementation of the systemic Kentucky reforms, according to Murphy (1994b, forthcoming). Generally, their role changed from leading a school system to creating a system of schools. Murphy noted change in three general areas. In all three areas, Lawler (1992) found similar changes in senior executive leader behavior in high-involvement managed firms; Lawler also identified some additional areas of leadership that did not emerge in the Murphy study in Kentucky.

First, superintendents in the Kentucky restructuring efforts began "orchestrating from the background." Rather than making and getting others to implement centrally made decisions, superintendents spent time gathering input and facilitating a variety of collaborative decision-making efforts. They began to manage by consensus rather than command, and assumed a facilitative rather than control orientation. Indeed, they engaged in much less actual decision-making but considerably more negotiation, discussion, and enabling the collaborative decision-making of others. The more successful superintendents also were adopting a more democratic style of leadership. In short, they began to lead by helping others make the important decisions for the key organizations in the system—school sites.

Lawler's studies of executives in companies imply that superintendents also could role model *participative management behavior.* Superintendents must themselves possess participatory management skills and be able to engage in them. Superintendents also could include principals as members of the district's management team, rather than just central office staff, thus directly involving the site in key system level decision activities, and by implication, modeling how the principal could include teachers in decision making at the site.

In addition, Lawler (1992) suggests that this component of the senior executive role pertains both to the purposes of system meetings and how they are run. In traditional, more hierarchically run organizations, the purpose of most meetings is to communicate information downward. But in a high-involvement organization, information flows are handled through a variety of other channels, as discussed both above and below. Thus, the purpose of meetings is to make decisions. Meetings, at both the system and site levels, then could entail substantive discussion of issues and then the making of key decisions.

Second, in the Kentucky study Murphy (1994b, forthcoming) found that superintendents played new roles of enhancing informed participation of a greater number of groups and constituencies in each schools decision-making processes. Superintendents spent more time helping schools involve teachers, parents, businesses, and the broader community in school councils that had authority to make important decisions for the school.

To strengthen this involvement, Murphy found that superintendents spent considerable time getting information to the new constituencies so that their decisions were based on data. Indeed, superintendents had to create a variety of new structures to ensure a flow of a wide range of information not just to the district's school board, but to the many new bodies and individuals involved in and engaged in decision-making activities. Information brokering became a new but very important new role for the superintendent.

Drawing from Lawler, superintendents also could engage in two types of information flow: *communication and feedback.* The first would be downward and address how the district was doing with respect to key goals, financing, and parental satisfaction. Communication on these issues should be systematic and periodic, not just once a year. Indeed, this type of broad report on the "health" of the system could be a linchpin communication function for superintendents, as it is for chief executives in the private sector.

The second concerns soliciting upward feedback on the functioning of the district office and the district's management team. In a high-involvement district, this would entail soliciting comments from principals, who in turn would obtain feedback from teachers and other key actors at the school site, on the role of the central office and superintendent.

Third, Murphy found that the managerial job of the superintendent in Kentucky was enhanced. The leadership and management role was enlarged even though the superintendent was engaged in less actual decision making! They were involved in overseeing and managing the implementation of Kentucky's education reform program, probably the most ambitious education reform program in the country. The policy, financial, monitoring, political, organizational, educational, and knowledge dimensions of managing reform and restructuring were exponentially greater than any one had expected. As a result, their managerial roles were dramatically expanded and demanded much more intellectual, political, and other expertise for handling them effectively.

Just as for the principal, however, this enhanced management role came at a cost of being pushed away from direct interaction with the core of the educational program, which through decentralized management had been placed more in the hands of teachers.

The findings on executive leadership behaviors in high-involvement firms (Lawler, 1992) imply several other key superintendent roles for schools moving to more decentralized management. Superintendents need to provide both symbolic and technical support for *ongoing training*. They need to be the first to participate in training on participative leadership styles, on collaborative decision-making, performance management, and development of high-involvement organizational structures. In addition, superintendents could participate in training sessions for central office staff and principals, and in some cases, actually conduct the training themselves. Since the bulk of the budget for training is controlled by work units, schools, in high-involvement school districts, the superintendent and senior managers role in training is symbolic—recognition of and support for training.

Further, superintendents need to *monitor the decision making processes at the school site*. Superintendents ultimately are responsible for the decisions made by principals and teachers in schools. Thus, they need to help manage the decisions that are made, by developing mechanisms that enhance the effectiveness of decision-making processes, including support for substantial training in team skills. Superintendents also could create more "fluid" flows of information that provide a "sensing of the organization" function, such as administering formal surveys, being accessible through e-mail for ongoing dialogue, having open door policies, and eating lunch with central office and school staff. They also need to select and promote principals on the basis of their expertise and skill in running schools characterized by collaborative decision-making.

The results of such activities would be more extensive upward flows of information, including information on managerial behavior, and widespread teacher and principal discussion of the academic condition of the school and its educational programs, the way resources are deployed toward system results, the satisfaction of parents and the business community, and progress towards attaining school goals. The discussion would not center on the requirements of any one's particular job but about what all faculty and administrators can do to make their school more effective.

An additional role for superintendents, as well as boards of education, would be *direction setting*. Direction setting is similar to creating a vision. In high-involvement managed school systems, superintendents need to identify the key business of the school, teaching and learning, and lead the direction-setting process so teachers and all other employees know that these elements are the business of schools. Superintendents need to create consensus on this focus by creating a variety of communication mechanisms. The superintendent can ensure that school district meetings, publications, symbolic activities, and external communications emphasize this central focus. Further, central district staff could meet with all new employees to socialize them into the district by explaining the centrality of teaching and learning, and the goals of student achievement. Finally, superintendents could develop communication mechanisms, including downward flows of information, describing how the district as a system is doing on accomplishing its strategic goals, including benchmarking data on other districts with similar students.

It is important to note that in the Murphy (1994a, 1994b, forthcoming) studies, neither principals nor superintendents saw their jobs get easier when a decentralized management approach that put teachers and other site staff in decision-making roles was implemented. If decision making is equated with power, these findings suggest that the role of system and organizational leaders becomes more complex, more challenging, and more intellectually demanding when power and authority, as well as information, knowledge, and rewards, are decentralized. Indeed, being a leader in a decentralized system is harder than being a leader in a bureaucracy; high-involvement leaders need to be smarter, they need more energy, they need more political skills, and they need more interpersonal skills. There is both "more" to lead and "more" to manage. The irony: delegating decision making, the quintessential function of a leader in a bureaucracy, made the job of being leader in a decentralized organization more demanding, and hopefully over time, more satisfying as well.

SUMMARY

School, government, and general corporate restructuring appears to imply new views of teachers, their roles in schools, the types of organizational structures appropriate for schools of the 1990s, as well as notions of very different roles for principals and superintendents. Teachers who work in schools engaged in restructuring efforts are being thrust into key leadership and decision-making roles; nearly all studies (Goldring and Rallis, 1993; Murphy, Joseph, 1991, 1994a, 1994b, forthcoming) document a devolution of power, at least in terms of curriculum and instruction decision-making, to teachers.

In other words, individuals who, prior to these restructuring initiatives were at the bottom of the organizational hierarchy and generally excluded from decision making, are now at the center of the organization and the lead individuals who make important decisions about how the school will operate. Principals and superintendents, who before were at the top of the organizational structure making decisions, now function in the middle of a vortex of collaborative human effort where others are engaged in numerous decision-making processes. The new role for both principals and superintendents is to help the individuals comprising these other groups to make good decisions, because all have a stake in whether the organization accomplishes its new, ambitious student learning goals.

The organization depicted is one with a flattened structure, surely different from any traditional notion of a hierarchically structured bureaucracy. The outlines of the organizational picture being developed and the roles of service providers and leaders are consistent with the tenets of high-involvement management that places service providers teachers in the case of education, in positions of power and authority. Indeed, power at least in terms of general decision-making does appear to be decentralized in school restructuring efforts, though when compared to the private sector more groups in education, teachers, parents, and community leaders, seem to have a role in these decision-making activities. Although the restructuring efforts cited previously are unclear about whether the dimensions of power devolved include authority over the budget and personnel, components of power which Lawler (1986) claims is one of the four key aspects that must be decentralized in order to make decentralized management work, other research on school-based management is finding that increasing amounts of budgetary and personnel power are being decentralized to schools (Mohrman and Wohlstetter, 1994; Wohlstetter and Buffett, 1992).

Thus, it seems that restructuring entails the devolution of power and decision making, and commensurate changes in the role of leaders of schools and school systems from decision making to helping others make decisions. Moreover, principals, central offices, and superintendents have become more engaged in two other sets of activities also critical to decentralized management—devolving information and knowledge. All the above studies on restructuring found principals, central offices, and superintendents involved not only in getting more information to the decision-making groups in the schools, but also in creating a series of new information channels to keep the broader constituencies involved with the schools informed. While the research was not clear on whether an upward flow of information from the school to system levels of the organization also was occurring, the expansion of information flow down to the schools was apparent, and upward information flows could be created.

Further, the studies showed that the central office and system leaders were becoming much more engaged in developing knowledge and expertise for the individuals engaged in school decision-making. Expanded professional development and training to teachers, member of school-site councils, and others at the school were a clearly identified change that was part of most restructuring efforts. These actions are important because, according to Lawler (1986, 1992) good decisions can only be made by individuals who are informed and knowledgeable. Thus, decentralizing information and knowledge are critical for effective decentralized approaches to management.

Research, however, has found that education has been pretty silent on the degree to which rewards are being decentralized. In the private sector, rewards mean change in the structure of compensation which can include skills-based pay as well as group-or team-based dollar bonuses for meeting targets for improved organizational outcomes. None of the studies cited above involved changes in teacher compensation structures.

However, if the notion of rewards can be expanded beyond compensation, it could be argued that at least some dimensions of rewards are being decentralized. Assuming that school restructuring efforts are producing improvements in curriculum, instruction, and student learning, teachers could be rewarded simply by knowing their professional expertise is being enhanced and seeing that student achievement is rising. Indeed, there is a strong body of educational research that claims that increased student learning is rewarding to teachers (Lortie, 1975; Rosenholtz, 1985, 1989). Further, McLaughlin and Yee (1988) found that career-oriented teachers viewed opportunities to engage in professional development activities as rewards for working hard at teaching. Thus, the more that school restructuring includes expanded amounts of professional development and training, the greater teachers might view the rewards for engaging in these activities. Although group-based salary bonuses could potentially strengthen the rewards component of school restructuring, this dimension might have to be added in the future. One version might be adopted in Kentucky since the Kentucky education reform also called for a revised way to pay teachers (Adams, 1993; Mohrman, Mohrman, and Odden, 1994).

In high-involvement managed schools, teachers have a wide range of new responsibilities. As importantly, principals, other site administrators, central office staff, and superintendents also have a dazzling array of new roles and responsibilities. Generally, new leadership roles center around strategies to ensure that information, knowledge, power, and rewards are developed in school sites. The more superintendents and principals are successful in engaging in these new roles, the better the decisions of teachers and the greater the likelihood of schools meeting and even exceeding improvements in student achievement.

Local Leadership and Policy

Implementing the change process described in the preceding chapter, which includes fundamental restructuring of curriculum, instruction, and school organization can be helped or hindered by the local, state, and federal education policy systems. Three chapters address the role, capacity, and new directions needed by the education policy system. This chapter reviews the local role in education leadership, politics, and policy. It discusses the issue of "local control," both its myths and realities; changes in local educational institutions that influence the way local control will become structured in the 1990s; the rationale for local districts, central offices, and traditional local governance in an era of state, national, and emerging professional educational standards; and highlights the key roles for school boards, central offices, and educational professionals in the evolving, more "standards" directed but decentralized managed education system, in which all levels of government play key and interconnected roles.

LOCAL CONTROL OF EDUCATION

Local control has been a strong "tenet" of the American public school system for over two centuries. However state, federal, and sometimes even local governments intruded into the life of schools, strong traditions of local control supposedly kept schools close to the people and reflected the values of the local community. As educational centralization grew, beginning with creation of state education systems in late nineteenth and early twentieth centuries, and continuing through desegregation and development of state and federal categorical programs for special populations in the postWorld War II era, the unwritten agreement was that local districts had "control" over what was taught. States could create a statewide education system, license teachers, accredit schools according to common inputs standards, and provide general operating aid, but local districts made decisions about education goals and the nature of the school curriculum. Indeed, when the federal government began creating categorical programs in the 1960s, it explicitly left the nature and character of the curriculum program to local discretion (Murphy, Jerome, 1991). Even in the late 1960s when the federal government created National Assessment of Educational Progress (NAEP) the nation's only student testing system, there were explicit agreements that it could in no way constitute a national curriculum. In the "theological" perspective of local control, school districts were independent entities that were or should be protected from outside influence, districts decided on specific education goals, the nature and content of their curriculum program, and measured student progress through local selection, if not design of tests.

Strong versions of local control existed around the country. Until quite recently, states as diverse as Arkansas, Colorado, Connecticut, Minnesota, Oregon, South Carolina, and Texas deferred to local school districts and pretty faithfully focused their activities on licensing teachers, accrediting schools, and providing general education aid (Wirt, 1980). While other states such as California, Florida, and New York took a more activist role in education, local control of curriculum, instruction, and testing was nevertheless quite strong. In other words, whatever variation in local control existed across the country, the common perception was that local control of schools was a value imbued in the American public education system that legitimately curtailed outside influence and had to be recognized and respected.

Idealized Local Control

The reality of local control, however, falls somewhat short of this idealized vision. Indeed, it could be argued that local control as commonly perceived never actually existed. First, school districts are and always have been creations of state governments and, thus, have never been completely independent. Under the federal constitution, only states are recognized and given separate and independent powers. Most states, indeed today all states have created many forms of local government—counties, cities, towns, villages, and, except Hawaii, school districts—to provide a wide array of services. But, the particular nature of local government and school district design varies across each state; no particular structure is required by the federal constitution. The fact that Hawaii created a state-run education system and has no local school districts is evidence of the degree to which the federal constitution is silent on local government and school district structure. Put directly, local school districts have no independent standing as governmental bodies; they have been created by state governments and constitutions and can be changed, eliminated or altered at will by them.

Second, there always have been segments of an informal national curriculum. Through the influence of commercial textbooks that are used nationwide and the proliferation of norm-referenced, standardized achievement tests, large elements of the school curriculum, from grade 1 to grade 12, look the same across states and districts and schools, from Maine to California, and from Idaho to Florida. Third grade arithmetic focuses on the basic algorithms of addition, subtraction, multiplication, and division, with numerous drill and skill textbooks, workbooks, and ditto sheets. Reading, spelling, and writing dominate the language arts curriculum. Little science and social studies is taught. At the secondary level, students take algebra in grade 9, geometry in grade 10, and algebra 2 in grade 11. U.S. and world history, and even literature courses stress names, dates, places and times, over ideas, concepts, and applications (Cohen, 1993; Goodlad, 1984).

Moreover, until recently schools were generally organized pretty much the same way: elementary schools with age and grade-grouped students in classes of 25 to 30 pupils with kindergarten through sixth grade, junior high schools for grades 7 through 9, and high schools for grades 10 through 12. Junior and high schools tended to have 45- to 50-minute periods, and students changed classrooms and teachers for each period in the day. The "biggest" school organization change has been the shift to grade 6 through 8 middle schools, with grade 9 through 12 high schools and grade kindergarten-5 elementary schools (Alexander and McEwin, 1989; Gruhn and Douglass, 1956).

Schools even tend to use money the same way—by hiring more teachers and education specialists and thus reducing the number of children in each classroom. Indeed, this common use of education dollars is stunningly similar across the country (Picus, 1994). Between 1950 and 1990, for example, real spending rose from $1,519 to $6,015 (in 1991–92 dollars) and the number of pupils per teacher dropped from 27.5 to 16.3 (National Center for Educational Statistics [NCES], 1992); moreover, teacher salaries, while rising, nevertheless retained their relative rank to other professions.

Third, the alleged independent nature of local schools and districts belies the long, gradual, but nevertheless consistent centralization of the nation's and each state's education system (Kaestle and Smith, 1982). For the past 100 years, local school and district autonomy has been systematically curtailed (Kirst, 1992b). The creation of state school systems at the beginning of the decade brought order and uniformity to many local education functions including length of school day and year, minimum qualifications of teachers, input standards for school accreditation, and sometimes even textbooks and high school graduation requirements. Beginning at the turn of the decade but accelerating by the middle of it, the consolidation movement, directed by state policy, eliminated more than 100,000 school districts, in perhaps the most drastic "attack" on local control. During the 1960s and 1970s, courts as well as federal and state governments created mandates and categorical programs that required districts to integrate schools and provide extra services to several categories of students. Finally, the 1980s education reforms began reaching right into the school house and classroom door to upgrade curriculum standards, improve discipline, impact student counseling, and (at least attempt) to change school culture (Cohen, 1982; Fuhrman and Elmore, 1990; Kirst and Meister, 1985), arenas that even local governments had respected as "off limits" to external policy interference. Individually and collectively, these were large intrusions on local autonomy and simply underscored the mythical nature of local schools and districts as separate from the influence of state and federal governments, or the courts.

Another concept surrounding local control is that it is a zero sum political game, that if the state or federal government gains power or influence, the cost is less power and authority for local districts and schools. In other words, if one level of government, or the courts, enhances its role, another level must lose something in the process. The notion is that power and influence exists in some fixed amount. But this notion is both outmoded and empirically unjustified. Cohen (1982) and Murphy (1982) showed how federal policy initiatives in the 1960s and 1970s expanded both state and local policy reach educational capacity and organization complexity.

Prior to these initiatives, most state governments engaged primarily in teacher licensing, accrediting schools and allocating state equalization aid. Departments of Education generally were small, ran few programs, and had a small number of organizational units. But, by 1980, all Departments had grown substantially in size, administered a multitude of programs (desegregation, compensatory, bilingual, and special education, gifted, and talented programs), had numerous new divisions and organizational units, and were staffed by individuals with considerable expertise. Each categorical program itself often became a large organizational unit within the department, with subdivisions focused on student eligibility, funds allocation, program quality, compliance review, and auditing. During this same time period, most state education departments created program evaluation units, and many also initiated new large scale (statewide) student testing programs. From small relatively unsophisticated institutions that had bungled program implementation at the beginning of the 1960s (Murphy, Jerome, 1991), state departments of education grew to become complex institutions, staffed with a wide variety of new, sophisticated professional expertise, and engaged in a dazzling array of education initiatives (Murphy, 1982; Peterson, Rabe, and Wong, 1986).

Similarly, Cohen (1982) and Elmore and Fuhrman (1990) showed how, over a 20-year time period, both federal and state policy initiative expanded local policy purview, organizational size, general capacity, institutional complexity, and professional competence (see also Peterson, Rabe, and Wong, 1986). As a result of these initiatives, local boards, central offices and sites became involved in desegregating schools, providing special services to a variety of students including the poor, physically handicapped and limited English proficient, developing and implementing school improvement initiatives, and evaluating new program endeavors. These efforts required more complex local education organizations, vastly expanded professional expertise, new involvement in interest group education politics, and leadership on a range of new issues.

Although it required the prod of governmental and court actions, and despite the inconsistencies of many rules and regulations that were promulgated, local educators ultimately had to weave the disconnected state and federal policy initiatives into something coherent, sensible, and that fit with local curriculum and instruction priorities (Cohen, 1982). This dependence on local ingenuity and, if you will, local control, is one reason why state and federal initiative expanded the overall dimension of local educational power and influence and ultimately enhanced rather than reduced local control. While the new directions required by state and federal action changed the nature of local control, it did not reduce the quantity of local control. The actions increased the amount of political influence, power, and control. The result was that local as well as state and federal power and authority expanded.

A similar scenario occurred with the state education reforms of the 1980s. Research on the impact of the 1980s state education reforms, which began direct state influence on the nature of curriculum and teaching, theretofore protected arenas of local control, showed that such initiative, rather than blunting local initiative, reinforced and emboldened many local education leaders in their attempts to improve, make more rigorous, and upgrade the local curriculum and instruction program. While many state reforms were broad, fragmented, and partially inconsistent in their design, local leaders nevertheless were able to take both their substance and symbolic messages and weave them into local visions of education improvement (Odden and Marsh, 1988; Fuhrman, Clune, and Elmore, 1991). Just as federal initiatives expanded state and local power and control, the 1980s state education reforms also expanded local power and control.

Finally, the education dollars that local districts and schools have to provide educational services have enjoyed a long-term rise in real value. As Chapter 13 will detail, per pupil revenues, after adjusting for inflation, have risen between 25 and 65 percent every decade since World War II, and even rose substantially before then. Thus, one impact of the frenetic actions of all levels of governments has been to increase the size of the educational fiscal pie. Since nearly all education money in the United States is spent at the local level, this impact itself is testimony to how state and federal initiatives have enhanced local power and authority.

The lesson from this history is that local control is not a zero sum game. Influence by one level of the education system does not come at the expense of influence of a lower level. In part because of the interconnected nature of political and education systems in the United States, actions by higher levels of government expand power and control of the lower levels, and money as well in education. Yes, higher level government actions can impact both substantively and politically the nature of lower level education policies and programs. For example, court decrees outlawed segregated schools, but the response required local districts immediately to become engaged in the more complex tasks of racially integrating schools, teaching effectively more diverse classrooms and spending more money for these activities.

The result of this accumulation of intergovernmental initiatives is a local educational system today that has a broader span of operations, is involved in a wider array of education issues, has greater knowledge and expertise, wields more power and influence, has a more professional staff, and spends more money in nominal and real terms than would have occurred if state, federal, and court activity had stayed at their levels of 1960 (Cohen, 1982; Fuhrman and Elmore, 1990; Peterson, Rabe, and Wong, 1986). While the result is certainly not a neat national system as in many other countries, the current United States education system is a more coordinated and interconnected system of schools, districts, and states and federal government agencies across a range of services and issues including education, civil rights and health and social services than any notion of "local control" would have predicted. In the U.S. education system, no individual level is autonomous, no level is significantly more powerful than another, and no function is completely independent of others. While schools are run by teachers and site administrators, and districts by school board and system leaders, they function not alone but as part of a vast and interconnected intergovernmental structure, that only America could create.

CHANGES IN LOCAL EDUCATIONAL INSTITUTIONS

The preceding section argued two points: (1) that the traditional rationale for school districts as the "local control" control mechanism in the country's education system has been somewhat exaggerated or at least misunderstood; and (2) that districts today are more sophisticated and capable bodies than in the past. But past and current capabilities might be neither necessary nor sufficient for the future. In an education system which has goals set by national and state political actions, and implementation devolved to school sites, it becomes reasonable to ask about the nature of the future roles and functions of boards, districts, central offices, indeed all the components of local educational institutions. This section describes in more detail the evolution of local education institutions and discusses the rationales for schools boards and districts in the future American education system. The last section describes new roles for these institutions in the context of systemic reform (Smith and O'Day, 1991).

School Districts

Independent school districts are a phenomenon of the progressive governmental reforms of the early nineteenth century and the attempt to separate education from local politics (Kirst, 1992b; Skowronek, 1982; Wilson, 1989; Wirt and Kirst, 1992). Districts generally were created as a form of centralized administration during the progressive period of governmental reform. They were contrived in part to bring standardization, rationality, and professionalism to schools that theretofore had been characterized as idiosyncratic, fragmented, and politicized local entities. This development within education also paralleled the creation of the large, standardized bureaucratic organizations that served well the industrial era. Education organization design in fact paralleled industrial organizational design, which made sense to the degree that schools were preparing students for the workforce in those expanding new industries. Indeed, the progressive form of government bureaucracy, while an antidote to the cronyism and nepotism of "Boss Tweed" local politics, also was rooted in the developing industrial organizational form—the bureaucracy. Another purpose was to protect schools from politics. Independent school boards were designed in order to separate education and politics (Elmore, 1993; Kirst, 1992b; Tyack and Hansot, 1982; Wirt and Kirst, 1992).

The structure of school districts today is about the same as it was years ago. They constitute the largest number of local governmental bodies. Generally, they are not coterminous with any other local government—cities, towns, or counties. They are creatures of the state; usually, legislatures can consolidate them, expand their number or modify what they do at will.

Most school districts are fiscally independent of any local government and have separate taxing and expenditure authority. In several states, including Connecticut, Maryland, North Carolina, and Virginia, school districts are fiscally dependent on other local governments, and must obtain their budget from these local, noneducation governmental authorities. The vast majority of school districts, however, are independent of other local governments.

School districts also are the only lay controlled governmental bodies in the country, perhaps even the world. They represent a unique aspect of the American governmental system. The rationale for this feature was to ensure public review of the values inherent in the curriculum and instruction program. As education became less a private and more a governmental function, lay control of school boards would help ensure that government actions would not depart radically from what local parents and communities wanted schools to teach their children.

The most notable phenomenon surrounding school districts per se in the twentieth century has been the decline in their numbers. Between 1900 and 1950, the number of school districts dropped from over 130,000 to 84,000; the number then dropped to 18,000 by 1970. Over the latter time period, an average of 3,300 school districts were consolidated into larger ones each year. Viewed any way, these numbers represent large change. Today, there are a stable number of approximately 15,000 districts and only a few consolidate each year.

As a result of the decline in numbers and the simultaneous increase in number of students, school districts today are larger than they have ever been, even though the bulk of districts today enroll less than 1,000 students. Although there were many rationales for the school district consolidation movement, cost reductions, expanded program offerings, better student achievement, greater fiscal equity, few have been supported by research (Guthrie, 1979; Sher, 1977). While the pace of school district consolidation slowed considerably after 1970, many today still believe small districts lead to inequities and are expensive to operate.

School District Roles. Elmore (1993) identified four key rationales for districts. One is that school districts are catalysts for local democracy. Local school districts are the governmental form closest to parents and children, and can act to buffer intrusive forays of state and federal governments. Districts also can serve to mobilize support generally for public schools. The engagement of nearly 100,000 individuals as local school board members and the numerous local bond issue referenda for building schools are examples.

Second, as education is a state function, school districts can function as local "laboratories of democracy" similar to how states have played that role vis-à-vis the federal government (Osborne, 1988). In this role, districts can take the lead in experimenting with new forms of education governance and new strategies of education reform. The trial of private school vouchers in Milwaukee (Witte, Bailey, and Thorn, 1993), new forms of collective bargaining and teacher/management relationships in Rochester, New York, Dade Country, Florida, Cincinnati, Ohio, and several other school districts (Kerschner and Koppich, 1993), and the school-site decentralization being tried in Chicago (Hess, 1991) and East Harlem (Fliegel, 1993) are all examples of "radical" initiatives being "piloted" at the local level.

Third, local governments such as school districts have a competitive edge in the developmental (curriculum and instruction) and allocative (specific resource use) functions of government, whereas state and federal governments have the advantage in redistributive policies (ensuring that minorities, the poor, handicapped, and other special-needs students are served). Local governments, such as school districts, have the strongest incentives to increase productivity and value with their resources. They are critical institutions in the type of interconnected, intergovernmental system the U.S. political structure favors.

Finally, local districts have played the role of molding and adapting to local conditions and implementing the proliferation of state and federal education initiatives and programs. Cohen (1982), Kaestle and Smith (1982), and Cohen and Spillane (1993) show quite clearly how districts and schools have had to make sense of the numerous and often times conflicting rules and regulations that accompany state and federal education programs. Indeed, it could be argued that the costs of providing this coordination at the federal or state level would be prohibitive if not impossible, and that cohesion and integration can happen only at the local level.

The District Role in Curriculum and Instruction. Given the restructuring and curriculum change that is needed at the school site for the remainder of the 1990s, the question that emerges is whether these difficult site tasks can be aided by existence of school districts. According to Elmore (1993), the answer in part depends on the potential for district involvement in curriculum and instructional improvement.

Although the research base is not extensive, the problem is that research portrays a timid and weak district role in curriculum and instruction issues. District organization and staff tend to emphasize finance, budget, collective bargaining, and categorical programs over the core curriculum and instruction program. Floden et al. (1988) showed that the district influence on curriculum was slight. Hannaway and Sproull (1979–79) argued that interactions between districts and schools rarely focused on curriculum and instruction. Chubb and Moe (1990) concluded that districts were in political gridlock and had trouble concentrating on any substantive issue. Although delegating curriculum issues to the school is no panacea because, as Chapter 7 discussed, site administrators also rarely provide much curriculum and instructional leadership, schools at least are closer to curriculum and instruction issues.

Despite this rather discouraging research base, there are arguments for a district role in the education restructuring efforts of the future. First, if the private sector can be taken as a guide, restructuring to a decentralized, high-involvement form of management and organization slims down central bureaucracies and dramatically changes their roles but generally does not eliminate them (Lawler, 1992); thus, the decentralizing trend in education does not, and perhaps should not, mean that there are no roles for districts or that they should be eliminated. Second, there are emerging examples of the roles central offices can play in school restructuring efforts (David and Jane, 1989; Murphy, 1994b, forthcoming) and the findings identify roles similar to those performed by corporate staff in private sector restructuring efforts, as Chapter 7 discussed. Further, such functions (described in Chapter 10) entail new initiatives on finance, budget, collective bargaining, and the information infrastructure, areas that have dominated past central office activity and areas in which central offices have a strategic advantage. Third, research has identified some positive examples of central offices involved in curriculum change (Cunningham, 1994; Marsh and Bowman, 1989; Murphy and Hallinger, 1988; Odden and Marsh, 1988); thus, there is some precedent for and knowledge about how a district role in curriculum and instruction can be structured. But this role should be designed with caution because it also appears that sites, not central offices, must take the key leadership positions in restructuring both curriculum and school organization (Marsh and Odden, 1991; Murphy, Joseph, 1991; Murphy and Hallinger, 1993). Fourth, district actions can help create and sustain site-based professional communities which are key to improving individual practice and commitment, both of which are needed to accomplish the nation's ambitious education goals (McLaughlin, 1992b; Talbert and McLaughlin, 1994).

From these findings it would be safe to conclude that it is feasible and necessary to design a new central office role for the education reform challenges of the 1990s. Before describing what these roles could be, it is necessary to visit the issue of school boards themselves, because school districts and school boards come as a package in the current way the county organizes its education system. So if there is a rationale and role for districts, the rationale and role for boards must be articulated as well.

Local School Boards

School boards are a unique American invention. Lay member, i.e., nonprofessional individuals, govern the American school system at the local level. Technically, school boards are the local policymaking body; their formal role is to set education goals, decide on the curriculum, hire superintendents, and allocate local district fiscal resources. Actually, school boards perform executive, legislative, and judicial functions, perhaps the only American political institution that performs all three governmental functions (Kirst, 1993).

School boards are a fairly recent phenomenon. In the seventeenth and much of the eighteenth centuries, education powers were vested in local legislatures and local governments. Separate, independent, and lay controlled school boards emerged in the late nineteenth and early twentieth centuries both as a way to reflect local public values in the local school program as state education systems were created, and to separate and insulate education from the "Boss Tweed," patronage, nepotism, and corrupt aspects of local politics.

Over time, school board roles changed dramatically. Initially, they were the administrative arms of school systems. They hired teachers, kept the books, and performed administrative functions. As the size of districts grew, however, and the amount of administrative work expanded, boards withdrew into more policy making roles and hired professional school administrators to manage the local education system and perform administrative duties. Over time, moreover, Boards tended to defer decision about important education policy to the professional staff, and spent much of their time on managerial details—reviewing the appointment of all staff (generally a formal legal requirement), reviewing budgets and making decisions about detailed expenditures, approving even the smallest contracts, and mediating disputes and grievances (Campbell et al., 1990; Kirst, 1992b; 1993; Wirt and Kirst, 1992).

Until the 1960s, boards functioned in a relatively calm political environment. They typically had between 3 and 7 members. While some were appointed, most were elected to "at large" positions in nonpartisan elections, i.e., they represented the interests of the entire district, not just a portion of the district. They generally were well educated. Most board members were male, white, and professionals or businessmen. They engaged in a "rational" policymaking process and governed by consensus. Most votes were unanimous, from selecting a superintendent to deciding on substantive policies (Campbell et al., 1990).

By midcentury, however, school boards and school board members came under fire and became embroiled in complex and divisive issues. First came school integration. Then collective bargaining and teacher militancy. In quick succession, inadequate finance, proliferation of state and federal laws and mandates, and finally broadly based community demands for more involvement of low-income and minority parents in school decision-making came to dominate the once tranquil agendas of local school boards.

By the close of the 1980s, the nation's political leaders (the President and 50 state governors) had adopted education goals for the country. Professional groups and state governments (sometimes with federal government support) were creating curriculum standards and leaning towards an American style national curriculum (Smith, O'Day, and Cohen, 1991) and there were calls for a national testing system (National Council on Educational Standards and Testing, 1992), all areas that had heretofore been the purview of local school boards. Indeed, proposals for systemic education reform in which goals, curriculum standards and testing would be set nationally or at the state level, and more power and authority would be devolved to schools was becoming the nationwide reform agenda (Smith and O'Day, 1991). These reforms had major implications for changes in local education governance and school board roles and functions. These initiatives together with proposals for public school choice and even vouchers raised centrally the question about the roles of the local school board (Danzberger, Kirst, and Usdan, 1992; First and Walberg, 1992), with more than one voice calling for their elimination (Doyle and Finn, 1984; Finn, 1991b).

In the late 1980s, a study by the Institute for Educational Leadership (1986) conducted by Jacqueline Danzberger, Michael Kirst, and Michael Usdan began what has become nearly a decade long reanalysis of school boards in the U.S. education system. That report concluded that boards were becoming less relevant. They tended not to be providing educational leadership. While boards might have had broad education goals (educate all students to their full potential), they lacked the capacity for more substantive goal setting (student achievement in complex subject matter) and the planning required to have their education systems accomplish specific goals. Boards were not providing the politically risk taking leadership for education reform required to be a "player" in the rapidly developing reform movement. Boards were "out of the loop" on education reform, were not spending sufficient time educating themselves on education issues or on education policymaking, and given the changing conditions of children, were not developing collaboration with other agencies and organizations to meet the social needs of students in their schools. Finally, as part of the local systems implementing state defined education reforms, local boards were not exercising adequate policy oversight nor did they have adequate accountability processes. While the IEL report concluded that boards needed to be reinvigorated, their report implied that without major change, school boards could become dangerously irrelevant to the major education issues the country faced.

In an early 1990s report, Danzberger, Kirst, and Usdan (1992) identified a series of additional problems with school boards. In no particular order, they argued that:

- The turnout for school board elections was embarrassingly low, many times less than 15 percent of eligible voters, calling into question the degree to which boards and their members represented local democracy.
- Too many board members were elected to represent specific portions or wards of school districts rather than the entire district, resulting in too many board members championing single or narrow issue agendas.
- Boards were politically unconnected to broader local and state governments and had little influence on the education policy these bodies were enacting, and also were politically fragmented themselves so experienced extreme difficulty functioning together to make policy.
- Constructive board superintendent relationships had collapsed. As evidence, the authors showed that in 1990, 20 of 25 largest districts had superintendency vacancies and most of those districts had recently hired superintendents.
- Boards were too bogged down in the minutia of routine administration decisions, i.e., embroiled in micromanagement. An example was the Tucson, Arizona school board which had met 172 times in one year!
- Despite the broadening needs of public school children, few school boards collaborated with general purpose local governments, a crucial initiative if coordinated children's services and social services were to become a reality
- Boards were less impressive than their rhetoric in devolving decision making to schools, thus seemingly holding on to power and authority when that was seen as a deterrent to school improvement.

In a survey of a large sample of board members conducted as part of the study, moreover, Danzberger, Kirst, and Usdan found that board members themselves rated their performance least effective in the above areas where they were being criticized. In the same survey, board members also rated themselves ineffective in areas in which they most needed to act: leadership, planning and goal setting, involving parents and the community, influencing others (general government, state policymakers agencies serving children and families, the private sector), policy oversight, and board operations and development.

The IEL report admitted that this rather strong criticism might not apply to all school boards. The major school board problems, Danzberger, Kirst, and Usdan stated, were in big city, urban districts not all districts across the country. Further, school boards were bogged down in local micromanagement largely because of the requirements of state and federal laws. In most states, law required boards to approve line budget items and hire all personnel; in some states, the chief state school officer was the final arbiter of local school-site grievances. Further, both states and the federal government required boards to create intrusive regulations for categorical programs. Third, even to the degree that general criticism of boards was true, there was a wide variation in effectiveness among the 15,000 school boards across the country, so the general indictment could not be applied at will to any specific board. Finally, the report cautioned that despite any shortcomings, school boards were a part of the intergovernmental education system, were unlikely to be eliminated, and were the local unit of democratic governance for education.

The IEL study team suggested "fixing" school boards rather than eliminating them. Although IEL considered more radical proposals for reconstituting school boards, such as developing "boards" or parent councils at each school site such as in Chicago, merging the school board into general government as was done in Boston, and even eliminating boards as part of radical choice plans, they took a more modest stand of calling for a reconstruction of school boards into policy boards, discussed more in the next section.

But, in making proposals for significant change, the study team claimed that reconstituted school board roles would need to address not only the identified extant problems plaguing boards, but also the longer term trends of more external forces on education policy including political actors and the business community, and the need to forge linkages with local general government in order to provide coordinated social services for children (Kirst, 1992a, 1993).

Local school boards no longer are the preeminent, or only policymaking education entity. Education governance for the remainder of the 1990s will be much more complicated, will include more delegating of decision making, and will entail more power sharing both within education (in terms of school-based management) and between education and other governments (coordinated children's services). Future school boards will need to be involved in setting goals and directions; engaging in strategic planning to implement them; stimulating curriculum development aligned with national, state, and professional curriculum standards and creating staff development structures to enable teachers to teach them; and designing mechanisms for restructuring education systems and changing school management.

By the beginning of the 1990s, then, the role and place of school boards in the evolving education policy system was clearly a topic for discussion. While only a few argued seriously for eliminating this institution that engaged nearly

100,000 lay Americans in the country's public school system, the difficulties boards had in making education policy, their lack of engagement in the education reform movement of the 1980s and their alleged micromanagement of local school systems (Danzberger, Kirst, & Usdan, 1992) suggested that they were ill equipped for the challenges of the 1990s. A new vision for school boards that thrust them into influential roles affecting the important education issues of the day was needed.

Central Offices

A good news, bad news scenario characterizes the maturation and development of central district offices over the past several decades. Again the story is one of growth in size, complexity, and expertise. Just as state departments of education expanded during the proliferation of the categorical programs of the 1960s and 1970s so also did most central school districts offices. New units were created generally for each new categorical program so central offices in medium and large size districts had compensatory education, bilingual education, special education, and vocational education units, each with a separate and protected funding source, specific rules and regulations protecting its new activities, and external interest groups, sometimes including the courts, that supported and lobbied for attention to its specific concern. During this time, many local research and evaluation departments were created, adding yet another professional dimension to central office organizational complexity and staff expertise. As a result, central offices gained staff with specialized professional expertise that simply had not existed in years past (Peterson, Rabe, and Wong, 1986).

As the 1980s evolved, curriculum staff, many of which had been cut during the growth of the special categorical program days, again rose to new prominence as the national curriculum reform efforts began to take root. During this time, central office staff expanded in the curriculum areas and thus gained additional expertise in mathematics, science, language arts, history, and social studies, and even fine arts and foreign language. In recognition that new curriculum required significant change in classroom practice, many central offices added professional development staff and often also created new staff development units, organizational entities that had never existed in most districts. In many districts, these new units were organizational solidification of the effective teaching, effective schools, and school improvement activities that had begun in the early 1980s but from a mixture of places in the central office, not a specific organizational unit.

Thus, the end of the 1980s saw central offices that were experienced, expert in curriculum, special-needs programs, staff development, evaluation, and a whole range of complementary expertise that had been required for the educational initiatives of the previous three decades.

The problem, however, was that central offices were still organized in a hierarchy and governed by bureaucratic rules and regulations. Despite the array of talent in them, central offices often were quite distant from the school site, sites often felt unsupported for the many changes they were required to make, and the gulf between the large, expert, professional central office and the school site was as large as ever. The problems were especially acute in large urban districts, but even where central offices sought aggressively to support school change efforts, site demand for assistance simply overwhelmed central office capacity to respond (Marsh and Odden, 1991).

Finally, as proposals for school-based management multiplied, particularly as a component of the second wave of the 1980s reforms (Elmore, 1991; Murphy, Joseph, 1990, 1991) and of systemic reform (Smith and O'Day, 1991), bureaucratically structured central offices simply were hard pressed to respond. The irony was that in many ways the institution of the central office had grown in stature, maturity, expertise, and capability, but in ways that often were insufficient for the substantial support needs of local school sites and organized in manners that were at odds with a decentralized approach to education management that seemed more tailored to the fast-tracked quality changes needed in the nation's schools.

Superintendents

Superintendent roles and strategies also have evolved rapidly during the past 100 years, although greater change occurred in the latter half than in the first half of this century. From the late nineteenth through the midtwentieth century, the superintendent's role often assumed a moral, even evangelic tone as superintendents defined their goal as helping to create an American public education system that would transmit the country's culture and be the unifying force in a nation of immigrants. While superintendent's were first hired by big city districts, and their role evolved from bookkeeper to educational manager, many assumed with almost a missionary zeal this developmental role to construct the American public education system (Tyack and Hansot, 1982).

After World War II, this creationist stance evolved into a business manager role as superintendents became the leaders of systems raising the funds, passing the bond levies, and constructing the school buildings needed to educate the children who became the baby boom generation. This rapid two decade growth of the public school system required focused managerial attention and good business and fiscal skills.

During this time, professional administrators and superintendents enjoyed tremendous influence at both local and state levels. Policy at both state and local levels was made almost consensually. Superintendents were deferred to for recommendations on state school finance and local fiscal policy (Bailey et al., 1962). This was the time when the "good old boy" network emerged. Superintendents, nearly all white men, retired into universities and staffed departments of educational administration, which trained the new entrants to the administrative world who became future superintendent leaders. This network was effective and largely responsible for building the postwar American school system and managing its rapid growth.

But the 1970s and 1980s became a period of change and transformation as the inward-focused operational style of the superintendent as dominant decision maker atop the hierarchical pyramid of the school district organization clashed with collective bargaining, demands for involvement of more diverse constituencies in the education policy process, new roles for women administrators, increased decision making by state and federal political leaders, and, by the end of the 1980s, single issue citizens, and the religious right. These new political forces strained the hegemony of the "good old boy" network. Education decision-making became a contentious process, board decisions were nearly always split with majorities changing quickly, and job tenure became shorter (Campbell et al., 1990).

By the 1980s and early 1990s, superintendent's roles had evolved more towards a more chief executive officer position. The superintendent was not only constantly involved in education reform, but also faced with the need to dramatically improve student learning for an increasingly diverse student body. The superintendent needed political skills to handle the board, the teacher union, special interest groups that had grown up around categorical programs, the local and state political process, and the religious right (McCarthy, 1993). The superintendent also was engaged in school restructuring, major curriculum reform, and implementing new forms of student testing, demanding education transformations that required new substantive knowledge. And despite significant average funding increases across the country, many superintendents also faced fiscal challenges to accomplish new, ambitious education goals without the large increases in dollars that they would have liked.

By the 1990s, then, the superintendent's role and the individuals in them had emerged as a sophisticated multifaceted position, far beyond the more unitary role of the evangelical builders of the public education system in the first half of the century and the school builders and system expanders of the immediate postWorld War II period. In the 1990s, the superintendent was the leader of education systems that had to "reinvent" themselves, decentralize their organizational structures, transform their curriculum, and raise a more diverse group of students to levels of learning heretofore reached by only a small portion of the population. This mission fell not only to Anglosaxon males, but also many to females and to a wide variety of minorities.

Professional Educational Organizations and Teacher Unions

The National Education Association was founded as a professional "association" and not a union in the nineteenth century. The American Federation of Teachers (AFT) was founded as a Union in 1916, initially representing teachers primarily in city districts. As the National Education Association (NEA) evolved, it was run by the superintendent leaders who also ran the other components of the education system (Kerchner and Mitchell, 1988). Indeed, in the early decades of the NEA, all educators—teachers, principals, central office administrators, and superintendents—joined the NEA if they wanted to become part of an education association.

But this hegemony and harmony changed dramatically and quickly in the latter half of this century. As collective bargaining emerged, tensions between teachers and managers grew and soon caused a rupture within the NEA; administrators split off and the American Association of School Administrators as well as associations for elementary and secondary principals grew as the primary professional groups for school administrators. Only teachers remained within the NEA. Overtime, however, the NEA evolved from a staid educational association to a powerful teacher union that, in the late 1970s, helped transform the U.S. Office of Education into a full-fledged cabinet department (Radin and Hawley, 1988).

New professional groups also were created to parallel the growth and development of categorical programs, such as the national association of directors of special education, bilingual education, compensatory education, etc. Political interest groups also formed around these programs and were active at local, state, and federal levels supporting the intent and separate nature of these programs (Campbell et al., 1990; Wirt and Kirst, 1992).

While subject matter associations, such as the National Association of Teachers of Mathematics (NCTM) and the National Council of Teachers of English, had existed for many decades, they tended not to be centrally involved in the education policy process. When the national curriculum standard setting movement of the late 1980s began, however, largely catalyzed by publication of the NCTM 1989 mathematics standards, these groups suddenly became quite influential (Furhman and Massell, 1992) and literally took a center role on the evolving education reform stage. Together with other organizations that emphasized curriculum and instruction concerns, such as the Association for Supervision and Curriculum Development (ASCD), state ASCD affiliate organizations, and the National Staff Development Association, these professional groups with a core interest in curriculum and instruction formed a large part of the infrastructure needed to advance school restructuring and curriculum change.

While new but more informal structures of such professional associations began to evolve in the 1990s, such as the teacher networks surrounding a new approach to mathematics in California (Adams, 1992), the Bay Area Writing Project, AFT sponsored teacher centers in New York City, the NEA National Center for Innovation and several others around the country, it was becoming clear that such teacher-led associations and networks were key to accomplishing the bold education reforms of the 1990s; what shape such networks would take was not clear, but it was clear that the teacher expertise and leadership developed through such associations were key to accomplishing reform goals (Lieberman and McLaughlin, 1992; Little, 1993; Massell and Goertz, 1994).

Local Taxing Maturity

To help finance their new capacities and actions, local governments including school districts also had a much more sophisticated revenue raising capacity by the 1990s than at the beginning of the century. Indeed, in the early 1990s, virtually the only source of local education revenues was the property tax. But in the 1990s, a multitude of additional revenue raising options had been made available.

In many states, including Maryland, Ohio, and Pennsylvania, states enabled school districts to raise additional revenues by imposing a surcharge on the state's income tax. Such a strategy also was being pursued in California as revenues were scarce and there was little hope of undoing Proposition 13 which had severely limited the property tax in 1978 (Kirst, 1994). There were even proposals to add an income surcharge at the school site, as part of a revised school finance structure for public school choice programs (Odden and Kotowski, 1992a).

Several other states including California, Missouri, and Nevada had allowed either school districts or counties to enact sales taxes in order to raise new educational resources; when this option was provided at the county level it required political cooperation across all districts in the county to run a campaign from which they all would benefit. In California, moreover, proceeds from the county sales tax surcharge also were shared with county governments, thus requiring political skills not only to determine the county-education share (which was not set by state law) but also to convince the people to vote for such a tax increase.

Finally, many districts and individual schools had begun to create private, nonprofit foundations as a fund raising vehicle outside the realm of just tax policy. Although these efforts rarely raised large sums in terms of the overall budget, they raised dollars that could be spent any way the district or school wanted to use them, and they became an additional new and creative revenue raising mechanism for a public school site or district.

Summary

As the 1990s dawned, therefore, the local landscape was quite different from how it looked at the beginning of the century, even quite different from the middle of the century. From a set of rather simple organizations and institutions with limited professional expertise and modest revenues, the local education context could be described as a series of interconnected and highly capable array of organizations and institutions. To be sure, there were problems, with the roles and functions of both school boards and central district offices. But both institutions were unlikely to vanish and, indeed, good arguments could be made for key, but different roles for both in the future. The issue today is what role boards, central offices, and educational professionals should play in an education system increasingly characterized by goals set by political leaders at the top, curriculum standards determined by nationwide professional groups if not governmental entities, state, and perhaps even national performance-based student assessment systems, and substantial school-based management. The concluding section addresses these issues.

LOCAL ROLES IN THE 1990S AND BEYOND

It is clear that changes in local school governance and local policy leadership and roles are needed. This chapter has argued that despite shortcomings, school boards are likely to continue, there are strategic (as well as democratic) rationales for school districts, and central offices can and should play crucial roles in the curriculum change and school restructuring efforts required for the remainder of the 1990s. This section briefly outlines the directions these changes should take.

School Boards

Danzberger, Kirst, and Usdan (1992) suggest (see also Danzberger, 1993; Kirst, 1993; Usdan, 1993), that school boards should be retained but restructured by state law into local educational policy boards. They should retain their executive functions, devolve to schools their previous legislative functions, and hire outside authorities, such as administrative judges, to perform their previous legal functions. But state legislatures are the key to making these changes; they need to alter state laws to enable boards to function in such new roles.

Danzberger, Kirst, & Usdan recommend that states should repeal all laws on the duties and function of boards, including those on finance, personnel, and grievances. States should move board elections to the same time as general elections, and make the majority of board members elected to "at large" positions. These changes hopefully would remove boards from their involvement in the details of local education systems, increase the percentage of the public selecting board members, encourage more board members to represent the entire district rather than portions of it, and focus the board on broad policy issues.

As part of the policy orientation, Danzberger, Kirst, & Usdan recommend that boards should be required to develop specific local education goals, consistent with state and federal education goals; implement an assessment and indicator system that tracks school and district policy towards accomplishing the goals; create policy coherence around local curriculum, categorical program requirements, student testing, and teacher professional development that are linked to the goals; and design school-based management and organization structures consistent with the need to create high-performance schools across the entire district. Danzberger (1993) also suggests that boards hire administrative law judges to hear complaints and grievances, and to establish mechanisms for collaborating with local governments to provide coordinated children's noneducation services.

Finally, Danzberger, Kirst, & Usdan suggest that boards should engage in strategic planning, develop a process for periodically reviewing each school's performance, and designing phased assistance/intervention programs when performance lags, and mount strategies to keep abreast of the rapidly evolving education reform agenda.

Following suggestions developed in previous chapters on decentralized management, boards also would need to sanction, design, and implement a more decentralized approach to managing school districts, which devolved more power, authority, and accountability to the school level. As part of this process, boards would need to negotiate different types of collective bargaining agreements with teacher unions, agreements that would specify the dimensions of school-based decision making, the nature of a knowledge and skills-based compensation structure if that were implemented, and the district policies on professional development, a key component to effective decentralized, high-involvement management. Many of these changes would entail alterations in the state's collective bargaining statutes which now proscribe what can be bargained, and the nature of teacher compensation.

Districts and Central Offices

Chapter 7 described the new types of roles for superintendents, stressing new superintendent roles in school restructuring efforts that included substantial school-based, high-involvement management. These suggestions placed superintendents more in the role of creating an education vision and new district culture within which to provide new leadership for a decentralized, site-based managed system. Superintendents would diminish their role in making decisions, a function that would be largely devolved to the school site. The role of the superintendent would be direction setting to accomplish ambitious student achievement goals and implementing a new system of site-based high-involvement management appropriate for organizational restructuring. In this structure, superintendents would help structure the decision-making processes of site-based administrators and teachers, provide opportunities for site-directed professional development, and get more information to school faculty so they could make good decisions.

Central offices likewise need to change their roles. They need to shift from mandating and monitoring, to providing service and technical assistance. Specifically, central offices need to help sites in the processes of school-based budgeting, personnel recruitment and selection; function as a broker to help sites find appropriate professional development expertise; redesign the district's information system to get fiscal, student, community, and other information to schools in an on-line computer format; and, perhaps negotiate with the teacher union new structures and policies to create a knowledge and skills-based pay structure (Lusi, 1994).

Note that these roles play to the historic strength of central offices, and are somewhat silent on curriculum and instructional leadership. The assumption is that each school needs to tailor a specific curriculum suited to the unique needs of its children; schools might suggest district roles and functions, but those roles might evolve in quite different ways within each district. The focus of the above suggestions for both boards, superintendents, and central office staff is to structure policies and procedures that help schools engage successfully in the decision-making and implementation processes required for changing the curriculum and restructuring school organization.

In this decentralization strategy, it is important to collaboratively decide what functions will be retained at the district level and which functions will be delegated to schools. At this point, it seems that the central office would maintain the fiscal accounting system but make fiscal (as well as other) data available on a school by school basis, build schools, provide transportation (although this could be accomplished on a regional basis and sometimes in collaboration with public transportation systems), administer common student assessments across schools and make the results public, and design the overall compensation structure. Schools would assume the key roles in developing curriculum aligned with state and professional standards, recruit, select and develop staff, and control the professional development of all teachers. Operation and maintenance of school plants could remain a central function, or be decentralized to schools; many ardent school-based management supporters would argue for the latter (Hentschke, 1988). Although extant research implies that teachers do not desire more than control over curriculum and instruction (Conley, 1991; Wohlstetter, Smyer, and Mohrman, 1994), lessons from the private sector suggest that once a decentralized, high-involvement structure is implemented successfully, workers and service providers want more rather than less control over all aspects of operations, not just the technical side (curriculum and teaching in education) (Mohrman, 1993).

Implementing these changes for the central office probably will require a downsizing of central offices as well. Since many service functions formerly performed by the central office would be performed in schools, both the resources and probably the staff formerly in the central office will need to be devolved to schools. Further, since many control functions will also be assumed by schools, through the high-involvement approach to management, many of these resources and staff also would be dropped from the central office. At the same time, central offices could become more entrepreneurial in their orientation and create units that provide professional development and other services that schools might want to purchase. If central offices were successful in designing high-quality services that schools needed and would purchase, staff size in the longer term might not have to decline. But the funding and governance structure for the services would be altered; funding would be under the control of sites and central office receipt of those resources would come through selling services rather than receiving a central budget appropriation.

Teacher Unions

The nature of education restructuring in the 1990s also posits several new roles for teacher unions as well. Since teacher unions developed along with the bureaucratic nature of the local school district, their roles have been conceived as protecting teacher interests by making decisions with central office leaders and school boards. Put another way, unions have bargained centrally with management over the details of general working conditions for teachers in schools. In the results driven, professional standards-oriented, and site-managed system of the 1990s, however, perhaps teacher unions too need to reconsider both what they seek to bargain and how they structure the bargaining process.

In high-involvement managed systems, Lawler (1992) suggests that unions do not bargain the specifics of local working conditions but the structures that would allow workers, teachers in education, to decide on how work is organized and structured in their school and team. Drawing on other Lawler suggestions, teacher unions would bargain for a wide range of decision making for site-based teacher teams, for the right of site teachers to recruit and select staff, for budget set-asides, for ongoing professional development, for a rich array of information and communication channels with and across schools and between schools and the central office, for the structure of a skill-based compensation structure, and for long-term commitments for site-based performance bonuses if they are added to the compensation structure. Unions also could provide professional training to teachers, a function which could vastly expand if the level of training actually needed by teachers is funded in the future.

Professional Educator Roles

The preceding suggestions for boards, central offices, and teacher unions are based on the supposition that teachers and administrators at school sites would assume the important leadership and management roles in education, a conclusion from both Chapter 6 on the new logic of structuring high-performance, high-involvement organizations and from Chapter 7 on the administrative roles required for such an approach. In addition to supporting a more decentralized approach to school management and organization, the conclusions in this book posit much stronger site-based roles for the curriculum and instruction program.

Research shows that the leadership and support needed for the sweeping nature of curriculum change proposed for the public schools simply outpaces what most districts can provide, and that the ongoing, coaching needs of teachers engaged in the curriculum change process can best be provided at the site level (Little, 1993; Marsh and Odden, 1991; McLaughlin, 1991b). Related research also shows that new types of teacher professional networks can have much more impact on new teacher curriculum and instruction practice than even good, centrally provided training (Adams, 1992; Lieberman and McLaughlin, 1992). Other research on more successful school-based management and school restructuring efforts also support the need for teachers and administrators in school sites to play the leading roles in these endeavors (Hallinger, 1992; Mohrman, 1993; Murphy and Hallinger, 1993; Wohlstetter, Smyer, and Mohrman, 1994).

These suggestions are further undergirded by the movement within special education, the "regular education initiative," which holds that the regular classroom teacher must play a stronger role in the education of children with physical and educational handicaps. Indeed, given the rapidly changing demographics of students and their multiple needs for stronger discipline and emotional, health, and physical supports, as well as special learning requirements, teachers in the future need an array of talents now provided often only by specialized personnel. For effective schools in the future, these teaching competencies need literally to be part of the professional expertise virtually all teachers posses. The only other option would be to staff schools with just specialized experts; even if that were fiscally affordable, it likely would be unworkable.

It is clear that these many new roles for teachers: managing the school, changing the curriculum, teaching the curriculum successfully to a more diverse student body, restructuring school organization and management, and engaging in additional functions such as professional development and school improvement, will require development of much new professional expertise. Many private sector organizations that have needed their workers to develop such a broad range of new expertise have shifted their compensation system to one that provides rewards for particular knowledge and skills (Mohrman, Mohrman, and Odden, 1993; Odden and Conley, 1992). Developing and implementing such a new way to pay teachers might be an even additional task in which teachers and their unions could be heavily involved in the future.

Summary

In short, the high-performance, high-involvement managed schools of the future require talented teachers and site administrators to engage in key leadership roles over a variety of functions, clearly all those functions currently performed in schools and many of the functions now performed by the central office. The local expertise that has been developed within education over the past 3 to 4 decades suggests that there is sufficient capacity to govern and manage schools this way, even though considerable additional capacity will need to be developed (Cohen 1991; Little, 1993). Boards will need to be reconstituted into broad policy boards, prohibited from engaging in micromanagerial decision-making, but required to set specific student achievement goals for their schools, and to monitor school-site performance and progress towards accomplishing the goals. Central offices will need to be restructured to provide the information and supports needed to help site professionals engage in this type of decision making to restructure school organization, management, curriculum, and instruction. Teacher unions will need to engage in a new form of collective bargaining that will put into contract language the key structures of a decentralized management structure. Unions also will need to ensure that professional development funds are available to site staffs every year. Teachers and their unions also might need to redesign teacher compensation structures that reward teachers for the ongoing development of new skills and competencies needed to effectively teach a new thinking-oriented curriculum to all students and to successfully engage in good management and other decision-making roles required by a high-involvement managed school.

State Education Leadership and Policy

State governments have the constitutional responsibility for education in the United States. While the "nation" might have been at risk in the 1980s (National Commission on Excellence in Education, 1983), the point governmental level for education was and is the state, not the federal government or even local school districts. As the saying goes, education is a state function, a federal interest, and a local administrative responsibility. On the other hand, this formal distinction between constitutional powers belies the connected nature of the country's intergovernmental education system that was described in the previous chapter. Although states assumed a key leadership role in education by the beginning of the 1980s, and likely will play critical roles in education reform throughout the decade, all levels of government as well as professional education organizations and the business community are major actors in both creating education policy and changing education practice.

One of the most fundamental changes in education leadership and policy of the last three decades has been increased involvement of the state, including governors, state legislatures, and state departments of education. Prior to the 1960s, few states played major substantive roles in education policy or administration; indeed, the leaders and policybrokers were the superintendents who had helped develop the country's public education system and who were turned to by legislatures for advice even on state school finance policy (Bailey et al., 1962; Tyack and Hansot, 1982). As this chapter will show, however, that as the local leadership on education policy that was so strong in the first half of the century and which rather quickly declined and the past four decades, governors, legislators, and state departments of education became the leaders championing education policy and reform (Fuhrman, 1994a; Fuhrman and Elmore, 1994; Odden and Wohlstetter, 1992).

Today, states are the focal governmental entities in designing a systemic reform strategy for the country (Massell and Fuhrman, 1994; Pechman and LaGuarda, 1993; Smith and O'Day, 1991). Even though the federal government can spur the development and implementation of systemic reform, federal initiatives in the 1990s such as those embodied in the Clinton Administration's Goals 2000 program (discussed more in the next chapter) and the State Systemic Initiative of the National Science Foundation work through state governments. And as Chapter 8 found, local school boards have been conspicuously uninvolved in the education reform initiatives of at least the past decade.

The purpose of this chapter is to outline the evolution of the state role in education over the course of the century, to show how the institutions of state government have matured over this time to a point where today all key actors at the state level are heavily involved in education leadership and policy, to identify both problems and challenges with this state activity, and to suggest new roles and strategies that state governments can undertake during the remainder of the decade to help implement a systemic reform agenda designed to dramatically improve student achievement.

CHANGES IN STATE GOVERNMENT INSTITUTIONS

This section traces the changes in the state role in education over the past century, from the development of state governments generally, to changes in governors' offices and legislatures, state tax structures, state courts, state departments of education, state-based national organizations, and the shift from education to children's policy. The story portrayed is one of a government that played a passive role (a time when states were called the "sometimes" governments) licensing teachers, accrediting schools, and providing general revenues until midcentury, that quickly turned to the activism of the second half of the century. The activist period began with the accountability, competency testing, collective bargaining, and school finance reforms of the 1970s, which then expanded to the comprehensive education reform decade of the 1980s. This was followed by the sophisticated and national leadership roles states are playing in the 1990s—designing the emerging systemic reform strategy (Massell and Fuhrman, 1994), monitoring the National Education Goals (National Education Goals Panel, 1993), and creating children's policy as a broader policy umbrella for considering education policy (Kirst, 1991). In the 1990s, it appears that states have risen to the lead position among governments championing children, schools, and education reform.

State Government

States only recently have assumed the respected role they are playing not only in education but in many functions. The history of government in the country has been more one of local and federal dominance. Local governments, including school districts, were generally the lead governmental entities during the first half of this century. Both states and the federal government tended to devolve most substantive leadership across nearly all functions (except defense) to local governments—counties, cities, towns, villages, and school districts.

The paucity of state leadership is documented in several treatises that chronicled a low level of state activities up through the early 1960s (Gray, Jacob, and Albritton, 1990). Indeed, with legislatures meeting for short terms (the "long" session in South Dakota was just eight weeks until quite recently), governors holding office for only one, two-year term, lack of staff in both governors offices and state legislatures, and few categorical programs to administer, states simply did not engage in much administration or substantive policy making. This unassuming approach to governing led one scholar of state governments to characterize states as the "sometime" governments (Burns, 1971).

This unpretentious involvement in the country's governmental system and social issues that needed attention put the states in a weak position to act when the more tranquil times of the postWorld War II eras became more agitated beginning largely with the 1954 U.S. Supreme Court decision in *Brown v. Board of Education* finding racially segregated schools unconstitutional under the Fourteenth Amendment of the nation's constitution. Initial state resistance to this decree under the rubric of "states' rights" created even further skepticism about the role state governments could play in policy leadership. Indeed, in assessing governmental institutions in the 1950s, it was easy to conclude that states were neither capable nor willing to assume leadership roles in addressing social issues and solving the country's problems, i.e., states more likely were part of the problem rather than part of the solution.

In part as a result, it was the federal courts together with federal government program creation that began the activist period of governmental initiative in the postWorld War II period. Not only had it been national leadership that had helped the country begin to lift itself up from the economic malaise that accompanied the Great Depression of the 1930s and then to win two world wars, but now it was up to federal governmental institutions to address a wider variety of the nation's social issues, beginning with racial segregation in the South.

Federal initiatives arose on a variety of fronts: desegregation of schools after the 1954 *Brown* decision; the National Defense Education Act of the late 1950s designed to gain leadership in mathematics and science after the Russians launched the first satellite; the War on Poverty in the Kennedy and Johnson Administrations that included new initiatives in education, economic development, housing, food stamps, and revised welfare programs; in public transportation, legal aid for the poor, and a host of other programs. Moreover, states often became the administrative agencies for these programs, a requirement that over time necessitated the expansion and growth of state bureaucracies and state governments generally.

As the previous chapter argued for both state and local governments, federal initiative into new social service areas, therefore, did not come at the expense of state (or local) government influence; it expanded their power, capacity, and activity as well. Thus, the story of state government change during the 1960s and 1970s is one of growth and maturation, from governments that had avoided roles in thorny as well as controversial social issues, to governments that within two decades had grown severalfold in size, administered a comprehensive array of new programs, and possessed a wide range of new substantive expertise (Doyle and Hartle, 1985; Gray, Jacob, and Albritton, 1990; Murphy, 1982).

If the 1960s and 1970s could be called the adolescent period of modern state government, the 1980s could be characterized as early adulthood. During this decade, a time when *national* political leaders were trying to catalyze a retrenchment of the federal government, *state* governments continued the growth spurt of the previous two decades by creating on their own new initiatives in economic development, stimulating development of high-technology industries, reforming schools, improving universities, and redesigning social programs (Osborne, 1988). During this decade, states again became the "laboratories of democracy" in the country's intergovernmental system, not just responding to federal government initiatives and administering their programs, but striking out in new directions and designing new strategies and policies on their own (see also Doyle and Hartle, 1985).

In the 1990s, many of these new state directions continued as attempts to "reinvent" government (Barzelay, 1992, Osborne and Gaebler, 1992). This concept means that states became engaged in the intellectual and policy reformulation process of restructuring government to the needs as well as the realities of the 1990s, and the next century. Three underlying notions characterize these efforts. The first is a shift from an input to an outcomes orientation, in which government initiatives are assessed on the results produced not just on the services provided. The second is that there may be limits to the level of tax revenues governments can take from citizens, and that governmental organization and service strategies need to be restructured and redesigned in order to produce more with less, the same or not much more money; these pressures are paralleled in the private sector as well (Lawler, 1992). Third, governments might need to identify problems, set goals, and monitor outcomes but that entities other than just the government can be involved in delivering the services. To use Osborne's phrase, governments need to "steer" the systems toward public goals, but the "rowing" to get there can be done in a variety of ways by a variety of actors, both public and private.

This dramatic change from "sometimes" governments to leading governmental bodies attempting to "reinvent" government represents a startling but welcome transformation of state governments across the country. Not only must state governments be recognized as important players in the country's efforts to reform education and many other functions (such as healthcare) but also state governments can be counted on to set strategic directions, provide new visions, and lead the country into the twenty-first century. As the remainder of these chapters argues, this leadership already is occurring in education.

Governors and Governors' Offices

In 1992, the nation elected one of the country's leading governors to the office of President of the United States. Although governors had been elected President before, and had run for the Presidency, they usually were from the big urban states of California, Illinois, Michigan, or New York. Bill Clinton, however, was from Arkansas, a small state which only a few decades ago would have represented anything but progressive government. But during the 1992 election, Clinton talked about how his successes in Arkansas in economic development and education reform could be accomplished for the nation as well. His election represented another evolution within the American political system: of governors, particularly southern governors, into key political leadership roles for the country. Several political analysts in the early 1990s had identified state governors as comprising the bulk of the new political leadership in the country (Broder, 1980).

This evolution of governor's offices paralleled that of state government generally. In the early part of the 1900s, few state governors provided leadership that could catapult them into national roles. Most governors sat for only two years, and could not succeed themselves. They had little budget authority. They were assisted by only a few staff members. Numerous state agencies ran state government; the structure was broad and shallow. Governors made literally hundreds, even thousands, of appointments to commissions and agencies but the structure was so expansive that it was difficult if not impossible to govern. State government was broad but not deep, spread across everything, and unimportant as well as important (Bele, 1990).

In the second part of the decade, all that began to change (Bele, 1990; Gray, Jacob, and Albritton, 1990). Most governor terms were extended to four years, and in most states today state governors can be elected to at least two successive terms. Thus, most governors have a chance to govern for at least an eight-year time period.

Second, governors were given more power over the budget. They often were given line item veto authority, a strong fiscal power. They were asked to submit budgets to the legislature each year (or every two years in states with biennial budgets). To respond to this latter requirement, many states created administrative divisions or offices of budget and management, similar to that office at the federal level. These units were staffed with individuals who knew public finance and the state fiscal structure, could make reasonable estimates of state revenue growth, and could analyze agency budget proposals. The line item veto and budget development process not only provided the governor with substantive expertise to engage in budget allocation decision making with knowledge and intelligence, but also gave governors "raw" political power, because power over the purse is the essence of political power.

Third, state governments often were reorganized into more cohesive and larger agency units. The multiple number of commissions were consolidated into a much smaller number. Service agencies were consolidated into larger bodies such as education, social services, health, transportation, and economic development. An individual was appointed to head each agency. Often that individual became part of the governor's cabinet, another new organizational innovation, which also included the attorney general, head of the management and budget division, and state treasurer. Thus the governor could govern with a "cabinet" form of government and have periodic meetings with key staff in charge of agencies that administered all state services.

Finally, governors' offices themselves were provided funds to hire staff. Personal and policy staff provided the governor with yet another capability to engage in substantive analysis and to approach policy formulation with knowledge, expertise, and independent information (see also Doyle and Hartle, 1985; Gray, Jacobs, and Vines, 1983).

As a result, many governors became expert on important state and national issues. Governor-created approaches to economic development were proposed for federal policy as well. In the mid1980s the governors made respectable reform proposals to Washington on such complex issues as welfare, immigration and health, many of which were adopted.

Governors also assumed leadership roles in education policy. In fact, at the beginning of the 1990s, governors could claim a solid two decades of active leadership in education policy formulation. In the 1970s, several governors provided leadership for complex school finance reforms; Bill Milliken in Michigan, Wendell Anderson in Minnesota, Ruben Askew and then Bob Graham in Florida represented both Republican and Democratic governors that were "out front" in changing school finance policy to provide more equity. Gubernatorial leadership for education continued into the 1980s; Jim Hunt of South Carolina, Lamar Alexander of Tennessee, Dick Riley of South Carolina, Bill Clinton of Arkansas, Tom Keane of New Jersey, Joe Frank Harris of Georgia, Rudy Perpich of Minnesota, and Roy Romer of Colorado represent just a few of the nation's governors, from both parties, who were prominent in both state and national education reform efforts.

Some would argue that nearly all governors from the old "South" had become leaders of education reform as they realized that an upgraded education system was a prerequisite for their state's economic development (Task Force on Education for Economic Growth, 1983). When Lamar Alexander became Chair of both the Education Commission of the States and the National Governors' Association (NGA) in the mid1980s, he encouraged the latter group to focus on key issues for governors, the main one being education, and had the NGA commit to a five-year education reform program (NGA, 1986; Fuhrman and Elmore, 1994).

From this list of education governors, several assumed direct national leadership roles. Lamar Alexander become Secretary of Education in the George Bush Administration, the first time a governor had headed that department. Subsequently, Dick Riley became Secretary of Education when Bill Clinton was elected President; Riley's deputy was another former governor, Madeline Kunin of Vermont. And Roy Romer led the National Education Goals Panel in the first two years after the Education Summit of October 1989 when the national education goals were written by the governors (then led by Bill Clinton) and President George Bush.

In summary, Governors and their offices have developed into much stronger institutions since the midpoint of the century. Governors are now viewed as strong, substantive leaders within their states, and many have assumed leadership positions at the national level as well. For education in particular, governors have become key leaders at both the state and federal levels. By the mid1990s, governors in many ways provided the central political and policy leadership for education reform across the entire country (Fuhrman and Elmore, 1994).

Legislatures

Among all the institutions of state government, legislatures wield considerable power because they have the plenary function to make state laws. Policies and programs do not even reach the governor's desk until they have been enacted by both the senate and house of state the legislature, except for Nebraska which has a unicameral legislature.

The active state legislatures of today have not always been that way. Legislatures also have evolved and matured as political institutions in a manner that parallels general state government and governors' offices (see Doyle and Hartle, 1985; Fuhrman, 1994a; Gray, Jacob, and Vines, 1983; Gray, Jacob, and Albritton, 1990; Rosenthal, 1981; Rosenthal and Fuhrman, 1981a). In the early years of this century up to the 1950s, most legislatures met for very short periods (2 to 4 months) and often met only every other year. Thus, they simply did not have enough time to engage in policymaking for complex social issues. During the next two decades, however, legislative sessions were expanded, with several legislatures today meeting nearly year round. While being in session does not necessarily improve policymaking, it at least provides the time needed to engage seriously in policy analysis and policymaking for the many complex problems states face (Rosenthal, 1981).

Over this same time period, legislatures were organized into more cohesive committees and subcommittees, that in many ways paralleled the larger agencies that had been created to administer state government programs. These new committees became staffed with nonpartisan individuals who often were trained in schools of public affairs, and thus had considerable policy analysis expertise in general and often specific expertise in functional areas such as education, health, transportation, welfare, etc. Legislators themselves were provided offices and individual staff (Rosenthal and Fuhrman, 1981b).

Beginning in the 1960s with court-required reapportionment each decade, the character and expertise of individual legislatures began to change as well. From bodies dominated by rural interests, legislatures gradually became comprised of well-educated, substantively expert individuals who truly represented the population in each state (Rosenthal, 1981).

Legislative expertise was well-represented in education policy. In fact, many legislative education leaders were powerful legislative figures apart from their interest in education, and over time many moved from heading education committees to heading appropriation and revenue committees as well. Some even became governors. For example, Rosenthal and Fuhrman (1981a) found that many of the top legislative leaders in education, such as Senator Joe Harder in Kansas, Representative Wayne Goode in Missouri, Senator Guilbert Bursely in Michigan, were senior members of the legislature sometimes with 15 to 20 years in office, and thus high in the formal and informal political powers of the legislature. Bob Graham moved from the Senate to Governor of Florida in the 1980s, and then to the U.S. Senate.

By 1990, legislatures also could claim a solid two decades of leadership on education policy; 35 states had enacted school finance reforms (Odden and Picus, 1992), 45 had increased high school graduation requirements, and 40 had created new student testing programs (Fuhrman, 1983, 1988, 1994a). By any measure, legislatures had amassed an impressive volume of education policymaking. Further, many legislators had taken proactive leadership positions on these issues; for example, Florida's Graham, Kansas' Harder, Michigan's Bursley, and Missouri's Wayne Goode led school finance reform in their states during the 1970s, and California's Gary Hart and Missouri's Annette Morgan led more general education reform in their states during the 1980s.

By the dawn of the 1990s, then, legislatures generally and numerous legislators individually were firmly entrenched in education policymaking (Fuhrman, 1994a; Odden and Wohlstetter, 1992a). Although the latter part of this chapter will identify some problems with this comprehensive involvement, the point here is simply that from a body that was essentially uninvolved in substantive education issue at midcentury and had little capacity for becoming involved, state legislatures at the start of the 1990s had considerable expertise, over three decades of active involvement in numerous important and complex education issues, and had been making policy on these issues for the same 30-year time period. While buffeted by forces that made it difficult to provide coherent policy leadership (Smith and O'Day, 1991), legislatures had clearly staked out a critical position in the education policymaking process.

State Tax Structures

Two other key components of state government institutions, tax structures and the courts, also developed in breadth and capacity during the past 40 years. Today all but a few states have balanced state and local fiscal structures, with comprehensive sales, income, and property taxes producing revenues for both state and local governments. States began reforming unbalanced and regressive tax structures in the 1960s as part of their general efforts to modernize state government (Gray, Jacob, and Vines, 1983). Tax reform activities continued as part of the school finance reforms of the 1970s; indeed, school finance reform often was accompanied by enactment of a state sales or income tax, as well as reforms both to reduce the level of property taxes and to make the incidence of the overall state tax system less regressive (Callahan and Wilken, 1976; Odden and Picus, 1992; Odden and Wohlstetter, 1992).

Many states passed lottery programs that dedicated all or the bulk of money to education. Although public debate during creation of these programs suggested they would produce large new sums of dollars, the actual proceeds were generally meager, usually only an extra 1 to 3 percent of the overall education budget (Clofelter and Cook, 1989; Odden and Picus, 1992).

The new robustness of state fiscal structures was one reason states were able to accommodate the federal program and fiscal cutbacks that occurred during the beginning of the 1980s. During that time period, states were even able to raise rates on many taxes both to compensate for lost federal dollars and to cover state budget shortages caused by the recession of the early 1980s (Gold, 1983). By the end of the 1980s, moreover, states again took the initiative on tax reform to go beyond what they had accomplished during the previous 30 years. Following the national efforts to reform the income tax and make it much more progressive, states too initiated a broadly based set of tax reform initiatives removing many low-income families from all income tax liabilities, modernizing and indexing rate brackets, expanding the sales tax base, and revisiting property tax relief (Gold, 1986, 1988). These reform initiatives solidified state sophistication on tax policy; while not equal partners with the federal government in terms of the dollars raised, states at least were equal partners in the tax issues addressed and the comprehensiveness of the reforms attempted.

For education in particular, states exemplified knowledgeable fiscal leadership. During the 1970s, states restructured school finance policy, which had largely been an issue of distributing state education dollars, to a mechanism providing property tax reform and relief, thereby reflecting a new understanding of the close linkages between education dollars, the property tax and overall state/local fiscal and tax policy (Callahan and Wilken, 1976). Thus, not only did states master the complexities of a modern day tax and state/local fiscal structure, but also they became fully aware of the inextricable linkages between school finance and overall state and local tax policy.

In addition, states provided schools large increases in education revenues (Odden and Picus, 1992; Odden and Wohlstetter, 1992). In the 1970s, the new money came for school finance reform. In the 1980s, several states enacted tax increases to finance expensive omnibus education reforms, again showing the capability to move on the parallel fronts of education and tax policy (Odden and Dougherty, 1984; Odden, 1990b). By the early 1990s, the states had taken the lead role in financing schools. States provided nearly 50 percent of all education revenues, local districts about 44 percent and the federal government just 6 percent (Odden, 1990b, 1992b). As most political pundits know, he who pays the bill also wields power. Thus, if for no other reason than its dominant fiscal role, state governments and their political leaders, governors and legislators, take a keen interest in education policy (Fuhrman, 1983, 1988, 1994a).

State Courts

State courts also launched into new arenas in the 1970s and 1980s thus adding yet another leg to the chair of sophisticated state government. The U.S. Supreme Court began the postWorld War II period of judicial activism through its many ruling on the requirements of the Fourteenth Amendment to the U.S. Constitution beginning with desegregation of schools in the 1954 *Brown* v. *Board of Education* decision and then extending itself into many other areas including voting rights and abortion. State courts, which for years had deferred to federal courts in plowing new judicial territory, soon followed their lead and began to make advances on these same judicial arenas, but on the basis of state constitutional requirements, including state equal protection clauses.

School finance was a beginning. The initial school finance court cases were brought on the basis of the Equal Protection Clause of the U.S. Constitution (Coons, Clune, & Sugarman, 1970; Odden and Picus, 1992). For the first two years after an opinion in the first successful case was rendered in California, all cases were based on the federal constitution. But when the U.S. Supreme Court overturned the *San Antonio* v. *Rodriguez* school finance case in Texas, finding that while inequitable the Texas school finance system did not violate the Equal Protection Clause of the U.S. Constitution, litigation returned to state courts, based on state constitutional requirements (both equal protection and state education clauses) and continued in intensity (McUsic, 1991). By the early 1990s, moreover, another round of school finance suits had been launched (Dively and Hickrod, 1993).

During the 1980s, moreover, when there was a retrenchment in the new ground being plowed by the federal courts, many state courts, in part emboldened by the successful expansion of equal protection litigation related to school finance, began expanding into new issues including race, sex, education, and abortion (Gray, Jacob, and Albritton, 1990). From courts that had historically been timid initiators of new judicial reach, these actions represented a new activism at the state court level, which included a multiple of courts across the land. Within education itself, state courts were not only advancing the substance of school finance issues, but also were tackling such complex topics as student rights, tuition vouchers, private school aid, the rights of handicapped students and children of illegal immigrants, and condoms in the schools.

Thus, the 1990s includes yet another state institution that has grown, matured, and become more expansive during the past four decades. And this new state judicial activism has not been reserved for just noneducation functions; it has affected education in many substantive areas and will remain a policy force wielding influence for at least the rest of the decade.

State Departments of Education

The modern state department of education is a late twentieth century phenomenon. While the roots of state departments of education reach back to the early 1800s, for the first 200 years there were neither separate local school districts, distinct state departments of education, nor chief state schools officers. During the first two centuries of the United States, education was run by general governments—local city and town governments, and state general government. Two reasons for this approach was that education then was a small and simple operation, which could be handled by general government officials, and much of education was privately provided (Campbell et al., 1990).

The first chief state school officer, called a superintendent of public instruction, was created by New York in 1812, but then was quickly disbanded only to be recreated towards the middle of the century. Other states experienced this same start and stop creation of a chief state education official. But by the late 1900s, all states admitted to the union had a chief state school officer, as do all today.

New York also led the country in creation of state boards of education, this time in the late eighteenth century creating the Board of Regents which initially controlled the state's colleges and universities and was not given purview over elementary and secondary schools until 100 years later in 1904, early in the twentieth century (Campbell et al., 1990). State boards of education and their accompanying state departments of education began to receive strong support beginning in 1837 with the pioneering and visionary leadership of Horace Mann, who was appointed secretary to the State Board of Education in Massachusetts. Mann, together with visionary chief state schools officers in a few other states, Henry Barnard of Connecticut, Calvin Wiley of North Carolina, and John Swett of California, literally started a crusade for the development of a public education system. These men all argued for an education system open to all children in the state and paid for by public funds. Their goal was to create a free, public education system that would educate and acculturate all children in America. While their brilliant leadership helped the country to implement their vision over time, state departments of education have not always been served by individuals with the distinction that has characterized these individuals (Campbell et al., 1990).

Originally, state boards of education were strongly tied to state political leaders. In fact, at their creation many state boards consisted only of ex officio members and included the governor, attorney general, and chief state school officer. The state board of education in Florida has retained this structure. Over time, however, boards became less directly politically connected. Board members became political appointments, primarily appointed by the governor but members became elected to those positions in some states. Despite the development of state boards of education and growth of state departments of education, legislatures retained their plenary, i.e., lawmaking authority for education, a division of power that remains in all states today.

Until the past few decades, state departments of education, which provide staff assistance to chief state school officers and state boards of education and also administer state education functions, were small, ran few programs, and had only a few organizational units. Most state departments of education were engaged primarily in teacher licensing, accrediting schools, and allocating state equalization aid. A few produced rules, regulations, and guidelines about the instructional program but these usually entailed length of the school year and day, requirements for providing kindergarten as well as programs for children in grades 1 through 12, and mandates to serve some handicapped students. A few states, such as California and Texas, adopted textbooks at the state level which added another function to the state department. Other states provided guidelines for courses of study, but generally curriculum was left to local school board determination.

This rather passive role began to change rapidly in the mid1960s when the federal government enacted the Elementary and Secondary Education Act (ESEA). This new federal program required state departments to administer a large, complex federal education program, monitor local districts for compliance with federal program regulations, engage in research and development to identify successful strategies for teaching economically disadvantaged children, and to begin evaluating the impact of many of these programs. In recognition of the lack of capacity in most state departments to engage effectively in these new functions, ESEA also included a section, Title V, that provided funds specifically for the purpose of expanding state departments in size and capacity. Although the impact and use of Title V funds in the early years fell short of expectations for transforming state departments (Murphy, 1974), they nevertheless began the process of transformation and development.

Cohen (1982), Murphy (1982) and Peterson, Rabe, and Wong (1986) document how, overtime, federal policy initiative in the 1960s and 1970s ultimately expanded the policy reach of state departments of education, their professional capacity and expertise, and their organization complexity. By 1980, all Departments had grown substantially in size, administered a multitude of programs (desegregation, compensatory, bilingual and special education, and gifted and talented programs), had numerous new divisions and organizational units, and were staffed by individuals with considerable expertise. Each categorical program itself often became a large organizational unit within the department, with subdivisions focused on student eligibility, funds allocation, program quality, compliance review, and auditing. During this same time period, most state education departments created program evaluation units, and many also initiated new large scale (state wide) student-testing programs. From small relatively unsophisticated institutions that had blunted program implementation at the beginning of the 1960s (Murphy, Jerome, 1991), state departments of education grew to become complex institutions, were staffed with a wide variety of new, sophisticated professional expertise, and became engaged in a dazzling array of education initiatives (Murphy, 1982; Peterson, Rabe, & Wong, 1986).

Thus, when the education reforms of the mid1980s were created and followed by the more complex reforms of the latter part of that decade and the beginning of the 1990s (Murphy, 1990b), state departments of education were much better positioned to provide leadership for reform implementation; in fact, in a few states it was a new chief state school officer and a restructured state department of education that were the point leaders for ambitious reforms (Massell and Kirst, 1986).

And states did indeed respond to the 1980s reform fervor. Bill Honig in California, Gordon Ambach in New York, Richard Mills in Vermont, Ted Sanders in Illinois and then Ohio, and Tom Boysen in Kentucky are a few examples. California, Kentucky, and Vermont created new and complex performance-based student assessment programs that probed not only what students knew but what they could do with that knowledge. California, Kentucky, and South Carolina created new curriculum standards that reflected the type of high standards, thinking, and problem-solving-oriented curriculum implied by the new findings of cognitive research, and reflected the curriculum standards developed by the nation's professional content groups (see Chapter 4). South Carolina, Florida, Pennsylvania, and Texas created new school incentive programs designed to reward school sites producing improvements in student performance (Richards and Shujaa, 1990). Other states devised new ways of licensing teachers, new forms of professional development, and new strategies for structuring technical assistance (Darling-Hammond and Berry, 1988). While these actions were not visible in all states, they reflected cutting edge practices and they all were initiated by states and their more sophisticated departments of education.

However, when the beginning of the 1990s produced a new and long-term national economic downturn that depressed state revenues across the country, many states curiously responded by substantially cutting the state department of education funding, thus seriously blunting the leadership and assistance roles departments could and needed to provide for implementing the increasingly complex reform programs (Massell and Fuhrman, 1994).

Today, and while not uniform across all states, expertise in state departments of education comprises an unrecognized and, in too many cases, an untapped capacity for implementing the ambitious education reform agendas of the 1990s. While many departments are still too hierarchically organized, even in states that have decided on a strongly decentralized managed approach to education reform (Lusi, 1993, 1994), state departments need to be involved in several aspects of today's systemic reform agenda. Departments can be focal points for developing new curriculum frameworks, new performance-based student-testing programs, new educational indicator systems, and new strategies for licensing teachers. Elaboration of these and other key roles state departments of education can play in furthering the goals of education reform are provided in the next section.

State-Based National Education Organizations

Another salutary development supporting state education policy leadership has been the creation and maturation of several organizations whose purpose is to help state political and education leaders make better education policy. There are five key organizations, nearly all created in the 1960s. The NGA was created to assist governors organize their offices and discharge their executive roles. As discussed previously, the NGA became very engaged in education reform in the mid1980s and education reform is still one of its primary emphases (NGA, 1986, 1990, 1991). It played a key role in establishing the National Education Goals Panel which reports to the nation each fall on progress towards accomplishing the national education goals (National Education Goals Panel, 1993).

The National Conference of State Legislatures (NCSL) was created to help legislators organize and run effective state legislatures. NCSL provides institutional support to legislatures and also engages in policy analyses on a wide variety of key issues. NCSL has had a major education program division since the school finance reforms of the 1970s (Callahan and Wilken, 1976; Gold, 1988).

The Council of Chief State School Officers (CCSSO) is an organization of all the top state education officials and was organized to help chiefs provide executive agency leadership and to help them organize and strengthen state departments of education. During the past decade, the CCSSO has taken a leadership role in several areas, three significant initiatives being their Assessment Center which is collecting valid and comparable data on the conditions of education in each state (CCSSO, 1990), their task force identifying knowledge and skills for beginning teachers (Interstate New Teacher Assessment and Support Consortium, 1992), and a multistate task force to help design a performance testing system.

The National Association of State Boards of Education was created to provide assistance to the hundreds of members of state boards of education. State boards developed regulations for implementing the myriad of state and federal categorical programs, and in the early 1990s began to focus policy on the declining conditions of children and the need to broaden education's horizons from schools to all the government programs and services that impact children, from early childhood through at least high school.

Finally, in 1966 the NGA helped create the Education Commission of the States (ECS) an interstate compact organization which states join by enacting a law to become part of the interstate compact for education. ECS serves all major education and political leaders at the state level: governors, legislators, chief state school officers, state higher education executive officers, and state board of education members. Although the original impetus for ECS was a state antidote to a potentially overly strong federal influence on education, a political concern of the mid1960s when ESEA was first enacted, ECS has matured as an organization that plays a much broader role. ECS addresses a wide range of education reform issues and is not just a counterforce to Washington, D.C. initiatives. Today the governor chair of ECS is also the Chair of the Education Committee of the NGA. President Bill Clinton was a chair of ECS during his tenure as chair of the NGA when he was governor of Arkansas in the 1980s.

One key role played by these national education organizations has been to raise important education issues and to identify and sanction cutting edge education policy options that states could enact. This role assumed new prominence during the 1980s when education reform was attempting to improve the overall education system. State policymakers could argue that their bold, omnibus reform proposals had been suggested and were supported by influential and knowledgeable national organizations. Indeed, one of the reasons for swift state response to the 1983 National at Risk report (National Commission on Excellence in Education, 1983) was that governors and legislators had convinced themselves of the efficacy of omnibus state education reform programs that had been discussed at the annual meetings of NGA, NCSL, and ECS (McDonnell and Fuhrman, 1986). In the mid1980s the NGA (1986) report sanctioned both public school choice and an outcomes orientation to education policy, which offered less regulation for improved results (meaning increased student achievement). Finally, at the beginning of the 1990s the NGA outlined ambitious strategies for accomplishing the national education goals, restructuring the education system and implementing systemic reform (NGA, 1990, 1991, 1993). In addition to describing a workable state policy strategy, a major function of these reports has been to provide external support for bipartisan gubernatorial and legislative action across the country on important education reform issues.

Children's Policy

Finally, as the 1980s closed and the 1990s began, a shift in state education policy towards a broader focus on children's issue generally began to occur. In part catalyzed by the ongoing reports of the national Children's Defense Fund (1994) and the California report on the conditions of children (Kirst, 1989), both educators and political leaders were beginning to realize that education reform was partially constrained by the deteriorating conditions of children, described in Chapter 2. As a result, some began to argue for a more focused policy orientation on children generally as the broader umbrella within which education policy should be constructed (Kirst, 1991; McLaughlin and Heath, 1989; Kirst, 1989). Arguments were made for providing an array of children's social services on or at locations close to schools, since children were in schools most of the day during the work week. Proposals for financing these innovations also were made (Kirst, 1992a), and states began to enact initiatives for such coordination of services (PACE, 1993).

Summary

As the previous chapters in the book have made clear, producing new and high levels of student cognitive capabilities in complex subject matter is a difficult challenge. It will require insight, hard work, and change throughout the education system. The point of this section is simply that states are not only playing key leadership roles in forwarding the country's progress towards these ambitious education goals, but that the machinery of state government generally and state education capacity in particular is much more advanced than it was at the midcentury point. Indeed, this section has argued that a considerable degree of expertise, knowledge, experience, technical know how, and fiscal capacity are embodied in these elements of state government. These state capabilities should be relied on as central components of the overall strategies to bring the goals to fruition if not by the end of the decade at least early in the twenty-first century.

Another aspect of the new prominence of the state in education policy is that while general politicians, governors and legislators, assumed the key leadership positions for education policy during the 1970s and 1980s, educational leadership is rebounding in the 1990s. Many would argue that although governors and legislators eclipsed educators in providing education policy leadership for the past 25 years (Fuhrman, 1983, 1988, 1993a, 1994a; Odden and Wohlstetter, 1992), state education leaders and professional content groups are assuming more leadership today. This represents a major change from the first half of the century during which local educators, primarily superintendents, were the prominent individuals who proposed education policy and school reform (see Chapter 8). Further, during the 1980s, another group of noneducators, business leaders, also became noticeable in framing education reform policy (Committee for Economic Development, 1985, 1987; Geranios, 1992; Odden and Wohlstetter, 1992). Some educators today do not necessarily like nor are very comfortable with the strong role of these noneducators in setting educational agendas. But their central involvement plus the new face of educational leadership portends a policy setting process that includes a wide range of actors, beyond those in education, and is characterized by collaboration among the many groups, certainly not the hegemony that characterized local education leadership in the earlier part of this century.

PROBLEMS WITH AND CHALLENGES TO STATE EDUCATION POLICY LEADERSHIP

The argument for the considerable capacity state government to play a key leadership role in furthering the nation's education reform goals, however, should not be taken as an overly sanguine perspective about whether states will effectively use those capacities to impact the curriculum and school restructuring the country's education system must undergo. Although the capacity and will of states to govern has grown and matured, the track record for producing results is quite spotty and many political structures still mitigate against the type of coherent policymaking that is needed for successfully implementing systemic reform. This section briefly discusses these problems before proceeding to the next section that outlines how state leadership can be restructured to produce a bigger impact.

Meager Results From a Century Focus on Improving Equity

Although recent discussions of educational equity appear to make it an issue that emerged in the 1960s, states have been trying to provide equity, equal education opportunity or, to use the 1990s phrase, "opportunity to learn" during much of this century (Elmore and Fuhrman, 1993). All three concepts have their roots in the various state education clauses that require "general and uniform," "thorough and efficient," or just plain old "free common school" education systems. While opportunity to learn explicitly includes educational process and student results (Porter, 1993a, 1993b) and equity and equal educational opportunity traditionally emphasized educational inputs such as dollars and programs, the implicit goal of all three, as well as state education clauses, arguably is the same: good education for *all* children. But the equity focus of most of the century has produced meager results.

At the turn of the century, equity was embodied in state efforts to create the common school system required by new state education clauses. Thus, states enacted regulations for certifying teachers, accrediting schools, and financing districts according to common, statewide standards. While these requirements produced a macroform of uniformity, they left untouched large inequities in finance and student achievement.

From about 1920 to 1950, the quest for equal educational opportunity focused on school finance equalization. Primarily through minimum foundation general aid programs, the goal was to provide all school districts with a minimum level of dollars per pupil that would allow them at least to provide an adequate education program (Odden and Picus, 1992). While progress was made in providing such financial minimums, large inequities in school finance remained and many legislated minimums quickly became outdated (Coons, Clune, and Sugarman, 1970; Odden and Picus, 1992).

The next state effort was to consolidate school districts into larger bodies, both to expand, improve, and make more equitable the education program that could be offered as well as hopefully to make the overall system more efficient. As a result, between 1900 and 1950, the number of school districts dropped from over 130,000 to 84,000; the number then dropped to 18,000 by 1970. Many concluded that the consolidation movement was successful "either in cutting costs" or improving program quality (Guthrie, 1979; Sher, 1977).

In the 1960s and 1970s, the quest for equal education opportunity broadened to include special-needs students. States and the federal government created numerous categorical programs to desegregate students, educate the handicapped, serve the economically disadvantaged, and meet the needs of limited English proficient students. The goal was to provide additional educational services to help ensure that these special-needs students would achieve on a level with the "regular" student (Odden and Picus, 1992). While these programs ultimately were implemented in compliance with rules and regulations and extra services were provided (Odden, 1991a), their impact on student achievement was very modest (Odden, 1991b).

The next stage in the twentieth century journey towards educational equity was a renewed school finance reform in the 1970s and 1980s. Emboldened by legal challenges that overturned improved, but still inequitable, school finance structures, this effort sought to move beyond just providing a minimal educational opportunity to creating an overall "fiscally neutral" system in which all districts would operate as if they had the same local property tax base (Coons, Clune, and Sugarman, 1970). In response, states enacted new power equalizing school finance systems as well as higher level foundation programs (Odden and Picus, 1992), but equity was not dramatically improved (Wykoff, 1992).

While none of these embodiments of equal educational opportunity, or what is now called opportunity to learn in the 1990s, explicitly mentioned student achievement, a reasonable argument is that better achievement implicitly was their objective. Indeed, the original goal of the special-needs programs was to reduce income inequality by raising the educational achievement and thus earning potential of children from poverty backgrounds (Murphy, Jerome, 1991). While grandiose in its aims, the goal nevertheless was achievement-oriented. Though school finance reformers often "ducked" the outcomes issue, they believed the quality of the educational program and level of student achievement was determined by spending levels (Coons, Clune, and Sugarman, 1970). And the consolidation movement was fueled by a desire to ensure that rural children were educated as well as their urban peers.

The results of this century long emphasis on improving input equity have been modest. As Elmore and Furhman (1993) noted, even after an 80-year focus on equalizing inputs, fiscal disparities have not been eliminated; indeed, in the early 1990s over half the states were embroiled in school finance court suits because large disparities in fiscal capacity and educational expenditures per pupil existed across school districts (Dively and Hickrod, 1993). Further, there were equally large differences in educational achievement between minorities and nonminorities (Mullis, Owen, and Phillips, 1990), low-income and non-poor students (Mullis, Owen, and Phillips, 1990), girls and boys (Mullis, Owen, and Phillips, 1990), and among students in the 50 states (Mullis et al., 1991; Mullis, Campbell, & Farstrup, 1993) including rich and poor states (Odden and Kim, 1992). But simply abandoning any concern with inputs defies common sense because more equity of student achievement outcomes, particularly the current goal to educate all students to high standards, seems unattainable with the rampant disparities in fiscal resources that still exists in most states (Wykoff, 1992).

Carving out a new state role to both reduce these input inequities and to make larger percentages of students meet the new high proficiencies expected of all students will not be an easy task. Given the meager results of the country's century long history of trying to improve the equity of education inputs suggests that the state strategy for making real progress on equity of both inputs and student results requires redesigning future policy strategies, a task reserved for the last section of the chapter.

Problems with Effective Program Implementation and Impact

Another problem with past state strategies to improve the education system, as discussed in Chapter 10, has been the weak impacts of implementing state (as well as federal) categorical programs. Chapter 10 chronicled 25 years of research on the changing nature of program implementation. Although many still argue that state as well as federal initiative will be resisted locally (Boyd, 1987), the research findings on both implementation of the early 1980s state education reforms (Fuhrman, Clune, and Elmore, 1991; Odden and Marsh, 1988) as well latter curriculum restructuring efforts (Cohen and Peterson, 1990; Marsh and Odden, 1991) found surprisingly little local resistance. In fact, research found local educators embracing these state initiatives and often going beyond what they required (Fuhrman, Clune, and Elmore, 1988). Some argued that the reason the majority of early 1980s reforms were implemented was that they were relatively simple, required little structural change, and could be implemented with traditional skills (Firestone, 1990). Whatever the reason, the research is consistent in showing little resistance.

The major problem of program implementation up to about 1985 turned out to be lack of impact on student learning. Odden (1991b) reviewed several 1970s and 1980s evaluations of the degree to which state and federal categorical programs improved student achievement and found only a small effect; the general conclusion was that students in the programs improved their performance a small degree but only for a short period of time, and that improvement atrophied quickly when the student no longer received program services. A more recent study of the impact of federal Chapter I program services reached similar conclusions about the impact of Chapter I programs (U.S. Department of Education, 1993). Similar conclusions were found for the early 1980s education reforms (Firestone et al., 1992).

For the curriculum change and school restructuring reforms of the 1990s, research is showing lack of sufficient knowledge and skills for full implementation. Cohen and Peterson (1990), Marsh and Odden (1991), and Ball et al., (1994a, 1994b, 1994c) found that teachers embraced the curriculum standards included in the new California curriculum frameworks (again, there was little if any local resistance), but lacked sufficient knowledge of the content included in the frameworks as well as the pedagogical strategies needed to teach them well. Teachers implementing the programs, moreover, had attended as many staff development opportunities as they could find. The implementation problem implied by these studies was not local resistance, but insufficient local capacity and inadequate attention of the education system to providing the magnitude of professional development teachers and administrators needed.

These findings are very important because the goals of the 1990s education reform agenda will not be accomplished unless an adequate and correctly focused implementation strategy is created. Conceiving of the problem as the futility of any initiative taken outside the school, either by the state or even by professional groups, misconstrues the issue if local teachers and administrators support that initiative and the problem is lack of local knowledge and skills and insufficient supply of quality professional development to create that expertise.

Assuming the curriculum that is the focus of implementation is of sufficient quality to impact student achievement, i.e., a curriculum of the sorts described by Chapter 4 and included in developing national curriculum standards (Lewis, 1990: Chapter 4), the implementation issues become ones that must include a powerful capacity development strategy. This will require that state reform efforts include a much stronger focus on capacity development, which means going far beyond the mandates and incentives that have characterized the bulk of state initiatives for the past thirty years (Elmore and McDonnell, 1991). Elmore and Fuhrman (1993) suggested that an emphasis on professional development should be a key state focus for providing students the "opportunity to learn" a high-standards curriculum program in the 1990s, Little (1993) showed how such professional development should be restructured for the more ambitious curriculum change and school restructuring agenda of the 1990s, Massell and Goertz (1994) recommend developing professional learning communities as part of a comprehensive strategy for implementing the ambitious new science curriculum of Project 2061, and Odden (1994c) and Monk and Brent (1994, forthcoming) supported that recommendation and identified the potential costs of such professional development.

In short, a quick review of the findings on education policy and program implementation suggests very strongly that new state policy supports for professional development are critical for the 1990s. The implementation problem is less resistance and inadequate curriculum, and more a teacher and administrator learning problem. Unless states invest heavily in professional development structures, such as those described in Chapter 5, it will be difficult for each state to accomplish its education goals.

Problems with the Political Structure and Policymaking Process

Several features of state and local government and finance function jointly to frustrate coherent state policymaking in education (Furhman and Elmore, 1994; Fuhrman, 1993a, 1994b; Fuhrman and Massell, 1992). The structure and operational features of state and local political system represent one problem. Education is governed within a multilayered and fragmented structure. To begin, there are three levels, local, state, and federal, of education governance. Within each level, there are separate branches—legislative, judicial, and executive. Each branch of government has its own structure, its own incentives and its own unique role in the overall system. In addition, for education only, the country has created at the state and local levels a separate, fourth branch divorced formally from general government—local school districts and state boards of education. Actors within and across these levels have different motivations, different expertise, and usually different education and political agendas. The structure was deliberately created by the founding fathers to provide checks and balances within and across government levels, and to ensure that power was concentrated nowhere but with the people. Trying to bring order to and frame coherent education policy within this incredibly mixed system, purposely designed to frustrate coordination, is difficult. In short, the political structure governing education mitigates against developing a bold, rational, and interconnected systemic reform education policy (Smith and O'Day, 1991), and supports the incremental and slow to change pattern that characterizes not only education but all government action (Lindblom, 1959).

Further, strong traditions of local control work against a strong state (or federal) education role. Even though the rhetoric of local control exceeds the reality and state government initiatives does not necessarily occur at the expense of local control, as Chapter 8 argued, strong feelings about local control act as a constraint on state initiative. Although the norms of local control in each state can be changed, change is produced by action of state political leaders not educators (McDonnell and McLaughlin, 1982). Indeed, Arkansas and Texas used to be strong local control states, but those norms were altered during the past decade as political leaders assumed leadership of education reform. Nevertheless, state education leadership and initiative swim against the tides of local control norms, however strong, weak, or altered from the past.

Third, the way money is raised and distributed also curtails state influence. About 46 percent of all education funds are raised locally, and not directly controlled by state policymakers. But even though state revenues comprise a somewhat larger portion of total revenues, about 48 percent, the bulk of state money is distributed to local districts through the equalization aid formula, and thus provided in a block grant format with virtually no restrictions on how it should be used. Thus, local districts control how the vast bulk of education dollars are spent. This reality is true even with the various restrictions that are tied to the numerous state and federal categorical programs, and even though local funds must be used to pay some of the costs of those programs. The fact remains that the vast majority of education dollars are subject to virtually no state or federal restrictions. In government, the government body making the key budget decisions tend to be in the powerful positions. Put differently, states have only modest control over how education dollars are used.

Fourth, state policymakers, governors and legislators, have incentives to enact a large number of policies that can be connected personally to them rather than fewer policies that cohere together to improve the system slowly over time. To maintain high profiles as education legislators or governors, policymakers seek to design and enact programs that have their stamp and for which they can take credit. Indeed, often this pressure induces the dismantling of programs created by previous political figures before new initiatives are made, a reality that was played out to some degree in South Carolina in the early 1990s (Massell and Fuhrman, 1994).

The result is an increasing volume of policies and programs that get layered into the already dense education policy system and which often send mixed signals to local education leaders. States toughen standards for teacher licensure but then enact alternative routes to licensure that bypass the standards. Finance reform provides more dollars with few ties to key state programs, while new programs are enacted and often underfunded (Jordan and McKewon, 1990; Odden and Dougherty, 1984). Higher education, which trains individuals who work in public schools, are absent from K–12 education reforms.

Another problem with state policy initiative is that it emphasizes mandates and incentives over capacity building (Fuhrman, 1994b; Fuhrman and Elmore, 1994). Yet, school improvement occurs through the interaction of policy, administration, and practice (McLaughlin, 1991b; McDonnell and Elmore, 1991). Although policy can set the stage for local improvement, indeed systemic reform seeks to upgrade achievement goals for students as well as curriculum and assessment standards, capacity is required at the local level in order to meet these ambitious aspirations. But for change to occur, capacity must be developed and that development requires considerable investment. Relative to total education spending, though, investments in capacity development at the state (as well as local and federal levels) are quite small (Monk and Brent, 1994, forthcoming) and the few capacity development programs that have been created have small impacts and are not ambitious enough for the capacity development needs of current education reforms (Little, 1993).

In summary, the structures and pressures of the political mechanisms at the state level work against the new roles that the state education community needs to play in designing and supporting an education reform strategy that can accomplish the nation's ambitious learning goals for all students. Thus, in making suggestions for what states should do to advance the progress of education reform for the remainder of the 1990s, these inhibiting pressures need to be considered. Expecting state political leaders simply to ignore these pressures is naive, yet as the last section of this chapter will show, there are strategies that can be attempted that both produce better policy and counter these natural and fragmenting political realities.

FUTURE ROLES FOR STATE LEADERSHIP AND POLICY IN EDUCATION

If state leadership in education reform matured during the 1980s, it became solidified in the early 1990s. The fact is that states have assumed the lead, although not the preeminent position in making education policy. States are not acting in isolation from other government levels or from education professional groups; nevertheless, states are the governmental entity looked to for designing coherent education policy for the remainder of this decade (Fuhrman, 1993a, 1993b). What is needed is a new vision for education, the type of education that can develop advanced cognitive capabilities for nearly all students—the bottom as well as the top half, those from poverty backgrounds, minorities, women and girls in science and technological areas, and children of recently arrived immigrants. State policymakers and education leaders will need to play new roles and functions in this endeavor, as will local leaders as described in the preceding chapter.

State Systemic School Reform

Systemic reform is emerging as a strategy states can use to formulate a powerful and cohesive education reform plan for the 1990s (Smith and O'Day, 1991; Fuhrman, 1993b). Systemic reform includes several components: an understanding of the nature of problems with the current education system; a vision of what a high-performance school could look like; a series of state policies supporting that vision including student academic goals, curriculum frameworks, instructional materials, performance-based assessment, revised teacher training and licensure, and new forms of professional development; and restructured governance and finance systems, including new forms of accountability.

Common Understanding of an Education Problem. The transformational nature of systemic reform requires that political and education leaders agree that there is a deep, fundamental education problem that needs to be resolved. As the beginning chapters in this book articulated, the problem is not that the education system has failed. Indeed, the country's education system is performing at many all time highs. The problem is that the cognitive expertise of graduating students is sufficient neither for the high-skill, high-wage jobs in the workplace nor for solid postsecondary education (Chapter 1 and 2). Without embarrassment and without placing the blame on educators, many state policymakers have come to believe that the performance of all students falls short of what is required for the country's economic and social agendas of the future (NGA, 1990, 1991). Many state policymakers also agree that the cognitive expertise of students in the "bottom half" is particularly problematic and needs close attention (NGA, 1986).

A Compelling Vision. The systemic reform vision includes ambitious goals for all students' achievement. It is not an elitist vision but a vision for all students. The goal is to move students, including the bottom half, up from the lowest to the highest levels in the international "intellectual" Olympics. Admittedly, this is a grandiose ideal. The goal is to produce individuals who can think, gather and analyze data, solve problems, communicate findings, and work effectively in teams.

State education and political leaders have articulated this vision in alternative ways. Some states have embodied this vision in descriptions of high-performance schools (Superintendent's Advisory Task Force on Middle Schools, 1989); the NGA has argued that this requires dramatic school restructuring (NGA, 1991, 1993); the Education Commission of the States launched a program, ReLearning, which seeks to join state policy with the school vision of the Sizer Coalition of Essential Schools (see Chapter 6); many states have joined in supporting middle school reform (Lewis, 1993); other states have joined the New Standards Project or the National Alliance for School Restructuring; and nearly all states have begun to create a new vision through curriculum frameworks and new student assessment systems.

Whatever particular form these visions take, they provide an ambitious goal for the state's education system to attain, they paint a picture of what a future high-performing education system or school will look like, and they provide a beacon that guides the hard work of educators towards a common goal. They help define the end state of the "steady work" of education reform for the 1990s (Elmore and McLaughlin, 1990).

Curriculum Frameworks. New curriculum frameworks or standards are becoming the linchpin to which several state policies are being connected in state education reform. Cohen and Spillane (1993) and Smith and O'Day (1991) view new curriculum frameworks as a critical ingredient in the instructional guidance role of systemic reform. As articulated in Chapter 4, curriculum frameworks identify the key concepts of school curriculum in each content area, suggest the general competencies that should be developed in students at key points in their academic career (such as grades 4, 8, and 10), and often provide general pedagogical strategies that can be used to teach them in classrooms. Evolving curriculum frameworks stress engaging students in the active construction of knowledge, and creating data analysis, problem solving, application, and communication expertise in the core-content areas of mathematics, science, language arts, and history/social science. Curriculum frameworks identify what students should know and be able to do.

State development of curriculum frameworks have generally followed the standards produced by the national curriculum professional groups such as the National Council of Teachers of Mathematics (1989), National Council of Teachers of English (1989), National Commission on Social Studies in the Schools (1989), and National Science Teachers Association (1989), although in the 1990s a plethora of additional (and complementary) new standards development activities were inaugurated. These developments, though, represent a convergence of standards-setting activities within the profession and those by education's key political leaders. State-sanctioned curriculum frameworks identify the new and high-standards school curriculum to which all students should be exposed (Curry and Temple, 1992). By the end of 1993, 45 states had become involved in various stages of creating new curriculum frameworks (Pechman and LaGuarda, 1993).

State curriculum frameworks are receiving support from more than education professional content groups. The National Science Foundation's State Systemic Initiative supports state framework development for mathematics and science. The federal government's Goals 2000 program provides funds to states that can be used to develop frameworks, as well as other key elements of systemic reform. And new requirements of the reauthorized ESEA requires that states and local districts use Title I funds to help low-income students develop the cognitive skills in the new curriculum. The NGA also supports state creation of content standards for school curriculum (NGA, 1993).

Instructional Materials. Since the curriculum embodied in new curriculum frameworks represent a large change from current practice, many states also have developed strategies for revising instructional materials as part of their systemic reform strategy. Textbook adoption states such as California, Florida, and Texas have urged publishers to make major revisions in their textbooks so they align with the content and skills outlined in the curriculum frameworks. Other states and local districts are encouraging publishers to develop manipulative materials to use in new mathematics courses, laboratory materials and equipment for hands on science experiences, and nontextbook instructional materials, such as novels, books, and minicurriculum units that can be used by teachers to implement the new curriculum frameworks. Another strategy, used by California to develop materials for their Math A program (a new and more rigorous program for high school students not ready for algebra [Adams, 1992]), has been to fund teacher networks to develop minicurriculum units that over time can be compiled into a course of instruction.

Performance-based Assessments. New types of student-testing systems comprise a further dimension of system reform. The 1990s education goals are to produce students who can actively construct knowledge, solve problems, and apply cognitive expertise to real life situations. These cognitive skills cannot be measured by traditional, norm-referenced, standardized achievement tests; paper and pencil, multiple choice exercises are not sufficient for assessing the advanced cognitive skills included in the new curriculum frameworks (Resnick and Resnick, 1992).

In response, states have launched a variety of activities to develop performance-based testing systems, that identify not only what students know but also what they can do. Such assessments have students perform "fat" tasks—solve a multiple-step mathematics problem, write a persuasive essay, do a complex science experiment, or answer an integrated question about U.S. or World History. To do well, students must understand the major concepts in the content area, have mastery over an array of knowledge and facts, and apply that knowledge to the task at hand.

The most common approach states have taken, such as California, Connecticut, and Kentucky, is to create an "on demand" performance assessment, i.e., the program has students do the tasks at some specified time of year, either early in the Fall or late in Spring. Students are usually assessed at grades 4, 8, and 10 in at least four content areas: mathematics, science, language arts, and social studies. The assessments take about a week to administer. After administration in some states, copies of students' work are left with the teacher who can review the results immediately themselves; copies also are taken to the state for external scoring. This procedure ensures both that the teachers see how their students did and that the state gets neutral, objective scores. By making all test items public each year after test administration, a state can stimulate statewide conversation about the tasks and have public discussions about what students are expected to know and be able to do. In some states, teachers, guided by subject matter experts, play key roles in developing the assessment tasks, and claim it is one of the most powerful professional development activities they have experienced.

Several states have joined the New Standards Project (Resnick, 1992–93) to collaboratively create a performance-assessment system. This project is emphasizing the use of student portfolios and projects. These are usually compiled over the course of a year. New Standards also is developing performance tasks that would not be given "on demand" but "curriculum-imbedded," i.e., given throughout the year after curriculum units for which the tasks would be appropriate. The efforts of this project require considerable research and development because the psychometric knowledge to create valid and reliable portfolios and curriculum-imbedded tasks is only in the beginning stages of creation. Vermont was the first state to try a portfolio approach to student assessment and continues to work at making the results valid across all students and districts (Rothman, 1992b; Koretz et al., 1992).

Changes in Teacher Development. A final core component of systemic reform is new approaches to teacher development. These approaches can include changes in teacher preservice training, shifting to licensure on the basis of what teachers know and can do, and restructured and expanded professional development opportunities and structures, as reviewed in Chapter 5. This component of systemic reform is critical to the new capacity development component of education reform. Only by taking seriously teacher development, from preservice to inservice, can states hope that by the end of the 1990s major progress can be seen in restructuring curriculum and instruction and producing higher levels of learning for all students.

Changes in Governance, Management, Organization, and Finance. These dimensions of systematic reform often are overlooked. They include changes in roles and functions of both state political and education leaders, as well as local school boards. At the state level, it includes shifting to a systemic reform policy agenda with more coherent policies directing and guiding the system, and fewer programs and mandates. At the local level, it entails devolution of more power, authority, and accountability to school sites. Within schools, it means redesigning how work is provided and schools are managed, and implementing a high-involvement approach that would involve more teachers in managing the school and restructuring its curriculum and instruction program. Indeed, several original framers of the systemic reform approach (Furhman and O'Day, 1994) see it as a strategy to support school-based restructuring (Chapter 13 outlines in considerable detail the implications of systemic reform for a new school finance structure).

Coordinated Children's Social Services. Some states also include in their systemic reform vision efforts to have the school play a role in coordinating social services many at-risk students need in order to perform well on the effortful learning systemic reform requires (Adams, 1993; Kirst, 1992a; Guthrie, Kirst, and Odden, 1992). This emphasis substantially broadens the education reform agenda to a wide range of health, social and family services, welfare, parole, and other noneducation services, and for that reason is not always included in articulations of systemic reform. Whether included or not, states as well as the federal government have begun several initiatives to make collaboration around social services more feasible. Some states, such as Missouri, enacted laws that facilitate districts making low-income children Medicaid eligible, thus triggering federal financial support for several needed noneducation social services.

A New General Approach to Policy

Systemic reform requires state political leaders to shift from a concentration on educational inputs, dollars, services, mandates, rules, and regulations, to a results perspective. As the 1986 NGA report proposed, it is time for education results. Policymakers can neither control what local educators do nor mandate improvement of practice (McLaughlin, 1991b). But policymakers can set goals and hold the system accountable for concrete results. States can build on the national goals, which became formal federal government education policy with passage of the Clinton Administration's Goals 2000 program. Setting more specific student-performance goals for each state would constitute a first step towards this restructuring of the strategy of state policymaking.

To accomplish this new orientation, states need to take a longer term perspective on education policy and reform. Implementing the changes needed in local practice to produce the high levels of hoped for student achievement will take many years. Demands for short-term accomplishments, specialized programs, and a new round of mandates will need to be overcome by a compelling vision of a transformed education system, an understanding that accomplishing the vision rests on the shoulders of local teachers and other local education leaders, and a commitment to policies that support long-term capacity development (Fuhrman, 1994a; Fuhrman and Elmore, 1994).

This perspective needs to cast governors, legislatures, and chief state school officers into the managerial roles of education policymaking, in which they concentrate on bringing coherence to a currently fragmented state education policy system. The general push should be to prune the underbrush of current state policies and programs, trim the remaining programs into a series of key, integrated policies, and resist the temptation to simply add a 1990s layer of new initiatives on an already cluttered education policy landscape (Fuhrman and Elmore, 1994).

This managerial role includes delegation of more power, authority, and autonomy to local educators for implementing the new policies and accomplishing the ambitious student-performance goals. Indeed, school sites, where teaching is provided and learning takes place, become the focal unit in the education system (Elmore, 1991; Furhman and O'Day, 1994; Odden, 1992c, 1994a: Chapter 6).

In this new education reform process, state education and political leaders can draw support from their national support organizations—the NGA, NCSL, CCSSO, ECS. These organizations, comprised of their peers in other states, can both help design coherent state policy and sanction systemic school reform that governors, legislators, and state education leaders might propose in their own states. Indeed, leadership in these organizations can even be publicized "back home" as a new way to give politicians high-profile images as education reformers.

Governors' Roles

Governors play critical roles in the formulation and support of systemic reform. As the formal as well as symbolic leader of each state, governors can both initiate a systemic reform agenda and work to keep the state focused on this way of framing a reform agenda that sends coherent signals to local educators. The governor becomes a lead player on this front because of all the political leaders, the office of the governor is charged with the managerial task. Governors have the executive function and are expected to manage the administrative activities of all state agencies. They formulate budgets for all agencies, which represents a key component of the managerial role.

Thus, it helps to have governors step forward and support a systemic reform agenda. Bill Clinton in Arkansas, Jim Hunt in North Carolina, Bob Graham in Florida, Pete Wilson in California, Booth Gardner in Washington, and Mel Carnahan in Missouri are examples of governors who became leaders of an education reform agenda consisting of education goals, curriculum frameworks, new assessments and, in the case of California, coordinated children's policy as well.

In providing the managerial education reform function, governors can serve as role models for not personalizing the education reform agenda. Instead of selecting a particularly attractive piece of the education reform agenda, and having a Governor X program, governors taking their managerial role seriously will attempt to provide a broad overview vision of the new directions the state's education system can and should take, and help orchestrate all initiatives towards that new direction.

Gubernatorial leadership of this type can be reinforced, and even profiled within the state, by gubernatorial leadership at the national level either through the NGA or the National Education Goals Panel. Bill Clinton played this role as governor of Arkansas when he helped write the national education goals at the 1989 Education Summit between then President George Bush and the 50 state governors. Colorado Governor Roy Romer gained both national and Colorado education leadership recognition for the role he played in chairing the National Education Goals Panel for the first two years after promulgation of the national education goals in early 1990, and in his work with the National Council on Education Standards and Testing (1992) which called for national curriculum and assessment standards linked to the goals. Carroll Campbell of South Carolina gained similar recognition as co-chair and then Chair of the Goals Panel.

Further, successive reports from the NGA (1990, 1991, 1993) have all been connected to the national education goals, a systemic reform state strategy, and school-based restructuring. Many governors use these reports within their particular state both to design their reform leadership positions as well as to buttress their programs when questions or criticisms may arise. Further, governors can ask the NGA to help them design policy alternatives when unanticipated problems and issues arise when their states move forward on a systemic reform agenda. In this way, governors have access to nationwide policy analysis and design talent, and can tailor NGA suggestions to the unique contexts of their own state.

Governors also can take the lead in forging stronger cooperative ties with their state legislatures and chief state school officers, all of whom need to work together and subsume personal agendas in order to advance a cohesive systemic reform agenda forward. This cooperative role with these other key players, especially chief state school officers who are elected statewide, is complex. All are elected to office and have their own mandates. Yet all must work together in order to foster consistent policies on education reform and encourage local leaders to move in clear, state and professionally sanctioned new directions. This cooperative role obviously is made more difficult when members of different parties lead either house of the legislature or head the education office. But state leaders are finding that education policy is key to the economic growth of the state and that bipartisan cooperation can provide political benefits for all involved (Fuhrman, 1994a, 1994b; Furhman and Elmore, 1990).

Finally, many governors with the cooperation of state legislatures are experimenting with new structures to help them and all key state education and political leadership shape coherent state education policy (Fuhrman, 1993a; 1994b). As governor of South Carolina, Dick Riley created the South Carolina Business-Education SubCommittee, which reviews the progress of education reform and proposes changes and enhancements to the reform program. The Pritchard Committee, on which several former governors sit, and which is supported by the current governor, plays a similar role in Kentucky.

Missouri's systemic reform law of 1993 created a Performance Commission that is chaired by the governor, and includes in its membership the speaker of the house, president pro tempore of the senate, chairs of both the house and senate education committees, the chief state school officer, members of the state board of education, representatives of the teachers' unions, site administrators, school superintendents, and members of the public. Its charge is to monitor the development of the elements of systemic reform in Missouri: performance standards, curriculum frameworks, new performance-based assessments, and a finance structure linked to these program initiatives.

Furhman (1993a, 1994b) is optimistic of the power of systemic reform and the use of these new structures to help sustain a state's long-term commitment to the tough, coherent requirements of systemic reform. Indeed, she finds that these elements have helped several state political leaders resist the fragmentation, incremental, and "politics as usual" approach to education policy. Clearly, experience in implementing systemic reform will differ by state. Strong gubernatorial leadership in the managerial role that is unique to the governor, however, is an important dimension of the success of systemic reform.

Even before discussing the role of legislators and legislatures in setting education policy during the 1990s, it is clear that political leaders, in addition to education leaders, will continue to be strongly involved in the education policy process. Although some educators might have hoped that the incursion of politicians into education that began in the 1960s might abate over time, the fact is that political involvement in education has intensified. Governors and legislators have a record characterized by greater and deeper involvement in education policy. There are few if any signs that they are willing to "hand back" education policy leadership to education professionals. This reality also means that educators must develop the skills to interact effectively with political leaders.

Education policymaking and education leadership have become a much more collaborative process. And often the point person in that collaboration is the governor, either in a formal role as chair of an oversight committee, such as the Missouri Performance Commission, or simply by making education reform a priority issue for state governance and being the manager that helps the state create and sustain a coherent education reform direction.

Roles for Legislators

Because of their plenary power in education and their awareness of the importance of an improved education system for the economic health of the state (and country), legislators also will remain active in education policymaking for the remainder of the 1990s. There are eight dimensions of this continued role that legislatures should emphasize.

First, the collaborative nature of education policymaking suggests legislators could create new mechanisms for collaborative education policy formulation both within legislatures and among the legislature, governor, and education leaders. Legislatures might be wise to create joint task forces, with members from both the house and senate and from both political parties, to formulate major new legislative education initiatives. Such task forces can help to make the state approach to education policy bipartisan, and can help mitigate against each legislator proposing a narrowly focused program to which his or her name might be attached. A joint task force might have an easier time devising a more cohesive and systemic reform strategy for which all legislators could claim authorship.

In addition, legislators need to interact with both the governor and chief state school officer, and other state and education leaders in formulating key new initiatives, to facilitate an even broader collaborative process. This reaching out beyond the legislature not only can be another support for framing coherent education policy, but, since the education community ultimately has the professional expertise for designing effective policy and is responsible for implementing new initiatives, their involvement in the policy formulation process can help both to strengthen policy design and firm educator ownership at the implementation stage.

Second, following the proposals in Chapter 8, legislatures need to take the lead in transforming local school boards into policy boards. Legislatures have the power to rescind current state requirements for the fiduciary responsibility of boards, their role in hiring personnel, and their judicial role as the arbiter of grievances and appeals. The Institute for Education Leadership (IEL) in Washington, D.C. has prepared the outline of a draft bill legislatures could use to restructure school boards. The specific responsibilities that need to be rescinded varies by state, but the IEL model bill identifies the areas that need to be addressed and also outlines a proposed set of new responsibilities for a local education policy board. Unless legislatures take the initiative to legally alter the membership, electoral process, and roles and responsibilities of school boards, the danger is that they will continue to play the passive and many times unhelpful roles that have characterized their behavior for the past decade or so.

Third, legislatures can enact systemic education reform programs, such as the Kentucky legislature did in 1990 and the Missouri legislature did in 1993. While the governor can propose such an education reform program, and while the state education agency and local educators will implement it, legislatures play the critical role of enacting education reform programs into state law. A coherent reform program would identify ambitious student-achievement goals in the core-content areas, and then set forth a mechanism for developing curriculum frameworks, better instructional materials, performance-assessment systems, and revised teacher development policies. Through the process of enacting systemic reform, moreover, legislators gain a clearer understanding of what coherent state education reform strategy is. The legislative process of enactment also brings to systemic reform wider spread political support and less political pressure for fragmented program enactment that has characterized legislative education policymaking in the past (Fuhrman, 1994a, 1994b).

Systemic reform also requires many new educational investments in framework development, student testing, instructional materials, professional development, and school finance restructuring. One important spin-off of legislative enactment of systemic reform is awareness of and support for the significant new investments required in these areas.

Fourth, as part of teacher development, legislatures can create state boards of professional teaching standards and give them the power to license teachers (Wise and Darling-Hammond, 1987). Today, this licensure responsibility generally is given to state departments of education. But several states, including Connecticut, Kentucky, and Minnesota, have created state teaching boards that have a majority of teachers as part of efforts both to professionalize teaching and to license teachers on the basis of their knowledge and skills rather than just passing a set of courses in a college or university program (Darling-Hammond, Gendler and Wise, 1990; Darling-Hammond, 1993b; Wise and Darling-Hammond, 1987; Wise and Leibbrand, 1993). Such a licensure policy would fit well with Board Certification of experienced teachers by the National Board for Professional Teaching Standards (1989).

Yet a fifth new role for state legislatures is to view a strong state education agency as a crucial ingredient for successful implementation of systemic reform. Compared to the budget cutting that legislatures visited on many state agencies in the early part of the 1990s, this understanding would suggest the need to increase funds for these agencies (Massell and Fuhrman, 1993). No state in the process of implementing education reform has been able to bypass the state department of education. Departments must lead the process of developing curriculum frameworks, are centrally involved in developing and administering performance-based assessment systems, and design and administer school-site incentive programs. Many state departments also can provide new and more complex technical assistance to local districts and sites. While it is true that many state departments need restructuring themselves as well as new expertise to fulfill these new roles and functions (Lusi, 1993, 1994), cutting their funding or ignoring the need to strengthen them likely will prove to be a fatal oversight. By the end of the 1990s strong state education agencies should be the goal for all states, and legislatures can lead in supporting this goal.

Sixth, legislatures can reconsider the school finance structure and redesign it to better reinforce the policy strategies of systemic reform. Most school finance structures are district and not school-based and have few incentives for accomplishing high levels of student achievement; they need to be restructured to support the thrust of systemic reform. The details of this dramatic policy restructuring are developed more in Chapter 13.

Seventh, legislatures should take seriously the need to focus more on designing new education policy that supports capacity development. One simple way to imbed the needed financing into the infrastructure of education policy is to set aside 2 to 4 percent of state and local revenues for ongoing professional learning. In 1993, Minnesota and Missouri enacted such a policy. Missouri's systemic reform set aside one percent of the equalization formula for state-determined professional development activities, and another one percent for districts. Minnesota set aside one percent for 1993–94, to be augmented by another percent in 1994–95. While devolving the bulk of professional development to the site is more consonant with new understandings of how powerful professional development must be structured to develop the professional expertise needed for systemic reform (Little, 1993; Massell and Goertz, 1994; see also Chapter 5), these set asides provide the type of ongoing financing that can make an aggressive capacity development strategy possible.

Finally, state legislatures might need to revisit the state's collective bargaining laws to determine the degree to which changes are needed if systemic reform includes more delegation of power and authority to school sites, as well as new forms of knowledge and skills-based teacher compensation (see Chapter 13). The scope of bargaining laws might need to be modified in order for the contract to include language structuring the key elements of: (1) a high-involvement management strategy (Lawler, 1992); (2) teacher roles in managing and governing schools; (3) school-based incentives; and (4) compensation that is based on knowledge and skills, not education and experience (Mohrman, Mohrman, and Odden, 1994; Odden and Conley, 1992).

From this list, it should be clear that legislatures will have agendas full of "large" issues as they continue to improve the public schools in the 1990s. The above list of potential initiatives underscores the central role legislatures must play in this process. Many current state laws need to be rescinded and many complex new laws need to be enacted. Only the legislature can enact these statutory changes. Since the issues are so complex, and need to be supported by both the governor and educator community, a collaborative process for formulating education reform policies can be helpful in producing proposals that are both stronger substantively and more widely supported. In the final analysis, however, the legislature will have the last say on the specifics of the laws.

Roles for State Departments of Education

It should be clear that there are several important and, many would say, critical roles state departments of education can play in the support of systemic education reform. Ultimately governors and legislatures will devolve responsibility for designing and implementing systemic reform to state departments of education, together with local districts and school sites. Whatever criticisms political leaders might have of state departments, and despite their penchant for slashing state department budgets during the first years of the 1990s, there is virtually no way that ambitious systemic reform can be achieved without strong departments of education engaging in numerous new and cutting edge practices (Massell and Furhman, 1993). Thus, as stated in the above sections on governors and legislatures, strengthening departments should be viewed as a critical component of systemic reform.

At the same, chief state school officers and state departments of education need to hone their skills for working collaboratively with political leaders on education reform. Education leaders in the 1990s gain very little by believing that they carry the torch of education improvement and must "stand up" to political incursions, although this in many ways was a hallmark of education leadership in the first part of this century (Tyack and Hansot, 1982). Indeed, state educator roles in the 1990s might be "fleshing out" directives that are given to them by state political leaders. For example, states moving on the systemic reform agenda might ask departments to take the lead in developing academic goals for student learning, curriculum frameworks, and performance-based testing systems. In most instances, these political communities want goals, frameworks, and assessment systems anchored in the traditional subject matter areas—mathematics, science, language arts, and history. Often they have become aware of the content standards set by the various national professional subject matter groups, and have participated nationally in discussions of systemic reform (Massell, 1993; National Council on Education Standards and Testing, 1992; Massell and Fuhrman, 1994). If state departments insist on going in different directions, such as generic-thinking skills or outcomes-based education that give prominence to affective outcomes and other potentially value-laden goals, they risk not only violating trust that political leaders have given them but also their efforts very likely will be defeated by lack of political support within the legislature (Massell, 1993).

Just as governors and legislators need to see chief state school officers and state departments of education as co-equal collaborators in framing a state's education reform strategy, so also must chiefs and departments view the intense involvement of political (as well as business) leaders in education as legitimate. In the 1990s, chiefs and state education leaders need to reach out to political leaders, keep them briefed on the progress of reform implementation, and design mechanism to ensure close collaborative interaction on all aspects of education policy formulation, enactment, implementation, and evaluation.

State departments should place five major issues on their agendas for the 1990s. First, they need to analyze their organization and management style to determine the degree to which fits with a goals and directions at the top, but implementation at the site approach to state education policy. Most state departments have adopted a hierarchical organizational structure and have operated in a manner in which they make rules and regulations and monitor local districts and schools for compliance. The tenets of systemic reform are inconsistent with this traditional approach to educational management. As previous chapters have described, systemic reform requires a more decentralized, high-involvement form of educational management, in which school-site personnel, teachers and administrators, play much stronger and broader roles in education organization and management.

Just as superintendents and even site administrators must play different roles in this way of running the education system, as described in Chapter 7, so also must state departments of education change roles and functions as well. They need to shift from command and control bodies to service centers that provide information and technical assistance. Their role should be to support actions that help sites make better decisions; these roles could be more direct retraining of superintendents and administrators in skills for working in a high-involvement managed system, or more indirect activities designed to get information, professional development, power, and rewards to professionals at the school site. If state departments continue to operate in a traditional, top down management style, they at best send mixed signals to local educators, and at worst function to inhibit the successful implementation of systemic reform at school sites (Lusi, 1993).

A first task for many state departments, then, is to reorganize to support site-based implementation of systemic reform. In some states such as Minnesota, this reorganization has included crossdisciplinary and crossfunctional teams who work with a fixed number of districts in the state (Odden, 1993c). In other states like California, the reorganization included developing strength in curriculum, textbook, and assessment divisions. There is no one template for state department reorganization. But it is likely that most departments will need to undergo some organizational restructuring.

A second set of new activities for state departments is in developing curriculum frameworks, sometimes better instructional materials, new forms of performance-based assessments, and new strategies for teacher development. In nearly all states working to implement systemic reform, state departments are asked to create curriculum frameworks for the state. Though states never simply adopt another state's framework or even a framework from a professional group, they often begin with those materials and adapt them to their particular context. This ensures both connections with the broader, professionally driven reform movement and tailoring to the needs and values of each specific state. To accomplish this task well, state departments need staff who are respected subject matter experts in at least the content areas in which the state develops curriculum frameworks.

Similarly, numerous states are in the process of redesigning their student-testing systems to create more performance-based programs. Few states are working completely on their own in moving forward on these agendas. The many states that are members of the New Standards Project, which is developing a new performance-based assessment system, are not waiting for that project to give them a new assessment; most are developing their own systems, using tasks from New Standards, and calibrating their grading of tasks to national standards. This national collaboration is also being fostered by a cross-state testing collaborative sponsored by the CCSSO. The goal is to pool the talent in the country that is working to develop new ways of assessing what students know and are able to do, while allowing states to tailor their specific examination programs to their particular state curriculum frameworks and to produce results that can be compared to nationwide standards.

A third new agenda for state departments of education would be restructuring of administrative structures for categorical programs. Admittedly one of the accomplishments of state departments that resulted from the first 20 years of implementing the categorical programs of the 1960s and 1970s was the establishment of separate organizational units that administered and protected many categorical programs (Kirst and Meister, 1985; Odden, 1991a; Peterson, Rabe, and Wong, 1986). Overtime, however, this strategy often isolated these same programs from the regular curriculum and produced a categorical program curriculum that emphasized basic skills and often excluded more advanced skills (Odden, 1991a). If *all* students are expected to develop proficiencies in a new thinking, and problem-solving-oriented curriculum, the categorical programs must become reconnected to the core curriculum and instruction program. This could be signaled both through reorganization of state departments, which placed categorical program management units within the curriculum and instruction branch, and through regulations requiring that categorical program services needed to reinforce and support students' learning the core curriculum. California was one of the first states implementing such a reorganization in the 1980s (Odden, 1987).

The reauthorization of the federal ESEA, and Title I which provides extra services to poor children, explicitly sought to reconnect Title I to a thinking and problem-solving systemic reform curriculum. The language is clear that the new purpose of Title I is to develop advanced cognitive expertise in students eligible to be served. The new program reinforces this goal by, in the near future, requiring states to use performance-based assessments to evaluate the effectiveness of their Title I programs.

A fourth new component of strengthened state departments of education departments would be development of expanded research, development and dissemination capacities. Two initiatives should take priority. The first would be development of education indicator systems at least on educational inputs, processes, and results that would provide state policymakers with important data on the status of and changes in the education system over time (CCSSO, 1990; Odden, 1990b; Shavelson, McDonnell, and Oakes, 1989; Smith, 1988; Special Study Panel on Educational Indicators, 1991). The goal would be an intelligent monitoring of the system so that as conditions changed the policy system could be altered to shore up weak areas as well as expand investments in areas of strength. Given the intense concern with "opportunity to learn" that arose in legislative debate surrounding the Clinton Administration's Goals 2000 program (Porter, 1993a, 1993b), state initiatives to gather information on key school level processes and the curriculum actually taught (Porter, 1991, 1993a) should be one particular goal of a new indicator system, in addition to indicators of dollar inputs and student performance results.

Further, since new strategies for teaching all students a problem-solving-focused curriculum and for restructuring schools into high-performance organizations are required by all districts and schools, state departments could play important roles in developing new structures for disseminating these effective practices.

Finally, state departments might urge legislatures and governors to create state policy and research centers that would provide outside information on the condition of the state's education system and the progress of implementing new curriculum frameworks, the new testing systems, teacher development programs, and restructured school organizations. While a reasonable argument could be made for developing this capacity within state departments, nearly all departments suffer to some degree with skeptical responses to evaluation reports their staff might write. Having outside but university-based policy analysts produce the information ensures that it will be neutral and objective, and might also enhance the likelihood of it being taken seriously in the policy arena. This type of mechanism would establish yet another component of the collaborative policy analysis, development, and evaluation processes that is characterizing the 1990s.

SUMMARY

States are key players in the education landscape of the 1990s. States not only have the capacity and will to engage in aggressive education leadership for the remainder of the 1990s, but they also have the formal constitutional responsibility to do so. Moreover, as the next chapter shows the federal government's new Goals 2000 program reinforces the state role in designing a systemic reform strategy by providing funds for states to develop learning goals for all students, curriculum standards, performance-based student assessments, professional development strategies, and opportunity to learn standards. State officials—governors, legislatures, state school boards, chief state school officers, and state departments of education—will need to work in close cooperation in order to make these many interrelated efforts cohere into strategies at the local level to actually raise the performance of all students to high levels of thinking and problem solving in the core-content areas.

National Education Leadership and Policy

National education leadership and policy has changed dramatically over the course of the twentieth century. From a passive role at the beginning of the century, it appears with the passage of the Clinton Administration's Goals 2000 program that the federal government will end the century as a major influencer of the core of education at the state, district, school, and classroom level. This chapter describes the evolution of national education policy during this century, briefly reviewing federal government roles up to 1960. It then describes the activist period of the 1960s and 1970s. Finally, it discusses in more detail the new directions that began to emerge during the 1980s and continue in the 1990s. The chapter will argue that the passage of the Clinton Administration's Goals 2000 program in March 1994 represents an intensification of federal government involvement in education policy which likely will be the center of attention for the remainder of the decade. The last section of this chapter raises issues about the directions signaled by Goals 2000.

The chapter echoes four themes about federal involvement in education. The first is that the difference between the federal role at the beginning and end of the century is not one of sudden shifts and new departures, but of gradual and consistent evolution towards greater and more involvement. The second is that events outside education per se have served as the stimuli for this gradual but consistently increasing federal presence in education; in other words, the federal role in education expands as noneducation problems seek their resolution through the country's education system. The third is that the consistently expanding federal role reflects a victory of centralization over local control, i.e., the belief that only higher levels of government can ensure common values, experiences and equity in the provision of educational services. The fourth is that as federal government involvement in education increased, it was accompanied by involvement of an ever widening array of national groups and organizations so that one must consider both federal, governmental initiatives as well as national, but not governmentally connected influences on elementary and secondary education.

In the early years of the country, when education was largely a local responsibility, the federal role was minimal. Overtime, two major roles emerged: (1) gathering data and statistics to report on the condition of education in the country and (2) developing and supporting programs in the "national interest." The latter quite general role has had two emphases: national needs of the labor market and equity. The national interest mechanism has been the primary rationale for the growth of federal programs over the course of this decade. Because the "national interest" is such an "elastic" term, it has been used overtime to justify expanded federal education initiatives in response to numerous forces, factors, or events in the broader environment, as well as to undergird the federal role in equity and equal educational opportunity.

For example, in the early part of this century the federal government enacted the 1917 Smith-Hughes vocational education program. The act was considered a major, new federal program; it provided grants, initially on a matching basis, for schools to establish vocational and home economics programs in the secondary curriculum.

Two major factors contributed to this new federal initiative (Kaestle & Smith, 1982). The first was an international competition in developing an industrial economy, as the economy of that time was shifting from one based on agriculture to one based on industrialism and manufacturing; it was felt that a national emphasis on vocational education would enhance the United State's fate in that larger economic struggle. The second was linked to changes in school enrollments. At about the same time, states were beginning to mandate secondary school attendance. This requirement dramatically increased the number of students in high schools. But, many of the new students were not interested in the typical college preparatory curriculum of that time; they wanted and needed a different type of curriculum. Thus, the second factor for the support of a federal vocational education initiative was an equity argument; vocational education was needed as a curriculum alternative for students who wanted a more "practical" course of studies and who planned on entering the labor force, not college, after completing high school (Grubb and Lazerson, 1988).

Few substantial federal education initiatives in elementary and secondary education were undertaken over the next three decades. By 1950, the largest federal programs were in school lunch (funded primarily by the Department of Agriculture), vocational education, impact aid for children who were dependents of federal employees usually the military but attended local public schools, and programs for native Americans. Moreover, Congress appeared to be uninterested in creating a program of general aid. Federal support of data collection and research was very small. And at that time, the federal courts were not active in ruling on education issues (Kaestle and Smith, 1982).

The 1950s

The 1950s produced two new federal initiatives and both were stimulated by external events, one of which was the growing civil rights movement and the other the technological race spawned by the Cold War. The 1954 *Brown v. Board of Education* decision (see also Chapter 12) overturned de jure segregated education systems across the country, many of which had existed since the end of the nineteenth century. It required states and districts to integrate the schools with "all deliberate speed." Although the decision was a shock to the American education system and represented a new line in the sand of education policy, it was the endproduct of nearly 50 years of litigation on a variety of issues both within and outside education, and represented an evolutionary expansion of equal protection litigation. The decision overturned the practice of "separate but equal" schools for racial minorities. To be sure, the decision was more than a shot over the bow of state education systems; the decision impacted education policy in substantive ways up to current times. Nevertheless, it was action by the court, not the Congress, and thus almost by definition constituted a force outside education that drove the apparatus of federal education policy into a variety of new, complex, and politically charged issues related to both education policy and practice.

Similarly, the late 1950s National Defense Education Act (NDEA) produced large amounts of federal money to alter mathematics and science training in secondary schools, largely administered through a newly created National Science Foundation (see Atkin and House, 1981; Yee and Kirst, 1994). The NDEA was not an idea that germinated within education circles, but more a response to the technological needs required by the Cold War standoff between the Western democracies lead by the United States and the Eastern Bloc led by the Union of Soviet Socialist Republics (USSR). The 1957 Russian launch of the Sputnik satellite was one of the most visible indicators of a potential USSR technical advantage, and the then "wake up call" that encouraged the Congress to enact a new federal education program to close the technology gap, if one existed, and to ensure that the United States maintained its technical lead (Kaestle and Smith, 1982).

Both of these 1950s federal educational ventures reflect the overall themes that have characterized the ever expanding federal role in education. To begin, they were policies enacted in response to forces outside of education. They were justified on grounds of the "national interest," both to enhance equity (desegregation) or economic needs, i.e., technological prowess (NDEA). Furthermore, even though new departures, their impact did not immediately require major change. Indeed, while the *Brown* decision was dramatic in what it overturned, and thus represented a major departure from the past, it took many years for the federal government and the courts to put teeth into the decision, thus limiting the impact of the decision to gradual, incremental rather than sudden, dramatic change. Further, even the NDEA mathematics and science programs focused only on some students (the brightest) and at just a few grade levels in the education system (high school), thus representing change for only a small percentage of students. Both entailed new actors on the education front: the courts and a new, noneducation federal agency—the National Science Foundation. Further, the amount of money put into the NDEA initiatives were not that large, and below the levels of most other education programs at that time. Finally, it took nearly two decades for the federal government to support its desegregation mandates with financial assistance. And without money, large change often is difficult to produce.

Many have viewed the 1960s and 1970s as the activist period of federal involvement in education. Indeed, if measured by the number of new programs enacted, the magnitude of the dollars appropriated, and the impact of a variety of court decisions, these two decades represent considerable expansion of the federal role in education. Nevertheless, the thematic arguments being made, of a consistent but ever increasing federal presence driven by forces outside education per se, are reflected in the initiatives of these two decades as well.

Equity issues undergirded nearly all the major federal initiatives of these two decades. Many programs represented followthrough on the promise of desegregation embodied in the 1954 *Brown* decision. First, there were subsequent court decisions that required more action than the "all deliberate speed" language of Brown. The decision in *Green* v. *County School Board* (1968) ruled that the open enrollment programs of that era were inadequate for the federal desegregation mandates. The *Swan* v. *Charlotte-Mecklenburg* (1971) decision specifically stated that bussing students to different schools could be imposed by districts in order to meet requirements for desegregating schools. In other decrees, the court opened the North to desegregation suits in *Keyes* v. *School District No. 1* (1973) by ruling that actions of the school board in building schools and drawing school attendance boundaries directly crafted to segregate students by race were unconstitutional and would trigger a desegregation decree. But in *Bradley* v. *Milliken* (1972) the court ruled that bussing across district boundaries (between central cities and their suburbs) was not required for reducing racial isolation in large urban districts.

In concert with the courts were other federal initiatives focused on eliminating racial inequities within schools. First, the 1964 federal Civil Rights Act included Title VI, which allowed the federal government to write specific federal guidelines governing the use of federal education funds in formerly segregated school systems as well as requirements for schools and local education systems to desegregate. Second, the U.S. Office of Education invigorated the Office of Civil Rights (OCR) and thrust it into numerous investigatory roles as well as empowered it to make rulings on a variety of race related education issues. Third, The U.S. Commission on Civil Rights was organized and focused much of its attention on the schools. Fourth, during the early 1970s period of the Richard Nixon Presidential Administration, when Republicans launched their Southern strategy to court political support among that region's conservative voters (Shalala and Kelly, 1973), the Congress enacted the Emergency School Assistance Act (ESAA) which provided assistance to districts, primarily in the South but also in the North, that had already desegregated or as a stimulus to desegregate.

Thus, by the mid1970s a substantial federal apparatus focused on desegregating schools had been developed—legal decisions, technical assistance and monitoring bodies, and federal programs. The roots of these initiatives were in the expanding requirements of the Equal Protection Clause of the fourteenth amendment to the U.S. Constitution, the growing civil rights movement across the country, and ultimately the political interests of both the Republican and

Democratic parties. An issue which just a few years earlier had been fraught with contentious debate and acrimony, had become a mainstream focus and structured both to create substantial change as well as to meet political interests.

These advances should not be interpreted to mean that school desegregation was accomplished or that the education of racial minorities was dramatically improved (Kaestle and Smith, 1982; Orfield, 1969). Indeed, during the same time period, the Congress passed many regulations prohibiting the use of federal dollars for bussing. The education programs supported tended not to impact the regular curriculum and instruction program, providing funds to finance services on the periphery of local school programs. And the results of these many efforts had not by the end of these two decades clearly improved the educational achievement of racial minorities. Thus, the expanded federal interest and involvement was accompanied by continuity of many practices and procedures. Nevertheless, this period did represent a firm new beginning for dealing with segregated schools and their progeny of problems and education challenges.

Another national initiative that was born at this time was the War on Poverty program of President Lyndon Johnson. Launching initiatives and new programs on a variety of fronts just shortly after becoming President in late 1963, Lyndon Johnson sought to make his mark on history by rooting out poverty in America. Education became a major beneficiary of these initiatives; the belief was that the route to poverty reduction was through education, that if students from poor backgrounds could be provided a superb education, they could qualify for good paying jobs and thus bound out of their poverty conditions.

The major educational program that evolved from these efforts was the Elementary and Secondary Education Act (ESEA) of 1965. Originally sent up from the federal Budget Bureau as a 900 million dollar program, President Johnson returned it to staff allegedly saying, "I want a billion dollar education program," which back in 1965 was "real money." The program was passed in 1965, and funded at just over 1 billion dollars. Its objective was to provide extra educational services to underachieving students from poverty backgrounds.

The original ESEA had five titles. By far the largest, Title I provided on a formula basis a large infusion of federal funds to all districts which had children from poverty backgrounds; districts were to use the funds to provide innovative educational services to their lowest achieving students. Title II provided funds for a five-year program of enhancing school libraries, instructional materials, textbooks, and other teaching materials. Title III included funds for experimental and innovative programs, with the notion being to expand the array of programs and strategies that worked for children eligible for this new "compensatory education" program; this Title also provided for additional supportive services such as guidance counseling and health services. Title IV created a new research and dissemination capacity, providing funds for several new education research centers as well as for several new education laboratories that would disseminate the research results. Title V was a grant program for each state's education department; the intent was to enhance the size and capability of state departments of education both to administer this new federal program, to provide assistance and guidance to local districts and schools in their design of local compensatory education strategies, and to develop a research and evaluation capacity.

ESEA was revised and expanded in 1968 during which several new titles were added, including a Title VIII creating programs for limited-English proficient students, and another title creating programs for students of migrant agricultural workers. Although implementation of ESEA's Title I was contentious in the early years because it required districts to provide extra services to a select group of students, as Chapter 11 shows, overtime Title I was fully implemented in compliance with all rules and regulations created over a ten- to fifteen-year time period (Kirst and Jung, 1980; Odden, 1991a).

During these two decades, the general equity thrust in the broader political environment continued to be reflected in a rising number of federal education programs. ESEA was expanded by the Congress to 11 titles with over 100 programs (Kaestle and Smith, 1982). Title VI of the Civil Rights act helped lead to the *Lau* v. *Nichols* (1974) decision which required school districts to provide special programs for students who were not fluent in English; subsequently, the Office of Education issued regulations specifying the type of education services required by the *Lau* decision. Title IX of the Education Amendments of 1972 proscribed discrimination against women and girls in both elementary/secondary and postsecondary education; this was the education component of the country's overall efforts to provide full opportunity for women and girls in all sectors of life. Section 504 of the 1973 Rehabilitation Act, which made discrimination against handicapped individuals a federal violation, laid the foundation for Congressional enactment of the 1975 Education for All Handicapped Children Act (P.L. 94-142), another large federal education program providing federal support and funds for students with physical or mental handicaps.

By the end of the 1970s, federal education policy had expanded into numerous arenas. Again, nearly all initiatives followed broader thrusts to provide equal opportunity for many groups and conditions; in this sense, federal education policy remained connected to strong pressures outside education per se. Indeed, this attention to equal opportunity for minority groups was a worldwide phenomenon: countries under the colonial rule of Western powers were fighting for and being given political independence and freedom, the condition of oppressed groups in numerous other countries were being scrutinized in the press, and the women's movement spread worldwide. So the focus on equal opportunity was more than an American invention, and certainly not just an education concern. At the close of the decade, moreover, the catalogue of federal education programs covered scores of groups and scores of special issues, nearly all of which were accompanied by a federal education program, though some were large and some were small.

At the same time, two aspects of this expansion of federal involvement in education conspired to limit the federal impact. The first was that even when totaled, federal dollars were only a small portion of the total spent on public elementary and secondary education. While ESEA boosted the federal role from 4.4 percent in 1965 to 7.9 percent in 1966, the first year of implementation, that still represented a minority position; by 1979, when the federal financial role peaked at 9.8 percent, states and local governments were still providing over 90 percent of school funding. Thus, even an allegedly expansionist federal agenda was able to provide only a small portion of the education fiscal pie.

A second limiting feature of federal involvement was that nearly all programs remained outside of the core of local curriculum and instruction programs. In fact, a continuous feature about the debates surrounding nearly all new federal programs was disavowal of any notion of a national curriculum, a tendency to defer decisions about the nature and substance of the instruction program to local discretion, and a reluctance to position federal programs in places other than on the periphery of local school programs. Put differently, despite the proliferation of federal initiatives designed to enhance the condition of a variety of special populations, the poor, handicapped, limited-English proficient, native Americans, girls, etc., neither program design nor program regulations spoke to the core of the education experience at the local level—the regular curriculum and instruction program. This reluctance to position federal programs on anything but the periphery of what mattered locally both crippled the impact any of the federal programs individually as well as all of the programs collectively (Odden, 1991b), and maintained the consistency of local of the curriculum and instruction program. In other words, a critical aspect of how an expanding set of federal education programs maintained a consistency with past education conditions was deferral to local systems on nearly all issues related to the nature and substance of what was taught.

Two other initiatives "round out" the expansionary federal education agenda of this time. The first was creation of the National Institute of Education (NIE) in the early 1970s and the second the creation of the Department of Education in 1979. Although the promise of the magnitude of education research envisioned at the creation of NIE was never fulfilled, NIE nevertheless solidified a substantial federal role in education research. The expanded National Center for Education Statistics (NCES) provided the same function for the federal role in data collection. Moreover, while creation of the Department of Education did not carry with it an additional expansion of federal education funding or programs, it did identify education as a separate and independent function that deserved top policy and presidential attention (Radin and Hawley, 1988).

The end of the 1970s, thus, saw the federal role in education conceptualized along three primary dimensions:

- Gathering data and statistics through NCES, and sponsoring research through the NIE.
- Providing equal education opportunity for a variety of special-needs students, through numerous programs including civil rights requirements and active federal courts.
- Supporting other programs in the national interest, such as vocational education which remained a strong contender for increased funding even though created much earlier in the century.

The Federal Role in Education: 1980

The irony of the 1980s is that it began with a President determined to reduce if not eliminate the federal role in education, but initiatives launched during Ronald Reagan's administration not only strengthened the federal role but also thrust the Office of the President directly into education policy in a way few had predicted and even fewer had considered possible. Further, federal activities during this time continued the winning record of the cosmopolitan centralists, who pushed for strong state and federal government roles, over the local resistors who continued to lose the prerogatives of local control over school operations (Kaestle and Smith, 1982).

The decade started with President Ronald Reagan proposing that the Department of Education be eliminated, that federal education funding be dramatically reduced, and that several education programs be consolidated and others eliminated. Few of these proposals were acted on. The Department was not eliminated and grew in power and influence even during the first Reagan administration (Bell, 1988). Federal funding was reduced modestly but no major cuts were made (Verstegen, 1990; Verstegen and Clark, 1988). The largest federal programs remained in tact: Title I of ESEA and the Education for All Handicapped Children Act. Although Title I was somewhat restructured in the 1982 Education Consolidation and Improvement Act (ECIA: Chapter 1), and its regulations eliminated for a short-time period at the beginning of the 1980s, the regulations were quickly reinstated and remained strong throughout the decade. While nearly 40 very small categorical programs were consolidated into the ECIA Chapter 2 block grant, most analysts recognized that the bulk of the programs had been inconsequential and, with one exception, no substantial education policy objective had been compromised by consolidation. The exception was the Emergency School Assistance Act, (ESAA) desegregation program which was incorporated into Chapter 2, effectively gutting federal support for school desegregation (Verstegen, 1990; Verstegen and Clark, 1988).

Another complication that surrounded federal education policy at the beginning of the 1980s was the effectiveness of federal programs. Although the implementation debates had been settled as research found the bulk of federal programs and guidelines fully and compliantly implemented (Kirst and Jung, 1980; Knapp et al. 1983, 1991; Moore et al., 1983, 1991), other studies were showing that the programs had little impact on student achievement (Elmore and McLaughlin, 1981, 1983; McLaughlin, 1991b; Odden, 1991b). One of the key issues, therefore, was how to improve the quality of federal education programs. Although the "education excellence" movement was soon launched and represented a legitimate response to this issue of quality, many who had toiled in the previous two decades to develop and protect the array of equity programs initially felt the new initiatives might pull the federal interest away from these equity objectives (*Harvard Educational Review*, 1982), but subsequent research showed that excellence-oriented programs could be combined with and potentially enhance the impact of equity programs such as Title I (Odden, 1987).

The impetus that stimulated the education excellence movement and overtime pushed for continued and more expansive federal involvement in education during the 1980s was international economic competition. Just as the economic change from an agricultural to an industrial economy launched the federal government into vocational education at the beginning of the century, economic change from an industrial to an analytic, information processing, high-technology economy at the end of the century thrust the federal government into the era of education excellence and reform. The *Nation at Risk Report* (National Commission on Excellence in Education, 1983) released in April 1983 sparked this new federal involvement. Noted for its language about the "rising tide of mediocrity" that threatened to swamp the nation's schools, the impetus for the report was a decline in student achievement just at a time when the ability to think, analyze data, and solve problems seemed key to improving the productivity of the country's economy and position in international markets. Although there were debates about the connections between education and economic growth (as developed in Chapter 1), political leaders at both the federal and state (Task Force on Education for Economic Growth, 1983) believed in the connection and began to focus considerable attention on improving education performance.

The *Nation at Risk* report was written by a Commission created by a Secretary of Education who had been charged with eliminating the Department of Education (Bell, 1988). But the report struck a responsive chord around the country and quickly engaged the federal government, this time including the President, in a visible, prominent, and national education reform movement. The report was released from the White House, one of the first times in history that an education reform report was made public by the President and with Presidential imprimatur. President Reagan then toured the country over several months giving education reform speeches based on the findings and recommendations of his Secretary of Education's Commission report; each public appearance appeared on both local and national news broadcasts and was written up in local and national newspapers. For the first time in history, a President was spending considerable time championing the issue of education and the need for dramatic school change, thus thrusting education reform daily into the public eye.

While Reagan did not propose new federal initiatives, he nevertheless used his office to focus public and policy attention on the nation's schools, suggesting that change and reform was needed for the economic health of the nation. The message was a strong one. The message no longer sat on the periphery of the education program; it spoke to the heart of the curriculum and instruction programs in the nation's 100,000 schools calling them inadequate. To a certain degree, the message about the problem with the core of the education enterprise was more important than would have been a new federal program on the margin. The message was that America's public schools needed major change, from the inside out.

The symbolic form of federal education influence continued throughout the decade. Shortly after the Nation at Risk report, another education report was released from the White House. This report, entitled *What Works* (U.S. Department of Education, 1986), was a synthesis of education research; the goal was to compile the results of education research to communicate to the lay public and education professionals research-based findings about how to improve school performance and thus student achievement. By lending the prestige of the Presidency to the release of this report, the White House reinforced its role as influencing how the nation thought about education and the need for change, in addition to the traditional federal role of expressing interest in education by enacting another federal program.

Finally, a new Secretary of Education, William Bennett, continued to tour the nation and exhort educators, parents, policymakers, and the public to sustain the pressure for dramatic education reform. Bennett was blunt and direct in his approach, a style appreciated by few local education leaders. But, this Secretary of Education took a federal position that had little money, little influence on the core of a school's education program, and at that time little prestige, and transformed it into a "bully pulpit" to heighten the nation's consciousness about the need to dramatically change the school curriculum, how it was taught, and to inject into the system a striving for excellence in all schools (Jung and Kirst, 1986). In so doing, he also strengthened the office of the Secretary of Education.

Presidential involvement in education continued even during the presidential campaign of 1988, when both candidates, George Bush and Michael Dukakis, ran on a platform of becoming an education president. Again, never before in the history of the country had a presidential campaign included the issue of education so centrally. Indeed, even the primaries were focused on education; more than a half dozen contenders in the Democratic primary were education governors, and participated in a nationally televised debate on what they would do for education if elected president.

The connection between education and the economy was further reflected by the appearance of a new set of policy actors on the national education policy arena—the business community and their key national organizations including the Committee for Economic Development (CED), the National Alliance for Business and the National Business Roundtable. Throughout the 1980s, the CED issued reports on education reform (CED, 1985, 1987, 1991) and the conditions of children. The National Alliance for Business launched a nationwide education initiative, and the Business Roundtable (1991) outlined a nine-point plan for education reform and began analyzing the gaps between its reform points and the elements of state education policies. In addition, the National Center on Education and the Economy (1989, 1990), comprised of key business and political leaders, represented one more national group targeting education reform as a key to economic reform; sitting on its board was Hillary Rodham Clinton, wife of an education reform governor, both of whom would shortly live in the White House.

The ultimate political engagement in national education reform was the October 1989 Education Summit called by then President George Bush. In Charlottesville, Virginia, under the nation's and media eye, the President and 50 governors met for two days, discussing the importance of an improved education system for the future of the country. The end result was the construction of the nation's first ever education goals (see Table 1-1). Through this concrete expression of the national interest in education, the country's political leadership cemented the country to long-term education reform, which continues into the 1990s. Interestingly, the Governor from Arkansas, Bill Clinton, led the governors during that Summit and he, together with the President, were the key writers of the goals. When Clinton subsequently became President in 1993, it was no surprise that he maintained continuity with what began in Charlottesville by supporting the goals, even though they were presented to the nation by his Republican predecessor.

Finally, while the federal role in education had been stimulated by *political* initiative and new *legal* findings, and while education leadership at the state level had also been taken over in the 1960s, 1970s, and 1980s by *political* leaders, thus eclipsing education leaders at all levels, another 1980s national education phenomenon was a re-emergence of professional educators in deciding on the nature and substance of education reform. Three reports published in 1989 reflect this renewal from within the education profession itself. First, the National Council of Teachers of Mathematics (NCTM) (1989) published a widely respected document identifying standards for the elementary and secondary mathematics curriculum; subsequently, this report was referred to as an exemplar both in the process used to create the standards and in the type of curriculum it proposed. In the 1990s, the NCTM document was followed by similar curriculum standards documents promulgated by the other national professional content associations.

Second, the American Association for the Advancement of Science (1989) published a new vision of science. The report argued that science was needed for all Americans, not just the best and the brightest, and that science should be part of the elementary and middle school as well as high school program of studies.

Third, the National Board for Professional Teaching Standards (1989) issued a report outlining the high and rigorous standards to which all teachers should aspire and which, beginning in Fall 1994, would be the basis for National Board certification of experienced, expert teachers.

All three of these initiatives came from national education professional groups. Although at the time these reports were not widely recognized as the beginning of what would become a process of the profession taking back leadership of the profession, from the perspective of the middle of the 1990s it could be claimed that they represented that new phenomenon (Massell and Furhman, 1994).

In summary, the 1980s represent continued but new directions in federal and national education policy. As in the past, an outside force, this time international economic competition, stimulated new federal initiatives. Also as in the past, the expanded federal role represented the continued dominance of the centralists over the localists in education policy; indeed, it could be argued that creation and adoption of the national education goals represents the ultimate centrist triumph as goals and curriculum, up until the Summit of 1989, had always been considered a local prerogative. Finally, as in the past, these new federal initiatives reflected a continuity with the past because the only new focus for federal and national education policy could be on the heart of the curriculum and instruction program, the only educational arena allegedly left untouched by federal programs. Further, although the rationale for the excellence movement was driven by the needs of the labor market, it also had an important equity component; the argument was that all students needed to be educated to high standards. In this sense, the notion of the "national interest" which had been bifurcated up until the 1980s between an excellence and equity focus (Kaestle and Smith, 1982), became fused together in the excellence reforms as articulated in the national education goals.

As the 1980s ended it became clear that the national and federal interest had fully matured. The courts, the Congress and now the President were centrally connected to education issues and policies. The key national business leaders and their top organizations were centrally engaged in elementary and secondary education policy. The entire education program was the focus of attention. And fortuitously, since the entire sweep in education was targeted for change, educators themselves, through their national professional organizations and many state education leaders, were beginning to take the substantive lead within education. These movements were fortuitous because the overall education enterprise could not be reformed by political, legal, and business leaders, but only by educators themselves. The apparent resurgence of the education community, on a professional and not a political basis, offered hope that the desires of the political and business leaders, expressed through the national goals, would have some chance of success in the next decade.

FEDERAL AND NATIONWIDE EDUCATION POLICY IN THE 1990S

The 1990s are witnessing a dazzling series of new national and federal education initiatives, which should continue throughout the decade. As the previous chapters have indicated, there is a considerable amount of reinventing or restructuring taking place within education (as well as most other functions in our society), and similar repositioning and revisioning will occur at the national and federal levels for the next several years.

The 1990s began with President George Bush elucidating the six national education goals in his State of the Union address. This represented the President's substantive followthrough on the October 1989 Education Summit. Shortly thereafter, he appointed Lamar Alexander as Secretary of Education; Alexander had been a governor who had championed comprehensive education reform in Tennessee and had turned the National Governors' Association to the education reform agenda while he was chair of that group (National Governors' Association, 1986). In May 1991, Bush and Alexander proposed the American 2000 program as that administration's vehicle to dramatically reform American education. This proposal became intertwined in partisan politics in the Congress, which was controlled by the Democrats, and was never enacted.

A portion of American 2000 proposal, however, was created namely the New American Schools Development Corporation (NASDC). NASDC had been proposed as a government-initiated but privately funded organization to create "break-the-mold" schools that could serve as visions for the kinds of schools required to accomplish the ambitious student learning embodied in the national goals. NASDC was incorporated, it raised considerable amounts of money, and in 1992 awarded 10 contracts around the country for design teams to craft their versions of such high-performing schools.

But a new national role in education was also carved out by the governors in early 1990. They too wanted to continue the momentum begun by the October 1989 Summit and the aspirations contained in the national goals. Therefore, they constituted a new entity called the National Goals Panel, soon comprised of governors, representatives of the Congress, representatives of the administration, and members of the public. The mission of the Goals Panel was to track the progress of the nation, and each state, in accomplishing the national goals. And the Goals Panel performed that task well, issuing comprehensive reports each October on the status of education in the country and progress towards implementing the goals (National Education Goals Panel, 1991, 1992, 1993).

Also in 1990, the federal government completed the 25 or so national education research centers. As part of that competition, the Consortium for Policy Research in Education, which ran the federal education policy center and had studied in depth the many state education reforms that had been enacted during the 1980s, argued that those reforms had been flawed along several dimensions, including a lack of coherence, and that to substantially impact student achievement, a more systemic reform strategy was required (Elmore and Fuhrman, 1990; Fuhrman and Associates, 1991; Smith and O'Day, 1991). Systemic reform, as described in previous chapters includes three interrelated sets of policies:

- Ambitious goals for student achievement in the core-content areas.
- A set of policies connected to those goals including high-quality curriculum frameworks (such as those proposed by the NCTM), revised instructional materials, new forms of student assessment linked to the frameworks that would indicate what students know as well as what they can do, and revised teacher preservice and inservice development.
- Restructured and decentralized governance, management, organization, and finance.

These policy ideas quickly entered policy parlance and both states and the federal government began discussing what systemic reform entailed, whether it was a wise approach to policy, and how it could be designed and implemented. Though influenced by other ideas as well, the Business Roundtable's (1991) nine essential elements echoed most of the core themes of systemic reform.

In early 1992, moreover, the National Council on Educational Standards and Testing (NCEST), which had been created by Congress and co-chaired by the two governors who chaired the Education Goals Panel, issued a report sanctioning both the idea of national curriculum standards and a national, performance-based student assessment system. If there was any question about whether the 1989 Education Summit and the national goals that evolved from that meeting had stared down local control, this report represented the final challenge to the notion that curriculum and testing would primarily be a local concern. Though identifying numerous technical and political issues, NCEST nevertheless came quite unambiguously down on the side of developing national standards for curriculum and testing (NCEST, 1992).

Nevertheless, there continued to be a national debate about what the federal role should be in the new era of national education goals. In an influential article, Hill (1990) argued for a continuation of the equity focus of earlier decades: continued funding of the major equity programs (Chapter 1 and P.L. 94-142), assistance to urban school systems where the most acute education problems existed, support for research on effective practices for inner city secondary schools, and new initiatives to support education improvement planning at the site level.

Elmore and Fuhrman (1990) set their recommendations more directly into the context of the shortcomings of the 1980s education reforms, the primacy of states in leading education restructuring, and the emergence of the national goals. The context, they argued, was one of great ferment and change at the state and local level (points made in previous chapters), fragmentation of those reform efforts, and difficulties in having a real federal impact both because federal funding was a small part of the total and because, whatever the federal government championed, states, districts, and schools ran and controlled the education systems in the country.

They made three primary recommendations. The first was to raise the level of knowledge and discussion on how to define, measure, and use student performance; they recommended funding several efforts to create performance-assessment techniques. Secondly, they recommended that the federal government sponsor solutions to the problem of policy incoherence such as developing high-quality curriculum standards, new forms of professional development, and decentralized governance and management systems. Third, they recommended greater investment in education research but focused on key problems such as effective programs for the poor and urban underclass, linkages among categorical programs at the district and site level, and use of a small percentage of Chapter 1 money for program development since few Chapter 1 programs had produced the desired achievement impacts on the children served. Their suggestions were mirrored in a Brookings Institution report (Murnane and Levy, 1992a).

The Congressional Budget Office (1993) also weighed in with a series of options for conceptualizing the federal education role for the 1990s. Published in early 1993, they were discussed throughout 1992. The CBO outlined three options, appealing to all factions of the Congress. The first was to reduce the federal role by consolidating all federal programs into two block grants: one for special-needs students (the specific uses to be decided at the state and local level) and another for education improvement. The second was to refine the federal role by sanctioning the national goals, requiring all states and districts that received federal education dollars to adopt the federal goals, and focusing new efforts on fully funding current programs or adding new programs that covered special-needs students, such as those in the inner cities of big urban districts. The third was to enhance the federal role to promote a restructuring of the country's education system, both by codifying the national goals and by developing initiatives to have the country move forward in developing performance standards, content standards, new forms of assessment, and opportunity to learn standards.

All these events help set the stage for the presidential race between George Bush and Bill Clinton. When Clinton became President in 1993, for the first time the country had a President who had been deeply involved in education reform, had lead the nation's governors for several years on an education reform agenda, had been a key writer of the national education goals, was convinced that education improvement was linked to the nation's economic growth, and viewed development of the human resources of the country, young children, school-aged children, young adults, and those adults already in the workforce, as a driving force for his administration.

His cabinet appointments surprised some but reflected these priorities. Richard Riley, former education reform governor of South Carolina, was appointed Secretary of Education and Madeline Kunin, another education reform-oriented governor of Vermont, was appointed Deputy Secretary.[1] Donna Shalala, formerly a professor of education politics and policy and an advocate for children's policy, was appointed Secretary of Health and Human Resources. And Robert Reich, who had written extensively on the need to upgrade the nation's human resources in order to spur economic growth (Reich, 1991), was appointed Secretary of Labor. Together with the President, these three began to form a comprehensive human resources development strategy that would drive a large portion of the President's domestic agenda (Smith, 1993).

To the surprise of many in Congress who expected that a Democratic President would propose full funding of the equity programs of the 1960s and 1970s (which never had been funded at their authorized levels), in addition to proposing a set of new federal categorical programs, and perhaps even rejecting all the initiatives of the previous administration, Clinton instead signaled that he supported the notion of the national education goals and proposed strategic policies to help the country accomplish them.

Although experiencing some difficulties in gaining Congressional approval, with criticisms from both Democrats and Republicans, the Clinton Administrations Goals 2000 bill was enacted and signed into law in March 1994. It reflected the proposals of both Elmore and Fuhrman (1990), and well as the more ambitious CBO (1993) proposal. In broad sweep, it crafted a federal role in creating, nurturing, and sustaining state and local momentum on the systemic reform agenda. Goals 2000 contained several key elements related to elementary and secondary education. First, it codified into federal law the national education goals, and added two goals, one on professional development and one on parent involvement in schools. Second, it formally authorized the Educational Goals Panel as a federal body, charged it with monitoring national progress towards accomplishing the national goals, and provided it the authority to set criteria for voluntary state education standards and national model curriculum and assessment standards. Third, it created a new technical panel, the National Education Standards and Improvement Council (NESIC), to certify content (curriculum), performance (testing), and opportu-

---

[1]We should note that Riley had also been the chair of the Advisory Board of the Consortium for Policy Research (CPRE) and was well versed in the systemic reform strategy. His selection for Under Secretary, Marshall S. Smith, had been the representative from Stanford on the CPRE Management Committee and one of the original framers of the systemic reform approach (Smith and O'Day, 1991). Riley's selection for Assistant Secretary for Elementary and Secondary Education, Thomas Payzant, had been leading a systemic reform in his former school district and also was a member of the CPRE Advisory Board.

nity to learn (Porter, 1993b) standards. Fourth, it provided funds for both states and local districts to create systemic reform strategies; the funding was to be used for developing curriculum standards, performance assessments and learning standards, opportunity to learn standards, new forms of professional development, and school finance equity.[2]

In many respects, Goals 2000 was designed to provide an education umbrella policy for all other federal (and perhaps state and local) involvement in education. The purpose was to gear all federal policies towards the national education goals, which called for educating all students to high standards. The Administrations proposals for reauthorizing Chapter 1 reflected this strategy. Among many other proposals, it required refocusing Chapter 1 services to help eligible students learn the material in the new curriculum standards that had been developed by several states and that would continue to be developed under the Goals 2000 program.

Its most significant departure from the past was its sanctioning of the use of new performance assessments to evaluate the impact of Chapter 1 services. The previous program had mandated the use of norm-referenced, standardized achievement tests for Chapter 1 evaluations. But these were precisely the types of tests that systemic reform, Goals 2000 and the cognitive approach to learning (see Chapter 4) wanted to purge from school practice. Since the Chapter 1 mandate of norm-referenced tests had influenced local testing practice so heavily, a key to both the Clinton Administration's commitment to Goals 2000 as well as the possibility of moving forward on the systemic reform agenda was how this evaluation mandate would be addressed during the 1994 Chapter 1 reauthorization. An Independent Review Panel, comprised of many of the original designers of and long-term advocates for Chapter 1, recommended such a testing switch (U.S. Department of Education, 1993). In its original bill, the Administration proposed that states be allowed to substitute performance assessments for norm-referenced tests as they implemented such new forms of student testing.

By Fall 1994, it appeared that Congress would go along with this proposal. Both the Senate and House versions of the reauthorized program, which renamed Chapter 1 to its original Title I, contained language that would require states to use performance-based examinations to track the impact of Title I programs on student achievement. Both bills also required states to set the same high standards for student learning in the core content areas, and required states to align their assessment system for Title I to curriculum standards developed under the Goals 2000 program.

Alongside these federal initiatives from within the U.S. Department of Education has also been a major program of the National Science Foundation to reconstitute the mathematics and science that is taught at both elementary and secondary levels in the United States. Begun in 1990, the State Systemic

---

[2]We should note that in the last year of the Bush Administration, 1992, the Department of Education let several grants to a series of professional groups to develop content standards in numerous subject areas including English, science, geography, civics, history, the performing arts, and foreign language. Draft standards were available from many of these groups in early 1994 but final documents were not available at the time this book was completed.

Initiative (SSI) was based on the notion of systemic reform outlined by Smith and O'Day (1991). Rather than just sponsor isolated efforts at curriculum change, professional development, and instructional change unconnected to the state policies that govern education across the country, the SSI initiative was designed to "move beyond piecemeal efforts . . . carried out by relatively isolated curriculum developers or practitioners to support systemwide, coherent changes in all or most of the elements of the education system (e.g., assessment, teacher education, curriculum), designed and implemented with the cooperation of all key players in the mathematics and science communities (Shields, Corcoran, and Zucker, 1993: 1–3)."

SSI provided states with up to 10 million over a five-year time period to think through a systemic approach to completely altering their mathematics and science curriculum programs, including assessment strategies. It was different from the 1950s NSF curriculum reform efforts in focusing curriculum reform on all students at all levels of the system, attending to all related aspects including inservice teacher training and ongoing professional development, and organized in a way to have practitioners, policymakers, and experts work in collaborative and interactive ways. For mathematics and science in particular, it was a clear federal initiative that reinforces systemic reform and Goals 2000. It also represented a large federal initiative outside the Department of Education that was playing a major role in helping to implement the national goals nationwide.

FUTURE NATIONAL AND FEDERAL EDUCATION POLICY

The latter half of the 1990s will witness how the implementation of these bold initiatives unfolds, as well as their impact on education policy and practice at the state, district, school, and classroom levels. Several issues relating to successful implementation and impact need to be raised and monitored over the next several years. This section reviews several of these issues.

Balancing Top-Down and Bottom-Up Reform Strategies

One critical issue is the balance between the top-down instructional guidance provided by the standards to be created under Goals 2000 and the bottom-up change processes that must be developed at each school site to implement the standards (see also Chapter 11). While both of these components are embodied in the classical conceptualization of systemic reform (Smith & O'Day, 1991), it appears that Goals 2000 was somewhat selective in the elements of systemic reform that it incorporated. Clearly, Goals 2000 includes the ambitious student outcomes and standards components of systemic reform. But it is pretty silent on the third component of systemic reform—changes in governance and management with an emphasis on substantial decentralization.

Systemic reform, however, is best conceived as top level, instructional guidance support for school-based change (Fuhrman and O'Day, 1994). But, it reverts to just another set of top-down directives if the school-based change mechanisms are deleted. As Chapter 11 argues, what happens at the school level, including the knowledge, skills, and disposition of school faculties, is what matters and determines the degree of change in classroom and school practice. Without the school-based restructuring components, the first two elements of systemic reform are unlikely to alter classroom practice towards the curriculum and pedagogy described in Chapters 3 and 4, and generally expected by Goals 2000. Without such changes, Goals 2000 unlikely will boost all students' achievement to high levels.

Serious attention needs to be given to the bottom-up, school-site components of systemic reform as Goals 2000 is modified overtime. Unless the federal government sends the signal to states and local districts that school-based implementation is a critical component of the Goals 2000 strategy, this bold federal initiative could turn into a rigid, top-down program and not produce its intended impacts on school achievement.

Political and Fiscal Resolve

Another issue is whether political and education leaders have the will and the pocketbook to do what is necessary to support the strategies needed to educate all students to high standards. As states such as California and Kentucky administer new, performance-based assessments and only 20 to 25 percent of students score at or above proficiency levels, the untested issue is whether political leaders and the public will continue to support high standards for all or, as with the minimum competency tests of the past, they will lower standards so more students can pass (Shepard, 1991).

Further, Casserly and Carnoy (1994) have shown that not only is the nation far away from educating all students to high standards, but also that, as Chapter 2 described, the students who are increasing in numbers, the poor, the disabled, immigrants, minorities, etc., are those whose education achievement currently is the lowest and whose conditions in society are worsening.

Federal and state investments in policies to improve the conditions of children and to provide the extra resources required to enable all students to perform at high standards will be an ultimate fiscal test of the resolve embodied in Goals 2000. Fully funding the Head Start program and other programs guaranteeing inoculation and adequate prenatal and postnatal care, and supporting efforts to coordinate social and health services at single locations on or near school sites, issues addressed in Chapter 2, would reflect additional federal resolve on these important areas.

Professional Development

Another issue pertains to professional development. There is widespread agreement that a systemic reform such as that reflected in Goals 2000 requires a large investment in ongoing professional development (Little, 1993: Chapter 5). Indeed, professional development was a key issue discussed during Congressional debate on Goals 2000, and added as a national goal. As part of its overall proposals, moreover, the Clinton Administration recommended merging the large Eisenhower mathematics and science program of staff development and the Chapter 2 block grant, into an expanded and targeted program of federal support for professional development linked to Goals 2000.

That proposal was not adopted by the Congress and, as a result, Goals 2000 contained no major professional development program. Although states could combine funds from the two programs mentioned in the original Clinton proposals, doing so was made politically difficult by Congressional inaction on that agenda. Thus, an open-ended question is whether subsequent initiatives at the state or local level will produce the type of expanded professional development needed (as Chapter 5 described) to accomplish the aspirations of Goals 2000. Federal movement on this agenda, with renewed attempts to merge the numerous and fragmented professional development programs financed by federal dollars, would signal federal resolve on this important dimension as well.

Standard Setting

Another concern is the nature of standards that will be created and who will have the final decision about new standards. Although most professional content groups are proceeding to develop content standards and curriculum frameworks, these efforts are not without criticism. One concern is whether the standards represent high, ambitious but reasonable goals for the content area or shoot to high and set targets only a few can accomplish. The objective is to set high standards for all students, but not "Olympic" level standards because, by definition, "Olympic" level standards can only be accomplished by the very best and, in this case, the brightest.

Second, when all professional content groups publish content standards, a distinct possibility is that not all the standards can be implemented within a reasonable school day and year. The tendency will be for each content group to set more standards than are possible when all standards are pooled into a whole. The process as well as the criteria used to resolve both of these dilemmas are important issues.

Related to these dilemmas is the orientation that the U.S. Department of Education and NESIC will assume towards state and local standard setting processes. The language of a joint federal, state, local, and professional partnership in developing standards stands in stark contrast to past difficulties in resolving alternative perspectives on the specifics of needed education policy/program change. For example, after the Congress enacted Title I of ESEA, many states created state compensatory education programs with similar goals, but different programmatic details. States, though, have never been able to merge the funds from both programs and administer them in accord with state guidelines; the federal government has always insisted that its program design be dominant.

One would hope that this type of federal dominance will not be the pattern in the creation of content, learning, and assessment standards. Certainly, the federal Department of Education and NESIC will need to function in the dialectic between holding the states to leading edge standards but deferring to them on details and implementation specifics.

How this dialectic is handled is important. For example, Goals 2000 seeks to upgrade the science program, at all grade levels and for all students. But the type of upgraded science envisaged by the National Science Teachers Association (1989) is quite different from that of the American Association for the Advancement of Science (1989). Both represent high standards for science education. Will the U.S. Department of Education or NESIC force states to select one higher quality program over the other, or will they be content to allow states to select their own vision? Similarly, will the federal government come down on the side of a strengthened social studies curriculum as proposed by the National Commission on Social Studies in the Schools (1989) or require a history and geography approach to this content area, as reflected in the California curriculum frameworks (California State Department of Education, 1987) and efforts to develop history and geography standards?

The federal stance on these issues is crucial to how the federal, state, local, and professional partnership develops in the processes of creating content standards. Federal insistence on the perspective of the federal bodies over state and professional bodies will inject considerable friction into what should be a cooperative, professional set of activities. However resolved, curriculum standard setting is complex and difficult (Massell and Kirst, 1994).

Adding a Goals 2000 Program or Changing the Entire Education System

There also is the complex and potentially large issue of inconsistency between the letter and spirit of Goals 2000 (as well as any state systemic reform program) and the multitude of programs, rules, regulations, and laws that currently govern federal and state education policies and programs. Overtime, Goals 2000 cannot be just grafted onto the current system; the programs, rules, and regulations in the current system will need to be fundamentally altered in order to reinforce the approach of Goals 2000.

The federal government recognized this reality as it reauthorized Chapter 1, but all of the large federal programs need to be changed, as do most state categorical programs. Movement on these other programmatic fronts represent another set of very important signals about the seriousness of the country's education and political leaders in backing Goals 2000 and systemic reform. These reforms are not just another education program; they represent a restructured vision of the education system—results driven, standards-oriented, and site-based implemented. Unless the remainder of the education infrastructure is redesigned to support this new vision, it will severely limit the influence and impact wielded by Goals 2000.

State Department Capacity

It is also clear that Goals 2000 depends heavily on good implementation at the state and local levels. As the previous chapter noted, however, during the first portion of the 1990s, states cut deeply into the funding of state departments of education and reduced their staff and substantive capacity in many areas, most particularly in curriculum, assessment and technical assistance (Massell and

Fuhrman, 1994). This behavior will not only have to be stopped but also reversed.

Indeed, one could argue that a 1990s version of Title V of the original ESEA is required to develop sufficient state capacity to be the "point" government implementing Goals 2000. Given this need, one could hope that a significant portion of the substantial funds that will be provided to the states for administering Goals 2000 will be retained by State Departments of Education in order to construct the sophisticated capacity required to simultaneously develop ambitious student learning goals, top quality curriculum standards in several content areas, new forms of performance testing, and provide assistance to local education systems engaged in the same complex tasks. These tasks will not be accomplished without investment in state department of education staff capacity to orchestrate the process.

Fiscal Disparities

A financial issue looming around the national interest in accomplishing the nation's education goals and underneath the fiscal problems confronted by the federal government is the fact of large disparities in education funding both across the states and across districts within states. Although money is not the only solution to improving school performance, as all of the previous chapters in this book suggest, money nevertheless matters (Hedges, Laine, and Greenwald, 1994). Moreover, while Chapter 13 shows that money for education has been consistently growing for the past 50 years, these dollars are distributed quite unequally across states and districts (Picus, 1994). As a result, some states provide an average of $4,000 per pupil, while other states provide over $8,000, and within states spending can vary from $2,500 per child to over $15,000 per child. Furthermore, even when funding per pupil at the district level is quite equal, dramatic disparities in resources can exist across schools both within and across districts (Hertert, 1993).

The linkage between the aspirations in the national education goals and these funding disparities is finally emerging as a federal concern. In the summer of 1993, the Congress held a series of hearings to begin discussing a potential federal role in school finance equalization (Odden, 1993b). Nearly all assessments of the efficacy of Chapter 1, now Title I, suggested that school finance equity was a prerequisite for improving the impact of this large federal program (United States Department of Education, 1993).

Hertert, Busch, and Odden (1994, forthcoming) not only document the large dimension of the unequal distribution of education resources, but also the small price of providing full fiscal equity either for the bottom 50 percent of students within each state or for the bottom 50 percent of students across the entire United States. With an increase of just 7 percent of the total spent from local, state, and federal sources, all districts could be raised to the national median revenues per pupil. Yes, the politics of producing this quantum leap in fiscal equity are daunting, but the economics are not. Over the past five decades, a seven percent real increase in education dollars has taken at most 3 years to produce in any 10-year time period. Another indicator of the country's resolve to accomplish the national learning goals for all students, therefore, is whether the deep and large disparities in education resources across the country are brought substantively and permanently under more control in this decade.

The Role of State-Based Education and Political Associations

A final important issue concerning the national resolve to implement Goals 2000 is the role the state-based political and education organizations will play in this effort. The National Governors' Association, National Conference of State Legislatures, Council of Chief State School Officers, Education Commission of the States and National Association of State Boards of Education represent the state officials who are the "point" individuals in orchestrating implementation of Goals 2000 at the state level. In order for implementation to proceed effectively, these organizations will need to work well together to determine effective state strategies, as well as work well collectively with the federal government, the Administration, the Congress, the Departments of Education, Health, and Human Resources, and perhaps Labor, the National Goals Panel, and the National Education Standards and Improvement Commission, on all the thorny and complex issues of standards setting.

CONCLUSION

The country is embarking on a new venture—educating all students to high standards. A gradual but consistent evolution of federal education policy over this century has thrust the federal government and other bodies with a national interest in education centrally into the comprehensive set of activities needed to accomplish this aggressive education goal. Spurred by creation of the national education goals in late 1989, the new Goals 2000 program enacted by the Congress in 1994 articulated the federal role in this complex undertaking of developing a standards and results driven education system.

In many respects, this federal initiative undergirds the type of education reform described in the preceding chapters of this book. Although there are large problems to be resolved, tricky relationships to develop, and much hard work to be done, hopefully the Goals 2000 program, despite its shortcomings, can serve as the stimulus for the country to seriously engage in the process of accomplishing the nation's education goals for all its students. Even if only half the progress needed to fully implement the goals is made by the year 2000 that would represent a dramatic improvement of the nation's education system, it would prove to a skeptical country that progress can be made on such an ambitious education agenda, and it likely would stimulate the country to exert the additional effort to accomplish 100 percent of the goals.

Policy Implementation and Educational Change

Putting the approach to learning, the type of curriculum, the new form of school organization, the new roles for teachers and administrators and the new local, state, and federal policies described in the previous chapters into practice in local education systems will require large scale, fundamental change in what happens in typical classrooms and schools. This chapter discusses what is known about these processes of policy implementation and educational change. It has three sections.

Section one discusses the backward-mapping approach to policy development. The concept of backward-mapping was developed in the mid1970s as study after study identified problems with local implementation of federal and state categorical programs. Backward-mapping has been used as the conceptual rationale for sequencing the chapters in this book.

Section two reviews the evolution of educational policy implementation from the early 1960s to the late 1980s. It chronicles implementation from the difficult period in the 1960s as local districts struggled to implement new federal and state categorical programs, up to the surprisingly smooth implementation of the 1980s education reforms. Drawing on 25 years of implementation research (Odden, 1991a), this section argues that, despite lingering skepticism, most of today's new governmental programs can be implemented at the local level.

Section three reviews knowledge about the local educational change process and discusses our knowledge about how change in classroom practice occurs. The section first describes the consensus that developed in the mid1980s for single, focused change attempts such as altering a school's mathematics program. But section three admits that this knowledge is insufficient for the types of more fundamental restructuring needed to change the entire school organization as well as its overall curriculum program, what is essentially required by the 1990s education reforms discussed in the early chapters of this book. The latter portion of this section thus summarizes knowledge about this larger scale organizational change.

Elmore (1979–80) posits that there are two different approaches to policymaking: forward-mapping and backward-mapping. We remind the reader that in this book, we posit that policy is made by principals, central office staff, and superintendents as well as state and federal policymakers. Forward-mapping begins at the top of the system and emphasizes implementation of policies as conceived by policymakers. Implementation research largely has focused on this notion of policymaking. It asks the question: has the program as conceived in a state or federal capital been implemented at the local level in compliance with rules and regulations, and sometimes also in line with the "spirit" of the policy initiative. This perspective has dominated policy implementation research where, as section two of this chapter argues, there are two competing viewpoints: (1) conventional wisdom that policy implementation rarely occurs well at the local level (Pressman and Wildavsky, 1973, 1984), and (2) a new view that relatively complete policy implementation occurs overtime and today can be quite swift (Odden, 1991a; Peterson, Rabe, and Wong, 1986).

Backward-mapping is a bottom-up versus top-down strategy for policy development. It focuses much more on the issues and needs at the point in the system that is closest to the presenting problem and to how local response impacts the problem that led to the policy initiative. For example, the first chapters in this book would argue that a leading education problem is a low level of student performance and that the goal is to dramatically improve the achievement of all students (to master complex subject matter); the book also argues that a fundamental part of the problem is the current basic skills curriculum and that there is a need to replace it with a curriculum more focused on developing thinking and problem-solving expertise in the key content areas. The backward-mapping approach to addressing the problem would be to first identify the level of the organization where services to address the problem are actually delivered, which in public education would be classrooms and schools. It then would describe what is known about effective practice at those levels. Chapters 2 through 7, which address how students learn, the curriculum and assessment implications of that knowledge, and the implied new teacher and administrator roles to implement it, attempt this description for current education challenges. Only then does backward-mapping begin the policy development process by moving step by step up the educational system and asking each successive level what it can do to help implement the identified effective practices at the service delivery level. That is the objective for this and subsequent chapters of the book.

From a backward-mapping perspective, the goal is to have educational leaders, administrators, and policymakers think of what works in classrooms and schools as the beginning step for engaging in policymaking whether the focus of policy is at the school, district, state, or federal level. The questions to be asked are: (1) what can policy at the school, district, state, or federal level do to help create and sustain effective practices at the classroom and school site level and (2) what resources are needed to implement these practices? The hoped for result would be to impact positively the policy problem: better achievement for all students. Thus, the issue that would be addressed in education, at least from the perspective of this book, is what is needed to implement the type of high-involvement school organization and analytically oriented curriculum described in previous chapters, and what is the subsequent impact on students.

The next two sections carry through with both the forward-mapping and backward-mapping approaches to policy, the next section summarizing implementation research that reflects the former and the last section covering the local educational change process that reflects the latter.

THE EVOLUTION OF EDUCATION POLICY IMPLEMENTATION

When implementation research began to analyze local response to the 1960s "War on Poverty" programs, the findings were sobering. Most studies found misuse of governmental funds, services provided to the wrong clients, and in some cases, outright local resistance to these new governmental initiatives. Subsequently, a large body of implementation research emerged and essentially argued that federally (or state) initiated programs, for education or other social services, were doomed to failure because of local implementation resistance, and that the priorities, orientations, and pressures of local governments (school districts in the case of education) were simply at odds with those of higher level of governments (Derthick, 1976; Pressman and Wildavsky, 1973, 1984). These findings became "conventional wisdom" for several years and led to skepticism about the efficacy of the state education reform movement that began in 1983 with publication of *A Nation at Risk* and large numbers of subsequent state commission reports calling for major overhauls in the country's elementary and secondary schools.

Early Implementation Results

Jerome Murphy's (1971, 1991) study of the early implementation of Title I of the Elementary and Secondary Education Act (ESEA) is a widely cited article on this early stage of implementation. Murphy concluded that neither local, state, nor federal education bureaucrats had the capacity or the will to implement the Title I program, which required that extra services be provided to low-achieving students in low-income schools. The federal program violated local education norms because many local education leaders were generally opposed to treating some students differently than others. Many other local educators had never before created a categorical program that was to serve some but not all students and simply did not have the expertise to design and administer such a new educational arrangement. Other local educators had thought Title I was providing general not categorical financial assistance and simply used the funds for expanding services to all students. At that time, neither state education department officials nor staff in the US Office of Education were sufficient in numbers or expertise to monitor state and local compliance with federal program aims. Indeed, many of these individuals also had thought ESEA Title I was to be a program of general aid and believed it was "proper" to defer all decisions about design and implementation to states and local school districts, even if local officials made decisions ostensibly at odds with federal program intent (Murphy, 1971).

In short, the capacity and will at the local level was not conducive to faithful implementation, and Murphy found that implementation faltered on the shores of local resistance and conflict. One conclusion from this and other research with similar findings was that there was inevitable conflict between local orientations, values and priorities, and state or federally initiated programs. The conventional wisdom which developed from this genre of research held that higher level government programs simply did not work, that ongoing and continuous conflict was inevitable, and that local governments would never faithfully implement higher level government programs (Boyd, 1987; Pressman and Wildavsky, 1973).

Implementation: 1970 to 1980

But several subsequent implementation studies, largely ignored by adherents of the conventional wisdom and the initial critics of the 1980s state education reforms, provided evidence that policy implementation took place overtime and, in the 1980s, provided hope to some that state education reform initiatives might not be dashed by local implementation resistance. First, late 1970s studies showed that many of the categorical programs that experienced problematic implementation at the beginning of the 1970s were pretty well implemented by the end of that decade (Kirst and Jung, 1980; Odden, 1991b; Peterson, Rabe, and Wong, 1986, 1991). Second, while almost totally ignored by state education critics, several states in the early 1980s had enacted a variety of school improvement programs (Dougherty and Odden, 1982), often based on the then emerging effective teaching and schools research (Cohen, 1983), and studies showed that several of these early efforts had substantial impact on local school operations (Anderson et al., 1987). Fifteen years of implementation research began to show that implementation problems and findings changed overtime.

Kirst and Jung (1980) produced one of the first articles addressing education program implementation at this stage, focusing on Title I of ESEA. They concluded that the Title I implementation problems identified by the late 1960s and early 1970s research had essentially abated by the late 1970s. A combination of new rules and regulations that "tightened up" Title I, a political support system of interest groups, and Title I political "protectors" in the Congress helped overtime to shape a clear Title I program structure that helped solidify compliant implementation over the decade of the 1970s. By the close of the decade, Kirst and Jung found that local school districts not only had learned how to administer Title I in compliance with rules and regulations, but also had even begun to sanction the education priorities embodied in it.

Their claim was substantially strengthened by publication of a series of research studies in the early 1980s that investigated the state level interaction and local implementation of several similar federal and state categorical programs including compensatory education, special education, bilingual education, vocational education, and other civil rights rules and regulations (Knapp et al., 1983, 1991; Moore et al., 1983, 1991). These studies found, at both state and local levels, that the federal (and state) programs: (1) were being implemented in compliance with legislative intent and accompanying rules and regulations; (2) were providing extra services to students who needed them and who probably would not get them if the state and federal programs did not exist; (3) did not cause curriculum fragmentation in local schools and, in fact, allowed local educators to create a set of relatively integrated services for eligible students; and (4) while creating some extra paperwork were, in the minds of local educators, worthwhile because they provided needed extra services.

Shortly thereafter, Peterson, Rabe, and Wong (1986) produced an implementation book about this implementation stage that provided both a new theory of program implementation and empirical data for programs in education and for other functions to support the theory. Peterson et al. identified two types of higher level governmental programs, developmental and redistributive, and argued that the implementation process differed for each.

Developmental programs, such as community development, transportation, and, in education, curriculum, instruction, and vocational education, are those in which most local governments are involved anyway. Thus, federal and state policies in these areas tend to reinforce local initiatives and program priorities as well as provide extra resources for them, usually with marginal new program requirements. Based on several case studies of such programs, Peterson et al. showed that developmental programs typically get implemented fairly quickly and with a relatively uncontentious implementation process.

Redistributive programs, such as compensatory education, special education, and desegregation assistance in education, require local governments, school districts in the case of education, to engage in activities in which they had not been involved and to provide more service to some clients, students, than to others. Through an analysis of multiple case studies of a number of these programs, Peterson et al. (1991) concluded that redistributive programs experience a relatively contentious, initial implementation process but that, overtime, these programs also get fully implemented in compliance with legislative intent, rules, and regulations.

The important overall conclusion from stage two implementation research is that higher level government programs eventually get implemented at the local level, that the initial conflicts associated with redistributive programs get worked out overtime, and that the opportunity for bargaining ultimately produces a workable program for both parties.

These research results show that the nature of education policy implementation evolved over a 25-year time period. Stage one began with the expansion of intergovernmental grant programs in the 1960s and is characterized by early implementation problems and "inherent conflict" in federal (or state) initiated but locally implemented programs. Stage two, which began about a decade later, showed that programs ultimately get implemented, but through a mutual adaptation process.

Stage two includes implementation of the state education reforms of the 1980s, which are discussed next. Stage three began in the early 1980s with concern about the results of federal and state categorical programs. Rather than just focusing on implementation per se of new governmental programs, stage three focuses more on whether programs improve local education systems and increase student performance and achievement, including such current policy initiatives as major curriculum change, school restructuring, and now systemic reform. Stage three, thus, focuses more on the quality of policies and programs and addresses the nature of the local educational change process and is discussed in the last section of this chapter.

1980s Education Reform Implementation

The implementation pattern for the 1980s state education reforms reflected the pattern for Peterson, Rabe, and Wong's (1986) developmental programs. Despite skepticism (Boyd, 1987; Timar and Kirp, 1988), there was widespread and swift implementation of these reforms. The Consortium for Policy Research in Education (CPRE) studied implementation of early 1980s education reforms in six states (Fuhrman, Clune, and Elmore, 1988, 1991). Synthesizing earlier implementation research, they made several predictions about local implementation behaviors, largely based on conventional notions about implementation. Their findings, however, countered most of their major predictions. CPRE predicted that:

- Local response would vary, with some districts refusing to comply, others complying fully, and most "adapting" reforms to local goals and agendas.
- Local educators would more readily adopt policies that matched local capacity, i.e., technical expertise, and reject those that did not.
- There would be little short-term response, that it would take time for local educators to transform reform programs into local practice.
- The reforms themselves and local response would be more symbolic than substantive and that local educators would give more an appearance of change than meaningful change in students' experience.
- Local ownership would depend on the degree to which local educators were involved in the policymaking process, that low involvement would lead to little ownership and that little ownership would produce contentious implementation processes.
- Implementation success would be enhanced when reform programs sent clear signals about policy intent.

Instead, CPRE found that:

- Local response was remarkably uniform, with little apparent local resistance.
- There was little adaptation.
- Local response was swift. The reform programs were implemented in the short-term. It did not take several years to transform reform programs into local practice.
- Local response was substantive and not just symbolic and that many districts had begun to revamp local curriculum and instruction programs before state education reform began.
- Local involvement in the policy development process was not so impor-

tant in part because the reforms were developmental in nature. Educators rarely were involved in the reform development activities, but were active in designing policy responses to reform programs. The reforms seemed to reinforce educator engagement in curriculum and instruction change.

- Policy clarity was less critical than predicted. While some policies appeared more straightforward than others (increased student standards, for example), all policies had ambiguities and multiple meanings. Local districts coped nevertheless, responding to the spirit of nearly all policy elements. Local education leaders were able to take the various and disparate components of state education reform policies and weave them into an integrated local vision of new curriculum and instruction policy.

Odden and Marsh (1987) found similar results in a more comprehensive analysis of the implementation of California's 1983 education reform. In a broader review of several studies of education reform implementation, Murphy (1990b) came to the same conclusion. All studies seemed to show that state-sponsored education reform legitimated local initiative. Rather than resistance (predicted by the conventional wisdom), local response typified a developmental program and was characterized more by "strategic interaction" with state reform direction, both in responding to and affecting the content of state policy locally. Indeed, the studies found that many districts were "active users" of reform (Firestone, 1989), i.e., had begun reform initiatives before state programs were enacted and went beyond several state standards and requirements.

Problems with Program Effects

Beginning in the early 1980s, however, these more upbeat findings about program implementation were tempered by increasing evidence that while many programs had been fully implemented in compliance with rules and regulations, they appeared not to improve student performance very much. There was increasing evidence that while categorical programs had expanded services to special-need populations, the achievement levels of those students reflected few if any long-term improvements (Odden, 1991b). As these findings about minimal program impact began to emerge, another implementation conclusion that began to develop was that the issue was less about program implementation and more about program quality and impact (Elmore and McDonnell, 1991; Elmore and McLaughlin, 1981, 1983; McLaughlin, 1991b). Indeed, even though the first waves of the 1980s state education reforms, which were specifically designed to improve student performance, were swiftly implemented, they too appeared to have little impact on student achievement (Fuhrman and Associates, 1991).

While positive local response to program implementation was a step forward from conflict and resistance, the objective of government initiatives was to improve student learning. If teachers and administrators worked hard to faithfully implement new government initiatives, whether categorical programs for special-needs students or state education reforms designed to improve learning for all students, but student learning was unaffected, there was still an implementation (or policy) problem though not the conventional one of conflict and resistance.

Programs to Improve Achievement

In part as a response to the modest impacts of the first wave of 1980s state education reforms, a new series of policies were initiated in the late 1980s that included fundamental curriculum change, school restructuring, school-based management, and teacher empowerment (Murphy, Joseph, 1991; Murphy and Hallinger, 1993). Findings from implementation research on these initiatives also produced a set of sweet and sour results similar to those for the first wave of reforms.

California was one of the first states to publish curriculum frameworks that embodied a new vision of school curriculum (see Guthrie, Kirst, and Odden, 1991), stressing development of thinking and problem-solving skills within the content areas for all students. The frameworks represented a large departure from traditional school curriculum. Marsh and Odden (1991) found strong, positive local response to these California curriculum initiatives. Their study also found substantial change in district, school, and classroom practice. Districts adopted the California mathematics and science curriculum frameworks as the curricular visions for their education systems. Schools took the broad frameworks and wove them into more specific mathematics and science programs for the site. Within classrooms, teachers covered new mathematics and science topics, used new textbooks that reflected the frameworks, were beginning to use a variety of manipulatives in mathematics and "hands-on" laboratory/project activities in science, and incorporated new teaching strategies such as inquiry methods, cooperative learning, and teaching for understanding. The study did not cover a sufficiently long enough time period to document the full degree of change in teacher practice, but the evidence of change in practice was nevertheless impressive. The findings provided evidence to suggest that state-initiated curriculum reform could penetrate districts, schools, and classrooms in substantial ways, far beyond what some had predicted about the efficacy of curriculum reforms (Atkin and House, 1981; Kirst and Meister, 1985).

Alongside these more upbeat conclusions about curriculum reform, however, was a subsequent, more indepth study of curriculum implementation that came to somewhat more pessimistic but not necessarily conflicting conclusions. Over several months and years, a research team led by David Cohen and Penelope Peterson (1990) observed teachers in several California classrooms attempting to implement the California mathematics curriculum framework. They too found strong local acceptance of these visions of curriculum change, as well as considerable change in classroom practice. But Cohen and Peterson concluded that teachers had not understood the full meaning of the nature of the curriculum change embodied in the frameworks and, rather than restructuring their mathematics program, had grafted a set of new strategies onto their battery of traditional classroom practices, thus only partially implementing the intent of the new curriculum. Their longer term observations on classroom practice enabled them to move beyond the initial findings of the Marsh and Odden study to point out a new, deeper, and more complex aspect of curriculum reform—that considerably more teacher learning was needed in order to produce full and complete implementation of the new curriculum reflected in the California frameworks.

These findings were particularly salient because by the time the results were published, the National Council of Teachers of Mathematics (1989) had published their new mathematics curriculum standards, which were similar in vision to that in the California frameworks. Further, the national education goals had been agreed to by the President and the nation's governors. Several other initiatives had been inaugurated to develop new curriculum standards in several core-content areas (Lewis, 1990). And states had launched a systemic reform strategy that was based on ambitious student achievement goals and high-quality curriculum standards (Fuhrman, 1993b).

The Cohen and Peterson findings suggested that putting such a new curriculum in place was an ambitious challenge but that the problem was not one of resistance and conflict, but of teacher expertise and learning. Teachers and administrators liked the curriculum embodied in the California frameworks; they felt they represented professional, state-of-the-art visions of good school curriculum. Both the Marsh and Odden, and Cohen and Peterson studies showed that teachers would engage in nearly all opportunities for professional development to learn the content in the new curriculum and the pedagogical strategies needed to teach it. Both studies showed that teachers altered classroom practice as a result. But Cohen and Peterson showed that substantially more change in classroom practice was needed, that much more teacher professional development was needed, and that even after several years of hard work, the new frameworks were being only partially implemented.

Research on other aspects of the second wave of education reform, such as school restructuring (Marsh and Crocker, 1991; Murphy, Joseph, 1991; Murphy & Hallinger, 1993; Prestine, 1994), teacher empowerment and professionalism (McDonnell, 1991), and school-based management (Wohlstetter and Odden, 1992) also concluded that implementation, while often uncontentious, was nevertheless partial and produced modest if any impacts on student learning. As the studies mounted in number, it began to become clear that the nature of the implementation problem in the 1990s had changed.

It was no longer sufficient to ask whether schools could implement program X or program Y. The issue was how to transform schools into high-performance organizations, defining high performance as developing advanced cognitive capabilities for all students. These are the types of educational results embodied in the Goals 2000 program enacted by the Congress in early 1994. Professional initiatives outside the school, such as those embodied in the curriculum standards promulgated by the National Council of Teachers of Mathematics (1989) and being developed by other professional bodies (Lewis, 1990) undergird these governmental pressures to dramatically change school organization and curriculum. Indeed, the previous chapters in this book have argued that schools must dramatically change their curriculum, organization, professional development, and leadership and that political leaders must change policy in order to create schools that can develop the high levels of advanced expertise required by the country's education goals.

Responding effectively to these challenges requires an understanding of implementation that is more sophisticated than old claims of ongoing conflict and resistance, and broader than just developing the knowledge to implement a new curriculum program, difficult as that objective is. Not only does such an understanding of implementation need to focus on the issue as one of individual and system learning, but also it must address the nature of a local change process within school organizations that can create the expertise needed simultaneously to restructure school organizations and curriculum programs along the lines suggested in previous chapters. The next section of the chapter addresses this broader need.

THE EDUCATIONAL CHANGE PROCESS

Altering classroom and school practice is produced through a more local, microimplementation process usually referred to as a local change process. This section addresses two approaches to effecting local educational change: (1) one focused on putting "innovations" into place in a school or district, and (2) another concerned with fundamentally transforming all aspects of a school, from its organization and management, to its entire curriculum and instruction program.

The Innovation Orientation

In the mid-1980s, a rough consensus began to emerge about the key elements of the local change process for implementing and institutionalizing innovations. Innovations usually were single programs such as a new writing program, an effective teaching project, a career education initiative, or an approach to student discipline. Overviews by several individuals, including Fullan (1982, 1985, 1991), the Dissemination Study Supporting Local School Improvement (DESSI) by Crandall and Associates (1982), Huberman and Miles (1984), Crandall, Eiseman, and Louis (1986), Odden and Marsh (1989), McLaughlin (1991a) and Miles (1993), identified remarkably similar key factors associated with an effective local change process for these types of programs. Eight factors seemed to be critical.

1. *Ambitious efforts were better.* Ambitious efforts had more impact on classroom change than did either narrowly focused projects or projects to change the entire local education structure. Ambitious efforts also were effective in stimulating teacher interest, engagement, and involvement.
2. *The microimplementation/change process was key.* The specific change processes were more important than the type of change pursued, geographical location, or ethnic characteristics of districts or schools. How a change effort was conducted was more important than what it was, where it was attempted, or for whom it was attempted.
3. *High-quality, proven-effective programs worked better.* Research-based programs with a track record of success produced more outcome success than locally created programs. This finding was somewhat different from the

RAND conclusion that local, teacher developed materials were important (Berman and McLaughlin, 1974–78). Subsequent studies (e.g., Huberman and Miles, 1984) showed that externally developed programs that had been shown by research to be effective for a particular problem could be "exported" to other districts and, with modest tailoring at the margins to the new local context, could be effective in the new setting. Indeed, one risk local program development took was in creating a program that did not work.

4. *Top-down initiation could work.* While the RAND change agent study (Berman and McLaughlin, 1974–1978) suggested that bottom-up initiation seemed to work better, Huberman and Miles (1984), for example, showed that top-down initiated efforts not only could work, but actually were successful in more instances than bottom-up initiated change efforts. Yin and White (1984) also found that top-down initiated efforts to install microcomputer systems reached more advanced implementation stages than did bottom-up initiated efforts. In a reassessment of RAND findings 10 years later, McLaughlin (1991) agreed with this conclusion. It seemed that top administrators more often were able to involve teachers and obtain their commitment than teachers were able to involve top administrator and obtain their commitment, and both administrator and teacher commitment were needed for implementation success. Top-down success was conditional, though. Top-down "worked" only if a proven-effective program was adopted, if top adoption was followed by teacher involvement in designing implementation strategies, and if intensive ongoing assistance was provided to teachers in classrooms and schools (see also Fullan [1985, 1991] and Purkey and Smith [1985]).

   These postRAND findings seemed to sanction district initiation, leadership, and orchestration of curriculum change efforts. Beginning with the DESSI study, district leadership and direction were resurrected, to overstate the case, as a key factor in successful change efforts. These findings, it turned out, emboldened district leaders across the country who saw from this research a more proactive role for administrative leadership.

5. *Central office support and commitment, as well as site-administrator support, commitment, and knowledge were needed.* These factors are somewhat different from initiation, leadership, and orchestration. Nearly all studies found that administration commitment at the beginning, middle, and late implementation stages, was important for successful implementation and institutionalization. Administrators pass new policies (which can support the change effort), allocate money, time, and personnel resources, schedule activities, and conduct an entire array of administrative functions that can help or hinder the change process. Without district and site-administrator support throughout the change effort, successful implementation was hindered.

6. *Teacher participation, especially in designing implementation strategies, mattered.* Teacher involvement usually occurred through a variety of "cross-role" teams of teachers, site administrators, central office curriculum staff, and central office line staff. Teacher involvement helped engage teachers in the overall change effort, provided key teacher input into designing the spe-

cific implementation strategies that would be used, and helped to develop teacher commitment to the change effort.

7. *Extensive, ongoing, intensive training and classroom-specific assistance was critical.* At the initial stages, training could emphasize awareness or some specific component of new knowledge or expertise needed for implementation. Ongoing assistance included a variety of actions such as concrete, teacher-specific help, classroom assistance from local staff, teacher observation of similar efforts in different classrooms, schools, or districts, and regular project meetings to sort out practical problems. Assistance also included coaching with feedback, a key to successful classroom change (Joyce and Showers, 1988). Ongoing assistance was the sine qua non for effective implementation when change in classroom practice was needed to put a new program into place. All studies, including RAND and post-RAND studies, documented the importance of this factor.

8. *Teacher commitment also was critical.* Few successful change efforts reached advanced stages unless teacher commitment to the project was developed. The RAND study concluded that teacher commitment must be built "up-front," before implementation began by involving teachers in identifying the change focus, in selecting the change program, and in developing materials. The argument was that this initial involvement developed teacher commitment to the change program itself. Guskey (1986) and Huberman and Miles (1984) expanded this conventional wisdom. They and other postRAND research found that teacher commitment could also emerge at the end of the implementation cycle when teachers gained mastery over the professional expertise needed to implement the new program and saw that the program improved student performance. This research suggested that teacher commitment came after mastery and after teachers saw that the program "worked". In her reanalysis, McLaughlin also agreed that "belief (i.e., commitment) could follow practice."

While the findings of the initial RAND study and the innovation-focused research seemed in conflict, they differed only at the margins. First, all studies identified teacher commitment as necessary to successful educational change efforts. At the time of the RAND study, there were very few high-quality, proven-effective programs so teacher up-front involvement in identifying topics to work on and in developing materials was crucial to initiating change efforts. But RAND also found that teacher skills mastery and positive program effects on students were necessary for complete implementation and institutionalization.

There also were two different kinds of commitment: commitment to try the new program and commitment to the new program. Commitment to try the new program needed to be developed upfront; without it, teachers would not become engaged in trying to implement the program. This type of commitment was probably built through awareness sessions on what the program was and in responding to teachers' personal concerns about how the program might affect them individually. Commitment to the program usually emerged at the end of the implementation process as teachers developed the expertise needed to implement the new program and saw that it, indeed, resolved the problem to which it was applied, i.e., that it "worked."

McLaughlin (1991a) raised two other issues concerning aspects of effective local implementation practices. First, she recommended less of a focus on policy implementation per se, which had been the traditional focus, and more of a focus on actions, from whatever source, designed to improve classroom practice—the behavioral change that must occur before most educational innovations (such as curriculum reform) can be effective. As the beginning sections of this chapter argued, we agree with this perspective.

Second, McLaughlin suggested that using teacher professional networks might be a powerful strategy for accomplishing the goal of enhancing classroom practice. She hinted that the usual formal mechanisms of district or county staff development and training related to policy implementation often are unconnected to the formal and informal networks in which teachers participate on a day-to-day basis and from which they develop professional norms focused on expanding professional expertise. She argued that getting inside these networks, whether they are the department structures of secondary schools or informal activities from participating in activities external to the school, offer high potential for enhancing teachers' professional classroom practice and expertise. Chapter 4 agreed with these recommendations and took them even further.

The above consensus around the local change process, though, was developed for "innovations," i.e., relatively focused change efforts that entailed putting a single new program into practice, such as a hands-on science curriculum, a school improvement program, an effective teaching program, a career education program, and even a parent involvement program. This research consensus tended not to derive from efforts to change the fundamental organization of the school or to alter the curriculum for *all* subject areas. Although the innovations attempted were individually ambitious and difficult to implement fully, the goal nevertheless generally was to incorporate them into the regular school program.

Large Scale Organizational Change

Little's (1993) discussion of the type of professional development required for the demands of today's education reforms provides a good argument by analogy for suggesting that such reforms also require a fundamental new and more ambitious approach to the local educational change process. Little argued that while good training was appropriate for many change efforts of the past, it was insufficient for the more grandiose changes entailed in the types of education reform described in the earlier chapters of this book. Schools are being asked to change their entire curriculum program, administer a new performance-based student assessment system, restructure their organization and management system, take on through high involvement several management and control activities previously performed by central office staff, and potentially incur a change in the way they are compensated, if not putting some of their compensation "at risk" to performance incentives. These are monumental—widespread, deep, fundamental—changes. They require simultaneous changes in roles, the nature of work tasks, and organizational norms, as well the more technical but nevertheless sweeping changes in the curriculum and instruction program. Just as the professional development needed to implement these changes is different, so also must the change process itself be different from that which was sufficient for putting one new program in place.

Fullan (1985) began raising these questions as the consensus around the more focused local change process began in the mid 1980s to be applied to schoolwide improvement projects. He wondered if attempts to improve schools as organizations needed a more ambitious and differently structured change strategy than that developed for changing a single curriculum program or implementing an effective teaching program. He echoed these hesitancies in his early 1990s update of research on the change process (Fullan, 1991). But shortly thereafter he stated firmly and directly that the depth of education reform contemplated for the 1990s simply required a new and more grandiose change strategy (Fullan, 1993). His most recent argument (Fullan, 1993: vii) is that "we are at the beginning of a new phase [of the educational change process] which will represent a quantum leap—a paradigm breakthrough—in how we think about and act in relation to change." We agree with this new perspective.

Mohrman (1994) argues that the dynamics of such pervasive and deep organizational change, entails four interrelated segments:

- Recognizing the need for fundamental change.
- Forming an organizational strategy to respond.
- Redesigning the work and structure of the organization.
- Implementing the design, assessing impacts, and refining and changing overtime.

Mohrman's four components incorporate the more detailed suggestions of several other authors (Beer, Eisenstat, and Spector, 1990b; Fullman, 1993). The remainder of this chapter discusses these four components in more detail.

Mobilizing Understanding of the Need For and Developing the Commitment to Engage in Fundamental Change. Creating the type of pervasive and deep change required by the sweep of current education reforms is exceedingly difficult. It requires individuals to dramatically alter their professional behavior. Such change requires a shedding of old assumptions, roles, and professional practices, and engaging in the hard, uncertain, and effortful process of creating new roles, learning skills, and competencies to engage in new behaviors, and developing and then working according to a new set of norms and values.

Few individuals want to engage voluntarily in this type of awesome change. The journey is simply too difficult, the endpoint too unknown, and often the rewards to meager. Indeed, the landscape of school reform is littered with many partial and abandoned large scale reform efforts (Fullan, 1993). One reason for these failed efforts has been lack of clarity about the goals of the proposed reform; indeed, many restructuring efforts have been initiated under the assumption that goals would emerge from the simple process of engaging in restructuring. But the research shows that such nonclearly guided restructuring efforts often fail to find a clear direction and tend to avoid engagement in the complex issues of changing the curriculum program in ways that would produce high levels of student learning (Easton, 1991; Fullan, 1993; Prestine,

1994; Wehlage, Smith, and Lipman, 1992; Weiss, 1992), which is the goal of the education reform suggested by this book.

Although more of the 1990s restructuring efforts have begun to address curriculum and instruction (Murphy and Hallinger, 1993), an important issue still is whether a deep enough understanding of the need to change has been created to sustain the long-term efforts required to produce the comprehensive education system changes described in the first 10 chapters of this book. As Mohrman (1994) puts it, the first step in the large-scale organizational change process is to have the participants recognize the need for deep, fundamental organizational change. Beer, Eisenstat, and Spector (1990a, 1990b) suggest that the first step in an effective change process is to mobilize commitment to fundamental change through a joint diagnosis of the problem. In education, the question therefore becomes: What is the problem to which the deep and fundamental reforms argued for in this book are directed. The answer we have been arguing is low-student achievement, and the need to produce much higher levels of advanced learning for *all* students.

However, as Chapter 1 described, there is a large contingent within education that believes the education system is as good as it has ever been, and that while improvements are needed, wholesale restructuring is not necessarily required (Bracey, 1991, 1992, 1993). The previous chapters in the book have argued, however, that major education reform is needed and that in order to produce high levels of new learning for all students, major transformations are required in understanding how students learn advanced cognitive skills, in reformulating the entire curriculum program, in changing to a more decentralized, high-involvement managed school organization, and in creating new roles for both teachers and administrators. But in order to believe sufficiently in the need for these dramatic changes, one must believe that there is a deep, fundamental, and pervasive problem with the way current schools are organized and structured, and the low-level student achievement results they produce, in order to push forward to create new and different school organizations.

In the private sector, according to Mohrman (1994), Lawler (1992), and Beer, Eisenstat, and Spector (1990b), pressures to engage in fundamental change derive from the environment and international competition. Corporations and work teams within them either understand that in order to stay in business, they must deliver services or make products that are better and lower priced, or they quickly lose market share and are forced out of business. Those authors would note that numerous corporations that were members of the Fortune 500 thirty years ago do not exist today, and that the bulk of those that remain have engaged in fundamental restructuring, such as AT & T, the Ford Motor Company, GE and Hewlett Packard, to name a few successful examples.

The issue in education is what can create a similarly strong pressure to urge educators to engage in the deep and fundamental school transformation efforts we argue are needed. One possibility is simply clear and ambitious signals from the policy community, such as those embodied in Goals 2000. Another possibility is creation of new performance assessments, that indicate what students know and can do but calibrated to world class standards (Finn,

1991a; Resnick, 1992–93). Kentucky is trying this approach with its new KIRIS student testing system as has California with its new CLAS student performance assessment system. In both states, only small proportions of students are performing at proficiency levels in any subject. In response, there has been pressure to reduce the demands of the test as well as efforts to accelerate school reform to produce higher levels of student learning. The unknown in both states is the degree to which policymakers will continue to support the higher expectations required by these assessments and whether the low scores will induce parents to pressure schools to get their children's performance up to the high standards of the tests.

Another possible strategy for creating external pressure for school reform has been school choice, both public school choice such as provided in Minnesota and other states (Odden and Kotowski, 1992a), charter schools (Wohlstetter, 1994), as well as vouchers (Chubb and Moe, 1990). While not taking a position on any of these proposals, we simply note that one of their rationales is to motivate schools to higher performance.

An additional nominee for building the pressure to dramatically change schools, argued both by Fullan (1993) and others (e.g., Sizer, 1992), is to create teams of teachers who have a moral passion to change schools to higher performing organizations, that produce high levels of thoughtful learning for all students.

What combination of strategies is sufficient to create a high level of external pressure for school change is not known. The first chapters of this book have tried to develop a rationale for why such change is needed. It may or may not be convincing. The chapters certainly show that achievement is low, that achievement differs across income, family, ethnic, and gender lines, and that advanced cognitive capabilities are needed for the evolving work environment. These arguments could be sufficient to induce some schools to engage in fundamental restructuring.

Whatever external pressure for change exists, an important step in the site change process is to devise mechanisms that involve wide numbers of teachers and administrators in diagnosing the education problem on which their education reform will focus. As this process unfolds, we would hope that the signals from the country's new education policy in Goals 2000, which sets high levels of advanced learning for all students as the national goal, as well as from increasing number of state systemic reform efforts (Pechman and Laguarda, 1993), would lead them to understand that current student achievement levels fall short of these goals and that to accomplish these ambitious objectives, the widespread change in curriculum, school organization, new roles, and government policies described in previous chapters, or similar sets of pervasive and deep change in schools, would be required.

Forming an Organizational Strategy to Respond. After diagnosing the problem, Mohrman (1994) suggests that the next step is determining an organizational strategy for responding to the problem. In previous times when the environment was relatively stable, a traditional hierarchical organizational response was adequate. Top level management could devise solutions and gradually change the organization. But in today's rapidly changing environment, most analysts have concluded that such an organizational structure tends to be more of an obstacle to fast-paced, large scale change and suggest a more decentralized, team-driven organizational response (Beer, Eisenstat, and Spector, 1990b; Fullan, 1993; Hammer and Champy, 1993; Katzenbach and Smith, 1993, Lawler, 1986; 1992).

Fullan and Miles (1992) state that the type of fundamental change envisioned for education reform today requires management which is best done by crossfunctional teacher and administrator decision-making teams, not by the formal management team of the district or school. In the private sector, Beer, Eisenstat, and Spector (1990a, 1990b) concluded that redesigning the workplace through crossfunctional workteams also appeared to be the most successful strategy. Fullan (1993) implied this type of new organization by several stipulations in his eight key lessons for fundamental education reform. He talked about teacher workgroups developing shared visions that would guide their organizational change efforts, about putting the control function into self-regulating workteams who through problem solving and decision making would devise their own solutions, and argued for both strong bottom-up and top-down pressures for change. Fullan (1993) cited Senge (1990) often, and Senge too argued for the efficacy of self-regulated work teams.

All of these aspects of organizations are included in the high-involvement approach to management (Chapter 6 and Lawler, 1992; Mohrman, 1994). High involvement is a change from a bureaucratic hierarchy to a more participative way of working. It entails creating work teams that have full responsibility for delivering a service or making a product. The goal of high-involvement management is to increase the commitment of employees to organizational performance (high levels of student learning), to give employees (teachers and administrators) the strategies, tools, knowledge, and skills to improve organizational performance, and to shift the control activity from the hierarchy to the self-managed work teams.

The essence of high involvement is to decentralize decision making to workteams actually providing services, teachers in schools, and through a variety of mechanisms (such as providing access to information and investing heavily in training) to help them make good decisions, and then hold them accountable for results. Again, research from both school (Fullan and Miles, 1992; Fullan, 1993; Smylie, 1994) and nonschool settings (Beer, Eisenstat, and Spector, 1990a; Katzenbach and Smith, 1993; Lawler, 1986, 1992) concludes that this is the most effective way to organize for functions such as education for which the work is complex, is best done collegially, and exists in a changing environment (see also Mohrman, Lawler, and Mohrman, 1992).

Under a high-involvement approach, which this book outlined and argued for in Chapter 6, power, knowledge, information, and rewards would be decentralized to school sites. The decentralization of these resources would set the stage for allowing a variety of teacher decision-making teams to engage in the process of diagnosing the problem and then redesigning the school organization, the curriculum and instruction program in it, and the nature of teacher work in order to accomplish the system goals of educating students to new, higher levels.

Both Odden and Odden (1994) and Wohlstetter, Smyer, and Mohrman

(1994) show how the high-involvement approach can be accomplished in the school setting. Schools in Victoria, Australia have numerous teacher decision-making teams for the overall curriculum program, for each individual curriculum-content area, for subschools and grade levels, for student discipline and welfare, and for school operations and administrative matters; each team actually makes decisions for these areas and usually has a budget as well (Odden and Odden, 1994).

Redesigning the Work and Structure of the Organization. A critical task of teacher workteams under a high-involvement management strategy is to redesign the work that takes place within schools (Smylie, 1994), as well as the structure of the school as an organization. As indicated above, a beginning step in this redesign process would be developing a joint understanding of the nature of the performance problem that they are addressing. Thus, both before deciding to engage in large scale change and after setting up a new organizational design for doing so, school-based teacher and administrator teams would need to engage in the collaborative process of determining the nature of the student learning problem that their particular school needs to confront.

Since agreeing on addressing a fundamental problem is contingent at least in part on being aware that something can be done about the problem, an aspect of this initial joint diagnosis process would be visiting other places that have identified similar problems as well as designed effective strategies to remedy them. Indeed, the beginning stages of private sector change processes are replete with visits to other companies and subunits within them to see a different way of doing business (Mohrman, 1994; Senge, 1990). Within education, this component of the change process is beginning to gain some acceptability. One of the first activities of new faculties joining the Coalition of Essential Schools is to visit other Coalition Schools to see the new program in action; this cross visiting often is done in the Accelerated Schools program as well.

An additional component of this "seeing it done differently" phase would include visiting classrooms in which teachers were successfully implementing teaching strategies according to the precepts of the cognitive approach to learning. Research on teacher learning has concluded that having teachers actually see teachers teaching in a fundamentally different way is a key ingredient for inducing many teachers to engage in the process of shedding their former way of instruction and engaging in the hard work of constructing a new set of pedagogical strategies suitable to teaching for understanding (Cohen and McLaughlin, 1993).

These steps are important because the objective of this stage of the restructuring change process is to have individuals understand that the nature of the student learning problem is so problematic that, in order to improve it, teachers individually and collectively will need to be willing to challenge existing professional practices and create new ones. In a sense, according to Mohrman (1994), this means shedding what had given one a sense of professional identity as well as personal and organizational satisfaction, and working hard to create a new professional persona. Seeing real examples of what that new identity could be helps to move individuals through this difficult stage of the large scale organizational change process.

But as Mohrman (1994) and many others note (e.g., Fullan, 1993), this stage can produce resistance, considerable negativism, uncertainty, the identification of problems, and disagreements. The existence of a student learning problem and the need for substantial education reform must be agreed to; as Chapter 1 showed, not all educators accept that premise. The question of "can all students learn to high levels" must be answered with substantive soundness; and as Chapter 3 discussed, outdated understandings of intelligence question whether all students can learn to high levels, and research on teacher learning finds that many teachers believe that advanced cognitive ability is attainable only by the "bright" student (Cohen and McLaughlin, 1993; Prawat and Jennings, 1994). Even less complex change efforts can experience resistance and questioning—how does this innovation impact me—in the early stages (Huberman and Miles, 1984). Unless these issues, problems, and concerns are recognized and dealt with in some way, making progress on the pathway of deep and fundamental educational change is difficult. At the same time, the predictability of initial problems should give faith to those orchestrating a substantial process that progress can be made despite the initial choppy waters.

After development of a shared understanding of the problem, becoming aware of alternative ways of addressing the problem, and dealing with predictable resistance, school-based teacher teams then need to begin constructing a vision of the kind of school organization they would like to create. This vision would include the nature of the curriculum and instruction program, the organization of students and the work of teaching and learning, and the organizational design of the new school. Mohrman (1994), Fullan (1993) and Beer, Eisenstat, and Spector (1990b) argue that this new vision must be a creation of decentralized work teams, not of any central management team.

This notion of the decentralized, high-involvement approach to change is different from the vision directed change described in many recent literature (Bennis and Nanus, 1985; Deal and Peterson, 1990; Manassee, 1984; Nanus, 1992; Peters and Waterman, 1992; Rutherford, 1985; Sergiovanni, 1984). The specific vision must be created by the work team, i.e., the faculty in a school for education. The goal to accomplish can be set externally, either by the policy system (Fullan 1993) or for businesses through competition (Lawler, 1986, 1992), but the vision for addressing the solution to the problem has to be crafted by the work team itself, which means teachers and administrators in schools must design their own new school.

Fullan, Beer, Eisenstat, and Spector, and Mohrman further conclude that the vision should not be viewed as full or complete or unalterable overtime. Indeed, at this point for both schools and many private sector organizations, there rarely are "proven-effective programs" that work teams could adopt; the visions and new programs must be constructed more than adopted or adapted from other contexts. While faculty work teams need to draw both on their experience and professional knowledge during this phase, the vision created should be viewed as tentative, as something with high potential that will be tried, but that likely will need to be redesigned and modified more than once overtime.

Currently, there are many examples of teams trying to create visions of high-performing school organizations. The Coalition of Essential Schools,

Accelerated Schools, and Developmental Schools are three examples discussed in Chapter 6. Groups around the country in nearly a dozen states designing charter schools comprise another example of this effort. The Edison Project of the Whittle Corporation, the New American Schools Development Corporation efforts to create "break-the-mold" schools, and Education Alternatives which is managing several schools in Baltimore, Maryland, and Dade County, Florida represent several private sector attempts to create new visions of schools. Each one of these examples use time, teachers, technology, and other school resources differently than most traditional schools. Reports on elementary schools (California Department of Education, 1992a), middle schools (Carnegie Council on Adolescent Development, 1989; Superintendent's Advisory Task Force on Middle Schools, 1989) and high schools (California Department of Education, 1992b) also provide alternative visions of effective schools. Miles (1994) also shows how teacher resources could be used very differently and more effectively in urban schools. Only time will tell whether these efforts or models actually produce new and higher levels of student learning, but they nevertheless represent concrete attempts to create new visions for elementary, middle, and secondary schools.

We would hope teacher teams engaged in developing new school visions would incorporate the type of curriculum and instruction program outlined in Chapter 4 in this vision creation phase. As Project 2061 has shown (American Association for the Advancement of Science, 1991), there are many different ways to design a curriculum to create thinking and problem-solving skills in the key content areas, so no template is implied by Chapter 4.

In addition to the curriculum and instruction program, a critical part of this vision setting task is redesigning the organizational pieces of the overall structure of the school. As Fullan and Miles (1992) and Fullan (1993) stated, work teams need to take a systemic approach at this point and redesign curriculum, teaching, staff development, structure, policy, and culture altogether. Smylie (1994) sees the task as fundamental "reinvention" of work roles, responsibilities, authority relationships, and technical tasks and activities. Mohrman (1994) agrees and is specific about what redesigning the school organization entails; she suggests it means redesigning six important aspects of the organization.

First, teams need to redesign the core technology of the organization, i.e., the process by which raw materials are transformed into outputs. In education, this means redesigning the curriculum, teaching, and learning process. It could include substantial use of microcomputer technologies. It could entail team teaching or differentiated staffing (Odden and Odden, 1994). It could entail longer or different school days and years (National Commission on Time and Learning, 1994). It would include attention to how students and teachers are grouped and how teacher time is used (Miles, 1994) and student time is spent. Again, the various school redesign efforts discussed above have been engaged in this process.

Second, attention would need to be given to the organizational structure of the school. This design effort concerns how work tasks would be put into organizational units, and what the coordinating and communicating mechanisms would be to help the organization function. Decentralized, high-involvement managed organizations generally place all functions within a self-managing work group, and give the group responsibility for providing the full array of services or making the complete product. In the private sector, this often means creating work teams with workers up and down the assembly line, and including design, engineering, manufacturing, sales, and marketing individuals in the same work team.

For education, this would include decentralizing several central office functions, such as professional development, curriculum development, textbook selection, student scheduling, personnel recruiting and selecting, etc. to each school site. Within the school, teams of teachers could then be created and given the responsibility to provide all school services for a group of students, including instruction in the content areas, guidance counseling, disciplining, and coordinating social services if they were required. This is the notion of the "house" in the Coalition School. Such a way of organizing teacher work would require individuals to posses a much broader array of knowledge and skills, including a willingness to take responsibility for all the learning needs of children under their responsibility.

Third, work teams also would need to work on new cultural norms and values. A decentralized, high-involvement managed school would be characterized by a new organization, new work processes and new behaviors for both teachers and administrators; Chapters 6 and 7 identified many of these changes. Cultural norms and values would need to change to support these new behaviors. A belief that all children can achieve at high levels would characterize such a school. Norms of collegiality, shared decision-making, continuous improvement, and high quality would need to be created. Values related to constructivist learning, multiple correct answers, engagement in real problems, and doing academic work for a purpose would need to be sanctioned. Letting teacher work teams actually make decisions reflects another norm, and articulating the principal role as helping others make good decisions would be another. In short, such a school organization would be characterized along a new set of norms, beliefs, and values, and these would need to be identified, articulated, and explicitly developed and modeled over time.

Fourth, teams would need to develop new information sharing and decision-making processes. High-involvement managed organizations are characterized by decentralized, shared, and participative decision-making, usually through a wide variety of both horizontal and vertical decision-making (not just advisory) teams. Odden and Odden (1994) discovered rich and multiple examples of such teams in the decentralized system in Victoria, Australia, and Wohlstetter, Smyer, and Mohrman (1994, forthcoming) found a similarly wide array of teacher decision-making teams in more advanced site-based managed schools in North America. Teams are keys to improving performance in the private sector as well (Katzenbach and Smith, 1993).

Fifth, therefore, Mohrman (1994) states that a high-involvement organization will need a new type of worker, i.e., teacher. Since many central office functions would be decentralized to schools, faculty would need to be multiskilled, not only in curriculum and instruction but also in staff development, curriculum development, assessment and monitoring, running decision-making teams, etc. Further, in a Coalition School for example, faculty would need to have multidisciplinary skills. Individuals in decentrally managed schools also would need good team and collegial skills, willingness to continually engage in skill development and expansion, and commitment to taking responsibility for school impacts on student learning.

Sixth, thus, the entire human resource system of such a school would need to be redesigned. The selection and hiring process would need to focus on hiring individuals with the above skills and include teachers centrally in the recruitment and selection processes (Lawler, 1992). Teacher participation in recruitment and selection would be the norm for a high involvement organized school.

Training and professional development would need to be viewed as a core program of the school and provided on a continuous, ongoing basis. Professional development would need to focus not only on curriculum and instructional skills, but also on team skills, breadth skills (for the decentralized central office functions), and the business skills needed for running the management, control and fiscal functions entailed with decentralized school operations. As argued in Chapter 4, such training would need to be long-term and structured in a variety of new ways—summer institutes, teacher networks, and other intensive mechanisms schools might develop. As a guideline, schools could consider setting aside 2 to 4 percent of their annual budget for ongoing training.

Schools and the education system also should consider a substantial investment in training as part of the regular, annual budget. As the research on implementing just the new curriculum embodied in several state new frameworks has shown, successful implementation will require several years and will need to be accompanied by large scale and long-term training (Ball et al., 1994a, 1994b, 1994c). Moreover, curriculum and instruction knowledge is not static; as new information and strategies are learned, they too must infiltrate professional practice. That can only occur through commitment to ongoing training.

Finally, research on decentralized, high-involvement management is finding that schools which focus training on the entire faculty experience more successful school restructuring (Odden and Odden, 1994; Wohlstetter, Smyer, and Mohrman, 1994). Put differently, professional development should not be viewed as an individualistic activity in which teachers engage on just a voluntary basis. As Fullan (1993) notes, each professional in a high-performance school needs to view themselves as a change agent. For teacher decision-making teams to be effective, all members of the team must have sufficient knowledge and skills in order to make good decisions. Further, if curriculum reform is to be a schoolwide phenomenon, then all faculty in the school must be able to teach a thinking-oriented curriculum effectively. In short, training should be viewed as a schoolwide activity in which all individuals in the school are heavily involved.

The compensation system also would need to move towards one that bases individual salary on knowledge and skills; schools might also experience with lump sum bonuses based on school as well as subschool team performance (see Lawler, 1990, 1992; Mohrman, Mohrman, and Odden, forthcoming; Odden and Conley, 1992). Changing current salary schedules to these new forms requires major change in design, finance, and politics. Yet, such a new form of compensation fits with a high-involvement management system. Also, as states begin to license teachers on the basis of a beginning set of knowledge and skills, and the National Board for Professional Teaching Standards certifies expert teachers on the same basis, there will be the technical tools for assessing knowledge and skills from beginning to advanced status. This would facilitate implementing such a new approach to educator pay. The Teacher Compensation Project of the Consortium for Policy Research, the National Education Association, the American Federation of Teachers, and the National Board for Professional Teaching Standards is investigating how such a new approach to salary could be accomplished in education.

Each of these six aspects of reorganizing the structure of a school is a complex and major undertaking. But combined they identify the issues that need to be worked on as a school would move to a decentralized, shared decision-making form of operation. Moreover, as both Fullan (1993) and Mohrman (1994) argue, these issues would need to be worked on simultaneously. Mohrman (1994) suggests that one strategy would be to have various teams with specific responsibilities, various teams redesigning the work, one team designing new information channels, another team re-engineering the human resources system, etc.

Implementing the Design, Assessing Impacts, Refining, and Redesigning Overtime. The final stage in large-scale, organizational change is implementation. Beer, Eisenstat, and Spector (1990b) suggest that implementation can be phased-in with a variety of task forces, work teams, both large and small. As all the new elements begin to be phased-in, they need to be monitored, assessed, and adjusted (Beer, Eisenstat, and Spector, 1990b; Fullan, 1993; Mohrman, 1994). At this stage, all authors state that it is important to take very seriously the idea of creating a learning organization, i.e., an organization that is continually seeking new information and knowledge and assessing organizational performance in light of such new data (Cummings and Mohrman 1987; Senge, 1990). Substantial funds need to be provided for ongoing training and professional development; the quality of both design and implementation is conditioned on providing continuous access to ideas and knowledge, information about the broader environment including the policy system, and ongoing training for knowledge and skill development. In addition, organizations need to develop mechanisms to provide feedback data on the implementation process: surveys, meetings, problem identification sessions, retreats are continually needed to monitor implementation of both what is working, what needs work, and what needs redesign.

Beer, Eisenstat, and Beer (1990b) suggest that as implementation proceeds, as new procedures become clear, as new roles and procedures become new standard practice, the organization should only then consider institutionalizing the new practices and behaviors in new organizational policies and standard operating procedures. They strongly suggest that such new policies not be created at the beginning of the process, but only towards the end of the process as the work teams and new organization "figure out" how new work tasks will be conducted, and how the many activities of the overall system will be coordinated under the new structures. The authors also caution against being too definitive and dogmatic about new policies, because change is a continuous and not static phenomenon, and what the organization does in any one year might be quite different in future years.

Given the rapidly changing nature of the environment, which for schools would include both rapid changes in student population as well as new signals from the policy community, Cummings and Mohrman (1987) also argue that organizations will constantly be engaged in the redesign business, that change is a constant and no set of organizational strategies will be sufficient in the medium to long term. Fullan (1993:4) agrees: "The new problem of [educational] change . . . is what it would take to make the educational system a learning organization—expert at dealing with change as a normal part of its work, not just in relation to the latest policy, but as a way of life."

CONCLUSIONS

Three arguments have been put forth in this chapter. First, policymakers at the school, district, state, and federal levels should take the backward-mapping approach to developing education policy. The initial step in this approach is to identify the nature of the educational problem and then identify knowledge about effective practice at the classroom and school level. Policy, then, should be created in ways that support and sustain use of these practices by teachers and education leaders in schools.

Second, policy implementation today should not be so focused on getting sites to implement state and federal program initiatives. Over the past 30 years, the local education system has learned how to implement specific program initiatives. But too often such programs do not improve student performance, which usually is their rationale in the first place. The "implementation" issue today envelopes a larger and more important range of issues focused on improving professional practice in each school.

The way professional practice can be improved and schools restructured requires a rich set of strategies that must be created at the site. Site teachers and education leaders need to redesign the curriculum and instruction program, change the entire way schools are organized, structured, and managed, restructure the use resources, and alter the work tasks of teachers. No template will work for this process. The specifics will differ from school to school. In order to enhance the likely success of this developmental process, faculties need to engage in these tasks, and to enhance the success of such faculties, they need to be provided information, knowledge, power, and rewards.

The intriguing aspect of the new approach to educational change in the 1990s described in section 3 is that its basic tenets harken back to the findings of the original RAND change agent study (Berman and McLaughlin 1974–78; McLaughlin, 1991a). Commitment to engage in the deep, difficult, and widespread restructuring that is required for accomplishing the educational goals of the 1990s must be developed "up-front" by teacher diagnosis of the deep nature of the learning problem. In responding to the problems, there are powerful "ideas" to pursue, such as those embodied in the Coalition of Essential

Schools, and ambitious goals to accomplish. While there is professional knowledge and wisdom that derives from experience, there are no research, proven-effective programs. Thus, schoolwide strategies, organizational structures, curriculum programs, instructional materials, and teaching strategies, need to be developed by each school site, just as teacher involvement in program and materials development was crucial in the original RAND study. The journey for such change will require hard work and good thinking, but the rewards, teaching all students to high standards, should be well worth the effort.

The Courts and Judicial Impact on Education Policy

The United States has created a three-part system of government with executive, legislative, and judicial branches. The executive branch, i.e., the President, governors, superintendents, and the various functional agencies, develop and propose policies and implement programs and strategies. The legislative branch, i.e., the Congress, state legislatures, and school boards enact laws and make policies. The judicial branch serves as a review body, and can decide whether policy, regulation, program, procedure, or practice violates constitutional provisions or legal requirements; it was the 1803 *Marbury* v. *Madison* decision that gave the courts the power of "judicial review" over legislative actions. Although controversial at times, court decisions have made fundamental impacts on the development of the American governmental apparatus including education (Yudof, Kirp, and Levin, 1992).

Before the second half of this century, the federal courts played a fairly silent role in education policy. Prior to 1850, there was a laissez-faire attitude of the courts towards education; education was viewed as a local matter and neither state nor federal courts intervened. The period from about 1850 and 1950 was a time of more judicial intervention, but on the part of state rather than federal courts. This was an era of state control of education (and other public policies) and few issues reached the U.S. Supreme Court (Campbell et al., 1990). There were a few important Supreme Court decisions approving expenditure of public funds for secondary schools in addition to the common school (*Stuart* v. *School Districts No. 1 of the Village of Kalamazoo*, 1874), allowing private school enrollment under state compulsory school attendance laws (*Pierce* v. *Society of Sisters*, 1925), and some late 1940s decisions on state aid to private schools (*Everson* v. *Board of Education*, 1947), but the more activist period of direct judicial involvement in the structure, nature, and substance of education policy and practice did not occur until the second half of the twentieth century.

During the second 50 years of this century, the courts, primarily but not exclusively the federal court system and U.S. Supreme Court Decisions, have had major and fundamental impacts on public education. As the last chapter discussed, judicial involvement in education policy began with the *Brown v. Board of Education* (1954) decision when the U.S. Supreme Court overturned de jure segregation, separate but equal education systems for African-Americans, ruling that separate was inherently unequal. Court rulings related to race and desegregation have been rendered often since that initial decision. Since then there have been a multitude of court decisions on a wide variety of topics including race, gender, school prayer, Christmas programs, freedom of speech, censorship of student newspapers, the right to demonstrate, student suspension and expulsion, creation science, home schooling, minimum competency testing, and school finance, to name a few.

The purpose of this chapter is to help organize these judicial entanglements in public education policy by arranging them according to several key constitutional principles, describing the constitutional principles and their legal requirements, showing how the constitutional principles were applied to the issues addressed, and indicating what the court decisions required or disallowed for both education policy and practice. This chapter emphasizes the constitutional requirements embodied in two amendments to the Constitution— the first amendment, included in the original Bill of Rights, and the fourteenth amendment which was added in the period immediately after the Civil War.

Under the first amendment, this chapter first discusses issues related to religion and the schools and second issues related to freedom of speech. Under the fourteenth amendment, this chapter addresses issues related to the "due process" clause and then issues related to the "equal protection" clause of that Amendment. Under equal protection, this chapter emphasizes the desegregation and school finance court decrees.

The activist period for court involvement in education policy in the second half of the twentieth century was during the 1950s, 1960s, and 1970s. The 1980s was a time of court quiescence or retrenchment. But in the 1990s, the courts have taken on a renewed activism, first in response to changes required for decisions rendered in the 1950s and 1960s, second in response changes in judicial orientation due in part to more conservative justices appointed during the many years of Republican party control of the White House, and most recently, in response to a bevy of new issues raised by the education reforms of the 1990s. Each section of this chapter addresses the evolution of the various issues caused by the first two of these influences, because they have produced court decrees. Each section ends with some ruminations on the potential new types of constitutional and legal issues raised by the standards-driven reform movement described in earlier chapters of this book. Thus, this chapter seeks to not only convey the important requirements of several constitutional stipulations and how they have impacted education policy and practice in the past, but also how they might impact education reform as it proceeds to unfold during the 1990s. Wise education leaders and policymakers would take heed of these legal concerns and seek to design policy and practice that fits with judicial requirements and thus legitimately circumvents the need for court interference.

THE FIRST AMENDMENT, PRIVATE SCHOOLS, AND RELIGION

The first amendment to the Constitution of the United States is one of the shortest, most misunderstood, controversial, and often used constitutional amendments. It states:

> Congress shall make no law respecting an establishment of religion or prohibiting the free exercise thereof; or abridging the freedom of speech, or of the press, or the right of the people peaceably to assembly and to petition the Government for a redress of grievances.

The roots of the first amendment reach back to religious persecution in Europe which led to the flight of many to what became the United States, a place where freedom of religion was a pillar of the new country and where government was prohibited from becoming entangled in religion of any sort. The roots of this amendment also derive from many European governments' control of the press, their curtailment of freedom of speech, and their opposition to public demonstration against governmental rule and policy. The founders of this country believed that individuals should be allowed to engage in such actions without governmental interference. These activities were created as fundamental, constitutional rights of all people in the United States by the first amendment (see Alexander and Alexander, 1985).

Two major issues related to the first part of this amendment concerning religion have been the subject of judicial actions impinging on education: attendance at and public support of private schools, and school prayer and religious activities in public schools. Each is discussed briefly below.

Private Schools

The bulk of private schools in this country are religious. At the beginning of the country, as developed in other parts of this book, most education was provided by private schools, and most of those were affiliated with various religions. Indeed, good education in older times included instruction in religion and the teaching of Greek and Latin, the former a language critical for Christian religious study. Such schools were primarily accessible only by the wealthy.

In the nineteenth century, the United States began to create a public school system that made education available to all children without charge. As state public school systems developed into their modern forms during the late nineteenth and early twentieth centuries, one of the large questions that had to be settled was the role that private schools would play in the U.S. education system. A series of court decisions over this century have given some answers to that large question, but there are still issues that have not been settled.

The first issue with private schools arose around state compulsory attendance laws, which required all children of a given age to attend school. Did such laws require attendance at just a public school or could attendance at a private school, including a private school affiliated with a religion, satisfy the compulsory attendance mandate? *Pierce* v. *Society of Sisters* (1925) answered this question. The U.S. Supreme Court affirmed the legitimacy of sectarian schools, i.e., religiously affiliated private schools, as an education organization a student could attend in response to state compulsory attendance laws.

The next issue concerned governmental support of private schools, again including sectarian schools. Since such schools functioned at least in part to provide a publicly desired service, the question was whether the public, i.e., governments, could provide resources to such institutions. This issue is not yet fully settled but numerous decisions have helped shape the answer over time.

The first decision was in *Cochran v. Louisiana State Board of Education* (1930). In this case, the U.S. Supreme Court ruled that it was constitutional for the state to purchase textbooks for use in private, sectarian schools. The decision established the "child benefit" theory, that government assistance could be provided if the child was the primary beneficiary of the action. This decision allowed the state to provide an educational resource, textbooks, to a private, sectarian school, but not necessarily money.

Nearly 20 years later, in *Everson v. Board of Education* (1947) the court ruled that paying for transportation of students to religiously affiliated schools, as part of a state's or district's overall transportation policy, was also allowable. Thus, by about 1950, states could not send money to private, sectarian schools, but they could assist them in providing educational resources, textbooks and transportation, as long as the resource was provided to both public and private schools on an equal basis.

After about another 20 years, during which the court turned down several more generous state attempts to support private schools, the court ruled in *Board of Education of Central School District No. 1 v. Allen* (1968) that providing funds to be used for textbooks, as compared to just providing the textbooks, was also permissible and did not violate the establishment clause of the first amendment. In this decision, the court added language that attempted to explain its findings. The opinion stated that private, sectarian schools served a public purpose and performed secular as well as religious functions; as a result, it was permissible for governments to assist them in their secular functions, as long as the primary beneficiary of the action was the child and not religion. This decision put forth a "secular purpose" standard and appeared to allow the state to provide financial assistance for the secular functions of private, sectarian schools.

In the wake of *Allen*, several states enacted laws to provide financial support for a wide variety of "secular" education services provided by private schools—salaries of regular teachers, special education services, operation and maintenance costs, etc. But the court overturned these actions, in the process creating a new and tougher standard, called "excessive entanglement." This standard was promulgated in the *Lemon v. Kurtzman* (1971), which addressed the constitutionality of two state programs that paid for the salaries of parochial school teachers. In ruling on the case, the court outlined a three-part test to determine whether that or any other state action ran afoul of the establishment clause. In order to be constitutional, *Lemon* held that:

- The statute must have a secular legislative intent.
- Its principal or primary effect must be one that neither advances nor inhibits religion.
- It must not foster excessive governmental entanglement.

The standard required any policy to pass each of these tests; if it failed on any one, it would be ruled unconstitutional. In applying the tripartite test, the court found that the practice of paying sectarian school teacher salaries involved excessive entanglement of the state in religion and overturned the state laws.

Using this more stringent standard in a series of subsequent cases, the court overturned a state law reimbursing parents for private school tuition (*Sloan* v. *Lemon*, 1973), as well as state support for the following: counseling, testing and special education services, and field trips to public buildings (e.g., museums) (*Meek* v. *Pittenger*, 1975). On the other hand, the court continued to allow public support for transportation and textbooks, and added the following as activities that could qualify for public subsidy: state-required standardized testing, treatments for speech and hearing problems, and dental services (Alexander & Alexander, 1985). Despite these advances made by the U.S. Supreme Court, many states interpreted their own constitutional requirements more tightly and disallowed financial support of parochial school services that met the *Lemon* test of the federal court.

As part of the series of decisions in the wake of *Allen*, the Supreme Court also ruled on a New York policy that provided tax deductions for low-income parents attending private schools, including parochial schools. In *Committee for Public Education and Religious Liberty* v. *Nyquist* (1973), the court ruled this policy unconstitutional largely because it provided a benefit only to parents of children attending private schools; the decision stated that neutrality toward religion could not be squared with such a targeted action. Although not that clear at that time, this wording, coupled with other decisions that allowed public support for services provided equally to public and private schools, began to suggest a set of criteria for constitutional state support of private school activities.

The next big step occurred a decade later in *Mueller* v. *Allen* (1983) when the U.S. Supreme Court upheld a Minnesota tax law that extended tax deductions to parents of all students, those in public as well as private schools, for educational expenses including not only textbooks and transportation but also tuition. In this decision, the court noted the basis for finding *Nyquist* unconstitutional, extension of the privilege to parents of students only in private schools, did not apply to the Minnesota law which extended the privilege to all parents, thus singling out neither private nor religiously affiliated schools as the only beneficiaries. The *Mueller* decision could very well signal a new view of the courts on state financial assistance for private and sectarian schools. It appears that if the aid is provided to parents rather than the institution itself, and if the aid is provided to parents of children in any school, public and private, then the proviso will be upheld.

The previous 40 years of rulings on public support for private, sectarian schools, thus, can be differentiated along two lines: what the court will allow in terms of direct public support to private, sectarian schools, and what the court will allow in terms of payments to parents. In terms of direct support, the court has upheld payments for transportation, textbooks, testing, some health and dental services, and, as shown below in the 1993 *Zobrest* v. *Catalina* case, for specialized services for handicapped students. How far the court will continue to expand this list is unknown, but the list has been consistently expanded each decade over the last 50 years. Although it is unlikely the court would allow support for a regular teacher, such as a first grade teacher, it is very likely that additional, specialized services could be approved. Tutoring for low-income, low-achieving students; services for learning disabled and mildly handicapped students; second language instruction for limited-English proficient students; and additional health and family services potentially could be added to the list that passes constitutional muster. The fact is that while the court has been struggling with how to maintain a separation between church and state, the trend has been to be more and more liberal in its interpretation of what separation means.

In terms of support to parents, the court in *Mueller* seems to be signaling that it will uphold financial aid to parents when the parents choose the school, when all parents can participate in the program, and when parents have children in either public or private, even private, sectarian schools. Although the amount of public support in Mueller was small, the deduction was limited to $700 which means the actual state cost was a small percentage of that amount, the language in the court decision appeared not to imply that the policy also was permissible because the level of public support was low. Clearly, however, a more generous state program could be found unconstitutional by the current court.

Application to Education Reforms of the 1990s. In the context of the 1990s, these decisions can be thought of as applying to three new types of education policies: (1) vouchers for private schools not including private, parochial schools, (2) vouchers for private schools including parochial schools, and (3) charter school programs (Wohlstetter & Anderson, 1993).

Although there was much action in the late 1980s after the *Mueller* decision, with then President Reagan supporting voucher programs and proposals in many states to enact them, no state except Wisconsin succeeded in enacting a voucher program, and a test of that policy has not yet reached the U.S. Supreme Court. Wisconsin's voucher program is a small, pilot program for a maximum of 1,000 students in Milwaukee; the state law provided the parents of students from low-income backgrounds a voucher in the amount of $2,987 to allow them to attend a private school, as an alternative to the Milwaukee public schools. In a general challenge to this policy, the Wisconsin Supreme Court ruled that the vouchers were constitutional for use in private, nonsectarian schools, thus upholding the principle of state support for private schools. Although the law prohibits use of the voucher in a sectarian school, the legality of extending the program to parochial schools was at the hearing stage in early 1994 and had not yet reached either the Wisconsin or U.S. Supreme Courts.

The logic in *Mueller* would suggest that if Wisconsin expanded the Milwaukee voucher program to private, sectarian schools, the U.S. Supreme Court could find the policy acceptable. The funds would then be provided to parents not directly to the school, parents could choose without restriction the school their child attended, and parents could choose both public and private schools; indeed, since the voucher amount is much less than that supporting each child in a public school, the state could argue that the policy, while including parochial schools, certainly was not singling them out for special support. How the U.S. Supreme Court would rule on a voucher program, though, will not be known until a state enacts one into law and supports it through the inevitable challenge that will bring it to the attention of the top court.

Charter schools pose another new situation for the courts. Charter schools are quasi-public and quasi-private schools. Charter schools are choice schools. Generally, any parent can choose to send their child to a charter school, as long as there is space; if demand exceeds supply, selection is usually by lottery. Charter schools provide a choice between a regular public school and a charter alternative. Charter schools are public because they receive their charter from a public entity—usually a local school district or the state board of education. They thus are accountable to the public for the goals they establish in their charter. But they generally are free from nearly all state education rules and regulations and thus function just like a private school; although they cannot charge additional tuition over and above the funds the state provides, they can engage in fund raising (Wohlstetter and Anderson, 1993).

The issue for state charter school programs is whether a school designed to meet state-stipulated performance standards could be eligible for a state charter, if it also provided religious instruction. In other words, would it be constitutional to provide a public charter to a school that fulfilled all the secular functions of a public school as well as provided activities that promoted a certain religion? Under *Mueller*, it would appear that such a school would be permissible. But the court could rule such a school ineligible because the state would send the money to the school rather than the parent. In response, however, it could be argued that that is just an accounting distinction, because for each additional student the charter school enrolls, it receives an extra per pupil amount so that in reality, the state is sending the per pupil check to the school on behalf of the parents of the child, and not as a general support for the school.

Only time will tell how the court will rule on vouchers or charter schools that have a religious component. At any rate, it is likely that both of these issues likely will be tested during the 1990s. If *Mueller* is an indication, such policies could be allowed, even though it could be argued that they bring the state closer to religion than appears to be implied by the first amendment. As the following section will show, however, the high wall of separation between the church and state built by *Lemon* has been consistently lowered in the years since the wall was erected. Approval of vouchers and sectarian charter schools could simply be a continuation of this process of deconstruction.

School Prayer and Religion

The lowering of the walls of separation between church and state over the last 30 years can also be seen in court attitude towards prayer and other religious activities within the public schools. From a stance of strict prohibition that emerged in the 1960s, which altered a century of tradition, the entanglement of school and church today is much more than in the late 1960s, but falls short of "excessive entanglement" according to recent court decrees.

Up to about 1962, at least a dozen states required Bible reading during school times, and other states and districts allowed voluntary prayer and Bible reading. These requirements and approved practices were allowed generally on the basis of tradition; they had been a practice for several years and were part of the American fabric, even though they were blatantly religious and clearly favored one religion, Christianity, over all others. In 1962, these practices came under constitutional attack. In *Engle* v. *Vitale* (1962), the U.S. Supreme Court held that prayer and Bible reading as part of the school program violated the first amendment.

This and numerous subsequent decisions prohibited a variety of creative state efforts to maintain the prayer tradition in schools, including several efforts to allow voluntary, nonsectarian prayers and moments of silence. Several related cases, drawing on the high wall erected by *Lemon,* found the court overturning the traditional practice of having Christmas programs performed in the public schools, prohibiting the display of crèches on public school or simply public, government property, giving prayers at commencement exercises and other blatant religious acts; other decisions forbade the use of classroom or other school space by religiously affiliated organizations for after school programs, such as release time for religious instruction (Alexander and Alexander, 1985).

Because these decisions overturned years of practice, they were controversial and many tried to circumvent their prohibitions. During the 1980s, the Ronald Reagan administration attempted to reverse these decisions both by promoting the idea of voluntary prayer in the schools, and by sponsoring a constitutional amendment that would allow such voluntary acts. The proposals, however, fell short of the required Congressional two-thirds majorities and were never sent to the people or state legislatures for approval.

Nevertheless, beginning in the 1980s justices to the Supreme Court appointed overtime by more conservative Presidents began to soften the edges of the standard set by *Lemon.* For example, in *Lynch* v. *Donnley* (1984) the court allowed both public financial support for and display of a nativity scene on public property; the court ruled that crèches were passive religious symbols and that the crèche in the case was not just a religious display because it also contained nonreligious items such as reindeer and a teddy bear. In subsequent decisions, the court has followed this line; many places allow nativity scenes that also have a symbol from another religion, such as the Menorah from the Jewish religion, and a secular symbol such as an American flag. With this bit of creativity, both governments and the courts have worked to preserve tradition but not make the practice overly noxious in its sanction of one religion.

Many schools, moreover, have switched from having Christmas performances to having holiday performances where songs, scenes, and traditions from several religions, Christian, Jewish, and Muslim, as well as secular winter celebrations are part of the program. In this way, schools have been able to maintain the tradition of a late December holiday performance but not run afoul of the Constitution by stressing only one religion or religious over secular themes.

In an additional softening of *Lemon,* the court also has rescinded its prohibition of religious group meetings on school property. The precedent was in the 1948 *McCollum* v. *Board of Education* case in which the court disallowed the release time program of religious instruction on school property. The problems with such a practice, the court then ruled, were both that the religious instruction occurred on school property and that the school administration was too involved in organizing the program. But 42 years later the U.S. Supreme Court in *Board of Education Westside Community Schools* v. *Mergens* (1990) found constitutional a 1984 federal law mandating that public high schools give political and religious groups the same access to facilities that was accorded to other co-curricular activities. The law was proposed by then President Reagan shortly after the constitutional amendment to allow voluntary prayer in the schools was defeated. While originally proposed as a law to allow access to school property for religious groups only, in its final versions it provided for access to political and philosophical groups as well. *Mergens* held that such access to school property did not run afoul of the excessive entanglement of the *Lemon* test. A key aspect of the law in its final form was that it neither favored nor hindered access by religious groups.

The chipping away of *Lemon* continued in a series of 1993 cases. The U.S. Supreme Court overturned a New York law that allowed civil and social groups to use school facilities but denied the same privilege to Christian groups that wanted to present speeches that emphasized family values. In this case, the court wrote that such a policy "discriminated" against religion and stated that laws needed to "neutral" towards religion.

Following this line of reasoning, the court in *Zobrest* v. *Catalina* (1993) overturned an Arizona ruling that public dollars could be used to provide a sign language interpreter for a deaf student attending a public, but not a parochial school. This decision was the first time the U.S. Supreme Court ruled that the constitution allowed public support of salaries for individuals providing educational services in private, religiously affiliated schools. The court ruled that prohibiting support for the service in a parochial school "discriminated" against religion and caused the student to suffer a disadvantage because of attending a nonpublic school. The court also ruled that public support for a "neutral" service inside a Catholic school did not offend the first amendment. This decision overturned rulings against this practice as recently as 1985 in *Aguilar* v. *Felton*, when the court overturned the 20-year practice of using federal Chapter 1 dollars to provide remedial programs to low-income students in private schools. In *Zobrest*, the court put forth the issues of neutrality and discrimination together with the tri-partite *Lemon* test. While maintaining that excessive entanglement was disallowed, the court also held that government action also could not discriminate against religious schools and had to be neutral in their impact. The result had the effect of softening what had been a decades long sharp-edged test for excessive entanglement.

Effects on Current Education Reforms. In terms of the applicability of these court decisions to issues related to the 1990s reform agenda, the key issues would be two-fold. The first, again, is whether vouchers could be provided to parents whose children attended private, religiously affiliated schools. As the last section concluded, this policy could very well receive a positive nod from the U.S. Supreme Court.

The second would be whether religious activity or functions could occur in a charter school; for example, could a prayer, voluntary or not, or other religious activity be an ongoing component of a charter school program? At this point it would be difficult to predict a position of the country's top court on the latter issue. On the one hand, attendance at the school would be voluntary. The school would be run in a quasi-private manner. It would meet all the secular requirements of a state's public education system. And the court has been paring down the rigidity of *Lemon*. On the other hand, the school would be a public school, to which the tri-partite test of *Lemon* would apply, which has been used to overturn such practices in "regular" public schools, but also to which the "neutrality" and "nondiscrimination" standard would be applied. It is quite likely that some court will soon need to rule in a case involving a state charter school that included in its ongoing program some element of a direct religious practice. When such a case is decided, there will be a more definitive judicial message on this issue. Until that time, one could argue both sides of the legality of such a practice, given the curtailment of *Lemon* in recent court rulings.

However, as both lines of cases have evolved, those dealing with aid to private and sectarian schools and those dealing with religion or the types of religious-related activities that would be allowed in the public schools, the trend line is clearly one of lowering the wall of separation between church and state. Today, the government can support many services provided in parochial schools. Under certain but not restrictive conditions, it can provide financial assistance to parents of children who attend sectarian schools. Religiously affiliated groups can use school property for meetings and gatherings. Students can lead private prayers at certain school gatherings. A period of silent meditation, which some can use to pray, is permitted in public schools. In short, from the high wall set up by *Lemon*, to the "nondiscriminatory" and "neutrality" standards of the 1990s, the court has gradually but consistently allowed a greater interaction between the state and sectarian schools. Many would predict the court would let stand a voucher program provided to all parents, even if some chose to use them at a parochial school. In short, if current trends continue, the United States could be closer to the practice of many other countries that includes substantial public support for the secular education that is provided in sectarian schools, or put differently, is content to allow the substantial exercise of religious activity in educational institutions supported largely by public dollars.

The First Amendment and Free Speech in the Schools

The first amendment also supports free speech stating that the "Congress shall make no law that . . . abridges freedom of speech." The primary topic addressed during the last 30 years under this topic has been the right of students, primarily high school students, to engage in unbridled free speech on school grounds. The activities addressed have ranged from demonstrations against governmental actions, particularly during the Vietnam War period of the 1960s and 1970s, to censorship of writings in student newspapers. The background is the degree to which schools can function as "in loco parentis," i.e., as surrogate parents as compared to functioning only as a governmental body. The constitutional issue is the degree to which students, i.e., citizens under voting age, have fundamental rights that constrain school restrictions on their behavior as compared to the prerogatives of schools to regulate student behavior in any manner they deem appropriate. The story is similar to that for prayer and state aid to parochial schools—an early "hard edge" that has been ground to a smoother surface overtime.

A seminal decision related to school restrictions on student behavior was *Tinker* v. *Des Moines* (1969). Students had wanted to wear black armbands to protest the Vietnam War. In response, the school district issued a ruling that they would suspend students who engaged in such a practice. Students sued on the basis that such a policy infringed on their right to free speech. In their decision in *Tinker*, the U.S. Supreme Court held that even though under age, students too had fundamental rights, in this case the right to freedom of expression, which entitled them to wear armbands as long as the action produced no substantial disruption in school activities.

This was a major decision that implied a challenge to a range of school regulation of student behavior, from dress codes, typical of many schools across the nation, to school sponsored newspapers. However, the student behavior protected by the court included only that related to social, political and economic issues, not behavior in the classroom nor disrespect shown for teachers. In the wake of *Tinker*, though, numerous dress codes were rescinded; columns in student newspapers began to include articles with sexually explicit topics, partisan political perspectives, with clear racial or ethnic bias, and other forms of freedom of speech and expression; and school officials became concerned about which rules curtailing student behavior were constitutional and which were not.

By the mid-1980s, however, again with a more conservative court, the unbridled behavior allegedly unleashed by *Tinker* began to be curtailed. In *Bethel School District* v. *Fraser* (1986) a student had used an explicit sexual metaphor in a nominating speech for president of a high school club during a school-sponsored student assembly. By so doing, the district decided that he had violated a school rule against obscene language, suspended him for three days, and barred him from speaking at commencement. The student protested on the basis of *Tinker* but the court ruled that the district action was constitutional, holding that the rules for obscenity outside the school, which have to meet general community standards, were less than the standards administrators could require for obscenity within the school. In so ruling, *Fraser* held that while student had rights inside the school, they were not co-equal with adult rights outside the school.

Two years later, the court continued the grinding down of *Tinker* in *Hazelwood School District* v. *Kuhlmeier* (1988). In this instance, the U.S. Supreme Court upheld censorship actions of a school district in eliminating two articles in a school-financed and widely circulated newspaper, one on three pregnant girls and another on a child whose parents had just gone through a divorce. The court supported district officials' actions seeking to inculcate society's values as perceived by the adults in the school, over the rights of students to experience the vortex of ideas by engaging in freedom of expression.

What impact both *Fraser* and *Hazelwood* will have overtime on district control of student behavior, newspapers, yearbooks, etc. is unknown. After *Hazelwood*, California, Massachusetts, and Iowa passed laws protecting the right of student newspaper editors to freedom of expression, subject to limitations of obscenity, libel, encouragement to violate school regulations or public laws, and the substantial disruption test of *Tinker* (Yudof, Kirp, and Levin, 1992). But other school curtailment of student behavior had not reached the high court by mid-1994.

Linkage to Current Education Reforms. It is not clear how these decisions will impact the education reforms of the 1990s. At first blush, they would appear to allow public schools, public choice schools, and charter schools, to have stricter student codes of behavior, perhaps even dress codes. For choice and charter schools, the argument for a court's sustaining a stronger code of behavior would be that students only attended the school on their own initiative, that they selected the school given its code of behavior. For public schools more generally, dress codes could be argued as needed in order to reduce the disruptions caused by the wearing of "gang-related" colors and dress in the classroom. Indeed, the Long Beach Unified School District in California adopted a dress code in 1994. Given the increased power provided to school authorities by *Fraser* and *Hazelwood*, and the increasing freedom of local school sites to craft education programs that fit local tastes, albeit including a core, high-standards curriculum, a reasonable scenario would be that more regulation of student behavior could creep back into schools supported by public funds, especially choice and charter schools, but also site-based managed schools.

THE FOURTEENTH AMENDMENT

The fourteenth amendment to the U.S. Constitution was adopted in 1868 and has several clauses. The equal protection and due process clauses read as follows:

> No state shall make or enforce any law which shall . . . deprive any person of life, liberty, or property, without due process of law; nor deny to any person within its jurisdiction the equal protection of the laws.

Over the nearly 150 years since their enactment, these two straightforward clauses have been used with tremendous force to challenge a host of actions on the part of local, state, and federal governments. In the latter half of this century they also began to be used to curtail and thus impact a range of traditional education policy and practice. This section discusses several but not all education issues related to these two clauses, beginning with due process, and then moving to equal protection—first as it relates to desegregation and second as it relates to school finance. For these two equal protection topics, an argument will be made that as both are becoming fully enveloped in the standards-driven education reform movement in the 1990s, they also are becoming intertwined with each other.

Due Process

The due process clause requires that a constitutionally sanctioned procedure must be followed if someone is to be deprived of something in the conceptual frame of life, liberty, or property. Three basic practices are included in procedural due process: (1) the individual must have proper notice, (2) she or he must be given the opportunity to be heard, and (3) the hearing must be conducted fairly. Under the due process case, the court decides both whether the above tri-partite procedure has been followed and whether the action of the government produces a deprivation for the individual. Courts have not been rigid in their interpretation of procedure, looking mainly for fairness in the processes used to determine whether the views of both sides were heard. Without a deprivation, though, a violation of due process does not occur, even if the process was not according to the above standards. Although for years the due process requirements were applied only in judicial settings, in the more recent past, the last 50 years, they began to be applied to governmental and private agencies as well, including the schools (Alexander and Alexander, 1985).

In addition, the due process clause has been used to eliminate inflexible standards that govern behavior or process. On the latter for example, courts have overturned the inflexible regulation many districts had that forced any teacher who was pregnant to stop teaching school; in its place, the court has required school regulations to speak to the abilities required to engage in teaching and to allow replacement only when an individual did not have the requisite expertise.

The context for application of the due process clause in education can be seen in the process begun with *Tinker,* a process in which the court began ceding to students constitutional rights that were provided to adults. The primary difference was in the constitutional clause, or handle, that was used to extend the right; the impact was the same—infringement of school regulation of student behavior. The due process shot over the bow of education practice was in *Dixon* v. *Alabama State Board of Education* (1961). Students had been expelled for participating in a sit-in at a lunch counter as part of a civil rights protest during the 1960s. This behavior had not been proscribed by the college nor had a hearing been held. In overturning the expulsion action by education administrators, the court ruled that such a significant deprivation required procedural due process including both notice and a fair hearing.

In the *Goss* v. *Lopez* (1975) decision, the court extended this requirement both to public school students and to the act of suspension in addition to expulsion. In this case, students had spiked a punch at a school-sponsored party and were summarily suspended for 10 days. The students sued on the basis of a violation of due process both because the district did not have a policy on this behavior (there was no notice) and because the suspension was invoked summarily (there was no hearing). The court concurred with the students, writing that depriving students of the right to attend school constituted a liberty deprivation which therefore required some type of notice and hearing. Although state law had required written notice and a hearing for expulsion, there had been no such policy for suspension. But the court ruled that minimal procedural safeguards, notice and hearing, were required even for deprivations less severe than expulsion.

P.L. 94-142, the 1975 Education for All Handicapped Children Act, is a further example of how due process mechanisms are being incorporated into the American public education system. This law included several due process principles as central mechanisms for determining resolutions over disagreements about the placement of children in different programs. Rather than allow each state, district, and school to devise the principles on their own, the law itself included the principles when it was enacted (Yudof, Kirp, and Levin, 1992).

In an issue that relates centrally to regular education practice, the *Debra P. v. Turlington* (1979) case constituted a landmark decision over the issue of due process for what is today called high-stakes testing. In the 1970s, many states began to administer minimum competency tests that assessed whether students had mastered the basic skills in reading and writing; most states also then required students to earn a passing mark on the tests as one condition for high school graduation. Florida initially provided about four years of notice for this requirement. After high percentages of African-Americans failed to pass the test, even after several retakes, the requirement was challenged. The court held that because of the vestiges of a separate but equal education system, a longer period of notice was required, and that the test could not be used until all students who had been subject to a segregated education had graduated from the school system.

While the basis for this ruling was equal protection (discussed below), subsequent concerns with such testing requirements have been related more to due process. A state would not be able to design a high school graduation, or middle school entrance examination, in one year and implement it the next. Students and parents would have to be given notice that the test would be implemented at some future time, and that adequate provision, including supplementary education services, would need to be provided to enable all students to earn passing scores.

Impact on Education Reform. These requirements are especially relevant to the 1990s education reforms and the conversation surrounding high-stakes tests. Not only is the country in the process of shifting away from norm-referenced, standardized achievement tests and towards more authentic, performance-based assessments, but also many states would like to attach "stakes" to the tests. Stakes could include requirements for certain performance levels as a condition of entering middle school or high school, for graduating from high school, as well as for college admission or job placement and salary determination. All of these "high stakes" would be based on test scores.

Due process requirements will mean that states will need to give adequate notice for the implementation of such high-stakes testing, which would include at least six years for elementary school students, assuming middle school would begin at grade 6, three years for middle school students, and four years for high school students. Indeed, if such high-stakes tests are based on new curriculum standards, it might be possible to invoke the consequences only for students who experience the new curriculum from the time they entered kindergarten; otherwise, as in *Debra P.,* students could argue that their previous school years had deprived them of an opportunity to perform well on a test that assessed such new and different cognitive competencies.

An additional issue that could be raised is whether even given adequate notice, students had actually been systematically exposed to a curriculum that would allow them to perform well on such tests. Put differently, due process requirements could include not only adequate notice but also provision of opportunity to learn (Porter, 1993a, 1993b). In other words, due process requirements could well go far beyond the reach of *Dixon* and *Goss* in the 1990s and to the core of notions involved centrally in system reform. In a sense, this should be expected. Systemic reform itself speaks to the core of the education enterprise. Thus, constitutional stipulations surrounding the use of high-stakes testing might "force" states to ensure the provision of opportunity to learn rather than just the voluntary provision that is now included in the Goals 2000 legislation.

Equal Protection—The Constitutional Argument

In holding that the government shall not deny any individual of the equal protection of the law, the constitution provides a widespread, blanket guarantee of citizens against the capricious actions of the government. But the exact meaning of the term has had to be defined and reinterpreted over the course of U.S. history.

If taken literally, the phrase could suggest that the government must treat all individuals equally, that in no case could the government treat one individual differently than another. But everyone knows that that is not the case. Some individuals can drive, work as a lawyer, or teach in the public schools, and others cannot. These differential government treatments of individuals, moreover, are constitutional. Why?

Judicial rulings under the equal protection clause have created three primary tests to determine whether and under what conditions differential treatment of individuals by governmental actions are permissible or not. The first test is the rationale test. Under this test, the government simply has to have a "rationale" or a reasonable justification for its variable treatment. For driving it would argue that restricting drivers to those that have a drivers license, and thus have shown some expertise in handling a car, serves the public interest and protects citizens against harm from individuals who did not know how to drive. Restricting the practice of law and teaching to those with licenses in those fields again would protect the public by ensuring that those who engaged in those practices had the requisite education, training, knowledge, and expertise.

The second test that was developed is called strict scrutiny. This test is used in very restrictive circumstances and it is a strict test. When a fundamental interest is involved (such as the right to vote, to engage in freedom of speech, or to appeal a decision in a criminal test) or when governmental action creates a "suspect class" of people (such as race), then the court applies the strict scrutiny test. Under this test, the state must show that there is a "compelling state interest" involved in its actions and that there is no less discriminatory approach that could be taken. In nearly all instances when the court has dealt with cases involving either a fundamental right or a suspect classification, it has overturned the governmental action (Yudof, Kirp, and Levin, 1992).

The third test has been developed recently and used primarily for cases involving differential treatment based on gender. It provides for an intermediate degree of scrutiny, less than strict scrutiny but more than the rationale test. Under this test developed for *Craig* v. *Boren* (1976), the constitution requires the state to show that its action serves some "important" state objective and is "substantially" related to achieving those objectives. The intermediate test has been used primarily in cases addressing equity between the sexes.

The remainder of this section addresses two major issues raised under the strict scrutiny test: desegregation and school finance.

Equal Protection and Desegregation

The 1954 *Brown* v. *Board of Education* was noteworthy not only because it overturned de jure segregated system of schools in the South, but also because it represented an advance in Equal Protection litigation. To comply with the Equal Protection requirement, several states allegedly had created "separate but financially equal" education systems, one for whites and another for African-Americans. The policies barred minority students from attending the white schools. The policy was upheld by the 1896 *Plessy* v. *Ferguson* U.S. Supreme Court Decision. In *Brown*, however, plaintiffs raised the issue of whether separation of children for public education created a "suspect class of individuals," arguing that separate was inherently unequal.

The 1954 Court agreed with their argument, thus for the first time in modern history identifying race as a suspect class and outlawing all actions of governments that had the impact of treating individuals differently according to their race. This decision was part of a time when the federal courts seemed sympathetic to broadening the reach of equal protection litigation, and to overturning long time governmental practices such as de jure segregated schools and the poll tax. As a result, the ruling opened the court to a flood of cases seeking equal protection clause against governmental actions that treated individuals differently.

Chapter 1 chronicled the series of desegregation cases rendered by the court in the wake of *Brown;* litigation on segregation related issues continued into the 1980s. But sometime in the 1980s, a new desegregation issue began to arise. The new issue pertained to school districts that had faithfully and fully implemented desegregation plans in response to *Brown* and its progeny. Many of these districts were monitored by the court for compliance with the court decrees; in the process, most key district policies were reviewed by the courts and often required court sign-off before they could be implemented. After desegregating their schools systems for several years, often covering over 20 years and almost two generations of students, districts and policymakers began to wonder when court review would be terminated and the school systems could be labeled "unitary," that is, one system for all races.

Many petitions for a ruling of unitary status grew from desegregation decrees rendered in the early 1960s. By the late 1980s, all students in the school systems had been attending under a desegregation plan. Districts began to petition for relief by claiming that desegregation had been implemented, the vestiges of segregation eliminated, and court review was no longer necessary. Although several if not the bulk of schools in many places were primarily minority, districts argued that this fact was due to housing and other economic patterns and not a result of direct actions of school boards or state policy. Initially, federal circuit courts produced mixed decisions, ultimately blocking the finding of unitary status. But in 1990 a case on this issue finally was heard by the U.S. Supreme Court and a decision was rendered on when and how unitary status could be declared.

In *Board of Education of Oklahoma City Public Schools* v. *Dowell* (1991) the court concluded that Oklahoma City could be given unitary status; it had faithfully implemented a desegregation plan over a period of nearly 25 years, it had a transfer program that allowed any student in a school with a high concentration of minorities to transfer to another school, and the court agreed that racial characteristics of schools were due to housing patterns and demographics and not actions of the state or local school officials. The court also suggested that rather than the burden of proof falling on districts to show that all vestiges of segregation had been eliminated, after some time period when all students were attending under a desegregation policy, the burden of proof reverted to plaintiffs, who were subject to the standards of *Keyes* (1973), i.e., having to show that actions of the current school officials produced the racial characteristics of schools.

In another case one year later [*Freeman* v. *Pitts* (1992)], the court came to the same conclusion. In *Freeman*, moreover, the court reiterated its stance that desegregation efforts needed to focus as much on the quality of education programs and their impacts on student performance, as on racial balance. These words undergirded the court's comments in *Milliken* v. *Bradley* (1977) that matters other than student assignment, such as the nature and quality of the education program including student achievement, could be addressed by federal courts as aspects of the vestiges of prior segregation that need to be eliminated. The language in both decisions, especially the recent expression in *Freeman*, brings desegregation much closer to the goals of current education reform, for which the rhetoric of educating all students to high standards includes elimination of current achievement differentials along racial lines.

Linkage to Reforms of the 1990s. There are several issues related to race that can be raised in the context of the reforms of the 1990s: Afro-centered curriculum that could be the focus in a charter school; all African-American, single sex schools that have been proposed by community and education groups in some cities; choice versus neighborhood schools, etc. Two will be discussed: the emerging overlap between desegregation goals and education reform, and more particularly, the persistent problem of the racial patterns characteristic of student-achievement differentials in general but particularly on high-stakes tests.

Tatel (1992–93) and Kazal-Thresher (1994) have both argued that there is a growing overlap between desegregation and education reform that likely will create both opportunities and conflicts during the 1990s. While desegregation has been required in many types of districts across the country, most of the country's largest urban districts have also been put under a desegregation decree (Tatel, 1992–93) and are the places where the opportunities and conflicts are most prominent. The largest 45 districts enroll 12 percent of the nation's total school population and one-third of all minorities. Successfully implementing both desegregation and education reform in these districts is critical for the success of each.

Doing so will be difficult. These and other large districts are becoming more and more minority, with the minority percentage often rising above 90 percent. Even if such districts desegregate, schools will still be primarily minority. Second, most urban districts are under fiscal stress (Cibulka, 1991) even when their expenditures are above the state average; this suggests a linkage also with school finance reform, an issue which will be addressed in the next section. Third, educational quality and performance in these districts is poor; they are beset by poor facilities, weak curriculum programs, and low-teacher quality; academic achievement is low, dropout rates are high, and performance seems to be declining rather than rising (Kozol, 1991; Slavin, 1991).

These types of educational problems are precisely the target of the educational changes for which the preceding chapters in this book have argued. Although the specifics of pupil assignment and racial balance as part of court mandates could raise administrative glitches in linking education reform and desegregation, and while there are other potential conflicts in the details of the two agendas (see Tatel, 1992–93), the fact is that recent desegregation decrees, the language in *Freeman*, and the overall *educational* objectives of current desegregation are the same as education reform—increased educational performance and elimination of race (as well as income, gender, and language background) as a correlate of educational attainment.

Indeed, as Tatel (1992–93) and Kazal-Thresher (1994) argue, the federal courts could become an ally of education reform in districts that are under court desegregation orders. The ingredients of education reform could be incorporated into court definitions of what constitutes acceptable strategies for eliminating the vestiges of segregation (Tatel, 1992–93). Courts could order provision of decent facilities, more expert teachers, high-quality curriculum standards, and higher graduation rates as part of the education program that must be provided in urban schools; these elements are quite the same as those embodied in education reform and even Goals 2000. Courts also could mandate provision of "opportunity to learn" (Porter, 1993a, 1993b). Choice programs could be designed, as they already have been in many areas, to further desegregation goals as well as to further the decentralized management aspect of education reform. Further, in many districts where schools often revert to high-minority status after a unitary decree, provision of the above program elements could be a requirement for maintaining unitary status.

In short, as desegregation addresses education objectives more centrally in the 1990s and as education reform continues to proffer ambitious learning goals for *all* students, including minority students, the objectives of both overlap. The connections between these two education arenas likely will strengthen over the 1990s. The interconnections will not always occur smoothly; developing and maintaining the connections will require ingenuity and administrative creativity by those in both camps. But effort to make these connections would be effort worth expending. In addition to producing more racial interaction, the long-term goal of desegregation is better education for minority students. This objective might become the only objective if the court insists on declaring unitary status to districts in the 1990s, even if that produces more segregated schools because of housing patterns and demographics.

A more particular issue linking desegregation with education reform in the 1990s, however, will likely be performance assessment and high-stakes testing. One key element of systemic reform and Goals 2000 is a new type of student assessment, one based more on student performance. Early results show that low-income and minority students might perform less well on these tests (O'Day and Smith, 1993). If the arguments being made generally and in this book are correct, that advances in understandings about how students learn should allow teachers to reduce if not eliminate the linkage between income, race, and gender in student achievement (see Slavin et al., 1994; Slavin, Karweit, and Wasik, 1994), it is possible that for some case in the future a court could very well require schools and districts to provide educational services in a manner that eliminates any relationship between student achievement and race. This would put a court requirement behind the current rhetoric of education reform and place the legal system in the position of requiring certain education results, which would raise the "ante" for both desegregation and education reform.

Further, if a state actually implemented a new type of "high-stakes" assessment and the performance of minorities was lower than that for other students, a suit could be filed. The argument could be that such a test violated the equal protection clause because there was sufficient knowledge to eliminate the connection between low scores and race. Indeed, a case making pretty much this argument was filed in 1994 challenging the results of such a new Ohio test. Court responses could prevent states from implementing the "stakes" portions of their assessments if minorities performed less well; court rulings also could require that districts provide certain services, preschool, full-day kindergarten, one-to-one tutoring in the early grades, lower class size, and a host of other interventions including enacted systemic reform, which have been shown to eliminate the linkage between race and achievement (Slavin et al., 1994; Slavin, Karweit, and Wasik, 1994)—as a condition for implementing a high-stakes testing system. Such a mandate also would raise the "ante" for both desegregation and education reform, as well as the cost of such policies.

In short, as the strategy of systemic reform and Goals 2000 become a national and state policy, and as this strategy is based increasingly on arguments claiming the knowledge base is sufficient to implement such a strategy in a way to make it successful for all students, the impact on minority students becomes very important. If the impacts on minority students are not as good as for nonminority students, the courts could enter the conversation and hold the education system accountable for producing better results, even if this meant the provision of more resources. Were this to happen, desegregation and education reform would also be linked to school finance, a topic addressed in the next section and Chapter 13.

Equal Protection and School Finance[2]

School finance cases have been brought on two primary bases: the equal protection clause (of both the U.S. Constitution and of state constitutions) and education clauses in state constitutions. The initial cases in the late 1960s and early 1970s were brought under federal Equal Protection. The problem was widely varying educational expenditures across school districts in a state. The spending differentials produced significant differences in the quality of educational programs and services, thus providing state-required educational services differentially to students attending public schools. In addition, the fiscal and programmatic differences generally were related to local school district property wealth and not education need.

In bringing the issue to court, plaintiffs claimed that both a fundamental right, education, was involved and that state policy created a suspect classification, district property wealth per pupil, and argued for a structural change. These cases attempted to have the court continue its expansion of what could be litigated under the equal protection clause. Plaintiffs sought to have the court recognize both a new fundamental interest, education, and a new suspect class—property wealth per pupil. Further, the nature of the suspect class, district property wealth per pupil, was different from other suspect classes in that it applied to a political jurisdiction, a school district, and not an individual.

While initially successful in some state courts, neither argument proved successful when the issue reached the U.S. Supreme Court in March of 1973. The U.S. Supreme Court in the *San Antonio Independent School District* v. *Rodriguez* (1973) held that education was not a fundamental right under the U.S. Constitution and, though inequitable and unfair, that the Texas school finance system did not create a suspect class. As a result, it upheld the Texas school finance system. It invited plaintiffs to take their case to state courts by writing that state courts could decide that education was a fundamental right since education is mentioned in nearly all state constitutions.

The *Rodriguez* decision eliminated the federal Equal Protection clause as an avenue for challenging state school finance systems. As a result, since that time, nearly all cases have been brought on the basis of state equal protection and state education clauses. Chapter 13 provides more detail on school finance litigation in state courts, including the more recent education "adequacy" cases.

Linkages to Education Reforms of the 1990s. Chapter 13 also discusses several issues that connect school finance to the evolving education reform agenda. In this chapter, three additional issues are addressed: (1) the overlap of school finance, desegregation, and education reform, (2) the potential impact of school finance on urban districts, and (3) interstate fiscal disparities.

Chapter 13 shows how the most recent education adequacy cases in school finance have legally linked school finance to education reform. Courts in

---

[2]More detail on the nature and problems of state school financing is provided in Chapter 13. More detail on school finance litigation can be found in Odden and Picus (1992), Chapter 2, and Underwood and Verstegen, (1990).

school finance cases have held that states must enact finance structures and education programs that create standards for student performance, curriculum content, and student opportunity to learn. It appears that in writing these judgments, judges are simply taking the standards developed in the educational professional and reform communities and requiring states to include them as part of redesigned education and school finance systems (see *Harper* v. *Hunt* [1991] and *McDuffie* v. *Secretary of Education* [1993]). One reason for these actions is that courts need standards for making legal decisions. The standards being developed by the reform movement, then, provide courts an ideal mechanism to include in a decree. Since the standards emanate from the education and not legal community, their use by the courts is viewed as professionally legitimate.

Lurking behind these general school finance decrees are the education problems in low-income and minority districts and big cities, including those under desegregation mandates. For example, Alabama is under an education adequacy school finance decree. This means that each district under a desegregation order now has two court decrees, one on desegregation and one on school finance, requiring major changes in the educational program it offers. Moreover, in Alabama it could be argued that the school finance order deals with the school building and educational program vestiges of segregation, thus further cementing the connections between the two court mandates.

In Massachusetts, the adequacy court decree applies to all districts, including the city of Boston, which is under a desegregation decree. Thus, in this state also the school finance decree puts an ambitious court mandate behind the type of education program that must be offered in Boston, and which meets the educational quality required by desegregation.

The point is that as both school finance and desegregation litigation and court decrees have evolved to include the major education standards components of systemic reform (and Goals 2000), education reform becomes intertwined with both school finance reform and the educational components of desegregation. Further, as these types of school finance decrees hit states (several adequacy suits are under way in Southern states) and districts under desegregation decrees, it is likely that the three issues will need to be worked out in tandem rather than individually (see also Kazal-Thresher, 1994).

A second issue linking school finance and education reform concerns urban districts. Trends in school finance decisions could portend new fiscal support for large, urban districts experiencing financial shortages. For example, the 1990 *Abbot* v. *Burke* decision in New Jersey required that state to not only raise the revenues per pupil in New Jersey's poorest cities to that in the wealthiest suburbs, but also required the state to provide an even additional amount of compensatory education funds for the low-income students in those cities. It will probably take this type of language to make sure that all states inject the level of financial resources into big city school districts that will enable them to offer the high quality educational programs of systemic reform. Without such additional fiscal help, many big city districts would be unable to implement such a program.

Third, as the country works to implement the national education goals in part through the Goals 2000 legislation, there is the possibility that cases will be brought to the U.S. Supreme Court both challenging intrastate fiscal disparities as well as interstate disparities. Hertert, Busch, and Odden (1994) showed that disparities across the 50 states are substantial, and that disparities across all districts in the country irrespective of state borders are greater than the fiscal disparities within any individual state. In an era of national goals and the rhetoric of educating all students to high standards, it will be difficult forever to keep the nation's high court from revisiting the issues of these dramatic disparities in school financing. A good prediction will be that someone in a poor state, with above average tax effort, below average education spending, and low-achievement levels for its minority children, will file a school finance case in the federal courts arguing that such inequities are unconstitutional under the equal protection clause especially in the context of Goals 2000. How the court will respond is not known, but it would be smart for policymakers and educators, including the President and the Congress, to brace themselves for such a revisitation of school finance by the U.S. Supreme Court.

CONCLUSION

Though not obvious at first blush, the bold education reforms of the 1990s could very well stimulate a wide array of new federal court decisions on education policy, drawing on requirements in both the first and fourteenth amendments to the U.S. Constitution. The most ominous is the overlap between education reform and desegregation that could ultimately find courts requiring districts and schools to implement a systemic reform program for all students and eliminate differentials in education results across racial boundaries. With similar court mandates for systemic reform coming from school finance cases as well (see Chapter 13), the courts could become the surprise partner of education reform in the future. While this possibility is not attractive to all, it clearly suggests that education leaders should pay close attention to evolving court decrees on education issues.

School Finance in the 1990s[1]

School finance is always a big issue. There never seems to be enough money. Recessions and slow economic growth put fiscal squeezes onto school districts. The demands of reform seem impossible without large dollar infusions. Further, the sweeping state supreme court decisions overturning school finance structures in Kentucky, Massachusetts, New Hampshire, New Jersey, and Texas between 1989 and 1994, aggressive decisions by lower courts in Alabama, Missouri, and Rhode Island, and active or planned cases in nearly half the states (Dively and Hickrod, 1993), have continued active court pressure to change the way we finance our schools. In short, dollar shortfalls, education finance litigation, fiscal inequities, and school finance reform are firmly established on state education policy agendas (Massell and Fuhrman, 1994). This chapter discusses the complex contours of education finance, and outlines both short-term and long-term policy options for school finance reform. The longer term options link new directions in school finance to the systemic reform directions of education policy (Business Roundtable, 1991; Smith and O'Day, 1991; National Alliance for Business, 1994).

The chapter is divided into three sections. The first discusses the scope of public school funding and the nature of changes in education finance in recent decades; this section shows that for most of the century education funding has been growing at rates far surpassing what most would predict. The next section provides an overview of traditional school finance issues and the evolution of litigation attacking school finance fiscal disparities. The last section addresses strategies for redesigning school finance as a support for state systemic reform and as an antidote to education's productivity problem of rising resources with flat student achievement.

---

[1]This chapter draws from and expands three previously published articles: Odden, 1992b, Odden, 1994a, Odden 1994b.

Public school funding is a big fiscal business that has grown by large amounts throughout this century. In 1930, the country spent 2.1 billion for its schools. That amount grew to 195.2 billion in 1990 and is estimated to grow to nearly 300 billion by 1994 (all numbers in nominal terms). As Table 13-1 shows, education revenues comprised 3.6 percent of the country's gross national product in 1990, having risen from 2.0 percent in the early parts of the century. Odden and Picus (1992) presented data that showed education dollars per pupil, after adjusting for inflation, rose by 375 percent in the 30 years from 1920 to 1950 and another 51 percent between 1950 and 1960.

But predictions for education funding changes always seem to be pessimistic. At the end of the 1970s, Kirst and Garms (1980) wrote that the optimistic fiscal scenario for the 1980s would be a steady fiscal state—enough funds to cover enrollment growth and inflation, but no real increases. When the *Nation at Risk* report (National Commission on Excellence in Education, 1983) was issued, several articles (e.g., Odden, 1984) suggested that implementing its recommendations would require an extra 20 to 25 percent in real per pupil resources, too high a price, and recommended lower cost strategies for education improvement. When the Carnegie Forum on Education and the Economy (1986) issued its *A Nation Prepared* report for transforming teaching into a full profession, the recommendations were priced at an additional 26 percent in real per pupil spending; few were confident that the nation would put that level of new resources into public schools, even during an era of education reform.

While school funding increased by more than these amounts by the end of the decade (Odden, 1990a), the proposals of neither report were fully implemented. The country, educators, education policymakers, and teachers simply did not believe that the funds for these ambitious reform programs would be provided. If a poll were taken of superintendents, administrators, teachers, and

TABLE 13-1. Educational Revenues, GNP, and Personal Income (billions), 1930–1990

Year	Total Educational Revenues	(GNP)	Revenues as percent of GNP	(PI)	Revenues as percent of PI
1930	$2.1	$104	2.0	$84	2.5
1940	2.3	100	2.3	78	3.0
1950	5.4	288	1.9	228	2.4
1960	14.7	515	2.8	409	3.6
1970	40.3	1,015	4.0	832	4.8
1980	96.9	2,732	3.6	2,259	4.3
1990	195.2	5,471[a]	3.6	4,672	4.2

[a]Estimated.

Abbreviations: GNP, gross national product; PI, personal income.

Source: Data from NCES, 1989a and NCES, 1989–90.

even most public education policymakers today, it likely would show that most believe school funding will not increase much during the 1990s, and that education will do well to keep its nose above the fiscal water line, i.e., to stay even fiscally. Indeed, as the 1991 recession hit state revenue coffers and education aid was cut along with aid for other functions, the fiscal scenario for education looked bleak, making the "steady fiscal state" scenario seem optimistic. This assumption of few new dollars can dampen local willingness to adopt an ambitious and perhaps expensive reform program. If inaction on education reform in the 1990s is coupled with yet another decade of rising education revenues, a "golden" opportunity for using new dollars more productively will have been lost.

Despite protestations to the contrary, education funding for public elementary and secondary schools has continued to increase at substantial rates. For each of the past three decades, funding per pupil after adjusting for inflation has risen by a minimum of one-third and a maximum of two-thirds, continuing the long trend of rising education dollars. The facts are shown in Tables 13-2 and 13-3.

These numbers show that relatively high levels of new fiscal resources have been provided for education nationally and in most states for the past 30 years. Nationally, expenditures per pupil increased by 1,223 percent in nominal terms between 1960 and 1990, and by 205 percent in real, i.e., inflation adjusted, terms over this 30-year time period. The inflation adjusted per pupil rise was 69 percent during the 1960s, 22 percent during the 1970s, and 48 percent during the 1980s. Put differently, per pupil funding about doubled between 1960 and 1980, and then increased severalfold, thus tripling between 1960 and 1990. Further, this pattern has occurred during periods of enrollment growth (the 1960s), enrollment decline (1970s) and enrollment stability (1980s). Moreover, this pattern is true despite the occurrence of recessions which, before the 1980s, tended to happen about every seven years. While some of these funds have been used to build schools, and provide new services for handicapped, poor, and other students with extra education needs, the bottom line is that the country consistently, overtime, has injected large levels of new resources into the public schools.

Two caveats should be mentioned concerning the overall patterns of school funding changes. First, because of the state and local financing of education which produces different levels of resources across states and districts, a large overall national average increase can be much larger or much smaller, including a decrease in specific states and districts. In other words, the fiscal disparities that have plagued American school finance for the entire twentieth century (Odden and Picus, 1992) undercut much of the positive side of the overall funding increases.

Second, education's fiscal increases over the past decades generally occurred in small increments. Indeed, over a 30-year time period, a 205 percent overall real increase averages just over two percent a year, not a large annual amount. Thus in any one year, real increases in resources tend to be small, but as anyone familiar with compounding interest knows, small amounts can compound over decades into quite large amounts. This phenomenon seems to have been the case for education.

The implications of these fiscal trends for the 1990s are nevertheless not so clear. Unless history completely reverses itself, public school funding per pupil could rise again during the 1990s. Despite the slow economic recovery for the first few years of the 1990s, the pattern of increases in education dollars for the beginning of the 1990s was better than that in the 1980s, when real education revenues dropped during the recession of 1981 and 1982 but then rebounded handsomely for the remainder of the decade. Table 13-4 shows that per pupil education spending in this decade has exceeded inflation each year from 1990 to 1994, although not by much.

Only time will tell what the real, per pupil funding change will be by the end of the decade of the 1990s. History would suggest significant increases. Indeed, the federal government predicts that education funding will rise by another 42 percent between 1993 and 2003, after adjusting for inflation, largely based on historical patterns of growth and traditional assumptions about the course of the economy. But there are some indications that this might be an overly rosy prediction. If the economy does not pick up or, as the next section argues, there is resistance to increased public sector spending, education funding increases in the 1990s could be modest.

Challenges to These Stable Sources of School Funding

Despite the impressive historical fiscal record, an argument can be made that continued education funding increases will be harder to produce in this decade. Several factors are behind this more pessimistic perspective.

First, one source of increased revenues in the 1970s and 1980s—the state—may not be a viable source for increased school funding during the 1990s. Indeed, the shift of funding from local to state sources seems to have stabilized in the late 1980s with states providing about 50 percent of revenues, locals about 44 percent, and the federal government about 6 percent. Actually, the state share dropped a couple of points to 48 percent during the early 1990s while the local share rose to 46 percent. Today, moreover, state tax rates generally are not being increased for schools; greater state dollars are being provided more for closing state budget gaps, building prisons, and funding Medicaid.

State tax rates were raised throughout the 1980s both in response to a drop in federal aid for many functions and to finance ambitious education reforms; income taxes also were indexed to inflation to keep their natural increases under control (Gold, 1983, 1986; Odden, 1990b). There is little sentiment across the country for higher state sales or income tax rates (Gold, 1993b). While state tax bases could be broadened, expanding the sales tax to services for example, or new revenue sources could be provided, by giving schools or local governments authority to enact sales or income taxes, all face both technical and political obstacles (Gold, 1993b; Kirst, 1994; Odden and Picus, 1992).

States that do not have one of the three major tax sources, such as a sales tax in Oregon or an income tax in Texas, could enact such a new tax. But today the proceeds might be used more to reduce the tax burden on the other two taxes, particularly the property tax, than to increase funding for any function, such as education. This scenario happened in the early 1990s in Connecticut

TABLE 13-2. Change in Current Expenditure Per Pupil In Average Daily Attendance In Public Elementary and Secondary Schools, By State: 1959–60 to 1989–90

State	Exp. Per ADA 1959–60	Exp. Per ADA 1969–70	% Change 1959–60 to 1979–80	Exp. Per ADA 1979–80	% Change 1969–70 to 1979–80	Exp. Per ADA 1989–90	% Change 1979–80 to 1989–90	% Change 1959–60 to 1989–90
United States	375	816	117.60	2,272	178.43	4,960	118.31	1,222.67
Alabama	241	544	125.73	1,612	196.32	3,327	106.39	1,280.50
Alaska	506	1,123	121.94	4,728	321.02	8,374	77.12	1,554.94
Arizona	404	720	78.22	1,971	173.75	4,057	105.83	904.21
Arkansas	225	568	152.44	1,574	177.11	3,485	121.41	1,448.89
California	424	867	104.48	2,268	161.59	4,391	93.61	935.61
Colorado	396	738	86.36	2,421	228.05	4,720	94.96	1,091.92
Connecticut	436	951	118.12	2,420	154.47	7,604	214.21	1,644.04
Delaware	456	900	97.37	2,861	217.89	5,696	99.09	1,149.12
D.C.	431	1,018	136.19	3,259	220.14	8,904	173.21	1,965.89
Florida	318	732	130.19	1,889	158.06	4,997	164.53	1,471.38
Georgia	253	588	132.41	1,625	176.36	4,187	157.66	1,554.94
Hawaii	325	841	158.77	2,322	176.10	4,448	91.56	1,268.62
Idaho	290	603	107.93	1,659	175.12	3,078	85.53	961.38
Illinois	438	909	107.53	2,587	184.60	5,118	97.84	1,068.49
Indiana	369	728	97.29	1,882	158.52	4,549	141.71	1,132.79
Iowa	368	844	129.35	2,326	175.59	4,453	91.44	1,110.05
Kansas	348	771	121.55	2,173	181.84	4,752	118.68	1,265.52
Kentucky	233	545	133.91	1,701	212.11	3,675	116.05	1,477.25
Louisiana	372	648	74.19	1,792	176.54	3,855	115.12	936.29
Maine	283	692	144.52	1,824	163.58	5,373	194.57	1,798.59
Maryland	393	918	133.59	2,598	183.01	6,196	138.49	1,476.59
Massachusetts	409	859	110.02	2,819	228.17	6,237	121.25	1,424.94
Michigan	415	904	117.83	2,640	192.04	5,546	110.08	1,236.39
Minnesota	425	904	112.71	2,387	164.05	4,971	108.25	1,069.65

TABLE 13-2 *(cont.)*

State	Exp. Per ADA 1959–60	Exp. Per ADA 1969–70	% Change 1959–60 to 1979–80	Exp. Per ADA 1979–80	% Change 1969–70 to 1979–80	Exp. Per ADA 1989–90	% Change 1979–80 to 1989–90	% Change 1959–60 to 1989–90
Mississippi	206	501	143.20	1,664	232.14	3,096	86.06	1,402.91
Missouri	344	709	106.10	1,936	173.06	4,507	132.80	1,210.17
Montana	411	782	90.27	2,476	216.62	4,736	91.28	1,052.31
Nebraska	337	736	118.40	2,150	192.12	4,842	125.21	1,336.80
Nevada	430	769	78.84	2,088	171.52	4,117	97.17	857.44
New Hampshire	347	723	108.36	1,916	165.01	5,304	176.83	1,428.53
New Jersey	388	1,016	161.86	3,191	214.07	7,991	150.42	1,959.54
New Mexico	363	707	94.77	2,034	187.69	3,518	72.96	869.15
New York	562	1,327	136.12	3,462	160.89	8,062	132.87	1,334.52
North Carolina	237	612	158.23	1,754	186.60	4,268	143.33	1,700.84
North Dakota	367	690	88.01	1,920	178.26	4,189	118.18	1,041.42
Ohio	365	730	100.00	2,075	184.25	5,136	147.52	1,307.12
Oklahoma	311	604	94.21	1,926	218.87	3,512	82.35	1,029.26
Oregon	448	925	106.47	2,692	191.03	5,521	105.09	1,132.37
Pennsylvania	409	882	115.65	2,535	187.41	6,061	139.09	1,381.91
Rhode Island	413	891	115.74	2,601	191.92	6,249	140.25	1,413.08
South Carolina	220	613	178.64	1,752	185.81	4,088	133.33	1,758.18
South Dakota	347	690	98.85	1,908	176.52	3,732	95.60	975.50
Tennessee	238	566	137.82	1,635	188.87	3,664	124.10	1,439.50
Texas	332	624	87.95	1,916	207.05	4,150	116.60	1,150.00
Utah	322	626	94.41	1,657	164.70	2,730	64.76	747.83
Vermont	344	807	134.59	1,997	147.46	6,227	211.82	1,710.17
Virginia	274	708	158.39	1,970	178.25	4,612	134.11	1,583.21
Washington	420	915	117.86	2,568	180.66	4,681	82.28	1,014.52
West Virginia	258	670	159.69	1,920	186.57	4,359	127.03	1,589.53
Wisconsin	413	883	113.80	2,477	180.52	5,524	123.01	1,237.53
Wyoming	450	856	90.22	2,527	195.21	5,577	120.70	1,139.33

Abbreviations: Exp, expenditure; ADA, average daily attendance.
Source: From the National Center for Educational Statistics, 1992, used by permission.

TABLE 13-3. *Change in Real Expenditure Per Pupil In Average Daily Attendance In Public Elementary and Secondary Schools, By State: 1959–60 to 1989–90 (Constant 1989–90 Dollars)*

State	Exp. Per ADA 1959–60	Exp. Per ADA 1969–70	% Change 1959–60 to 1979–80	Exp. Per ADA 1979–80	% Change 1969–70 to 1979–80	Exp. Per ADA 1989–90	% Change 1979–80 to 1989–90	% Change 1959–60 to 1989–90
U.S.	1,621	2,743	69.22	3,345	21.95	4,960	48.28	205.98
Alabama	1,042	1,828	75.43	2,281	24.78	3,327	45.86	219.29
Alaska	2,361	3,773	59.81	5,978	58.44	8,374	40.08	254.68
Arizona	1,744	2,421	38.82	2,980	23.09	4,057	36.14	132.63
Arkansas	973	1,908	96.09	2,190	14.78	3,485	59.13	258.17
California	1,832	2,915	59.12	3,351	14.96	4,391	31.04	139.68
Colorado	1,712	2,480	44.86	3,154	27.18	4,720	49.65	175.70
Connecticut	1,884	3,197	69.69	3,816	19.36	7,604	99.27	303.61
Delaware	1,969	3,025	53.63	3,711	22.68	5,696	53.49	189.28
D.C.	1,863	3,423	83.74	4,361	27.40	8,904	104.17	377.94
Florida	1,373	2,461	79.24	3,198	29.95	4,997	56.25	263.95
Georgia	1,095	1,976	80.46	2,586	30.87	4,187	61.91	282.37
Hawaii	1,403	2,825	101.35	3,378	19.58	4,448	31.68	217.03
Idaho	1,252	2,028	61.98	2,491	22.83	3,078	23.56	145.85
Illinois	1,895	3,057	61.32	3,717	21.59	5,118	37.69	170.08
Indiana	1,593	2,447	53.61	2,731	11.61	4,549	66.57	185.56
Iowa	1,589	2,837	78.54	3,086	8.78	4,453	44.30	180.24
Kansas	1,503	2,592	72.46	3,114	20.14	4,752	52.60	216.17
Kentucky	1,007	1,833	82.03	2,218	21.00	3,675	65.69	264.95
Louisiana	1,607	2,178	35.53	2,771	27.23	3,855	39.12	139.89
Maine	1,222	2,328	90.51	2,717	16.71	5,373	97.75	339.69
Maryland	1,697	3,087	81.91	3,838	24.33	6,196	61.44	265.11
Massachusetts	1,767	2,888	63.44	3,630	25.69	6,237	71.82	252.97
Michigan	1,794	3,038	69.34	3,737	23.01	5,546	48.41	209.14
Minnesota	1,837	3,037	65.32	3,785	24.63	4,971	31.33	170.60

TABLE 13-3 *(cont.)*

State	Exp. Per ADA 1959–60	Exp. Per ADA 1969–70	% Change 1959–60 to 1979–80	Exp. Per ADA 1979–80	% Change 1969–70 to 1979–80	Exp. Per ADA 1989–90	% Change 1979–80 to 1989–90	% Change 1959–60 to 1989–90
Mississippi	890	1,684	89.21	2,149	27.61	3,096	44.07	247.87
Missouri	1,486	2,382	60.30	2,816	18.22	4,507	60.05	203.30
Montana	1,775	2,628	48.06	3,313	26.07	4,736	42.95	166.82
Nebraska	1,456	2,475	69.99	3,115	25.86	4,842	55.44	232.55
Nevada	1,860	2,586	39.03	2,913	12.65	4,117	41.33	121.34
New Hampshire	1,501	2,430	61.89	2,893	19.05	5,304	83.34	253.36
New Jersey	1,675	3,416	103.94	4,371	27.96	7,991	82.82	377.07
New Mexico	1,567	2,376	51.63	2,731	14.94	3,518	28.82	124.51
New York	2,427	4,460	83.77	5,659	26.88	8,062	42.46	232.18
North Carolina	1,025	2,058	100.78	2,677	30.08	4,268	59.43	316.39
North Dakota	1,585	2,318	46.25	2,724	17.52	4,189	53.78	164.29
Ohio	1,577	2,454	55.61	2,862	16.63	5,136	79.45	225.68
Oklahoma	1,346	2,032	50.97	2,517	23.87	3,512	39.53	160.92
Oregon	1,937	3,108	60.45	3,826	23.10	5,521	44.30	185.03
Pennsylvania	1,769	2,964	67.55	3,712	25.24	6,061	63.28	242.62
Rhode Island	1,786	2,996	67.75	3,933	31.28	6,249	58.89	249.89
South Carolina	951	2,059	116.51	2,531	22.92	4,088	61.52	329.86
South Dakota	1,499	2,319	54.70	2,626	13.24	3,732	42.12	148.97
Tennessee	1,029	1,903	84.94	2,429	27.64	3,664	50.84	256.07
Texas	1,436	2,098	46.10	2,607	24.26	4,150	59.19	189.00
Utah	1,393	2,105	51.11	2,510	19.24	2,730	8.76	95.98
Vermont	1,486	2,713	82.57	3,348	23.41	6,227	85.99	319.04
Virginia	1,185	2,379	100.76	2,941	23.62	4,612	56.82	289.20
Washington	1,817	3,077	69.35	3,419	11.11	4,681	36.91	157.62
West Virginia	1,117	2,252	101.61	2,567	13.99	4,359	69.81	290.24
Wisconsin	1,785	2,967	66.22	3,454	16.41	5,524	59.93	209.47
Wyoming	1,946	2,877	47.84	3,496	21.52	5,577	59.53	186.59

Abbreviations: Exp., expenditure; ADA, average daily attendance.
Source: From the National Center for Educational Statistics, 1992, used by permission.

TABLE 13-4. Education Expenditures Per Pupil in the 1990s (1992–93 dollars)

	1989–90	1990–91	1991–92	1992–93	1993–94	
Real expenditures per pupil	$5,570	$5,582	$5,645, est.	$5,721. est.	$5,747, proj.	3.

Abbreviations: est., estimated; proj., projected.
Source: From the National Center for Education Statistics, used by permission.

when it finally enacted an income tax, in 1994 in Michigan when it cut the property tax and replaced it with new state sales and cigarette taxes, and is predicted for Wisconsin which must reduce property taxes by over 1 billion in 1997.

Recently, moreover, Colorado and Oklahoma joined the large list of states that limit state expenditures; each year, there continue to be such proposals put to the voters or debated in state legislatures. When these proposals are approved, the most likely scenario overtime is a reduction in state spending which also usually produces fewer school revenues (Picus, 1991; Theobald and Hannar, 1991, 1992). The more these types of state measures are approved, the more tenuous becomes the ability of states to hike education revenues.

Second, the federal government is a potential but unlikely source of new education revenues. It already spends much more than it collects and any significant new spending likely will occur in health rather than in K–12 education.

Third, there may be a brewing local tax revolt. Nationally, local taxes were the fastest rising revenue source in the country between 1985 and 1993 (Gold, 1993a), outpacing both state and federal taxes. Rising local taxes included not only increasing property taxes, but also many new local sales and income taxes approved over the past decade when there was resistance to raising state and federal taxes. As a result, local taxes in the aggregate rose at rates above both inflation and personal income. Rising property values were exacerbated by shifts of property taxes from nonresidential property and business inventory onto residential property.

The bulk of the rise in local taxes was pumped into the schools. Indeed, one of the unmentioned secrets of the revenue rise for schools during the 1980s was rising property taxes. Many states, particularly southern states, saw the property tax as an untapped revenue source, and increased property tax rates as a major component of their education reforms (Odden, 1990b). Thus, the antitax property tax fever could express itself as an antischool movement as well. Growing school tax bills together with flat student achievement could increasingly become irritating to local tax payers.

The law enacted by the Michigan legislature in July 1993 that eliminated the local property tax as a school revenue was the clearest indicator of current dissatisfaction with property tax burdens. That action cut about 6.3 billion from Michigan's total 10 billion public school budget. This drastic action emerged from 20 years of unhappiness with high property taxes. Their strategy for replacing that lost revenue hinged at least partly on taxpayers approving an increase in the sales tax from 4 to 6 percent, a change that had been voted down by large majorities 11 times during the past 20 years.

In a somewhat less drastic initiative in 1990, Oregon taxpayers enacted a substantial reduction in property taxes that was to be phased-in over five years; the lost property taxes were to be covered by new state revenues. By 1993, the third year of the phase-down, neither the legislature nor the people had approved a sales tax to cover the lost revenue; as a result total education revenues were down.

These combined events suggest the time might be ripe in many states for a 1990s round of property tax relief and reform, much as happened during the early 1970s. While it would be wise for policymakers to respond to public dissatisfaction with rising property tax burdens, throwing out the property tax is risky because replacement state revenues rarely cover the lost property tax revenues. Further, as just argued, the fiscal resources today for reducing property taxes are fewer than in the 1970s. Not only is there resistance either to enacting new taxes or raising existing tax rates, strategies used in the school finance reforms of the 1970s (Callahan and Wilken, 1976), but also there is no "free" revenue source such as the federal revenue sharing dollars that first became available to states in 1973. Responding to the current cry for property tax relief, therefore, will be very hard to do fiscally in the 1990s.

These realities could portend a "flattening" of the public sector, or at least a lower increase than has been experienced during the past. The result would be much slower growth and potentially even decline in school revenues. Such a scenario would be at odds with the consistent rise in education funding over the past 70 years and would represent a new departure for school finance, as well as for government funding in general. Some "read into" the events in Michigan, Oregon, and California a potential watershed change in school finance.

Only time will tell whether such a pessimistic scenario becomes a future reality. But what could be predicted is somewhat slower growth in education revenues caused by the overall sluggishness of the national and most state economies, together with stiffened resistance to raising tax rates, and increasing property tax burdens. Until economic growth picks up, tax revenues flowing into government coffers, including those of school districts, could be in very limited supply.

A Productivity Problem

Another aspect of education finance is the fact of steadily rising resources and flat outcomes, i.e., only small aggregate changes in student achievement. Nearly all analyses of student achievement over the past decades conclude that while there have been changes, student achievement in 1990 was at about the same level as in 1970. Koretz (1986; 1987) concluded that there was indeed a decline in average test scores in the late 1960s and early 1970s. He concluded that the declines occurred for all students, in public and private schools, and in all regions of the country. Further, he concluded that the declines were documented by all types of tests, Scholastic Aptitude Test (SAT) and the American College Test (ACT) scores, and scores on standardized achievement tests.

Finally, the decline, which lasted about ten years, was immediately followed by a widespread and significant rise, so that by the mid-1980s achievement was back to where it had started. The silver lining within these results was that about half the achievement gap between minorities and nonminorities was closed over this same time period. All of Koretz's major findings are essentially corroborated by 20 years of results from the National Assessment of Educational Progress (Applebee, Langer, and Mullis, 1989; Mullis, Owen, and Phillips, 1990).

The bottom line conclusion is that while education dollars have risen substantially over the past few decades, average achievement generally has stayed flat, thus leading to an educational productivity problem—increases in dollar input resources with flat outcomes. The productivity problem is particularly urgent because current reform notions posit a new and higher level of outcomes for all students that the education system is supposed to meet (National Governors' Association, 1990). While educators tend to be uncomfortable with applying the concept of productivity to education, questions about flat student performance amidst rising resources are nevertheless being raised.

In assessing the fiscal inequities that are discussed in the next section and that have been the target of school finance policy over the bulk of this century, therefore, two implications of the above discussion should be kept in mind. First, despite unacceptable inequities in the distribution of dollars discussed in section two, overall fiscal support for the public schools has consistently increased and is likely to continue to do so to some degree in the 1990s as well. Second, funding rose even though the key result of the education system, student achievement, did not. Thus the education system is presented with some degree of a productivity problem. If the bold goals for the education system of raising the achievement of all students to new, high levels can be accomplished, not only would more equity of student results be produced but also the chronic productivity problem in education might also be reversed, a very salutary accomplishment!

TRADITIONAL SCHOOL FINANCE ISSUES

The average, national increases in educational funding do not hold for all states, nor for school districts within states. Tables 13-2 and 13-3 show that there are major differences in what is spent per pupil for public elementary and secondary schools across the 50 states, and that changes in state revenues per pupil are both above and below the national average. Hence, the data show that there are inequities across the states. These inequities exist even when the numbers are adjusted for differences in prices of educational services (Barro, 1992).

Within states, moreover, school finance is characterized by dramatic fiscal differences across school districts, that recently were characterized as "savage inequalities" (Kozol, 1991). These fiscal inequities (see Hertert, Busch, and Odden, 1994, for a recent quantification of these inequities) have been the primary focus of school finance analysis and policy for most of this century (Odden and Picus, 1992). Traditional school finance inequities derive from the way states finance public elementary and secondary schools. In most states, local property tax dollars are the major source of school revenues. Indeed, early in the twentieth century, property taxes provided nearly all school revenues, with states providing only small amounts, and the federal government providing barely any revenues.

Nationally, local revenues comprise about 46 percent of education revenues, states provide about 48 percent and the federal government 6 percent (National Council on Educational Standards and Testing, 1992). Heavy reliance on local property taxes produces fiscal inequities because the property tax base is not distributed equally across school districts. As a result, some districts have a large, while others have a small property tax base per pupil. At a given tax rate, therefore, districts high in property wealth per pupil raise more money per pupil than districts low in property wealth per pupil. In many states, this unequal ability to raise local revenues varies by as much as ten to one.

While a variety of school finance programs can eliminate these local revenue raising inequities (Odden and Picus, 1992), typical state programs reduce but do not eliminate them. As a result, revenues (from local and state sources) per pupil vary considerably in most states, with a high correlation between per pupil revenues and the local per pupil property tax base. High revenue per pupil districts usually are rich in property wealth per pupil and levy below average tax rates, while low revenue per pupil districts usually are poor in property wealth per pupil and levy above average tax rates.

School Finance Reform During the 1970s

These fiscal disparities were the subject of several court suits in the 1970s, beginning with *Serrano* v. *Priest* in California (Odden and Picus, 1992: Chapter 2). Using both the Equal Protection Clause of the Fourteenth Amendment to the U.S. Constitution and state constitution education clauses, cases were filed in several states arguing that it was unconstitutional for local property wealth to be linked with revenues per pupil. The suits proposed the fiscal neutrality standard for the courts: that education quality (as measured by dollars per pupil) should be a function of state but not local wealth (defined as property wealth per pupil). While the U.S. Supreme Court decision in *San Antonio Independent School District* v. *Rodriguez* (1973) held that these inequities did not violate the fourteenth amendment to the federal constitution, cases continued in state courts on the basis of both state equal protection and state education clauses. In about half of the cases, state courts overturned school finance structures; in the other cases, state courts found that school finance systems, with similar fiscal disparities, did not violate constitutional requirements (Odden and Picus, 1992).

A direct result of a court mandate or the threat of such a mandate led over 35 state legislatures to enact fundamental changes in their school finance structures between 1971 and 1985 (Odden and Wohlstetter, 1992). These reforms had five major characteristics. First, they revamped the school finance equalization formula sending more state funds to property poor, lower spending districts. Second, they increased the overall state role in funding schools. Third, they increased state funding for special needs student programs—compensatory, special, and bilingual education programs. Fourth, the reforms often increased aid for the extraordinary needs of large urban, city districts. Fifth, many reforms were accompanied by education tax and spending limitations that restricted local fiscal control over tax rates, and curbed annual increases in expenditures per pupil.

The reforms during the 1970s also produced change in the sources of school revenues, as shown in Table 13-5. Local revenues dropped from over 50 percent of total revenues in 1970 to 43.4 percent in 1980, while state revenues rose from about 40 to 47 percent. The expanded state role is not surprising since only the state can equalize local education tax bases or school spending across districts.

But despite the attention focused on them, school finance inequities across the country did not change that much from the mid-1970s to the mid-1980s. The disparity in expenditures per pupil rose modestly (with the average coefficient of variation increasing from 0.16 to 0.19) and the relationship between revenues and wealth declined a bit (with the average correlation coefficient dropping from 0.55 to 0.50), but both statistics remained high (Schwartz and Moskowitz, 1988). Another study indicated that expenditure per pupil disparities decreased moderately from 1980 to 1987 (Wyckoff, 1992).

While riveting attention on the fiscal inequities that derived from unequal property tax bases, school finance court cases and subsequent school finance policy reforms left a major policy issue unresolved. Was the policy issue variation in the tax base, i.e., variation in ability to raise revenues, the traditional school finance issue? Or was the policy issue differences in spending per pupil, a more restrictive view of the school finance problem (Wise, 1969)? Each implies a different solution.

The remedy for resolving variation in the local tax base is to enact a Guaranteed Tax Base (GTB) program (or district power equalizing program) in which all districts are guaranteed a minimum tax base by the state (Coons, Clune, and Sugarman, 1970; Odden and Picus, 1992: Chapter 7). Then, school tax rates will produce equal revenues per pupil from state and local sources for districts with per pupil property wealth below or equal to the state guaranteed level. All districts, rich or poor, would raise substantially the same amount of money per pupil if they levied the same tax rate. GTB programs let local districts decide how high a tax rate to levy. Different tax rates produce

TABLE 13-5. Percent Revenues by Source for U.S. K–12 Public Education: 1960 to 1990

Government Level	Year			
	1960	1970	1980	1990
Federal	4.4	8.0	9.8	6.1
State	39.1	39.9	46.8	47.2
Local and Other	56.5	52.1	43.4	46.6

Source: From the National Center for Educational Statistics, 1992, used by permission.

different expenditures per pupil. Thus, *GTB programs allow for spending differences,* but differences are related to tax effort not local property wealth. In 1993, conditions in Michigan and Wisconsin documented this point as, in both states, expenditures per pupil varied substantially even though the states guaranteed a fairly high property tax base.

If, however, the school finance problem is defined as differences in spending per pupil per se for whatever reason, differences in tax bases or differences in local preference for education, the remedy is a school finance system that mandates equal spending across all school districts (albeit with appropriate adjustments for different pupil needs and different education prices). California, Florida, Hawaii, and Washington have systems that restrict local spending above a common base per pupil funding level.

Lack of clarity over the nature of the problem has plagued school finance policy for decades. State policymakers and education leaders need to decide if their definition of the school finance problem is unequal ability to raise local revenue, or unequal expenditures per pupil per se. The former requires a school finance program that provides equal access to a tax base while allowing for differences in local per pupil spending, while the latter requires a program to mandate equal spending, a focus of more recent school finance court cases.

School Finance During the 1980s and 1990s

Despite the school finance reform ferment that begun in the 1970s, school finance did not change much during the 1980s, particularly with respect to sources of revenues and the typical fiscal inequities. As Table 13-5 shows, sources of education revenues at the end of the 1980s were about the same as at the beginning, although local sources rose a bit, to 47.7 percent, and federal sources dropped from 9.8 to 6.1 percent.

The focus was on providing more money, but school finance structural changes were dormant or at least secondary. Even the school finance changes made in response to the turn of the decade court mandates in Kentucky, New Jersey, and Texas were quite traditional and broke little new school finance policy design ground (Odden, 1993d).

But more change is probably in store for the 1990s. First, there is a push for education reforms but with limited fiscal increases; this either requires local restructuring or alteration in how states fund the schools. Second, there are more state actions creating new local revenue sources for the schools, such as local income and sales taxes that have been provided to Ohio and California school districts, respectively. Third, there is a strong push to link school finance to student achievement results and systemic reform (National Alliance for Business, 1994; Odden, 1993b, 1994b). Finally there has been a series of new school finance court cases moving court decrees and legislative responses far beyond the fiscal neutrality standards of the cases in the 1970s.

School Finance Litigation

One of the 1980s and 1990s surprises was the resurgence and new directions taken in school finance litigation. The small amount of legal action in school finance at the dawn of the 1980s rose to a crescendo by the end of the decade, as court cases had been filed or were being planned in about 25 states. Also, the 1980s state supreme court school finance cases overturning school finance systems in Arkansas, Kentucky, Montana, New Jersey, and Texas began a process of raising new issues, that then accelerated in the 1990s with decisions in Alabama, Minnesota (later overturned by the state supreme court), Massachusetts, New Hampshire, and Rhode Island. The Texas and New Jersey cases represented a "second round" of litigation, each state having experienced a court suit during the 1970s as well. The 1989 school finance case in Kentucky broke new ground by overturning the state's entire education system, its organization, structure, programs, and governance systems, as well as its school finance system. The 1993 Alabama case was equally sweeping in its legal findings, holding that the state's finance structure was inadequate and did not provide sufficient funds for districts to meet state set educational standards. As important, plaintiffs in the 1990s tended to win most cases brought to trial, as compared to the 33 percent success rate of the 1970s (Odden and Picus, 1992).

Second Decisions. Interestingly, courts have not been adverse to rendering a "second decision." Even during the 1970s, courts in Connecticut and Washington found systems unconstitutional in a second case. In the 1980s, courts in both New Jersey and Texas ruled school finance systems unconstitutional in a second round of litigation. The Texas case was noteworthy in two ways. First, it was the earlier Texas case, *Rodriguez,* that in 1973 reached the U.S. Supreme Court which, by upholding the Texas system, eliminated the federal courts as a route for challenging school finance inequities. Second, prior to the 1989 ruling, several new, conservative justices had been elected to the Texas Supreme Court earlier that year, yet the court surprised the state and the country by unanimously finding the Texas school finance structure unconstitutional. Moreover, about 18 months later, the court again unanimously overturned the reform enacted by the Texas legislature in mid-1990 (Picus and Hertert, 1993).

Focus on Spending Disparities. Nearly all school finance court cases challenge the linkage between per pupil spending and per pupil property wealth, the traditional school finance legal issue. But, several of the late 1980s and early 1990s legal decisions suggested an emerging focus on spending differences per se, rather than just on the relationship between spending and wealth. The Texas decision revolved around differences in spending between the bottom 50 and top 50 districts. The Kentucky court required a much higher per pupil spending base across all districts. The New Jersey decision required that spending in the bottom districts be equal to that of the top spending districts. The Alabama case stated that differences in spending between even the very top and very bottom spending districts were constitutionally invalid, since these districts were part of the *state* education system and enrolled a significant number of students. It appears the balance in school finance court decrees may be tipping toward a standard of equal expenditures per pupil (with legitimate adjustments for pupil need and education price differences), and away from the fiscal neutrality standard that required just equal access to local property tax bases.

Further, courts seem to have become more restrictive in the magnitude of fiscal disparities allowed. In both the Kentucky and Texas cases, the vast majority of districts spent close to the state average and the court still overturned the finance systems. The lower court in the Minnesota case overturned spending differences that were only 10 percent higher for the wealthiest 10 percent of school districts. Disparities were not that large in the Alabama case either. Further, in nearly all cases today, plaintiffs show how spending differences lead to large variations in numbers of teachers and thus class size, quality of facilities, and level and quality of instructional materials. Plaintiffs show that even rather modest differences in dollars per pupil can produce notable differences in the levels of these educational inputs. Clune (1992) also proposed a new litigation standard for courts that are moving away from the simpler fiscal neutrality standard, and toward a more restrictive equal spending requirement.

New Issues. The New Jersey, Kentucky, Alabama, and Massachusetts cases, moreover, raised intriguing new issues. In New Jersey, the court focused its decision on the poorest 28 school districts and found the system *unconstitutional only for those districts.* Those 28 districts were primarily large urban school systems with low-property wealth per pupil, and high concentrations of poverty and minority students. The decision required the state to make the per pupil spending in these districts "substantially equal" to the spending in the highest wealth suburban districts.

In Kentucky, the court went far beyond ruling on the school finance system. By holding the entire education system unconstitutional, the Kentucky court may have set a precedent for the direction of school finance litigation, as well as education policy, during the 1990s. The court essentially ruled that disparities in local tax bases and dollar inputs were only part of the problem and required the state to redesign the entire education system—structure, governance, program, and finance.

The 1993 Alabama and Massachusetts cases, although not overturning the entire education system per se, nevertheless challenged several aspects of the state's overall education structure. These cases, together with the Kentucky case, may represent a transition of the courts away from a dollar input approach and towards an educational outcomes orientation. Language in these three court decisions discussed the nature of student achievement and stated explicitly or implied that the purpose of an education system is to prepare individuals to participate in the labor force and/or a postsecondary education experience. The language suggested that the court viewed a fair school finance system as a means to prepare all students to achieve at high standards.

The Alabama case, *Harper v. Hunt* (1991), may foreshadow what this language could mean. The Alabama court found that while the school finance structure was not that inequitable across districts, the overall level of funding was inadequate and, in a move similar to the late 1980s Kentucky case, ordered the state to redesign the overall education system and to fund it with more money. In an implementing mandate, the presiding judge required the state to include several elements of the evolving national educational standards in its response.

The explicit inclusion of national standards could be the legal mechanism for connecting school finance and program policy in the 1990s. Courts need standards to guide the creation of new policy in response to court decrees. In the 1970s, the school finance standard was fiscal neutrality, which just required that expenditures or revenues per pupil *not* be statistically related to property wealth per pupil. In the 1990s, the standards could be curriculum content standards, student performance standards on new assessment systems, as well as opportunity to learn standards (Odden, 1994c), which requires some version of an implemented systemic reform program together with an adequate finance package. In other words, as the education profession as well as state education policy provide standards for the education system, courts might very well mandate that the standards be provided for all districts, sites, and students. If school finance architects or state policymakers are reluctant to formally link school finance to the evolving education reform movement, courts might force the connection by the close of the century.

Another implication of the new directions in these court cases, according to University of Wisconsin Professor William Clune, is new legal recognition of the extra educational needs of children in poverty especially given research in many states that shows these students often have average or below average fiscal resources behind them and achieve at low levels. Indeed, Clune references both the New Jersey and Kentucky cases as specifically calling for a state responsibility to provide extra services to children from poverty backgrounds. The result is that courts may be moving towards recognizing poverty background as a legal mandate for services similar to how physical and mental handicaps or limited-English proficiency produces entitlements to educational services.

National Education Goals. The emergence of bold new national education goals has begun to focus the education system on student performance, on what students know and can do. The goals include bringing all students to high levels of thinking, problem solving, and communication in all basic content areas, and to have U.S. students rank first in the world in mathematics and science. As the school finance court cases move more directly to issues of student achievement results, it may be difficult for school finance and school finance litigation to limit itself to the fiscal and dollar input issues of the 1970s and 1980s. School finance policy in the 1990s may have to address directly issues related to student outcomes and school strategies required to produce those outcomes.

LINKING SCHOOL FINANCE TO SYSTEMIC REFORM

Thus, not only the arguments in the beginning chapters of this book but also court decrees in school finance suggest that the pressing need in education is to identify a set of strategies that will propel all students to levels of thinking and problem solving required for full participation in the workforce and society of the next century. The school finance challenge is to craft an education finance structure that would be an integral part of this overall strategy.

As discussed in previous chapters, nationally and in many states systemic reform is now identified as one potentially powerful way to produce these newer and higher levels of student achievement (Business Roundtable, 1991; National Council on Educational Standards and Testing, 1992; Smith and O'Day, 1991). Briefly, systemic reform includes the following key components:

- Ambitious student expectations that all students will perform at high levels on thinking and problem-solving skills.
- High-quality curriculum standards.
- New forms of performance assessment, strongly linked to the curriculum standards.
- Development of teacher expertise to teach this curriculum.
- Restructured management (including site-based implementation) and finance.

Determining just what restructured management and finance means is complex, but there are lessons that can be learned from nonschool organizations.

The Implications of Systemic Reform for Governance and Finance

In the private and public sectors where the challenge has been to dramatically improve outcomes and often times at reduced costs, the most effective strategy has been to set clear performance targets at the top of the system, flatten the organizational structure, move decision making down to work teams actually providing the service, and hold them accountable for results. Indeed, high-involvement or decentralized management is *the* rapidly rising organizational strategy used in the nonschool sectors of our economy to enhance organizational effectiveness and productivity (Barzelay, 1992; Lawler, 1986, 1992; Lawler and Mohrman, 1993; Osborne and Gaebler, 1992).

As Chapter 7 argued, a decentralized, high-involvement management system seems appropriate for education too. Research discussed in Chapter 7 concludes that decentralized management works best when four resources are developed in the decentralized unit:

- Information
- Knowledge
- Power
- Rewards—the compensation structure

Implications for a New School Finance

The above imply five new structural aspects of a new school finance system that would support a systemic education system designed to produce higher levels of student achievement:

- A focus on the school as the key organizational unit.
- Devolution of power over the budget and personnel to schools.
- Development of a comprehensive school level information system.
- Investment of dollars in professional development and training.
- Redesign of teacher compensation.

A School-based Policy System. Most states now have a district finance system. In the nineteenth century, most states created local school districts. Money was raised by districts and distributed by states and the federal government to districts. Schools received resources, teachers, books, transportation, etc., but they rarely received money. This district emphasis needs to change to a school orientation if systemic reform is implemented. This policy emphasis fits with the dozen or so states that have mandates for school-based decision making; most of those states assume that, over some time period, dollars will be decentralized to schools as well.

The school emphasis is undergirded by other research and policy trends. The school effectiveness research, which is broader than just the effective schools research and evolved during the 1970s and 1980s, clearly identified the school as the key organizational unit, the unit where educational services are provided and student learning occurs (see for example, Chapter 6).

Policy interest in public school choice, charter schools, and new school designs also target the school. In most states that have public school choice programs, students can select schools outside their district. In response, states had to determine how to reallocate dollars. Today, most states count the student as a pupil in the school/district attended, a policy that transfers the entire foundation or base level of funding from the sending to the receiving district. The point is that public school choice plans required states to face the issue of how much money per pupil would support each *school,* not just each *district* (Odden and Kotowski, 1992a).

States enacting Charter School programs, California, Colorado, Georgia, Massachusetts, Minnesota, New Mexico, and Wisconsin, also had to decide how much money would flow to each school. Charter school programs finance schools not districts and give school personnel total discretion over use of funds and selection of staff (Wohlstetter, 1994).

Finally, the New American Schools Development Corporation is an initiative directed to designing schools; each team must be explicit about the cost of the school design, which cannot exceed the national average expenditure per pupil.

In short, there are several substantive arguments for directing policy to the school and many policy initiatives actually doing so. Changing the finance system from one with the district as the key unit financed to one with the school as the key unit would seem to follow from these trends.

Move Budget and Personnel Power to the School. Power over the budget and personnel would then need to shift to the school. This shift would entail budgeting most dollars in a lump sum to schools. The more radical approach would be for states, or perhaps districts, to fund schools directly. A less dramatic approach would be for states to follow the lead of the United Kingdom and by law require that 85 to 90 percent of all dollars, both general and categorical, now allocated to districts be sent by the district to schools in a lump sum. This budgetary authority would need to be accompanied by devolving authority to the school for recruiting and selecting staff as well.

There could be three components to the level of money allocated to each school. First, each school should receive an equal base level of dollars per pupil. The preferred approach would be for the state to determine the base spending level. Following the new legal remedy for school finance inequities proposed by Clune (1992), the per pupil funding level should be put at the 90th to 95th percentile of spending in a state. Alternately, a state could enact a combined foundation-GTB structure (Odden and Picus, 1992). The foundation expenditure would be set at a level close to the median that would allow nonurban districts to develop the advanced cognitive proficiencies for their students; the GTB would be set at the 95th percentile to cover expenditures up to the 95th percentile, for districts/schools that wanted to spend above the foundation amount. Whatever the spending level guaranteed, moving budget authority to the school would entail having the state require each district to budget a large portion of per pupil revenues directly to the school.

Since some schools have poor children who need additional services in order to learn the core curriculum, the base allotment should be augmented by a substantial amount for every poor child. The dollar amount for this add-on should be sufficient for the school to raise the achievement of low-income children to acceptable levels of proficiency on thinking and problem solving tasks. The amount should be at least $1,000 for each poor student, the cost of implementing the Success for All program, which has been quite successful in producing substantial achievement gains (Madden et al., 1992). However, the cost of that program might be closer to $2,000 per pupil (Clune, 1993) which suggests an adequate compensatory education add-on could approach $2,000 for each low-income child.

Third, the purchasing power of the educational dollar varies across districts and labor market regions. Equal funding per pupil discriminates against urban districts, where prices are higher, and advantages nonmetropolitan districts, where prices are lower. Thus, states should modify all dollar allocations by some regional labor market index that adjusts for the varying purchasing power of the educational dollar (Chambers, 1982; Monk and Walker, 1991).

This finance structure would produce fiscal equity across not only school districts in a state but also schools. In one major sweep, fiscal equity could be accomplished. But it would result from a new finance structure designed as part of an overall systemic strategy to help schools produce high levels of student learning, not as part of a fiscal equity agenda.

Develop a School-based Information System. The data implication of school-based financing and decentralized management is a school-based fiscal accounting structure that would provide schools with detailed information on revenues, budgets, and expenditures by object, function, and program. At a minimum, this would technically mean moving current education fiscal accounting information systems down from the district to the school level. It also would require information on student performance, periodically over the course of the year, feedback from parents and the community on school satisfaction, benchmark information with schools in similar communities, and up-to-date information on the sociodemographics of the school context. For the most effective implementation, it would entail developing an on-line, personal computer-based, interactive system that would provide each school with accurate, up-to-date fiscal information, as well as all of these other data on teachers, students and the community.

Invest in Knowledge Development Activities. Effective decentralized management requires development of a new and wide range of knowledge and expertise for faculty in a school. This requires substantial investments in professional development and training. Training would need to focus on the knowledge and skills needed to teach the new thinking-oriented curriculum, on the expertise needed to engage in school-based fiscal decision making and budgeting, a broader range of competencies for teachers if many specialized jobs are eliminated (such as guidance counselors, curriculum supervisors, etc.) and those functions are taken on by teams of teachers in schools, and skills to engage in interpersonal, collegial activities. While lump sum budgeting could allow school faculty to allocate new funds for professional development, a state also could target 2 to 4 percent of the total school revenue for ongoing professional development and training, as Minnesota and Missouri set aside 2 percent in 1993.

Redesign Teacher Reward—Change Teacher Compensation. This dimension of new school finance would include changes in the reward or compensation structure for teachers. It would entail changing the base of teacher compensation from the indirect measures of education and experience to direct measures of individual knowledge and skills, i.e., what teachers know and can do. Such a structure also could include a salary increase for Certification from the National Board for Professional Teaching Standards. The revised compensation system also could include group-based (usually school faculty) performance awards, including bonuses for meeting improvement targets and cost-reduction gain sharing programs. Odden and Conley (1992) and Mohrman, Mohrman, and Odden (1993) outline in much more detail how such a new compensation structure could be designed, what the skill block components could include, and how to make a transition from the current to such a proposed system.

Further, new approaches to teacher compensation are of strong interest to the American Federation of Teachers and National Education Association, and to the National Board for Professional Teaching Standards (NBPTS), which hopes Board Certified teachers receive a pay increment. Moreover, rapid advances are being made in developing a technology that could be used to validly and reliably assess teacher knowledge and skills. The work of the NBPTS to assess what experienced teachers know and can do will significantly add to this technology. The work of the Educational Testing System, the Council of Chief State School Officers, and several states to license teachers on the basis of a beginning set of knowledge and pedagogical skills represent other contributory efforts. By the time a state or district becomes engaged in the processes of designing a skills-based pay structure, these technologies could be tapped and used for implementation.

Choice and Deregulation. Two other issues should be linked to such a new approach to school finance: choice and deregulation. The type of decentralization described above produces choice among educational professionals in how to accomplish education achievement targets. Different schools likely would take on different characteristics—some math and science oriented, some more humanities oriented, some using standard curriculum frameworks, others taking a more thematic approach, etc.

Some of these strategies might not be good for some children or liked by some parents. As a result, it would be inappropriate to require everyone to attend his or her neighborhood school. Thus choice of school, at least *within the public sector,* should also be provided. Put differently, public school choice within and across districts is a side effect of dramatic school-based management and decision making. Further, charter schools, which now are in vogue, can provide perhaps even more choice. In short, a wide range of choice options should accompany the above approach to school finance and education policy reform.

In Minnesota, a set of comprehensive public school choice programs, including charter schools, has not only empowered parents but also has induced schools to pay closer attention to their parent and children customers. Schools now assess what they offer in terms of what parents want and, in the main, parents want a quality curriculum program and high standards for student achievement. Further, although pressed for resources, schools responding to these new pressures are rethinking how they use current revenues and devising strategies for reallocating revenues to focus funding on core programs (Hertert, 1994).

Another ingredient of such a new structure would be substantial regulatory relief. It is hard to unleash the creativity of school professionals to redesign educational services to produce higher and more ambitious student learning results, while holding them to all the federal, state, local and union contract rules and regulations that now govern and proscribe their behavior. A serious results-oriented system would de-emphasize regulations and focus accountability on what students actually learned. Clearly, minimum antidiscrimination and handicapped regulations need to be retained, but the bulk of other process regulations, including class size requirements in union contracts, would need to be dramatically reduced if not rescinded.

Complementary Programmatic Strategies

The last component of school finance in the 1990s concerns financing several nonschool or nontraditional school programs. These programs largely concern the goal of having all students come to school ready to learn. Several programs could be included in this category; all have price tags but nearly all have been shown by research to have both short- and long-term pay offs.

Pre-school. Nearly all studies show that early childhood education programs have long-term impacts and, even when future benefits are discounted to present values, have significant net benefit-cost ratios (Barnett, 1985; Grubb, 1989a). Early childhood education programs for poor children improve student academic performance in the basic skills in elementary through high school, decrease failure rates and below grade level performance at all grade levels, decrease discipline problems, and improve high school graduation rates (Slavin, Karweit, and Wasik, 1994). Early childhood education programs can provide long-term returns of four dollars for every one dollar invested (Barnett, 1990).

Extended-day Kindergarten. Kindergarten was a full-day program until World War II when teacher shortages cut it to a half day. Research syntheses suggest that students from poverty backgrounds who receive a full-day kindergarten program perform from 0.5 to over 1.0 standard deviations better on basic skill activities in the early elementary grades than those who do not (Puleo, 1988; Slavin, Karweit, and Madden, 1989; Slavin, Karweit, and Wasik, 1994). Both expanded early childhood education and extended-day kindergarten cost more money and they give students from poverty backgrounds a substantial boost in successfully learning the basic skills in early elementary grades.

Child-care for Working Parents. As women increasingly enter the workforce in full time jobs, there is a growing need to provide child care for students both before and after traditional school hours (Grubb, 1989b). While there is only scant research on the educational achievement effects of variations in level and quality of child care services, the fact remains that rising numbers of children are not under the supervision of an adult after school ends during the midafternoon. Whether from public or private sources, child-care services will consume expanding percentages of the nation's personal income in the future, unless the work behavior of women and men change dramatically (Carnegie Task Force on Meeting the Needs of Young Children, 1994).

Integrated Children's Services. A child's ability to experience success in school depends to a substantial degree on other nonschool conditions such as the home environment, health, mental health, etc. Further, students "at-risk" usually are at-risk along several dimensions. Yet a growing body of research shows that the structure of delivering noneducation services to children, health, family, psychological, parole, medical, preschool, child and day-care, etc., is fragmented and increasingly ineffective (Kirst, 1989). Integrated children's services is a policy proposal being recommended across the country. The idea, generally, is to have all or at least a great variety of children's non-education services provided at one location. The school is a prime candidate because nearly all children spent large portions of each day at a school. Schools then could employ "case brokers" who would work with individual students and broker-needed services from the various service providers. The Carnegie (1989) report on middle schools, for example, proposed having a health coordinator at each school.

The "New Beginnings" project in the San Diego public schools is one of the most recent attempts to provide school-based integrated services for children (Cohen, 1991). California's Governor Pete Wilson proposed a similar program for all California schools in his 1992 budget. Integrating social and education services in one location, with schools being a prime locale in most states, is very likely to add a new dimension to school finance during the 1990s. The key issue is how to create such a program without further financial burdening schools; the policy trick is to direct the flow of resources for children's noneducation services, primarily but not solely funded by the federal government, to some central locality, such as the school (Kirst, 1992a).

Poverty and Health Programs. While the governors and the President did not raise the issue of reducing poverty as a means of having more children come to school ready to learn, the growing rate of children in poverty (Pallas, Natriello, and McDill, 1989), the increasingly sophisticated understanding of policies that would dramatically reduce poverty, especially children in poverty (Ellwood, 1987), and the continued linkage of low-student performance with poverty suggest that reducing children's poverty, a laudable objective in itself, would also help accomplish the country's and each state's education goals during the 1990s. Further, programs such as the Women, Infant, and Children's Program, that provide prenatal care for pregnant mothers are highly cost-effective in producing healthy children and reducing the incidence of learning disabilities. In short, reducing poverty and expanding research proven effective health and nutrition programs that enhance the child's family environment and result in healthy children entering school are noneducation and pre-school programs that will help schools accomplish their tasks once children begin formal schooling.

New School Finance Equity Issues

These changes in school finance for the 1990s require that the traditional definition of school finance equity stated in terms of dollar inputs at the district level, must be dramatically transformed during the 1990s. While the Berne and Stiefel (1984) framework helped bring conceptual, intellectual, and technical clarity to school finance equity discussions during the 1970s and 1980s, that framework now needs expansion (Odden and Picus, 1992: Chapter 3).

First, school finance equity analysis needs to link indicators of school finance equity to the developing work in educational indicators more generally (Council of Chief State School Officers, 1990; Odden, 1990c; Shavelson, McDonnell, and Oakes, 1989; Smith, 1988). There is renewed interest in improving national data bases in school finance, enhancing interstate measures of the status of state school finance systems, and including finance and other related data in broader attempts to provide indicators of the current and changing status and condition of the U.S. and state education systems. These events place the earlier attempts to define and measure school finance equity into a broader policy context in which finance indicators are part of a set of more comprehensive educational indicators (Oakes, 1986).

Second, school finance equity frameworks need to move beyond expenditures and revenues as indicators of educational resources and look at the curriculum and instructional educational resources into which dollars are transformed. Indeed, while fiscal inequities have dominated school finance for decades, dollars are used by school districts to purchase educational resources. Further, the curriculum and teaching to which students are exposed are key determinants of what students learn (Bryk, Lee, and Smith, 1990; McKnight et al., 1987; Schwille et al., 1982). Since a key goal of the education system is student learning, knowledge of the equity of the distribution of the key resources most directly linked to student learning, curriculum and instruction, ought to be expressly part of a comprehensive school finance equity framework.

Third, school finance, and curriculum and instruction data need to be developed on *a school basis,* not just at the district level as is common practice today. Indeed, the major thrust of education policy in the 1990s will be directed at the school site. Site-based budgeting, performance incentives, management, and data on student performance all require that detailed fiscal and resource information will be needed on a school-by-school basis. Expenditures by function and program, and curriculum and instruction resources actually provided are key school-based data needed to implement both new education policy initiatives as well as analyze the functioning of the system, including school productivity.

The school-based finance structure described above would provide opportunities to significantly expand the level of fiscal equity in state school finance systems as well as the dimensions of resource equity that could be assessed. First, financing schools could enhance school fiscal equalization within districts since the bulk of general fund dollars would be distributed on an equal per pupil basis. If states funded schools directly, fiscal equity across schools would be produced.

At the school, moreover, equity concerns could move beyond measures of dollar equality and include the issue of opportunity to learn standards, an issue surrounding systemic reform that is being hotly debated. Opportunity to learn standards arose in the deliberations of the National Council on Educational Standards and Testing (1992), are inextricably part of systemic reform (O'Day and Smith, 1993), and were controversial parts of the passage of the Federal Goals 2000 Legislation. The idea is that if the nation or a state implements a new form of performance testing for students and uses the results to make important decisions for students, whether to promote to the next schooling level, admit into postsecondary education, or hire in the job market. The schools then need to have the resources, broadly conceived, to allow students the opportunity to achieve at the expected levels (Porter, 1993a, 1993b).

While defining such standards is a complex issue, philosophically, technically, and statistically, what is desired is a set of variables strongly linked to student learning, in addition to dollar equality. Porter (1992, 1993a, 1993b) suggests three key school process variables:

- Measures of the enacted curriculum, i.e., the curriculum actually delivered and covered in the classroom.
- Measures of the teaching strategies actually used. Emphasis would focus on strategies that engaged students in problem solving and activities that had students construct resolutions to problems and experiments.
- Measures of curriculum-imbedded resources, such as computers, access to laboratories, laboratory equipment, and manipulatives in mathematics classrooms.

Further, both Porter (1993a, 1993b) and Guiton and Burstein (1993) believe it would be possible to collect the above data through periodic surveys, coupled with a small number of case studies to validate the survey results.

It could very well turn out that disparities in fiscal resources would be related to disparities in these education process variables which are closely linked to student learning. If so, it would provide a new understanding of how fiscal disparities across schools within states, or within schools across states, were connected with variation in student learning. This could transform education resource discussions from just simple attacks on dollar differences to sophisticated understandings of how resources are linked to student learning, which is the real target of systemic reform, school finance, and the use of educational dollars (see also Odden, 1994c).

CONCLUSION

Education faces a dilemma since resources have been rising for the past several decades, but school finance inequities remain, and student performance today is about where it was 20 to 30 years ago. In the future, achievement needs to rise faster than educational spending, and inequities in both achievement and fiscal resources need to be reduced. Systemic reform has been identified as a potentially powerful strategy for raising the achievement of all students to levels attained by only a small percentage of students today, and thus is a strategy that if implemented with a redesigned finance structure could remedy the inequities.

Findings from multiple strands of research suggest that a decentralized, high-involvement organization and management strategy, i.e., should explicitly be made part of systemic reform. The research concludes this strategy would work most effectively if information, knowledge, power, and rewards are decentralized to the school level. This suggests that a school finance system aligned with systemic reform would: (1) target the school as the key unit to be financed; (2) budget the bulk of revenues in a lump sum to schools and give schools power to recruit and hire personnel; (3) include an extensive on-line, computerized information base with revenues, expenditures, achievement and other data; (4) set aside 2 to 4 percent of school revenues for ongoing professional development and training; and (5) restructure teacher compensation to pay teachers individually on the basis of their knowledge and skills, and as a group for achievement gains made by students in each school. Such a system could simultaneously enhance fiscal equity across both districts and schools, help produce higher levels of achievement for all students, and turn the education system from a low to a high performance system.

Bibliography

Abbot v. *Burke*, 110 N.J. 575 A. 2d 359, 367 (1990).

Adams, Jacob. (1992). *Policy Implementation Through Teacher Professional Networks: The Case of Math A in California.* Palo Alto, CA: Stanford University, Unpublished Ph.D. dissertation.

Adams, Jacob. (1993). School Finance Reform and Systemic School Change: Reconstituting Kentucky's Public Schools. *Journal of Education Finance,* 18(4), 318–345.

Adams, Marilyn. (1989). Teaching Thinking to Chapter 1 Students. Cambridge, MA: Center for the Study of Reading, Illinois University, Urbana.

Adams, Marilyn Jager. (1990). *Beginning to Read: Thinking and Learning About Print.* Champaign, IL: Center for the Study of Reading, University of Illinois.

Adler, Louise, and Sid Gardner. (1994). *The Politics of Linking Schools and Social Services.* Philadelphia: Falmer Press.

Aguilar v. *Felton*, 473 U.S. 402 (1985).

Alexander, Kern, and M. David Alexander. (1985). *American Public Schools Law.* St. Paul, MN: West Publishing.

Alexander, W., and C.K. McEwin. (1989). *Schools in the Middle: Status and Progress.* Macon, GA: Panaprint.

Allington, Richard L., and Ann McGill-Franzen. (1989). School Response to Reading Failure: Chapter 1 and Special Education Students in Grades 2, 4 and 8. *Elementary School Journal,* 89(5), 529–542.

American Association for the Advancement of Science. (1989). *Science for All Americans* (A Project 2061 report on Literacy Goals in Science, Mathematics, and Technology.). Washington, D.C.: American Association for the Advancement of Science.

Anderson, Beverly, Allan Odden, Eleanor Farrar et al. (1987). State Strategies to Support Local School Improvement. *Knowledge: Creation, Diffusion, Utilization,* 9(1), 42–86.

Anderson, Charles W. (1991). Policy Implications of Research on Science Teaching and Teachers' Knowledge. In Mary M. Kennedy, ed., *Teaching Academic Subjects to Diverse Learners.* New York: Teachers College Press, pp. 5–30.

Anderson, C., and K. Roth. (1989). Teaching for Meaningful and Self-Regulated Learning of Science. In Lauren Resnick and Leopold E. Klopfer, eds., *Toward the Thinking Curriculum: Current Cognitive Research.* Washington, DC: Association for Supervision and Curriculum Development, pp. 265–309.

Anderson, L. (1989). Implementing Instructional Programs to Promote Meaningful, Self-Regulated Learning. *In Advances in Research on Teaching, Vol. 1.* Greenwich, CT: JAI, pp. 311–343.

Apple, Michael K. (1990). *Ideology and Curriculum,* 2nd ed. New York: Routledge.

Apple, Michael K. (1991). The politics of the textbook. In Michael W. Apple and Linda K. Christian-Smith, eds., *The Politics of the Textbook.* New York: Routledge.

Apple, Michael W. (1993). *Official Knowledge: Democratic Education in a Conservative Age.* New York: Routledge.

Applebee, Arthur N., Judith A. Langer, and Ina V.S. Mullis. (1989). *Crossroads in American Education.* Princeton, NJ: Educational Testing Service.

Ashton, Patricia, Linda Crocker, and Stephen Olrjnik. (1986). Does Teacher Education Make a Difference? Tallahassee, FL: Florida State Department of Education, Student Assessment Section.

Association for Supervision and Curriculum Development. (1987). *Building an Indivisible Nation: Bilingual Education in Context.* Alexandria, VA: Association for Supervision and Curriculum Development.

Atkin, Myron, and Ernest House. (1981). The Federal Role in Curriculum Development: 1950–1980. *Educational Evaluation and Policy Analysis,* 3(5), 5–36.

Au, Kathryn H. and Jana M. Mason, (1981). Social Organizational Factors in Learning to Read: The Balance of Rights hypothesis. *Reading Research Quarterly,* 17(1), 115–152.

Bailey, Stephen, Robert T. Frost, Paul E. Marsh, and Robert C. Wood. (1962). *Schoolmen and Politics: A Study of State Aid to Education in the Northeast.* Syracuse, NY: Syracuse University Research Corporation.

Bailey, Thomas. (1990). *Changes in the Nature and Structure of Work: Implications for Employer-Sponsored Training.* Berkeley, CA: National Center for Research in Vocational Education.

Baker, Eva L., M. Freeman, and S. Clayton. (1991). Cognitive Assessment of History for Large-Scale Testing. In Merlin C. Wittrock and Eva L. Baker, eds., *Testing and Cognition.* Englewood Cliffs, NJ: Prentice Hall.

Baker, Eva L., and D. Niemi. (1991). *Assessing Deep Understanding of History and Science Through Hypertext.* Paper presented at the annual meeting of the American Educational Research Association, Chicago.

Baker, Eva L., Harold F. O'Neil, Jr., and Robert L. Linn. (1993). Policy and Validity Prospects for Performance-Based Assessment. *American Psychologist,* 48(12), 1210–1218.

Balfanz, Robert. (1991). Local Knowledge, Academic Skills and Individual Productivity: An Alternative View. *Educational Policy,* 5(4), 343–370.

Ball, Deborah Loewenberg. (1991). Teaching Mathematics for Understanding: What Do Teachers Need to Know About Subject Matter? In Mary M. Kennedy, ed., *Teaching Academic Subjects to Diverse Learners.* New York: Teachers College Press, pp. 63–83.

Ball, Deborah Lowenberg. (1992). *Implementing the NCTM Standards: Hopes and Hurdles.* East Lansing, MI: Michigan State University, National Center for Research on Teacher Learning.

Ball, Deborah Lowenberg, David K. Cohen, Penelope L. Peterson, and Suzanne M. Wilson. (1994a). *Understanding State Efforts to Reform Teaching and Learning: Learning from Teachers About Learning to Teach.* Papers presented at the annual meeting of the American Educational Research Association, New Orleans.

Ball, Deborah Lowenberg, David K. Cohen, Penelope L. Peterson, and Suzanne M. Wilson. (1994b). *Understanding State Efforts to Reform Teaching and Learning: School Districts and State Instructional Policy.* Papers presented at the annual meeting of the American Educational Research Association, New Orleans.

Ball, Deborah Lowenberg, David K. Cohen, Penelope L. Peterson, and Suzanne M. Wilson. (1994c). *Understanding State Efforts to Reform Teaching and Learning: The Progress of Instructional Reform in Schools for Disadvantaged Students.* Papers presented at the annual meeting of the American Educational Research Association, New Orleans.

Barnett, Stephen W. (1985). Benefit-Cost Analysis of the Perry Preschool Program and Its Policy Implications. *Educational Evaluation and Policy Analysis, 7*(4), 333–342.

Barnett, Stephen W., (1990). Developing Preschool Education Policy: An Economic Perspective, *Education Policy, 4*(3), 245–265.

Barro, Steve. (1992). *What Does the Education Dollar Buy? Relationships of Staffing, Staff Characteristics, and Staff Salaries to State Per Pupil Spending.* Madison, WI: University of Wisconsin, Wisconsin Center for Education Research, Consortium for Policy Research in Education-The Finance Center.

Barzelay, Michael. (1992). *Breaking Through Bureaucracy: A New Way for Managing in Government.* Berkeley, CA: University of California Press.

Bass, B.M. (1990). *Bass & Stodghill's Handbook of Leadership: Theory, Research, and Managerial Applications.* New York: Free Press.

Beck, Lynn G. and Joseph Murphy. (1993). *Understanding the Principal.* New York: Teachers College Press.

Beer, Michael, Russell A. Eisenstat, and Bert Spector. (1990a). Why Change Programs Don't Produce Change. *Harvard Business Review, 68,* 158–166.

Beer, Michael, Russell A. Eisenstat, and Bert Spector. (1990b). *The Critical Path to Corporate Renewal.* Boston: Harvard Business School Press.

Bele, Thad. (1990). Governors. In Gray, V.H. Jacob and R.B. Albritton, eds., *Politics in the American States: A Comparative Analysis.* Glenview, IL: Scott, Foresman & Co, pp. 63–69.

Bell, Terrell. (1988). *The Thirteenth Man.* New York: Macmillan.

Bellack, Arno. (1970). Structure in the Social Sciences and Implications for the Social Studies Program. In William E. Gardner and Fred A. Johnsons, Eds., *Social Studies in Secondary Schools: A Book of Readings.* Boston: Allyn and Bacon.

Bennis, Warren and Bert Nanus. (1985). *Leaders: The Strategies for Taking Charge.* New York: Harper and Row.

Bennis, Warren. (1989). *On Becoming a Leader.* Reading, MA: Addison-Wesley.

Bereiter, Carl. (1994). Implications of Postmodernism for Science, or, Science as Progressive Discourse. *Educational Psychologist, 29*(1), 3–12.

Bereiter, Carl and Marlene Scardamalia. (1989). Intentional Learning as a Goal of Instruction. In Lauren Resnick, Ed., *Knowing, Learning and Instruction* Hillsdale, NJ: Lawrence Erlbaum Associates, pp. 362–392.

Berliner, David. (1990). If the Metaphor Fits, Why Not Wear It? The Teacher as Executive. *Theory Into Practice.* 24(20), 85–93.

Berman, Paul and Milbrey Wallin McLaughlin. (1974–1978). *Federal Programs Supporting Educational Change, Vol. I–VII.* Santa Monica, CA.: The Rand Corporation.

Bernstein, Aaron. (1994). Why Americans Need Unions But Not the Kind it Has Now. *Business Week,* May 23, 70–82.

Berryman, Sue E. and Thomas R. Bailey. (1992). *The Double Helix of Education and the Economy.* New York: Teachers College Press.

Bethel School District v. *Fraser,* 478 U.S. 675 (1986).

Birman, Beatrice F., Martin E. Orland, R. K. Jung et al. (1987). *The Current Operation of the Chapter 1 Program: Final Report from the National Assessment of Chapter 1.* Washington, DC: U.S. Government Printing Office.

Bishop, John and Shani Carter. (1991). The Worsening Shortage of College-Graduate Workers. *Education Evaluation and Policy Analysis.* 13(3), 221–246.

Blackburn, McKinley L., David L. Bloom, and Richard B. Freeman. (1990). The Declining Economic Position of Less Skilled American Men. In Gary Burtless, ed., *A*

Future of Lousy Jobs: The Changing Structure of U.S. Wages. Washington, DC: The Brookings Institution, pp. 31–76.

Blinder, Alan. (1990). *Paying for Productivity.* Washington, DC: The Brookings Institution.

Bluestone, Barry and Bennett Harrison. (1986). *The Great American Job Machine: The Proliferation of Low-Wage Employment in the U.S. Economy.* Washington, DC: U.S. Government Printing Office.

Board of Education of Central School District No. 1 v. Allen, 392 U.S. 236 (1968).

Board of Education of Oklahoma City Public Schools v. Dowell, 111 U.S. 630 (1991).

Board of Education Westside Community Schools v. Mergens, 493 U.S. 182 (1990).

Boyd, William. (1987). Public Education's Last Hurrah? Schizophrenia, Amnesia, and Ignorance in School Politics. *Educational Evaluation and Policy Analysis,* 9(2), 85–100.

Bracey, Gerald W. (1991). Why Can't They Be Like We Were? *Phi Delta Kappan,* 73(2), 104–117.

Bracey, Gerald W. (1992). The Second Bracey Report on the Conditions of Public Education. *Phi Delta Kappan,* 74(2), 104–117.

Bracey, Gerald W. (1993). The Third Bracey Report on the Conditions of Public Education *Phi Delta Kappan,* 75(2), 104–112.

Bradley v. Milliken, 345 F Supp 914 (1972).

Bransford, John. (1979). *Human Cognition: Learning, Understanding and Remembering.* Belmont, CA: Wadsworth.

Bransford, John, Susan Goldman, and Nancy Vye. (1991). Making a Difference in People's Abilities to Think: Reflections on a Decade of Work and Some Hopes for the Future. In Lynn Okagaki and Robert J. Sternberg, eds., *Directions of Development: Influence on Children's Thinking.* Hillsdale, NJ: Erlbaum, pp. 147–180.

Bredeson, Paul. (1993). Letting Go of Outlived Professional Identities: A Study of Role Transition and Role Strain for Principals in Restructured Schools. *Educational Administration Quarterly,* 29(1), 34–68.

Bredo, E. (1994). Reconstructing Educational Psychology: Situated Cognition and Dewey Pragmatism. *Educational Psychologist,* 29(1), 23–36.

Broder, David S. (1980). *Changing of the Guard: Power and Leadership in America.* New York: Simon and Schuster.

Brophy, Jere E. (1983). Classroom Organization and Management. *Elementary School Journal,* 83(4), 265–286.

Brophy, Jere. (1988). Research Linking Teacher Behaviors to Student Achievement: Potential Implications for Instruction to Chapter 1 Students. *Educational Psychologist,* 23(3), 235–286.

Brophy, Jere. (1989). *Advances in Research on Teaching,* Vol. 1. Greenwich, CT: JAI Press, Inc.

Brophy, Jere. (1990). Teaching Social Studies for Understanding and Higher-Order Applications. *Elementary School Journal,* 90(4), 351–418.

Brophy, Jere. (1991). *Advances in Research on Teaching: Teachers' Knowledge of Subject Matter as it Relates to Their Teaching Practice,* Vol. 2. Greenwich, CT: JAI Press, Inc.

Brophy, Jere. (1992). Probing the Subtleties of Subject-Matter Teaching. *Educational Leadership,* 49(7), 4–8.

Brophy, Jere and Thomas Good. (1986). Teacher Behavior and Student Achievement. In Merlin Wittrock, ed., *Handbook of Research on Teaching.* New York: Macmillan, pp. 328–375.

Brown v. Board of Education of Topeka, 347 U.S. 483 (1954).

Brown, J. S. and R. R. Burton. (1978). Diagnostic models for procedural bugs in basic mathematical skills. *Cognitive Science,* 2, 155–192.

Brown, Rexford G. (1991). *School of Thought: How the Politics of Literacy Shape Thinking in the Classroom.* San Francisco: Jossey-Bass.

Bryk, Anthony S. and Driscoll, Mary Erina. (1988). *The School as a Community: Theoretical Foundations, Contextual Influences and Consequences for Students and Teachers.* Madison, WI: University of Wisconsin, Wisconsin Center for School Research, National Center on Effective Secondary Schools.

Bryk, Anthony S. and Valerie Lee. (1993). *Catholic Schools and The Common Good.* Cambridge, MA: Harvard University Press.

Bryk, Anthony S. Valerie E. Lee, and Julia B. Smith. (1990). High School Organization and Its Effects on Teachers and Students: An Interpretive Summary of Research. In William J. Clune and John F. Witte, eds., *Choice and Control in American Schools, Vol. 1.* Philadelphia: The Falmer Press, pp. 135–226.

Bryson, Mary and Marlene Scardamalia. (1991). Teaching Writing to Students At Risk for Academic Failure. In Barbara Means and Michael S. Knapp, eds., *Teaching Advanced Skills to Educationally Disadvantaged Students.* Washington, DC: U.S. Department of Education, Office of Planning, Budget and Evaluation, pp. 43–64.

Burns, John. (1971). *The Sometime Governments.* New York: Bantam Books.

Burtless, Gary, ed. (1990a). *A Future of Lousy Jobs: The Changing Structure of U.S. Wages.* Washington, DC: The Brookings Institution.

Burtless, Gary. (1990b). Earnings Inequality over the Business and Demographic Cycles. In Gary Burtless, ed., *A Future of Lousy Jobs: The Changing Structure of U.S. Wages.* Washington, DC: The Brookings Institution, pp. 77–122.

Business Roundtable. (1991). *Essential Elements of a Successful Education System,* Washington, D.C.: The Business Roundtable.

Byrne, John A. (1993). The Horizontal Corporation. *Business Week,* December 20, pp. 76–81.

Calfee, Robert. (1991). Schoolwide Programs to Improve Literacy for At-Risk Students. In Barbara Means and Michael S. Knapp, eds., *Teaching Advanced Skills to Educationally Disadvantaged Students.* Washington, DC: U.S. Department of Education, Office of Planning, Budget and Evaluation, pp. 71–92.

California Department of Education. (1992a). *It's Elementary!* Sacramento, CA.

California Department of Education. (1992b). *Second to None.* Sacramento, CA.

California State Department of Education. (1987). *History-Social Science Framework.* Sacramento, CA: California State Department of Education.

California State Department of Education (CSDE). (1988). *English-Language Arts Framework.* Sacramento, CA: California State Department of Education.

California State Department of Education. (1990). *Science Framework for California Public Schools.* Sacramento, CA: California State Department of Education.

California State Department of Education. (1992). *Mathematics Framework for California Public Schools.* Sacramento, CA: California State Department of Education.

Callahan, John and William Wilken. (1976). *A Legislators Guide to School Finance.* Washington, DC: National Conference of State Legislatures.

Callahan, Raymond E. (1962). *Education and the Cult of Efficiency: A Study of the Social Forces that Have Shaped the Administration of the Public Schools.* Chicago: University of Chicago Press.

Campbell, Roald E., Luvern I. Cunningham, Ralph O. Nystrand, & Michael D. Usdan. (1990). *The Organization and Control of American Schools,* 6th ed. Columbus, OH: Merrill Publishing Company.

Canell, John J. (1987) *Nationally Normed Achievement Testing in America's Public Schools: How All Fifty States Are Above the National Average.* Daniels, WV: Friends for Education.

Carnegie Council on Adolescent Development. (1989). *Turning Points: Preparing American Youth for the 21st Century,* New York: Carnegie Corporation.

Carnegie Forum on Education and the Economy. (1986). *A Nation Prepared: Teachers for the 21st Century.* New York: Carnegie Corporation.

Carnegie Task Force on Meeting the Needs of Young Children. (1994). *Starting Points: Meeting the Needs of Our Youngest Children.* New York: Carnegie Corporation.

Carpenter, Thomas P. and Elizabeth Fennema. (1991). Research and Cognitively Guided Instruction. In Elizabeth Fennema, Thomas P. Carpenter, and Susan J. Lamon, eds., *Integrating Research on Teaching and Learning Mathematics.* Albany, NY: State University of New York Press, pp. 1–16.

Carpenter, Thomas P., Elizabeth Fennema, Penelope L. Peterson et al. (1989). Using Knowledge of Children's Mathematics Thinking in Classroom Teaching: An Experimental Study. *American Educational Research Journal, 26*(4), 499–531.

Carpenter, Thomas P., J. Moser and R. Romberg, eds. (1982). *Addition and Subtraction: A Cognitive Perspective.* Hillsdale, NJ: Lawrence Erlbaum.

Carson, C.C., R. M. Huelskamp and T.D. Woodall. (1991). *Perspective on Education in America.* Albuquerque, NM: Sandia National Laboratories.

Carson, C.C., R. M. Huelskamp and T.D. Woodall. (1993). Perspectives on Education in America: An Annotated Briefing. *Journal of Educational Research, 86*(5), 259–310.

Casserly, Catherine M. and Martin Carnoy. (1994). *The National Education Goals 2000, Changing Demographics of the Under 17 Population and U.S. Achievement Trends: Are They Compatible?* New Brunswick, NJ: Rutgers University, Consortium for Policy Research in Education.

Cazden, Cortney B. (1988). *Classroom Discourse: The Language of Teaching and Learning.* Portsmouth, NH: Heinemann.

Chambers, Jay G. (1982). Cost and Price Level Adjustments to State Aid for Education: A Theoretical and Empirical Review. In K. Forbis Jordan and Nelda H. Cambron-McCabe, eds., *Perspectives in State School Support Programs.* Cambridge, MA: Ballinger, pp. 39–86.

Chapman, Judith. (1990). School-Based Decision-Making and Management: Implications for School Personnel. In Judith Chapman, ed., *School-Based Decision-Making and Management.* London: Falmer.

Children's Defense Fund. (1994). *State of America's Children Yearbook 1994.* Washington, DC: Children's Defense Fund.

Christenson, G. (1992). *The Changing Role of the Administrator in an Accelerated School.* Paper presented at the annual meeting of the American Educational Research Association, San Francisco.

Chubb, John E. and Terry M. Moe. (1990). *Politics, Markets and America's Schools.* Washington, DC: Brookings Institution.

Cibulka, James G. (1991). Urban School Finance: Diversity in Urban Schools. In James G. Ward and Patricia Anthony, eds. *Who Pays for Student Diversity? Population Changes and Educational Policy.* Newbury Park, CA: Corwin Press, pp. 21–47.

Clemons, Herbert. (1991). What Do Math Teachers Need to Be? In Mary M. Kennedy, ed. *Teaching Academic Subjects to Diverse Learners.* New York: Teachers College Press, pp. 84–96.

Clotfelter, Charles T., and Phillip J. Cook. (1989). *Selling Hope: State Lotteries in America.* Cambridge: Harvard University Press.

Clune, William. (1992). New Answers to Hard Questions Posed by *Rodriguez:* Ending the Separation of School Finance and Educational Policy by Bridging the Gap Between Wrong and Remedy. *Connecticut Law Review, 24*(3), 721–755.

Clune, William. (1993). The Shift From Equity to Adequacy in School Finance. *The World and I, 8*(9), 389–405.

Cochran v. *Louisiana State Board of Education,* 281 U.S. 370 (1930).

Cohen, David. (1982). Policy and Organization: The Impact of State and Federal Educational Policy on School Governance. *Harvard Educational Review, 52*(4), 474–499.

Cohen, David. (1993). America's Children and Their Elementary Schools. *The Public Interest, or Daedalus, 122*(1), 177–207.

Cohen, David K. (1991). Revolution in One Classroom. In Susan Fuhrman and Betty Malen, *The Politics of Curriculum and Testing*. Philadelphia: Falmer Press.

Cohen David and James P. Spillane. (1993). Policy and Practice: The Relations Between Governance and Practice. In Susan H. Fuhrman, ed., *Designing Coherent Education Policy*. San Francisco: Jossey Bass, pp. 35–95.

Cohen, David and Milbrey McLaughlin. (1993). *Teaching for Understanding*. San Francisco: Jossey-Bass.

Cohen, David and Penelope Peterson. (1990). *Educational Evaluation and Policy Analysis*, September 1990, Entire Issue.

Cohen, Deborah L. (1991). San Diego Agencies Joint to Ensure 'New Beginning' for Families, *Education Week*, January 23: 1.

Cohen, Michael. (1983). Instruction, Management, and Organizational Issues in Effective Schools. In Allan Odden and L. Dean Webb, eds., *School Finance and School Improvement: Linkages for the 1980s*. Cambridge, MA: Ballinger.

Coleman, James, Carol J. Hobson, James McPartland et al. (1966). *Equality of Educational Opportunity*. Washington, DC: U.S. Government Printing Office.

Collins, Allan, John Seely Brown, and Susan E. Newman. (1989). Cognitive Apprenticeship: Teaching the Craft of Reading, Writing, and Mathematics. In Lauren B. Resnick, ed., *Knowing, Learning and Instruction: Essays in Honor of Robert Glaser*. Hillsdale, NJ: Lawrence Erlbaum.

Collins, Allan, Jan Hawkins, and Sharon M. Carver. (1991). A Cognitive Apprenticeship for Disadvantaged Students. In Barbara Means and Michael S. Knapp, eds., *Teaching Advanced Skills to Educationally Disadvantaged Students*. Washington, DC: U.S. Department of Education, Office of Planning, Budget and Evaluation, pp. 173–194.

Comer, James. (1987). New Haven's School-Community Connection. *Educational Leadership*, 44(6), 13–16.

Comer, James. *School Power*. (1980). New York: Free Press.

California Commission on Teacher Credentialing. (1992). *Draft Framework of Knowledge, Skills and Abilities for Beginning Teachers*. Sacramento, CA: Commission on Teacher Credentialing.

Committee for Economic Development. (1985). *Investing in Our Children*. New York: Committee for Economic Development.

Committee for Economic Development. (1987). *Children in Need*. New York: Committee for Economic Development.

Committee for Economic Development. (1991). *The Unfinished Agenda: A New Vision for Child Development and Education*. Washington, DC: Committee for Economic Development.

Committee for Public Education and Religious Liberty v. *Nyquist*, 413 U.S. 756 (1973).

Conference Board of the Mathematical Sciences *National Advisory Committee on Mathematical Education*. (1975). *Overview and Analysis of School Mathematics Grades K–12*. Washington, DC: National Council of Teachers of Mathematics.

Congressional Budget Office. (1993). *The Federal Role in Improving Elementary and Secondary Education*. Washington, DC: Congressional Budget Office.

Conley, Sharon. (1991). Review of Research on Teacher Participation in School Decision Making. In Gerald Grant, ed., *Review of Research in Education*. Washington, DC: American Educational Research Association, pp. 225–266.

Conley, Sharon C. and Bruce S. Cooper, eds. (1991). *The School as a Work Environment*. Boston: Allyn & Bacon.

Conley, Sharon and Allan Odden. (1994). *Linking Teacher Compensation to Teacher Career Development: A Strategic Examination*. Madison, WI: University of Wisconsin, Wisconsin Center for Education Research, Consortium for Policy Research in Education—The Finance Center.

Coons, John, William Clune, and Stephen D. Sugarman. (1970). *Private Wealth and Public Education.* Cambridge, MA: Belknap Press of Harvard University Press.

Corcoran, Thomas B. (1985). Effective Secondary Schools. In Regina M. J. Kyle, ed., *Reaching for Excellence: An Effective Schools Sourcebook.* Washington, DC: U.S. Government Printing Office.

Corcoran, Thomas B. and Bruce L. Wilson. (1986). *The Search for Successful Secondary Schools: The First Three Years of the Secondary School Recognition Program.* Philadelphia: Research for Better Schools.

Council of Chief State School Officers. (1989). *State Education Indicators, 1989.* Washington, DC: Council of Chief State School Officers.

Council of Chief State School Officers. (1990). *State Education Indicators: 1990.* Washington, D.C.: Council of Chief State School Officers.

Craig v. *Boren,* 429 U.S. 190 (1976).

Crandall, David and Associates. (1982). *A Study of Dissemination Efforts Supporting School Improvement,* Volumes 1–10. Andover, MA: The Newwork.

Crandall, David P., Jeffrey Eiseman, and Karen S. Louis. (1986). Strategic Planning Issues that Bear on the Success of School Improvement Efforts. *Educational Administration Quarterly,* 22(3), 21–53.

Crawford, James. (1989). Bilingual Education: History, Politics, Theory, and Practice. Trenton, NJ: Crane Publishing.

Cresswell, Anthony and Michael Murphy. (1980). *Teachers, Unions and Collective Bargaining in Public Education.* Berkeley, CA: McCutchan.

Cuban, Larry. (1985). *How Teachers Taught: Constancy and Change in American Classrooms, 1890–1980.* New York: Longman.

Cuban, Larry. (1988). A Fundamental Puzzle of School Reform. *Phi Delta Kappan,* 69(5), 340–344.

Cuban, Larry. (1990). Reforming Again, Again, and Again. *Educational Researcher.* 19(1), 3–13.

Cuban, Larry. (1992). Why Some Reforms Last: The Case of Kindergarten. *American Journal of Education,* 100(2), 166–194.

Cummings, Thomas G. and Susan A. Mohrman. (1987). *Self-Designing Organizations.* Reading, MA: Addison-Wesley.

Cummins, James. (1981). The Role of Primary Language Development in Promoting Success for Language Minority Students. In Office of Bilingual Bicultural Education, ed., *Schooling and Language Minority Students: A Theoretical Framework.* Los Angeles, CA: California State University, Evaluation, Dissemination, and Assessment Center.

Cummins, James. (1983). *Heritage Language Education: A Literature Review.* Toronto: Ministry of Education, Ontario.

Cummins, James. (1989). *Empowering Language Minority Students.* Sacramento, CA: California Association for Bilingual Education.

Cummins, James and Merrill Swain. (1986). *Bilingualism in Education: Aspects of Theory, Research, and Practice.* London: Longman.

Cunningham, Shalee. (1994). *State Curriculum and School Improvement: Policy Impact on the Content and Process in Science and Mathematics Reform.* Unpublished Ph.D. dissertation, University of Southern California.

Curry, Brian and Tierney Temple. (1992). *Using Curriculum Frameworks for Systemic Reform.* Alexandria, VA: Association for Supervision and Curriculum Development.

Cyert, Richard & James G. March. (1963). *A Behavioral Theory of the Firm.* Englewood Cliffs, NJ: Prentice Hall.

Cyert, Richard. (1988). *The Economic Theory of Organization and the Firm.* New York: New York University Press.

Danzberger, Jacqueline P. (1993). Governing the Nation's Schools: The Case for Restructuring Local School Boards. *Phi Delta Kappan, 75*(5), 367–373.

Danzberger, Jacqueline P., Michael W. Kirst, and Michael D. Usdan. (1992). *Governing Public Schools: New Times, New Requirements.* Washington, DC: Institute for Educational Leadership.

Darling-Hammond, Linda. (1984). *Beyond the Commission Reports: The Coming Crisis in Teaching.* Santa Monica, CA: RAND Corporation.

Darling-Hammond, Linda. (1992). Teaching and Knowledge: Policy Issues Posed by Alternative Certification for Teachers. *Peabody Journal of Education, 67*(3), 123–154.

Darling-Hammond, Linda. (1992–93). Creating Standards of Practice and Delivery of Learner-Centered Schools. *Stanford Law and Policy Review, 4,* 37–52.

Darling-Hammond, Linda. (1993a). *Professional Development Schools.* New York: Teachers College Press.

Darling-Hammond, Linda. (1993b). Reframing the School Reform Agenda. *Phi Delta Kappan. 74*(10), 753–761.

Darling-Hammond, Linda and Barnett Berry. (1988). *The Evolution of Teacher Policy.* Santa Monica: RAND Corporation.

Darling-Hammond, Linda, Tamar Gendler, and Arthur E. Wise. (1990). *The Teaching Internship: Practical Preparation for a Licensed Profession.* Santa Monica, CA: The RAND Corporation.

David, Jane. (1990). Synthesis of Research on School-Based Management. *Educational Leadership, 46*(8), 45–53.

Deal, Terrence E. and A.A. Kennedy. (1982). *Corporate Cultures: The Rites and Rituals of Corporate Life.* Reading, MA: Addison-Wesley.

Deal, Terrence E. and Kent Peterson. (1990). *The Principal's Role in Shaping School Culture.* Washington, D.C.: U.S. Government Printing Office.

Deal, Terrence E. & Lynn D. Celotti. (1980). How Much Influence Do (and Can) Educational Administrators Have on Classrooms? *Phi Delta Kappan, 61*(7), 471–473.

DeBevoise, Wynn. (1984). Synthesis of Research on the Principal as Instructional Leader. *Educational Leadership, 41*(5), 14–20.

Debra P. v. *Turlington,* 474 F. Supp. 244 (M.D. Fla. 1979).

Deming, Edward W. (1986). *Out of the Crisis.* Cambridge, MA: Addison-Wesley.

Derthick, Martha. (1976). Washington: Angry Citizens and an Ambitious Plan. In Walter Williams and Richard Elmore, eds., *Social Program Implementation.* New York: Academic Press, pp. 219–239.

Dively, John A. and G. Alan Hickrod. (1993). *Status of School Finance Constitutional Litigation.* Normal, IL: Illinois State University, College of Education, Center for the Study of Educational Finance.

Dixon v. *Alabama State Board of Education,* 368 U.S. 930 (1961).

Dole, Janice A., Gerald G. Duffy, Laura R. Roehler, and P. David Pearson. (1991). Moving From the Old to the New: Research on Reading Comprehension Instruction. *Review of Educational Research, 61*(2), 239–264.

Dougherty, Van and Allan Odden. (1982). *State School Improvement Programs.* Denver, Colo.: Education Commission of the States.

Doyle, Denis and Chester E. Finn, Jr. (1984). American Schools and the Future of Local Control. *The Public Interest, 77,* 77–95.

Doyle, Denis and Terry Hartle. (1985). *Excellence in Education: The States Take Charge.* Washington, DC: American Enterprise Institute.

Doyle, Denis P. and Bruce S. Cooper. (1988). *Federal Aid to the Disadvantaged.* Philadelphia: The Falmer Press.

Doyle, Walter. (1986). Classroom Organization and Management. In Merlin Wittrock, ed., *Handbook of Research on Teaching* New York: Macmillan, pp. 392–431.

Driver, Rosalind E., Edith Guesne, and Andree Tiberghien. (1985). *Children's Ideas in Science.* Philadelphia: The Open University Press.

Duignan, Patrick. (1980). Administrative Behavior of School Superintendents: A Descriptive Study. *Journal of Educational Administration,* 18(1), 5–26.

Easton, John. (1991). *Decision Making and School Improvement: LSCs in the First Two Years.* Chicago: Chicago Panel on Public School Policy and Finance.

Edison Project. (1994). *Partnership School Design.* New York: The Edison Project.

Edmonds, Ronald. (1979a). Effective Schools for the Urban Poor. *Educational Leadership,* 37(1), 15–24.

Edmonds, Ronald. (1979b). Some Schools Work and More Can. *Social Policy,* 9(5), 28–32.

Edmonds, Ronald. (1982). Programs of School Improvement: An Overview. *Educational Leadership,* 40(3), 4–11.

Education Week. Special Report: By All Measures: The Debate Over Standards and Assessments. June 17, 1992.

Elementary School Journal. (1993). 93(5). Entire Issue.

Elley, Warwick B. (1992). *How in the World Do Students Read?* Hamburg, Germany: Grindeldruck GMBH for the International Evaluation of Education.

Ellwood, David. (1987). *Family Poverty in America.* New York: Basic Books.

Elmore, Richard F. (1979–80). Backward Mapping: Implementation Research and Policy Decisions. *Political Science Quarterly,* 94(4), 601–616.

Elmore, Richard F. (1991). *Teaching, Learning and Organization: School Restructuring and the Recurring Dilemmas of Reform.* Address presented to the annual meeting of the American Education Research Association. Chicago, IL.

Elmore, Richard F. (1993). The Role of Local School Districts in Instructional Improvement. In Susan H. Furhman, ed., *Designing Coherent Education Policy.* San Francisco: Jossey Bass, pp. 96–124.

Elmore, Richard F., and Associates. (1991). *Restructuring: The Next Generation of Education Reform.* San Francisco: Jossey-Bass.

Elmore, Richard F. and Susan H. Fuhrman. (1990). The National Interest and the Federal Role in Education. *Publius: The Journal of Federalism,* 20: 149–162.

Elmore, Richard F. and Susan H. Fuhrman. (1993). *Opportunity to Learn and the State Role in Education.* Paper prepared for the National Governors' Association, Washington, DC.

Elmore, Richard F. and Lorraine M. McDonnell. (1991). Getting the Job Done: Alternative Policy Instruments. In Allan R. Odden, ed., *Education Policy Implementation.* Albany, NY: State University of New York Press, pp. 157–183.

Elmore, Richard F. and Milbrey W. McLaughlin. (1981). Strategic Choice in Federal Policy: The Compliance-Assistance Trade-off. In Ann Lieberman and Milbrey McLaughlin, eds., *Policymaking in Education.* Chicago: Chicago University Press, pp. 159–194.

Elmore, Richard F. and Milbrey W. McLaughlin. (1983). The Federal Role in Education: Learning From Experience. *Education and Urban Society,* (15)3, 309–330.

Elmore, Richard F. & Milbrey W. McLaughlin. (1990). *Steady Work: Policy, Practice and The Reform of American Education.* Santa Monica, CA: RAND Corporation.

Emmer, Ed. T., Carolyn M. Evertson, & L. M. Anderson. (1980). Effective Classroom Management at the Beginning of the School Year. *Elementary School Journal,* 80(5), 219–231.

Engle v. *Vitale,* 370 U.S. 421 (1962).

Englert, Carol S., and Taffy E. Raphael. (1989). Developing Successful Writers Through Cognitive Strategy Instruction. In Jere Brophy, ed., *Advances in Research on Teaching,* vol. 1. Greenwich, CT: JAI Press, pp. 105–151.

Etzioni, Amatai. (1961). *Modern Organizations.* Englewood Cliffs, NJ: Prentice Hall.

Etzioni, Amatai. (1964). *Comparative Analysis of Complex Organizations.* New York: Free Press.

Everson v. *Board of Education,* 330 U.S. 1 (1947).

Evertson, Carolyn M. (1985). Training Teachers in Classroom Management: An Experimental Study in Secondary School Classrooms. *Journal of Educational Research,* 79(1), 51–57.

Evertson, Carolyn M. (1989). Improving Classroom Management: A School-Based Program for Beginning the Year. *Journal of Educational Research,* 83(2), 82–90.

Evertson, Carolyn M. and Ed T. Emmer. (1982). Effective Management at the Beginning of the School Year in Junior High Classes. *Journal of Educational Psychology,* 74(4), 485–498.

Evertson, Carolyn M. and Arlene H. Harris. (1992). What We Know About Managing Classrooms. *Educational Leadership,* 49(7), 74–78.

Evertson, Carolyn, Willis Hawley, and M. Zlotnik. (1985). Making a Difference in Educational Quality Through Teacher Education. *Journal of Teacher Education,* 36(3), 16–19.

Fennema, Elizabeth, Thomas P. Carpenter, and Penelope L. Peterson. (1989). Learning Mathematics with Understanding: Cognitively Guided Instruction. In Jere Brophy, ed., *Advances in Research on Teaching, Vol. 1: Teaching for Meaningful Understanding and Self-Regulated Learning.* Greenwich, CT: JAI Press.

Ferris, James and Donald Winkler. (1986). Teacher Compensation and the Supply of Teachers. *Elementary School Journal,* 86(4), 389–404.

Finn, Chester E. (1991a). *We Must Take Charge: Our Schools and Our Future.* New York: Macmillan.

Finn, Chester E. Jr. (1991b). Reinventing Local Control. *Education Week.* January 23, 1991.

Finnan, Christine and Henry M. Levin. (1993). *Bringing School Organization and Culture into Studies of School Effectiveness.* Stanford, CA: Stanford University, Center for Educational Research at Stanford.

Firestone, William and Robert E. Herriott. (1982). Prescriptions for Effective Elementary Schools Don't Fit Secondary Schools. *Educational Leadership,* 40(3), 51–53.

Firestone, William A. (1989). Using Reform: Conceptualizing District Initiative. *Educational Evaluation and Policy Analysis,* 11(2), 151–164.

Firestone, William A. (1990). Continuity and Incrementalism After All: State Responses to the Excellence Movement. In Joseph Murphy, ed., *The Educational Reform Movement of the 1980s.* Berkeley, CA: McCutchan, pp. 143–166.

Firestone, William A., Beth Bader, Diane Massell, and Sheila Rosenblum. (1992). Recent Trends in Educational Reform: Assessment and Prospects. *Teachers College Record,* 94(2), 254–277.

Firestone, William A., Susan H. Fuhrman, and Michael W. Kirst. (1989). *The Progress of Reform: An Appraisal of State Education Initiatives.* New Brunswick, NJ: Rutgers, The State University of New Jersey, Consortium for Policy Research in Education (CPRE).

First, Patricia F. and Herbert J. Walberg. (1992). *School Boards: Changing Local Control.* Berkeley, CA: McCutchan Publishing Corporation.

Fliegel, Seymour. (1993). *Miracle in East Harlem.* New York: Times Books.

Floden, Robert E., Andrew C. Porter, Linda E. Alford et al. (1988). Instructional Leadership at the District Level: A Closer Look at Autonomy and Control. *Educational Administration Quarterly,* 24(2), 96–124.

Frase, Mary. (1989). *Dropout Rates in the United States: 1988.* Washington, DC: U.S. Department of Education.

Freeman v. *Pitts,* 112 U.S. 1430 (1992).

Fuhrman, Susan H. (1983). State Level Politics and School Financing. In Nelda Cambron-McCabe and Allan Odden, ed., *The Changing Politics of School Finance.* Cambridge, MA: Ballinger, pp. 53–70.

Fuhrman, Susan H. (1988). State Politics and Education Reform. In Robert Crowson and Jane Hannaway, eds., *The Politics of School Administration.* Philadelphia: Falmer Press, pp. 61–75.

Fuhrman, Susan H. (1993a). The Politics of Coherence. In Susan H. Fuhrman, ed., *Designing Coherent Education Policy.* San Francisco: Jossey Bass, pp. 313–322.

Fuhrman, Susan H., ed. (1993b). *Designing Coherent Education Policy.* San Francisco: Jossey Bass.

Fuhrman, Susan H. (1994a). Legislatures and Education Policy. In Richard F. Elmore and Susan H. Fuhrman, eds., *The Governance of Curriculum.* Alexandria, VA: Association for Supervision and Curriculum Development, pp. 30–55.

Fuhrman, Susan H. (1994b). *Politics of Coherent Policy.* New Brunswick, NJ: Rutgers, the State University of New Jersey, Eagleton Institute of Politics, Consortium for Policy Research in Education.

Fuhrman, Susan H., and Associates. (1991). *Final Report: Center for Policy Research in Education.* New Brunswick, NJ: Rutgers University, Consortium for Policy Research in Education (CPRE).

Fuhrman, Susan H. and Richard F. Elmore. (1990). Understanding Local Control in the Wake of State Education Reform. *Educational Evaluation and Policy Analysis,* 12(1), 82–96.

Fuhrman, Susan H. and Richard F. Elmore. (1991). *Takeover and Deregulation: Working Models of New State and Local Regulatory Relationships.* New Brunswick, NJ: Rutgers University, Consortium for Policy Research in Education (CPRE).

Fuhrman, Susan H. and Richard F. Elmore. (1994). Governors and Education Policy in the 1990s (pp. 56–74). In Richard F. Elmore and Susan H. Fuhrman, eds., *The Governance of Curriculum.* Alexandria, VA: Association for Supervision and Curriculum Development.

Fuhrman, Susan H. and Diane Massell. (1992). *Issues and Strategies in Systemic Reform.* New Brunswick, NJ: Rutgers, the State University of New Jersey, Eagleton Institute of Politics, Consortium for Policy Research in Education.

Fuhrman, Susan H. and Jennifer O'Day. (1994). *Systemic Reform as Support for School Based Change.* New Brunswick, NJ: Rutgers, the State University of New Jersey, Eagleton Institute of Politics, Consortium for Policy Research in Education.

Fuhrman, Susan H., William Clune, and Richard Elmore. (1988). Research on Education Reform: Lessons on Implementation of Policy. *Teachers College Record,* 90(2), 237–258.

Fuhrman, Susan H., William Clune, and Richard Elmore. (1991). Research on Education Reform: Lessons on Implementation of Policy. In Allan R. Odden, ed. *Education Policy Implementation.* Albany, NY: State University of New York Press, pp. 197–218.

Fullan, Michael. (1985). Change Processes and Strategies at the Local Level. *Elementary School Journal,* 85(3), 391–422.

Fullan, Michael G. (1982). *The Meaning of Educational Change.* New York: Teachers College Press.

Fullan, Michael G. (1991). *The New Meaning of Educational Change.* New York: Teachers College Press.

Fullan, Michael G. (1993). *Change Forces.* New York: Longman.

Fullan, Michael G. and Matthew B. Miles. (1992). Getting Reform Right: What Works and What Doesn't. *Phi Delta Kappan,* 73(10), 744–752.

Fusan, K. S. (1988). *Children's Counting and Concepts of Numbers.* New York: Springer-Verlag.

Gage, Nate and Margaret Needels. (1989). Process-Product Research on Teaching: A Review of Criticisms. *Elementary School Journal, 89*(3), 253–300.

Galbraith, Jay R., Edward E. Lawler, III, and Associates. (1993). *Organizing for the Future.* San Francisco: Jossey-Bass.

Gamoran, Adam. (1987). The Stratification of High School Learning Opportunities. *Sociology of Education*, 60, 135–155.

Garcia, Georgia and P. David Pearson. (1991). Modifying Reading Instruction to Maximize Its Effectiveness for "All" Students. In Michael S. Knapp and Patrick M. Shields, eds., *Better Schooling for the Children of Poverty: Alternatives to Conventional Wisdom.* Berkeley, CA: McCutchan, pp. 31–60.

Gardner, Howard. (1983). *Frames of Mind.* New York: Basic Books.

Gardner, Howard. (1991). *The Unschooled Mind: How Children Think and How Schools Should Teach.* New York: Basic Books.

Gerald, Debra E. and William J. Hussan. (1991). *Projections of Education Statistics to 2001.* Washington, DC: National Center for Education Statistics.

Geranios, John. (1992). *The Impetus and Effect of Private Sector Involvement in Legislative Agenda Setting: Application of the Kingdom Model to Education Reform in California, South Carolina and Texas.* Unpublished Ph.D. dissertation. University of Southern California, Los Angeles, CA.

Ginsburg, Herbert P. (1983). *The Development of Mathematical Thinking.* New York: Academic Press.

Ginsburg, Herbert P. (1989). *Children's Arithmetic.* Austin, TX: Pro-Ed.

Gold, Steven D. (1983). *State and Local Fiscal Relations in the Early 1980s.* Washington, DC: The Urban Institute.

Gold, Steven D. (1986). *Reforming State Tax Systems.* Denver, CO: National Conference of State Legislatures.

Gold, Steven D. (1988). *The Unfinished Agenda for State Tax Reform.* Denver, CO: National Conference of State Legislatures.

Gold, Steven D. (1993a). *State Fiscal Brief, Revised No. 11.* Albany, NY: State University of New York, Rockefeller Institute of Government.

Gold, Steven D. (1993b). *Tax Options for States Needing More School Revenue.* Washington, DC: National Education Association.

Goldring, Ellen B. and Sharon F. Rallis. (1993). *Principals of Dynamic Schools.* NewBerry Park, CA: Corwin Press.

Good, Thomas L. and Jere Brophy. (1986). School Effects. In Merlin Wittrock, ed., *Handbook of Research on Teaching.* New York: Macmillan, pp. 570–602.

Goodlad, John. (1984). *A Place Called School.* New York: McGraw Hill.

Goss v. *Lopez*, 419 U.S. 565 (1975).

Gray, Virginia, Herbert Jacob, and Robert B. Albritton. (1990). *Politics in the American States: A Comparative Analysis*, 5th ed. Glenview, IL: Scott, Foresman & Co.

Gray, Virginia, Herbert Jacob, and Kenneth N. Vines. (1983). *Politics in the American States: A Comparative Analysis*, 4th ed. Boston: Little Brown & Co.

Green v. *County School Board*, 391 U.S. 430 (1968).

Greenberg, James D. (1983). The Case for Teacher Education: Open and Shut. *Journal of Teacher Education, 34*(4), 2–5.

Greenfield, William, ed. (1987). *Instructional Leadership: Concepts, Issues and Controversies.* Boston: Allyn & Bacon.

Grimshaw, William J. (1979). *Union Rules in the Schools: Big City Politics in Transformation.* Lexington, MA: Lexington Books.

Grossman, Pamela. (1989). Learning to Teach Without Teacher Education. *Teachers College Record, 91*(2), 191–208.

Grubb, Norton. (1989a). Young Children Face the State: Issues and Options for Early Childhood Programs, *American Journal of Education,* 97(4): 358–397.

Grubb, W. Norton and Marvin Lazerson. (1988). *Broken Promises.* Chicago: University of Chicago Press.

Gruhn, William T. and Harl R. Douglass. (1956). *The Modern Junior High School.* New York: Ronald Press.

Guiton, Gretchen and Leigh Burstein. (1993). *Indicators of Curriculum and Instruction.* Paper presented at the annual meeting of American Educational Research Association, Atlanta, GA.

Guskey, Thomas. (1986). Staff Development and the Process of Teacher Change. *Educational Researcher,* 15(5), 5–12.

Guskey, Thomas, ed. (1994). *High-Stakes Performance Assessment.* Thousand Oaks, CA: Corwin Press.

Guthrie, James W. (1979). Organizational Scale and School Success. *Educational Evaluation and Policy Analysis,* 1(1), 17–27.

Guthrie, James W. (1988). *Understanding School Budgets.* Washington D.C.: U.S. Department of Education.

Guthrie, James W., Michael W. Kirst, and Allan R. Odden, eds. (1991). *Conditions of Education in California: 1990.* Berkeley, CA: University of California, School of Education, Policy Analysis for California Education (PACE).

Guthrie, James W., Michael W. Kirst, and Allan R. Odden, eds. (1992). *Conditions of Education in California: 1991.* Berkeley, CA: University of California, School of Education, Policy Analysis for California Education (PACE).

Guthrie, James W., George B. Kleindorfer, Henry M. Klein, and Robert T. Stout. (1971). *School & Inequality.* Cambridge: Cambridge Press.

Guthrie, James W. and Rodney J. Reed. (1986). *Educational Administration and Policy.* Boston: Allyn & Bacon.

Halinger, Phillip. (1992a). School Leadership Development: Evaluating a Decade of Reforms. *Education and Urban Society.* Entire Issue. 24(3).

Halinger, Phillip. (1992b). The Evolving Role of American Principals: From Managerial to Instructional to Transformational Leaders. *Journal of Educational Administration,* 30(3), 35–48.

Hallinger, Phillip and Joseph Murphy. (1983). The Social Context of Effective Schools. *American Journal of Education,* 94, 328–355.

Halpin, Andrew W. (1966). *Theory and Research in Administration.* New York, Macmillan, Inc.

Hammer, Michael and James Champy. (1993). *Reengineering the Corporation.* New York: Harper Business.

Hannaway, Jane and L. Sproull. (1978–79). Who's Running the Show? Coordination and Control of Instruction in Educational Organizations. *Administrator's Notebook,* 27(9), 1–4.

Harper v. Hunt, CV-91-0117-R (1993).

Harvard Educational Review. (1982). 52(4). Entire Issue.

Hawley, Willis and Susan Rosenholtz. (1984). Good Schools: What Research Says About Improving Student Achievement. *Peabody Journal of Education,* 61(4), entire issue.

Hazelwood School District v. *Kuhlmeier,* 484 U.S. 260 (1988).

Hedges, Larry V., Richard D. Laine, and Rob Greenwald. (1994). Does Money Matter? A Meta-Analysis of Studies of the Effects of Differential School Inputs on Student Outcomes. *Educational Researcher,* 23(3), 5–14.

Hentschke, Guilbert C. (1986). *School Business Administration: A Comparative Perspective,* Berkeley, CA: McCutchan Publishing Company.

Hentschke, Guilbert C. (1988). Budgetary Theory and Reality: A Micro-View. In David

H. Monk and Julie Underwood, eds., *Microlevel School Finance: Issues and Implications for Policy.* Cambridge, MA: Ballinger, pp. 311–336.

Hersey, Paul and Kenneth H. Blanchard. (1982). *Management and Organizational Behavior: Utilizing Human Resources.* Englewood Cliffs, NJ: Prentice-Hall, Inc.

Hertert, Linda. (1993). *School Finance Equity: An Analysis of School Level Equity in California.* Unpublished Ph.D. dissertation, University of Southern California, Los Angeles.

Hertert, Linda. (1994, forthcoming). *Local Response to Minnesota's Education Reforms.* Madison, WI: University of Wisconsin, Wisconsin Center for Education Research, Consortium for Policy Research in Education.

Hertert, Linda, Carolyn Busch, and Allan Odden. (1994). School financing inequities among the states: The problem from a national perspective. *Journal of Education Finance, 19*(3), 231–255.

Hess, Fred. (1991). *School Restructuring: Chicago Style.* Newbury Park, CA: Corwin Press.

Hill, Paul T. (1990). The Federal Role in Education: A Strategy for the 1990s. *Phi Delta Kappan, 71*(5), 398–402.

Hill, Paul T., Gail E. Foster, and Tamar Gendler. (1990). *High Schools With Character.* Santa Monica, CA: RAND Corporation.

Hillocks, G. Jr. (1987). Synthesis of Research on Teaching Writing. *Educational Leadership, 44*(8), 71–82.

Hillocks, George Jr. (1991). The Knowledge Necessary to Teach Writing Effectively. In Mary M. Kennedy, ed., *Teaching Academic Subjects to Diverse Learners.* New York: Teachers College Press, pp. 142–162.

Hodgkinson, Harold. (1985). *All One System: Demographics of Education, Kindergarten through Graduate School.* Washington, DC: Institute for Educational Leadership.

Hodgkinson, Harold. (1992). *A Demographic Look at Tomorrow.* Washington, DC: Institute for Educational Leadership.

Hopfenberg, Wendy S., Henry M. Levin, and Associates. (1993). *The Accelerated Schools Resource Guide.* San Francisco: Jossey Bass.

Houston, W. Robert, ed. (1990). *Handbook of Research on Teacher Education.* New York: Macmillan, Inc.

Huberman, Michael and Matthew Miles. (1984). *Innovation Up Close.* New York: Plenum Press.

Hudson, Lisa, David W. Grissmer, and Sheila Nataraj Kirby. (1991). *New and Returning Teachers in Indiana: The Role of the Beginning Teacher Internship Program.* Santa Monica, CA: The RAND Corporation.

Hull, Glynda Ann. (1989). Research on Writing: Building a Cognitive and Social Understanding of Composing. In Lauren Resnick and Leopold E. Kolpfer, eds., *Toward the Thinking Curriculum: Current Cognitive Research.* Washington, DC: Association for Supervision and Curriculum Development, pp. 104–128.

Independent Review Panel. (1993). *Statement of the Independent Review Panel of the National Assessment of Chapter 1.* Washington, DC: U.S. Department of Education.

Institute for Educational Leadership. (1986). *School Boards: Strengthening Grass Roots Leadership.* Washington DC: Institute for Educational Leadership.

Interstate New Teacher Assessment and Support Consortium. (1992). *Model Standards for Beginning Teacher Licensing and Development: A Resource for State Dialogue.* Washington, DC: Council of Chief State School Officers.

Jacobson, Stephen L., and Robert Berne, eds. (1993). *Reforming Education: The Emerging Systemic Approach.* Thousand Oaks, CA: Corwin Press.

Jencks, Christopher, Marshall Smith, Henry Acland et al. (1972). *Inequality: A Reassessment of the Effect of Family and Schooling in America.* New York: Basic Books.

Johnson, Susan Moore. (1986). Incentives for Teachers: What Motivates, What Matters. *Educational Administration Quarterly,* 22(3), 54–79.

Johnson, Susan Moore. (1990). *Teachers at Work: Achieving Success in Our Schools.* New York: Basic Books.

Johnston, William. (1987). *Workforce 2000.* Indianapolis, IN: Hudson Institute.

Johnston, William B. (1991). Global Work Force 2000: The New World Labor Market. *Harvard Business Review,* 69, 15–127.

Jordan, K. Forbis and Mary McKeown. (1990). State Fiscal Policy and Education Reform. In Joseph Murphy, ed., *The Educational Reform Movement of the 1980s.* Berkeley, CA: McCutchan, pp. 97–120.

Joyce, Bruce and Beverly Showers. (1982). The Coaching of Teaching. *Educational Leadership,* 40(1), 4–10.

Joyce, Bruce and Beverly Showers. (1988). *Student Achievement Through Staff Development.* New York: Longman.

Jung, Richard and Michael Kirst. (1986). Beyond Mutual Adaptation, Into the Bully Pulpit: Recent Research on the Federal Role in Education. *Education Administration Quarterly,* 22(3), 80–109.

Kaestle, Carl F. and Marshall S. Smith. (1982). The Federal Role in Elementary and Secondary Education, 1940–1980. *Harvard Educational Review,* 52(4), 384–408.

Kaplan, George R. and Michael D. Usdan. (1992). The Changing Look of Education's Policy Networks. *Phi Delta Kappan,* 37(9) 663–672.

Kaplan, Rochelle G., Takashi Yamamoto, and Herbert P. Ginsburg. (1989). Teaching Mathematics Concepts. In Lauren Resnick and Leopold E. Kolpfer, eds., *Toward the Thinking Curriculum: Current Cognitive Research.* Washington, DC: Association for Supervision and Curriculum Development, pp. 59–82.

Katzenbach, Jon R. and Douglas K. Smith. (1993). *The Wisdom of Teams: Creating the High-Performance Organization.* Boston: Harvard Business School Press.

Kaufman, Phillip and Marilyn M. McMillen. (1991). *Dropout Rates in the United States: 1990.* Washington, DC: U.S. Department of Education.

Kay, Alan C. (1991). Computers, Networks and Education. *Scientific America.* 265(3), 138–146. September 1991.

Kay, Alan. (1992). Open School Article. *Scientific America.*

Kazal-Thresher, Deborah M. (1994). Desegregation Goals and Educational Finance Reform: An Agenda for the Next Decade. *Educational Policy,* 8(1), 51–67.

Kellog, John B. (1988). Forces of Change. *Phi Delta Kappan,* 70(3), 199–204.

Kennedy, Mary M. (1991). *Teaching Academic Subjects to Diverse Learners.* New York: Teachers College Press.

Kerschner, Charles T. and Douglas E. Mitchell. (1986). Teaching Reform and Union Reform, *Elementary School Journal,* 86(4), 449–470.

Kerschner, Charles T. and Douglas E. Mitchell. (1988). *The Changing Idea of a Teachers' Union.* Philadelphia: Falmer.

Kerschner, Charles Taylor and Julia E. Koppich. (1993). *A Union of Professionals.* New York: Teachers College Press.

Keyes v. *School District No. 1,* 413 U.S. 189 (1973).

King, Jennifer. (1994). Meeting the Educational Needs of At-Risk Students: A Cost Analysis of Three Models. *Educational Evaluation and Policy Analysis,* 16(1), 1–20.

Kirp, David. (1992). Open School Article. *Los Angeles Times Magazine.*

Kirp, David L. (1992). Good Schools in Bad Times. *Los Angeles Times Magazine.* January 5, 1992.

Kirst, Michael W. (1989). *Conditions of Children in California.* Berkeley, CA: University of California, Policy Analysis for California Education.

Kirst, Michael W. (1991). Improving Children's Services: Overcoming Barriers, Creating New Opportunities. *Phi Delta Kappan,* 72(8), 615–618.

Kirst, Michael W. (1992a). Financing School Linked Services. In Allan R. Odden, Ed., *Rethinking School Finance: An Agenda for the 1990s*. San Francisco: Jossey Bass, pp. 298–321.

Kirst, Michael W. (1992b). *Recent History of U.S. Education Governance*. Paper prepared for the U.S. Department of Education, Office of Educational Research and Improvement.

Kirst, Michael W. (1993). A Changing Context Means School Board Reform. *Phi Delta Kappan*, 75(5), 378–381.

Kirst, Michael W. (1994). *Using an Equalized Local Income Tax Surcharge for Education*. Berkeley, CA: University of California, School of Education, Policy Analysis for California Education (PACE).

Kirst, Michael W. and Walter I. Garms. (1980). The Political Environment of School Finance Policy in the 1980s. In James W. Guthrie, ed., *School Finance Policies and Practices*. Cambridge, Mass.: Ballinger.

Kirst, Michael W. and Gail Meister. (1985). Turbulence in American Secondary Schools: What Reforms Last? *Curriculum Inquiry*, 15(2), 169–185.

Kirst, Michael W. and Allan Odden. (1992–93). National Initiatives and State Education Policy. *Stanford Law and Policy Review*, 4:99–111.

Kirst, Michael W. and Richard Jung. (1980). The Utility of a Longitudinal Approach in Assessing Implementation. *Educational Evaluation and Policy Analysis*, 2(5), 17–34.

Knapp, Michael, Maria Stearns, Brenda Trunbull, et al. (1983). *Cumulative Effects of Federal Education Policies on Schools and Districts*. Menlo Park, CA: SRI International.

Knapp, Michael S., Marian S. Stearns, Brenda J. Turnbull, et al. (1991). Cumulative Effects of Federal Education Policies at the Local Level. In Allan R. Odden, ed., *Education Policy Implementation*. Albany, NY: State University of New York Press, pp. 105–123.

Kochan, Thomas A. and Paul Osterman. (1990). *Human Resource Development and Utilization: Is There Too Little in the U.S.?* Cambridge, MA: Massachusetts Institute of Technology, Sloan School of Management.

Koppich, Julia E. (1993). Getting Started: A Primer on Professional Unionism. In Charles Taylor Kerschner and Julia E. Koppich, eds., *A Union of Professionals*. New York: Teachers College Press.

Koretz, Daniel. (1986). *Trends in Educational Achievement*. Washington, DC: Congressional Budget Office.

Koretz, Daniel. (1987). *Educational Achievement: Explanations and Implications of Recent Trends*. Washington, DC: Congressional Budget Office.

Koretz, Daniel, D. McCaffrey, S. Klein, et al. (1992). *The Reliability of Scores from the 1992 Vermont Portfolio Assessment Program*. Los Angeles: University of California, National Center for Research on Evaluation, Standards and Student Testing.

Kotter, John P. (1982). What Effective General Managers Really Do. *Harvard Business Review*, 60, 156–167.

Kozol, Jonathan. (1991). *Savage Inequalities*. New York: Crown Publishers.

Krashen, Stephen. (1981). Bilingual Education and Second Language Acquisition Theory. In Office of Bilingual Bicultural Education, ed., *Schooling and Language Minority Students: A Theoretical Framework*. Los Angeles, CA: California State University, Evaluation, Dissemination and Assessment Center.

Krashen, Stephen. (1982). *Principles and Practice in Second Language Acquisition*. Hayward: CA: Alemany Press.

Krashen, Stephen. (1985a). *The Input Hypothesis: Issues and Implications*. New York: Longman.

Krashen, Stephen. (1985b). *Inquiries and Insights: Essays on Second Language Teaching, Bilingual Education and Literacy*. Hayward, CA: Alemany Press.

Krashen, Stephen. (1992). *Fundamentals of Language Education*. Torrence, CA: Laredo Publishing Co., Inc.

Krashen, Stephen and Douglas Biber. (1988). *On Course: Bilingual Education's Success in California,* Sacramento, CA: California Association for Bilingual Education.

Krashen, Stephen and Terry Terrell. (1983). *The Natural Approach: Language Acquisition in the Classroom.* Hayward, CA: Alemany Press.

Kucer, Stephen B. and Cecilia Silva. (1989). The New California English-Language Arts Framework: A Step in the Right Direction but . . . . *California Journal for Supervision and Curriculum Improvement,* 2(2), 14–25.

Kyle, Regina, ed. (1985). *Reaching for Excellence: An Effective Schools Sourcebook.* Washington, D.C: The National Institute of Education.

Lampert, Magdalene. (1991). Connecting Mathematical Teaching and Learning. In Elizabeth Fennema, Thomas P. Carpenter and Susan J. Lamon, eds., *Integrating Research on Teaching and Learning Mathematics.* Albany, NY: State University of New York Press, pp. 121–152.

Lapointe, Archie E., Janice M. Askew, and Nancy A. Mead. (1992a). *Learning Mathematics: The International Assessment of Educational Progress.* Princeton, NJ: Educational Testing Service.

Lapointe, Archie E., Nancy A. Mead, and Gary W. Phillips. (1989). *A World of Differences.* Princeton, NJ: Educational Testing Service.

Larkin, Jill H. & Ruth W. Chabay. (1989). Research on Teaching Scientific Thinking: Implications for Computer-Based Instruction. In Lauren Resnick and Leopold E. Kolpfer, eds., *Toward the Thinking Curriculum: Current Cognitive Research.* Washington, DC: Association for Supervision and Curriculum Development, pp. 150–172.

Latimer, John Francis. (1958). *What's Happened to Our High Schools?* Washington, DC: Public Affairs Press.

Lau v. Nichols, 414 U.S. 563 (1974).

Lawler, Edward E. (1986). *High Involvement Management.* San Francisco: Jossey-Bass.

Lawler, Edward E. (1990). *Strategic Pay: Aligning Organizational Strategies and Pay Systems.* San Francisco: Jossey-Bass.

Lawler, Edward E. (1992). *The Ultimate Advantage: Creating the High Involvement Organization.* San Francisco: Jossey Bass.

Lawler, Edward E. and Susan A. Mohrman. (1993). *A New Logic for Organizing: Implications for Higher Education.* Los Angeles: University of Southern California, Center for Effective Organizations.

Lawler, Edward E., Gerald E. Ledford, and Susan A. Mohrman. (1989). *Employee Involvement in America.* Houston, TX: American Productivity and Quality Center.

Lawler, Edward E., Susan A. Mohrman, and Gerald Ledford. (1992). *Employee Involvement and Total Quality Management.* San Francisco: Jossey-Bass.

Lawrence, Paul R. and Jay W. Lorsch. 1969. *Organization and Environment: Managing Differentiation and Integration.* Homework, Ill. Richard D. Irvin, Inc.

Lawson, Anton E. (1991). What Teachers Need to Know to Teach Science Effectively. In Mary M. Kennedy, ed. *Teaching Academic Subjects to Diverse Learners.* New York: Teachers College Press, pp. 31–60.

Lee, Valerie E., Anthony S. Bryk, and Julia B. Smith. (1993). The Organization of Effective Secondary Schools. In Linda Darling Hammond, ed., *Review of Research in Education.* Washington, DC: American Educational Research Association, pp. 171–268.

Leinhardt, Gaea. (1992). What Research on Learning Tells Us About Teaching. *Educational Leadership,* 49(7), 20–25.

Leinhardt, Gaea and Isabel L. Beck. (1994). *Teaching and Learning in History.* Hillsdale, NJ: Lawrence Erlbaum Associates.

Leithwood, Kenneth A. (1992). The Move Toward Transformational Leadership. *Educational Leadership,* 49(5), 8–12.

Leithwood, Kenneth A. and D. Jantzi. (1990). Transformational Leadership: How Principals can Help Reform School Cultures. *School Effectiveness and School Improvement,* 1(4), 249–280.

Lemon v. *Kurtzman,* 403 U.S. 602 (1971).

Levin, Henry. (1987). Accelerated Schools for Disadvantaged Students. *Educational Leadership, 44*(6), 19–21.

Levin, Henry. (1988). *Accelerated Schools for At-Risk Students,* New Brunswick, NJ: Center for Policy Research in Education, Eagleton Institute of Politics, Rutgers University.

Levin, Henry. (1989). Financing the Education of At-Risk Students. *Education Evaluation and Policy Analysis,* 11(1), 47–60.

Levin, Henry and Russell Rumberger. (1983). The Low Skill Future of High-Tech. *Technology Review, 86,* 18–21.

Levin, Henry and Russell Rumberger. (1987). Educational Requirements for New Technologies: Visions, Possibilities, and Current Realities. *Educational Policy, 1*(3), 333–354.

Levin, Henry M. and Carolyn Kelley. (1994). *Can Education Do It Alone?* Economics of Education Review, 13(2), 97–108.

Levin, Henry, David Leitner and Gail Meister. (1987). Cost Effectiveness of Computer Assisted Instruction. *Evaluation Review,* 11(1), 50–72.

Levy, Frank and Richard J. Murnane. (1992). U.S. Earnings Levels and Earnings Inequality: A Review of Recent Trends and Proposed Explanations. *Journal of Economic Literature.*

Lewis, Anne C. (1990). Getting Unstuck: Curriculum as a Tool of Reform. *Phi Delta Kappan,* (7), 534–538.

Lewis, Anne C. (1993). *Changing the Odds: Middle School Reform in Progress, 1991–1993.* New York: Edna McConnell Clark Foundation.

Lieberman Ann and Lynne Miller, eds. (1992). *Staff Development for Education in the '90s.* New York: Teachers College Press.

Lieberman, Ann and Milbrey W. McLaughlin. (1992). Networks for Educational Change: Powerful and Problematic. *Phi Delta Kappan,* 73 (9), 673–677.

Lieberman, Myron. (1980). *Public Sector Bargaining: A Policy Reappraisal.* Lexington, MA: Lexington Books.

Lightfoot, Sara Lawrence. (1983). *The Good High School.* New York: Basic Books.

Likert, Renis. (1961). *New Patterns of Management.* New York: McGraw Hill.

Lindblom, Charles E. (1959). The Science of Muddling Through. *Public Administration Review,* 19:257–264.

Linn, Robert L. and Stephen B. Dunbar. (1990). The Nation's Report Card Goes Home: Good News and Bad About Trends in Achievement. *Phi Delta Kappan,* 71(2), 127–133.

Lipsitz, Joan. (1984). *Successful Schools for Early Adolescents.* New Brunswick, NJ: Transaction Books.

Little, Judith Warren. (1982). Norms of Collegiality and Experimentation: Workplace Conditions of School Success. *American Educational Research Journal,* 19, 325–40.

Little, Judith Warren. (1993). Teachers' Professional Development in a Climate of Educational Reform. *Educational Analysis and Policy Analysis,* 15(2), 129–152.

Little, Judith Warren, William H. Gerritz, David S. Stern; et al. (1987). *Staff Development in California.* Berkeley, CA: University of California, Policy Analysis for California Education.

Lortie, Daniel. (1975). *School Teacher.* Chicago: University of Chicago Press.

Lusi, Susan Follett. (1993). *Systemic School Reform: The Changes Implied for SDEs and How One Department Has Responded.* Paper presented the annual meeting of the American Educational Research Association, Atlanta, GA.

Lusi, Susan Follett. (1994). Systemic School Reform: The Challenger Faced by State Departments of Education. In Richard F. Elmore & Susan H. Fuhrman (eds.), *The Governance of Curriculum* (pp. 109–130). Alexandria, VA: Association for Supervision and Curriculum Development.

Lynch v. *Donnelly,* 465 U.S. 668 (1984).

MacIver, Douglas J. and Joyce L. Epstein. (1990). *How Equal Are Opportunities for Learning in Disadvantaged and Advantaged Middle Schools?* Baltimore, MD: Johns Hopkins University, Center for Research on Effective Schooling for Disadvantaged Students.

Madden, Nancy, Robert Slavin, Nancy Karweit, et al. (1992). *Success for All: Fourth Year Results.* Paper presented at the annual meeting of the American Educational Research Association, San Francisco, CA.

Madden, Nancy A., Robert Slavin, Nancy Karweit, et al. (1993). Success for All: Longitudinal Effects of a Restructuring Program for Inner-City Elementary Schools. *American Educational Research Journal,* 30(1), 123–148.

Maeroff, Gene I. (1991). Assessing Alternative Assessment. *Phi Delta Kappan,* (4), 272–281.

Magaziner, Ira and Hillary Rodham Clinton. (1992). Will America Choose High Skills or Low Wages? *Educational Leadership.* 49(6), 10–13.

Malen, Betty and Rodney T. Ogawa. (1988). Professional-Patron Influence on Site-Based Governance Councils: A Confounding Case Study, *Educational Evaluation and Policy Analysis,* 10(4), 251–270.

Malen, Betty, Rodney T. Ogawa and Jennifer Kranz. (1990). What Do We Know About School-Based Management? A Case Study of the Literature—A Call for Research. In William H. Clune and John F. Witte, eds., *Choice and Control in American Education, Volume 2: The Practice of Decentralization and School Restructuring.* Philadelphia: Falmer Press. pp. 289–342.

Maloy, Kate. (1993). *Toward a New Science of Instruction.* Washington, DC: U.S. Department of Education, Office of Educational Research & Improvement.

Manasse, A. Lorri. (1984). Principals as Leaders of High-Performing Systems. *Educational Leadership,* 41(5), 42–46.

Manasse, A. Lori. (1985). Improving Conditions for Principal Effectiveness: Policy Implications of Research. *Elementary School Journal,* 85(3), 439–463.

Marbury v. *Madison,* 5 U.S. (1 Cranch) 137, (1803).

March, James. (1978). American Public School Administration: A Short Analysis. *School Review,* 86, 217–250.

Marsh, David and Greg Bowman. (1989). State Initiated Top-Down versus Bottom-Up Reform, *Education Policy,* 3(3), 195–216.

Marsh, David D. and Patricia Crocker. (1991). School Restructuring: Implementing Middle School Reform. In Allan R. Odden, ed., *Education Policy Implementation.* Albany, NY: State University of New York Press, pp. 219–239.

Marsh, David D. and Allan R. Odden. (1991). Implementation of the California Mathematics and Science Curriculum Frameworks. In Allan R. Odden, ed., *Education Policy Implementation.* Albany, NY: State University of New York Press.

Marshall, Ray and Marc Tucker. (1992). *Thinking for a Living: Education and the Wealth of Nations.* New York: Basic Books.

Massell, Diane. (1993). *Setting Content Standards.* New Brunswick, NJ: Rutgers, the State University of New Jersey, Eagleton Institute of Politics, Consortium for Policy Research in Education.

Massell, Diane and Susan H. Fuhrman. (1994). *Ten Years of State Education Reform: Overview with Four Case Studies.* New Brunswick, NJ: Rutgers: The State University of New Jersey, Eagleton Institute of Politics, Consortium for Policy Research in Education.

Massell, Dianne and Margaret Goertz. (1994). *Project 2061 Policy Blueprint.* New Brunswick, NJ: Rutgers, the State University of New Jersey, Eagleton Institute of Politics, Consortium for Policy Research in Education.

Massell, Diane and Michael Kirst. (1986). State Policymaking for Educational Excellence: School Reform in California. In Van Mueller & Mary McKeown, eds., *The Legal, Fiscal and Political Aspects of the Reform of Elementary and Secondary Education.* Cambridge, MA: Ballinger, pp. 121–144.

Massell, Diane and Michael Kirst. (1994). Setting National Content Standards. *Education and Urban Society.* February 1994, Entire Issue.

Mayeske, George. (1969). *A Study of Our Nation's Schools.* Washington, DC: U.S. Office of Education.

Mayo, Elton. (1933). *The Human Problems of an Industrial Civilization.* New York, Macmillan, Inc.

McCarthy, Martha. (1993). Much Ado over Graduation Prayer. *Phi Delta Kappan,* 75(2), 120–125.

McCollum v. *Board of Education,* 333 U.S. 203 (1948).

McDonnell, Lorraine. (1991). Ideas and Values in Implementation Analysis: The Case of Teacher Policy. In Allan Odden, ed., *Education Policy Implementation* Albany, N.Y.: State University of New York Press, pp. 241–258.

McDonnell, Lorraine and Richard Elmore. (1987). Alternative Policy Instruments. In Allan R. Odden, ed., *Education Policy Implementation.* Albany, NY: State University of New York Press.

McDonnell, Lorraine and Susan H. Fuhrman, (1986). The Political Context of Education Reform. In Van Mueller & Mary McKeown, Eds. *The Fiscal, Legal, and Political Aspects of State Reform of Elementary and Secondary Education.* Cambridge, MA: Ballinger, pp. 43–64.

McDonnell, Lorraine E. and Milbrey W. McLaughlin. (1982). *Education and the Role of the States.* Santa Monica, CA: RAND Corporation.

McDonnell, Lorraine and Anthony Pascal. (1988). *Teacher Unions and Educational Reform.* Santa Monica, CA: RAND Corporation.

McDonnell, Lorraine, Leigh Burstein, Ormseth, James Catterall, and D. Moody. (1990). *Discovering What Schools Really Teach: Designing Improved Coursework Indicators.* Santa Monica, CA: RAND Corporation.

McDuffie v. *Secretary of Education,* (1993).

McGregor, Douglas. 1960. *The Human Side of Enterprise.* New York: McGraw Hill.

McKnight, Curtis C., F. Joe Crosswhite, John A. Dossey, et al. (1987). *The Underachieving Curriculum: Assessing U.S. School Mathematics from an International Perspective.* Campaign, IL: Stipes Publishing Company.

McLaughlin, Milbrey and Shirley Heath. (1989). Policies for Children with Multiple Needs. In Michael W. Kirst, ed. *Conditions of Children in California.* Berkeley: University of California, School of Education, Policy Analysis for California Education.

McLaughlin, Milbrey and Sylvia Yee. (1988). School as a Place to Have a Career. In Ann Lieberman, ed. *Building a Professional Culture in Schools.* New York: Teachers College Press, pp. 23–44.

McLaughlin, Milbrey W. (1991a). The Rand Change Agent Study: Ten Years Later. In Allan R. Odden, ed., *Education Policy Implementation.* Albany, NY: State University of New York Press.

McLaughlin, Milbrey W. (1991b). Lessons From Past Implementation Research. In Allan R. Odden, ed., *Education Policy Implementation.* Albany, NY: State University of New York Press.

McLaughlin, Milbrey W. & Joan E. Talbert. (1993). How the World of Students and

Teachers Challenges Policy Coherence. In Susan H. Fuhrman, ed. *Designing Coherent Education Policy* (pp. 220–249). San Francisco: Jossey Bass.

McLaughlin, Milbrey Wallin. (1982). States and the New Federalism. *Harvard Educational Review, 52*(4), 564–583.

McLaughlin, Milbrey Wallin. (1992a). Enabling Professional Development. In Ann Lieberman and Lynne Miller, eds. (1992). *Staff Development for Education in the '90s.* New York: Teachers College Press, pp. 61–82.

McLaughlin, Milbrey Wallin. (1992b). How District Communities Do and Do Not Foster Teacher Pride. *Educational Leadership, 50*(1), 33–35.

McUsic, Molly. (1991). The Use of Education Clauses in School Finance Reform Litigation," *Harvard Journal on Legislation, 28*(2), 307–340.

Means, Barbara and Michael S. Knapp. (1991). Models for Teaching Advanced Skills to Educationally Disadvantaged Students. In Barbara Means and Michael S. Knapp, eds., *Teaching Advanced Skills to Educationally Disadvantaged Students.* Washington, DC: U.S. Department of Education, Office of Planning, Budget and Evaluation, pp. 1–20.

Medrich, Elliott A. and Jeanne E. Griffith. (1992). *International Mathematics and Science Assessments: What Have We Learned?* Washington, DC: U.S. Department of Education, Office of Educational Research and Improvement, National Center for Educational Achievement.

Meek v. *Pittenger*, 421 U.S. 349 (1975).

Miles, Karen Hawley. (1994). *Finding Time for Improving Schools: A Case Study of Boston Public Schools.* Paper presented at the annual meeting of the American Educational Research Association, New Orleans.

Miles, Matthew B. (1993). Forty Years of Change in Schools: Some Personal Reflections. *Educational Administration Quarterly, 29*(2), 213–248.

Milliken v. *Bradley*, 433 U.S. 267 (1977).

Milsap, Mary Ann, Marc Moss and Beth Gamse. (1993). *The Chapter 1 Implementation Study.* Washington, DC: The U.S. Department of Education.

Minstrell, James A. (1989). Teaching Science for Understanding. In Lauren Resnick and Leopold E. Kolpfer, eds., *Toward the Thinking Curriculum: Current Cognitive Research.* Washington, DC: Association for Supervision and Curriculum Development, pp. 129–149.

Mintzberg, Henry. (1973). *The Nature of Managerial Work.* New York: Harper and Row.

Mintzberg, Henry. (1977). The Manager's Job: Folklore and Fact. *Harvard Business Review, 53*(4), 49–61.

Mohrman, Susan Albers. (1992). *High Involvement Management: An Overview of Practice in the Private Sector.* Los Angeles, CA: University of Southern California, Center for Research in Education Finance, Consortium for Policy Research in Education.

Mohrman, Susan Albers. (1993). *School Based Management and School Reform: Comparisons to Private Sector Organizational Renewal.* Paper presented the annual meeting of the Association for Public Policy Analysis and Management, Washington, DC.

Mohrman, Susan Albers. (Forthcoming). Large-Scale Organizational Change Processes: The Transition to High Involvement. In Susan Albert Mohrman and Priscilla Wohlstetter, eds., *School-Based Management: Organizing for High Performance.* San Francisco: Jossey Bass.

Mohrman, Susan Albers, Edward E. Lawler III, and Allan M. Mohrman, Jr. Applying Employee Involvement in Schools. (1992). *Education Evaluation and Policy Analysis.* 14(4), 347–360.

Mohrman, Allan, Susan Albert Mohrman, Gerald E. Ledford, et al. (1989). *Large-Scale Organizational Change.* San Francisco: Jossey Bass.

Mohrman, Susan Albers, and Allan Odden. (Forthcoming). Aligning Teacher Compensation with Systemic School Reform: Skill-Based Pay and Group-Based Performance Rewards. *Educational Evaluation and Policy Analysis.*

Mohrman, Susan Albers and Priscilla Wohlstetter, eds. (1994). *School-Based Management: Organizing for High Performance.* San Francisco: Jossey Bass.

Monk, David and Billy Walker. (1991). The Texas Cost of Education Index: A Broadened Approach. *Journal of Education Finance.* 17(2), 172–192.

Monk, David, and Brian O'Neil Brent. (1994 forthcoming). Financing Teacher Education and Professional Development. In *Handbook of Research on Teacher Education.* New York: Macmillan.

Moore, Mary T., Margaret Goertz, Terry Hartle, et al. (1983). *The Interaction of Federal and Related State Education Programs.* Executive Summary, Princeton, NJ: Educational Testing Service.

Moore, Mary T., Margaret E. Goertz, and Terry W. Hartle. (1991). Interaction of State and Federal Programs. In Allan R. Odden, ed., *Education Policy Implementation.* Albany, NY: State University of New York Press, pp. 81–104.

Mueller v. *Allen,* 463 U.S. 388 (1983).

Muller, Thomas and Thomas Espenshade. (1985). *The Fourth Wave.* Washington, DC: Urban Institute.

Mullis, Ina V.S., Jary R. Campbell, and Alan E. Farstrup. (1993). *The NEAP 1992 Reading Report Card for the Nation and the States.* Washington, DC: U.S. Department of Education.

Mullis, Ina V.S., John A. Dossey, Eugene H. Owen, and Gary W. Phillips. (1991). *The State of Mathematics Achievement: NAEP's Assessment of the Nation and Trial Assessment of the States.* Washington, DC: U.S. Department of Education, Office of Educational Research and Improvement.

Mullis, Ina, Eugene H. Owen, and Gary Phillips. (1990). *Accelerating Academic Achievement.* Princeton, NJ: Educational Testing Service.

Murnane, Richard J. and David K. Cohen. (1986). Merit Pay and the Evaluation Problem: Why Some Merit Pay Plans Fail and a Few Survive. *Harvard Educational Review,* 56(1), 1–17.

Murnane, Richard J. and Frank Levy. (1992a). Education and Training. In Henry J. Aaron & Charles L. Schulltz, eds., *Setting Domestic Priorities.* Washington, DC: The Brookings Institution, pp. 185–222.

Murnane, Richard J. and Frank Levy. (1992b). *The Growing Importance of Cognitive Skills in Wage Determination.* Cambridge, MA: Harvard Graduate School of Education.

Murnane, Richard J., Judith D. Singer, John B. Willett, et al. (1991). *Who Will Teach? Policies That Matter.* Cambridge: Harvard University Press.

Murphy, Jerome T. (1971). Title 1 of ESEA: The Politics of Implementing Federal Education Reform. *Harvard Educational Review,* 41(1), 35–63.

Murphy, Jerome T. (1974). Title V of ESEA: The Impact of Discretionary Funds on State Education Bureaucracies. *Harvard Educational Review,* 43(3), 362–385.

Murphy, Jerome T. (1982). Progress and Problems: The Paradox of State Reform. In Ann Liebermann and Milbrey McLaughlin, eds., *Policymaking in Education.* Chicago: Chicago University Press, pp. 195–214.

Murphy, Jerome T. (1991). Title I of ESEA: The Politics of Implementing Federal Education Policy. In Allan R. Odden, ed., *Education Policy Implementation.* Albany, NY: State University of New York Press, pp. 13–38.

Murphy, Joseph. (1990a). Principal Instructional Leadership. In Paul Thurston and Linda Lotto, eds., *Advances in Educational Administration, Vol I, Part B: Changing Perspectives on the School.* Greenwich, CT: JAI Press, pp. 163–200.

Murphy, Joseph. (1990b). *The Educational Reform Movement of the 1980s.* Berkeley, CA: McCutchan.

Murphy, Joseph. (1991). *Restructuring Schools: Capturing and Assessing the Phenomena.* New York: Teachers College Press.

Murphy, Joseph. (1994a). Transformational Change and the Evolving Role of the Principal: Early Empirical Evidence. In Joseph Murphy and Karen Seashore Louis, eds., *Reshaping the Principalship: Insights from Transformational Change Efforts.* Newbury Park, CA: Corwin Press.

Murphy, Joseph. (1994b, forthcoming). Restructuring in Kentucky: The Changing Role of the Superintendent and the District Office. In Keith Leithwood, ed., Perspectives on Effective School District Leadership: Transforming Politics into Education. Albany: State University of New York Press.

Murphy, Joseph and Phillip Hallinger. (1993). *Restructuring Schooling: Learning From Ongoing Efforts.* Newberry Park, CA: Corwin Press.

Murphy, Joseph and Phillip Hallinger. (1986). The Superintendent as Instructional Leader: Findings from Effective School Districts. *Journal of Educational Administration, 24(2), 213–236.*

Murphy, Joseph and Phillip Hallinger. (1988). Characteristics of Instructionally-Effective School Districts. *Journal of Educational Research,* 81: 175–181.

Murphy, Kevin and Finis Welch. (1989). Wage Premiums for College Graduates: Recent Growth and Possible Explanations. *Educational Researcher,* 18(4), 17–26.

Nanus, Burt. (1992). *Visionary Leadership.* San Francisco: Jossey-Bass.

National Alliance for Business. (1990). *A Blueprint for Business on Restructuring Education.* Washington, DC: National Alliance for Business.

National Alliance for Business. (1994). *Linking the Education Finance System to Improved Student Learning.* Washington, DC: National Alliance for Business.

National Board for Professional Teaching Standards. (1989). *Towards High and Rigorous Standards for the Teaching Profession.* Detroit, MI: National Board for Professional Teaching Standards.

National Center for Educational Statistics. (1989a). *Digest of Educational Statistics: 1989.* Washington, D.C.: U.S. Department of Education.

National Center for Educational Statistics. (1989–90). Key Statistics for Public Elementary and Secondary Education: School Year 1989–90. Washington, DC: United States Department of Education.

National Center for Educational Statistics (NCES). (1991). *Digest of Educational Statistics: 1991.* Washington, DC: U.S. Department of Education.

National Center for Educational Statistics. (1990). *Digest of Educational Statistics: 1990.* Washington, D.C.: National Center for Education Statistics.

National Center for Educational Statistics. (1992). *Digest of Educational Statistics: 1992.* Washington DC: U.S. Government Printing Office.

National Center for Educational Statistics. (1993a). *Projections of Educational Statistics to 2002.* Washington, DC: U.S. Department of Education.

National Center for Educational Statistics. (1993b). *Condition of Education 1993.* Washington, DC: U.S. Department of Education.

National Center for Educational Statistics. (1993c). *NAEP 1992 Reading Report Card for the Nation and the States.* Washington, DC: U.S. Department of Education.

National Center for Educational Statistics. (1993d). *NAEP 1992 Mathematics Report Card for the Nation and the States.* Washington, DC: U.S. Department of Education.

National Center for Improving Science Education. (1989). *The Reform of Science Education in Elementary Schools.* Washington, DC: National Center for Improving Science Education.

National Center for Research on Teacher Education. (1991). *Findings from the Teacher Education and Learning to Teach Study.* East Lansing, MI: Michigan State University, National Center for Research on Teacher Education.

National Center on Education and the Economy. (1989). *To Secure Our Future: The Federal Role in Education.* Rochester, NY: National Center on Education and the Economy.

National Center on Education and the Economy. (1990). *America's Choice: High Wages or Low Skills.* Rochester, NY: National Center on Education and the Economy.

National Commission on Excellence in Education. (1983). *A Nation At Risk.* Washington, DC: U.S. Government Printing Office.

National Commission on Social Studies in the Schools. (1989). *Charting a Course: Social Studies for the 21st Century.* Washington, DC.

National Commission on Time and Learning. (1994). *Prisoners of Time.* Washington, DC: U.S. Department of Education.

National Council of Teachers of English. (1988). *Report Card on Basal Readers.* Champaign, Il: National Council of Teachers of English.

National Council of Teachers of English. (1989). *Democracy Through Language.* Champaign, Il: National Council of Teachers of English.

National Council of Teachers of Mathematics. (1989). *Curriculum and Evaluation Standards for School Mathematics.* Reston, VA: National Council of Teachers of Mathematics.

National Council on Education Standards and Testing. (1992). *Raising Standards for American Education.* Washington, DC: National Council on Educational Standards and Testing.

National Education Goals Panel. (1991). *Measuring Progress Toward the National Education Goals: Potential Indicators and Measurement Strategies.* Washington, DC., National Education Goals Panel.

National Education Goals Panel. (1991). *The National Education Goals Report.* Washington, DC: National Education Goals Panel.

National Education Goals Panel. (1992). *The National Education Goals Report.* Washington, DC: National Education Goals Panel.

National Education Goals Panel. (1993). *National Education Goals Report: Building a Nation of Learners.* Washington, DC: National Education Goals Panel.

National Governors' Association. (1986). *Time for Results.* Washington, DC: National Governors' Association.

National Governors' Association. (1990). *Educating America: State Strategies for Achieving the National Educational Goals.* Washington, D.C.: National Governors' Association.

National Governors' Association. (1991). *From Rhetoric to Action: State Progress in Restructuring the Education System.* Washington, DC: National Governors' Association.

National Governors' Association. (1993). *Transforming Education: Overcoming Barriers.* Washington, DC: National Governors' Association.

National Research Council. (1989). *Everybody Counts.: A Report to the Nation on the Future of Mathematics Education.* Washington, DC: National Academy Press.

National Science Teachers Association. (1989). *Essential Changes in Secondary Science: Scope, Sequence, and Coordination.* Washington, DC: National Science Teachers Association.

Newman, L. and S. Buka. (1990). *Every Child a Learner: Reducing Risks of Learning Impairment During Pregnancy and Infancy.* Denver, CO: Education Commission of the States.

Newmann, Fred. (1988). *Higher Order Thinking in High School Social Studies: An Analysis of Classrooms, Teachers, Students and Leadership.* Madison, WI: University of Wisconsin, National Center on Effective Secondary Schools.

Newmann, Fred. (1991). Higher Order Thinking in the Teaching of Social Studies: Connections Between Theory and Practice. In D. Perkins, J. Segal, and J. Voss, eds., *Informal Reasoning and Education.* Hillsdale, NJ: Lawrence Erlbaum.

Nickerson, Raymond S. (1988). On Improving Thinking Through Instruction. In Ernst Z. Rothkopf, ed., *Review of Research in Education.* Washington, DC: American Educational Research Association, pp. 3–57.

O'Day, Jennifer and Marshall Smith. (1993). Systemic Reform and Educational Opportunity. In Susan Furhman, ed., *Designing Coherent Education Policy.* San Francisco: Jossey-Bass, pp. 250–312.

O'Neil, John O. (1992). On Education and the Economy: A Conversation with Marc Tucker. *Educational Leadership.* 49(6), 19–22.

Oakes, Jeannie. (1985). *Keeping Track: How Schools Structure Inequality.* New Haven, CT: Yale University Press.

Oakes, Jeannie. (1986). *Educational Indicators: A Guide for Policymakers.* Santa Monica, Calif.: The Rand Corporation.

Oakes, Jeannie. (1990). *Multiplying Inequalities: The Effects of Race, Social Class and Tracking on Opportunities to Learn Mathematics and Science.* Santa Monica, CA: The RAND Corporation.

Oakes, Jeannie and M. Lipton. (1990). Tracking and Ability Grouping: A Structural Barrier to Access and Achievement. In John I. Goodlad and Pamela Keating, eds., *Access to Knowledge: An Agenda for Our Nation's Schools* (pp. 43–58). New York: College Entrance Examination Board, pp. 43–58.

Oakes, Jeannie, Adam Gamoran and Reba N. Page. (1992). Curriculum Differentiation: Opportunities, Outcomes and Meanings. In Phillip W. Jackson, ed., *Handbook of Research on Curriculum.* New York: Macmillan, pp. 570–606.

Odden, Allan. (1983). *School Finance Reform in the States, 1983.* Denver, CO: Education Commission of the States. With the assistance of C. Kent McGuire and Grace Belsches Simmons.

Odden, Allan. (1990a). Class Size and Student Achievement: Research-Based Policy Alternatives. *Educational Evaluation and Policy Analysis, 12*(2), 213–227.

Odden, Allan. (1990b). School Funding Changes in the 1980s, *Educational Policy, 4*(1), 33–47.

Odden, Allan. (1990c). Educational Indicators in the United States: The Need for Analysis, *Educational Researcher, 19*(4), 24–29.

Odden, Allan. (1993a). *The Local Response to School Finance Reform: Findings from Kentucky, New Jersey and Texas.* Madison, WI: University of Wisconsin, Wisconsin Center for Education Research, Consortium for Policy Research in Education.

Odden, Allan. (1993b). *Redesigning School Finance in an Era of National Goals and Systemic Reform.* Madison, WI: University of Wisconsin, Wisconsin Center for Education Research, Consortium for Policy Research in Education.

Odden, Allan. (1993c). The Shift Towards Outcomes: The Evolution of Education Reform in Minnesota. In Massell, Diane and Susan H. Fuhrman. (1993). *Ten Years of State Education Reform: Overview with Four Case Studies.* New Brunswick, NJ: Rutgers: The State University of New Jersey, Eagleton Institute of Politics, Consortium for Policy Research in Education, pp. 153–171.

Odden, Allan. (1993d). School Finance Reform in Kentucky, New Jersey and Texas, *Journal of Education Finance, 18*(4), 293–317.

Odden, Allan. (1994a). Decentralized Management and School Finance. *Theory Into Practice.*

Odden, Allan. (1994b). *Including School Finance in Systemic Reform Strategies: A Commentary.* Madison, WI: University of Wisconsin, Wisconsin Center for Education Research, Consortium for Policy Research in Education.

Odden, Allan. (1994c). *Preliminary Thoughts on the Costs of Measuring and Providing Opportunity to Learn.* Paper prepared for the National Center for Education Statistics.

Odden, Allan and Beverly Anderson. (1986). How Successful State Education Improvement Programs Work. *Phi Delta Kappan, 67*(8), 578–581.

Odden, Allan and Sharon Conley. (1992). Restructuring Teacher Compensation Systems. In Allan R. Odden, ed., *Rethinking School Finance: An Agenda for the 1990s.* San Francisco: Jossey-Bass, pp. 41–96.

Odden, Allan and Lori Kim. (1992). Reducing Disparities Across the States: A New Federal Role in School Finance. In Allan R. Odden, ed., *Rethinking School Finance: An Agenda for the 1990s.* San Francisco: Jossey Bass, pp. 260–297.

Odden, Allan and Nancy Kotowski. (1992d). Financing Public School Choice: Policy Issues and Options. In Allan R. Odden, ed., *Rethinking School Finance: An Agenda for the 1990s.* San Francisco: Jossey Bass, pp. 225–259.

Odden, Allan and Nancy Kotowski. (1992b). *Implementing California's Language Arts Framework,* Policy Brief #4. Berkeley, CA: University of California, Policy Analysis for California Education.

Odden, Allan and David D. Marsh. (1988). How Comprehensive Reform Legislation Can Improve Secondary Schools. *Phi Delta Kappan, 69*(8).

Odden, Allan and David D. Marsh. (1989). State Education Reform Implementation: A Framework for Analysis. In Jane Hannaway and Robert Crowson, eds., *The Politics of Reforming School Administration.* Philadelphia: Falmer Press, pp. 41–59.

Odden, Allan and William Massy. (1992). *Education Funding for Schools and Universities: Improving Productivity and Equity.* New Brunswick, NJ: Rutgers, the State University of New Jersey, The Eagleton Institute of Politics, Consortium for Policy Research in Education.

Odden, Allan and Eleanor Odden. (1994). *Applying the High-Involvement Framework to Local Management of Schools in Victoria, Australia.* Paper presented at the annual meeting of the American Educational Research Association, New Orleans, LA.

Odden, Allan and Van Dougherty. (1984). *Education Finance in the States, 1984.* Denver, CO: Education Commission of the States.

Odden, Allan and Priscilla Wohlstetter. (1992). The Role of Agenda Setting in the Politics of School Finance: 1970–1990. *Educational Policy.* 6(4), 355–376.

Odden, Allan R. (1984). Financing Educational Excellence, *Education Finance in the States: 1984,* 65(5), 311–319.

Odden, Allan R. (1987). Education Reform and Services to Poor Students: Can the Two Policies Be Compatible? *Educational Evaluation and Policy Analysis.* 9(3), 231–244.

Odden, Allan R. and Lawrence O. Picus. (1992). *School Finance: A Policy Perspective.* New York: McGraw Hill.

Odden, Allan R., ed. (1991a). *Education Policy Implementation.* Albany, NY: State University of New York Press.

Odden, Allan R. (1991b). Thinking About Program Quality. In Allan R. Odden, ed., *Education Policy Implementation.* Albany, NY: State University of New York Press, pp. 125–143.

Odden, Allan R. (1992b). School Finance and Education Reform: An Overview. In Allan R. Odden, ed., *Rethinking School Finance: An Agenda for the 1990s.* San Francisco: Jossey-Bass.

Odden, Allan R. (1992c). Towards the Twenty-First Century: A School-based Finance. In Allan R. Odden, ed., *Rethinking School Finance: An Agenda for the 1990s.* San Francisco: Jossey Bass, pp. 322–344.

Office of Technology Assessment. (1992). *Testing in American Schools: Asking the Right Questions,* OTA-SET-519. Washington, DC: U.S. Government Printing Office.

Orfield, Gary. (1969). *The Reconstruction of Southern Education: The Schools and the 1964 Civil Rights Act.* New York: Wiley.

Osborne, David and Ted Gaebler. (1992). *Reinventing Government: How the Entrepre-*

neurial Spirit is Transforming the Public Sector. Reading, MA: Addison-Wesley Publishing House, Inc.

Osborne, David. (1988). *Laboratories of Democracy.* Cambridge: Harvard Business School Press.

Ouchi, William G. (1981). *Theory Z: How American Business Can Meet the Japanese Challenge.* Reading, MA: Addison-Wesley.

Packer, Arnold H. and John G. Wirt. (1991). *Restructuring Work and Learning.* Paper presented at the annual meeting of the Association for Public Policy and Management, Bethesda, MD.

Packer, Arnold. (1992). Taking Action on the SCANS Report. *Educational Leadership,* 49(6), 27–31.

Palinscar, Annemarie S. and Ann L. Brown. (1984). Reciprocal Teaching of Comprehension-Fostering and Comprehension-Monitoring Activities. *Cognition and Instruction,* 1(2), 117–175.

Palinscar, Annemarie S. and Ann L. Brown. (1989). Instruction for Self-Regulated Reading. In Lauren Resnick and Leopold E. Kolpfer, eds., *Toward the Thinking Curriculum: Current Cognitive Research.* Washington, DC: Association for Supervision and Curriculum Development, pp. 19–39.

Palinscar, Annemarie Sullivan and Laura J. Klenk. (1991). Learning Dialogues to Promote Text Comprehension. In Barbara Means and Michael S. Knapp, eds., *Teaching Advanced Skills to Educationally Disadvantaged Students.* Washington, DC: U.S. Department of Education, Office of Planning, Budget and Evaluation, pp. 21–34.

Pallas, Aaron M., Gary Natriello and Edward L. McDill. (1989). The Changing Nature of the Disadvantaged Population: Current Dimensions and Future Trends. *Educational Researcher,* 18(5), 16–22.

Pechman, E. M. and K. G. Laguarda. (1993). *Status of New State Curriculum Frameworks, Standards, Assessments and Monitoring Systems.* Washington, DC: Policy Studies Associates.

People of the State of Illinois ex rel. McCollum v. *Board of Education of School District No. 71, Champaign Co., Ill., et al.,* 333 U.S. 203 (1948).

Peters, Thomas and Robert Waterman. (1982). *In Search of Excellence.* New York: Harper and Row.

Peters, Thomas J. (1992). *Liberation Management.* New York: Alfred Knopf.

Peterson, Kent. (1982). Making Sense of Principals' Work. *Australian Administrator,* 3(3), 1–4.

Peterson, Paul, Barry Rabe, and Kenneth Wong. (1986). *When Federalism Works.* Washington, DC: Brookings Institution.

Peterson, Paul, Barry Rabe, and Kenneth Wong. (1991). The Maturation of Redistributive Programs. In Allan R. Odden, ed., *Education Policy Implementation.* Albany, NY: State University of New York Press, pp. 65–80.

Peterson, Penelope L., Elizabeth Fennema, and Thomas Carpenter. (1991). Using Children's Mathematical Knowledge. In Barbara Means and Michael S. Knapp, eds., *Teaching Advanced Skills to Educationally Disadvantaged Students.* Washington, DC: U.S. Department of Education, Office of Planning, Budget and Evaluation, pp. 103–128.

Piaget, Jean and Wadsworth, Barry J. (1979). *Piaget's Theory of Cognitive Development.* New York: Longman.

Picus, Lawrence O. (1991). Cadillacs or Chevrolets?: The Evolution of State Control Over School Finance in California. *Journal of Education Finance,* 17(1), 33–59.

Picus, Lawrence O. (1993a). *The Allocation and Use of Educational Resources: District Level Analysis from the Schools and Staffing Survey.* Los Angeles, CA: University of Southern California, Consortium for Policy Research in Education.

Picus, Lawrence O. (1994). *The $300 Billion Question: How Do Public Elementary and Secondary Schools Spend Their Money?* Paper presented at the annual meeting of the American Educational Research Association, New Orleans.

Picus, Lawrence O. and Linda Hertert. (1993). Three Strikes and You're Out: Texas School Finance After Edgewood III. *Journal of Education Finance,* 18(4), 366–389.

Pierce v. *Society of Sisters,* 268 U.S. 510 (1925).

Pitner, Nancy and Rodney Ogawa. (1981). Organizational Leadership: The Case of the Superintendent. *Educational Administrative Quarterly,* 17(2), 45–66.

Plessy v. *Ferguson,* 163 U.S. 537 (1896).

Pogrow, Stanley. (1990). Challenging At-Risk Students: Findings from the HOTS Program. *Phi Delta Kappan,* 71(5), 389–397.

Policy Analysis for California Education. (1993). *Conditions of Education in California, 1992.* Berkeley, CA: University of California, Policy Analysis for California Education.

Popkewitz, Thomas S. (1988). Educational Reform: Rhetoric, Ritual, and Social Interest. *Educational Theory* 38(1), 77–93.

Porter, Andrew C. (1991). Creating a System of School Process Indicators. *Educational Evaluation and Policy Analysis,* 13(1), 13–29.

Porter, Andrew C. (1992). *School Delivery Standards.* Madison, WI: University of Wisconsin, Wisconsin Center for Educational Research.

Porter, Andrew C. (1993a). *Defining and Measuring Opportunity to Learn.* Paper prepared for the National Governors' Association. Washington, DC.

Porter, Andrew C. (1993b). Opportunity to Learn. *Educational Researcher.* 22(5), 24–30.

Porter, Andrew C. and Jere Brophy. (1988). Good Teaching: Insights from the Work of the Institute for Research on Teaching. *Educational Leadership,* 45(8), 75–84.

Porter, Andrew C., Doug A. Archbald, and Alexander K. Tyree, Jr. (1991). Reforming the Curriculum: Will Empowerment Policies Replace Control? In Susan Fuhrman and Betty Malen, eds., *The Politics of Curriculum and Testing.* Philadelphia: Falmer Press, pp. 11–36.

Powell, Arthur, Eleanor Farrar, and David Cohen. (1985). *The Shopping Mall High School.*

Prager, Karen. (1993). Collegial Process versus Curricular Focus: Dilemma for Principal Leadership. *Brief,* 5. Madison, WI: University of Wisconsin, Wisconsin Center for Educational Research, Center on Organization and Restructuring of Schools.

Prawat, Richard S. and Nancy Jennings. (1994). *Learners as Context in Educational Reform: The Story of Karen and Joe.* Paper presented at the annual meeting of the American Educational Research Association, New Orleans.

Prawat, Richard S. (1992). Teachers' Beliefs about Teaching and Learning: A Constructivist Perspective. *American Journal of Education.* 100(3):454–495.

Presseisen, Barbara Z. (1987). *Teaching Thinking and At-Risk Students: Understanding the Problem.* Philadelphia: Research for Better Schools.

Pressman, Jeffrey and Aaron Wildavsky. (1973). *How Great Expectations in Washington are Dashed in Oakland, or Why It's Amazing that Federal Programs Work at All.* Berkeley: University of California.

Pressman, Jeffrey L. and Aaron Wildavsky. (1984). *Implementation,* 3rd ed., Berkeley: University of California Press.

Prestine, Nona. (1991). *Shared Decision Making in Restructuring Essential Schools: The Role of the Principal.* Paper presented at the conference of the University Council for Educational Administration, Baltimore.

Prestine, Nona. (1994). *A Five Year Study of Four Schools Attempting to Restructure Using the Nine Precepts of the Coalition of Essential Schools.* Paper presented at the annual meeting of the American Educational Research Association, New Orleans.

Puleo, Vincent T. (1988). A Review and Critique of Research on Full-Day Kindergarten, *Elementary School Journal,* 88(4), 425–439.

Purkey, Stewart C. and Marshall S. Smith. (1983). Synthesis of Research on Effective Schools. *Educational Leadership,* 40(3), 64–69.

Purkey, Stewart C. & Marshall S. Smith. (1983). Effective Schools: A Review. *Elementary School Journal,* 83(4), 427–452.

Purkey, Stewart and Marshall Smith. (1985). The District Policy Implications of the Effective Schools Literature. *The Elementary School Journal,* 85(3), 353–388.

Putnam, Ralph, Magdalene Lampert, and Penelope Peterson. (1990). Alternative Perspectives on Knowing Mathematics in Elementary Schools. In Courtney Cazden, ed., *Review of Research in Education,* Vol. 16. Washington, DC: American Educational Research Association, pp. 57–150.

Radin, Beryl and Willis Hawley. (1988). *The Politics of Federal Reorganization.* New York: Pergamon Press.

Ramirez, J. David, Sandra D. Yuen, and David K. Billings. (1991). *Longitudinal Study of Structured English Immersion Strategy, Early-Exit, and Late-Exit Transitional Bilingual Education Programs for Language Minority Children.* San Mateo, CA: Aguirre International.

Ravitch, Diane and Chester E. Finn, Jr. (1987). *What do Our 17-Year-Olds Know?* New York: Harper and Row.

Ravitch, Dianne. (1987). Tot Sociology, Or What Happened to History in the Grade Schools. *American Scholar,* 56, 343–354.

Reed, Sally and R. Craig Sautter. (1990). Children of Poverty: The Status of 12 Million Young Americans. *Phi Delta Kappan,* 71(10), K1–K12.

Reich, Robert B. (1991). *The Work of Nations.* New York: Alfred Knopf.

Reich, Robert. (1983). *The Next American Frontier.* New York: Times Books.

Resnick, Lauren. (1987). *Education and Learning to Think.* Washington, DC: National Academy of Education.

Resnick, Lauren. (1988). Learning in School and Out. *Educational Researcher,* 16(9), 13–20.

Resnick, Lauren. (1991). *Testimony Before the Senate Committee on Labor and Human Resources, Subcommittee on Education, Arts and Humanities,* March 7, 1991.

Resnick, Lauren. (1992–93). Standards, Assessment, And Educational Quality. *Stanford Journal of Law and Policy,* 4: 53–59.

Resnick, Lauren, ed. (1989). *Knowing, Learning, and Instruction.* Hillsdale, NJ: Lawrence Erlbaum.

Resnick, Lauren and Daniel P. Resnick. (1992). Assessing the Thinking Curriculum: New Tools for Educational Reform. In Bernard R. Gifford and Mary Catherine O'Conner, eds., *Changing Assessments: Alternative Views of Aptitude, Achievement and Instruction.* Boston: Kluwer Academic Publishers, pp. 37–75.

Resnick, Lauren and Leopold E. Klopfer, eds. (1989). *Toward the Thinking Curriculum: Current Cognitive Research.* Washington, DC: Association for Supervision and Curriculum Development.

Resnick, Lauren and S. Omanson. (1986). Learning to Understand Arithmetic. In Robert Glaser, ed., *Advances in Instructional Psychology,* vol. 3. Hillsdale, NJ: Lawrence Erlbaum.

Resnick, Lauren B., Victoria Bill, Sharon Lesgold, and Mary Leer. (1991). Thinking in Arithmetic Class. In Barbara Means and Michael S. Knapp, eds., *Teaching Advanced Skills to Educationally Disadvantaged Students* (pp, 137–160), Washington, DC: U.S. Department of Education, Office of Planning, Budget and Evaluation.

Reynolds, Anne. (1992). What is Competent Beginning Teaching: A Review of the Literature. *Review of Educational Research,* 62(1): 1–36.

Reynolds, Maynard C. (1988). *Knowledge Base for the Beginning Teacher.* Oxford: Pergaman Press.

Richards, Craig and M. Shujaa. (1990). State-Sponsored School Performance Incentive Plans: A Policy Review, *Educational Considerations, 17*(2), 42–56.

Richards, Craig and Tian Ming Sheu. (1990). *The South Carolina School Incentive Reward Program: A Policy Analysis.* New Brunswick, NJ: Rutgers University, Consortium for Policy Research in Education (CPRE).

Richards, Craig and Tian Ming Sheu. (1992). The South Carolina School Incentive Reward Program: A Policy Analysis. *Economics of Education Review, 11*(1), 71–86.

Richards, Craig, Daniel Fishbein, and Paula Melville. (1993). Cooperative Performance Incentives in Education. In Stephen L. Jacobson and Robert Berne, eds., *Reforming Education: The Emerging Systemic Approach.* Thousand Oaks, CA: Corwin Press, pp. 28–42.

Richardson, Joanna. (1994). In First Changes Since '87, NCATE Revises Teacher Training Standards. *Education Week, 13*(25) (May 25).

Riley, M. S., James G. Greeno, and J. I. Heller. (1983). Development of Children's Problem' Solving Ability in Arithmetic. In H. P. Ginsburg, ed., *The Development of Mathematical Thinking.* New York: Academic Press, pp. 153–196.

Rosenholtz, Susan J. (1985). Effective Schools: Interpreting the Evidence. *American Journal of Education, 93*(3), 352–388.

Rosenholtz, Susan J. (1989). *Teachers' Workplace: The Social Organization of Schools.* New York: Longman.

Rosenshine, Barak and Robert Stevens. (1986). Teaching Functions. In Merlin C. Witrick, ed., *Handbook of Research on Teaching.* New York: Macmillan, pp. 376–391.

Rosenthal, Alan. (1981). *Legislative Life: People, Process, and Performance in the States.* New York: Harper and Row.

Rosenthal, Alan and Susan Fuhrman. (1981a). *Legislative Education Leadership in the States.* Washington, DC: Institute for Education Leadership.

Rosenthal, Alan and Susan Fuhrman. (1981b). Legislative Education Staffing in the States. *Educational Evaluation and Policy Analysis, 3*(4), 5–16.

Rotberg, Iris. (1990). I Never Promised You First Place. *Phi Delta Kappan, 72*(4), 296–303.

Rothman, Robert. (1992a). KY Reformers Await Reaction to Results of Tough Tests. *Education Week*, September 23, 1992.

Rothman, Robert. (1992b). RAND Study Finds Serious Problems in Vermont Portfolio Program. *Education Week*, December 16, 1992.

Rothman, Robert. (1993). State Consortia to Join Forces to Develop Assessments. *Education Week*, February 10, 1993.

Rowan, Brian. (1994). Comparing Teachers' Work with Work in Other Occupations: Notes on the Professional Status of Teaching, *Educational Researcher, 23*(6). 4–17, 21.

Rowan, Brian and Larry F. Guthrie. (1989). The Quality of Chapter 1 Instruction: Results from a Study of Twenty Four Schools. In Robert Slavin, Nancy Karweit, and Nancy Madden, eds., *Effective Programs for Students at Risk.* Newton, Mass.: Allyn and Bacon, pp. 195–219.

Rutherford, William. (1985). School Principals as Effective Leaders. *Phi Delta Kappan, 67*(1), 31–34.

Rutter, Michael, B. Maughan, Peter Mortimore, et al. (1979). *Fifteen Thousand Hours: Secondary Schools and Their Effects on Children.* Cambridge, MA: Harvard University Press.

San Antonio Independent School District v. *Rodriguez, 411 U.S. 1* (1973).

Scardamalia, Marlene and Carl Bereiter. (1986). Written Composition. In Merlin Wittrock, ed., *Handbook of Research on Teaching.* New York: Macmillan, pp. 778–803.

Schlechty, Phillip and Cyrus Vance. (1983). Recruitment, Selection and Retention: The Shape of the Teaching Force. *Elementary School Journal,* 83(4), 469–487.

Schoenfeld, Alan H. (1985). *Mathematical Problem Solving.* New York: Academic Press.

Schoenfeld, Alan H. (1987). *Cognitive Science and Mathematics Education.* Hillsdale, NJ: Lawrence Erlbaum.

Schoenfeld, Alan H. (1989). Teaching Mathematics Thinking and Problem Solving. In Lauren Resnick and Leopold E. Kolpfer, eds., *Toward the Thinking Curriculum: Current Cognitive Research.* Washington, DC: Association for Supervision and Curriculum Development, pp. 83–104.

Schwartz, Myron and Jay Moskowitz. (1988). *Fiscal Equity in the United States.* Washington, D.C.: Decision Resources.

Schwille, John, Andrew Porter, Gabriella Belli, et al. (1982). Teachers as Policy Brokers in the Content of Elementary School Mathematics. In Lee Shulman and Gary Sykes, eds., *Handbook of Teaching and Policy.* New York: Longman, pp. 370–391.

Secada, Walter G. and Lisa Byrd. (1993). School-Level Reform and the Teaching/Learning of Mathematics. *NCRMSE Research Review,* 2(2), 5–7.

Secretary's Commission on Achieving Necessary Skills. (1992). *Learning a Living: A Blueprint for High Performance.* Washington, DC: U.S. Department of Labor.

Sedlak, Michael and Steven Schlossman. (1986). *Who Will Teach?* Santa Monica, CA: RAND Corporation.

Senge, Peter. (1990). *The Fifth Discipline.* New York: Doubleday.

Sergiovanni, Thomas. (1984). Leadership and Excellence in Schooling. *Educational Leadership,* 41(5), 4–13.

Shalala, Donna E. and James A. Kelly. (1973). Politics, the Courts, and Education Policy. *Teachers College Record,* 75(2), 223–238.

Shavelson, Richard J. and Gail P. Baxter. (1992). What We've Learned About Assessing Hands-On Science. *Educational Leadership,* (5), 20–25.

Shavelson, Richard J., Gail P. Baxter, and Jerry Pine. (1992). Performance Assessments: Political Rhetoric and Measurement Reality. *Educational Researcher,* 21(4), 22–27.

Shavelson, Richard, Lorraine McDonnell, and Jeannie Oakes. (1989). *Indicators for Monitoring Mathematics and Science Education.* Santa Monica, Calif.: The Rand Corporation.

Shedd, Joseph. Collective Bargaining, School Reform, and the Management of School Systems. In Samuel B. Bacharach, ed., *Educational Reform: Making Sense of It All.* Boston: Allyn & Bacon, pp. 92–102.

Shepard, Lorrie A. (1991). Will National Tests Improve Student Learning? *Phi Delta Kappan,* (3), 232–238.

Sher, Jonathan, ed. (1977). *Education in Rural America: A Reassessment of Conventional Wisdom.* Boulder, CO: Westview Press.

Shields, Patrick M., Thomas B. Corcoran, and Andrew A. Zucker. (1993). *Study of NSF's Statewide Systemic Initiatives (SSI) Program: First-Year Report.* Menlo Park, CA: SRI International.

Sizer, Theodore. (1984). *Horace's Compromise: The Dilemma of the American High School.* Boston: Houghton-Mifflin.

Sizer, Theodore. (1990). Educational Policy and the Essential School, *Horace,* 6(2). Providence, RI: The Coalition of Essential Schools, Brown University.

Sizer, Theodore. (1992). *Horace's School: Redesigning the American High School.* Boston: Houghton Mifflin.

Skowronek, Stephen. (1982). *Building a New American State: The Expansion of National Administrative Capacities, 1877–1920.* Cambridge, England: Cambridge University Press.

Slavin, Robert E. (1990). *Cooperative Learning: Theory, Research and Practice.* Englewood Cliffs, NJ: Prentice Hall.

Slavin, Robert E. (1991). *Funding Inequities Among Maryland School Districts: What Do They Mean in Practice?* Baltimore, MD: Johns Hopkins University, Center for Research on Effective Schooling for Disadvantaged Students.

Slavin, Robert E., ed. (1989). *School and Classroom Organization.* Hillsdale, NJ: Lawrence Erlbaum Associates.

Slavin, Robert E., Nancy Karweit, and Nancy Madden. (1989). *Effective Programs for Students at Risk,* Newton, Mass.: Allyn and Bacon.

Slavin, Robert E., Nancy L. Karweit, and Barbara A. Wasik. (1994). *Preventing Early School Failure.* Boston: Allyn and Bacon.

Slavin, Robert E., Nancy A. Madden, Lawrence J. Dolan et al. (1994). 'Whenever and Wherever We Choose' The Replication of 'Success for All.' *Phi Delta Kappan,* 76(8), 639–647.

Slavin, Robert E., Nancy A. Madden, Nancy L. Karweit et al. (1990). Success for All: First-Year Outcomes of a Comprehensive Plan for Reforming Urban Education. *American Education Research Journal,* 27(2), 255–278.

Sloan v. *Lemon,* 413 U.S. 825 (1973).

Smith, Frank. (1992). Learning to Read: The Never-Ending Debate. *Phi Delta Kappan.* 73(6), 432–441.

Smith, Marshall S. and Jennifer O'Day. (1988). *Teaching Policy and Research on Teaching.* Stanford, CA: Stanford University, Center for Policy Research in Education.

Smith, Marshall S. and Jennifer O'Day. (1991). Systemic School Reform. In Susan Fuhrman and Betty Malen, eds., *The Politics of Curriculum and Testing.* Philadelphia: The Falmer Press, pp. 233–268.

Smith, Marshall S. and Jennifer O'Day. (1991a). Educational Equality: 1966 and Now. In Deborah A. Verstegen and James G. Ward, eds., *Spheres of Justice in Education.* New York: Harper-Collins, pp. 53–100.

Smith, Marshall S. (1993). Speech given to the 1993 meeting of the Cleveland Conference, Chicago.

Smith, Marshall S., Jennifer A. O'Day, and David K. Cohen. (1991). A National Curriculum in the United States. *Educational Leadership,* 49(1), 74–81.

Smith, Marshall S., Susan H. Fuhrman, and Jennifer O'Day. (1994). National Curriculum Standards: Are They Desirable and Feasible? In Richard F. Elmore and Susan H. Fuhrman, eds., *The Governance of Curriculum.* Alexandria, VA: Association for Supervision and Curriculum Development, pp. 12–29.

Smith, Marshall. (1988). Educational Indicators, *Phi Delta Kappan,* 69(7), 487–491.

Smylie, Mark A. (1994). Redesigning Teachers' Work: Connections to the Classroom. *Review of Research in Education.* Washington, DC: American Educational Research Association, pp. 129–177.

Sparks, Dennis and Susan Loucks-Horsley. (1990). Models of Staff Development. In W. Robert Houston, ed., *Handbook of Research on Teacher Education.* New York: Macmillan.

Sparks, Dennis. (1994). Staff Development Implications of National Board Certification: An Interview with NBPTS's James Smith. *Journal of Staff Development,* 15(1), 58–59.

Sparks, GeorgeAnn. (1983). Synthesis of Research on Staff Development for Effective Teaching. *Educational Leadership,* 41(3), 65–72.

Special Study Panel on Education Indicators. (1991). *Education Counts.* Washington, DC: National Center for Education Statistics.

Spring, Joel. (1988). *Conflict of Interests.* New York: Longman.

Spring, Joel. (1994). *American Education* (6th Edition). New York: McGraw Hill.

Sternberg, R. J. (1985). *Beyond I.Q.: Toward a Triarchic Theory of Intelligence.* Cambridge, MA: Cambridge University Press.

Stevenson, Harold W. and James W. Stigler. (1992). *The Learning Gap: Why Our Schools are Failing and What We Can Learn From Japanese and Chinese Education.* New York: Summit Books.

Stodgill, Ralph M. and Alvin E. Coons, eds. (1957). *Leader Behavior: Its Description and Measurement.* Research Monograph 88. Columbus, OH: Ohio State University, Bureau of Business Research.

Stodgill, Ralph M. (1948). Personal Factors Associated with Leadership: A Survey of the Literature. *Journal of Psychology,* 25, 35–71.

Stodgill, Ralph M. (1974). *Handbook of Leadership: A Survey of Theory and Research.* New York: The Free Press.

Stuart v. *School District No. 1 of the Village of Kalamazoo,* 30 Mich. 69 (1874).

Superintendent's Advisory Task Force on Middle Schools. (1989). *Caught in the Middle,* Sacramento, CA: California State Department of Education (1988).

Swann v. *Charlotte-Mecklenburg,* 402 U.S. 1, 29 (1971).

Talbert, Joan E. and Milbrey W. McLaughlin. (1994). Teacher Professionalism in Local School Contexts. *American Journal of Education,* 102(2), 123–153.

Task Force on Education for Economic Growth. (1983). *Action for Education Excellence.* Denver, CO: Education Commission of the States.

Tatel, David S. (1992–93). Desegregation Versus School Reform: Resolving the Conflict. *Stanford Law and Policy Review,* 4: 61–72.

Taylor, Frederick Winslow. (1911). *The Principles of Scientific Management.* New York: Harper and Row.

Tharpe, R.G. (1982). The Effective Instruction of Comprehension: Results and Descriptions of the Kamehameha Early Education Program. *Reading Research Quarterly,* 17(4), 503–527.

Theobald, Neil D. and Faith Hanna. (1991). Ample Provisions for Whom?: The Evolution of State Control Over School Finance in Washington. *Journal of Education Finance,* 17(1), 7–32.

Thurow, Lester. (1992). *Head to Head: The Changing Economic Battle Among Japan, Europe and America.* New York: William Morrow.

Timar, Thomas and David Kirp. (1988). *Managing Educational Excellence,* Philadelphia: Falmer Press.

Tinker v. *Des Moines,* 393 U.S. 503 (1969).

Tyack, David. (1974). *The One Best System.*

Tyack, David. (1991). Public School Reform: Policy Talk and Institutional Practice. *American Journal of Education,* 100(1), 1–19.

Tyack, David and Elizabeth Hansot. (1982). *Managers of Virtue: Public School Leadership in America, 1920–1980.* New York: Basic Books.

Tyack, David, Michael W. Kirst, and Elizabeth Hansot. (1980). Educational Reform: Retrospect and Prospect. *Teachers College Record,* 81(3), 253–269.

Underwood, Julie and Deborah Verstegen, eds. (1990). *The Impacts of Litigation and Legislation on Public School Finance: Adequacy, Equity and Excellence.* Cambridge, MA: Ballinger.

United States Department of Education. (1986). *What Works: Research About Teaching and Learning?* Washington, DC: United States Department of Education.

United States Department of Education. (1993). *Reinventing Chapter 1: The Current Chapter 1 Program and New Directions: Final Report of the National Assessment of the Chapter 1 Program.* Washington, DC: United States Department of Education.

United States Department of Education. (1993a). *Achieving World Class Standards: The Challenge for Educating Teachers.* Washington, DC: United States Department of Education.

Usdan, Michael D. (1993). The Relationship Between School Boards and General Purpose Government. *Phi Delta Kappan,* 75(5), 374–377.

Villasenor, A. (1990). *Teaching the First Grade Mathematics Curriculum From a Problem-Solving Perspective.* Unpublished doctoral dissertation. University of Wisconsin-Milwaukee.

Verstegen, Deborah A. (1990). Educational Fiscal Policy in the Reagan Administration. *Educational Evaluation and Policy Analysis,* 12(4), 355–374.

Verstegen, Deborah A. and David L. Clark. (1988). The Diminution in Federal Expenditures for Education During the Reagan Administration. *Phi Delta Kappan,* 70(2), 134–138.

Warren, Donald. (1990). Passage of Rites: On the History of Educational Reform in the United States. In Joseph Murphy, ed., *The Educational Reform Movement of the 1980s.* Berkeley, CA: McCutchan, pp. 57–81.

Wasley, Patricia A. (1991). *Teachers Who Lead: The Rhetoric of Reform and the Realities of Practice.* New York: Teachers College Press.

Weber, Max. (1947). *The Theory of Social and Economic Organization.* (Talcot Parsons, translator). New York: Free Press.

Wehlage, Gary, G. Smith, and P. Lipman. (1992). Restructuring Urban High Schools: The New Futures Experience. *American Educational Research Journal,* 29(1), 51–93.

Weick, Karl. (1982). Administering Education in Loosely Coupled Schools. *Phi Delta Kappan,* 63, 673–676.

Weiss, Carol. (1992). *Shared Decision Making About What? A Comparison of Schools With and Without Teacher Participation.* Paper presented at the annual meeting of the American Educational Research Association, San Francisco.

Westbury, Ian. (1992). Comparing American and Japanese Achievement: Is the United States Really a Low Achiever? *Educational Researcher,* 21(5), 18–24.

White House, The. (1991). *America 2000: An Education Strategy.* Washington, DC.

Willig, Ann E. (1985). Meta-Analysis of Studies on Bilingual Education. *Review of Educational Research,* 55(3), 269–318.

Willower, Daniel and H. Fraser. (1979–80). School Superintendents and Their Work. *Administrator's Notebook,* 28(5).

Wilson, Bruce and Thomas Corcoran. (1988). *Successful Secondary Schools,* Philadelphia: The Falmer Press.

Wilson, Bruce L. and Thomas B. Corcoran. (1987). *Places Where Children Succeed: A Profile of Outstanding Elementary Schools.* Philadelphia: Research for Better Schools.

Wilson, James Q. (1989). *Bureaucracy: What Government Agencies Do and Why They Do It.* New York: Basic Books.

Wilson, Woodrow. (1887). The Study of Public Administration. *Political Science Quarterly,* 197–202.

Wirt, Frederick and Michael W. Kirst. 1992. *Schools in Conflict.* Berkeley, CA: McCutchan.

Wirt, Frederick M. (1980). Does Control Follow the Dollar? School Policy, State-Local Linkages and Political Culture. *Publius,* 10(2), 69–88.

Wise, Arthur. (1969). *Rich Schools-Poor Schools: A Study of Equal Educational Opportunity.* Chicago: University of Chicago Press.

Wise, Arthur and Jane Leibbrand. (1993). Accreditation and the Creation of a Profession of Teaching. *Phi Delta Kappan,* 75(2), 133–136.

Wise, Arthur and Linda Darling-Hammond. (1987). *Licensing Teachers: Design for a Profession.* Santa Monica, CA: RAND Corporation.

Witte, John F, Andrea B. Bailey, and Christopher A. Thorn. (1993). *Milwaukee Parental Choice Program.* Madison, WI: University of Wisconsin, Department of Political Science and the Robert LaFollette Institute of Public Affairs.

Wohlstetter, Priscilla and Allan R. Odden. (1992). Rethinking School-Based Management Policy and Research. *Educational Administration Quarterly,* 28(4), 529–549.

Wohlstetter, Priscilla and Leslie Anderson. (1993). Charter Schools. *Phi Delta Kappan,* 75(6), 486–491.

Wohlstetter, Priscilla. (1994). Charter Schools. In Susan Albers Mohrman and Priscilla Wohlstetter, eds., *School-Based Management: Organizing for High Performance.* San Francisco: Jossey Bass.

Wohlstetter, Priscilla and Leslie Anderson. (1993). Charter Schools. *Phi Delta Kappan,* 75(6), 486–491.

Wohlstetter, Priscilla and Thomas M. Buffett. (1991). Promoting School-Based Management: Are Dollars Decentralized Too? In Allan R. Odden, ed. *Rethinking School Finance: An Agenda for the 1990s.* San Francisco: Jossey Bass, pp. 128–165.

Wohlstetter, Priscilla and Thomas M. Buffett. (1992). Decentralizing Dollars Under School-Based Management: Have Policies Changed? *Educational Policy,* 6(1), 35–54.

Wohlstetter, Priscilla and Susan Albers Mohrman. (1993). *Site-Based Management: Strategies for Success. Finance Brief.* New Brunswick, NJ: Rutgers, the State University of New Jersey, The Eagleton Institute of Politics, Consortium for Policy Research in Education.

Wohlstetter, Priscilla and Allan R. Odden. (1992). Rethinking School-Based Management Policy and Research. *Educational Administration Quarterly,* 28(4), 529–549.

Wohlstetter, Priscilla and Roxane Smyer. (1994). Decentralization Strategies: A Review of the Effective Schools Literature. In Priscilla Wohlstetter and Susan Albert Mohrman, eds., *Creating High Performance Schools.* San Francisco: Jossey Bass.

Wohlstetter, Priscilla, Roxane Smyer, and Susan Albert Mohrman. (1994). New Boundaries for School-Based Management: The High Involvement Model. *Education Evaluation and Policy Analysis,*

Wykoff, James. (1992). The Interstate Equality of Public Primary and Secondary Education Resources in the U.S., 1980–1987. *Economics of Education Review,* 11(1), 19–30.

Yee, Gary and Michael Kirst. (1994). Lessons From the New Science Curriculum of the 1950s and 1960s. *Education and Urban Society,* 26(2), 158–171.

Yee, Sylvia Mei-Ling. (1984). *Careers in the Classroom: When Teaching is More Than a Job.* New York: Teachers College Press.

Yudof, Mark G., David L. Kirp & Betsy Levin. (1992). *Educational Policy and the Law.* St. Paul: West Publishing Co.

Yukl, Gary. 1981. *Leadership in Organizations.* Englewood Cliffs, NJ: Prentice-Hall, Inc.

Yukl, Gary. 1982. Managerial Leadership. In *The Effective Principal: A Research Summary.* Reston, Va.: National Association of Secondary School Principals.

Zobrest v. *Catalina,* 113 S. Ct. 2462 (1993).

Zuboff, Shoshana. (1988). *In the Age of the Smart Machine: The Future of Work and Power.* New York: Basic Books.

Author Index

Subject Index